His Holiness:
John Paul II and the History of Our Time
(with Marco Politi)

Loyalties: A Son's Memoir

The Final Days
(with Bob Woodward)

All the President's Men
(with Bob Woodward)

A WOMAN
IN CHARGE

A WOMAN IN CHARGE

THE LIFE OF

Hillary Rodham Clinton

CARL BERNSTEIN

ALFRED A. KNOPF   *New York*   2007

For Christine

CONTENTS

A WOMAN
IN CHARGE

Prologue

What I did and said in the next days and weeks would influence not just Bill's future and mine, but also America's. As for my marriage, it hung in the balance, too, and I wasn't at all sure which way the scale would, or should, tip.

—Hillary Rodham Clinton, *Living History*

TOWARD NOON on February 12, 1999, Hillary Rodham Clinton, wearing sensible pants, a simple top, flat shoes, and a smile, strode into her sitting room, with its majestic view of the capital's great Mall. The meeting she was about to convene would change the course of her life and (to an extent yet to be determined) the history of her country. Since the day she had met Bill Clinton in 1970, she had stood by her man through all manner of harrowing twists and turns, including (most famously and most recently) the national out-of-body experience known as the Lewinsky affair, on this day reaching its long overdue denouement. More than a year had passed since she (and the country) had first heard the name Monica Lewinsky, a year in which her world had been turned upside down, and Washington with it. Now Hillary Clinton was about to cut loose—though not from her marriage, necessarily, or from Washington, or from her tether to the national consciousness. Rather, a profound alteration in her relationship to all three was reaching critical mass: she was moving toward a final decision on whether to run for the United States Senate from the state of New York, where she had never lived, and to become the first first lady to run for office.

Downstairs in the Oval Office, the president was receiving reports from aides glued grimly to television pictures of the chamber to which his wife aspired. As the Senate's one hundred members were called to order by the chief justice of the United States, the relative solemnity of the occasion was indicated by the special robes William H. Rehnquist had designed for himself to wear at the president's trial. Their gold-embroidered, striped, and ruffled sleeves had been inspired, appropriately, by a Gilbert and Sullivan operetta.

On each senator's desk lay a red leather folder containing the formal, printed charges—perjury and obstruction of justice—against the president, and a tally sheet to track the vote. The result of the roll call about to begin was a foregone conclusion. A two-thirds majority was required to convict, and it was known that only Republicans would cast ballots in favor: forty-five on the first charge, fifty on the second. Clinton, the first president to be impeached by the House of Representatives since Andrew Johnson in 1868, would be acquitted of high crimes and misdemeanors.

Clinton would survive in office due principally to the actions of his wife, just as their tangled relationship—more than any other factor, arguably—was central to his being impeached in the first place.

Seven years later, Bill Clinton was trying to figure out what to do with his life. She, meanwhile, was trying to become president. After a single term in the Senate, she had transformed herself from first lady–cuckold to the most talked about and important leader of her party, the most polarizing politician in the land, a senator like no other, a celebrity like no other, taking the country on another wild Clintonian ride as she became close to omnipresent in what passed for sociopolitical dominance—on TV, in arguments every night at dinner tables all over America, in the foreign press, among her Senate colleagues, in the precincts of the supposed vast right-wing conspiracy that had tried to kill Clintonism. By the time of her overwhelming reelection to the Senate in 2006, she had inspired a nonstop national and international dialogue about herself—her politics, her business acumen, her future, her morals, her sexuality, her religion, her looks, her marriage (still). Single-handedly, she had reanimated the enemies of Clintonism to new heights of fear and frenzy. The public attention drawn to her person, abetted by a press whose hunger she fed unabatedly, at times exceeded even that of the incumbent president, who had been declared elected in 2000 by the same chief justice who wore the Gilbert and Sullivan robes and his colleagues on the Supreme Court. George W. Bush, winner of the first presidential election in American history to be decided not by the electorate but by the judiciary, had prevailed following a campaign promising voters that he would restore honor and traditional American values to the White House after its desecration by the Clintons. *Plural.*

Yet, as the disastrous presidency of her husband's successor neared expiration, Hillary Clinton, in a nation besotted with celebrity, had come to a prominence unique in her time—settling in a rarefied place never populated even by FDR, Princess Diana, Ike, Oprah, or Eleanor Roosevelt as, in a great cacophony, people from every station and walk of life (plus talk show hosts and the *National Enquirer*) fulminated, debated, and screamed at one another about her. Those abroad asked Americans they encountered: Who is she? Do you like her? Will she become president? Is she gay? Meanwhile, she continued to play the U.S. Senate like a flute, charming her colleagues on both sides of the aisle, raising record funds for members of her own party (and preparing the financial ground for her own presidential campaign), entertaining the troops in Iraq, and carefully supporting their mission while looking for ways to separate herself from the policies of the president who sent them there, and from her own vote that had helped dispatch them.

In all this, Bill Clinton had become her biggest booster as, roles now reversed, the gears of the Clinton apparat shifted and another Clinton sought the presidency. He was now a constant presence in the background as her counsel, consultant, strategist, and, finally, the elemental part of *her* process as a woman in charge.

A FEW MINUTES after the Senate had voted to acquit her husband and the thump of the chief justice's gavel had ended his trial in the Capitol, Hillary had finished up her meeting in the White House with Harold Ickes. Hillary and Ickes, her unofficial deputy, had been the architects of successful strategies to save the Clinton presidency at various points. It had been Hillary, who, at the darkest moment, while others were floundering, had assigned a fanatically loyal entourage of men and women to report Sunday mornings to plan for the battle ahead as the impeachment process hurtled down the tracks, braked in a deafening screech, and came to a halt in the Senate chamber. Ickes, the president's former deputy chief of staff, is the son of Harold Ickes, one of the most distinguished elders of the Democratic Party. It had been Harold Sr., FDR's confidant and secretary of the interior, who in 1945 had met with Eleanor Roosevelt shortly after her husband's death to urge her to enter electoral politics and run for governor in New York. After intense examination, political and emotional, she had rejected the idea.

Ickes Sr., like his son, had been equally close to the president and first lady, and had helped Eleanor adjust to the hatred and enmity engendered by her principles, politics, and participation in the presidency of her husband—the last Democratic president to be elected and reelected before Bill Clinton.

Harold Jr., a master of New York's ice-pick-pointed politics, was ambivalent about whether Hillary should run for the Senate to succeed Daniel Patrick Moynihan, and he was forthright that afternoon about presenting all the obstacles of such a course, not least of which would be inevitable stories about the hostility (finally diminishing as Moynihan neared retirement) between the outgoing senator and the first lady. In the end, Harold Jr. had a much more willing and motivated candidate than his father had had a half century earlier with Eleanor—whom Hillary Clinton idolized. Hillary was seeking not just a seat in the Senate, but redemption: hers, her husband's, and the Clinton presidency's.

THE YEARS OF the Clinton presidency delineated what many friends and associates regarded as the most profound difference of character between Hillary and Bill Clinton: her capacity for personal growth and change. "Emotionally, he's still the same guy who got off the boat after Oxford," a worn-out presidential assistant said as the Clintons left the White House on January 20, 2001. Hillary, sworn in January 3 as New York's junior senator, had, on the other hand, demonstrated extraordinary capability for change and evolutionary development—from Goldwater Girl to liberal Democrat, from fashion victim to power-suit sophisticate, from embattled first lady to establishmentarian senator.

The ultimate demonstration of her ability to change was her transformation as the Lewinsky experience moved relentlessly through her life, and her decision to cut loose in its wake. She acted on "what even on its face is a preposterous idea," said a deputy who had served both her and her husband. "A sitting first lady of the United States was going to the state of New York where she had never lived and run for the Senate— while she was in the White House. And pull[ed] it off. Every political consultant in the world would say, Preposterous, it's goofy. Where did that come from? And she did it."

She had never really aspired to public office, despite all the chatter in the press to the contrary over two decades, and the entreaties of close friends who wanted her to run. She had looked forward after her years as first lady to a life with books and policy advocacy, perhaps becoming a college president or the head of a foundation. Only once had she given even the briefest consideration to seeking elective office, in 1989, after she'd learned that her husband believed himself to be in love with another woman. She had thought then about divorce, and running for governor of Arkansas the following year, when his term ended. The few people who knew about that possibility said the idea was largely born of anger and hurt. Instead, Hillary and Bill had reconciled with great difficulty, and in 1991 she had told him (and he agreed) it was finally his time to run for president, that he could win in 1992.

After he had won, Hillary intimated to her closest friend, Diane Blair, that once in the White House, her husband's sexual compulsions—the source of so much of her rage and anguish over the years—would by necessity be tempered by the office itself; if not by the grandeur of the presidency, then by the fact that he would be locked up in the White House, a golden cage with the nosiest press corps in the world constantly on the prowl.

Inevitably, when the impeachment ugliness arrived, like so many of the crises and battles of their life together, she and their relationship were at its root, the underlying factors, the unstated casus belli, at home and in the Congress—Lewinsky was only the most recent catalyst. The impeachment of the president was a direct reflection of the choices she had made, the compromises she had accepted, however reluctantly, and the enmity engendered by *their* grand designs, successes, and failures.

Robert S. Bennett, Bill Clinton's lawyer in the Paula Jones sexual harassment case, which had led to the special prosecutor's discovery of Monica Lewinsky, said later that the outcome of the Jones matter ultimately turned on what he called "the Hillary question." Bennett was certain that his client had refused to heed sensible legal counsel and settle out of court with Jones (who claimed that Clinton, without invitation, had exposed himself to her) only out of fear of Hillary's wrath and abandonment. The president, his other women, Hillary, and the Clinton presidency had become inextricably intertwined.

Hillary, too, had instinctively recognized the dangers in the Jones case and that something ruinous lay underneath, portending the further destruction of the Clintons' carefully constructed world. Not many days before the suit was filed in court against her husband, Hillary telephoned Bill's former Arkansas chief of staff, Betsey Wright, and, her voice breaking, begged that a way be found to head off further legal process. But the Clintons' enemies had by then taken control of the case. Her husband had dug himself in, the case went forward, and the predictable dynamic of the Clinton marriage in extremis took over once again: Bill didn't dare acknowledge to his wife that *something* had transpired with Jones, so he rolled the dice and risked his presidency on the outcome—just as he would when he denied for months that he had had a sexual relationship with Lewinsky.

As those who knew the Clintons best could testify, this was for him the only way forward. Hillary was the one person he could not do without,

the single irreplaceable part of his past, his process, and his presidency—
and his heart.

In the course of the twenty-two years that took them from Yale Law
School to the governorship of Arkansas to the presidency, the Clintons
had formed *their* politics, a very specific set of values and calculations
arrived at from their separate experiences, expertise, and backgrounds:
joined, tempered, and perfected in endless discussion, always with the
understanding that they were on a journey together. And though her
intellectual firepower was not nearly as spectacular as his, and her political instincts could be clumsy, she was in every sense his political partner,
the person with whom he discussed every significant matter of policy,
strategy, ideology, or ambition.

In the summer of 1974, a week after her work had ended (with
Richard Nixon's resignation) as a staff member of the House Judiciary
Committee's impeachment inquiry, she had packed her belongings into
a Volkswagen and left Washington to join Bill in Arkansas, to partake in
his campaign for election to the U.S. Congress. It had taken her another
year to make up her mind to marry him, knowing full well that the odds
of his becoming monogamous could be less favorable than his becoming
president. Almost all her close friends had tried to dissuade her: Could
she really live in backwater Arkansas while he pursued a political career
there? Was she really willing to tie her fate to his future and abandon
her own potential as a political supernova? How could this square with
the feminism of the era? To all these questions she always answered, "I
love him," and reminded herself that he was the most dazzling person
she—or her friends (who conceded the point almost universally)—had
ever met.

Bill and Hillary's marriage would prove to be an uninterrupted dialogue of ideas and aspirations and a lasting love—often punctuated by
passionate argument. Her counsel was the constant of his method and
political development, though in the Little Rock governor's mansion and
later the White House he would, on occasion, sometimes to her frustration, follow a course at variance from the one she advised.

The "Journey"—their term—was at once endlessly romantic and
unapologetically ambitious, a trek across the political landscape in which
they intended to inspire the expansion of their country's social consciousness, based on their own ideas and ideals, and those of their generation. There is no question, judging from their own words and those of
their friends, that since their courtship, each had come to regard the
other as the brightest star in their universe; that this fusion of energy and
purpose was never just about *him*, but about *them* and the art of the possible. They would change the American story. To their opponents and

enemies, who grew ever more numerous and outraged as the Clintons marched toward the summit, seemingly unbowed by humiliation and unfazed by peril, ambush, and attacks that would have felled lesser mortals, their journey was an act of hubris such as modern American politics had never witnessed.

WHEN THE DEFINITIVE history of the Clinton journey is written, its Thucydides will be hard pressed not to portray the White House years 1993–2000 as a co-presidency. The concept was at first proudly proclaimed by candidate Clinton at a campaign rally in New Hampshire in 1992; then hastily retracted as impolitic; and, in the early days of his presidency, stealthily put into effect—dictating, for the next eight years, the basic terms of American political life and civic amusement. Ultimately, the most essential and yet elusive dynamic of the Clinton presidency came to be the relationship between the two of them—the sand in the gears in bad times, the grease that moved the machinery in good ones, the factor that almost no one else in the White House could get a grip on. Sometimes not even the president himself knew how to handle the Hillary factor.

With the notable exception of her husband's libidinous carelessness, the most egregious errors, strategic and tactical, of the Bill Clinton presidency, particularly in its infancy, were traceable to Hillary—not just her botched handling of their health care agenda, or the ethical cloud hovering like a pall over their administration, but so many of the stumbles and falls responsible for sweeping in the Congress led by Newt Gingrich in 1994 and ending the ambitious phase of their presidency, as well as what had seemed almost a permanent Democratic congressional majority, in place with irregular interruptions since FDR. The inept staffing of the White House, the disastrous serial search for an attorney general, the Travel Office fiasco, the Whitewater land deal, the so-called scandal over her commodities trading, the alienation of key senators and congressmen—all this can be traced in large measure to Hillary.

For the first time in American history, a president's wife sent her husband's presidency off the rails. At the end of two years in office, their dual administration seemed wrecked, repudiated. The first lady feared—and faced—possible indictment. Both the president and his wife were experiencing serious emotional depression. Heralded on inauguration day 1992 as an icon, yet endlessly beset by enemies, she now found herself loathed not only by right-wing zealots, but by millions of voters who had never registered Republican. In the capital, she was loved by few and feared by many more. While Bill sought solace in his familiar escapes, she read the Bible of her Methodist childhood and considered anew the explicit message of service in John Wesley's teaching: "Do all the good you can, by all the means you can, in all the ways you can, in all the places you can, at all the times you can, as long as ever you can." She dabbled in New Age spiritualism, almost always carried with her an underlined and dog-eared book of celestial axioms, and welcomed into the White House Solarium a pair of feminist oracles who channeled her into Eleanor Roosevelt's soul. All of this as she found herself—unimaginably to her—with no choice but to remove herself (or be removed) from the White House chain of command before two full years had passed. She then fled Washington for weeks at a stretch as she sought purpose and redemption in solidarity with women of the Third World.

Her climb back—and his—was long and arduous, but abetted by Gingrich's arrogance, which brought about a government shutdown (which produced Monica Lewinsky's pizza delivery service), the Clintons triumphed magnificently with Bill's overwhelming reelection in 1996, something few political analysts would have predicted in the gloom left behind. A few months later, the special prosecutor who had pursued them for two years announced he was leaving Washington (and his sputtering investigation) to become a law school dean in Malibu, California.

At her husband's second inaugural on January 20, 1997, the Journey finally seemed back on track, a repudiation of those who had hounded and harassed them, and a powerful endorsement by the American people for the policies and politics of the Clintons.

A year later, disaster arrived. The *Washington Post*, *The Drudge Report*, and ABC News reported that the reinvigorated special prosecutor, having been persuaded on grounds of unseemliness not to retire before the formal end of his investigation, had belatedly discovered that the president had been having an affair with a White House intern for sixteen months, and he had allegedly lied and conspired about it under oath in a deposition taken in the Paula Jones case. That afternoon, as the firestorm threatened to consume his presidency, Bill Clinton confided to a trusted adviser that he was not sure he could survive the week in office, and that he would probably be forced to resign. But his wife had gone on television six days later, on NBC's *Today* show, and lent connubial credence to his contention that he "did not have sexual relations with that woman, Ms. Lewinsky." Her support as a wife saved his presidency. She had done much the same thing in the presidential campaign of 1992, appearing on CBS's *60 Minutes* to assure the nation that another of her husband's supposed lovers was a piece of trailer trash (as she called Gennifer Flowers in semiprivate) trying to turn a tabloid trick and land a book deal.

Almost alone among her family and friends and his aides, Hillary actually believed his protestations about this latest and most devastating allegation of his infidelity, believed him for the next seven months, until he'd had his lawyer prepare her for the rumbling ground beneath, and then (on the same day that he confessed to the nation and the world) informed her that he had (once again) lied.

And again, at perhaps the lowest point of both their lives, she had rescued him, intent on redeeming *their* legacy. First, tentatively, she had decided to stay in the marriage. She had brought in ministers of divinity and psychological counselors to attend him. Then she had thrown her weight and intellect into the battle to survive the impeachment crusade. In her fury and anguish she was convinced he had undermined virtually all they (and the Clinton presidency) had achieved together. Yet her credentials—as his wife, as a lawyer, and as a political strategist uniquely positioned to salvage the Clinton epoch—were unimpeachable. "Everything I had learned [working on] the Watergate investigation convinced me that there were no grounds to impeach Bill," she wrote later.

Seen in the light of all these events, Hillary's ascent after her husband's presidency seems all the more remarkable.

I

Formation

I adored [my father] when I was a little girl. I would eagerly watch for him from a window and run down the street to meet him on his way home after work. With his encouragement and coaching, I played baseball, football and basketball. I tried to bring home good grades to win his approval.

—*Living History*

HILLARY RODHAM's childhood was not the suburban idyll suggested by the shaded front porch and gently sloping lawn of what was once the family home at 235 Wisner Street in Park Ridge, Illinois. In this leafy environment of postwar promise and prosperity, the Rodhams were distinctly a family of odd ducks, isolated from their neighbors by the difficult character of her father, Hugh Rodham, a sour, unfulfilled man whose children suffered his relentless, demeaning sarcasm and misanthropic inclination, endured his embarrassing parsimony, and silently accepted his humiliation and verbal abuse of their mother.

Yet as harsh, provocative, and abusive as Rodham was, he and his wife, the former Dorothy Howell, imparted to their children a pervasive sense of family and love for one another that in Hillary's case is of singular importance. When Bill Clinton and Hillary honeymooned in Acapulco in 1975, her parents and her two brothers, Hughie (Hugh Jr.) and Tony, stayed in the same hotel as the bride and groom.

Dorothy and Hugh Rodham, despite the debilitating pathology and undertow of tension in their marriage (discerned readily by visitors to their home), were assertive parents who, at mid-century, intended to convey to their children an inheritance secured by old-fashioned values and verities. They believed (and preached, in their different traditions) that with discipline, hard work, encouragement (often delivered in an unconventional manner), and enough education at home, school, and church, a child could pursue almost any dream. In the case of their only daughter, Hillary Diane, born October 26, 1947, this would pay enormous dividends, sending her into the world beyond Park Ridge with a steadiness and sense of purpose that eluded her two younger brothers. But it came at a price: Hugh imposed a patriarchal unpleasantness and ritual authoritarianism on his household, mitigated only by the distinctly modern notion that Hillary would not be limited in opportunity or skills by the fact that she was a girl.

Hugh Rodham, the son of Welsh immigrants, was sullen, tight-fisted, contrarian, and given to exaggeration about his own accomplishments. Appearances of a sort were important to him: he always drove a new Lincoln or Cadillac. But he wouldn't hesitate to spit tobacco juice through an open window. He chewed his cud habitually, voted a straight Republican ticket, and was infuriatingly slow to praise his children. "He was rougher than a corncob and gruff as could be," an acquaintance once said. Nurturance and praise were left largely to his wife, whose intelligence and abilities he mocked and whose gentler nature he often trampled. "Don't let the doorknob hit you in the ass on your way out," he frequently said at the dinner table when she'd get angry and threaten to leave. She never left, but some friends and relatives were perplexed at Dorothy's decision to stay married when her husband's abuse seemed so unbearable.

"She would never say, That's it. I've had it," said Betsy Ebeling,* Hillary's closest childhood friend, who witnessed many contentious scenes at the Rodham dinner table. Sometimes the doorknob remark would break the tension and everybody would laugh. But not always.

By the time Hillary had reached her teens, her father seemed defined by his mean edges—he had almost no recognizable enthusiasms or pretense to lightness as he descended into continuous bullying, ill-humor, complaint, and dejection.

In fact, depression seemed to haunt the Rodham men. Hugh's younger brother, Russell, a physician, was the "golden boy" of the three children of Hannah and Hugh Rodham Sr. of Scranton, Pennsylvania. When Russell sank into depression in 1948, his parents asked Hugh to return to Scranton to help. Only hours after his arrival, Russell tried to hang himself in the attic, and Hugh had to cut him down. Afterward,

*Ebeling is Betsy's married name. Her maiden name was Johnson.

Russell went to Chicago to stay with Hugh, Dorothy, and their baby daughter in their already overcrowded one-bedroom apartment. For months, Russell received psychiatric treatment at the local Veterans Administration hospital. Eventually he moved to a dilapidated walk-up in downtown Chicago, worked as a bartender, and declined into alcoholism and deeper depression until he died, in 1962, in a fire that was caused by a lit cigarette. Hillary deeply felt her father's pain over the tragedy, she wrote.

Hugh's older brother, Willard, regarded as the most gregarious and fun-loving of the three, never left home or married, and was employed in a patronage job for the Scranton public works department. He resolved after his mother's death to take care of his father. He dedicated himself completely to the task for the next thirteen years, and when his father died at age eighty-six in 1965, Willard was overwhelmed by despair. He died five weeks later of a coronary thrombosis, according to the coroner's report, though Hillary's brother Tony said, "He died of loneliness. When my grandfather died, Uncle Willard was lost."

Hugh Rodham, himself broken of spirit, his brothers and parents dead, soon thereafter shut his business and retired. Not yet fifty-five, he continued to withdraw. Later, both of Hillary's brothers, to varying degrees, seemed to push through adulthood in a fog of melancholia.

In 1993, after Hillary's law partner, close friend, and deputy White House counsel Vince Foster committed suicide, she approached William Styron, who had chronicled his own struggles with depression in his acclaimed book *Darkness Visible*. The conversation was not only about Foster's suicide, but also touched on the depression that seemed to afflict members of Hillary's family.

Hillary's mother, a resilient woman whose early childhood was a horror of abandonment and cruelty, was able to overcome adversity, as would her daughter. Dorothy persevered through five years of dating Hugh Rodham—during which time she worked as his secretary and suspected he was continuing a relationship with another woman—before she agreed to marry him, according to family members. She and Hugh waited another five years to have their first child. (Chelsea Clinton, too, was born in the fifth year of her parents' marriage.)

As intellectually broad-minded as her husband was incurious and uninterested, as inclined to reflection as he was to outburst, she fulfilled her lifelong goal of attending college in her late sixties (majoring in psychology), after she and her husband moved to Little Rock in 1987 to be near their daughter and grandchild. Constantly evolving and changing (like her daughter), she managed almost invariably to find a focus for her energy and satisfaction despite the dissonance of a difficult life at home.

As her husband descended, she even became something of a free spirit, at turns sentimental, analytical, spiritual, and adventurous. (Her favorite movies were not those of her childhood, but *The Adventures of Priscilla, Queen of the Desert*—an Australian drag queen romp—and the bloody classic *Pulp Fiction*.) Dorothy taught classes at Sunday school (as would her daughter); Hugh didn't go to church on Sundays, saying he'd rather pray at home.

Life in the Rodham household resembled a kind of boot camp, presided over by a belittling, impossible-to-satisfy drill instructor. During World War II, as a chief petty officer in the Navy, Rodham had trained young recruits in the U.S. military's Gene Tunney Program, a rigorous phys-ed regime based on the champion boxer's training and self-defense techniques, and on the traditional skills of a drill sergeant. After the war, in which Hugh had been spared overseas duty and was assigned to the Great Lakes Naval Station because of a bad knee, he replicated the barracks experience in his own home, commanding loudly from his living room lounge chair (from which he rarely rose, except for dinner), barking orders, denigrating, minimizing achievements, ignoring accomplishments, raising the bar constantly for his frustrated children— "character building," he called it.

His control over the household was meant to be absolute; confronted with resistance, he turned fierce. If Hillary or one of her brothers had left the cap off a toothpaste tube, he threw it out the bathroom window and told the offending child to fetch it from the front yard evergreens, even in snow. Regardless of how windy and cold the Chicago winter night, he insisted when the family went to bed that the heat be turned off until morning. At dinner, he growled his opinions, indulged few challenges to his provocations, and rarely acknowledged the possibility of being proved wrong. Still, Hillary would argue back if the subject was substantive and she thought she was right. If Dorothy attempted to bring a conflicting set of facts into the discussion, she was typically ridiculed by her husband: "How would you know?" "Where did you ever come up with such a stupid idea?" "Miss Smarty Pants."

"My father was confrontational, completely and utterly so," Hugh Jr. said. Decades later, Hillary and her brothers suggested this was part of a grander scheme to ensure that his children were "competitive, scrappy fighters," to "empower" them, to foster "pragmatic competitiveness" without putting them down, to induce elements of "realism" into the privileged lifestyle of Park Ridge. Her father would tepidly acknowledge her good work, but tell her she could do better, Hillary said. But there is little to suggest that she or her brothers interpreted such encouragement so benignly at the time. When Hillary came home with all As except for one B on her report card, her father suggested that perhaps her school was too easy, and wondered half-seriously why she hadn't gotten straight As. Hillary tried mightily to extract some unequivocal declaration of approval from her father, but he had tremendous difficulty in expressing pride or affection.

At the dinner table, Betsy Ebeling recalled, "Hillary's mom would have cooked something good, and her dad would throw out a conversation topic, almost like a glove on the table, and he would always say something the opposite of what I thought he really believed—because it was so completely provocative and outrageous. It was just his way. He was opinionated, and he could be loud, and what better place to [be that way] than in his own home?"

Unleashed, his rage was frightening, and the household sometimes seemed on the verge of imploding. Betsy and the few other girlfriends whom Hillary brought home could see that life with Hugh Rodham was painfully demeaning for her mother, and that Hillary winced at her father's distemper and chafed under his miserliness. Money was always a contentious issue, ultimately the way in which he could exercise undisputed control, especially in response to Hillary's and Dorothy's instinctive rebelliousness and the wicked sense of humor they shared.

Sometimes his tirades would begin in the kitchen and continue into her parents' bedroom. Hillary would put her hands over her ears. But the experience of standing up to her father also prepared her for the intellectual rough-and-tumble that honed Hillary and Bill Clinton's marital partnership, and helped inure her in the arena of political combat.

"I could go home to two parents who adored everything I did," said Betsy. "Hillary had a different kind of love; you had to earn it."

As a child, Hillary was affected by her parents' often-conflicting values, and her politics borrowed from both, she said later. Dorothy was basically a Democrat, although she never told Hugh or anyone else in Park Ridge, according to Hillary.

Hugh Rodham was a self-described rock-ribbed conservative Republican of the Taft-Goldwater school who despised labor unions, opposed most government aid programs, and fulminated against high taxes. He had tried his hand briefly in politics in 1947 when, as a Democratic-leaning independent, he ran for alderman in Chicago. He had wanted to ingratiate himself with, or even become part of, the fabled Democratic machine then being assembled by the young Richard Daley, and be in a position to exploit an investment he'd made in a downtown parking lot.

He was swamped in the election by the candidate on the regular Democratic line. Some members of his extended family believe the experience contributed to his strident disdain of Democrats. Every four years, during the Republican National Convention, he would instruct his children to watch the proceedings on television; when the Democrats convened, he ordered the set turned off.

To a child, Hugh seemed an unusually big character—loud, broad-shouldered, dominating psychologically as well as physically (he was six foot two, the same height as Bill Clinton, and weighed more than 230 pounds), a former varsity football player and physical education major at Penn State whose hopes of turning pro, he said, had been wiped out by a knee injury that was further aggravated in the Navy.

In all likelihood, though, he had never been a first-stringer at Penn State or a serious professional prospect. He was often described in news stories during the 1992 Clinton presidential campaign as a standout high school quarterback who had been awarded a college football scholarship. However, there were no football scholarships awarded at Penn State during his years there (1931–1935), and he played third-string tight end, according to university newspaper records. Evidence of his exaggerations in regard to his curriculum vitae is extensive. "He was a bullshit artist," said one member of the Rodham family who eventually became alienated from him. In high school, he was known as a braggart; in college, he developed a reputation for embellishing tales about himself.

His only conspicuously humble traits were his origins in Scranton, a tough town of factories, mills, coal dust, prostitution, and political corruption. His father was a loom operator in the big Scranton Lace Works on the Lackawanna River, one of eleven brothers and sisters, almost all of whom had worked on the floor of the factory. His mother, Hannah Jones Rodham—she used all three names—was "hard-headed, often gruff," Hillary remembered, and dominated the life of her family. Hugh was afflicted by self-doubt while growing up.

Despite his college diploma, embittered and disappointed perhaps because of the effects of the Great Depression on his own prospects, Hugh had remained in the same industry in which he'd worked since childhood—the same as his immigrant father—lace-making and embroidering. But he also had a great skill: like the man Hillary would marry, he could talk a great game. "Dad was the world's greatest salesman," said Tony Rodham. "You never saw him lose a sale. Our father was the best closer I've ever met in my life."

His business acumen was also considerable, and he became quite successful as an entrepreneur. He manufactured drapes, window shades, and lace curtains that he sold to hotels, offices, movie theaters, and airlines—printing and cutting and sewing the fabric himself. His only employee was a black man he'd found drunk on the doorstep in 1958 and offered a part-time job. His wife served as his bookkeeper at the start. The shop, near the Merchandise Mart in downtown Chicago, was stifling hot in summer, and the workroom gave off a whiff of tobacco. There was also a showroom. He invested wisely and saved prodigiously. He was fascinated with the how-to's of making money—how money makes money, and how he could keep it.

When Hillary was three years old, he bought the mock-Georgian house in Park Ridge, moving from the one-bedroom apartment in downtown Chicago where he and Dorothy had lived since their wedding. The house at 235 Wisner was purchased for $35,000, all cash. Hugh did not believe in borrowing.

Most days, he was back home by 3 or 4 P.M. When the children were growing up, he could usually be found after work sitting in his easy chair with his bad leg stretched out on an ottoman or low table, complaining about something or silently drinking a beer as he watched television, preferably a sports event. He rarely rose from the chair to greet guests or even uttered a welcome, but his presence dominated the room.

When the boys returned from school, he issued their orders for the rest of the day—chores, studying, then lights out early, the same that had been expected of him as a boy in Scranton. Rather than hire tradesmen for regular upkeep of the house, Tony and Hughie were conscripted to patch and paint as required. As a result, the house gradually sank into structural disrepair and headed toward deterioration, so much so that it was described as "a wreck" by the real estate saleswoman who eventually handled its sale—for about $200,000—when Dorothy and Hugh moved to Little Rock. At the time, it still had antiquated sixty-amp electrical wiring.

Hugh Rodham did not pay his children on those weekends when they came downtown to "help work on a big order." Often he'd drive them through Chicago's aggregation of skid row neighborhoods to remind them of how fortunate they were. He freely expressed prejudices against blacks in the most denigrating terms. He never had a credit card, taught Hillary and her brothers to read the stock tables in the *Chicago Tribune*, and counseled the wisdom of thrift. The bitterness never left, despite the accoutrements of prosperity and his children's devotion.

Rodham had chosen to settle his family in a tranquil neighborhood of two-story, brick-and-frame houses painted in subtle hues, with copses of maples and elms shading the macadam, and small gardens and grassy curbsides lovingly tended. The house was on a corner, its front and side yards seeded green, its sizable front porch directly under the second-floor bedroom-and-sundeck that was Hillary's.

The house was not large. Downstairs there was a living room; a dining room with space sufficient for a table and eight chairs; a cramped kitchen with a breakfast nook; a TV den perhaps fifteen feet square; and a tiny powder room. Upstairs were three bedrooms—none large. The basement was unfinished and used for storage. Across the backyard was a garage, only slightly wider than Hugh's Cadillac but with room for a few bicycles.

In "town," a single stoplight hung like a pendant from wires over the intersection of Main Street and South Prospect Avenue, Park Ridge's commercial center—candy store, art deco theater, public library, wedding photography studio, pharmacy, coffee shop. Nearby, planes bound for new O'Hare Airport descended like buzzing drones in the twilight. Park Ridge, then as now, was an altogether different type of suburb from the communities along Chicago's exclusive North Shore, the houses newer, built mostly in the 1930s and 1940s, without pretension of the grand manner. The breadwinners of Park Ridge in the 1950s and 1960s were mainly first-generation professionals or successful merchant-tradesmen like Hillary's father. They were disposed to exhibiting the ripe fruits of their good fortune and hard work, which had lifted their generational climb from working-class wages: Cadillacs, golf handicaps, gadgets, leisure wear, and leisure time. Many had moved their families from Chicago to escape the incursion of Negroes from the South whose numbers were tipping the city school system. The high school Hillary would attend through eleventh grade, Maine East, was the largest all-white high school in the nation.

To reach Park Ridge, you drove or took the Northwest Rail train past the synagogues of Skokie or the tract houses and little apartments in Niles and then, before you got to O'Hare, you turned and skirted some vegetable farms just outside town. Park Ridge had no Jews (at least none that Hillary knew of), blacks, or Asians, or legal liquor sales, or, so far as Hillary was aware, divorce. Dorothy Rodham was one of the few women in the community who didn't stay home all day, who could be found in the library's reading room, or downtown at a museum. Almost all the Rodhams' neighbors were Methodist, Catholic, or Lutheran, and voted Republican.

After each of Hugh's children was born, he drove the family back to Scranton for a baptism at Court Street Methodist Church, where he had been baptized in 1911, and his brothers before and after him. Every summer the Rodhams drove across the Alleghenys for a two-week vacation at a cabin he and his father, with their own hands, had built on Lake

Winola, near Scranton, in the rolling Pennsylvania hills. The cabin had no heat, bath, or shower. It was a far different environment than the luxurious vacation cottages of many Park Ridge children on the shores of Lake Michigan or the Wisconsin dells.

Hugh meant the vacation to connect his children to a past not as privileged as the one they knew in Park Ridge, as well as to maintain a strong sense of family. On one of their summer vacations, he insisted they visit a coal mine in the anthracite fields nearby. Whatever her discomfort with such gestures at the time, Hillary's later political identification with working-class values and the struggles of average wage-earners was not something acquired at Wellesley or Yale as part of a 1960s countercultural ethos.

As Hillary and her mother increasingly expressed mixed feelings about the prospect of another Lake Winola vacation, their objections were met with Hugh's promises of a shopping spree somewhere on the return trip, where they could spend money on clothes and personal items. After one summer holiday in Pennsylvania, Hugh drove to Fifth Avenue in New York and told Dorothy and Hillary they could buy whatever they wanted before the stores closed at five o'clock. Mother and daughter had only twenty-five minutes so they took off their shoes and ran.

While their Park Ridge schoolmates dressed according to the current fashions, the Rodham children rarely got new clothes until they'd outgrown or worn out the old ones; Tony was occasionally dressed in his brother's hand-me-downs. Neither Hillary nor her mother had much success in persuading Hugh that girls sometimes needed to consider more than the practical in matters of dress. Dorothy herself dressed indifferently.

During summers, the Rodham children were paid pennies for plucking dandelions from the grass. The fact that other kids in the neighborhood received regular allowances failed to impress their father. "They eat and sleep for free. We're not going to pay them for it as well," he told Dorothy. He seemed to have an aphorism for every means of denying his wife and children the smaller, store-bought pleasures of their neighbors. Under her breath, Dorothy had epithets for her husband, like "cheapskate" and "the SOB." Hillary began earning money as a babysitter for neighbors and at a day care center, and later as a salesgirl in a store on Main Street.

As Hugh Rodham increasingly came to be regarded as an oddity in Park Ridge, he seemed to go to extra lengths to put distance between himself and his neighbors. He almost never showed up at a community barbecue or a PTA meeting. He did not join the local country club or participate in civic enterprises. When Hugh Jr. was quarterback of his high school football team, his father would sit by himself on the sidelines during games, following the action close-up rather than joining the other parents, students, and fans in the stands. Characteristically, when his son had his best day as quarterback, completing ten of eleven passes and throwing several touchdowns, Hugh told him only that he "should have completed the other one."

Usually the children could recognize when their father was serious and when he was just being cantankerous. But it was a fine line, especially hard to distinguish because he could not bring himself to be demonstrative in an obviously loving way, and because of his violent streak. According to Hillary, "Occasionally, he got carried away when disciplining us, yelling louder or using more physical punishment, especially with my brothers, than I thought was fair or necessary. But even when he was angry, I never doubted that he loved me." Her father was "not one to spare the rod,"* she wrote.

The Rodham brothers as adults described their father as "critical" and "pretty tough," but also as "kindhearted." Certainly Hugh Rodham was proud of the accomplishments of his children, but if his methodology was intended to convey tough love in an era before the term became fashionable, the results were mixed at best.

His constant pushing of Hillary's brothers to follow his example—so they, too, might be successful and respected in business—did not always take. Hillary, alone among the Rodham children, seemed to possess his self-discipline.

Tony seemed to adjust to his father's difficult philosophy of parenting better than Hugh Jr., who responded by trying endlessly to please his dad, an impossible task. The more he pandered to his father, the more his father seemed to push him away.

"Hugh was toughest on Hughie because he's his first-born son—and he was very tough on him," said a member of the Rodham family. "I don't think he approved of everything he did. But Hughie always wanted that approval, and very much tried to follow in the footsteps of his father. He went to Penn State like his father. He played football like his father." Yet there was always the feeling that he didn't measure up. "Tony, on the other hand, didn't care. Tony just did what he wanted to do, and got Hugh's respect very early on as a younger child."

At age nine, Tony was diagnosed with rheumatic fever and spent an entire school year bedridden, during which Dorothy nursed and tended

---

*How severely Hugh Rodham beat his children has never been directly addressed publicly by Hillary, her brothers, or her mother.

to him. Even as adults, Tony and Hughie would seek solace from their mother during difficult times. Though sometimes dour, she was regarded by the children as the heart and soul of the Rodham household. For the most part unflappable in the company of others, she served as referee between the children and her husband, intervening when Hugh became unusually callous or hurtful in his remarks or demands, or too physical.

"They got ridden, treated like men from the time they were three years old," said a relative. Hillary "was the girl in the house with two crazy little boys," Betsy Ebeling said. "The first time I walked into that house, Hughie was seven and Tony was four. Hughie threw Tony over the balcony onto the curb and Tony bounced and came up with a smile. They're street scrappers, which Hugh loved. They were just physical. They smashed things in the house playing. And Hugh loved that." Dorothy didn't.

Hugh Jr. and Tony were also the beneficiaries of their sister's protection. Even in her teens (as in her years in the White House) she came to their aid when they got into scrapes that required some artful intervention—whether to mollify their father or, later, to quiet a nosy press corps. Though grateful for her intercession, they were also terrified of her, especially of her disapprobation.

Until her teenage years, Hillary could get away with many of the minor infractions for which they were penalized. Often the Rodham children engaged in pranks around the house, engineered by Hillary, but it would be the boys who were punished more severely. " 'Little Hillary' could do no wrong," said Tony. "She was Daddy's girl, there's no doubt about it." Her brothers called Hugh "Old Man," but Hillary called him Pop-Pop (as would Chelsea Clinton, who also could do no wrong in her grandfather's eyes). Toward their sister, at least, their father was capable of a modicum of tenderness. He taught her to play baseball, making her swing at his pitches until she connected with the ball solidly; fished with her at the lake; showed her (like her brothers) how to play pinochle; lingered some evenings over her math homework; told her tales of his childhood (including one about a blind mule that worked in the mines and walked outside to find his sight restored, and others about the freight trains he'd supposedly hopped); and exempted her from some of the heavier tasks assigned to her brothers. When he offered praise—in very pointed fashion—it was eagerly accepted because it was so rare.

It was expected that she excel at school, of course. Education was the bedrock of both Hugh's and Dorothy's divergent philosophies of parenting, and of their aspirations for their children. "Learning for earning's sake," said Hugh. "Learning for learning's sake," said Dorothy, or so their children recalled many years later.

Dorothy, said Hillary, also often told her, "Do you want to be the lead actor in your life, or a minor player who simply reacts to what others think you should say or do?" She remembers her father, on the other hand, focusing on her problems, often asking her how she would dig herself out of them—which she said always brought to mind a shovel.

DOROTHY HOWELL RODHAM had been abandoned by her own parents at age eight. Hillary and her brothers knew little of this history while they were growing up; Dorothy revealed the full story only when Hillary interviewed her for her first book, written during the White House years, *It Takes a Village*. The Rodhams were a family of secrets (first from one another, then from prying journalists), just as Bill Clinton's family was. Complicated feelings of hurt and confusion were never matters for family discussion in the Rodham house.

Dorothy's mother, Della Murray Howell, one of nine children, was only fifteen when Dorothy was born, in Chicago. Her father, Edwin Howell, a fireman, was seventeen. The young couple divorced when Dorothy was eight and her sister, Isabelle, three. Both girls were put on a train and sent without escort to live with their father's parents in Alhambra, California. In their new home, Dorothy told Hillary, they were constantly criticized, ridiculed, and severely punished by their grandmother, while their grandfather seemed totally removed from their lives. At one point, Dorothy said, her grandmother had ordered her confined to her room for a year during nonworking hours.

At fourteen, she left and became a babysitter in the home of a close-knit family who treated her well, sent her to high school, and encouraged her to read widely. Without this experience of living with a strong family, Dorothy told Hillary, she would not have known how to manage her own household or take care of her children.

After graduation from high school, Dorothy returned to Chicago because of the marriage of her mother to Max Rosenberg, four or five years her senior. He was well-to-do, owned several Chicago apartment buildings, as well as property in Florida, and was involved in the hotel business. According to members of the Rodham family, Rosenberg had persuaded Della—who could hardly read and write—to send for her children and to try to make amends for the past. It was the first time in ten years that Dorothy had been contacted by her mother, wrote Hillary. "I'd hoped so hard that my mother would love me that I had to take a chance and find out," Dorothy told her.

When Dorothy and Isabelle returned to Chicago, Rosenberg offered to send Dorothy to secretarial or vocational school—but not college, as she had expected. Della, meanwhile, intended Dorothy to be her house-maid. Dorothy refused to stay with her mother and stepfather and found a job and room of her own; Isabelle moved in with the Rosenbergs.

"My [step]grandfather, Max, for sure wanted her to have an education—I'm sure he promised her some form of education, but she was anticipating a whole lot more," said Hillary's first cousin Oscar Dowdy, Isabelle's son. "I think Dorothy felt she was deceived, but proba-bly more by her mother."

Today a rift remains in the Rodham family related to these events, and only a few facts are indisputable. The role of Rosenberg in the life of Hillary and her family has always been clouded. The first time Hillary mentioned her stepgrandfather publicly was in 1999, during her Senate campaign in New York, after his existence was disclosed by the *Forward*, a secular Jewish weekly. (She did not include the information in her first book.) "I have nothing but fond memories of Max Rosenberg," Hillary said in response to the *Forward*'s story, and recalled family get-togethers at the home of Della and Max. In *Living History* she wrote only a single sentence about him, simply acknowledging he was Jewish.

Dorothy supported herself by doing office work. When she met Hugh Rodham, she was eighteen, he was twenty-six. Hillary claimed her mother was attracted by his gruff personality, however unlikely that seems.

In the last years of his life, Hugh would tell one of his daughters-in-law that, at first sight, he thought Dorothy was absolutely beautiful. Tony Rodham was amazed when he heard what his father had said; he had never known him to openly express such affection for his wife. She also seemed strong and intelligent to Hugh, qualities that he sometimes seemed unsure of in himself.

After Dorothy and Hugh's marriage in 1942, and Hugh's discharge from the Navy in 1945, he and Dorothy moved into a one-bedroom apartment in a building owned by Rosenberg—probably rent-free, according to Oscar Dowdy and others. Isabelle and her husband also lived in the building. Hillary and Oscar played together as children.*

Hillary described Della as "weak and self-indulgent," addicted to soap operas, and "disengaged from reality." She could occasionally "be enchanting." When Hillary visited her she would be taken to amusement parks and the movies. She died in 1960, unhappy and still "a mystery," according to Hillary.

---

*Today Hillary and Oscar Dowdy Jr. do not speak to each other, ostensibly because Oscar—a real estate speculator, like his grandfather Max—failed to provide adequate financial assistance to a brother with health problems.

Dorothy Rodham never took kindly to Max Rosenberg, but Hugh Rodham apparently did, accepting his offer of an apartment, and of advice in financial matters. "They were both hustlers," said Oscar Dowdy. "They understood each other. And I think Max admired Hugh. Max realized that Hugh was trying to do something with his life, and Hugh would listen to Max and take Max's advice. . . . Over the years, Max helped Hugh with financial matters and gave him business advice and probably loaned him money."

Rosenberg agreed to back Hugh in his parking lot venture, counseling him to run for alderman and, if elected, initiate a change in the zoning laws favorable to their investment.

PERHAPS AS A RESULT of her own grim childhood without a real home, being a competent homemaker was important to Dorothy. At the cabin in Pennsylvania, she assembled a collection of stained glass. Other small collections materialized, which Hugh Rodham grudgingly—and gradually—agreed to let her purchase. She took pride in her visual sense through paint colors and choices of inexpensive department store furniture for the house on Wisner Street. Though Hugh told endless stories about his boyhood and family in Pennsylvania, Dorothy rarely spoke of early life. "I realized that there was a sadness about Dorothy," said Betsy Ebeling. "I don't know if 'beaten down' is the term—isolated sometimes. She lived through her children a lot. It was very important to her that her children be happy. I don't think she thought she could be happy, though she could laugh a lot." Some visitors to the Rodham home noted a certain fear in Dorothy—fear of being left alone.

Dorothy made her own uneasy peace with her husband ("Mr. Difficult," she called him) and, when the children were still young, had decided to stay in the marriage. Keeping the family together was more important than pursuing independent aspirations or escaping her husband's indignities, though she had to witness much harshness toward the children. "Maybe that's why she's such an accepting person," Dorothy said of Hillary. "She had to put up with *him*."

The same, obviously, could be said of Dorothy.

She did not believe in divorce except under the most dire of circumstances, as she first told Hillary in the 1980s. "It was drummed into me by Dorothy that nobody in this family gets divorced," said Nicole Boxer, who was married to Hillary's brother Tony from 1994 to 1998—when they divorced. "From Dorothy—and Tony—I heard divorce is not an option. She'd say, 'You can work it out.' She said, 'You have to talk to him on a level he can understand. Don't give up on him. *You do* *not leave the marriage.'** She was supportive of us going to counseling, which we did."

Hillary, after considering whether to divorce Governor Bill Clinton in Arkansas, wrote several years later that "children without fathers, or whose parents float in and out of their lives after divorce, are precarious little boats in the most turbulent seas." Her mother would agree. Given the hardships of her mother's childhood and Hillary's own experiences growing up, her decision to devote so much of her professional life to defending and asserting the legal rights of children seems like a natural choice.

Hillary and Bill's difficult but enduring marriage is perhaps more easily explained in the context of her childhood and the marriage of her parents, dominated by the humiliating, withholding figure of her father, whom she managed nonetheless to idolize and (later) to idealize, while rationalizing his cruelty and indifference to the pain he caused his family. "I grew up in a family that looked like it was straight out of *Father Knows Best*," Hillary said in *It Takes a Village*, and also referred to "the stability of family life that I knew growing up." Hillary's first boyfriend in college, upon visiting the Rodham house, wondered almost immediately why Dorothy had not walked out of the marriage, and how Hillary had endured her father's petulance. But Hillary somehow found a way in difficult times to either withdraw or focus on what her father was able to give her, not what was denied. Hillary knew she was loved, or so she said.

As a child, Hillary had tried every way she knew to please him and win his approval, and then spent years seething at his treatment of her. The pattern seemed to repeat itself in her marriage. Both Hugh and Bill Clinton, who came to like and respect each other, were outsized personalities whose presence inevitably dwarfed others around them. In Clinton's case, this dominance was seductive, mesmerizing, fascinating. Rodham's effect on people, especially outside his immediate family, was usually the opposite—alienating, forbidding, unpleasant. As she later did with her husband, Hillary eventually took an almost biblical view in her forgiveness and rationalization of her father's actions: "Love the sinner, hate the sin." The lesson came directly from Hugh Rodham: "He used to say all the time, 'I will always love you but I won't always like what you do,'" said Hillary (which cynics might regard as understated shorthand for how Hillary came to view her husband). "And, you know, as a child I would come up with nine-hundred hypotheses. It would always end with

---

*Boxer also sought advice from Bill Clinton, then president, who advised her to stay married and to try to work things out, especially since she and Tony had an infant son.

something like, 'Well, you mean, if I murdered somebody and was in jail and you came to see me, you would still love me?'

"And he would say: 'Absolutely! I will always love you, but I would be deeply disappointed and I would not like what you did because it would have been wrong.' "

One of Bill and Hillary's principal aides came to a less theological interpretation after years of watching (and listening to) the Clintons— and the Rodhams, who often stayed at the White House. Hillary, said the aide, devolved into "kind of the classic bitchy wife . . . not quite putting her hand on her hip and finger-wagging at him, but practically. *Nah-nah-nah*. . . . She has a derisive tone that is very similar to the way she sometimes sounds publicly—a sing-songy tone, like, 'I guess I could have stayed home and baked cookies and had cheese.' That tone only more so. . . . It's very much directed at him, his faults, his shortcomings; that he's let her down again."

The same tone, others have observed, characterized the way Dorothy Rodham sometimes responded to her husband's failings.

"Hillary hates the fact that Bill Clinton cheats on her, and that he doesn't need her as much as she wants," said the aide. "And he's weak. She's a very judgmental Methodist from the Midwest. As much as they talk about loving the sinner, they actually also despise a part of the sinner. They hate the weakness. They hate the part of the person who can't toe the puritan line."

Dorothy and Hugh were polar opposites—temperamentally, intellectually, emotionally—and their children could see that each grew increasingly exasperated with the other's evident ambivalence, antipathy, and obvious resentment. The more Hugh Rodham disparaged and heaped scorn on his wife, the more she resolved to stay out of his way and ignore his provocation. And the more she spurned him, keeping to her own projects and agenda and interposing herself as a buffer between him and the children, the more resentful he became.

As the chasm between Hillary and her father broadened during adolescence, Hillary and her mother drew closer. "Dorothy is the person who shaped Hillary more than any other, and there is no way to see Dorothy and not see how she fashioned her daughter," said Linda Bloodworth-Thomason, the Hollywood producer who is among Hillary's closest long-standing friends. But matters are hardly so simple. Hillary could, in fact, "be either her father or mother at different times, in different situations," said Betsy Ebeling. Hillary's cousin Oscar Dowdy, who regularly visited the Rodham home as a youngster, concluded more succinctly that Hillary had inherited her mother's orderly mind and her father's bluster.

· · ·

DOROTHY WANTED to name her daughter Hillary because to her it sounded exotic and unusual, and she liked the fact that "Hillary" sounded like a family name. That could be considered daring in 1947, especially in the Midwest. Hillary was born at Edgewater Hospital on Chicago's North Side. She weighed more than eight pounds. "Very mature upon birth," Dorothy liked to say. Hillary, meanwhile, insisted illogically into the White House years that she was named after Sir Edmund Hillary, the first man to climb Mount Everest. (Sir Edmund did not make his ascent until 1953, and until then he was hardly known beyond his native New Zealand, where he lived in relative obscurity as a beekeeper in Auckland.)

Dorothy was determined that her daughter would have none of the disadvantages of her own childhood nor experience hesitancy in speaking her mind or pursuing her goals. If someone tried to muzzle Hillary or get in the way, Dorothy counseled, "don't let it happen." When four-year-old Hillary was getting pushed around by a bigger girl known as a bully in the neighborhood, her mother supposedly told her, "There's no room in this house for cowards." Though Hillary was scared, Dorothy instructed her to strike back the next time. Hillary encountered the bully soon afterward, hit her in the face in front of several boys, ran back to her mother, and proclaimed, "I can play with the boys now." The story is basically true, Dorothy insisted.

Characteristically, she urged Hillary to set lofty objectives, and suggested she might become the first female Supreme Court justice. (Hillary preferred the idea of being an astronaut, and wrote to NASA at age fourteen to volunteer; she was told no women need apply.) Dorothy also wanted her children to be able to maintain their equilibrium, however great the chaos. To make her point, she showed Hillary how the bubble in a carpenter's level moved to dead center. "Imagine having this carpenter's level inside you," she said. "You try to keep that bubble in the center. Sometimes it will go way up there"—she tipped the level so the bubble drifted—"and then you have to bring it back." She straightened the level.

Hillary took easily to school from the start, bringing home almost straight As from Eugene Field Elementary School. She was also nearsighted in the extreme, and thick glasses were prescribed for her at age nine—a defining experience for a young girl growing up in the 1950s and 1960s. Hillary's spectacles, usually with red or purple frames, remained an essential part of her appearance until she got her first pair of contact lenses at age thirty-three. Sometimes she was vain enough to leave her glasses at home and needed someone to help her get around, "like a seeing-eye dog," wrote Hillary. (At a school reunion many years afterward, she asked Betsy, repeatedly, "Who is this person? Do I know him? Who's that one?" Betsy would remind her and Hillary would reply, "Oh, I never knew what they looked like.")

By her own account and those of her schoolmates, she was a tomboy in grade school. Though she could sometimes be a clumsy athlete, her father's instruction in baseball and football, and repeated practice sessions with her mother, gave her enough skill to at least stay in the game with the boys. She was also a strong swimmer. Her mother batted tennis balls at her regularly on the public courts of Park Ridge, but her game remained underdeveloped. One playmate, Jim Yrigoyen, was fond enough of her to give her his dog tags to wear briefly.

Hillary's capacity for making deep friendships, especially with girls and, later, women (though hardly to the exclusion of boys or men) was already evident in elementary school. In sixth grade, Betsy Ebeling transferred to Eugene Field and she and Hillary became the closest of friends. They took piano lessons from the same teacher (after Hugh Rodham relented and paid for an upright that sat in the living room), passed their lifesaving swimming tests together, helped each other with homework, and treated each other's homes almost as their own. During the summer, the girls and their mothers would put on white gloves and go into the city to have lunch at Marshall Field's, spend the afternoon at the Art Institute, and then return to suburbia on the train. Gloves were an essential part of feminine apparel and both Hillary and Betsy had fully stocked glove drawers in their bedroom vanities.

In elementary school, Hillary became known as a teacher's pet, because of her desire to please, her willingness to work hard, and her ability to stay alert. By eighth grade, classmate Art Curtis said, he and Hillary were the two biggest overachievers in the class. The first time they met, Art and Hillary stood outside her house on the corner and talked about Barry Goldwater. Her father's politics still held considerable sway in Hillary's schema—as they would until after she reached college. "I was immediately taken with her," Art recalled. He liked her competitiveness. While most girls talked about makeup and boys, Hillary was "absolutely political" at a stage when "politics wasn't cool."

Even in adolescence, her self-confidence was evident. Hillary was definitely not a worker bee; she was disposed to running things, whether it was in her Girl Scout troop or the neighborhood carnival. Her assemblage of merit badges was formidable, and she looked forward to wearing her uniform to school on the days when her Scout troop met. But the combination of being teacher's pet, self-assurance, and the occasional inability to recognize classmates because she wasn't wearing glasses led some students to regard her as conceited. She was aware of this view of her. Few assertions could be as hurtful, but she was never known to complain.

By the time she reached Maine East High School, John F. Kennedy was president, the population of the Chicago suburbs was bulging from the baby boom, and *American Bandstand* was on TV. Though some students at Maine East smoked and occasionally drank, Hillary and Betsy and their crowd were not among them. Both girls moved in the more popular circles of the school and were generally well liked. Hillary seemed to be involved in almost every extracurricular activity featured in the Maine East yearbook: student government, school newspaper, cultural values committee, the Brotherhood Society, prom committee, member of the *It's Academic* quiz show team that competed on local television. She also became one of the school's eleven finalists for a National Merit Scholarship. She wanted to be a doctor, an ambition she retained through her early Wellesley semesters, when she recognized that her discomfort at the sight of blood would make such a career impossible.

By tenth grade, Hillary had realized she was by no means the smartest member of her class, and that to compete at the top level of academic achievement she would have to work harder than others. She was an honor roll student by force of will, intense preparation, and dutiful study. Even with such extraordinary effort, her grade point average was too low to be among the top ten students in her class. But the term "well-rounded," an important accolade of the era, understated her achievement. In classroom debates, her prodigious memory and preparation made her formidable. Her competitive sense was highly developed, to say the least, both on the athletic field and in student government. She rewrote the student assembly constitution and, in eleventh grade, became class vice president. In her senior year of high school, she ran for what she called "the presidency." In a letter to the youth minister of her church, she wrote that her opponent's campaign manager had begun "slinging mud" at her, but that "we did not retaliate. We took the high road and talked about motherhood and apple pie." She was overwhelmingly defeated on the first ballot. She now understood how rough student politics could be. In another letter, she noted that she had run "against several boys and lost, which did not surprise me but still hurt, especially because one of my opponents told me I was 'really stupid if I thought a girl could be elected president.'" One of her heroes was Margaret Chase Smith, then a senator from Maine, the first woman to be elected to both houses of Congress and the first woman to be placed in nomination for president by a major party (the Republicans).

Because of overcrowding at all-white Maine East, Hillary and her classmates from Park Ridge were transferred in their senior year to

Maine South, a racially mixed and ethnically diverse school. Until then, their school lives had been relatively untouched by urban reality. Hillary and other students from her neighborhood had never had a black teacher or minister or close black friends. As Betsy Ebeling said, "We were ignorant . . . until we went into the city and saw that people did not live in houses like ours." Betsy's mother, who had grown up on Lakeshore Drive, told her that she had never seen a Negro shopping in Marshall Field's until after World War II.

In 1961, unbeknownst to Hillary's parents, Betsy's grandfather, who described his politics as "progressive," took her and Hillary to hear Dr. Martin Luther King Jr. speak at the Chicago Sunday Evening Club. King talked about racial segregation in the North as well as the South. It was the first time Hillary, then fourteen, grasped the notion of Negro children being the country's poorest and most vulnerable.

If there is a single defining thread of Hillary's political, religious, and social development, it is her belief and determination, from her teenage years onward, that the tragedy of race in America must be made right. What in part first attracted her to Bill Clinton was her perception that he was an unusual, enlightened Southerner who wanted to go into politics and help right the country's greatest wrong. And even more than her husband, Hillary formed many of her closest friendships with blacks; her mentor as a professional was a black woman, Marian Wright Edelman, founder of the Children's Defense Fund, for whom she went to work as a legal advocate for neglected and impoverished children; later, in the White House, Hillary chose several African Americans as senior aides, including her chief of staff. (Hillary and her subordinates on the first lady's staff frequently referred to the president and his aides, half-jokingly, as "the white males in the West Wing.")

In Hillary's junior year in high school, she and Betsy both became Goldwater Girls, assigned by local campaign aides to check for voter registration fraud in minority neighborhoods in Chicago. Hillary's father raised no objection to his daughter knocking on doors in the slums to find out the registration status of voters whom the Goldwater campaign might be able to disqualify. Hillary's territory included the new (and later infamous) Robert Taylor Homes housing project, bulldozed into oblivion as a symbol of poverty and racism eight presidencies later. She was a privileged suburban teenager seeing, close up, how thousands of poor black people lived, and it made a transforming impression.

As Hillary's school life and expanding social concerns became sources of great personal satisfaction, her life at home—at least with her father— was deteriorating. He adamantly refused to allow her to take ballroom dancing lessons in seventh grade and eighth grade, despite the fact that most Park Ridge boys and girls of Hillary's age attended dance class every Friday night, and were encouraged to do so by their parents. Initially, her friends thought this was another example of his not wanting to spend money. But in fact money, for a change, wasn't the issue. Rather, Rodham didn't want his daughter dancing with boys, did not want his daughter in the dating game, though in Hillary's circle most of the kids had known one another since kindergarten, had traded dog tags, entertained preteen crushes on one another, and long enjoyed going to the movies together in groups on weekends.

By high school, boys seemed to have two different views about Hillary and her unusual kind of appeal. "Guys didn't think she was attractive," said one of her male classmates. "They liked girls who were 'girlish.'" Hillary was "womanish." Her ankles were thick. She had a reputation for being bossy. Though she displayed an easy humor with Betsy and some of the other girls, boys often perceived her as too earnest and aloof and, by implication, uninterested in sex. So much so that the Maine newspaper wrote "humorously" that she would become a nun, one day, with the name "Sister Frigidaire." But some boys, usually older ones, were attracted by her seeming self-possession. She did not go out on dates often, but it wasn't for lack of invitations. Partly it was because she was more interested in other pursuits, and partly because she seemed anything but confident about herself with the opposite sex.

Some of the difficulty was the way she dressed. Her face, without her glasses, was unquestionably pretty, though she had something of an overbite. And when she dressed up, it was said she had a certain tasteful look of refinement and sophistication. But she didn't dress up often, and style did not come to her naturally. Hillary was convinced that her father's penurious attitudes and his tendency to overrule her mother in decisions affecting her as a young woman forced her to dress unattractively. "He didn't want to give her money to do things that she wanted to do," said Betsy. "We were all clothes crazy and he didn't see that as a good reason for spending a lot of money or time." Betsy and others at school believed his attitude undermined Hillary's sense of femininity, making it difficult for her to feel comfortable or popular with boys.

The essential rite of passage to young adulthood in suburban America of the 1950s and 1960s was getting a driver's license. Hugh Rodham forbade it. "You don't need to drive a car, you have a bike," he insisted. Besides, Betsy, who did drive, picked Hillary up whenever they needed to get somewhere together.

Embarrassed to have to continue riding her bicycle while her classmates drove (and, in some instances, even owned) cars, Hillary took matters into her own hands. Lori Jo Hansen, a classmate, surreptitiously helped her get her driver's license. Hillary's father was incensed at first, but after some lobbying by her mother he finally agreed that she could sometimes drive his Cadillac. She turned out to be an awful driver.

As Hillary's senior prom approached, her anger and disillusionment with her father became almost uncontrollable (or as uncontrollable as Hillary could get). She and Betsy were to double-date, chaperoned by the Rodhams. Hillary was clearly embarrassed by the dress her father had permitted her to buy. "Looking at it, I think everyone else next to me will think they are overdressed, it is so modest," she wrote to Don Jones, the former youth minister of her church.

Betsy fixed Hillary up with Jim Van Schoyck, whom Ebeling had once dated back in tenth grade. Van Schoyck balked at the idea initially, saying Hillary was a bit too nerdy for him. But he agreed to call her, and took her out on a "practice date" a couple of weeks before the prom. They went for a drive and Jim stopped the car at the top of the Lutheran General Hospital's winding driveway, brought out his skateboard, and asked Hillary whether she'd ever ridden on one. She hadn't, but not wanting to say no, Hillary said she could do it. Jim handed her the skateboard and Hillary stepped on.

"[He] put her on the skateboard, and down she went," Ebeling said. "And she made it to the bottom of the hill and didn't wipe out. So, she was the date."

Hillary's next problem was her hair (which she has struggled with ever since). It was as strong-willed as she was. Betsy, who regularly had the difficult task of trying to tame her friend's mane, described it as having a mind of its own. The most famous model of the day, Suzy Parker, fashioned her hair with a curl over her forehead, but Hillary could not achieve that effect no matter how hard she tried. The afternoon of the senior prom proved no exception. Hillary, who almost never paid attention to (or had the money for) brand-name goods, had a favorite mock tortoiseshell Revlon comb. She grabbed it angrily from Ebeling and cracked it. This was as riled as Betsy had ever seen her, and she was near tears. Finally, her mother came into Hillary's room, pulled her daughter's hair back, and put a blue bow in it and the three agreed it looked wonderful.

The prom crisis reflected Hillary's developing perfectionism, which revealed itself in many different ways. If she couldn't get something right, she felt surprisingly exposed and vulnerable. If men were involved, she could be especially sensitive to even implied criticism. Her face would become flushed or she would get angry and turn away. She didn't like to be questioned, leading one of her friends to observe, perhaps too simply, "She didn't like not to have the upper hand with men." It reminded her of the way her father treated her, said the friend. Gradually, the conflicts over money and boys, and Hillary's chagrin at her father's prevailing demeanor and attitudes, led to an almost complete breakdown of their relationship. The rupture carried over to her college years and to matters far removed from his refusal to buy (or allow her to buy) the clothes she thought she needed. She and her father could hardly agree on the most elemental of questions, not to mention political ones, and his tone with her became increasingly intolerant.

After Hillary's father died in 1993, she wrote that during this period she hardly knew what to say to him, and often argued with him over issues of the day, like feminism, the war in Vietnam, or the counterculture. "I also understood that even when he erupted at me, he admired my independence and accomplishments and loved me with all his heart."

IN 1961, while Hillary was in tenth grade and the conflict with her father became more tense, there arrived in a red Chevy Impala convertible a dashing, transforming figure who, until she met Bill Clinton, would become the most important teacher in Hillary's life. He was a Methodist youth minister, the Reverend Don Jones, twenty-six, who had completed four years in the Navy and had just graduated from the Drew University seminary in New Jersey. Hillary had never met anyone like him. Jones became something between a father figure, adored brother, and knight-errant. He had an ally in Dorothy Rodham, who regarded him as a kindred sprit.

Lissa Muscatine, Hillary's chief White House speechwriter, who helped her work on *Living History*, once said of Hillary: "She's a prude, she's hokey, she's a fifties person who grew up Methodist in the Chicago suburbs." It wasn't quite as simple as that.

Hillary had been confirmed at the First United Methodist Church of Park Ridge in the sixth grade. (Hugh Rodham's parents claimed that John Wesley himself had converted members of the Rodham family to Methodism in the coal-mining district near Newcastle in the north of England.) Dorothy taught Sunday school at United Methodist. Hillary attended Bible classes and was a member of the Altar Guild. "[My family] talked with God, walked with God, ate, studied and argued with God," Hillary said.

But until Jones showed up, Hillary's sense of politics and her sense of religion existed on two different planes. Now they began to meld into one as he promoted what he called the "University of Life" two evenings a week at the church. Jones brought a message of "faith in action," based on the teachings of Wesley and twentieth-century theologians, including

Reinhold Niebuhr and Dietrich Bonhoeffer, who believed that the Christian's role was essentially a moral one: balancing human nature, in all its splendor and baseness, with a passion for justice and social reform. He assigned Hillary and other members of the Methodist Youth Fellowship in Park Ridge readings from T. S. Eliot and E. E. Cummings; showed them copies of Picasso's paintings, which he sometimes explained in theological and geopolitical terms; discussed the significance of Dostoyevsky's Grand Inquisitor in *The Brothers Karamazov*; played "A Hard Rain's a-Gonna Fall" from Bob Dylan's new LP, and on weekends shepherded the privileged Protestant children of Park Ridge to black and Hispanic churches in Chicago as part of exchanges with their youth groups. On one visit, Jones had brought with them a big reproduction of Picasso's *Guernica,* which he set up in front of the Park Ridge teenagers and members of a Chicago teenage gang. Picasso's masterpiece portrays the horror of the Spanish Civil War in all its agony and misery. According to Jones, the ostensibly less-educated and less-sophisticated children from the city's streets were far more articulate and candid in relating to the work than those from Park Ridge.

His interpretation of the Gospels, inevitably, ran afoul of Hillary's high school history teacher, Paul Carlson (she was his favorite student), who shared Hugh Rodham's unwavering belief in the coming of the Red Menace. In Hillary's class, Carlson played excerpts of Douglas MacArthur's farewell speech to the Congress ("Old soldiers never die . . .") and introduced students to refugees from communism who told of the horrors of the Soviet system. Carlson took it upon himself to warn the parishioners of United Methodist that the minds of their children were being poisoned by the new youth minister in the red Chevy convertible.

Jones had taken up his assignment in Park Ridge in 1961, during the summer of the Freedom Rides in Mississippi and elsewhere in the Deep South. That fall, when Martin Luther King Jr. again came to preach in Chicago, Jones took Hillary and other members of his youth group to Orchestra Hall to hear him.

Some parents had refused to let their children go, believing that King was a "rabble-rouser," a view held by Hugh Rodham. Dorothy had granted Hillary her permission. After the program Jones took his awed students backstage to meet Dr. King. King's sermon, "Sleeping Through the Revolution," had woven the message of God with the politics of conscience: "Vanity asks the question Is it Popular? Conscience asks the question Is it Right?" He also cited Jesus' parable about the man condemned to hell because he ignored his fellows in need.

Jones became not only the most important teacher in young Hillary's life, but also a counselor over the decades whose ministrations would show her ways to cope with adversity, and to "give service of herself" at the most difficult moments: to "salve [her] troubled soul" through the doing of good works. At almost every juncture of pain or humiliation for the rest of her life, she would return—in her fashion—to this lesson. For more than twenty years she would maintain a fascinating correspondence with Jones in which they discussed the requirements of faith and the vagaries of human nature. During the Clintons' White House years, Jones and his wife were frequent visitors there.

Aside from her family, Hillary's Methodism is perhaps the most important foundation of her character. As one of her aides said during the winter's night of the Lewinsky epoch, "Hillary's faith is *the link*. . . . It explains the missionary zeal with which she attacks her issues and goes after them, and why she's done it for thirty years. And, it also explains the really extraordinary self-discipline and focus and ability to rely on her spirituality to get through all this. . . . She's a woman of tremendous faith. Again, not advertised. She's not one of those people who's out there doing the holy roller stuff. But that's how she gets through it: some people go to shrinks, she does it by being a Methodist."

Other members of the White House staff believed she used her religiosity as a cover for her faults. Some saw it as a mask in her relationship with her husband. "She elevates her staying with [Bill] to a moral level of biblical proportion," said a presidential deputy. "I am stronger than he is. I am better than he is. Therefore, I can stay with him because it's my biblical duty to love the sinner, and to help to try to overcome his defects of character. His sins are of weakness not of malice."

After two years, Paul Carlson convinced the congregation of United Methodist that Don Jones's teachings were too "freethinking," and he was forced out. "We were fighting for [Hillary's] soul and her mind," Jones was to say years later.

Before he left, Jones gave Hillary a copy of J. D. Salinger's *The Catcher in the Rye* to read. She did not like it. Holden Caulfield reminded her too much of her brother Hughie. Salinger's coming-of-age novel seemed to stir up all kinds of difficult questions and feelings about family and family traits, including her own tendency toward aloofness and detachment. Over the decades some of Hillary's greatest admirers came to question whether she genuinely liked people, at least in the aggregate, or whether she merely preferred the company of a few and embraced the multitudes as part of her sense of Christian responsibility and political commitment.

Shortly after Jones left Park Ridge, Hillary seemed to raise the question herself, in a letter: "Can you be a misanthrope and still love or enjoy some individuals?" she wondered. She added, "How about a *compassionate* misanthrope?"

· · ·

By the time seventeen-year-old Hillary Rodham left Park Ridge, Illinois, for Wellesley College, almost all the essential elements—and contradictions—of her adult character could be glimpsed: the keen intelligence and ability to stretch it, the ambition and anger, the idealism and acceptance of humiliation, the messianism and sense of entitlement, the attraction to charismatic men and indifference to conventional feminine fashion, the seriousness of purpose and quickness to judgment, the puritan sensibility and surprising vulnerability, the chronic impatience and aversion to personal confrontation, the insistence on financial independence and belief in public service, the tenacious attempts at absolute control and, perhaps above all, the balm, beacon, and refuge of religion.

2

A Young Woman on Her Own

Nineteen sixty-eight was a watershed year for the country, and for my own personal and political evolution.

—*Living History*

ILLARY DIANE RODHAM arrived at Wellesley College in the fall of 1965 a Barry Goldwater conservative, her well-worn copy of his famous book *The Conscience of a Conservative* in her suitcase. A relatively sheltered, suburban Midwest teenager, she was suddenly in the company of formidable young women who had gone to private boarding schools, summered in Europe, spoke foreign languages with ease, and possessed sophistication of a sort that had long defined the Wellesley aura. That she had been in the top 5 percent of her class at Maine South meant little. Hillary was no longer considered brighter than most of her classmates. In fact, admission to Wellesley, even more than the other Seven Sisters colleges in the Northeast, was predicated on the assumption that, upon matriculation, you were demonstrably brilliant. Most of her fellow students had been in the top 1 or 2 percent of their high school graduating class. In 1965, Harvard, Yale, Columbia, Brown, and the other traditional Ivy League universities were still all-male bastions. Thus Wellesley had its pick of almost any girl in the country who aspired to the best possible education (and could afford it or win a scholarship).

In this rarefied environment, Hillary felt intimidated and lonely at the start, a foreigner in a strange place she had seen only in pictures. Her decision to go east to a women's college had been inspired by a high school teacher who had attended Wellesley; Hillary gave it preference over the other Seven Sisters schools partly on the basis of photographs of the campus: bucolic acres of rolling green, wooded horse trails, and crystal-clear ponds. Pictures of Wellesley's Lake Waban reminded her of Lake Winola, where she had summered in the Poconos. To this postcard scene, Hillary brought her suitcases packed full with Peter Pan blouses, box-pleat skirts, penny loafers, and knee socks. It became obvious soon after her parents had left her on the campus and had headed back home (her mother crying much of the way) that she had won admission to, and chosen to attend, a school in which more glamorous and accomplished young women—debutantes, many of them—were on the fast track. If she were to compete, it would have to be on her own terms. In this, she would be helped immensely by the country's changing mood, culture, politics, and philosophies of gender during her undergraduate years. There would be no need, as it turned out, for the girl with Coke-bottle glasses and complicated political notions to hold to the old model of a Seven Sisters perfectly mannered woman.

Robert Reich, who would become President Bill Clinton's secretary of labor, met Hillary when she was a Wellesley freshman wearing bell-bottoms, board-straight blond hair, and no makeup. "She and I were self-styled student 'reformers' then," said Reich, "years before the radicals took over administration buildings and shut down the campuses. We marched for civil rights and demanded the admission of more black students to our schools. Even then we talked of bringing the nation together. We were naive about how much we could accomplish."

In fact, the last thing on Hillary's mind at Wellesley seemed to be adherence to the old paradigms, either political or gender-based.

Hillary's mother had taught her that, above all else, she could do anything, aspire to anything, that there was no reason for a daughter to aim for less than her brothers. Hillary would later describe herself as a "transitional figure" in regard to the women's movement, caught between two epochs—pre-feminist and post-feminist—and the demands and opportunities of each. However, as one less-conflicted Wellesley graduate observed, Hillary might not have considered or understood another possibility: that "it is *not* hard to have it all; but it's hard to have it both ways."

Hillary's time at Wellesley was not made easier by whatever tendency toward depression she had either inherited or developed—a tendency that surfaced again in the White House. Periodically at Wellesley she fell into debilitating, self-doubting funks. During the early weeks of her freshman semester, she was so deflated that she called home and confessed failure and an inability to cope. She had never been away from home—even for a weekend—on her own before. She missed the comfortable precincts of Park Ridge, and insisted she was incapable of adjusting to the Wellesley milieu. Whatever her anger at her father, she briefly seemed to miss him. He said she could come back to Illinois, but

Dorothy said she didn't want her daughter to be a quitter. Her mother prevailed.

After Hillary decided to stay at Wellesley, she seemed to regain some of her old confidence and began making friends who would figure in the rest of her life. But even as she steadied her footing, there were stumbles and persistent signs of melancholy. In the winter of 1967, her junior year, she again experienced what she described in a letter as her recurring "February depression." Despite earning As, dating a Harvard man regarded as a good catch, and working off-campus with disadvantaged children (including a seven-year-old Negro girl she tutored and had formed a close bond with), she sometimes overslept, nodded off in her classes, and became concerned that her teachers regarded her as a washout. "Why am I so afraid?" she wrote to her high school friend John Peavoy. "Or why am I not afraid? Am I really not unique after all? Will I have a clichéd life? Is life merely absurd?" (Hillary now sounded like a character in *The Catcher in the Rye*.) She now called herself an "agnostic intellectual liberal" and an "emotional conservative." During Christmas break that year, she wrote to Peavoy again, expressing how alienated she felt from "the entire unreality of middle-class America," in which she included her family, who, because of her difficult first semester, had insisted she cancel plans to meet Peavoy in New York City over the Christmas holiday. The following winter break, she told her parents nothing of her holiday plans and headed for Dartmouth College and a round of parties where she stayed overnight after meeting a young man.

The most important man in her life during the Wellesley years, despite the distance between them, was Don Jones. By mail, he became her counselor, correspondent, confessor, partner in Socratic debate, and spiritual adviser. When depression struck, she turned to him, as she would for the next three decades, including the year of her husband's impeachment. He focused her on theologian Paul Tillich's sermon "You Are Accepted," in which he says that sin and grace coexist. "Grace strikes us when we are in great pain and restlessness," said Tillich. "It happens; or it does not happen." Hillary was convinced there would be grace in her life and meanwhile she would just carry on.

For the rest of her life, spiritual and quasi-spiritual axioms (some imbued with New Age jargon, others profound) would serve as soothing balms in painful times, and provide answers to questions and situations that seemed otherwise confounding. These comforting postulations would also be used by Hillary to justify, often publicly, her or her husband's less palatable actions or aspects of character.

. . .

WHEN HILLARY ENROLLED at Wellesley, the campus was edging toward great changes, pushed by the women's movement and pulled by the politics of the 1960s. Betty Friedan's *The Feminine Mystique* had been published in 1963. Its thesis, based largely on the experience of Friedan's fellow alumnae from the Smith College class of 1942, held that women were victims of a pervasive system of delusions and false values that urged them to find their fulfillment and identity vicariously, through their husbands and children. More radical feminists preached open hostility toward males. Hillary was in her freshman year when Friedan cofounded the National Organization for Women (NOW), dedicated to achieving equality of opportunity for women.

Until the mid-1960s, a visitor to the Wellesley campus might have concluded that the goal of a Wellesley woman was to find the brightest Harvard or Yale graduate, marry him and hitch her wagon to his politics or stardom, raise bright children, and become the person who could, at dinner parties, jump in to cleverly point out similarities between the opposing positions of guests fighting at the table. (The description is borrowed from an alumna of that period.) The Latin motto of the college was *non Ministrari sed Ministrare*, a New Testament exhortation to minister service, not receive it; invariably, it was interpreted by generations of Wellesley women as "not to be ministers but to be ministers' wives."

The most important aspect of Wellesley for Hillary and for thousands of others who had gone there before her was that it was an all-women's school. ("You don't have the thing where women don't put their hands up because someone might not take you out because you know the answer and they don't," noted a fellow graduate.) In *Living History*, Hillary agreed with that assessment and said that "psychic space" was created without men on campus. Throughout her four years there, she lived in Stone-Davis, an imposing mock-gothic pile that served both as a dormitory and a hub of sisterly conversation, activity, and purpose. The nexus of Stone-Davis was its glass-enclosed dining hall, where a community of women convened, socialized, and formed friendships. Risk-taking was easier in an all-female environment.

Though Hillary was the beneficiary of the "women's liberation" movement (as it was then known), she was hardly one of its pioneers or even a firebrand of its second wave. By the time of her graduation, she still reflected the traditions of her upbringing, but also had been hugely influenced by the movement's accomplishments, so visible on the two coasts of America especially. Moreover, what was happening in America in regard to women—literally liberating them in a fundamental sense— was consistent with her mother's ambitious aspirations for her daughter. Who better than Hillary Rodham to be the exemplar of Wellesley's transition? She could toe the line with one foot and drag the institution forward with the other.

Aspects of Wellesley seemed stultified for the age: incoming freshmen were forced to wear beanies; room assignments were made on the basis of race and religion—not just Jewish students with Jewish students, but Episcopalians with Episcopalians, and Catholics with Catholics. Wellesley wasn't nearly as politically engaged as many other schools in the era. "There was a teacher who used to rage at the class because they were so timid," recalled a graduate of only a few years before. "It was just a group of young women who didn't want to take a stand on anything, including, Is it a major chord or a minor chord?"

Hillary appeared to come late to embrace real solidarity with women as a class. Other women who encountered her over the next two decades, including some of her close friends, felt she could be oblivious to the obstacles impeding her gender, because her own experience was so singular. "She was neither intimidated nor inhibited by any barrier or stereotype—so much so that any weakness she might have is a lack of empathy for others, for whom those barriers have been more difficult. Hillary barged through with such force that she didn't even seem to take note," said Betsey Wright, one of the women with whom she was closest from the time of her law school graduation through her husband's governorship.

The evolution of Hillary's politics during her years at Wellesley—1965 to 1969—was characteristic of millions of her generation, especially Midwesterners from conservative families who went off to college in the East and found themselves moving toward (and sometimes beyond) liberalism as they grappled with the three great issues of the day: civil rights, the war in Vietnam, and the role of women. Some were radicalized (incongruously, many of the leaders of the Weathermen, for instance, were Midwesterners), but Hillary's progression was predictably even-keeled.

No doubt Hillary was a product of her time, an era in which many young people chose to protest violently, and others "turned on, tuned in, and dropped out," as Timothy Leary had put it. But she always followed a sensible course. Hillary's methodology and goals in terms of politics were reform, not radical change. A faculty adviser said, "I would argue that everything that Hillary has done in her adult life . . . strikes me as a classic Wellesley kind of graduate concern: families, children, and social reform."

Greg Craig, who knew Hillary well during her law school years and would become White House counsel to Bill Clinton a generation later, said, on the basis of his conversations with her, "It seemed that the

1960s had passed relatively by" at Wellesley. Hundreds upon hundreds of students from Harvard, Yale, Vassar, and Columbia mobilized and went south to participate in the Freedom Rides and voting drives of the so-called Mississippi Summer. But Wellesley's women were much more removed, and Craig concluded that, far from committing herself to such direct activism, "Hillary was in learning mode then and listening mode." He discerned little of the hardness that characterized so many later portraits of her. "I had no sense of the toughness, of the intensity. I didn't see it, I really didn't. And I was, I think, close enough to her to have seen it."

Detachment from politics was not the Wellesley way. Polite participation was. During Hillary's freshman year, she eased into the leadership of the Wellesley Young Republicans club, and by the end of the second semester was elected its president. Meanwhile she had begun questioning her party's policies on civil rights and the war in Vietnam. Barry Goldwater had been defeated for president in her last year of high school. Now she found herself moving toward the distinctly liberal (and minority wing) of the party. Her alienation from her father seemed exacerbated in their few discussions and letters, as he became typically dismissive and antagonistic to her increasingly feminist, egalitarian, and antiwar assertions. She had also begun reading—and citing—the *New York Times*, much to his consternation.

As a high school graduation present, Hillary's church in Park Ridge had given each of its senior class members a subscription to *motive* magazine, the official publication of the Methodist Student Movement. Its views were far different from her customary sources of information. The magazine echoed the call of John Wesley and his disciples to faith-rooted social activism, but also contained provocative articles by New Left theoreticians including Carl Oglesby, who later became head of the radical Students for a Democratic Society. Meanwhile, her ideas, old and new, were subjected to unfamiliar scrutiny as she came under the influence of professors whose outlooks were much less parochial than those of her teachers in Park Ridge, whether left or right, conservative or liberal. After a while, she would write later, her views were not Republican ones.

Peter Edelman, who knew Hillary before she met his wife-to-be, Marian Wright Edelman, thought Hillary's politics "reflected what you would expect in a certain kind of young person at the time . . . sort of on the liberal side. She was opposed to the war in Vietnam and she had a very instinctive interest in children's issues that had already manifested itself" before she graduated from Wellesley. She had caused a slight stir on the campus when she brought a black classmate—one of only ten at the college—with her to church services in town, a week after classes began during her freshman year. "I was testing me as much as I was testing the church," Hillary wrote to Don Jones. She appeared interested in her own motives, which was not something she often expressed curiosity about. For a person so focused on religion and spiritual notions, Hillary seemed to many acquaintances to be surprisingly devoid of introspective instinct, and when things went wrong, she habitually looked elsewhere for the reasons. It was only after she became a candidate for the Senate that she meaningfully acknowledged personal responsibility for the failure to reform health care during the Clinton presidency. She told Jones that, had she seen someone else make the same gesture a year earlier of taking a black classmate to an all-white church, she might have thought, "Look how liberal that girl is trying to be going to church with a Negro."

Once she had recovered her emotional equilibrium at Wellesley, fellow students, even those uncomfortable with her politics, were drawn to Hillary's natural warmth, humor, and obvious ability to get the job done. There was something both generous and gracious about her character that made people like being around her. She possessed a seemingly unselfish ability to praise others, recognize their personal concerns, remember meaningful details about their lives. These elements figured in the willingness of many of Wellesley's overprivileged young women to see Hillary as their leader, instead of other students whose prep school backgrounds they shared.

She was also notably direct in almost everything she did. This could be either an asset or intimidating. Her undisguised ambition for recognition and praise also figured in the equation, and she cultivated relationships unabashedly with well-connected students, influential members of the faculty, and administrators. "She already knew the value of networking, of starting a Rolodex, even back then," a Wellesley contemporary observed, not too admiringly. "While she was respected across the board, and she had her circle of friends, I would not say she was popular." (Others would dispute the latter assertion.) Some found her "not always easy to deal with if you were disagreeing with her," noted Wellesley's president at the time, Ruth Adams. "She could be very insistent." She also could be impatient and aloof. Yet she became a figure of almost unique stature on the campus: a leader, socially concerned, personable, articulate, hardworking, hard-studying, fun-loving. But she revealed little of her interior life to those around her. As in the White House years and beyond, some spoke of her in almost reverential fashion. Hillary seemed aware of this mystique, but even then she was never known to address it in discussion with others. She *carried* the notion as part of herself.

Hillary continued to follow the student leader path she had trod at Maine East and South. At a time when many of her contemporaries at

other colleges were directly challenging the authority of college administrators and of government structures, she carefully worked within the
system, joining peaceful marches for civil rights and against the Vietnam
War in Cambridge, New Haven, and New York. Rather than become a
leader in larger protest movements off the campus and work to fuse her
student constituency with them, she kept matters self-contained. She
steered the antiwar movement at Wellesley—and student rage after the
assassination of Martin Luther King in 1968—away from the kind of
confrontation with civil authorities and school administrators that convulsed many other campuses.

Still, Hillary and the members of her class were responsible for
greater changes at Wellesley than any in its history. When her class
arrived in the fall of 1965, men were not allowed in Wellesley's dorms
(except on Sundays), and students could not drive cars on campus or
wear jeans or slacks in the dining hall or on trips into town. By the time
she was chosen commencement speaker of 1969, the student body had
become politicized as never before; Black Studies was added to the curriculum and, under pressure from the student government, the college
had agreed to increase the number of black students and faculty members. The following fall, 104 blacks would be accepted and 57 would
enroll. At Hillary's insistence, a summer Upward Bound program for
inner-city children was initiated on campus, antiwar activities were conducted in college facilities, the skirt rule had been rescinded, grades were
given on a pass-fail basis, parietal rules were a thing of the past, interdis-
ciplinary majors were permitted for the first time. One of Hillary's
strengths as a leader, still evident today, was her willingness to participate
in the drudgery of government rather than simply direct policy from
Olympian heights. She attended committee meetings, became involved
in the minutiae (of finding a better system for the return of library books,
for instance), and studied every aspect of the Wellesley curriculum in
developing a successful plan to reduce the number of required courses.

Her political transformation was incremental. She spent the summer
of 1966 at a beach cottage on the Lake Michigan shore, babysitting and
working as a researcher for an ex-Wellesley professor who was editing
portions of a book about the war in Vietnam, *The Realities of Vietnam: A
Ripon Society Appraisal.* The Ripon Society was a liberal Republican movement, founded in 1964, which took its name from Ripon, Wisconsin, the
birthplace of the Republican Party; its statement of purpose declared that
the party's future would be found "not in extremism, but in moderation,"
a play on Barry Goldwater's declaration that "extremism in the defense of
liberty is no vice . . . moderation in the pursuit of justice is no virtue."
The professor for whom Hillary worked had been asked to leave Welles-

ley, ostensibly because of his antiwar activism but perhaps because he was an unusually nonconformist figure on the campus. That summer, he gave Hillary books to read by Marshall McLuhan and Walter J. Ong, both out-of-the-mainstream Catholics and revolutionary theorists in the field of media. The fact that they came from a Jesuitical tradition, with similarities to Hillary's Wesleyan orientation, appealed to her.

By summer's end, her opposition to the war in Vietnam was adamant—though the antiwar movement was still in its infancy—and she now identified herself as a Rockefeller Republican, at the very left of the party, some of whose younger adherents gravitated to the Ripon Society.

Her political interests were more expansive than the usual partisan agenda of either party, and reflected her idealism at the time. One day that summer, walking on the beachfront, she came upon hundreds of dead fish that had washed up on the polluted Lake Michigan shore. She buried them beneath the sand. That evening she wrote to her boyfriend, Geoff Shields: "It is really a shame that they are taking the beauty out of the beach and the fun out of the swimming. If I ever have any sort of influence I'm going to use a majority of it for human conservation and the rest for nature."

HILLARY'S EXPLORATION during her Wellesley years was focused just as intensely on men as it was on politics. She liked them. Geoff Shields, who had grown up in a much wealthier Chicago suburb, Lake Forest, on the North Shore, twenty minutes and light-years away from Park Ridge, was her first serious boyfriend (or, as Wellesley women were taught to say, beau). In high school, Hillary and members of her circle had usually socialized in groups of unpaired girls and boys who hung out together at the luncheonette on Main Street after school and went to the movies on weekends. Couples who "went steady" or were considered "in love" were exceptional, and tended to be sexually inexperienced, according to Betsy Ebeling. If Hillary had engaged even in heavy necking before she got to Wellesley, no one said so.

The rituals of a century of Ivy League life were very much part of the Wellesley experience: train rides to New Haven and Manhattan; football on weekends; concerts and museum exhibitions, and walks on the Common in Boston. Hillary and her classmates relied largely on being formally introduced to undergraduate men, usually from the New England Ivy schools, during weekend mixers that might lead to more serious dating. On Friday and Saturday nights, Route 9 out of Boston was jammed with traffic to Wellesley, Smith, and Mount Holyoke as young women hurried back to their dorms to beat 1 A.M. curfews. Men were allowed in the women's dorm rooms only on Sundays at Wellesley, from 2 to 5:30 P.M., with the door open. The "two feet rule" was in effect, or so legend had it: two feet out of four had to be on the floor throughout visits from men. Guests had to check in at the reception desk in the lobby of the women's dorm and were identified by bells and announcements. Women were "visitors." Men were "callers."

In her freshman year, Hillary met Shields on a double date at a Harvard party. Many years later he said he thought "she was attractive, interesting to talk to, and she was a good dancer." Shields, who was planning on becoming a lawyer (and did), was good-looking, interesting, politically aware, a jock—he had been an all-state football star—and more worldly than she. Her letters to him at Harvard reveal her to be soft, thoughtful, alive with the possibilities of youth, dreamy, romantic, passionate.

"The best place to start any adventure is in a daffodil field when the sun has come up. Did you ever see the field—the one behind the formal gardens? We were going to visit after canoeing but we never got there. . . ." She had gone back Sunday, "to sit in a congregation of yellow and white," and found herself mesmerized by the "attentive" flowers, their petals drawn to the sun and swaying in unison "to the preaching of the wind." She imagined the daffodil field to be a cathedral, its altar delineated by a roadway where a "choir" of flowers sang amen. "After the service, I walked out through the daffodil field" to the lake, just to watch, though lakes—essentially motionless—ordinarily did not interest her "as does the ocean or a fire. . . . A fire is always changing and the ocean—I will not even attempt to articulate how I feel about it."

Throughout her years as a public person there has been sexual innuendo about Hillary, implying that somewhere along her way—in the rumor it is usually at Wellesley—she experimented with lesbianism. (One wonders if a malleable male politician, say Bill Clinton, a former overweight band boy, would be accused of having "experimented" with being gay at Georgetown University, in the same manner as "tough, inflexible" Hillary at Wellesley.) When not whispered sotto voce, such innuendo about her reached its most incendiary and unsupportable in 2005 with Edward Klein's supposed biography, *The Truth About Hillary*, an ideological screed, which contains barely smidgens—and no context—about what its title promises. Little could be more contradictory to what is known about Hillary's actual character and history—and her manner, with, respectively, men and women who are her friends—than the notion of her as a lesbian. Her most deeply held personal values are conservative, and no letters to a woman such as she wrote to Geoff

Shields have come to light. No woman has come forward to claim a sexual relationship with Hillary. Her (and her husband's, for that matter) belief in, and commitment to, gay rights, and approval of gay lifestyles as a matter of individual choice, are hardly an indication of sexual preference. At Wellesley, her experimentation *is* known to have been with men. And to this day, she is playful, even flirtatious in an innocent manner with men she likes, and less likely to physically embrace female friends or be "touchy" with them or look deeply into their eyes in conversation, as she does with men.

Until she arrived on the Wellesley campus, men her age hadn't appeared all that important to her, unless it was in some unstated, unrequited longing, which Betsy Ebeling indicates was a part of Hillary's situation—rather typical for a suburban teenage girl of the period who was hardly regarded as among the prettiest or most popular in high school, not to mention one with a fearsome father.

Hillary and Shields dated for almost three years and remained friends afterward. Theirs was a full relationship—intellectual, social, sexual. They spent time together with each other's families during summers. It seems apparent from her correspondence with Shields that for a part of their time together Hillary thought herself in love. As with the other men she is known to have been romantically or sexually involved with before Bill Clinton, Hillary has never discussed publicly or written about her relationship with Shields, which, according to him, "was healthy," and "normal in every respect."

They saw each other almost every weekend of Hillary's freshman and sophomore years and into her junior year. Their relationship seemed to be moving toward a platonic friendship in the summer of 1968 when she met a dashing Georgetown University undergraduate, David Rupert, in Washington, D.C., whom she dated for the next three years—including a brief period during which she was also seeing Bill Clinton at Yale Law School. Rupert, who had attended a liberal Catholic prep school, the Christian Brothers Academy in Syracuse, became a conscientious objector after his graduation from Georgetown and performed his alternative government service in Vermont, where Hillary often visited him on weekends. Following a friend's wedding in the Midwest, she introduced Rupert—as she had Shields—to her parents as "my boyfriend" during a detour to Park Ridge on the way back to Wellesley.

Hillary and Rupert had "an intense love affair," according to Nancy "Peach" Pietrafesa, who shared a weekend house with them. "Hillary was always attracted to arrogant, sneering, hard-to-please men, like her father," she believed, and judged Rupert an example. Pietrafesa described

Hillary during the Wellesley years as "a kick: fun-loving, full of mischief, spunky, good-natured . . . a wonderfully warm and thoughtful friend," even though the two women later had a falling-out. (Her husband was fired from Bill Clinton's gubernatorial staff.)

Both Rupert and Shields indicated that Hillary had a physically passionate side, and Rupert later volunteered that "we always used birth control." Hillary came of age at a time in America when the sexuality of women, especially young women, was undergoing a profound change, in large measure because of the easy availability of "the Pill."

Geoff Shields, from the beginning of his romance with Hillary, was aware both of Hillary's desire for "responsible" sexual exploration and her extraordinary seriousness of purpose, discipline, and focus. That she was "personally very conservative" was obvious from the beginning of their relationship, which flowered through the height of late 1960s abandonment. (The *Sgt. Pepper* album, the Beatles' ode to psychedelic ecstasy, was released in the spring of 1967; the ensuing summer became known in the counterculture as the Summer of Love.) Shields never knew her to smoke marijuana (though the smell of pot wafted through the Stone-Davis hallways), never saw her drink to excess, and she was hardly promiscuous. Yet she was definitely not one of those Wellesley women who were considered "grinds." She enjoyed parties; dancing to Elvis, the Beatles, and the Supremes; cheering for the Harvard football squad; playing catch with a Frisbee or football; being on the water in a boat or a canoe and diving over the edge to swim. Hillary and Shields took frequent hiking trips to Cape Cod and Vermont. They and their friends engaged in long hours of political discussion. One of Geoff's roommates was black and active in civil rights campaigns; Hillary's solidarity was evident and enthusiastic, even excessively expressed. Being able to discuss intimately with a black friend the realities of black life and struggle in America represented "for both Hillary and I . . . a time of awakening," said Shields. When she expressed her views—and they tended to be firmly held—they were well argued and informed, whatever the issue: dorm rules, the feminist revolution, campus dress codes, the war in Vietnam, student power, racism. The time she seemed to light up the most was when there was a sharp, heated debate about the issues. She showed little interest in more abstract or philosophic concerns or even literature. One exception made an impression on Shields: a discussion about whether there was an absolute or only a relative morality. "She was very much into debating the basis of moral decisions," and more than a few Wellesley women and Ivy League men believed she had a self-righteous streak, though it was hardly the overwhelming aspect of her character.

Her correspondence with Shields, particularly, is full of desire for exploration—cultural, personal, professional, political, social. With Reverend Jones, it was more philosophical and reportorial.

When she sometimes found herself "adopting a kind of party mode," as she called it in a letter to Jones, she claimed herself capable of getting "outrageous . . . as outrageous as a moral Methodist can get." She defined herself at the time as "a progressive, an ethical Christian and a political activist."

One of Jones's letters to Hillary at Wellesley alluded to Edmund Burke's emphasis on personal responsibility and raised the question of "whether someone can be a Burkean realist about history and human nature and at the same time have liberal sentiments and visions." In her response, Hillary mused, "It is an interesting question you posed—can one be a mind conservative and a heart liberal?"

No description of the adult Hillary Clinton—*a mind conservative and a heart liberal*—has so succinctly defined her as this premonitory observation at age eighteen. She believed it was possible, though difficult, to be both. The question Jones asked was in the context of the civil rights movement, which Jones had first introduced her to. The travail and experience of black people in America touched something fundamental in Hillary Rodham, before she knew Bill Clinton. "Some people think you can't be critical of the black power movement and still be for civil rights," she wrote Jones. She supported Martin Luther King's nonviolent philosophy, but she was dubious about the increasing radicalism of Stokely Carmichael's SNCC, the Student Nonviolent Coordinating Committee, which was moving away from nonviolence in its embrace of Black Power. Her disinclination to go along with every aspect of movement dogma did not mean that she was in any way hostile to the movement itself.

"She was more interested in the process of achieving victory than in taking a philosophical position that could not lead anywhere," Shields said. "If challenged philosophically, she proclaimed, 'You can't accomplish anything in government unless you win!' " He described her as "very interested in exploring the process as opposed to the ideology of politics." When he met her, he judged her mind a clean slate ideologically, and compared her political transformation during the Wellesley years to his own, as she moved from rote membership in the Young Republicans to pronouncing New York a "saved city" with the election of liberal Republican John Lindsay as mayor ("See how liberal I'm becoming," she wrote to another friend), to supporting Eugene McCarthy's antiwar campaign for the presidency in 1968.

Even as early as eighteen or twenty, Hillary got tremendous gratification "from ideas and campaigns in the sense of getting something done in a way that was unusual with most women," Shields said. He described a "social intensity" that was weighted toward talking about ideas, going to serious movies, and serious conversation about issues. "Even then she had a real driving desire." Her method was to set goals for herself, whether personal or to advance a cause.

Recognition was important to her, and the most obvious outlet for her ambition at Wellesley was student government. All her myriad and frenetic campus activities seemed part of her preparation for becoming president of the student body, the ultimate sign of recognition. As a sophomore, she was a class representative to the student senate. The next year, she was not only selected a "Vil Junior," a particularly prestigious honor—Vil Juniors were chosen for their maturity and dependability and served as counselors to freshmen—but the campus chairman of all Vil Juniors.

By then, her extraordinary ability to speak in full sentences and paragraphs moving toward well-reasoned conclusions was already evident, and contributed to her aura as a leader with attributes rarely seen in an undergraduate. Part of her skill was finding a careful middle ground that brought progress without engendering unnecessary enmity. The minutes of college government meetings in which she presided demonstrate her method: November 1968—"Miss Rodham questions if it would be politic to approach individual faculty members and discuss the matter of student participation with them."

When she was elected by her fellows to be their president in February 1968, she did not disguise either her surprise or her exhilaration. Later, reporters would write about her husband's endless campaign for the presidency, even after he had been elected. The phrase aptly fit Hillary's activities at Wellesley. The formal campaign for student body president lasted three weeks, during which she made door-to-door appeals for votes in every dorm. But in the end, she won because of her tireless campaigning both before and during the allotted election period. On election day at Wellesley, she told a professor, "I can't believe what just happened! I was just elected president of the government. Can you believe it? Can you believe that happened?"

Notably, an hour-long debate with her two opponents was not definitive. The *Wellesley News* wrote of the three candidates, "They each expressed a desire for greater student jurisdiction in social matters and a more responsible role in academic decision-making, but all three were equally vague as to exactly how they would implement that change in power structure to achieve the second objective." It was the same kind of vagueness that would work to her advantage as a candidate for the U.S. Senate.

THE EVENTS OF 1968, of course, changed America and the world on a seismic scale. The very plates that had seemed to secure postwar Western democracy and American idealism appeared to shift with cataclysmic effect. Hillary Rodham, Bill Clinton, and Wellesley—like most American institutions of higher education and their students at the time—were shaken by the force of the concussion. The antiwar movement in the United States had, by 1968, become pervasive and angry, moving far beyond its student and leftist origins to become a mainstream cause that united millions of anguished working-class parents of draftees, students, intellectuals, and people of vastly differing political orientations. On March 31, Lyndon Johnson, already facing an unprecedented electoral challenge from within his own party to an incumbent president, announced he would not seek reelection. On April 4, Martin Luther King was assassinated by a bigot's bullet in Memphis. For days wide swaths of Washington and other cities burned with fire and rage. In May, European cities were overwhelmed by student radicals who battled police and took to the streets demanding not only an end to America's war in Vietnam, but insisting on unprecedented recognition of student power. American campuses were convulsed, many of them literally taken over by students who barricaded themselves in buildings in April and May in response to King's assassination, the wave of anarchy in the streets of Europe, fury at the war and the draft, and disgust with a prevalent system of education that had placed authority in tenured professors and slothful administrators with little regard to the changing will of the young people they were charged with educating. Antiwar demonstrations became increasingly violent, especially in Washington, New York, the Bay Area, and on university campuses. Many colleges and universities suspended classes by mid-semester and canceled formal graduation exercises. Senators Eugene McCarthy and Robert F. Kennedy had entered the race for the Democratic presidential nomination, mobilizing antiwar and student sentiment and a sense of political power outside the traditional party structure; Hubert Humphrey, meanwhile, campaigned as Johnson's loyal vice president, further inflaming the divisions in the party over the war. Then, on June 5, seemingly within reach of winning the nomination, Kennedy was assassinated in Los Angeles.

Even Wellesley, splendidly isolated by tradition and class from much of the radical student movement of 1968, did not escape being rocked by these events. The response of the women on campus to the explosions and turmoil outside was largely determined by the leadership of Hillary working with the college administration and her fellow students. While tens of thousands of young men and women within a hundred miles of Wellesley were yelling, "Fuck the pigs," Hillary's chosen means of protest and resistance were in the nonviolent, disciplined tradition of Dr. King, and reflected John Wesley's insistence on obeying the law. An expanding "Christian left," led by priests and ministers, was becoming an increasingly important element of the antiwar movement, helping to move organized opposition more and more into the mainstream of American politics and culture even as other elements became increasingly violent and radicalized. Hillary's evolving political sensibility drew from the tenets of Reinhold Niebuhr, Dietrich Bonhoeffer, and Paul Tillich, all of whom regarded Christian values and ethics as essential elements in the exercise of political power; from this heritage, and her continuing tutelage under the Reverend Jones, Hillary had no doubt that those values demanded spiritually based intervention in the political system.

The single event that seemed to galvanize Hillary's more militant instincts was the assassination of Dr. King. Hearing the news, she stormed into a dorm room, shaking and shouting. She threw her book bag against the wall. One witness said she screamed, "I can't stand it anymore! I can't take it!" King had been the embodiment of black America's hope, and white America's as well in many respects. King was perhaps the man she admired most in the country, if not the world. She had met him in 1962, shaken his hand, sat spellbound as he preached, twice; she had witnessed, on television, the hope and solidarity of the March on Washington in 1963, her sophomore year in high school. But since then she had watched that hope devolve into the fractious, violent confrontations of 1968, the failure of King's Poor People's Campaign in Washington the previous year, and his increasing isolation as a national moral leader as he tried, without success, to bring the civil rights and antiwar movements together. Now, it was clear, America would pay for King's death.

In the days following the assassination, many Wellesley students threatened to go on a hunger strike if the college did not give in to their demands to recruit more black faculty members and students, and use its influence with the town of Wellesley, Massachusetts, to demand immediate improvement of conditions in which black residents lived and worked. Hunger strikes were serious business, not to be taken lightly by institutional leaders. Some students wanted to close down the school by refusing to attend classes. This was by far the most heated campus protest of Hillary's time at Wellesley, the only one that threatened seriously to escape the control of the college administration. She proposed a solution that, in the end, avoided a dangerous clash: in her official position, she would work as a go-between with students, faculty, and the college administration to find a compromise. And indeed, the college gradually began to recruit minority faculty and students, and, as the most important institution in the town, exert pressure on local leaders to improve housing and job opportunities for blacks. Hillary's response had been totally in character. "Hillary would step in and organize an outlet that would be acceptable on the Wellesley campus. She co-opted the real protest by creating the academic one, which, looking back on it, I think was a mature thing to do," recalled a classmate.

That spring, she had begun volunteer work in support of Eugene McCarthy's candidacy. Weekends, she and a cadre of Wellesley women drove to New Hampshire to stuff envelopes and campaign for him in the state's primary, the first in the nation. His 42 percent of the vote (to Johnson's 49 percent) in the March primary was one of the factors leading the president to abdicate, and her fervor was further stoked when McCarthy came to thank student volunteers at his headquarters and she met him.

Ironically, Hillary had been one of thirteen students accepted the previous year to participate in Wellesley's Washington Internship Program for the summer of 1968—as a Republican, assigned to the party's apparatus on Capitol Hill. By the time she arrived in D.C. in June, she was anything but enthusiastic about her earlier choice of party affiliation. The capital seemed desperate and desolate; mourning another assassinated Kennedy and coping with the after-effects of its burning after King's assassination—on a scale unseen since the British burned the city in 1812. She spent nine weeks interning at the House Republican Conference, mostly answering telephones and delivering messages, and keeping her own counsel about her ties to the Democrats. Despite her misgivings, she found her situation manageable: she was one of thirty interns working in the office of the conference chairman, Melvin Laird, then a congressman from Wisconsin and subsequently secretary of defense under President Nixon. She made a lasting impression on Laird. "She presented her viewpoints very forcibly, always had ideas, always defended what she had in mind," he said. She worked on two projects for him, one a white paper called "Fight Now, Pay Later" that criticized Johnson's escalation of the Vietnam War without regard for the costs. She made clear to Laird that her opposition to the war was based more on the human costs than budgetary considerations. She also wrote a paper for the conference on revenue-sharing. She was for it. "Instead of the categorical fixed grants being dictated [from Washington] on how you spent every dollar, she felt it was better to return funds to the states and local communities where the decision could best be made," said Laird. Meanwhile, she got a field-level introduction to the ways of

Washington during a particularly divisive and violent time in the country's history.

For Hillary, the ugliness of the political atmosphere in Washington and the harsh divisions of the country were relieved somewhat by the excitement of her relationship with David Rupert, who was also interning at the GOP conference that summer. They had met on Capitol Hill at a mixer (the term was ubiquitous in certain academic and political milieux in the mid-1960s) for Republican interns. Later that evening, they headed for Georgetown for a drink and conversation. Many years later, Rupert said that he recognized almost immediately that Hillary's Republican credentials were thin, as his own increasingly came to be. She told him that she was president of the Young Republicans club at Wellesley, but she did not hide from Rupert her alienation from party orthodoxy. He, too, opposed the war, as did the congressman he worked for that summer, Charles Goodell of New York.

Near the end of her internship, Hillary attended the Republican convention in Miami as a volunteer in the effort to draft Nelson Rockefeller and derail Richard Nixon's nomination for president. She knew before she got there that Rockefeller's quest to be the nominee was hopeless, but she wanted to work against Nixon and participate in the excitement of a party convention. She shared a room with four other young women volunteers for Rockefeller at the opulent Fontainebleau Hotel on Miami Beach, where she placed her first-ever room service order (cereal and a fresh peach), shook hands with Frank Sinatra, and rode in an elevator with John Wayne. She had spent her summer in Republican politics while being a Eugene McCarthy Democrat, the kind of fence-straddling she accomplished in high school as well, when she was a member of Don Jones's youth group and her history teacher's anti-communist society simultaneously. It was a noteworthy pattern.

The Democratic convention, scheduled for August in Chicago, was certain to be far uglier than the GOP's meeting in Miami. With Robert Kennedy's death, McCarthy's candidacy was the only alternative to Hubert Humphrey's nomination. Humphrey was almost certain to win, but tens of thousands of antiwar demonstrators were heading to the convention, including followers of the band of neo-anarchists led by Abbie Hoffman and others who called themselves Yippies and were promising to disrupt the convention proceedings. Antiwar demonstrations had already turned unprecedentedly violent and virulent that spring. Police and military personnel in uniform were routinely subjected to hateful scorn. Many campuses remained shut down. In this atmosphere, Hillary returned to Chicago to stay with her family for the few weeks remaining before she was due back at Wellesley for her senior year.

With war in the streets between demonstrators and police erupting even before the convention was called to order, the nation's attention became fixed on Chicago. Hillary and Betsy Ebeling were adamant that they see for themselves what was happening downtown. On the first night of the convention, Betsy took her parents' car and the two of them, unbeknownst to Hugh and Dorothy, drove from Park Ridge to the barricades on the edge of Grant Park, where the carnage, tear gas, and fighting were the heaviest. As they drew nearer on foot, working their way through police lines and past emergency first-aid stations, they were struck incredulous at what they were seeing: Chicago's police, given full authority by Mayor Richard Daley to assault and arrest indiscriminately, were out of control, their fury as demonstrable as the demonstrators'. "It was kids our age with their heads being split open," said Ebeling. To Hillary and Betsy, the scene seemed horribly reminiscent of television pictures of the war in Vietnam itself—a battlefield, with blood, bandages, fires burning, and tear gas. Except in Chicago, people were throwing toilets out of the Hilton, and the police seemed to harbor special rage for young women in the crowd who taunted them.

The two young women returned to Grant Park the second and third nights of the convention as the battles grew more intense. As opposed to the war as they both had been, and as often as they had watched filmed scenes on television from Vietnam, the violence in Chicago somehow underscored the horror and reality of young Americans their own age dying in Southeast Asia; some were classmates from Maine South. (A friend from Park Ridge, Jeannie Snodgrass, was nursing the wounded in Grant Park.) The lesson Hillary and Betsy drew from what they had seen was recognition "that our government would do this to our own people"—both in Chicago and Southeast Asia, said Ebeling.

Though Hillary had turned twenty-one on October 26, she was ineligible to vote in the presidential election because of a thirty-day registration cut-off requirement in Illinois. Later she said she would have voted for Humphrey.

Hillary returned to Wellesley for her senior year determined to bring the campus more actively into the antiwar movement. As president of the student body, she did not want to see her college and classmates passively ignore the struggles—becoming more inflamed each month after Nixon's election—that would define so much of her generation and the future of the country. Yet she followed a cautious path, taking care to edge the campus and its women toward meaningful action without causing, literally, a riot. Instead of public demonstrations that would have brought police to the campus, she organized university-sanctioned "teach-ins" to protest the war. She was never in the leadership of any antiwar protests off-campus, nor did she choose to identify with the few women at Wellesley considered to be genuinely radical in their beliefs and actions. "She kept the student body focused on learning about the war, the pros and cons, being able to discuss it," said Professor Alan Schechter, who was her faculty adviser. Still, she found the substance of the teach-ins hollow, and their effectiveness disappointing.

That fall, Hillary began research on her senior thesis about a true American radical, Saul Alinsky, whose work Don Jones had lauded. What she found in the library stacks on Alinsky seemed to her insufficient and truncated. His philosophy was perhaps best summarized two years after she had completed her thesis, when Alinsky published his *Rules for Radicals*, a volume intended for Hillary's generation of student activists. In it, he enumerated a set of rules governing what he called "the science of revolution," based on an analysis of ends and means:

> Power is the very essence, the dynamo of life. . . . It is a world not of angels but of angles, where men speak of moral principles but act on power principles; a world where we are always moral and our enemies are always immoral; a world where "reconciliation" means that when one side gets the power and the other side gets reconciled to it, then we have reconciliation.

In pursuing "revolution," Alinsky continued, the advocate "asks of ends only whether they are achievable and worth the cost; of means only whether they will work." Hillary's research on Alinsky was largely based on her own academic visits to impoverished areas of Chicago, where she examined local community action programs in which poor people themselves set out the goals, developed the mechanisms of implementation, and controlled the purse strings. The concept "maximum feasible participation" was at the heart of Lyndon Johnson's Great Society anti-poverty programs and had been endorsed by, among others, Robert Kennedy. Hillary "started out thinking community action programs would make a big difference," Schechter said. Her on-site observations and extensive interviews (with Alinsky, among others) led her to conclude she had been too idealistic and simplistic in her expectations, and that the programs "might make a marginal but not a lasting difference" unless large infusions of outside funding and expertise, particularly by the federal government, were utilized.

When she and her husband settled into the White House, and Hillary was attempting to burnish a more conservative image, she said, somewhat disingenuously, "I basically argued that [Alinsky] was right. Even at that early stage I was against all these people who came up with these big government programs that were more supportive of bureaucracies than actually helpful to people. You know, I've been on this kick for twenty-five years."

THERE HAD BEEN no tradition of a student commencement speaker at Wellesley. But throughout the country in 1969, student protesters were demanding to be heard at their graduations or threatening to boycott them if they weren't. As president of the Wellesley student body, Hillary and a number of highly regarded classmates agreed they would urge Wellesley's president to have both a student speaker and, as was customary, a prominent leader from outside the college community.

Sensing the overwhelming will of the students, President Ruth Adams put aside her misgivings, particularly because it was clear who the student speaker would be. "There was no debate so far as I could ascertain as to who their spokesman was to be—Miss Hillary Rodham. She is cheerful, good humored, good company, and a good friend to all of us," Adams said in her introduction. It followed the address of Republican senator Edward Brooke of Massachusetts, at the time the highest-ranking black politician in American history and the only nonwhite member of the Senate. As president of the Wellesley Young Republicans in her freshman year, Hillary had campaigned hard for his election.

She had sought ideas from her fellow students about what she should say in her commencement address. But instead of delivering the speech she had drafted, she improvised a totally unscripted reproof to Brooke's rather bland and dispassionate remarks, in which he had professed "empathy" with some of the goals of antiwar demonstrators and civil rights workers, while implying disapproval of their tactics, which he described as "coercive protest." He seemed to defend the war itself, or at least Richard Nixon's approach to prosecuting it, and said nothing about the grievances that inspired the civil rights revolution—nor did he mention the assassinations of Dr. King and Robert Kennedy, two of the defining events of the graduates' time at Wellesley.

"I find myself in a familiar position," Hillary began, "that of reacting, something that our generation has been doing for quite a while now. We're not in the positions yet of leadership and power, but we do have that indispensable task of criticizing and constructive . . . protest, and I find myself reacting just briefly to some of the things that Senator Brooke said. Part of the problem with empathy, with professed goals, is that empathy doesn't do us anything. We've had lots of empathy; we've had lots of sympathy, but we feel that for too long our leaders have used politics as the art of the possible. And the challenge now is to practice politics as the art of making what appears to be impossible, possible." The most important part of that task, she then asserted, was to end the war.

Suddenly, a jolt of electricity seemed to startle the audience, and many in it wondered how far Hillary Rodham would go.

Some of what followed was a heartfelt, if hackneyed, litany of the era's anti-capitalist cant, combined with a verbally tangled commitment to a kind of blissful searching that would seem utterly foreign to the Hillary Rodham Clinton of today. ("We are, all of us, exploring a world that none of us understands and attempting to create within that uncertainty. But there are feelings that our prevailing acquisitive [culture], and some things we feel [about] corporate life, including, tragically, universities, is not the way of life for us. We're searching for more immediate, ecstatic and penetrating modes of living.")

Hillary's audacious response to Senator Brooke, and the passionate antiwar tone of her remarks (and perhaps the unintelligible part, too), seemed to the editors of *Life* magazine to exemplify what was happening on campuses that spring, and they chose to feature it, along with a photo of Hillary in her Coke-bottle glasses of the moment, wearing striped bell-bottom trousers, her hair a mangy tangle.

Though Geoff Shields was no longer her boyfriend and had moved to Vermont, they had remained close, and she called him shortly after the speech: "She said it had been hard for her to come around and make what was a political statement and a personal attack. There was some exhilaration but also nervous questioning about whether it had really been the right thing to do. She realized what she had done was important. But when it was over she wondered about what she had said. She asked, 'Did I go too far?' "

The least noticed parts of her speech were in many ways a vivid reflection of Hillary's values, the values of her family and of the placid, secure, suburban environment of Park Ridge. Hillary noted "a very strange conservative strain that goes through a lot of New Left collegiate protests" which "harken[ed] back to a lot of the old virtues, to the fulfillment of the original ideas." Her generation, like the country's Founders, had lost trust in government, and in powerful institutions. It extended even to the universities. Trust was "the one word that when I asked the class at our rehearsal what it was they wanted me to say for them, everyone came up to me and said, 'Talk about trust.' [But] what can you say about a feeling that permeates a generation and that perhaps is not even understood by those who are distrusted?"

Her answer was to return to the old verities, the values of her Methodist upbringing and her parents' teaching, expressed in words that sounded much like the anti-liberal rhetoric of the Goldwater campaign she had supported in 1964. She praised "that mutuality of respect where you don't see people as percentage points, where you don't manipulate people, where you're not interested in social engineering for people."

Her father, who had flown in for the day and then turned around and gone home, was among those listening in the audience, but not her mother. Hillary said her mother could not attend because a doctor had advised against her traveling due to health problems that required her to take blood-thinning medications. Hillary wrote she was very disappointed because of that. "In many ways, this moment was as much hers as mine."

She closed her commencement address with a poem from one of her classmates, Nancy Scheibner. It began:

> *My entrance into the world of so-called social problems*
> *must be with quiet laughter, or not at all.*
> *The Hollow Men of anger and bitterness*
> *The bountiful ladies of righteous degradation*
> *All must be left to a bygone age.*

3

Love and War at Yale

I was about to meet the person who would cause my life to spin in directions that I never could have imagined.

—*Living History*

BETSEY WRIGHT once noted that Hillary Rodham and Bill Clinton "both passionately share the sense that they're supposed to make a difference in this world—and they had that before they met each other." It was extraordinary how these two very different people meshed and enabled each other to better pursue their singularly huge ambitions. Neither likely had ever dreamed of finding such an ideal partner. A loving wife, a devoted husband, yes, a helpmate—but a fitting of gears such as these two exhibited was beyond the imagination (and certainly the experience in their own families) of either, according to those who had known Hillary or Bill before the two met. From the beginning of their relationship, their mutual friend Deborah Sale was aware of a consummate "sharing of values and ambitions that are really important." But Sale sensed another shared trait, perhaps equally telling: "a little bit of a level of naïveté about both of them." *Naive* is a word used with surprising frequency by those who know the two of them well.

At Yale, where they met in 1970, Bill and Hillary recognized almost immediately in the other the leavening and ameliorating attributes that would make for a partnership with limitless political possibilities. That Hillary would soon articulate, straight-faced and with total seriousness, what Bill had never been known to say aloud—her certainty that he would be president of the United States someday—underlies the point. But their falling in love—described by friends as real, rapid, and deep—was hardly part of some Faustian bargain. Until she met Bill, "Hillary was interested in her own capacity to help change the world," Sale knew, and had chosen a career in the law "because she thought that lawyers could change most of the world." The "female law-school virus," as some skeptical lawyers had half-mockingly named it, was sweeping through women's colleges in 1969, the year Hillary graduated from Wellesley; instead of working toward teaching credentials, thousands of women graduating from college were going on to study law. Yet law degree in hand, "ultimately Hillary made the decision to join Bill Clinton, and to help him change the world. That was probably a reasonable decision for a woman in the early 1970s," Sale believed.

Others who knew Hillary, especially those who identified themselves as feminists, disagreed. "The political world was ready for truly independent women," said a Wellesley alumna of the period. "It seems wildly tragic that we know she could have been president if she had just not even married him." By the time Hillary had graduated from Wellesley, she was already on her way to becoming a political meteor. She, not he, had been recognized in *Life* magazine, after all, as an emblem of her generation and its values. Betsey Wright, who would move to Washington in 1973 with the specific idea of advancing the electoral career of Hillary Rodham, had no doubt that Hillary could have reached the Senate or perhaps the presidency on her own. The question would be debated by millions of women, especially, during Hillary's White House years and even her first term in the Senate. In a common scenario, it was assumed that, without Bill Clinton's coattails, Hillary could have become head of a children's defense organization or legal aid program after law school and, by her early thirties, been drafted to run for Congress in Illinois or New York. "In fact, it's hard to think of a sadder example of a person who couldn't quite give up the old ideas," said the same Wellesley alumna. "Her way of moving toward electoral politics was to marry someone who was going to run."

Certainly upon her graduation from Wellesley that was not her intent. She was out to make her own mark on the world, her way. Until Hillary met and fell in love with Bill, she did not believe that her ambition could be fulfilled through marriage alone.

Hillary's ambition was always to do good on a huge scale, and her nascent instinct, so visible at Wellesley, to mediate principle with pragmatism—without abandoning basic beliefs—seemed a powerful and plausible way of achieving it. Bill Clinton, too, wanted to do good, and on a grand scale, but his gaze had always been fixed at the ground level of practical politics. Hillary's looked heavenward and toward John Wesley's message of service. Part of what Hillary brought to the union was an almost messianic sense of purpose, a high-mindedness and purity of vision that hovered above the conventionally political. Bill's political beliefs were strongly held, but "with Bill, you felt he just wanted to be president, whereas Hillary had this religious zeal," said a friend from law school days. Hillary had seemed to believe since her adolescence that her life was an unending search to determine what was right and seeking to make it happen.

Toward that end, she had applied to and was accepted at both Harvard and Yale law schools, but delayed a final decision on which to attend. From the start, she leaned toward Yale. Its law school, rather than Harvard's, was in the forefront of a movement in the 1960s that regarded the law as a primary instrument of social change, in the tradition of Thurgood Marshall and pioneering civil rights lawyers who recognized that the courts—not Congress, presidents, or state legislatures—had been the impetus for desegregating the nation, and protecting the civil liberties of its citizens. Hillary's choice of Yale was sealed during an exploratory visit to Harvard's law school, when she was introduced to an eminent professor whom she quoted as telling her, "Well, first of all, we don't have any close competitors. Secondly, we don't need any more women."

Hillary arrived at Yale in the fall of 1969, one of 27 women among 235 law students. She had brought from Wellesley a reputation as both a bold leader and an activist that was perhaps greater than justified by the facts. "We were awed by her courage," said Carolyn Ellis, one of her new classmates. "She arrived with many of us thinking of her as a leader already. We had seen her picture in the national magazine and here she was, three months later, in our class." Her fellow law students presumed that a career in electoral politics was inevitable for Hillary, and that she had chosen Yale as the optimal trajectory of her ambition. Her first year on campus seemed designed to give her a rocket-powered liftoff. She had no visible self-doubt. Hillary "knew she wanted to be politically influential and prominent. She wanted recognition," said a female classmate. As at Wellesley, her peers gravitated toward her, sensing that she was where the action was.

"Action," in fact, was perhaps the best description of the wild aura that had seized the once staid and stolid precincts behind the ivied-fortress walls of the university and its law school in New Haven. An almost dizzying anti-establishment ethic pervaded the place. In its main quadrangle, declared "a liberated zone" by students who took over the space during Hillary's first weeks on campus, tents were pitched by various factions who announced their countercultural ethos: hippies, Black Power preachers, earnest antiwar advocates, radical leftists. Though the tents were intended for teach-ins and distribution of literature, they also became free motels for homeless students and hangers-on. In the midst of this chaos, marijuana was freely consumed, students propelled themselves above the tents and teepees from an inflatable trampoline, and Frisbees floated through the airspace. Hendrix, hard rock, and sitar strains played incessantly. Later in the semester, members of author Ken Kesey's (*One Flew Over the Cuckoo's Nest*) Hog Farm commune arrived on their psychedelic bus. Abraham Goldstein, who became dean of the law school the following year, referred to this period of Yale's history as "the Dark Ages." Students had forced the faculty to institute pass-fail grading, and there was some truth to the statement that, if you could get admitted to Yale Law, it was almost impossible to flunk out. Lawyerly haberdashery had been replaced by tie-dyed shirts and dirty jeans.

For all the appearances of anarchy, however, there was something deadly serious about the atmosphere. The antiwar movement appeared sometimes on the brink of overwhelming the nation's established political process, and student leaders from Yale were among its most skilled strategists. Black Power advocates dominated the discussion of race in America—not proponents of integration or mere desegregation—and in Hillary's freshman year New Haven became the scene of a murder trial that objectified the country's twisted racial dynamic. Unbridled capitalism was also under philosophical and practical attack, spurred by young lawyers from Yale and elsewhere whose weapons were class-action lawsuits and other tactical matériel not favored in traditional law books.

As usual, Hillary carefully threaded her way through the extremes and patterned her own agenda. The notoriety she had achieved from her commencement speech at Wellesley led to an invitation from the League of Women Voters to join its Youth Advisory Committee. In October, she attended a league conference in Fort Collins, Colorado, convened to encourage young leaders to participate in mainstream politics, or at least in politics that respected traditional institutions and methods of discourse. Her participation left a lasting impression on some of her contemporaries. More important than the substance of the conference—on the question of lowering the voting age from twenty-one to eighteen, Hillary repeated the old slogan about young people being old enough to fight being old enough to vote—were the friends she made who would become part of the Rodham-Clinton constellation over the next three decades. They included Vernon Jordan, then heading a campaign to register black voters in the South as director of the Voter Education Project of the Southern Regional Council in Atlanta; David Mixner, a principal organizer of that year's Vietnam moratorium and later a leader of the gay rights movement; and Peter Edelman, then the associate director of the Robert F. Kennedy Memorial and chairman of the league's youth committee. Her meeting with Edelman was especially significant. He told her about the work of his wife-to-be, Marian Wright, a 1963 Yale Law graduate who had become the first black woman admitted to the Mississippi bar; now she was in the process of putting together an advocacy organization in Washington that would focus on the needs of the nation's poor children. Hillary was intrigued, and Peter urged that she and Marian meet soon. "You had an immediate sense you were in the presence of somebody who was just exceptionally impressive," he said of Hillary.

For millions of college and university students in the spring of 1970, traditional matters of learning and classwork were secondary to the larger issues facing the country generally and, more directly, young people subject to the draft and the war in Vietnam. Rather than move rapidly toward ending the war, as he had promised in the presidential campaign of 1968, Richard Nixon had intensified the conflict as part of his and Henry Kissinger's strategy to achieve "peace with honor"—meaning that the United States would not stand down in Indochina until it had won enough on the battlefield to impose a political settlement foreclosing an outright communist victory. Pursuit of that strategy would cost more than twenty-five thousand American lives and hundreds of thousands of Vietnamese and Cambodian casualties during the four years Hillary was at Yale. That spring of 1970, her second semester, America and its campuses especially were roiled by protest and violence. White, middle-class members of the Weathermen and other supporters of violent action were building bombs and exploding them at military recruiting centers, banks, and other symbolic institutions of the state. The FBI, under its director, J. Edgar Hoover, was engaged in deadly warfare with urban blacks who gravitated to the Black Muslim movement and the Black Panther Party. The bureau's own lawbreaking, and that of the Nixon administration in infiltrating and disrupting the antiwar movement, was manifest. At times it seemed like the government "was at war with its own people," Hillary said later. Constitutional guarantees of rights of assembly and free speech were being deliberately undermined from the top down.

The traditional route to student recognition in American law schools had always been appointment to the law review, and none was more influential or important than Harvard's and Yale's. But in the spring of 1970, an alternative law journal, *The Yale Review of Law and Social Action*, published its first issue, with Hillary listed on its board of editors. Its title proclaimed its purpose, as did an introductory note written by Hillary and her fellow editors: "This, the first issue of *Law and Social Action*, begins our exploration of areas beyond the limits of traditional legal concerns. For too long, legal issues have been defined and discussed in terms of academic doctrine rather than strategies for social change. *Law and*

Social Action is an attempt to go beyond the narrowness of such an approach, to present forms of legal scholarship and journalism which focus on programmatic solutions to social problems." The language seemed to pick up where her commencement speech ("for too long our leaders have used politics as the art of the possible . . .") had left off.

Hillary's interests "were not in the legal academy," a law school colleague noted. "They were in the legal profession and the use of law in the service of people." This was especially true of serving the legal needs of the poor—one of the founding principles of the new review. The inaugural issue was dominated by two other concerns: the war and the Black Panther movement, the center of which had moved from Northern California to New Haven, "the grim Connecticut port city that housed the Yale campus, a bastion of white middle-class guilt surrounded by a black ghetto," as one cynic put it. At the federal courthouse in downtown New Haven, Panther chairman Bobby Seale and seven of his comrades were on trial that spring for murdering a fellow Panther who had, supposedly, become a police informant. Thousands of protesters converged on New Haven for the trial, certain that the Panthers had been persecuted by Hoover's FBI and federal prosecutors under the thumb of Nixon's Justice Department. The trial ended in a hung jury.

The *Review*'s inauguration had been timed to coincide with a huge May Day protest and student strike called for New York and New England to demand that charges against the Panthers be dropped because of the supposed inability of black defendants to receive a fair trial in a "white man's justice system." The cover photo of the first issue of the *Review* pictured police wearing gas masks (and some armed with heavy weapons) to illustrate an article on "University and the Police: Force and Freedom on Campus." Another article, "Lawyers and Revolutionaries: Notes from the National Conference on Political Justice," exhaustively reported the remarks of Yippie Jerry Rubin, and of two of the most prominent radical lawyers of the era—William Kunstler, who had defended the so-called Chicago Seven organizers of the protests at the 1968 Democratic convention, and Charles Garry, the lead attorney for Bobby Seale.

Though Hillary has never spoken publicly of her view of the Panther trial, she was among student-observers from Professor Tom Emerson's civil liberties class who attended each day's courtroom proceedings to report possible abuses by the government, discuss them in class, write papers about them, and then prepare summaries for the American Civil Liberties Union. She took charge of scheduling the student monitors, to make certain that every minute of the trial was scrutinized. A subsequent issue of the *Review* that year—Hillary had become its associate editor by then—was devoted almost entirely to the trial, accompanied by pictures and drawings in which police were depicted as pigs. According to her friend and classmate Greg Craig, Hillary expressed her dismay to him at the choice of artwork; he was likewise appalled, though neither seemed to have tried to do anything about it.

The underlying rationale of the May Day protesters had been endorsed in a statement by Yale's president, Kingman Brewster, who, faced with the prospect of violent demonstrations, acceded to some student demands: classes were suspended, permission was granted to use dormitory dining rooms to feed protesters, and Garry was permitted to take up residence on campus during the trial. Brewster's statement is indicative of how mainstream the larger issues raised by the Panther trial had become: "I personally want to say that I am appalled that things should have come to such a pass that I am skeptical of the ability of black revolutionaries to achieve a fair trial anywhere in the U.S." President Nixon and Vice President Spiro Agnew, who already had their sights trained on Yale because of the antiwar leadership of the university's chaplain, William Sloan Coffin, were enraged by the remarks.

On the night of April 27, as the campus prepared for what organizers were calling the May Day "uprising," the International Law Library in the basement of Yale's grand, classicist law school building was set ablaze. Hillary rushed with a bucket brigade of students and library staff to extinguish the fire and save as many books as possible. The flames had already caused considerable damage; the water furthered the destruction. For the rest of the semester Hillary walked a beat as a member of round-the-clock security patrols protecting the university's resources and property.

The Panthers and some of their supporters had been doing their utmost to whip up trouble, announcing, "Come to New Haven for a burning on May Day." On campuses throughout the Northeast, leaflets were distributed, proclaiming, "All power to the good shooters . . . [to] create peace by destroying people who don't want peace"—an unsubtle reference to assassinating the police. The National Guard was mobilized in advance of the protests, with uniformed soldiers taking up positions on the Yale campus. The night before May Day, April 30, 1970, Nixon announced that American soldiers and South Vietnamese forces had begun an invasion—"incursion" was the word he used—of Cambodia.

Though its significance was unclear at the time, the May Day demonstration in New Haven contributed to the anti-establishment fury of the Nixon era. In the next week, the logic of the antiwar movement became even more interlocked with a sense among millions of citizens, particularly young people, many of them by now radicalized, that their government was hell-bent on a course in which a new kind of American imperialism abroad and extra-constitutional governance at home were undermining the basic nature of the country's democracy and historical progress. Millions of others believed that the nation was descending into anarchy.

True to form, Hillary identified with the larger goals of the May Day protests but aligned herself with those who were determined that the demonstrations remain peaceful, purposeful, pragmatic, and aimed at achieving longer-term objectives within the system. Though she was a first-year student, she was already a figure of unusual influence and respect at the law school. That week, when an ad hoc gathering of protest leaders arguing over tactics became unruly, Hillary skillfully managed to corral the crowd and moderate a discussion that calmed matters. Accounts and memories of exactly how she came to take over the meeting are sketchy, but there is agreement that she became a kind of mediator, damping down the vitriol of some of the heated presentations of various factions, restating rhetorical excess in less incendiary language, and more or less presiding in a Robert's Rules of Order fashion. She wore blue denim bell-bottoms and a work shirt and sat rather imperiously atop a table at the front of the fractious assembly. Tempers were unusually hot because so many law students and professors were incredulous that books had been burned. Her friend Kris Rogers remembered trying to push her "far more to the left," without success. Not for the first or last time, Hillary's forceful presence registered both with students and the administration hierarchy, as deans and demonstrators alike identified her as someone they could work with. "There was a lot of angry rhetoric being exchanged. Hillary showed extraordinary force for a very young woman," said Dean Goldstein.

Her method reflected the unusual combination of her temperaments: she could be in-your-face, soothing, mocking, abrasive, praising, sarcastic, analytical, enthusiastic, ebullient. Even students who, many years later, came to loathe her politics, recalled her during this period with grudging admiration, and commented on how she appeared to summon all these attributes during the protests of May. Meanwhile, in expectation of the worst, New Haven businesses were boarded shut, and word traveled that blasting caps were missing from a Yale chemistry lab. Not far away, on the Connecticut Wesleyan campus, a Molotov cocktail consumed a classroom building.

Fifteen thousand demonstrators gathered in view of the Yale quadrangle on May Day, some holding "Burn Yale" signs aloft. The demonstration turned out to be remarkably peaceful. There were teach-ins: "Arrest and Search," "Colonization and Race in Plantation Society." Jerry Rubin, one of the day's main speakers, exhorted the crowd with a chant of, "Fuck Nixon! Fuck Nixon! Fuck Nixon!"—the principal target that day of scourging remarks about his war policies, supposed racism, and "police state tactics." For Hillary, the substantive critique seemed more than justified. The next day, the *Yale Daily News* reported that the demonstration had brought together "the largest assemblage of long-haired youths, film crews, and National Guardsmen that New Haven has ever witnessed." Two days later, National Guard troops shot and killed four student antiwar demonstrators at Kent State University in Ohio. The famous photograph of a young woman stooped over a dead student brought Hillary to tears, she wrote.

Following the Kent State shootings, there were an average of a hundred demonstrations or student strikes per day in the country, and more than five hundred colleges and universities closed down.

In Washington on May 7, Hillary was one of the speakers at the fiftieth anniversary convention of the League of Women Voters, another indication of her increasing prominence. She wore a black armband at the podium, in memory of those killed at Kent State. Her emotions, she said later, were in evidence as she argued against the war's extension into Cambodia as "illegal and unconstitutional." To her elders, she tried to put into context the anguished protests taking place on college campuses. At Yale, she pushed for engagement, "not disruption or 'revolution,'" during the upheavals of 1970, she said years later. Hillary had moderated a meeting at which the law school students voted 329 to 12 to join the national student strike and to protest the American military action in Cambodia. She had called it "the unconscionable expansion of a war that should never have been waged."

Thirty-five years later, Senator Hillary Rodham Clinton, by then a potential presidential nominee of her party, would argue with less vehemence—and less convincingly—that there could be no withdrawal of American military forces from Iraq until more U.S. political and military objectives were accomplished. Then, as in the case of the Vietnam War, the U.S. Senate had given the president a blank check to fight a war in which he had misrepresented the underlying factors that he claimed justified American sacrifice. Hillary was among the overwhelming majority of senators who had voted to give George W. Bush the authorization he sought. A year later, she succeeded in winning appointment to the Senate Armed Services Committee, becoming—like Margaret Chase Smith (who had served as a lieutenant colonel in the Air Force Reserve)—an expert on military preparedness. Her continuing refusal to use her unprecedented influence to urge rapid withdrawal of American soldiers from Iraq alienated many of her supporters among the Democratic Party's left and others who questioned whether her evolution from Vietnam to Iraq represented evidence of youth versus maturity, or merely the political expediency of an ambitious politician who had abandoned the values and principles she had espoused in an era when she had no electoral agenda.

As a first-year law student, Hillary's oratory could still slip precipitously into vague and perplexing generalities if the subject required conceptual analysis. This seemed especially true in her appearance before the League of Women Voters, when she assumed the mantle of generational spokesperson. If she was speaking about a clearly defined subject, her thoughts would be well organized, finely articulated, and delivered in almost perfect outline form. But before the league audience she again lapsed into sweeping abstractions—though it was not hard to understand what she was getting at. "Here we are on the other side of a decade that had begun with a plea for nobility and ended with the enshrinement of mediocrity," she declared. "Our social indictment has broadened. Where once we exposed the quality of life in the world of the South and of the ghettos, now we condemn the quality of work in factories and corporations. Where once we assaulted the exploitation of man, now we decry the destruction of nature as well." In trying to connect with women in the audience, many of them two and three times as old as she, Hillary spoke of holding "our institutions . . . accountable to the people," suggesting that corporations were susceptible to pressure through "what kind of stock one owns." She asked, "What do you do with your proxies? How much longer can we let corporations run us?" Ironically, in the next decade she would be a member of the boards of two huge corporations and represent others in court.

She was still finding her way, cruising at times on a reputation that, in fact, derived more from the audacity of her challenge to a U.S. senator in a commencement speech than the sum of her accomplishments.

In less than a year, she had been interviewed on Irv Kupcinet's nationally syndicated television talk show from Chicago, been chosen by the league to be her generation's liaison to an earlier generation of civic-inclined women, and been written up in her hometown and New England newspapers. She liked the attention, the way it set her apart from the herd of her fellows, conveying to them and their elders that she was on a different, somehow more thoughtful track. She did nothing to publicly douse the accompanying speculation that electoral politics was where she saw her future. Especially given the abdication of congressional oversight of the war, electoral politics was neither her goal nor even something she had much faith in, nor felt particularly drawn to. She still believed in public service on behalf of those in society who were among the least powerful and most marginalized or discriminated against. The people she seemed naturally drawn to helping above others were children. They were the most vulnerable of citizens and the most powerless politically—the more so if they were poor and black. She believed that the law could be put to much stronger use on their behalf and that she could find ways to make it happen.

The league convention's keynote speaker was Marian Wright Edelman. Already Hillary regarded her as something of a hero for using the system, particularly the courts, on behalf of children. Edelman's father was a Baptist preacher whose message to his own five children was the same as to his congregation in Bennettsville, South Carolina: that Christianity required service in this world. Marian embraced many of the same traditional values—self-reliance, family, hard work, equal justice, universal brotherhood, the pursuit of knowledge—that Hillary had so tenaciously held on to through the turbulence of the 1960s. She and Edelman shared a religious interpretation of social and political responsibility. Edelman, like Hillary, was fond of proverbial language and aphorisms: "You really can change the world if you care enough." "Service is what life is all about." "Children don't vote, but adults who do must stand up and vote for them." The words could have just as easily rolled from Hillary's lips. Like the advocate Hillary would become, Marian also was focused, determined, winsome, and, if necessary, took no prisoners as she marched toward an imperative objective.

Edelman, eight years older than Hillary, had abandoned her plans to enter the foreign service after law school and instead chose to use her legal credentials in the struggle for civil rights in the South. She joined the staff of the NAACP Legal Defense Fund, first in New York and then in Mississippi. In 1967, while leading New York senator Robert F. Kennedy on a tour through the shacks of the Mississippi Delta, Marian met Peter Edelman—Brooklyn-born, Jewish, a former clerk for Supreme Court Justice Arthur Goldberg, and Kennedy's principal aide on matters of civil rights. Both Edelman and Wright had gone south during college to register black voters—a dangerous enterprise, especially for a Southern black woman and a Northern Jew. Kennedy, but not Wright or Edelman, "was shocked to see starving, hungry and listless children with bloated bellies and families who had no income and were unable to purchase food stamps that cost 50 cents a person," as she later noted in a report. Outraged, Kennedy sought immediate action from Secretary of Agriculture Orville Freeman, who professed incredulity that there were American families without income.

Marian and Peter married in 1968 and settled in Washington, where she continued her civil rights work. That year, she helped organize the Poor People's Campaign of Martin Luther King and his Southern Christian Leadership Conference. It was intended to be the most massive campaign of civil disobedience undertaken by the civil rights movement. Protest activities in Washington, including many intended to shut down the city, were to be supported by simultaneous demonstrations throughout the country. The campaign was meant to draw unusual attention to family issues and the punishing handicaps suffered by children born into poverty. But it failed to strike a national chord. Many of the fragile pitched tents and ramshackle huts erected by the campaigners, between the Capitol and the Lincoln Memorial on the Mall, were occupied that spring and early summer by poor black parents and their children. But internecine struggles in the civil rights movement, incessant rain and flooding that turned the encampment on the Mall into a village of mud huts, and the pall cast by Kennedy's and King's assassinations in the spring doomed the campaign.

From her experiences as an activist, her disappointment in the failed campaign, and her own intimate familiarity with black poverty in the South, Marian began to conceive the idea of a national organization that would become a voice for and legal defender of poor, minority, abused, and handicapped children. This was what Peter Edelman had talked to Hillary about in Colorado. When Marian came to Yale a few months later to speak about the state of the civil rights movement and her plans for a new organization dedicated to children's advocacy, Hillary introduced herself and raised the possibility of working for her when the school term finished in June. Edelman told her there was no money to pay her. Hillary persisted. What if she could figure out a way of getting paid? "Of course," Edelman responded.

Marian's speech at Yale seemed to touch on the themes of Hillary's most ardent social, political, and personal concerns—both those she articulated to others and some she sensed perhaps only through the deepest of her own feelings. Since childhood, Hillary had heard teachers, preachers, politicians, and theoreticians talk about the future of the country and the world being in the hands of the next generation—hers. Almost all of it sounded like lip service to her, which was what she had tried to express both in her commencement speech and to the League of Women Voters.

The only public woman Hillary had ever looked to as a plausible role model had been Margaret Chase Smith. But Smith's accomplishments, unlike Edelman's, had derived almost literally from following in her husband's footsteps. Smith had been his secretary while he was a member of Congress, and upon his death was elected to finish his term. When she first ran for the Senate, Smith leaned heavily on her qualifications for governance—as a housewife: she compared management of public affairs with running a household. "Women administer the home. They set the rules, enforce them, mete out justice for violations, thus, like Congress, they legislate. Like the Executive, they administer; like the courts, they interpret the rules. It is an ideal experience for politics." Increasingly, it seemed to Hillary that Smith was a fine role model—for a previous generation. Marian Wright Edelman was a woman of her own time.

Four weeks after the league convention, Hillary moved to Washington for the summer and went to work for her new mentor. Hillary had persuaded the Law Students Civil Rights Research Council to fund an internship—through a grant—for Edelman's new organization, the Washington Research Project. "I always liked people who could find ways to get things done," said Edelman.

She put Hillary to work developing information for a Senate investigation into the living and working conditions of migrant farm laborers and their families. The subcommittee conducting the inquiry was headed by Senator Walter Mondale, who had worked closely with Edelman to obtain passage of the Child and Family Services Act, a legislative milestone that required compensatory education and day care for poor infant and school-age children. Hillary knew something of the conditions that migrant workers faced from her days babysitting for some of their children in Illinois. Several had attended her elementary school for a few months each year, and on Saturday mornings during the fall crop season, she babysat at a migrant camp with other members of her Sunday school class.

Hillary's assignment in Washington built on that experience. She was asked to come up with hard information about migrant children's health and education difficulties. Her research focused on the South, where migrant children were confronted by, among other things, a particularly cruel form of discrimination. School districts in Virginia first, and then increasingly in other Southern states, had turned formerly all-white public schools into private, segregated academies to escape court-ordered desegregation. The white children of migrant workers could not afford tuition for the academies; black and Hispanic children of migrant workers were excluded by race. The Nixon administration was inclined to grant tax-exempt status to the academies as part of its strategy for achieving an "emerging Republican majority"—by appealing to Southern segregationists who had traditionally voted Democratic. For Hillary, her summer was an education in how the most powerless citizens were further punished by malevolent government and misuse of the law.

With her introduction to Marian Edelman and work with Mondale's subcommittee, Hillary could sense that her experiential path was finally leading toward a satisfying destination, even a kind of maturity, in which her life's passions and concerns could be used in the spirit that John Wesley had enunciated. She studied the filthy camps for migrant workers who serviced the Florida citrus groves and tended the green fields of adjacent states, where they made possible the South's bountiful harvest. As in the fields outside the Chicago of her childhood, the people who suffered most grievously were the children, whose preordained futures were the product of their parents' misfortune. Her documentation of extreme examples of the cruelties of migrant labor life, especially the plight of migrant children without schooling, sanitation facilities, or decent housing, was the basis for some of the most dramatic testimony compiled that fall in hearings convened by Mondale. Among the migrant camps Hillary scrutinized were ones serving the Coca-Cola Company, which had recently acquired the Minute Maid brand. Her strategy was to have Coca-Cola's president, J. Paul Austin, brought before the committee to testify, and held up as an egregious example of corporate callousness. Here was a recognizable villain for the piece. The effectiveness of Austin's example would become a basic component of her approach to political action over the next quarter-century. Still, no legislation resulted from the committee's work. That in itself reinforced her negative impression of electoral politics.

The hearings, however, had made for good Washington theater, timed to mark the tenth anniversary of Edward R. Murrow's celebrated *Harvest of Shame* broadcast, which had vividly revealed the despicable conditions in which migrant workers and their children subsisted. Hillary took great satisfaction from what she had uncovered for the committee's investigation, but in reality, what she had learned was that the lives of migrants hadn't improved. At the hearings, several fellow students from Yale Law School sat across the witness table from the senators: they were present as summer associates on behalf of corporate clients of the law firms where they were interning. She made her contempt for such lawyering clear, and upbraided them for their choice. "I'm not interested in corporate law. My life is too short to spend it making money for some big anonymous firm," she had said. Her summer working with Edelman became "a personal turning point." She would concentrate her studies on how the law affected children.

That fall, she commuted between New Haven and Washington, an ideal vocational and educational arrangement. On Capitol Hill she monitored hearings for Edelman and evaluated legislation that might have impact on the lives of children. In New Haven, she developed a unique curriculum and work program for herself, which combined aspects of law, medicine, and psychology. She audited classes at Yale's medical school and worked at the Yale–New Haven Hospital on problems of children's physical and mental health, including child abuse, which was being seriously studied for the first time as a significant sociological phenomenon. She helped establish the hospital's legal procedures dealing with incoming cases of suspected child abuse. At the Yale Child Study Center, she spent much of the academic year observing clinical sessions with children and attending subsequent case discussions with their doctors. The center's director, Dr. Al Solnit, and one of her law school professors, Joe Goldstein, asked her to become their research assistant on a book they were editing with Anna Freud, Sigmund's daughter. The work, *Beyond the Best Interests of the Child*, became a standard text of the era. As a result of Hillary's work on the book, "I began to think through a lot of the issues that affect children, both visible and invisible, and the role that the law can and cannot play." Like many law students, she was assigned to the local office of the federally funded National Legal Services Program, where a young legal aid lawyer named Penn Rhodeen instructed her on advocacy for neglected and abused children.

With Rhodeen, she represented a black foster mother in her fifties who had cared for a two-year-old since the child was born. The foster mother sought to adopt the girl, who was of mixed race. The woman had already raised two grown children of her own. However, the Social Services Department of Connecticut enforced its rule forbidding foster parents from adopting, and ordered the little girl placed with "a more suitable family." Hillary and Rhodeen drafted a lawsuit against the state, but lost.

Despite losing the case, a children's rights movement seemed to be on the horizon, in which the courts would protect the interests of children as an aggrieved class, much as civil rights law had addressed the inequities and cruelties of racial segregation. In the next few years Hillary would write a series of articles in scholarly journals, beginning with "Children Under the Law," published in 1974 in the *Harvard Educational Review*. It examined the legal problems and civic consequences of children suffering abuse or neglect, including those denied medical care by their parents or the right to continue school. Abused children, she argued, were "child citizens," entitled to the same procedural rights under the Constitution as adults. She saw a connection between her mother's mistreatment as a child and the horrible things some parents were doing to their children. She wanted to help those children.

Hillary's academic writings and work as a children's advocate would later become a target of attack by the Clintons' enemies. The caricature of her work and its "subversive" implications were seen as part of the makeup of a leftist ideologue. By the 1992 presidential campaign, she was being characterized as "anti-family," a woman who "believes that twelve-year-olds should have the right to sue their parents, and . . . compared marriage as an institution to slavery," in the words of Patrick Buchanan, addressing the 1992 Republican convention. In fact, her scholarly writings were carefully wrought, highly regarded in the field of family law, and not terribly controversial. Historian Garry Wills, reviewing some of her writings in *The New York Review of Books*, found them impressive enough to call Hillary "one of the more important scholar-activists of the last two decades."

Her decision to pursue children's studies at Yale and her work with Marian Edelman's Washington Research Project had left Hillary unusually settled and at ease with herself. Finally, she seemed to know what she wanted to do with her life. "I want to be a voice for America's children," she said.

IN HER FORTY-FIFTH YEAR, not long after deciding against divorcing her husband and soon before moving to the White House, Hillary was asked to recall the most ecstatic experience of her twenties. She answered without hesitancy. "Falling in love with Bill Clinton." There is no reason to disbelieve the spontaneity or substance of her response. Though *ecstasy* is a word not often associated with this most disciplined, controlled, and controlling of characters, it is perhaps the best explanation of the path she put herself on in the spring of 1971.

Having finally arrived at an exciting, satisfying choice of vocation, having settled into an easy relationship with an interesting, attractive man, and having seen her image burnished as one of her generation's brightest stars after only eighteen months of law school, Hillary suddenly allowed her life to be turned upside down in the most traditional of ways: by falling head-over-heels in love. Bill Clinton "was the wild card in her well-ordered cerebral existence," said a friend. She had been seduced. But so had Bill Clinton. "He was the first man I'd met who wasn't afraid of me," she said. His friends doubted his fearlessness. "I was afraid of us," he said. More likely, his friends believed, he masked his fear of her. She was so out of the realm of his previous girlfriends, and he was so captivated by her attributes, that his self-assurance was severely tested. Meanwhile, she confessed to feeling a degree of comfort she had never known previously.

Their own oft-told story of meeting and falling in love—a version suitably dramatic, unencumbered by awkward mention of mutual ambition, clouded by several degrees of self-generated myth—ignores the fact that they had already been introduced and hardly took notice of each other on the first day of classes at Yale in the fall of 1970.

Bill Clinton arrived at Yale Law School from Oxford two semesters shy of a graduate degree, determined to embellish his credentials among the brightest and best of his generation of Americans. He was looking forward to going back to Arkansas to run for public office and eventually get to Washington as a congressman. If he succeeded, the whole gaudy panorama of political possibility would spread before him. Since high school his friends had been saying that he was destined for the White House. But he understood that, after Oxford, to fulfill his ambitions he needed the American equivalent of High Church, establishment credentials of the kind that could never be found at the University of Arkansas Law School, where he had briefly considered alighting. Yale Law School in 1970 was the perfect perch from which to glide toward his destination.

He arrived at precisely the right place and at the most politically opportune moment. Though Eugene McCarthy had been swamped by traditional Democrats at Chicago, and Robert Kennedy was dead, a single Senate race that year—in Connecticut—had captivated the imaginations of their acolytes. Joseph D. Duffey, a former seminarian, thirty-eight years old, president of the liberal Americans for Democratic Action, a professor of ethics, and ardent campaigner for civil rights and peace in Vietnam, meant to revive the electoral hopes crushed by the nomination of Hubert Humphrey and the election of Richard Nixon. Fueled by the shootings at Kent State and the extension of the war to Cambodia, the itinerant irregulars of the antiwar army massed in New Haven to push Duffey's candidacy forward. The war would not be stopped unless opposition votes in Congress forced the president's hand, they believed. Duffey faced the same dilemmas that would confront Clinton throughout his career as a progressive, Southern Democrat: how to create a center from the competing elements within the Democratic Party and still attract independent votes; how to spur basic political and civic change without antagonizing middle-class white voters.

Though Duffey failed—in a three-way race against the incumbent senator, Thomas J. Dodd, running as an Independent; and Republican congressman Lowell P. Weicker Jr.—Bill Clinton did not. He acquired an encyclopedia of practical political knowledge and a retinue of friends who would make the jump enthusiastically from Duffey's candidacy to Clinton's in Arkansas, and later onto the national stage. Thus, Duffey's unsuccessful Senate campaign was invaluable in establishing the Clinton political network and philosophy. Its ethic was articulated by Duffey in a self-evaluation of his run:

It is always tempting to blame our defeat on those people who never understood what we were trying to say or who rejected our efforts to lead them. But the fact is that the search for a new politics in America is still at a very primitive stage. . . . Many of our policies have been formulated as if the nation were composed of only two major groups—the affluent and the welfare poor. But somewhere between affluence and grinding poverty stand the majority of American families living on the margins of social and economic insecurity. The new politics has thus far not spoken to the needs and interests of those Americans. We have forgotten that they, too, feel the victims of decisions in which they have no voice.

Until election day in November, Clinton had hardly attended his law school classes. He'd worked from dawn until past midnight on Duffey's campaign, and then returned from Third District congressional headquarters in New Haven to sack out in the rambling beach house he rented on Long Island Sound with three classmates. After election day, his study habits changed little. Roommates would find him reading a book after midnight, assume it was a law text, and then discover it was a novel. He slept less than five hours a night, wrote copious letters to former girlfriends (who were numerous), and, when he did study, managed an intensity that could push him successfully through an exam with barely a couple of hours of preparation.

Within weeks of his arrival in New Haven, it was obvious that he possessed an extraordinary appeal that attracted, in great numbers, individuals from the most disparate of backgrounds. He soaked up their stories and their knowledge and gave back from his sophisticated ideas and sense of history. He effused an uncommon empathy that left them fascinated and utterly charmed. Nancy Bekavac, a Yale classmate who would later become closer to Hillary than to Bill, was typically bowled over. "I'd never seen anyone with that much focus, that much brains, and that much charm. And, it was all focused. He was very efficient about getting what he wanted, and it was clear he had a kind of novelist's love for people. He remembered salient things about them. He listened to them. And, he played that back to them in more than an artful way. He was funny. He was observant. He paid attention to who was smart and who wasn't smart. . . . He made an effort to talk to them. It was so monumentally clear he was a politician. . . . [P]eople say, 'Well, is it true you thought he was going to be President?' Absolutely. I don't think I knew him two hours before it dawned on me."

Bekavac would become president of Scripps College in California.

She had spent the summer before law school in Vietnam as a journalist, working for the *Catholic Welfare News* and Metromedia. Bill Clinton, she believed, regarded his own life, too, in novelistic terms, with his surprising, simultaneous capacity for both self-awareness and denial, and—for someone so focused—his tortured road to decision-making.

And then there were the women.

"While law school and politics were going well," Clinton said later, "my personal life was a mess. I had broken up with a young woman who went home to marry her old boyfriend, then had a painful parting with a law student I liked very much but couldn't commit to. I was just about reconciled to being alone and was determined not to get involved with anyone for a while."

Enter Hillary Rodham.

"One day," he recalled, "when I was sitting in the back of Professor Emerson's class, I spotted a woman I hadn't seen before. . . . She had thick dark blond hair and wore eyeglasses and no makeup, but she conveyed a sense of strength and self-possession I had rarely seen in anyone, man or woman."

By then, it would have been almost impossible for Clinton not to have known about her. She was a recognizable star on campus, much discussed among the law school's students, known as politically ambitious, practical, and highly principled.

When they had been introduced on the first day of classes, neither had taken much notice. Clinton was at a table in the law school cafeteria with old friends, among them Bob Reich, who had been at Oxford with him and knew Hillary from her undergraduate days as a student leader. Reich remembered sitting next to Clinton, "And Hillary came up in back of us, and I just said, 'Hillary, it's great to see you.' Blah-blah-blah. Small talk. 'Let me introduce you. This is Bill Clinton. Hillary, Bill. Bill, Hillary,' and that was it. . . . Obviously my introduction didn't take."

Clinton was dating another woman at the time, and was perhaps preoccupied with his work on Duffey's campaign. Whatever the case, neither he nor Hillary seems to remember the introduction. But the impression she made on him the next semester in Professor Emerson's class, where her hand seemed always upraised and she invariably knew the right answers, was irrevocable.

He began conspicuously trailing her around campus. Hillary said she first took notice of him in the law school student lounge, "looking more like a Viking than a Rhodes scholar"—long hair, ragged beard, six foot two and a half and 220 pounds. He was talking to someone about how Arkansas grew the biggest watermelons in the world—something he talked about a lot.

Yet, according to their autobiographies, they didn't exchange a word until the spring of 1971 in the Yale Law library one evening. Clinton had spotted a friend in the stacks, Jeffrey Gleckel, and went over to say hello to him. As they conversed, Gleckel noticed that "little by little . . . his concentration was disappearing. He listened but was saying much less. His glance began to wander and he seemed to be looking over my shoulder. I was trying to find a way to look in an inconspicuous manner and so I sort of turned around halfway as an excuse to scratch my leg or something and there I saw, seated nearby at a desk with a stack of books and notepads, Hillary Rodham, who was also an acquaintance."

Gleckel "politely excused myself," leaving no other witnesses except the two protagonists.

Hillary, in *Living History*, said he had been glancing at her off and on so she went and introduced herself. Bill, who said he had been literally dumbstruck by the boldness of her approach, said hello and they soon parted company.

At the time, Hillary was still dating David Rupert and spending weekends with him and another couple in Bennington, Vermont, in a two-bedroom apartment carved out of the corner of a barn that they called the "chicken coop." Apparently two more months passed before she and Clinton spoke again.

On the last day of the spring term, while walking from a politics and civil rights class, Bill asked Hillary where she was headed. She said she was on her way to register for the next semester's classes. They arrived together at the office of the registrar, who asked why Bill was there since he had already registered.

Hillary laughed when Bill confessed it was a ploy to be with her, and they "went for a long walk that turned into our first date," Hillary wrote.

Bill suggested they walk to a Mark Rothko exhibit at the Yale Art Gallery, but they found the museum closed because of a campus-wide strike by unionized employees. He talked his way in by volunteering to remove the garbage that had piled up. Hillary was impressed. That night, he took her up on her invitation to come to an end-of-term party Hillary and her roommate, Kwan Kwan Tan, were giving in their dorm. Bill phoned a few days afterward and could tell from Hillary's voice that she was ill. He showed up thirty minutes later with some orange juice and chicken soup, Hillary said. She was impressed by his range of interests, everything "from African politics to country and western music." Hillary now knew that he "was much more complex than first impressions might suggest." They soon became a couple.

Nancy Bekavac was one of the first friends he introduced her to. "I remember being struck by this aggressive, ambitious, bright woman who studied child development and cared about children," she said. "It was unusual in some ways. Every young woman was running away from, you know, childhood and family issues. Jesus Christ, the last thing you wanted to do was family law. . . . It was very unusual. And you couldn't find an obvious biographical or autobiographical hook. For me, it was a given: That's where she was going."

Though Clinton later professed to not want another romantic involvement so soon after the breakup of his latest relationship, his housemates discerned in him almost a desperation that he not lose her. He coached them on helping him impress Hillary during her early visits to the beach house. His roommates—Douglas Eakeley, a friend from Oxford, Douglas Pogue, and William T. Coleman III (whose father was serving as secretary of transportation and was the only black in Richard Nixon's cabinet)—were amused at the unusual deference Clinton exhibited toward this new woman in his life. The pair seemed to be doing a kind of pas de deux, pushing and pulling yet with a lightness of step that was uncharacteristic of both of them. There was an ease. "They were very funny together, very lively," said Pogue. When Bill would lapse into his home-fried, good ole boy Southern caricature, she would affectionately mock him. "Get to the point, will you, Bill!" she'd say (she would do that throughout their lives together). It took some time for him to adjust to her straightforward Midwestern ways.

Early on, their discussions turned political. She sensed in him a commitment to public service that transcended mere ambition for office. He came from a state that lagged behind the rest of the country in education, economic prosperity, and cultural sophistication, but "he cared deeply about where he came from, which was unusual," she noted. "He was rooted, and most of us were disconnected."

Within a few weeks of their encounter in the library, Hillary and Bill were to be seen striding across campus hand in hand, obviously smitten. Deborah Sale encountered them early in their courtship. She had known Clinton since childhood days in Arkansas and Hillary as an undergraduate: "My response to them was, Well, of course. These are two people who obviously belong together. He was always very engaging, and very charming."

She "looked like a hippie," according to one close friend, dressed in blue jeans and sandals, her hair below her shoulders, her face enunciated by thick glasses, the frames of which she was constantly changing. Physically, it seemed she almost went to lengths to hide her more attractive features.

"Their values are the same. Their ambitions are the same," Sale recognized. "The passions that they have in life are the same. The kind of engagement that they have, intellectual and otherwise, is really something. And to my mind they were a perfectly reasonable couple." Sale could see that Hillary, despite disguising it, "was always very attractive in many ways," including physically, though her glasses tended to overpower some of her best features. Hillary's reputation was "of someone who was thoughtful . . . and deep. He really had the reputation of being quick." In fact, as Sale and others would come to recognize, he was the deeper one.

Some fellow students thought Clinton's attraction to Hillary was calculated, that he was trading on her renown to advance his own stature on campus and beyond. Hillary, meanwhile, conveyed an attitude that Bill's women had never confronted him with: *I don't need you.* It seemed to unnerve him.

Within weeks, Hillary told him that she planned to spend the summer in Oakland, California, as an intern at the law firm of Treuhaft, Walker and Burnstein. Clinton's plan had been to work in the South in George McGovern's presidential campaign, still in its infancy, for the Democratic presidential nomination. Now he told her he wanted to go with her to California instead.

When she pressed as to his reasons, he said it was because he loved her, according to Hillary's account in *Living History.* Hillary said later she was over the moon.

From the start, he was looking at the big picture. "I just liked . . . being around her, because I thought I'd never be bored with her. In the beginning, I used to tell her that I would like being old with her. That I thought that was an important thing."

Even then it was possible to glimpse aspects in their relationship that would become much more evident during their years in the governor's mansion and the White House. David Gergen, who worked with each during the first years of the Clinton presidency, observed: "The Bill Clinton I saw needed the emotional approval of his wife on a daily basis. He depended on her, spoke of her, and acted as if she were his Rock of Gibraltar. . . . When they were in balance, they complemented each other well. Their partnership energized his leadership. She was the anchor, he the sail. He was the dreamer, she the realist. She was the strategist, he the tactician."

For their friends, and virtually all of the law school's students, that carefully balanced equation would become evident six months later when Hillary and Bill were selected as one of the two debating teams in the renowned Barristers' Union Prize Trial.

In *Living History,* Hillary wrote: "He can astonish me with the connections he weaves between ideas and words and how he makes it all sound like music. I still love the way he thinks and the way he looks. One of the first things I noticed about Bill was the shape of his hands. His wrists are narrow and his fingers tapered and deft, like those of a pianist or surgeon." In an "autobiography" written in large part by ghostwriters, this is one of the few passages in which ecstasy comes through.

Early in their relationship, at the beach house on Long Island Sound, Hillary and Bill talked one night about what each would do after graduation. Bill said he intended to go back home to Arkansas and seek public office. Hillary's plans were still up in the air, except for her certainty that she wanted to pursue her interests in child advocacy and civil rights.

In Oakland, she would be working for the most important radical law practice on the West Coast, celebrated for its defense of constitutional rights, civil liberties, and leftist causes. "The reason she came to us," said Robert Treuhaft, the firm's senior principal, "the only reason I could think of because none of us knew her, was because we were a so-called Movement law firm at the time." In all probability, Hillary found her way to the firm through her professor, Tom Emerson, an old friend of Treuhaft and some of his partners. "There was no reason except politics for a girl from Yale" to intern at the firm, said Treuhaft. "She certainly . . . was in sympathy with all the left causes, and there was a sharp dividing line at that time. We still weren't very far out of the McCarthy era."

Treuhaft et al. had represented leaders of the labor movement on the West Coast who had been prosecuted for allegedly being members of the Communist Party. It also represented some of the Black Panther leadership. Of the firm's four partners, "two were communists, and others tolerated communists," Treuhaft said, but none acknowledged membership in the party until many years later.

Hillary's attraction to the firm was not ideology but rather its defense of constitutional causes and liberties. "All I can say is some people may have been bothered by being associated with my law firm, but she wasn't," said Treuhaft, who was married to the writer Jessica Mitford. Hillary stayed in touch with the Treuhafts, and when Mitford came to Arkansas for research on an article she was writing, she visited the Clintons in the governor's mansion. Characteristically, the note Hillary wrote to Treuhaft upon the death of his wife in 1996 was filled with personal touches. Equally characteristic, Hillary's description of her association with the Treuhafts and her summer interning in Oakland—"at Treuhaft, Walker and Burnstein, a small law firm in Oakland, California"—glosses over the suggestion of anything that could be construed as resembling a radical or leftist past.

She and Bill found an apartment near the University of California, Berkeley, campus, still the nexus of American student radicalism. She worked on a child custody case. Bill got to know the area and introduced Hillary to it. Bill read a lot and discussed *To the Finland Station* by Edmund Wilson and other books with Hillary. And they took long walks.

BILL CLINTON, as he was falling in love with Hillary, perceived that she possessed the one necessary quality that was not native to his soul: a kind of toughness, the significance and nature of which would be endlessly debated by the Clintons' friends, advocates, and adversaries. Without it, he could never have gotten to the presidency. There is truth in the observation that, after all, Bill Clinton would rather accommodate than fight and that it often took Hillary to push him into the ring. The Clintons' former pollster, Stan Greenberg, described this quality as a "fierceness," a "tough-mindedness," summoned by Hillary in pursuit of their shared goals because Clinton, unlike his wife, was preternaturally "conflict-averse . . . and by nature uncomfortable attacking. . . . He didn't get there instinctively. He'd rather persuade people. He'd like to persuade everybody in the room."

Their most important political counselor and consultant for two decades, Dick Morris, remarked—before he turned enemy—that "she has a quality of ruthlessness, a quality of aggressiveness and strength about her that he doesn't have. A killer instinct. Her genre of advocacy is always straight ahead—fight, battle, take the fight to the other side. There's no subtlety, there's none of the nuance that he has."

But Hillary's is not the caricatured, bitchy, ball-breaking toughness that their enemies like to attribute to her. She has almost always been much more thoughtful than they accorded. It is more like a kind of military rigor: reading the landscape, seeing the obstacles, recognizing which ones are malevolent or malign, and taking expedient action accordingly. Bill's process is different. He is slow to recognize the malevolence in others, he wants to assume the best about them, and he is willing to spend months trying to win their hearts and minds. Hillary means to cut off the enemy at the pass.

The first public glimpse of their political partnership, and indications of what Morris, Greenberg, and others later discerned, came during the 1972 Prize Trial at Yale. Hillary and Bill were assigned the role of prosecution team. They spent more than a month preparing their arguments, citations, and tactics. They had a tough case to prosecute, based on the murder trial of a Kentucky cop whose antipathy was on record toward young people who looked like hippies. "But is that enough motivation to beat and kill someone?" read posters advertising the trial and laying out the case.

Bill and Hillary failed to win the prize. But their preparation and performance were prototypical of a methodology they would perfect over the next quarter-century, carving out complementary roles that played to the strength and character of each. Their full partnership was apparent to their peers, who watched, fascinated, as they laid out their unusual division of labor. Nancy Bekavac described the dynamic perfectly: "Hillary was very sharp and Chicago, and Bill was very *To Kill a Mockingbird.*"

SENATOR GEORGE MCGOVERN's presidential campaign, which had grown out of the antiwar movement, was at the grassroots level a youth crusade. The candidate's campaign manager, Gary Hart, thirty-five, one of the movement's most talented organizers, chose Clinton to be McGovern's state co-coordinator in Texas with Taylor Branch, a fellow Southerner who had organized antiwar protests and worked as a political journalist for *The Washington Monthly.* (Later, Branch would write a classic three-volume biography of Martin Luther King and win a Pulitzer for one of its volumes.) In their Texas environment, Clinton and Branch looked a bit like Butch Cassidy and the Sundance Kid, Bill with his bushy hair and cowboy boots, and Taylor with a full mustache.

Bill had asked Hillary to come to Texas for the campaign, and she signed on to register voters in San Antonio. Clinton was physically and organizationally a dominating presence in the state campaign, but Hillary created an equally memorable impression. Many of the women in the campaign regarded her as the real luminary, with a more impressive résumé than Bill's. Given the likelihood of Richard Nixon overwhelming McGovern in the election, they looked to her as someone who could help pick up the pieces of the Democratic Party and, in the next few years, run for office herself.

In San Antonio she lived and worked with Sara Ehrman, who was fifteen years older. "We were two oddballs in San Antonio," Ehrman said of the two of them—a middle-aged Jewish housewife with the assertive edge of her native Brooklyn, and a hippie-looking Ivy Leaguer possessed with an intensity every bit the equal of her own. Hillary, recalled Ehrman, "came into campaign headquarters a kid—in brown corduroy pants, brown shirt, brown hair, brown glasses, no makeup, brown shoes. Her Coke-bottle glasses. Long hair. She looked like the campus intellectual that she was. She totally disregarded her appearance." Hillary's politics at the time were "liberal, ideological, the same as my own," Sara said. She described the Hillary she knew that Texas summer as a "progressive

Christian in that she believed in litigation to do good, and to correct injustices and to live by a kind of spiritual high-mindedness." Sara said Hillary was a compulsive reader: contemporary fiction, religious tomes, the Bible, academic materials about child psychology. Hillary seemed to have everything in balance—the gift of seriousness leavened by the ability to have a good time. She was witty, genuinely funny; there was nothing stuffy about her, Sara thought.

Hillary was vivid and pragmatic in approaching her task in San Antonio: trying to establish a strong connection between the local Mexican-American community and the McGovern campaign. Ehrman found her to be firm and indomitable, knocking on doors in tough neighborhoods to register Hispanic voters. Hillary was so un-intimidated that Sara took to calling her by the nickname "Fearless," the same quality that others had recognized in Hillary in her early teens, jumping on a skateboard to get a prom date or going into Chicago's ghettos on behalf of Goldwater's campaign.

Ehrman also noted another, less apparent aspect of Hillary's character—"I'd call it a kind of fervor, and self-justification that God is on her side." That summer Sara sensed Hillary was trying to reconcile her rigorous liberal political theology with her middle-class Methodist upbringing. She carried her Bible almost everywhere, marking in it and underlining as she read.

Ehrman had also met twenty-five-year-old Bill Clinton that summer, before Hillary had arrived. Sara judged him to be one of the most handsome young men she had ever seen, a conclusion many other women in the McGovern campaign seemed to share.

"Bill Clinton tapped into part of Hillary that no one ever had. Everybody else saw her as a terribly serious woman, very intense," Ehrman said. "He saw the side of her that liked spontaneity and laughter. He found her guttural laugh: it's fabulous—there's nothing held back. The public never sees that side of her. When she's laughing, that's when she's free."

Most of the McGovern volunteers in Texas were under thirty, dispatched there by Hart, and there was an easy camaraderie among the bunch, including a carefree sexual atmosphere that was reflective of the era. Evenings they would have a beer or go bowling. On weekends, Hillary was often with Bill in Austin, but they occasionally dated others, and were frequently seen arguing heatedly. More than a few women thought Bill was captivating and sexy. With his reputation as a political wunderkind, there were even groupies, and Hillary took note. After a fight, they decided to stop seeing each other. Franklin Garcia, a San

Antonio labor organizer who was tutoring Hillary about the Hispanic community, smoothed things over. Bill thanked him. "You really saved our relationship," he said.

She had a knack for making male friends, some of whom found her easier to talk to than Bill. Taylor Branch, who had recently separated from his wife, remembered that Hillary was "more focused on the grand cosmic questions" that troubled people of their generation. "Bill and I talked business," he recalled. "We laughed. We talked personalities, but we never sat down and philosophized. I was feeling rootless, unhinged, and it was easier to talk to Hillary about those things than to Bill."

To the women working in McGovern's Texas campaign, Hillary seemed to be on her way to an exceptional career in politics. Betsey Wright, a particularly industrious and ideological organizer from the West Texas hamlet of Alpine, became a true acolyte. Wright thought "women were the ethical and pure force" that could change American politics, and she and Hillary spent many of their spare hours discussing how to get more women into politics in a serious way. "It was a nascent feminist movement then. We had both read Simone de Beauvoir and Germaine Greer. And I'd just come off the heady experience of Sissy Far-enthold's campaign [for governor] in Texas," Wright said. Betsey was "less interested in Bill's political future than Hillary's. I was obsessed with how far Hillary might go, with her mixture of brilliance, ambition, and self-assuredness. There was an assumption about all the incredible things she could do in the world."

Hillary thought Wright's experience ought to benefit women outside Texas, and at Hillary's behest she moved to Washington after McGovern's crushing defeat (33 percent to Nixon's 67 percent in Texas, and similarly disastrous nationwide) to organize for the National Women's Political Caucus. From such a position, Betsey believed she could help Hillary eventually become America's first female president.

Though Ehrman and Wright formed easy friendships with Hillary, others remembered her intelligence or reserve more than any sort of effusive social interaction. Some found her aloof. There would be others, though not as many, who found her warm, gregarious, accessible, and sociable. This dichotomy always seemed to be the case with Hillary—in an organization, campaign, or even the Senate of the United States.

4

Making Arkansas Home

After all that has happened since, I'm often asked why Bill and I have
stayed together. . . . What can I say to explain a love that has persisted
for decades?

—*Living History*

WHEN HILLARY CLINTON met Bill Clinton she was no
fatalist. She fervently believed that a person could control
her own destiny and that she, Hillary, could never give herself over to vague forces, or to somebody else's dominating personality, as
she knew her mother had disastrously done. She did not believe that an
individual—particularly herself—was powerless to change either events
or the nature of other people, and she went about both tasks tenaciously.

But time after time, in Hillary's courtship and marriage with Bill
Clinton, she was confronted with the obvious: He was beyond her control when it came to other women. It wasn't his pursuit of extramarital
sex per se that so riled her, she once said. She had come to view her husband almost as an adolescent when it came to his sexual sensibilities and
compulsions, and attributed them to the pathology of his unusual childhood. "There are worse things than infidelity," she told a confidante in
1989, at a time when Bill believed himself to be in love with an Arkansas
divorcée, Marilyn Jo Jenkins. The source of Hillary's frustration and
anger, dating back to their courtship, was her knowledge that she was
powerless to change him, as she was reminded repeatedly during their
marriage. Hillary trusted in the power of rational thought and logic
above almost all else, yet he seemed immune to logical reasoning on the
subject, rather than defiant.

It took Hillary more than two years to make up her mind to marry
Bill. She had serious doubts not only about his womanizing but about

living in Arkansas, about the intensity with which he pursued his passions (including even his passion for her, which sometimes could be overwhelming). She wanted children, but she didn't want them to grow up in a strained marriage. The experience of her mother—both as an abandoned child and an abused wife (a term Hillary avoided)—weighed on her. Hillary's hesitant decision was reached only after dipping her toes in the Arkansas waters and calculating that she could learn to live there. She carefully positioned herself during those years to have a fallback plan in case their marriage or political journey ran aground. She knew that Bill's history of compulsive infidelity during their courtship meant the chances for a stable marriage, especially a marriage without adultery, were at best a crapshoot.

In the end, she married for love, and the shared dream of a grand political future someday in Washington. But that future would be focused on him, not her, she reluctantly conceded to friends who were urging her to pursue a more independent course and separate identity. Going to Arkansas meant forgoing a prestigious job in the capital or New York, and all but extinguishing her own flash in the season of her greatest promise. Since her graduation from Wellesley, she had been speeding toward national prominence.

In Arkansas, she would not be a woman in charge—something she knew was not necessarily antithetical to being married, but was antithetical to being married to Bill Clinton, on his turf. She would, by choice, inhabit the more traditional universe in which she would invest her talent, dedication, and energy to brighten her man's star—as her mother's generation had done. She would be the partner, the manager, the adviser. She would follow her heart.

HILLARY HAD ALREADY deferred her independent ambitions and made her first great sacrifice by remaining at Yale an extra year to be with Bill rather than graduate with her own class. She worked in the McGovern campaign until election day and studied children's development at the Yale Child Study Center. After their graduation from law school in the spring of 1973, she went with Bill on her first trip abroad, to England, and he showed her London, Oxford, and some of the places he had visited during his year as a Rhodes Scholar. At twilight one evening "on the shores of Ennerdale," in the English Lake District celebrated by the Romantic poets, he asked her to be his wife.

She said no. She didn't want to rush into a decision, she later explained. At that time she was afraid "of commitment in general and Bill's intensity in particular."

Many years afterward, Hillary said the marriage almost didn't happen. Bill proposed many times. "I never doubted my love for him, but I knew he was going to build his life in Arkansas. I couldn't envision what my life would be like in a place where I had no family or friends."

Not long after their return from Europe, Hillary made her first visit to Arkansas, in June 1973, almost as a consolation for saying no to his marriage proposal. Bill had asked her to come with him "to see how she liked it." He urged her to take the Arkansas bar exam. He picked her up at the Little Rock airport, choosing a picturesque (and symbol-heavy) route home to Hot Springs, first passing the state capitol and governor's mansion, then following the Arkansas River to Russellville, seventy miles from the capital, then south through the Ouachita Mountains where they stopped periodically to take in the view. Since they had first met, Bill had talked almost incessantly about his state, trying to make his enthusiasm infectious—a tough sell, the scenery notwithstanding. It was made tougher by Hillary's brief stay in Hot Springs, where Bill's mother and brother lived.

Hillary had first met Virginia Cassidy Blythe Clinton Dwire (later, Kelley) when she visited New Haven in 1972. Virginia and Hillary loved the same man, but from the beginning that didn't seem to sit well with either woman. Virginia thought Hillary was a fright—her hair badly cut (she had chopped it herself that semester, to save money), no makeup, and jeans, her preferred posture tending toward a hippie slouch. As someone with a pedigree from Park Ridge, Wellesley, and Yale—though that was hardly how she projected herself—Hillary might have concluded that Virginia, with her distinctive white-striped hair and fondness for fast men, fast horses, red lipstick, and false eyelashes had followed Route 1 straight north from Tobacco Road to New Haven. Virginia certainly didn't expect Bill to bring someone like Hillary home—a "Yankee," for good measure, albeit from Illinois.

Roger Clinton, Bill's younger brother, whom Hillary had not met prior to her arrival in Hot Springs, was quick to share his mother's parochial assessment: Hillary wasn't good-looking enough, for starters. And they thought she was bossy with Bill.

Hillary got along much more easily with Virginia's third husband, Jeff Dwire. From the time Jeff met her in New Haven, he treated her kindly and encouraged her efforts, unreciprocated for a long stretch, to reach out to Virginia. Hillary took note that he regarded Virginia with deep reverence. Dwire was a charming character, an ex-con beauty parlor proprietor who had served nine months in prison for stock swindling in the early 1960s. He was the person who had fashioned Virginia's distinctive hairstyle, taking the white stripe she'd already had and dyeing the area around it. Dwire told Hillary that Virginia would eventually come around, and embrace her as family. She did, but the turning was glacially slow.

In the two years Bill and Hillary had been together, he had recapitulated for her the vague history of his family origins as best he knew or understood them. But in Hot Springs, in Virginia's house, she would come for the first time to clearly comprehend the milieu Bill came from and, she once inferred, his sexual proclivities.

Virginia's family, the Cassidys, and the Clintons had always been religious, churchgoing people, but their faith didn't put much store in sexual restraint as an essential element of godliness. Virginia's mother, Edith, a nurse, regularly denounced her husband, Eldridge, for affairs with other women, and she was rumored to be involved sexually with some of the physicians in Hope, Arkansas. Bill's likely father, William Jefferson Blythe, had four or five wives before his death at twenty-eight. Roger Clinton, Bill's stepfather, whose last name was conferred on Bill, did not cease his philandering after marrying Virginia, and his drunken rages were sometimes fueled by jealousy—because of gossip about his wife, her flirting, or discovering her out on the town. In this environment, it might not be surprising that part of Bill's intensity was focused on women, flirting, and sexual conquests, Hillary believed.

Her confusion and ambivalence were evident the day she and Bill took the Arkansas bar exam, in Little Rock, when she ran into Ellen Brantley, who had been a year behind her at Wellesley and was also taking the exam. Brantley, who was born and raised in Little Rock, was surprised to see Hillary in a setting so jarringly out of context. "What are you doing here?" she asked.

"Oh, you know, I'm trying to get a job in Arkansas," Hillary said. Brantley could see that "she was kind of enigmatic about it, [and] didn't mention there was a romantic interest that had brought her here."

But Bill was already making calculations for both of them based on his political future, even evaluating whether there might be negative political consequences to him if they listed the same New Haven address on their individual bar applications. It had been nine years since he'd really lived in Arkansas, since he'd graduated high school and gone off to Georgetown. His plans were to teach law at the University of Arkansas while he adjusted to the political climate back home, and then to run for office.

If Hillary eventually moved to Arkansas, she would either join a law firm there or teach at the law school in Fayetteville—hardly roles commensurate with the scale of her ambition. Meanwhile, she had accepted an exciting job opportunity in Cambridge, Massachusetts, at the organization Marian Wright Edelman had recently founded, the Children's Defense Fund. When Bill and Hillary parted after her brief stay in Arkansas, their situation seemed totally unsettled.

Not long thereafter, on July 23 and 24, Hillary took the D.C. bar exam, according to records of the District of Columbia Bar Association. In Cambridge, she rented rooms not far from the Harvard campus. It was the first time in her life she had lived alone. She didn't like it.

Hillary found herself invigorated by her work for Edelman. There was a pioneering feeling about what she was doing. There had never before been a national organization devoted solely to defending the legal rights and interests of children. Hillary traveled to South Carolina to interview juvenile offenders, some as young as fourteen, who were housed in adult state prisons. The situation was all too common, she was learning, especially in the South. In Massachusetts, she went door-to-door in New Bedford to find out why there was such a discrepancy between the number of school-age children counted in the census and those enrolled in school. She studied the history of family law and the inherent and practical difficulties of asserting the rights of abused or neglected children. She was intellectually stimulated, and she enjoyed Cambridge, where many friends from her Wellesley and Yale years had gravitated, either to Harvard's campus or jobs in nearby Boston. But she missed Bill and confessed she was lonely.

On November 3, the District of Columbia Bar Association notified Hillary that she had failed the bar exam. For the first time in her life she had flamed out—spectacularly, given the expectations of others for her, and even more so her own. Of 817 applicants, 551 of her peers had passed, most from law schools less prestigious than Yale. She kept this news hidden for the next thirty years. She never took the exam again, despite many opportunities. Her closest friends and associates—Webb Hubbell, Jim Blair (Diane's husband), Nancy Bekavac, Betsey Wright, Sara Ehrman—were flabbergasted when she made the revelation in a single throwaway line in *Living History*. "When I learned that I passed in Arkansas but failed in D.C., I thought maybe my test scores were telling me something."

Those who knew her best speculated that she must have felt deep shame at her failure, and that her self-confidence—always so visible a part of her exterior—was shattered by the experience (though many first-rate lawyers, even Yale Law graduates, had flunked the bar on their first try). There can only be conjecture about what turn her life—and the nation's—might have taken had she *not* failed the exam.

There was a striking aspect to her failure. Her almost uninterrupted success to that point—including her academic career—had been based in large measure on interaction with the people who were evaluating her performance: teachers, employers, colleagues, interviewers, mentors, friends. Propelled by her character, personality, and drive, she was almost invariably very impressive. The D.C. bar examination, hardly one of the toughest in the nation but far more difficult than the Arkansas exam, was an impersonal test—no people skills were on display, no opportunity to influence the outcome with demonstrations of character or force of personality, or a winning way with strangers. This failure, a blow to her ambition, played a role in the decisions she now faced.

Bill flew to New England over the Thanksgiving holiday in 1973, and while they explored Boston together, they talked about their future. By then he had rented "the perfect place to live," as he called it, a singularly beautiful, small wood-and-glass house eight miles outside Fayetteville in the countryside, on eighty secluded acres bordered on one side by the White River. Clinton had always had an aesthetic gift, more developed than Hillary's in art, design, and music, their friends thought, and he'd rented a house created by one of the country's more remarkable mid-century architects, the Arkansan Fay Jones, whose Thorncrown Chapel outside Fayetteville, in Eureka Springs, is a tiny jewel justly celebrated for its simple, pared beauty. Fayetteville, on the edge of the Ozarks in northwest Arkansas, was only a few miles from the summer band camp Bill had attended as a boy, a forested annual respite from the tar-baked asphalt of Hot Springs. Sitting in a rocking chair on the porch of this little house, Clinton could gaze at cattle grazing on the property near the river, and the familiar forests beyond. Field mice regularly scurried into the kitchen, and when he gave up trying to keep them out, he put out breadcrumbs for them.

In Cambridge, Bill told Hillary how he loved the house, how he was enjoying teaching at the university—and that he was scouring his corner of the state to find a Democratic candidate who could take on Arkansas's only Republican member of Congress, John Paul Hammerschmidt. Hammerschmidt might be unusually vulnerable because of the toll Nixon's Watergate scandal was taking on members of the president's party as he fought to stay in office. Bill had been unable to persuade anybody to run. Hillary could tell he was thinking of doing it himself. She was relieved to be with him again, even elated. Their time together in Cambridge did little to clarify their situation, however. Her reservations about marriage and Arkansas remained.

Bill recognized that to be married to him "would be a high-wire operation," and that Arkansas was not her preferred residence. He'd been fortunate to rub elbows with the ablest people of his generation, but he regarded Hillary as "head and shoulders above them all in political potential. She had a big brain, a good heart, better organizational skills than I did, and political skills that were nearly as good as mine; I'd just had more experience." Her happiness was all-important to him, he said, and perhaps it was better if she proceeded without him. They agreed that during the upcoming Christmas holidays Hillary would visit Arkansas again, so they could work toward a decision, Hillary said.

She arrived in Fayetteville a few days after Christmas. She had hardly settled in when what must have seemed like Providence itself intervened, in the form of a phone call to Bill from John Doar, who had just been hired as chief counsel to the House Judiciary Committee's impeachment investigation of Nixon. Doar had served the previous year as a judge during the Barristers' Union Prize Trial at Yale—at the invitation of Hillary and Bill, who had admired him from afar. Now Doar was saying that Bill was at the top of his list of recommendations for young lawyers to join the impeachment committee staff. Would Clinton take off a year from teaching law and come to Washington, and suggest the names of other exceptional attorneys who might be available.

According to Hillary's version of events, Bill had already made up his mind to run for Congress before Doar's call, and she, too, was on the short list of Doar's candidates to join the impeachment staff. Bill, in his version, said that he was still undecided about running for office, but after talking with Hillary he made up his mind. He turned Doar down but recommended Hillary.

Whatever the exact version of events, when Hillary was offered the job, she jumped at the opportunity.

IF THINGS FELL into place, Doar's offer to Hillary represented a perfect solution to her and Bill's dilemma as a couple. Hillary did not want to move to Arkansas. But if Nixon were investigated by the Judiciary Committee, then impeached by the House and tried by the Senate (a real possibility, even likely), the process would almost certainly take more than a year. If Bill won election to the House of Representatives in November, he would begin the job in January 1975, about the same time the impeachment process was likely to end. Under such circumstances, Hillary's stature, at age twenty-seven, among the political cognescenti of the capital would be soaring (as indeed occurred after Nixon's resignation). They could accede in the capital as the city's golden young couple.

Hillary excitedly called Marian Edelman from Bill's house. Marian told her she could always return to the Children's Defense Fund, but that working on the impeachment inquiry was far more important.

Before leaving for Washington, Hillary accompanied Bill on a courtesy call to the home of former governor Orval Faubus in Huntsville, high on a ridge overlooking the Ozarks, about twenty-five miles from Fayetteville. Seventeen years after his famous (and shaming) refusal to permit the integration of Little Rock's Central High School and President Dwight Eisenhower's dispatch of federal troops to enforce the desegregation order of the Supreme Court, Faubus was still a canny operator, and as much as Clinton "disapproved of what he'd done at Little Rock," he knew a thing or two about Arkansas politics. In fact, Faubus was an amalgam of Arkansas political traditions—the son of a communist/socialist organizer, a populist, a New Dealer, and an unrepentant segregationist. Calling on him was a price that wise Democratic candidates still paid. Hillary remained virtually silent through the visit four or five hour visit, as did Faubus's second (and much younger) wife, Elizabeth, whose hair was piled in a beehive. Bill sought answers to practical and historical questions: How did Arkansans cope with the Depression? What was life like in World War II Arkansas? Why was Faubus insistent on still defending his segregationist stand of 1954? How did he think the impeachment investigation of Nixon—and the president's difficulties generally—would figure in the congressional election? (Not much, Faubus replied.)

Meanwhile, Bill called David Pryor, then running for governor, to ask whether his girlfriend's taking a job on the impeachment inquiry staff might prove a political liability. It might even be an asset, Pryor believed.

In Washington, Hillary moved into a spare room in the townhouse of Sara Ehrman, her friend from the McGovern campaign in Texas. The atmosphere in the capital felt to her electric. She was part of a historic enterprise in which her work and ideas would contribute to monumental events. There was a further, personal dividend: by doing what she did best—research, analysis, absorbing the experience of accomplished colleagues and stimulating them with her own ideas, engaging her keen political sensibility in the most meaningful public service imaginable— Hillary could rebuild her self-confidence after failing the D.C. bar examination.

Her work reflected Doar's unorthodox and clever methodology. Only three or four of his most trusted aides had a full picture of how the impeachment investigation was being put together, and of the materials that would be used to build the case against Nixon. At the staff attorney level—Hillary's—Doar assigned scutwork, nuts-and-bolts tasks that required procedural research about the rules and requirements for impeachment, even who would sit where during hearings. The last impeachment by the House had been in 1936, of a federal judge. Hillary's first responsibility was to collate procedural information about previous impeachment proceedings, both American and English, from which the concept had been borrowed. The proclamation of the sergeant at arms was duly noted in the materials she put together: "All persons are commanded to keep silent on pain of imprisonment while the House of Representatives is exhibiting to the Senate of the United States articles of impeachment against _____."

Hillary was one of three women on the staff of forty-four lawyers. The whole operation—ninety lawyers and secretaries, clerks, researchers, and typists—was directed by Doar on the faded premises of the old Congressional Hotel on Capitol Hill, which had been commandeered for the staff's exclusive use. Capital police patrolled the perimeter. Many bedrooms had been transformed into two-desk offices. Some of the larger bathrooms had been set aside for single-desk occupancy.

Like her colleagues, Hillary worked twelve- to eighteen-hour days, rising shortly after dawn. Doar's rules forbade the staff from making personal notes or keeping diaries or (not surprisingly) talking outside the office to any nonstaff members about the inquiry or their work. Given such strictures, colleagues tended to eat lunch and dinner together, then go home for a night's sleep and report back to the office in the morning.

One of the other women on the legal staff was Terry Kirkpatrick, an Arkansan who had been raised in Fort Smith and attended the University of Arkansas Law School in Fayetteville. As they got to know each other better, Hillary began asking Kirkpatrick about life in Arkansas and how a non-Southern woman like herself might fare there, especially in the state's tight-knit legal community. There weren't many female lawyers in the state, noted Kirkpatrick, so "you have to be three hundred percent better than any man to succeed. You have to pick your friends carefully. It's a very different culture. But the people when they accept you are loving and very supportive and very willing to accept new ideas once they get past the initial shock." Morover, it would be "easy to make an impact there. You can be a big fish in a small pond."

It was clear to Kirkpatrick that Hillary was "besotted," "absolutely, totally crazy about Bill Clinton"; the two or three times he was on his way to Washington to visit, Hillary's "face would change. It would light up."

Others regarded her as near-obsessed with her relationship with Bill to the extent that her moods were dictated by the frequency of her phone conversations with him and the vibes she was picking up over the line from Arkansas. Tom Bell, with whom she shared an office, saw her "come in some mornings mad because he wouldn't have called her. She would be cranky. But she would come in other mornings, hit me in the biceps, and say, 'You know, Tom Bell, Bill Clinton is going to be president of the United States someday.'"

Bernard Nussbaum, a former assistant U.S. attorney from New York, class of '61 at Harvard Law, was her immediate supervisor. One night when they were the last to leave the office, Nussbaum offered Hillary a ride home and she talked about Bill. Nussbaum, who regarded himself as Hillary's mentor, suggested that perhaps her young man needed some experience beyond law school before seeking a congressional seat.

"You don't understand," she said. Her umbrage was palpable. "He's going to be president of the United States." Nussbaum drew a deep breath, as he remembered it, and pronounced the idea absurd. Hillary remained unbowed. "You don't know him—I do. He is going to be president. You may think it's silly. It's not." He'd never seen her angry before. At Sara Ehrman's house, she got out without saying another word and slammed the car door. Nussbaum did not understand that much more than a seat in Congress was at stake in Bill's candidacy. His victory would mean a life in Washington for Hillary, and she wouldn't be tethered like an Arkansas prisoner on a ball and chain.

WHILE HILLARY was virtually locked up in a building on Capitol Hill, Bill declared his candidacy from the Third Congressional District of Arkansas on February 25, 1974, with press conferences in the state's four principal cities: Hot Springs, where he grew up; Little Rock; Fort Smith, with the biggest concentration of voters in the Third District; and Fayetteville, where he set up his campaign headquarters not far from the University of Arkansas campus.

From the outset, his campaign staff heard Bill speak rapturously and repeatedly about his politically savvy girlfriend who was working back in Washington on the impeachment inquiry, and how much he was in love with her. What he did not convey was the degree to which she was already his closest confidante and adviser. From Washington, Hillary became a significant player in the campaign, phoning advice almost daily to the candidate and making her weight felt with Bill's campaign managers. Hillary's political advice to the Arkansans, however, didn't necessarily rub well. "She started calling from day one, several times a day at first," campaign manager Ron Addington said. "She was telling me, You need to get this done, you need to get that done. What positions we had to fill." The campaign's senior staff recognized that her insights about Bill were incisive. Indeed, with her work in McGovern's Texas campaign and now in Washington, her political experience was greater than some of Clinton's managers. But Hillary knew comparatively little about Arkansas, its unique history and political environment. Still, she didn't hesitate to give Addington and his deputies detailed lists of what she thought needed to be done. When her ideas weren't acted on, she was quick to express her dismay. On several weekends when she flew to Arkansas to be with Bill she invariably made her presence felt at campaign headquarters.

Betsey Wright, who was also commuting on weekends from Washington to help Clinton, was amazed at Hillary's ability to do her job on the impeachment inquiry and devote so much time to the campaign. Wright believes there was another reason Hillary traveled to Fayetteville: to run off Bill's other women. Bill and Hillary sometimes fought openly about it. "I was very much aware that he was dating other women," Wright said.

At one point Hillary threatened in a phone call to go to bed with somebody in Washington if Clinton persisted in his womanizing. Campaign deputy Paul Fray said he overheard Bill's end of the conversation in which Clinton "about broke down and cried" and pleaded that Hillary not "go and do something that would make life miserable" for them both. Clinton had girlfriends in Little Rock and several towns in his campaign district, and, for several months, he had been seeing a young student volunteer from the University of Arkansas who worked at campaign headquarters. His staff, well aware of their candidate's propensities, turned a blind eye unless problems impeded on the campaign itself.

Wright, who for the next decade would devote herself to Bill Clinton's political life and the attendant task of minimizing damage to his future and his marriage from his sexual compulsions, described the environment of the 1974 campaign: "There were girls falling all over him like he was a rock star . . . just like they were for the rest of his life." Bill's attitude, Wright said, was to pretend there was no inherent conflict with his relationship to Hillary, as if he were saying, in effect, "Hillary is a very important person to me, and she is one of the most incredible people I've ever known. And, hey, isn't this girl falling all over me cute? That was the context." Wright didn't discuss it with Bill or Hillary. "I was chickenshit about it then, and I was chickenshit about it for the next twenty years of our lives."

IN WASHINGTON, bound by their mission, members of the impeachment staff formed extremely close relationships. "It had the characteristics of an intense political campaign but with much less sex," said one of Hillary's colleagues. As she always did, Hillary formed important friendships with men in her orbit, but it seems they remained platonic.

Still, Hillary and a few of her women colleagues reacted to what they regarded, not unreasonably, as the underlying sexist attitude of many men in the office. She was among those responsible for a sign on a coffee machine near the library, where many of the women worked, that read: "The women in this office were not hired to make coffee. Make it yourself or call on one of these liberated men to do so." There followed the names of male lawyers on the staff.

Albert Jenner, the committee's senior Republican counsel, found himself challenged by Hillary when he offhandedly remarked that there were no celebrated trial lawyers who were women. Terry Kirkpatrick remembered Hillary telling him that "the reason was because women generally did not have wives. She said that the reason male trial lawyers could be famous was because their wives packed their bags and ironed their clothes and were supportive of them while they were doing their work."

That spring, during a visit to Fayetteville, Hillary attended a dinner party with a group of Bill's law school colleagues, including the dean, who invited her on the spot to join the faculty. Bill had been lobbying the dean to make just such an offer. A few weeks later she scheduled a formal interview with a faculty review committee. "Hillary came dressed as if she had been shopping at Bloomingdale's the day before," one of the interviewers remembered. "It looked strange in Arkansas. She was wearing one of those long skirts and black stockings and horn-rimmed glasses. She did not look Arkansas." Hillary easily won over the faculty, but could this Ivy League–educated Yankee from the Midwest fit in?

Her taste in clothes was something that people who met her over the next twenty years always seemed to comment on. "She didn't care a flip about" clothes, said Kirkpatrick. Nor had she ever liked to shop. "But once she got started, she had a great time." Shopping was a manifestation of Hillary's inclination to sometimes go overboard with a new enthusiasm, not necessarily with great skill.

THE ARRIVAL in Fayetteville that summer of Hillary's father and brother Tony was believed by some campaign volunteers to be part of her effort to keep tabs on Bill, to prevent his chasing other women. But more than anything else it was a sign of how seriously Hillary was trying to make a commitment to him; the same attitude had been reflected in her willingness to interrupt her work and prepare for a job interview at the university, taking off three days (to Doar's displeasure) to do it.

Hillary had told Bill how difficult it would be for her to live in Arkansas without family and friends. When her father and Tony arrived in Hugh's Cadillac, campaign manager Addington was surprised. He had no memory of Hillary saying they were coming to town.

"Well, how long are you going to be here to visit?" Addington asked Hugh. "Hell, I don't know. Hillary told me I ought to come down here and help you out." The next day, the Cadillac was loaded with piles of "Clinton for Congress" signs, and father and son headed for the back roads of Arkansas's rural counties. Occasionally, calls were received at campaign headquarters about "the Yankees in the Cadillac."

Hugh Rodham had come a long way—for him—since Hillary had gone off to Yale. The first summer she and Bill dated, she'd brought him to meet her family at the cabin on Lake Winola, where her father promptly ordered his daughter's suitor, who was long-haired and bearded, to sleep on the porch—ostensibly because he didn't like the way Bill looked. In fact, her father's attitude at that time would have been the probable fate of any young man who came calling on his daughter, with whom he had made a grudging peace since Wellesley. He'd taken silent pride in her accomplishments, not least of which had been a gradual but obvious attempt at being less provocative toward him and more accepting of his rough edges. Bill's charm and ability to mix well with pretty much anybody, and enjoy it, helped win Hugh over.

There had never been a strong male figure in Clinton's family life— his probable father, William Jefferson Blythe, having died in a car accident before he was born, and his alcoholic stepfather, Roger Clinton, whom he came to love and understand only as he succumbed to cancer, died while Bill was at Georgetown University. Bill wanted very much to fit in with the Rodham family. He and Hugh Jr. would stay up late discussing the state of the world, while Bill taught him to play Hearts. Clinton enjoyed the sparring over politics (and almost any other subject) that seemed to be part of every meal at the Rodham dinner table, and exhibited much more patience with Hugh's dogmatic pronouncements than did his daughter. Bill could *explain* to him, as Hillary seemed incapable of doing calmly, the history and reasoning behind so many aspects of liberal and Democratic tradition. The fact that he was someone who had grown up in the conservative Deep South also carried weight. Hillary's father taught Bill (as he had taught his daughter at a very young age) to play pinochle, and Bill enjoyed telling Hugh tales about good ole boys from the piney woods back home, about high rollers and hellish women from Hot Springs, and the pols and mobsters who'd set the tone of life there in the 1930s, 1940s, and 1950s, the same kinds of characters who enlivened the underside of life in Hugh's native Scranton.

Dorothy was intrigued with Bill and his stories from the start. She judged him exceedingly interesting and sincere, and was surprised that he'd traveled so widely. When she asked him what he intended to do after Yale, and he said without blinking that he was planning to go back to Arkansas to help his home state, she was impressed, not "least [because] he knew what he wanted." However, when it came time for Hillary to decide whether to follow Bill back to Arkansas, she was unsure if it was the right choice for her daughter. "But you know, I've never told my children what to do. I had to rely on Hillary's judgment—there'd never been any reason not to."

JOHN DOAR regarded Hillary as among the most able of his young recruits and he tended to entrust her with a bit more responsibility than others at her level. Occasionally he would summon her to his office—his desk was invariably almost bare except for a notepad and pencil, which was indicative of the mysterious aura that surrounded him—and ask her opinion of something; it was never a major item affecting evidence or the totality of the case against Nixon, but important enough to signal his unusual confidence in her. The case he was assembling was meticulously registered on five-by-seven-inch cards of evidentiary materials that came to number more than half a million eventually, filed and cross-indexed (each was seven-ply) in card cabinets in the library. By design, only he and two or three of his "chiefs," as he called his principal deputies, knew the coherent story of what the collected entries told. But "the cards" became a famous symbol of the impeachment investigation, and indeed were the heart of Doar's process.

Doar, once nominally a Republican himself, had made his name as a courageous aide to Attorney General Robert Kennedy, protecting blacks and asserting their civil rights in the South. He was insistent that staff members maintain the appearance of absolute nonpartisanship and convey that no prejudgment of Nixon had been made. However, his own prejudgment had already been made, based on the abundance of facts already known from the Senate Watergate hearings and the fuller record assembled by the special prosecutor's office. His job was to protect the integrity and secrecy of the Judiciary Committee investigation, he believed, to assemble all the facts as they continued to develop, especially from analysis and transcription of Nixon's secret tapes. From these sources, he intended to build an airtight case that would convince the Congress that the president had grievously violated his oath of office and should be impeached. Conviction in the Senate, he was confident, would follow if Doar and his staff, and by extension, the Judiciary Committee, proceeded with sufficient care and meticulousness. Doar succeeded, in no small measure because of his methodology, which, among other attributes, resulted in virtually no information leaking to either the press or unauthorized members of Congress. His obsession about secrecy and security was extreme but well reasoned. Reporters were constantly trying to pry and wheedle information from staff members, from trash collectors (though Doar had instituted an elaborate and impregnable shredding and trash-burning procedure), and from friends and relatives of anyone who worked on the inquiry.

Upon her arrival for duty, Hillary had strong opinions about Nixon and his transgressions (since the McGovern campaign and Nixon's response to the war in Vietnam she'd described him as "evil") and had little doubt that he deserved to be impeached. Even many Republican staff members agreed. But from Doar she learned the value of working in extreme secrecy and of building a meticulous case to obtain a desired objective as well as the ability to keep *outsiders*, especially the press, from changing the internal dynamic of a working project. Unfortunately, over the ensuing decades, Hillary often applied these principles to situations that did not justify such control.

During the investigation, Hillary also learned a great deal from Bernie Nussbaum, whom she came to regard as a teacher and avuncular figure. At her age and level of experience, the difference of eleven years between them seemed particularly significant. Nussbaum was a partner in a high-class New York law firm, but his experience as a litigator had been forged in the U.S. Attorney's Office of the Southern District of New York, with its tradition of brilliant book-lawyering and tough-guy street smarts. He could be blustery and ball-busting and believed in scorched-earth tactics if they would bring about the desired result and did not extrude to the farther ethical reaches of the judicial swamp. He also could be sweet-talking if the strategy required it.

Following her initial assignment to research the procedures of impeachments, Doar and Nussbaum assigned her with some colleagues to determine what the precise grounds or standards had been for previous impeachments. The report she co-authored focused on the meaning of the phrase "high crimes and misdemeanors." It propounded that "to limit impeachable conduct to criminal offenses would be incompatible with the evidence concerning the constitutional meaning of the phrase . . . and would frustrate the purpose that the framers intended for impeachment." This was heady stuff.

Since March, Nixon's tapes had been arriving from the special prosecutor's office, to devastating effect for the president. In early July, members of the Judiciary Committee staff listened to the Oval Office tape recording in which Nixon's culpability and centrality to the cover-up was established beyond any doubt. "I don't give a shit what happens," Nixon had said to his top aides on March 22, 1973. "I want you to stonewall it, let them plead the Fifth Amendment, cover up or anything else. . . .

That's the whole point." There was no doubt in Hillary's mind, or hardly anyone else's in the office, that the conversation established that the president was guilty of high crimes and misdemeanors and would be impeached. On July 19, 1974, Doar formally presented articles of impeachment to the full Judiciary Committee. Three—citing abuse of power, obstruction of justice, and contempt of Congress—passed the Judiciary Committee with overwhelming bipartisan majorities.

When Nixon recognized he would be impeached by the full House and convicted by the Senate, he resigned, on August 9, 1974. Rather than make plans to stay in Washington and study for the bar (later, she would say she had been approached for a job interview by acquaintances at the firm of Williams & Connolly and at other Washington law offices), or even see the impeachment investigation through to its final report, Hillary that day accepted the job she had been offered to teach at the University of Arkansas Law School, and told Bill she would come to Fayetteville.

If Bill and Hillary were truly to be a couple, one of them had to compromise, said Hillary. "With the unexpected end of my work in Washington, I [could] give our relationship—and Arkansas—a chance."

LOOKING BACK over her life upon her arrival in Arkansas, she could have reflected on the path that brought her to this point. In an early letter to the Reverend Don Jones from Wellesley, Hillary had declared that her undergraduate days would be a period for her to "try out different personalities and lifestyles"; and in her junior year, she wrote to her boyfriend Geoff Shields at Harvard: "I want to go to Africa and then Europe and then back to the U.S. to travel—really 'bum around' for a year doing all the things which strike my bountiful fancy." She wanted to work at a crafts center in the Carolinas; try her skills at theater; head for Southern California or Mexico, to "work at a series of day jobs for about a month, just to meet various types of people." Northern California and "the Nevada caves where all the 'real' hippies are moving" also beckoned. She had been told that Mount McKinley "is the most beautiful sight in the world," and planned to get there (which she did). "Working in television or movies for a short while would really be fun." All of this she intended to pack into the year she was planning between Wellesley and graduate school.

By the time Hillary had met Bill at Yale, she was considerably more sophisticated than he. His romantic relationships with women were usually short, sexual, casual, one-dimensional. She'd had real romances before she met him, a few of them in which political, philosophical, and intellectual ideas were meaningfully exchanged. There was a maturity and wholeness that was lacking in Bill's relationships with women. She had come a long way since Park Ridge.

When Bill Clinton became president he had experienced life through the glands of a politician and the mind of an intellectual. With the formative exceptions of his empathic boyhood experience among Southern blacks and the European travels of his Oxford days, his most basic ideas and values evolved from reading, conversation, campaigning, and governing—and the experience of his wife.

Her detractors and enemies have long maintained that her huge ambition was rooted in the raw pursuit of power and bent severely toward a far-left or radically liberal agenda. But by the time she had graduated from Yale Law School in 1973, radicalism and fervent ideology held little appeal to her. She was, though, willing to experiment with radical ideas, borrow from them and seek to understand their impetus, the history behind them, and their relevance. Democracy, she asserted in her senior thesis at Wellesley, was "the most radical of political faiths."

As an undergraduate, "she was never truly left," in the words of a classmate. "Very much a moderate, very much a facilitator." Her gift for political pragmatism as a means of achieving what she believed was right—a gift she shared with Bill—was already evident.

Ultimately Hillary's real-life education and sense of right and wrong (which became more complicated and relativist as she grew older) guided her away from rigid ideology, led her to reject hard political dogma of any sort (including aspects of feminist theology), and to choose a career in mainstream law—to pay the bills—and a pro bono practice (the unconventional impetus) defending the rights of children. These were particularly interesting choices for the daughter of Dorothy Rodham, a woman who had been abandoned by her parents and marginalized financially by her husband, and the wife-to-be of a man whose mother had been beaten by his alcoholic stepfather and widowed by his wandering biological father.

By high school, the different approaches taken by Hillary and Bill had already emerged—her riskier, experimental, and experiential path was evolving; his more set, conventional track with its emphasis on good government, Boys Nation, and band was likewise identifiable. He loved Elvis, played the saxophone, and worshipped Jack Kennedy. Hillary chaired the Fabian fan club, accumulated batches of Girl Scout badges, was a certified swimming instructor for the recreation department, and cleaned the church altar on weekends—but she also canvassed Chicago's black housing projects for Barry Goldwater's candidacy and babysat migrant Mexican children whose mothers and fathers worked the fields in rural Illinois, west of Chicago. Hillary reached decisions through trial and error; participation and involvement was common to both Bill and Hillary. Her political development reflected more curiosity and openness.

Hillary put enormous faith in her own empirical compass, allowing it to guide her exploration of Wellesley and Yale, and eventually to get through the wilderness of her personal and political struggles in Arkansas. She might have been better served in the White House had she not wandered so far from her usual path of testing and experimenting with different routes before fixing on a destination. With her decision to run for the Senate, and her subsequent tack as a senator, she again turned confidently to the magnetic tug of her own experience.

Though she looked bookish and enjoyed studying, Hillary was far more inclined than Bill to augment study with firsthand reconnaissance and personal trial as the basis for action and belief. She was not a classic intellectual, one guided by received wisdom and consequent supposition. Characteristically, she had traveled to Chicago to personally examine the programs described in her senior thesis. Her college letters to Geoff Shields and Don Jones are a lode of rich descriptions of her own experiences, from trying out for a Wellesley production of Edward Albee's play *Who's Afraid of Virginia Woolf?* (in the role of foul-mouthed, emasculating Martha) to working in a cannery.

When she settled in Arkansas, her diverse undertakings were already remarkable. She'd worked at menial jobs (washing dishes at a lodge in Mount McKinley National Park and sliming fish in Alaska, where she wore knee-high boots in bloody water while removing the guts of king salmon with a spoon); studied law as it affected the wealthiest and poorest of clients; spent a summer interning at a California law firm noted for representation of the Black Panthers and the Communist Party; and been a summer intern for the House Republican Conference. Now she had been a lawyer in the congressional impeachment investigation of Richard Nixon.

And she could throw a football.

Before becoming president, Bill had held few real jobs outside of electoral politics: as a counselor in his teens at a summer youth camp and a summer clerk for the Senate Foreign Relations Committee as an undergraduate; and, to support himself at Yale, as an instructor at a community college teaching law enforcement personnel and a lawyer's assistant in New Haven. His later teaching and law practice were basically time-killers between running for office.

Through the years of their marriage, Hillary's experiential openness would further delineate her capacity for personal growth and change. As for Bill, only his political skills and judgments, as opposed to personal and emotional attributes, appeared to become more acute as he grew older.

HILLARY'S MOMENTOUS political journey with Bill began in earnest in Sara Ehrman's Volkswagen a week after Richard Nixon and his long-suffering wife, Pat, left the White House for exile in San Clemente, California. Hillary would never forget the experience of that first lady, and her wifely passivity at the trauma her husband put her through.

For the next uneasy twelve months, Hillary, now twenty-six, would vacillate about whether to marry Bill. Ehrman, who had been an important source of wisdom and encouragement in her life since their summer together in Texas, was deeply disappointed by Hillary's decision to leave the capital for Arkansas. To her, Hillary was the "brilliant and dazzling" embodiment of the women's movement and all its promise, and she tried mightily to persuade her not to surrender a limitless future in Washington for a man—even Bill Clinton, whom she knew—and become an assistant professor at a "hillbilly" law school. "You are crazy," Ehrman told her at one point, and asked why she would do something so out of character. Hillary, of course, was deeply ambivalent, "at sea about whether she wanted to move to Arkansas," according to one of their mutual friends, torn about "how hard to be, how careerist to be," for this was 1974, and she was hardly unaffected by the feminist movement.

Ehrman asked incredulously, "Why on earth would you throw away your future?" The Democrats in Washington looked ascendant and principled. The country seemed on the verge of a new age of reform. By virtue of Hillary's role in the most important investigation in Washington since the Army-McCarthy hearings in the 1950s, she was now at the top of the heap of America's young, public-service-minded lawyers, with an undimmed opportunity (or so Ehrman thought) to take a seat at any of Washington's or New York's top law firms, leading to a partnership. And though Ehrman regarded Hillary almost as a daughter, and as "a poster child of a liberated woman," she also knew from the incessant phone calls between Hillary and Bill that they were deeply in love.

Unsuccessful at persuading Hillary to stay in Washington, Sara had finally offered to drive Hillary to Arkansas, with another friend, Alan Stone, who was a native of the state. Hillary packed her books, stereo, and clothes into Ehrman's Volkswagen and they headed south. Her bicycle, which she had barely had a chance to ride in Washington, was strapped to the roof. When they crossed the Potomac that humid August morning, its banks were ablaze in yellow and red blossoms, Lady Bird

Johnson's lasting floral bequest to the nation before she and her husband had left the capital, disillusioned, with the country mired in an unwinnable war. Hillary's final glance back was of Memorial Bridge and Lincoln's marbled temple from the Arlington Heights, after which they drove through the Virginia countryside, past Middleburg, Warrenton, Culpeper, and into the Shenandoah Mountains, then down to Charlottesville. Hillary was in a hurry to get to Fayetteville, excited at the prospect of seeing Bill, but Ehrman stopped at Monticello, the home of Thomas Jefferson, and detoured to other historical sites as she renewed her campaign to persuade Hillary to turn around.

Hillary was unflinching.

"Are you sure?" Sara kept asking.

"No, but I'm going anyway."

Hillary was sure only that she loved Bill and wanted to take a chance. "My friends and family thought I had lost my mind. I was a little bit concerned about that as well," she said later.

Fayetteville seemed even farther away from Washington than the 1,225 miles between. When they finally reached the University of Arkansas campus, a rally was underway for the Razorbacks football team. The whole town had turned out, thousands upon thousands of fans wearing pig hats and yelling *Sou-ee, sou-ee, pig, pig, pig.* "I was just appalled," Sara recalled. The following day, however, when she and Hillary went to see Bill speak at a campaign stop, Sara recognized immediately those magnetic attributes that had pulled Hillary across the mountains. Sara could see now, for the first time, something else: that Hillary was not being preposterous when she said that this young man, only twenty-eight years old and seeking his first public office, might someday be president of the United States. And for the first time, Sara sensed that Hillary had given a lot of thought about how she could become something approaching an equal partner in the venture.

TWO DAYS AFTER her arrival in Fayetteville, Jeff Dwire died unexpectedly of heart failure at forty-eight, probably a consequence of the diabetes from which he suffered. Virginia, widowed for a third time, and Bill's brother, Roger (who had now lost two fathers, as Bill put it), were devastated by his death. Dwire had made Virginia happier than she'd been in all the years Bill could remember. Bill's closeness to his mother, his solicitousness and lifelong desire to please her, his caring and love for a troubled younger brother, affected Hillary, though she continued to chafe at Virginia's antipathy. Bill had conveyed to Hillary, with extraordinary tenderness, his longing to have with her the kind of family life he had lacked. Both of them carried scars from childhood. Each recognized some deep, unresolved hurt in the other.

Dwire had wanted to be cremated, but there was no crematorium anywhere in the state. This was the sort of thing that reinforced Hillary's fears about the smallness of the Arkansas world into which she had just arrived. Bill, who had driven to Hot Springs to take care of the funeral arrangements, had to ship Dwire's body to Texas for cremation; upon the return of Jeff's ashes, Bill would see that they were scattered over a lake outside town, near Dwire's favorite fishing dock.

Hillary had arrived on campus only a day before the term began at the law school and didn't learn what courses she'd be teaching until then. In addition to her classwork, she was assigned to run the local legal aid clinic and a prisoners assistance project.

By the end of the first week of classes, almost everyone at the University of Arkansas seemed to know that Hillary was Bill Clinton's girlfriend, and that she had just come from working on Nixon's impeachment. Her competence and high expectations of her students registered immediately, but not nearly as much as her personal style, her accent, and her manner of dress, which struck many on campus as Northern hippie. The ethos and impact of the counterculture were much less apparent in the nonurban South than cities like Atlanta and New Orleans and even Dallas; and the University of Arkansas hardly rivaled Duke or the University of Texas in terms of the general sophistication of its student body or faculty. Behind the barrier of the Ozarks there was almost a time warp, reflective of many aspects of the state itself.

Fayetteville, with its quaint town square lined on each side by small shops (including the Campbell-Bell department store run by Bill Clinton's cousin Roy) and the municipal post office in the middle, could not have been more removed from Hillary's experience since she'd left Park Ridge—her life in Washington and New England and even Texas, with their rhythms of drama and conflict. Since she'd left home for Wellesley in 1965, she'd been literally in the thick of things, which she craved. She had always aspired to be a major player. But there was something about Fayetteville that was reminiscent of Park Ridge—not just the little downtown with its soda shop and hangouts for the locals, but also the easy congeniality of the town. People seemed to recognize one another on the streets, to smile, to move more slowly. Not long after her arrival, Hillary dialed Information to obtain the phone number of a student who'd skipped an appointment. "He's not home," the operator told her. "He's gone camping."

To Hillary's surprise and relief, Fayetteville was home to an extraordi-nary, and worldly, group of women, some of them native Arkansans, oth-ers from big Northern and Western cities who had followed their men back home after college. Life in Fayetteville had a certain sweetness, they seemed to agree, and there was no shortage of things to do locally either politically or intellectually. "She was moving into an academic environ-ment," said Deborah Sale. "She wasn't moving to a plantation along the Mississippi in a town of twenty." Hillary learned to enjoy some of the town's Southern charm: eating barbecue, cheering from the stands at Arkansas Razorback football games—even yelling "Soo-ee!" to call the hogs. She moved into a stone-and-wood house—also designed by Fay Jones—that belonged to a renowned member of the faculty who had taught for many years both in Fayetteville and at New York University Law School.

Hillary taught criminal law and trial advocacy the first semester and criminal procedures the second semester. When Bill had decided to run for Congress, he had obtained permission from the dean to keep teaching through the campaign. He taught agency and partnership law, as well as trade regulation. Many students had both as professors. Hillary's style was confident, aggressive, take-charge, and much more structured than Bill's. "All business," a colleague said. Her questions to students were tough and demanding. Bill almost never put his students on the spot; rather, he maintained an easy dialogue with them. His conversational approach often gave students the run of the class, and he let them filibuster.

"If you were unprepared, she would rip you pretty good, but not in an unfair way," recalled Woody Bassett, who became a good friend of both, and worked in many Clinton political campaigns. "She made you think, she challenged you. If she asked you a question about a case and you gave an answer, well then—here comes another question. Whereas in Bill Clinton's classes, it was much more laid-back." In class Hillary never mentioned her work on the impeachment inquiry. Bill was far more open about discussing political issues with his students, whether Nixon's impeachment or *Roe v. Wade*, on which he spent several weeks. The sub-ject of his constitutional law course more naturally lent itself to political questions than Hillary's. He was regarded as the easiest grader in the law school. Hillary's exams were tough, and her grading commensurate with what she expected serious law students to know. There was little doubt that she was the better teacher, possessed with "unusual ability to absorb a huge amount of facts and boil them down to the bottom line," Bassett thought. Clinton was more likely to go at a subject in a circular way, looking at it from every angle and sometimes never coming to a conclusion. But usually his was the more interesting class, because of the passion and knowledge with which he addressed legal questions that related to everyday events.

HILLARY MADE GOOD women friends in Fayetteville, which helped put her at ease. One, Diane Kincaid (later Diane Blair), became what Hillary described as the closest friend of her life, a source of great joy, camaraderie, understanding, and mutual purpose. Two years before Hillary's arrival, not long after they had started dating, Bill had sought out Diane with the idea that she could help get Hillary to Arkansas.

> We walked over to the student union to have lunch [Diane recalled], and I was in the middle of a sentence, and he just stopped me and said, "You remind me so much of the woman that I'm in love with." And I said, "Tell me about her." And he went on to describe this paragon and the smartest person he had ever met, the most wonderful, innovative, luminating mind on any subject whatsoever and just on and on and on. He was just smitten. It was clear to me by that time that he was planning his political future in the state, and wanted to marry this woman, and bring her here. And he said, "I *hope* I can, that's what I want to do. But, if I bring her here it will be *my* state and *my* political life. And she could very easily have an amazing political career of her own. She could easily be a governor, a United States senator." I had never met at that point a man who was in politics, and who wanted to do politics, who could so easily envision a woman with a brilliant political future. So, it impressed me.

Diane, nine years older than Hillary, had also left Washington for Fayetteville to join an Arkansas man, her first husband, in 1965. She shared with Hillary a common political outlook and views about their generation of women, particularly women like themselves who wanted both careers and families. The daughter of a devout Irish Catholic father and a Polish, Orthodox Jewish mother, she was pleased to enlist another kindred spirit in the causes and movements of women who saw themselves as Southern progressives. Neither Hillary nor Diane was truly radical in her politics, but both were committed to concepts that situated them on the outer edges of Arkansas liberalism. They shared a belief in an activist government that asserted and protected the equal rights and opportunities of all Americans, including women and their reproductive rights.

With two children from a prior marriage, Diane was the partner of one of the most powerful (and richest) political figures in the state, Jim Blair, who would become a counselor to Bill and loom large in Hillary's life as well. Because Hillary had "somebody like me, what might have festered if you felt totally isolated would become an endearing eccentricity," Diane said. She connected emotionally with Hillary "because I had been through a very similar experience."

The smallest town I had ever lived in before was Washington, D.C. Fayetteville then had 25,000 people. The only place to eat downtown was Ferguson's Cafeteria, and if you really wanted to get fancy you drove up to Tontitown for spaghetti. Women still put on white gloves and had bridge parties and tea parties. People dressed up for football games. I just knew the kind of culture shock that she was going to go through because I'd had an Ivy League education and all that kind of stuff. I just knew what was coming. But, I also had been here long enough by the time she came to be able to see the positives and the sweetness to life here. So, I felt like I could be her guide, and more to the point, I think before she even came, Bill thought that I could. He wanted her to love it here.

Racial segregation, poverty, the psychological and physical barrier of the Ozarks themselves, had mired Arkansas in relative isolation, but the state also had a vigorous tradition of populism and progressivism. The legacy of the state's competing forces were reflected in the student body of the university where Diane taught political science to undergraduates, and its law school, where Hillary thought too many of her pupils were constrained by convention. "We both took teaching very seriously," Diane said. "We wanted to lift people's expectations. Arkansas kids, we thought, just didn't think big enough about the world and their place in it. And we were concerned about women students who were still thinking of themselves as having very limited existence." Both were amused but frustrated with their students' evaluations of their teaching. "Hillary and I got a lot of comments about the way we dressed, which we thought was hilarious," Blair said. Hillary was told that turtleneck sweaters made her look fat. "It was just so absurd to us that students who had this opportunity to critique ways in which you could improve your teaching instead [were focused on] dress code."

Hillary and Diane traded books, played tennis, and met regularly at the student union for lunch. There weren't many women on the university faculty. They took long walks and discussed their disappointment at the failure of ratification of the Equal Rights Amendment in the Arkansas legislature.

Hillary had the natural coordination of her father. Neither she nor
Diane had anything approaching good tennis form, but they thrived on
competing. "We'd go out and just whack balls at each other until we
drove each other into the ground," said Diane.

When Hillary would call Diane to tell her about some aspect of
Arkansas life she was experiencing for the first time, Diane would share a
similar anecdote from her first days in town and they would laugh
together. "There would be frustrations, but I never, ever heard her say,
Oh, I ruined my life. I could have done this, I could have done that," said
Diane.

Yet there were concessions Hillary had to make to Arkansas's conservative political and social milieu. The first was to continue to live
separately from Bill, an arrangement that left their friends from Yale flabbergasted.

VENOMOUS RUMORS and allegations would follow Bill Clinton throughout his political career—some of them true (his carefree sexual ways, his
elusive Selective Service status), some of them wildly exaggerated, many
of them outright false—and they were a major factor in his first campaign, a source of animated discussion in the Third Congressional District and political circles around the state, even on the University of
Arkansas campus. Though he had never sought election before, he
already had enemies. Max Brantley, one of the ablest journalistic
observers of his state's politics and traditions (his wife was Ellen Brantley), believed part of Bill's problem—and Hillary's eventually—was the
nature of the electorate itself. "There is a strong feeling in Arkansas, that
was taught in school a while ago, that you could build a wall around
Arkansas and we could survive without the rest of the world just fine,
thanks. And even though Clinton was a local boy, he'd gone away. He
had put on airs, going off to Eastern schools and even going abroad for
education. A lot of people read into that that somehow what we have
here isn't good enough. It's an implicit insult." Ideology was also a factor.
Clinton was running for a seat in a strongly Republican congressional
district, and he generated antipathy, on the far right especially, because
he allowed himself to be identified as a liberal in ways that he more successfully shrugged off in later campaigns, by which time his identity as a
centrist had solidified.

Some voters held it against Clinton that he had "imported" a Miss
Fancy Pants from New England and Washington. (Hillary's Midwest
credentials were often ignored.) Even Bill's band boy history became
freighted with sexual overtones: not only were there rumors that Clin-

ton was gay, but he was simultaneously said to be living in sin with a woman to whom he wasn't married (though he and Hillary lived apart). Conservative preachers around the state took to the pulpit to denounce the Clinton campaign as an iniquitous den of drug use and perfidious women.

Though Hillary became a dominating presence at headquarters upon her arrival, Bill fitfully continued his relationship with the student volunteer. He told his staff to watch for Hillary's car in the driveway and often sent the young woman out the back door to avoid confrontations. In fairly short order, Hillary succeeded in having the student banned from headquarters. Hillary made it known that she thought women from Bill's past, and by implication any others still in his orbit, were intellectually from another world than her and Bill's, and thus represented no serious competition. This would be her condescending assertion through many an election season, the degree of venom and how publicly she expressed it often dependent on the commensurate political danger to him and embarrassment to her.

Hillary's relationship with Bill during the period was often explosive. She was fiercely determined to keep her man—and make sure the political dream was kept on track, as much on her terms as possible. It was not unusual for the campaign's managers to stand by silently while Hillary and Bill shouted at each other, often about a matter of strategy, but there were obviously other underlying tensions. She was not exempt from the famous Bill Clinton temper that hundreds of campaign workers and even, occasionally, cabinet members were to be subjected to over the next quarter-century. Unlike them, she gave as good as she got, both in tone and language. On one such occasion, while being driven to a campaign stop, she angrily announced at a stoplight, "I'm getting out." After she did, she slammed the car door and began walking down the road.

"They would constantly argue, and the next thing you know, they'd be falling all over each other with 'Oh my darling . . . come here baby . . . you're adorable . . .' then throwing things at each other, and then they'd be slobbering all over each other," a disaffected Clinton aide said with exaggerated disdain. Yet this dynamic would persist.

As would happen when Bill ran for president in 1992, rumors about his sexual involvements intensified as election day drew near, most of them (in this instance) elaborated by his opponent's workers. Whatever her private discomfort at the situation—or perhaps because of it—Hillary overruled the Clinton campaign's managers when it was proposed that fire be fought with fire. They wanted to counterattack with a slogan used by Democrats in a previous campaign: "Send John Paul Hammerschmidt to Washington, the wife you save may be your own."

But Hillary was adamantly opposed. Bill, as he did several times in the closing weeks of the campaign, sided with her against his campaign manager. In all of Bill Clinton's subsequent campaigns, including for the presidency, her influence with the candidate was that of first among unequals, partly because of her often superior instincts and knowledge (especially about him), and partly because Bill did not like contravening her. On this occasion, for reasons she did not articulate, Hillary was insistent on taking the high road.

From the time of her arrival, the campaign's top managers clashed with her substantively and stylistically. Both sides seemed bewildered by the other. The three male principals—Clinton, Fray, and Addington—talked to each other in their own kind of mock-redneck patois that eluded her at first ("the Boy" was their name for Clinton).

"Our organization went to shit" after Hillary's arrival, said Addington. He felt her presence led to a general atmosphere of infighting and bickering. Hillary, however honorable her intentions, "managed to antagonize the entire staff," Clinton's press secretary complained in a memo to the candidate.

As election day approached, Bill was again caught between Hillary's high-minded ethical insistence and his managers' ground-level strategic realism. Desperate for last-minute funds, the campaign had been offered $15,000 from a lawyer who represented state dairy interests, earmarked for use in Sebastian County, where it was known voting results could be bought and certified. The contribution was also intended to help secure Clinton's agreement to serve the interests of the dairy industry once he was in office. But Hillary fought the deal during a heated election eve meeting. Clinton remained quiet, but, according to Fray, Hillary was unyielding, telling Bill: "No! You don't want to be a party to this!"

Did they want to win or did they want to lose? Fray asked.

"Well, I don't want to win this way. If we can't earn it, we can't go [to Washington]," Hillary answered, according to Fray.

In September, Bill had been behind 59 percent to 23 percent, according to the polls. By election day, he and Hammerschmidt were locked in a tight race, partly because Hammerschmidt hadn't felt it necessary to campaign until three weeks before the election, so confident had he been of coasting to victory. Bill had been doing door-to-door campaigning for eight months in every hamlet and hollow in the district. The Clinton camp was optimistic on election night. By midnight, Bill had pulled ahead in a close race, with only the votes from Sebastian County outstanding—long past the hour when they should have been reported. Hillary was seated at a desk, calmly working a calculator and trying to analyze the vote. Clinton volunteers at the county courthouse were hearing tales of chicanery with the ballot boxes. When Fort Smith, the county seat, fell to Hammerschmidt by a big—and unlikely—margin, Fray went on a tear, throwing things and swearing. "It was the goddamn money!" he shouted. Clinton had lost the election by six thousand votes. Fray claimed that Hillary's ethics kept Clinton out of Congress.

She processed the campaign's lessons. Subsequently, she would be far less committed to the high road and much more concerned with results. The question of Bill's other women would become a prominent feature of the Clinton electoral landscape and, when raised by opponents or when the women themselves surfaced, Hillary would set the strategy of response: to attack the women as gold diggers and lying opportunists trying to capitalize on her husband's prominence. By the time of her husband's reelection as president (and a decade after that, her own preparations for running for president), she would preside over a vast fund-raising apparatus and bowed to no one in her willingness to stretch the rules of campaign finance.

BILL'S CONGRESSIONAL race was a turning point in Arkansas politics. Though he had lost by 2 percentage points and agonized for days afterward about what might have been (seventy-five Democratic freshmen were elected to Congress on November 5, part of a generational transformation on Capitol Hill, in which he would have been a standout), he became the inevitable leading young man of the state Democratic Party for his challenge of Hammerschmidt, a four-term incumbent, who had previously been reelected with ease. The major question about his political future was now what office he would run for in 1976, two years hence, and how fast and far he could go.

Hillary, however, now had to deal with the practical consequences of his loss. She seemed more on the fence than ever about whether to marry Bill. They were not going to Washington together anytime soon. Their grand vision seemed to be derailed, and she was left with choices she had not wanted to face: remain with the man she loved or strike out on her own, either in New York practicing law (which meant yet another bar exam to study for) or moving back to Washington, which, compared with Manhattan or even Cambridge, was still tea-pouring country when it came to welcoming strong, able professional women.

She wondered if she could build a meaningful professional and politically influential life in Arkansas while her husband climbed the state electoral ladder, which she judged the likely course he would pursue, rather than trying to get elected to Congress again. She did not relish becoming a local politician's wife in a poor Southern state. Less talented women were getting plum jobs in New York and Washington, where the action was.

Two weeks after Bill's defeat, Nancy Bekavac, their law school classmate, arrived in Fayetteville to visit. Bekavac thought Bill seemed "oddly elated" as he launched into an analysis and explanation of his loss. "We know how to whip them next time," he said. Hillary was less upbeat, expressing particular disappointment that she and Bill wouldn't be going to Washington together to advance the causes—local and national—they believed were important. Bill sounded a lot like he intended to stay in Arkansas and run for statewide office. Hillary, sounding desultory, enumerated some reasons for her to stay, too. She really cared about her students. There were plenty of local issues to get involved in, education especially. The Arkansas education system was one of the weakest in the country. Many of her students lacked the requisite writing skills and vocabulary for a legal career. Arkansans desperately needed help on urban issues, women's rights, the stubborn rural poverty that afflicted the state, which ranked forty-ninth in per capita income and forty-ninth in educational achievement. There were many ways for her to contribute. But she was frank with Bekavac about her fear that Arkansas would smother her ambitions and chances for personal achievement such as she had once envisioned for herself.

Bekavac, given a guided tour of the local scene on her first night in town, was certain suffocation would come sooner rather than later. At a payback chicken dinner for campaign supporters, Bill arrived late and went to sit with the politicos. After the speeches, Bekavac started to move to the back of the room where the serious political discussions were going on. Hillary stopped her.

"Sit down. We sit here," she instructed. They had to remain seated with the women through dessert and coffee, until the event was over and the men had concluded their backslapping.

Bekavac was shocked. Later, the three could go to Bill's house for drinks, said Hillary, who was still living in town with her brother Tony.

Bekavac told Hillary she couldn't believe she was in modern America. "This is Australia in 1956," she said. "This is like mind Jell-O. You can't do this. It's like Antigone, you know, it's like, 'Jump in the tomb.' You can't do this."

Hillary responded: "Well, I know, but I love him."

"Hillary, you've got to love him a whole lot to do this," Bekavac said.

"I do," Hillary said. Her clear, measured way of discussing the matter convinced Bekavac that Hillary was carefully weighing her options, however unpalatable. She seemed inclined toward staying, but still undecided.

"When will you know if you can do this?" Bekavac asked.

"When I know," said Hillary.

It was a choice unlike any faced by Bekavac or Hillary's other friends. "Because you're buying this guy, and you're buying this life, which is not New Haven. It's not anything," Bekavac recalled thinking. She was stunned. "Because I identified with her. She was smart. She was funny. She was warm. She was ambitious. She had done all these accomplished things."

As Bekavac drove out of Fayetteville in her Pinto a few days later, she thought to herself: "This is a nightmare! . . . Thank God, it's not me."

BEKAVAC WAS IGNORING how good Hillary and Bill could be together, how much fun they had, how they reveled in each other's company, how they connected, the deep commitment they shared to an old-fashioned concept of public service, the belief of each, naive as it sounded, that together there was a way to make things better for people whose lives were not as blessed as their own. Bekavac knew they were, in their respective ways, the two most ambitious people she had probably ever met. Yet she felt the sharper edge of their ambitions seemed to become blunted, less threatening when they were together. Others found the joint ambitions of Hillary and Bill terrifying.

Their friends observed a remarkable chemistry. "She's the one that gets up in the morning with a dark cloud over her head, and he gets up with the bright sun," said a photojournalist who followed the Clintons in Arkansas and in Washington. "As the day goes on, he's the one who falls into a funk and she's the one who will refocus him. It's one of those things that if they had never met neither of them would have reached the heights that they did."

Bill supplied the passion and Hillary the focus, though obviously there was far more to the bond. "They're not whole without each other," said their friend Deborah Sale. "He is enormously dependent on her, and I think she on him as well. He loves getting up in the morning and seeing what the day's going to bring, seeing what he can do. Living with someone who has that kind of passion for life is wonderful. And she's someone who wakes up thinking about what she's going to accomplish that day, what she has to do, who she should be seeing, what she should be doing."

For a few days after his defeat Bill traveled through the Third Congressional District thanking voters for their support or if they hadn't voted for him, for merely considering the merits of his candidacy. Then, for the next six weeks, "I went into a funk," he said. He spent most of his time at Hillary's house lying on the floor and feeling sorry for himself. Then, as became the rhythm of their life, with her encouragement, he grasped her stronger, extended hand, picked himself up, and turned to action: in December Hillary coerced him to take her dancing and that seemed to lift his spirits. He also knew that only two sitting senators (and no House members) had been elected president in the twentieth century, Kennedy and Harding. Most of the others had been governors. He convinced himself that if he'd won and they'd gone to Washington, he might never have been elected president.

With renewed vigor, he set out to win over Arkansas voters, whatever office he decided to seek, and to win over Hillary as well. She wrote later that he asked her so many times to marry him that he finally said she should let him know if and when she was ready.

She sought counsel from Jim Blair, who was familiar with almost all of Bill's complexities and proclivities. "Well, Bill has asked me to marry him several times, and I've turned him down several times," Hillary said. "And he's asked me again and this is something I want to do someday— but just not right now." Abruptly, she switched gears: "On the other hand . . . I'm afraid that if I turn him down he will never ask me again." Innately, Hillary recognized that she was "happier with Bill than without him" and that her heart was still telling her "that I was going in the right direction."

"Oh hell, Hillary, go ahead and marry him 'cause if it doesn't work out you can always get divorced," said Blair.

She also sought advice from Ann Henry, who had married a state senator, was the mother of three young children, and was herself a prominent figure in the state Democratic Party. She was among the women Hillary felt closest to in Fayetteville. She had spent hours sitting by the Henrys' backyard swimming pool with Ann, Diane, and others, talking about their lives, the problems of their state, and issues of particular concern to women—and organizing to try to change things.

Ann elaborated for Hillary the constant compromises demanded of a politician's wife, especially in Arkansas. There was no way to fully pursue your own professional and political ambitions, or even express yourself adequately, without jeopardizing your husband's agenda and career, she said.

Hillary disagreed, and aggressively questioned some of the choices Henry had made as a political wife. "Whether I *wanted* to run for office myself or take a big public job was beside the point," Henry tried to explain to Hillary, "because I was married to somebody who was in politics. And I was not willing to take on a real public profile in some areas. It might get Morriss [her husband] defeated, and I would take the blame. And I didn't want that."

Hillary suggested that Ann's decisions had been far too accepting. "She wouldn't call me a coward, but she just thought I was wrong," Ann remembered. "But she was young and not married. And I was married with three children, and had already gone through campaigns where your lives are disrupted."

Hillary cited Eleanor Roosevelt in order to contradict Ann.

"That's right," said Ann, who had just finished reading Joseph Lash's recently published biography of Eleanor, documenting for the first time that FDR had had an affair with Lucy Mercer. Eleanor "never found her voice until after that marriage was over—until she didn't care about the marriage!"

Ann concluded that Hillary had already made up her mind to marry Bill. But the question of Arkansas, the character of the place (more than the character of Bill), its provincial outlook, its Southernness, continued to propel her doubt, especially when she listened to stories like Ann's and looked beyond the congeniality of a university town like Fayetteville and its bucolic setting. Little Rock beckoned, but it did not call to her.

Hillary took a long, soul-searching trip in the fall of 1975 to Boston, New York, Washington, and Chicago to assess what she was missing, including in the job market. Her trip may have been at least partially instigated by Bill's decision to seek election as Arkansas's attorney general, rather than run again for Congress. "I had lost my desire to go to Washington. I wanted to stay in Arkansas," he said. In New York, Carolyn Ellis, her law school friend who was raised in Mississippi, told her that Arkansas "wasn't Mars," and that "to love somebody and not marry them because of where they were living was the height of foolishness." Other friends thought she was on the verge of jumping off a marital cliff with Bill Clinton.

He sometimes gave the impression that he, too, had doubts. "All we ever do is argue," he told Carolyn Yeldell Staley, a friend since high school. However, he didn't tell her that underlying much of the fighting was Hillary's perception that he still wanted to see other women, which he did. Later, he claimed to Betsey Wright that he had actually tried to "run Hillary off, but she just wouldn't go," not because he worried about Hillary being hurt by his promiscuous ways, but because marrying him and living in Arkansas would restrict Hillary's career and political independence.

"He was surprised she really wanted to marry him because he felt that she could have so much more," Betsey said. Wright attributed part of this to "Bill Clinton's ongoing inferiority complex. . . . Bill Clinton has spent his whole life scared that he's white trash, and doing whatever he could to try to prove to himself that he isn't."

He had told his mother to "pray that it's Hillary. Because I tell you this: It's Hillary or it's nobody. I don't need to be married to a beauty queen or a sex goddess. I am going to be involved all my life in hard work in politics and public service, and I need somebody who is really ready to roll up her sleeves and work for me." He did not mention a corollary of the equation: that he had no money and, if he stayed in politics, would have little opportunity to amass any on his own. Hillary's earning potential as a lawyer was considerable, though the whole question of money was something he rarely considered.

Hillary's trip to Chicago and the East Coast rattled whatever complacency he might have been feeling. He told his friend Jim McDougal and McDougal's then girlfriend (and eventual wife), Susan, over a meal at Frankie's Cafeteria in Little Rock, that Hillary had totally won him over.

Bill and McDougal had worked together one summer in Washington, in the office of Senator J. William Fulbright, while Bill was at Georgetown. Jim encouraged Bill to do it. "Don't worry about marrying someone different," he said. "You'll need someone stronger to support you."

It seems likely that Bill's expressions of doubt were as much preparation for the possibility of being rejected than a genuine desire to send Hillary off to another life.

Bill sent a letter to a friend that contained a more plausible description of what was in his mind and his heart. The friend said that in the letter Bill talked about his shared values with Hillary, about how different she was from the other women he had dated. "That's not to say he hadn't known smart women," said the friend. "But, you know, he liked boobs and big hair and—I mean he liked lookers. He's from a state where beauty pageants are a big deal. There was a kind of Southern look that Bill was attracted to. But Hillary fit none of those, and had no cultural connection. She was as far and removed as if he had gone to a foreign country and found her."

When Bill picked Hillary up from the airport upon her return from the East Coast, he reminded her about a small brick house with a "For Sale" sign on it that they had passed on their way to the airport when she left for her trip. "Well, I bought it," he told her, "so now you'd better marry me because I can't live in it by myself."

Hillary said that was the moment she agreed to marry him.

Not long after she accepted, he told Betsey Wright that he and Hillary were going to be married. Wright was not pleased. "I really started in on how he couldn't do that. He shouldn't do that. That he could find anybody he wanted to be a political wife, but we'd [the women's movement] never find anybody like her" to run for political office. Wright promptly called Hillary and told her she hoped Hillary wouldn't marry Bill. Hillary laughed and said she was going to marry Bill and live in Arkansas. Elective office was not the only way to lead. She was going to make a difference wherever she was living.

Deborah Sale considered Hillary's decision the natural one. "I think she was happy to make it. I think she could have done something else, but she could not have done something else with him that would have been as satisfying. And she could not have done something else that would have so united her goals and her heart."

The wedding was set for October 11, 1975, in the front room of the house he had just bought at 930 California Street in southwest Fayetteville. Their new home, all of one thousand square feet, had a beamed A-frame ceiling, a fireplace, and a bay window. An attic fan and a screened porch compensated for the lack of air-conditioning. Bill took the first steps toward making the house a home by buying some old wooden furniture, an antique cast iron bed, and Wal-Mart sheets with green and yellow flowers. He had made a $3,000 down payment on the $20,000 house. The monthly mortgage was $174.

Hillary did not want an engagement ring, but she and Bill did have an engagement party in Hot Springs in early October. Guests remembered Bill sitting in a chair and Hillary sitting on the arm, and the two "holding hands and looking very much in love," as one described it.

Hillary seemed supremely uninterested in planning her own wedding. She happily accepted Ann Henry's offer to throw a reception in her backyard and left the details up to her. Hillary was "looking more at life to come than at the wedding itself," Henry concluded. No printed invitations were sent to the guests for either the ceremony or the reception. Hillary's conformity with wedding protocol was pretty much limited to registering at Dillard's department store for Danish modern dishware. It wasn't until the day before the ceremony, when Dorothy asked what her daughter's dress looked like, that Dorothy discovered Hillary hadn't bought one and didn't intend to. Dorothy insisted that they head to Dillard's, on the town square, the only place in town that sold bridal gowns. Hillary chose the first dress she took off the rack, in Victorian lace style, designed by Jessica McClintock. "This will be fine," she said.

The details Hillary seemed most concerned with were putting the finishing touches on her new home, which was to be the site of the ceremony. She and Dorothy were painting and putting in bookshelves and light fixtures until the day before the wedding—much to the horror of

Hillary's mother-in-law-to-be, who arrived with her guests and was appalled that the house was still such a mess.

When the minister said "Who will give away this woman?" at the beginning of the brief Methodist ceremony, everyone looked at Hugh Rodham, but he seemed frozen in place and continued to hold his daughter's arm. The minister finally said, "You can step back now, Mr. Rodham." Bill and Hillary exchanged old family rings in front of about twenty guests in their living room. Roger Clinton was the best man and Betsy Ebeling, who arrived late from Chicago, was Hillary's maid of honor. Both choices reflected an important fact in the lives of Bill and Hillary. They each had a large and devoted circle of friends but even the closest of their friendships were in some way restrained or compartmentalized. Neither had a real confidant, an intimate with whom deepest confidences were comfortably exchanged and to whom even dark secrets could be disclosed. The real intimacy in their lives was reserved for each other and perhaps always would be. But there would always be secrets.

More than two hundred relatives and friends—many from Yale, Oxford, Wellesley, Georgetown, Park Ridge, and Hot Springs—crowded into Ann and Morriss Henry's backyard, several blocks away, for the reception. There was a champagne fountain, a wedding cake decorated with yellow roses, and a piano player. The party was also something of a political rally. Many of Bill's students, but few of hers, attended. "It was like a big reunion," said Ann. "People like Don Tyson [of Tyson Foods, the state's biggest business enterprise], who were interested in Bill's future. A lot of business people who saw he was going somewhere. People who had money. . . . And a lot of the local Democratic Party people from all over the whole district."

Some thought Hillary was having a difficult time seeing her guests clearly since she wasn't wearing her glasses. She stunned the crowd—especially those from Arkansas—when she announced that she would not be taking her husband's name and would remain Hillary Rodham. Bill had told Virginia that morning, as she and a friend ate breakfast at the Holiday Inn coffee shop. Virginia had cried at the news. Paul Fray, already planning the next campaign, was upset about the political implications of Hillary's decision. When the *Arkansas Democrat-Gazette* printed their wedding announcement, and underscored the fact that Hillary was keeping her maiden name, Fray told Bill, "Hillary Rodham will be your Waterloo."

The whole saga of Hillary's name-changing was, for her, for Bill, and for the Clintons' friends, a dispiriting index of attitudes in Arkansas and (later, when he sought the presidency) much of the nation toward women in public life and independent women generally. Hillary had resolved to keep her maiden name as a young girl, even before the practice was encouraged by a nascent women's movement. To Hillary, her name was her identity—something, she told Ann Henry and others, that would always ensure she remained "a person in my own right," and not a "sacrificial" political wife.

HILLARY AND BILL spent their wedding night in their new house. At 4 A.M. they got a call from the Washington County Jail, where Tony Rodham had been incarcerated after departing the wedding festivities. His car had been pulled over by a state trooper who noticed that a passenger was dangling her feet through the back window and that Tony had been drinking. Bill bailed him out—not for the last time.

The Clintons' honeymoon was postponed for two months, until the end of the school term, when they took a penthouse suite at a hotel in Acapulco and, with the whole Rodham family (Dorothy had noticed a vacation package ad and booked the trip) and a girlfriend of one of Hillary's brothers, spent a week by the sea.

They saw far less of each other in the next year than most newlyweds. In January, Bill set up headquarters in Little Rock for his campaign for the Democratic nomination as attorney general of Arkansas. His old childhood friends Mack McLarty and Vince Foster helped him reach into the state capital's business establishment for support. Hillary continued her teaching. During the first six months of 1976, Bill crisscrossed the state, sometimes aided and attended by the Rodham brothers, both of whom had moved to Arkansas (Hugh Jr. had finished serving two years in the Peace Corps in Colombia) and enrolled at the university.

Some of the issues and political positions embraced by her husband's campaign were antithetical to, or harder-edged, than Hillary's own beliefs, and were touted by Bill as intended to "significantly improve the quality of life in Arkansas." This included capital punishment, which, for the first time, he publicly said he favored when he was asked about it in a television interview, and seemed to be caught off-guard. His platform for attorney general included mandatory "minimum prison sentences, victim compensation programs, improved work release, and rapid assistance to law enforcement agencies in interpreting the new criminal code, issues related to criminal justice and the office." More to Hillary's liking, Bill also ran on issues that would appeal to working- and middle-class voters: "fair utility rates, citizens' rights to consumer protection in small claims courts, effective antitrust laws, and a right to privacy." His campaign slogan was "Character, Competence, and Concern."

Clinton won the Democratic primary in May with 55.6 percent of the vote, a triumph against two opponents. His victory virtually ensured his election to the job that November. With the most difficult part of the race behind him, his political fortunes rising, Bill and Hillary attended the Democratic convention in New York that July, which nominated Jimmy Carter for president. They were a conspicuous presence at social and political events there, almost glamorous in their somewhat disheveled, youthful way, proud exemplars of the next generation of the New South of which Carter, the governor of Georgia, was the current embodiment. Already there was an assumption in Arkansas that Bill was in line to become governor of his state in the next few years. Part of Hillary and Bill's plan in going to New York was to talk to Carter and his deputies about working seriously in the campaign: Bill signed on as Arkansas state chairman and Hillary was named field coordinator for Indiana. Betsey Wright, working out of Washington, had urged campaign officials to give Hillary the top position in Indiana, but "she was to be the number two, which is what they always did to women," Betsey said.

Hillary was feeling far more hopeful about the future than when she'd embarked on her last trip north. From New York, they flew to Europe for a two-week vacation, the highlight of which was intended as "a pilgrimage" to the Basque town of Guernica, which inspired Picasso's emblematic masterpiece that Don Jones had cited in talking about both art and fascism. Generalissimo Francisco Franco had succeeded in persuading Hitler to send the Luftwaffe to level the town in 1937. The newlyweds explored its rebuilt streets and took coffee in the central plaza. Like many of their generation, they were still idealistic young thinkers and doers who wanted to influence their own time for the better. But there was something different (though not necessarily unique) about them from most people their age making their way through the ranks of either American political party: a powerful connection to the threads of the history of the century and their country, a deep feel for what had gone before, intimate knowledge of the conflicting currents that had defined the generation of their parents and the places of their own past. Their uniqueness, however, was in the intertwining of their dreams—as a political mission to be achieved together, conceptually premeditated, breathtakingly ambitious, a true partnership, and yet flexible enough to adapt to all manner of personal, political, and cultural upheaval and possibility.

THE CARTER CAMPAIGN was an opportunity for Hillary to increase her own considerable political knowledge, to help raise her husband's stature in the Democratic Party (and perhaps in the next presidency), and to get herself placed on the list of the most promising prospects for appointment to presidential boards and commissions. If Bill was going to stay in Arkansas, she wanted a foot in Washington. Upon returning from Europe, she went immediately to Indianapolis. As director of Indiana field operations, she would be in charge of executing the campaign's strategy in ninety-two counties, dispatching hundreds of volunteers to storefront offices throughout the state, and managing some very tight finances. She brought to the challenge a combination of useful political experience and received wisdom: from Texas during the McGovern campaign, from Bill's campaign and his tutelage, from Marian Edelman, and from John Doar and her time in Washington. She was in her element—though the odds of Carter winning Indiana were daunting. From her father's politics and her own Midwestern roots in neighboring Illinois, she understood Indiana's voters, their interests, and their prejudices with almost intimate familiarity. Her manner with subordinates and the state's top Democrats, from Senator Birch Bayh down, was direct and to the point, with little of the gift of her husband's gab. Yet she seemed comfortable whether dealing with Bayh or a ward-heeler, a company president or a union shop steward. And she was decisive, partaking in almost none of the agonizing temperature-taking and enervating debate with aides that Bill indulged in on his circumlocutious way to action. She imaginatively embraced the underdog mentality of Carter's situation in Indiana, luring phone-bank workers by offering the legal minimum wage and then hiring senior citizens or accused criminals, whose bond had been posted by the bail-bonding firm that had previously occupied the office space of Carter headquarters in Indianapolis.

Election day produced a double victory for Hillary. As expected, Carter did not carry traditionally Republican Indiana but he had captured a very respectable 46 percent of the vote, compared with Gerald Ford's 53 percent. He won the presidency with a popular vote majority of 50 percent to 48 percent, and 297 electoral votes to Ford's 240. In Arkansas, Bill Clinton overwhelmingly won the attorney general's race, carrying sixty-nine of seventy-five counties. Hillary chose to celebrate in Indianapolis—Bill agreed—with her comrades from the Carter campaign.

BILL'S ELECTION meant that he and Hillary would have to move to Little Rock. She had "slipped into Fayetteville like a duck to water," Jim Blair noted, but Fayetteville was not typical of Arkansas. Little Rock was a very different place, with a far more formal power and social structure, characterized by restricted country clubs, debutante balls, and business conducted in the tap room of the Capital Hotel, where state officials and overlords of the state's enormous deposits of private wealth broke bread together. Little Rock was a state capital but not really a big city, "an insulated big town, a place that ran according to unwritten rules," in the words of its mayor from 1979 to 1981, Webb Hubbell. He noted that "Rule 1 might well have been: Little Rock women don't have careers." Later the Clintons would move to another capital that was not really a big city, another insulated big town that managed according to its own unwritten rules. But their adjustment to Washington, D.C., would be much more difficult. Bill Clinton was a native Arkansan, and though he had moved away for college for a spell, he knew the people of his state and their ways inside and out. He was always one of them, and Hillary proved to be surprisingly adaptable. But during the Clintons' occupancy of the White House, he and Hillary remained rank outsiders, from the moment they ungraciously swept into town with ill-disguised contempt for the capital's unwritten rules and protocols. This, too, taught Hillary. When she ascended to the U.S. Senate, she kept her head down and deferred to the institution and the town and its ways—until the critical moment when she recognized it was time to raise her head, after which she outsmarted and outwitted just about everybody in the Senate chamber and the press in a New York minute, and made herself so outsized that the people who lived and breathed the capital's old rules didn't know what had hit them.

Hillary had adjusted to the town of Fayetteville far more easily than she could have envisioned. She made friends quickly—good friends— and a name for herself in the town's tight-knit academic and legal communities. She even lost some of her flat Midwest accent. After only four or five months, Woody Bassett could see that "she not only became very comfortable living here, but she enjoyed living here." When Richard Stearns, one of Bill's fellow Rhodes Scholars, came to visit, he was stunned to hear her talking about how the biggest watermelons anywhere came from Arkansas. "She could recite with pride all of these firsts that Arkansas accomplished. She had become at least by outward appearances a fanatic University of Arkansas football fan." What Stearns found most interesting was that "she had pretty much mastered an Arkansas accent. She had absorbed it." As she would do for the next quarter-century, she could turn it off and on.

She also took obvious satisfaction from her teaching. She was pleased that so many of her students seemed to respond to her rigorous standards. She had been put in charge, upon her arrival, of a moribund legal aid clinic. Her perseverance and government experience rapidly produced tangible results. By first semester's end she had obtained support from the county's judges and the bar association, and federal grants were approved to fund a new University of Arkansas legal clinic. In its initial year under her direction, the clinic served three hundred clients; student-lawyers, supervised by bar members, appeared in fifty court cases. With the help of Diane Blair and other women whom Diane had introduced to her, she was the leading force in creating Fayetteville's first rape crisis center, the consequence of a student coming to Hillary and telling of her experience after being raped. There seemed to be a prevalent attitude in town, held by older women as well as men, that the young victim had somehow been to blame for the incident because she had been wearing tight clothing and was walking alone at night.

As part of Hillary's faculty assignment to assist prison inmates seeking legal representation, she helped prepare the successful appeal of a prisoner on death row. Her opposition to the death penalty seemed unequivocal at the time, and during Bill's campaign for attorney general she was fortunate that no one asked her to address the question publicly. At some point between his service as attorney general and governor—when Bill was forced to consider, and sometimes subsequently denied, stays of execution—she changed her position.

While she would miss Fayetteville and university life, Arkansas was a small state, and she would constantly shuttle between the political, academic, and corporate worlds of Little Rock, Fayetteville, and northwest Arkansas. She came to understand, enjoy, and appreciate the role of college football, which, as in any Southern state, united the local population. Her father and brother had been football players, but she had never before considered football as a social leveler, a basic communal rite that, in the enthusiasm and energy it produced, transcended almost all else.

While Bill had become a very big fish in a small-state pond, she had learned to swim in the same waters—warm but still treacherous—with considerable command. Hillary, an outsider to the system, had prodded the male-dominated legal community to action. People took note. Her developing role underscored a division of labor that would endure between herself and her husband. She was the hands-on player, addressing with real-time practicality the social problems he approached through a politics emanating from his intuitive sensitivity, his voracious intellectualism, and his willingness to compromise. Whether by happenstance or design they were moving toward a synthesis in their unique joint political venture.

"IT WAS HILLARY who decided that she wanted to be financially secure, and took the steps to accomplish that," said Betsey Wright. "Those decisions you wouldn't expect Bill Clinton to make. Bill Clinton would live under a bridge—as long as it was okay with Chelsea. He just doesn't care."

Upon Bill's election as attorney general, Hillary faced the question of how to resume her legal career. Given the paltry salaries of Arkansas public officials, and Hillary and Bill's desire to have children, she was now willing to consider a career she had regarded previously with overt contempt: corporate law. Bill, trying to help her find a place in a major law firm, recommended his wife to the partners of Rose, Nash, Williamson, Carroll, Clay & Giroir—the Rose Law Firm.* The firm, which was founded in 1820—sixteen years before Arkansas became a state—had only nine partners, one of whom was his friend from childhood in Hope, Vince Foster.

Foster had met Hillary the previous year, as a member of the state bar association's committee on legal assistance, when Bill was campaigning and she was attempting to establish the university's legal aid clinic. "[Vince] came back to the firm raving, uncharacteristically, about a smart female professor he had worked with up there named Hillary Rodham," recalled Hubbell. "He came home from Fayetteville saying we should be thinking about hiring her—that surely they would move to Little Rock, and surely she would be looking for a job." At the time, the Rose Law Firm had no women lawyers. Foster argued that it was time for a change, and that another firm would move fast to lure Hillary, because her husband was about to become the state's chief legal officer and was already marked as the most promising young politician in Arkansas. Setting aside the conflict of interest question, Hillary was indeed an attractive candidate.

Before she reached a decision to practice corporate law, Hillary consulted with Jim Blair, who extolled its obvious financial advantages over public interest law, while touting its intellectual stimulation. Phil Kaplan, a Little Rock lawyer in private practice, had established a major public interest practice, but Hillary did not attempt to join his firm. Instead she decided to respond to Foster's siren song in hopes of joining the state's most well-connected blue-chip firm. It was a long way from Treuhaft, Walker and Burnstein, the only other law office she'd worked in.

Rose was the ultimate establishment law firm, representing the most powerful economic interests in the state: Tyson Foods, Stephens Inc. (the state's biggest brokerage firm), Wal-Mart, Worthen Bank, the *Arkansas Democrat-Gazette*, and the Hussman media empire in southwest Arkansas. In the capital of a small state in which business was a matter of backslapping and backscratching, its primacy was undisputed. Though the reforms of Watergate were putting pressure on politicians

---

*Over the years the firm went under a variety of names, formally becoming the Rose Law Firm in 1980.

in Washington to be more careful about conflicts of interest, such concerns remained muted in Arkansas's capital, where the line between public and private business had never been much delineated.

Foster dispatched Webb Hubbell to convince the other associates of the firm that hiring Hillary was a good idea. Others would later say that Foster—tall, with impeccable manners and a formal mien—worshipped Hillary from the start, or that he had been awed by her from the time they met in Fayetteville, or that he had never met a woman like her who was so whip-smart and almost sassy. What is unquestionable is that he and Hillary grew incredibly close. For the next twenty years, the relationship would confound Foster's wife (but not Bill Clinton), their colleagues at the law firm and the White House (but not Webb Hubbell), and women who had known Bill intimately and didn't like his wife.

OTHER PARTNERS in the firm were less enthusiastic about hiring Hillary than Vince and Webb. Some were perhaps more sensitive than Foster to the potential conflict of interest, which seemed inherent if a member of the firm were married to the state attorney general. Foster, however, argued that the firm had little business with state agencies and none with regulated utilities. Nor did it do criminal work, in which defendants were prosecuted in the name of the state by the attorney general. The argument seemed a bit hollow because the firm's major clients included the state's highest-earning corporations and manufacturing industries. The Rose Law Firm, at Foster's direction, was able to get an opinion from the American Bar Association holding that it could hire the wife of the attorney general, and specifying procedures to avert conflicts of interest. Their effectiveness was illustrated by a hearing early in that year's legislative session at the statehouse. Bill Clinton, representing the state, spoke against the particular piece of legislation being considered. Among the numerous witnesses arguing for the measure was Vince, with Hillary present as his co-counsel. All proceeded to conduct business as usual.

But the most powerful and hushed argument against Hillary joining the firm was that she was a woman. "How will we introduce her to our clients?" an associate asked Foster and Hubbell. All of Rose's important clients were male. "What if she gets pregnant?" The firm's partners were all white men, most of whom were already wealthy and graduates of the two Arkansas law schools. Hillary, with her Wellesley and Yale credentials and her view of the law as an instrument for social reform, would be a radical departure.

On the day of Hillary's interview, the law firm's partners were the

ones who were nervous, remembered Hubbell. As usual under such circumstances, her performance was near flawless. On February 1, 1977,
less than a month after her husband was sworn in as attorney general, she
became an associate at the firm. Her starting salary was just under
$25,000 a year, up from $18,000 as a law professor. On the third floor of
a former YMCA building, Hillary, Hubbell, and Foster occupied corner
offices. Bill's salary, recently raised by the state legislature, was $26,000.
She would earn more than he every subsequent year until he became
president. Meanwhile, he settled into a spacious office a stone's throw
from Hillary's, decorating his adjacent bathroom with a poster of a scant-
ily clad Dolly Parton.

THE ATMOSPHERE at the Rose Law Firm was not always welcoming.
Some secretaries made disparaging comments about Hillary out of her
presence. Much of the gossip was about her appearance, and some
reflected obvious envy of an accomplished woman in an executive position. Even her own secretary mocked Hillary's attempts at creating a
career woman image: "At first, she didn't wear stockings and the old
ladies in the firm were horrified. She was a comic figure as a lady lawyer.
Her hair was fried into an Orphan Annie perm. She had one large eye-
brow across her forehead that looked like a giant caterpillar. We laughed
until we cried. She tried to look good when she went to court, and she
would put on some awful plastic jewelry. She'd be wearing high heels she
couldn't walk in. There wasn't one stereotypically womanly or feminine
thing about her." Hillary's weight was a regular topic of conversation,
spurred by her inability to shed the few pounds that would have made her
more attractive. "She was on a perpetual diet. She would show up for
work with a big bag of lettuce and eat out of it all day," said her secretary.
    Hillary once represented a jewelry sales company whose representa-
tives were mostly women with beehive hairdos. Hubbell liked to recall
that "Hillary won their lawsuit, and the beehive ladies revered her as their
hero. Every one of them volunteered to give her a makeover. Even then,
Vince and I kidded her about it. She said she loved those ladies but didn't
want to look like them." Hillary's manner with other members of the firm
and their clients could be intimidating—not because she was particularly
aggressive, but because she was rarely, if ever, deferential. It had never
been her style nor would it ever be. "In our morning meetings she didn't
hold her tongue," Hubbell noted. "She was simply never intimidated by
anyone, partner or client, and that in itself is often intimidating to others." Would a new associate who was male be judged on similar grounds?
Probably not, and it took Hillary a long time to feel at ease in Little Rock

and at Rose, except with Vince and Webb—the Three Amigos, as they came to refer to themselves.

At office parties, wives of Rose partners and associates tended to ask her what it was like to work in a place full of men (which spoke volumes about their view of women who were secretaries and clerks there). They frequently tried to get Hillary to join them in working for their favorite local charities. "But if she spent time with the wives, the partners would reinforce their suspicion that she was, after all, a woman, not a real lawyer. And the wives would still cut her to shreds," said Hubbell. Still, more than a few of the partners' wives, particularly younger ones, had a certain admiration for Hillary, leading Foster and Hubbell to conclude that they, too, would like to live lives that weren't defined by the standards of 1970s Little Rock. "The real secret," said Hubbell, "was that Hillary hadn't escaped either."

Despite the sometimes tense atmosphere, Hillary came to enjoy her workdays, largely because of her relationship with Foster and Hubbell. They poked fun at her intensity, tutored her in the traditions of the capital (and how she might take advantage of them), and looked out for her like a little sister. The three often went to lunch together at the Lafayette Hotel. Sometimes they watched lingerie shows there, a popular form of lunchtime entertainment of the era, in which models from upscale lingerie stores showed off nightgowns and their bodies. Hillary simply laughed at her two partners and told them what Neanderthals they were. Physically Hubbell and Foster were polar opposites. Vince was rail-thin, elegant in perfectly tailored suits, and soft-spoken to the point of taciturnity. Hubbell was a whale of a man, a former college quarterback who (unlike Hillary's father) actually had been drafted to play pro ball, but was injured before his career could take off. Hubbell carried close to three hundred pounds, and his back suffered the load, requiring sometimes that he lie on the floor while working. Once, as the three prepared for a case, Webb was sprawled on the carpet airing hundred-year-old case law, while Hillary was dispatched to the library to produce the documentation.

The first case she handled solo involved a canning company Rose represented—against a man who claimed he'd found a rat's hindquarters in a can of pork and beans. Though he didn't eat the rat, he said, looking at it made him so sick he couldn't kiss his fiancée. For the jury's obvious benefit, he regularly spit into his handkerchief. The plaintiff was awarded only a small amount in damages. Aside from the obvious "rat's ass" jokes, the experience shook Hillary. Though her defense was reasonably able and well crafted, she was "amazingly nervous" in front of the jury, according to Hubbell. In fact, she was not a particularly good litigator, hardly light on her feet before judge and jury. There had been signs of it during the Barrister's Trial with Bill, and the Rose firm began steering her practice toward nonjury work, and she appeared in court only infrequently.

IN DECEMBER, a month before Bill was sworn in, he and Hillary found a house in the Hillcrest neighborhood of Little Rock, an upper-middle-class enclave not far from downtown. It was even smaller than the house in Fayetteville, a mere 980 square feet, and cost $34,000.

Though Bill's campaign had stressed the punitive side of the job, as attorney general he maintained a careful balance in which the interests of consumers and working people were accorded rhetorical, legislative, and enforcement priority. This reflected Hillary's counsel on both policy and staffing matters. On occasion, she made speeches in the state booked by his office and stressed his consumer-friendly policies. Much of the new attorney general's agenda was pure populist politics. He developed regulations to improve the quality of nursing home care, tried to maintain the price of a pay phone call at a dime, sued dairy companies for fixing milk prices, and took tentative, but ultimately ineffectual, steps to regulate lobbyists. He also took care not to alienate companies that he recognized were the most important part of Arkansas's tax base. And, from the beginning, he had fun. There was a juke-joint down the street from the statehouse, and on Fridays, when the legislature didn't meet, he encouraged casual dress in the office and invited the whole staff to join him for lunch there and play the pinball machine at the back of the restaurant.

Hillary was particularly pleased by the profile she and Bill were projecting inside the national Democratic Party and in Washington under a Democratic president. In Arkansas and at the national level, it was common knowledge that Bill was en route to the governor's mansion, unless he chose to run for the U.S. Senate in 1978. During his campaign, prospective contributors had been advised to "get on board early."

Bill and Hillary became somewhat regular dinner guests in Jimmy Carter's White House, and Bill traveled frequently to Washington for briefings and meetings with the president's staff and the Democratic National Committee. Carter gave him the authority—with Dale Bumpers, the state's Democratic senator, and Jackson Stephens, a Carter contributor—to vet presidential appointments and judgeships of Arkansans. However, Bill and Hillary were rebuffed in their attempt to get Jim Blair appointed as chairman of the Federal Home Loan Bank Board. Hillary did succeed in winning a seat for herself on the presidentially appointed board of the Legal Services Corporation. It was based on merit, as well as her political service to Carter in Indiana and Bill's in Arkansas.

She had continued her work in children's advocacy while at the Rose firm, taking a few pro bono cases, including that of a couple seeking to adopt the foster child for whom they'd cared for more than two years. She won it, and the case later served as a precedent used in the state for foster care adoptions.

The Legal Services Corporation, as any local journalist who had covered municipal court in an urban area knew, was genuinely important to keeping the American legal system functioning. Established in 1974, it was an extension of Lyndon Johnson's War on Poverty programs of the 1960s. The corporation's board decided how to distribute funding to the 335 local Legal Services offices around the country, which offered counsel to people who couldn't afford an attorney. In most big cities, this meant a majority of individuals charged with crimes and many others preyed upon by unscrupulous merchants. Hillary knew how important the program—originally called Neighborhood Legal Services—was to protecting the constitutional right to a fair trial of the most vulnerable defendants who passed through America's turnstile system of justice. The program's local lawyers tended to be young, diligent, and dedicated, and won a surprisingly high proportion of their cases, including many in which local prosecutors and police played fast and loose with the facts.

Many Republicans loathed the idea of using federal money to provide free legal services to the poor and lawsuits undertaken on their behalf, and when Richard Nixon became president he attempted to discontinue the program even before it was fully up and running. By the time Hillary was appointed to the board, the program had five thousand lawyers handling one million cases a year. A few months later, Carter named her to chair the board. After confirmation by Congress, she became the first woman ever to hold the position. Carter's choice was deft.

In 1980, while trying to become the Republican presidential nominee, Governor Ronald Reagan sought to drastically reduce funding for legal services for the poor in California. Hillary successfully persuaded the LSC board to reject Reagan's proposal. But when he became president, succeeding Carter, Reagan again tried to undercut the Legal Services program, this time attempting to get Congress to reduce its funding on a national basis and approve new members of the board who opposed the basic concept of free legal services for the poor. As chairperson, Hillary hired Vince Foster to seek a restraining order, prohibiting Reagan's nominees from meeting before they were confirmed by the Senate. Meanwhile, she enlisted Senate Democrats in a campaign against the nominees. Ultimately, the Senate refused to confirm them and instead forced the president to name more moderate members to the board. By the time Hillary's term as chairperson expired in 1982, funding for the

Legal Services Corporation had grown from $90 million to $300 million. She had not only saved the concept of federal funding for legal aid to the poor, but she had done it with crucial assistance from Foster working under her direction and going to court to defend the prerogatives she enunciated. More than a decade later in the White House, she would attempt the same with disastrous effect, this time instructing Vince to find a way to defend the secrecy of her health care task force against those who wanted its deliberations to be public.

BILL CLINTON couldn't care less about money, Hillary once said, confirming Betsey Wright's opinion. But because politics is hardly a sure thing, she knew they had to make some money and put it aside. She had come a long way from her rejection of "our prevailing acquisitive corporate life" that she condemned in her Wellesley commencement address. Though Arkansas ranked forty-ninth in per capita income, there were also huge fortunes in the state, not just in Little Rock, but in Hot Springs, Bentonville, Fayetteville, and towns barely known outside the state. Little Rock and northwest Arkansas were home as well to a new generation of concentrated wealth, some of it from fast money in the financial markets and some of it from servicing the industries and companies that were basic to the state's tax base. Brokers in the state were often averaging $50,000 a month and a few were making twice that. It was not uncommon in Springdale or the wealthiest parts of Little Rock to see Porsches, Cadillac convertibles, and Mercedes coupes in driveway after driveway. In Fayetteville, long before there were "Microsoft Millionaires," there were supermarket cashiers and filling station attendants who had become wealthy from stock in Wal-Mart and Tyson, where their relatives worked.

Until their arrival in Little Rock, Hillary had seemed almost as uninterested in money, not to mention wealth, as her husband. She had worked for Marian Edelman's nonprofit Children's Defense Fund at a nominal salary, earned a clerk's wages in the Watergate impeachment investigation, and received an assistant professor's salary at one of the lowest-paying law schools in the nation. Her most adamant action in Bill Clinton's congressional campaign had been to insist that he turn down dirty money from lobbyists.

What seems to have changed is that, with the need to support a family (and, later, perhaps be on her own if her marriage failed), she could justify in her moral construct financial opportunities that increasingly made her uncomfortable (judging from her subsequent, almost frenzied efforts to hide them) or perhaps led her into some state of denial in which she rationalized that "everyone" did it. She also operated in an easy atmosphere of conflicts of interest that, in a larger state, might not have been regarded as business as usual. Moreover, the Clintons certainly had the friends and the opportunities to skirt rules and procedures required of less-well-connected individuals.

Even before Hillary had decided to follow Jim Blair into the tricky cattle futures market in which he was making millions in 1978, she had engaged a well-connected financial adviser, William Smith, a broker in Little Rock at Stephens Inc., the largest investment firm in the United States off Wall Street. It was controlled by the Stephens family of Arkansas, and though the Clintons had little money to invest, Smith took them on as serious clients not least because Bill was Arkansas's attorney general. Hillary told Smith she knew little about the markets but that she wanted to earn a much greater return than Treasury Bonds would yield. She set up two accounts, a joint investment account with Bill, and a separate one for herself, and gave Smith discretionary authority to trade and invest in both. In occasional meetings with Smith to review the accounts, Hillary explored various investment strategies and asked Smith detailed questions, while Bill—if he appeared at all—seemed uninterested and talked politics.

Hugh Rodham had taught his daughter how to read the stock tables. Occasionally, Hillary and Blair, who was then engaged to Diane Kincaid, would talk about the market. Blair's law office was outside Fayetteville in Springdale, and though he was retained by Tyson Foods as its outside counsel, he made even more money in the financial markets—a considerable fortune by the time Diane, Hillary, Bill, and Jim had become close friends in the mid-1970s. The two couples met for frequent dinners, spent time at Jim and Diane's cottage on Beaver Lake, and would take numerous vacations together over the next fifteen years. Hillary served as "best person" at the Kincaid-Blair wedding (and wore a tuxedo). They discussed and argued any and all aspects of life: politics, life in Arkansas, where the country was headed, books, movies, rock and roll, Razorbacks football.

Jim had become something of an older brother to Bill Clinton. He had managed J. William Fulbright's last senatorial campaign, introduced Bill to the Tysons, helped raise funds for his first political campaigns, and contributed mightily to Bill's talents as a storyteller. Both Blair and Clinton had grown up in unusual circumstances. If a visitor to Fayetteville was given a tour of northwest Arkansas with Blair at the wheel of his white Cadillac, the first stop was likely to be a little brick building in which he was raised above a grocery store in the apartment of his paternal grandparents, after being abandoned by his mother. Blair was a match for Bill in his catholic interests and ability to do several things at once—including, in his case, lawyering and playing the financial markets. He graduated high school at age eighteen and law school at twenty-one. He had been ordained a Southern Baptist minister but left the church because it had supported segregation. After Bill had been elected governor, Jim would fly Hillary and Bill in his private plane from Little Rock to Fayetteville for football games and political events. Hillary and Jim had won first place in the Fayetteville Country Club's mixed doubles tennis tournament. If any couple could be considered closest to the Clintons in Arkansas, it was the Blairs.

By the end of summer in 1978, Blair was urging close friends and colleagues to follow him into the cattle futures bonanza. Hillary was looking for bigger returns than she was seeing on her Stephens accounts. Blair had had a knack for the stock market since he began trading at the age of twenty-one. "I made my first $1,000 in 1958, and in 1959, I made $30,000 trading American Motors stock when I was making $5,000 a year practicing law, so I think I'm a good trader," he said. In the next two decades, he earned far more from his trading than his law practice. His broker was Robert L. (Red) Bone, at Ray E. Friedman & Company (Refco), who specialized in futures and took Blair into the cattle business. Bone was another Tyson executive who'd started with the company young—driving a chicken truck—and eventually became a vice president. He then left to become a broker. He also was an inveterate gambler who had made it to the semifinals of the World Series of Poker in Las Vegas. At first, Red Bone made the cattle call decisions for Blair, no matter how large the trade. And though Blair still lacked the expertise to make trades himself, he was learning. "I was watching the [cattle] market by then. I would come down to Red's office sometimes and watch the board, and I got a pretty good sense of what was going on." He began sitting in on Bone's conference calls at the end of the day in which the broker would talk to pit-traders in Chicago, cattle buyers in Texas and Colorado, operators of feed lots in Nebraska, and the head of Refco, Thomas Dittmer, at the home office in Vegas.

Blair explained: "I thought I was a lot smarter than Red and I'd form my own opinion. I was taking so much time away from the law firm that I set up a commodity account for the law firm [and its partners]. We had a holding company called Lawyers Investment Company that held our real estate and stuff and I set the account up in that name. And, because some associates didn't participate in that I set up another account for them that I called the Pups Account, so I'd make them a little money. And then I set up an account for my ex-wife. I set up an account for Diane, who I was dating. I set up accounts for my kids. I set up accounts for her kids. I set up an account for a business associate of mine named Jim Brooks, dear friend, dead now. And then one day I made the fatal mistake. I was talking to Hillary and said, 'Why don't you let me set you up an account on this? I'm just making so much money it's unreal.' "

Over the next nine months, under Blair's influence and because of Red Bone's machinations, Hillary experienced the highs and lows of the futures market. Then, ahead of the game to the tune of $100,000, she was rescued from margin calls that would have wiped out other less-favored investors. She cashed out just as the cattle futures business was collapsing.

The combination of Blair's smarts and Bone's privileged information proved infallible. While the information Bone received was not necessarily considered insider information within the commodities market, he certainly benefited from Dittmer's position as the chairman of Refco; Dittmer also happened to be one of the country's largest cattle owners. Bone ran the Springdale office of Refco two miles down the pike from Fayetteville. And though at one point he was making a lot of people in Arkansas very wealthy, he ran an undisciplined operation that rarely bothered with the requisite record-keeping.

In October 1978, Hillary, through Blair, made an initial payment of $1,000 to Refco to open a trading account. Three months into her stint in the commodities market, Hillary had realized a stunning $26,000 gain. Other high yields followed—as well as frightening lows. She lost $16,000 in a single trade, a little less than half of Bill's annual salary by then. It would be another thirteen years before questions would arise about margin calls—in which investors are forced to sell stock to cover their losses, thereby restricting their purchasing power—that should have been imposed on her account. At one point Hillary owed more than $100,000 to Refco to cover losses. Bone had been sanctioned by the Chicago Mercantile Exchange in 1977 for failing to follow margin requirements, among other infractions. But Blair served as Hillary's protective barrier. Any client that Blair brought to Bone would be given the same sort of preferential treatment that was extended to Blair himself. Therefore, because Bone never demanded it, both Blair and Hillary were able to make large sums of money without being saddled with large margin call payments. They would simply ride out the lows. Blair was trading millions of dollars and Bone knew he was good for it if the bottom fell out. But they were all on a roll.

Finally, Hillary got cold feet. Blair correctly predicted a dip in the market and sold short, giving Hillary a $40,000 profit in an afternoon. The volatility in the marketplace, she later said, was too much for her, and she closed her account with Refco, keeping her $99,000 overall profit secret until she and Bill, under duress, revealed their tax returns during the second year of his presidency. Hillary returned to the commodities market for a short spell in October 1979, allowing William Smith, her broker in Little Rock, to trade for her. Far more conservative then, her futures account with Smith doubled a $5,000 initial investment. The month after Chelsea's birth Hillary moved her money from the commodities casino to a safer, more assured investment—U.S. Treasury Bonds. Hillary said to Blair that she had become so rattled about the markets that she was worrying about her sugar contracts with Smith as she went into labor with Chelsea.

She was not worried, however, about a nest egg she and Bill had been sitting on since 1978, around the same time she'd gone into the cattle futures business. It was a piece of land they had bought with Bill's old mentor from the Fulbright days, Jim McDougal. The 230-acre parcel on the White River was called Whitewater.

BILL CLINTON's dilemma in his thirty-first year was whether to run for governor of his state in 1978, or for the U.S. Senate and seize the opportunity to move himself and Hillary to Washington for the next six years, as Hillary would have preferred. If elected, he would be the youngest member of the Senate. She would be a significant, and desirable, candidate for a job in the administration of President Carter in the capital. Or she could resume her career as a powerful advocate for children with Marian Wright Edelman's increasingly influential organization, now relocated to Washington, or another nonprofit foundation.

It was perhaps a measure of how seriously Arkansas took its politics (and of the seniority system in the United States Congress) that a state with a population of fewer than two million people and an antediluvian economy produced five politicians (all Democrats) in two generations who were among the most powerful of the second half of the twentieth century: Bill Clinton, Orval Faubus, Congressman Wilbur Mills, and Senators J. William Fulbright and John L. McClellan. At age eighty-two, McClellan had announced his retirement, and Clinton was his choice to succeed him. When Bill had told McClellan that he was considering running for governor instead, McClellan said it was a bad idea, "that all you did in the governor's office was make people mad. In the Senate you could do great things for the state and the nation." The governor's office was "a short trip to the political graveyard," partly because it held a two-year term, and only two of its occupants since 1876—one of them Faubus, who became enormously popular because of his segregationist stand in the schoolhouse door—had served more than four years. The worst that could happen, said McClellan, was that if Bill lost, as the senator himself had done on his first try (early in the century), well, he was young and could win again. This was hardly Hillary's or Bill's outlook. One loss had been enough.

In the fall of 1977, Steve Smith, Clinton's chief of staff in the attorney general's office, phoned an obscure, thirty-year-old political consultant, Dick Morris, who was approaching every Democratic Senate or gubernatorial candidate across the country, seeking employment. Morris, a New Yorker, had never had an out-of-state client, and he was awed by Clinton; like himself, the young attorney general had sideburns, long hair, and a razor-sharp sense of politics. Clinton was fascinated with Morris's unusual polling techniques, recognizing that they were uniquely penetrating and advanced in terms of the underlying meaning of the numbers. Morris was certain he could help Clinton in his decision about whether to run for governor or the Senate. Which office would Bill really prefer? "I'd like to be governor; I feel there's a lot more I can do here," Clinton answered. "But the real action is in Washington." If he sought the Senate seat, he would probably have to run against three strong Democrats for the nomination, including then Governor David Pryor, a relatively popular figure.

Morris was aware of Hillary's preference that Bill roll the dice and try to get to Washington. He suggested that he poll Clinton's chances in the two races. The results showed that Clinton might be able to win the Senate race, but victory was hardly certain. He would start perhaps ten points behind Pryor, who (like most of his predecessors) had been weakened in his second term in office. The governorship seemed a clearer shot for Bill. Pryor was pleased when Clinton informed him he would not challenge him for the nomination—a decision that helped keep the state's Democratic Party in reasonably good order over the next decade.

Bill, with Hillary, his mother, and his brother at his side (in the state capitol building he'd driven past the first day Hillary set foot in Arkansas), announced his decision to an excited press corps (already the Clintons were good copy) and enthusiastic supporters, explaining that being governor was what he "really wanted because a governor can do more for people than any other office." He paused. "Any office except the president." It was a remark not lost on those present.

Compared with subsequent campaigns, Hillary's involvement in Bill's 1978 gubernatorial race was minimal, just as her fitful involvement in his first term as governor would contrast with her dominance in the two decades that followed. For now, they were a two-career family. "She had a law practice and he had politics," Morris noted. And she was enjoying her days spent in the company of Vince Foster and Webb Hubbell. At the Rose firm, they were forming almost a private subsidiary, so much did they enjoy each other's company and support. Morris perceived that she meant to keep her independence. "Working at the Rose Law Firm, she seemed no different from dozens of wives (or husbands) of other candidates," he said. "She wished Bill well, would help him in any way she could, but gave no appearance of having a personal stake in his professional accomplishments."

Though Hillary was not present for the polling and strategy sessions with Morris, she remained involved enough in Bill's campaign to critique his speeches and suggest how, as a candidate, what he did and said to get elected might smoothly lead to policy once in office. She knew how to look out for her husband's interests. But the experience of his first campaign for Congress, when his advisers had wanted him to steal the election if necessary, still cautioned her to put some distance between herself and his aides. "Bill sees the light and sunshine about people, and Hillary sees their darker side," Clinton's 1978 campaign manager and chief of staff in his first term, Rudy Moore, said. "She has much more ability than he does to see who's with you, who's against you and to make sure they don't take advantage of you. He's not expecting to be jumped, but she always is. So she's on the defensive." Later, her expectations invariably put her on the offensive.

All Bill had to do to coast to the governor's mansion, according to Morris's numbers, was keep the big lead he was starting with. Though Hillary's public contributions to the campaign were comparatively sedated—"She did not do so much on the campaign trail that year. A woman was expected to smile and not give speeches," Morris said—for the first time she herself became an object of considerable enthusiasm by many voters inclined to support Bill. Already, the Rodham-Clintons were being perceived in the electorate and the press as a package and a partnership, smooth, smart, and idealistic. The promise of what they might be able to do together to improve the lives of Arkansas made some people's skepticism fade away. Others seemed frightened, or incensed.

As would increasingly become the case over the next twenty years, Hillary was seen by many as a polarizing figure. For the first time, she became the object of intense dislike and verbal abuse. Clinton's opponents criticized him for having a wife with a career—a lawyer to boot—who was so independent-minded that she wouldn't take her husband's name. The "name issue" would become one of the most talked about of the campaign. Men and women around the state argued publicly and privately about it. "People thought even his wife didn't like him enough to take his name," said an acerbic political columnist for the *Arkansas Democrat-Gazette*, Meredith Oakley, who would make a name for himself writing about the Clintons. Within the campaign itself and among supporters, there were a number who urged Hillary directly to change her mind.

Despite the name issue, Clinton easily won the Democratic primary with 60 percent of the vote and was in a solid position to win the general election. In the final months before election day, Bill and his top campaign aides, Steve Smith, Rudy Moore, and Hillary, started planning Clinton's gubernatorial agenda. Hillary would perform the same role—formulating policy ideas and reviewing candidates for her husband's staff—that she would play during his transition from president-elect to president, with disastrous consequences. Increasingly, his staff would bear her imprimatur, to the point where it became impossible to see clearly where the influence of one Clinton began and the other ended.

Though Bill and Hillary were thrilled at the prospect of his imminent victory, two ominous events occurred in the final weeks before the election that would haunt them in the years to come. The first was a press conference by retired Air Force Lieutenant Colonel Billy G. Geren, who accused Clinton of dodging the draft during the Vietnam War. Geren, a Republican, charged that Clinton had obtained a draft deferment in 1969 by signing up for the University of Arkansas ROTC, but had broken this agreement by returning to Oxford University for a second year of study. Clinton denied that he received a deferment, saying that when he did not attend ROTC training his name had been placed back in the draft. Fortunately for Clinton in 1978, his history with the draft remained an issue in the governor's race for only two days.

Frank Lady, an evangelical Christian with backing from Moral Majority voters, meanwhile, became the first (but hardly the last, as Bill noted) Clinton opponent to attack Hillary both for being a lawyer (as Pat Buchanan would remind Republicans at their 1992 national convention) and keeping her maiden name. Here were some early traces of the vast right-wing conspiracy, fueled by Lady's charges that she had used her position as a corporate lawyer to win clients favors from the state government in which her husband served as attorney general.

In fact, the potential conflicts were obvious and almost unavoidable in a state in which a single law firm represented the enormously wealthy few ("the ArkoRomans," in local parlance) and maintained close friend-and-family relationships with members of the political class. Hillary had done work for the Little Rock Airport Commission, which was headed by Seth Ward, whose son-in-law was Hillary's colleague Webb Hubbell. Hillary herself represented a subsidiary of the Stephens empire in court, despite the regulation of many of the parent company's assets by Bill's office. Meanwhile, he was receiving campaign contributions from Tyson, Stephens, and other ArkoRoman enterprises his office had to deal with.

Hillary's presence next to Bill at campaign events—and the vigorous support of each for the Equal Rights Amendment—further inflamed the Moral Majority right, still in its infancy but, in Arkansas, motivated increasingly by Bill's and Hillary's rise. At a campaign stop in Jonesboro, a woman wearing a Frank Lady T-shirt started hollering angrily at Bill, "Talk about the ERA! Talk about the ERA!" The Clintons' friend Diane Kincaid had recently overwhelmed Phyllis Schlafly, the country's leading ERA opponent, in a debate over a second attempt in the Arkansas legislature to ratify the amendment (which nonetheless failed there again). "Okay," said Bill, "I'll talk about it. I'm for it. You're against it. But it won't do as much harm as you think it will or as much good as those of us who support it wish it would. Now let's get back to schools and jobs." But his interlocutor was unwilling. "You're just promoting homosexuality," she screamed. Bill looked back at her and smiled. "Ma'am, in my short life in politics, I've been accused of everything under the sun. But you're the first person who ever accused me of promoting homosexuality." The crowd roared, Bill noted later.

On election day, Clinton became governor-elect with 63 percent of the vote and became the youngest governor in America since Harold Stassen in 1938 (not necessarily a good omen, given Stassen's repeated and eventually quixotic failure to reach the presidency). The *New York Times* covered Bill's triumph as a story of major importance and described him as "the 31-year-old whiz kid of Arkansas politics." This was Clinton's first important national interview, with Howell Raines, then a thirty-five-year-old correspondent covering the South for the *Times*. There had been vague references during the campaign (not by the Clintons) to Camelot and the glamour of the Kennedys as a couple. In the interview with Raines, Bill described the people of his state in terms inspired by Hillary's often expressed view to him, in private: his victory, he said, represented the wishes of Arkansans to no longer "be perceived, especially by themselves, as being backward." There was no way to retract what he had said once it was out of his mouth, and it gave the impression that he—and she—held a condescending and patronizing view of the people he had been elected to serve. The experience with Raines would be a harbinger: as the *Times*'s Washington bureau chief during the 1992 presidential campaign and in the Clintons' first year in the White House, Raines—a fellow progressive Southerner from Birmingham, Alabama, 370 miles from Little Rock—would send his reporters out on the Whitewater trail with what Hillary and Bill thought was a vengeance. Others in journalism attributed it to some sort of good ole boy competition with Bill Clinton that motivated Raines. In any case, when Raines was promoted to editorial page editor of the *Times* in 1993, he would crusade without mercy against the Clintons and what he believed their unforgivable ethics—though against Bill's impeachment—until they left the White House.

On election night 1978, when the votes confirmed the magnitude of his triumph, Clinton became emotional in accepting victory, cheered by thousands of supporters and campaign workers, including many friends from his days at Georgetown, Oxford, and Yale. Looking at Hillary, who was standing next to Virginia, he said, "I am very proud of the campaign we have run."

The customary inaugural ball was preceded by an extravaganza of Arkansas entertainment they called "Diamonds and Denim," not too distant a concept from "The People's Inaugural" invented by Hillary and others for Bill's inauguration as president thirteen years later. Both events were intended to symbolize a new era of generational and philosophical change in political power and its use. All the entertainers for "Diamonds and Denim" were from Arkansas, among them soul singer Al Green, country singer Jimmy Driftwood, and Bill Clinton on sax. "The whole theme of the evening was country come to town—we're just Arkansas folks, but we're kinda sophisticated," said an aide to the new governor, but it came off less hokey than it sounded. Hundreds of Bill's and Hillary's friends, far more than on election night, from every phase of their lives since grammar school, had come to Little Rock for the festivities—and to watch the man many of them had long thought might someday be president take his first big step, with Hillary by his side.

THE ARKANSAS GOVERNOR'S mansion, though reasonably commodious, is not one of the nation's more distinguished. Built in 1950 in downtown Little Rock, on the site of a former school for the blind, with Greek revival columns and a facade of red bricks retrieved from the demolished school, it resembles—inside and out—a rather grand suburban spec house.

When Bill took the oath of office, a limitless future seemed to stretch out before him. "Our vote was a vindication of what my wife and I have done and what we hope to do for the state," he had said from the podium to cheers on election night. But the Clintons' first two years in the governor's mansion would be disastrous, marked by huge political mistakes, some of them a result of Hillary's tin ear, some the result of her refusal to

act like a traditional first lady, some the result of Bill's tendency to want
to do too much, too fast. Many of the same problems, especially those
related to Hillary's role, would also occur in the first two years of the
Clinton presidency. Later, Hillary would describe the years 1978 to 1980
as "among the most difficult, exhilarating, glorious and heartbreaking in
my life," which would fit as well her first two years in the White House.

What was so extraordinary about Hillary's failures in the White
House more than a decade later was that she seemed to have learned
almost nothing from her experience those first two years in the governor's mansion, though there were obvious differences in circumstances.
Hillary's finely tuned sense of her own evolution, the ability to learn from
her mistakes, to replay in her mind the macro- and micro-factors that
moved a project from conception to realization or collapse and then
rearrange them to get a more satisfactory result the next time, had always
been part of her makeup. These characteristics were among the most
valuable in her ability to help her husband, whose process and emotional
constitution were so different from hers. But her experience those two
years in Little Rock seemed to have hardly registered in her memory
bank when she got to Washington.

HILLARY, AS THE WIFE of the attorney general and (simultaneously) a
corporate lawyer in the capital of the state, had managed with purposeful
skill to keep comfortably below Arkansas's political radar. She could go
almost anywhere in the state and few people would recognize her, even
on the streets of downtown Little Rock. That was impossible as the governor's wife. Meanwhile, through her increasing work in Washington
during Bill's governorship, she purposefully raised her national profile.

Rather than attend to the traditional ceremonial and social role of
being first lady of Arkansas, she chose instead to work substantively with
her husband, and until shortly before the birth of Chelsea in 1980, she
hardly reduced her workload at the Rose Law Firm. "Hillary was very
active in shaping public policy, but not in being a political wife," recalled
Bev Lindsey, who worked for Bill Clinton during part of his governorship, and was married to (and then, after the White House years, divorced
from) Bruce Lindsey, Clinton's all-purpose factotum. "She thought then
that Bill could be governor and she could shape policy and be a corporate
lawyer, and not have to do the rest, not have to go to ladies' lunches, or
travel with him and not speak." *Arkansas Times* columnist John Brum-
mett said that during the first term Hillary wanted to make "no concessions to any obligations of the office. She just went her own way and got

a job, got involved in things she was interested in. . . . A lot of people thought she was remote, distant."

Bill and Hillary quickly formed their routines. Hillary didn't read newspapers or watch television news. Instead, she listened to National Public Radio or classical music in the morning. If there was anything else she really needed to know she figured she'd be told about it early in her day, either by Bill on the phone or Vince in the office. But even in her earliest days as first lady of Arkansas, "she didn't want to read about things that would bother her and about which she could do nothing," said Betsey Wright. "She saw it as an irritant."

Rather than be chauffeured in an official car by a state trooper, Hillary preferred to drive her own Oldsmobile Cutlass. She'd be at her desk at the Rose firm for coffee with Vince or Webb by 7:30 A.M. Bill awakened late, faded for a while in the afternoon, then got reenergized around the time Hillary was ready for bed; he stayed up until two or three conducting all manner of business, playing cards with friends, picking up the telephone, plowing through piles of paper—often simultaneously. Hillary didn't have his stamina, but she paced herself better. She knew when she needed rest and could easily fall asleep in a car or on a plane and wake up with her batteries recharged. Hillary didn't have her own staff in the governor's mansion. Instead, she was assigned someone from the governor's office to help her on specific projects. The mansion staff of five consisted of cook, assistant cook, maid, landscape-maintenance worker, and mansion manager, who, after Chelsea's birth, was enlisted to babysit so Hillary and Bill didn't have to pay a sitter out of their own pockets.

Clinton took office with enthusiasm, bold concepts (many from the dialogue he and Hillary had been embarked on since Yale), and an electorate that seemed relatively amenable to change. His agenda as governor was an ambitious extension of his campaign promises. But he was nowhere near as good governing—at least not yet—as running for office. His plans were full of ideas he'd been making notes on for years, based on the suggestions of academics, business people, friends ensconced in think tanks, and his voluminous reading from political economy to scientific tracts to day care manuals. But the ideas often clashed with budgetary realities, and with the priorities of legislators who were heavily indebted to the state's moneyed interests—just as Hillary's health care priorities would be at odds with the policies developed by his own presidential economic advisers, and put to death by moneyed interests and legislators in their thrall, and her own hubris.

The notion of Hillary and Bill Clinton as power-hungry acquisitors with little interest in the public weal save some sort of left-leaning ideology, however, has always been at odds with the facts. Even before they met, each believed fervently in the concept of public service, even the humble nobility of it, however unlikely the term might seem today in a declarative sentence that includes the names Bill and Hillary Clinton in it, however difficult this objective might be. The principles that they believed in upon Bill's election as governor are indicated by the programs he proposed, and the words he (and Hillary) spoke and wrote, especially in his inaugural address, even if a bit florid: "For as long as I can remember," he proclaimed, "I have believed passionately in the cause of equal opportunity, and I will do what I can to advance it. For as long as I can remember, I have deplored the arbitrary and abusive exercise of power by those in authority, and I will do what I can to prevent it. . . . For as long as I can remember, I have loved the land, air and water of Arkansas, and I will do what I can to protect them. For as long as I can remember, I have wished to ease the burdens of life for those who, through no fault of their own, are weak or needy, and I will try to help them." Bill, more than Hillary at first, believed also that his message needed to be informed by advanced models of economic development and fewer restraints on investment capital than traditional liberals had advocated. At the time of his accession in Arkansas, many governors and mayors, Democrats and Republicans, working at the ground level of American politics, not the Olympian heights of Capitol Hill in Washington, were trying to devise imaginative formulas that would break out of the old liberal-conservative stereotypes to deliver better services to constituents and bigger profits to business and industry, thus increasing jobs and the tax base to pay for civic improvement.

Bill's major spending priorities, he said, were meant to pull the old Arkansas into the modern era. Over the next two years Clinton would find himself walking a thin line between implementing policies that could dramatically contribute to improving the lives of his fellow Arkansans, and attempting not to rattle too hard the sensibilities of the ArkoRoman establishment and the good ole boys who ran the legislature. Indicative of his new-school approach (the term "policy wonk" had not yet been applied to Hillary or Bill), Bill used surplus funds from his campaign to hire Price Waterhouse to help him devise a budget and projections for its implementation. Other surplus funds went to Dick Morris to survey citizens about the ideas and programs called for in the budget. Bill wanted him to rank them in order of appeal to the voters, and then develop an overarching theme connecting them all. "He was left with a program that was thoroughly admirable but indescribable," said Morris.

There was no theme, but rather "a bit of everything. Like a kid in a candy store he wanted to do it all." Because he had won election by so large a margin, Hillary and Bill both were convinced he had a mandate to initiate wholesale change. (The same mistake was repeated in 1993, largely at her instigation, though Bill had won the presidency without even a majority of the popular vote.)

The budget book he presented to the state legislature was impossibly thick, in number of pages and density of factoids. But there were identifiable priorities: education, reorganizing school districts; providing a rural health care system in a state where doctors and hospitals were many miles away from people with little means of transportation; establishing new departments of economic development and of energy. Some legislators dismissed the Clinton program as the idealistic overenthusiasm of a boy governor. But in his two years in office, Clinton made some progress: a $1,200 annual raise for teachers; a 40 percent increase in education spending; an extension of public transportation; the maintenance of a 10-cent pay phone call (most neighboring states were up to a quarter); a study on the ill-effects of clear-cutting by the big timber companies that were setting up in the state (and then succumbing to their interests by appointing a forestry commissioner to their liking).

And he appointed Hillary to head his health care advisory committee. Characteristically, this came about when he ran into trouble, in the first year of his term. He had appointed a health commissioner from out of state (already a mistake) who had proposed that nurse-practitioners be permitted to serve as doctors in many areas of Arkansas where physicians were scarce. The state medical society—licensed doctors—were in an uproar that their fat Medicaid fees were about to get eaten up by a bunch of paramedics. He cleverly appointed Hillary to solve the problem of delivering expanded health care to the poorest counties and towns in Arkansas without taking a bite from doctors' fees; he was bypassing the bureaucracy so he would be able to reach a decision at home in the governor's mansion. It worked. Navigating the federal shoals as she had in getting funding for a rape crisis center in Fayetteville, Hillary used her contacts in Washington to obtain federal money to pay for rural health care services in Arkansas. Four rural clinics were opened almost immediately, construction began on three others, and the use of midwives and nurse-practitioners was expanded.

Despite her studied uninterest in ribbon-cuttings and formal dinner parties at the governor's mansion, Hillary carefully monitored guest lists for the occasional informal dinners she and Bill gave. "Think about who you really want to have dinner with because now anyone will come," a friend recalled her telling Bill. The friend speculated that instead Hillary "was going to continue to suffer his old friendships way long past their value stage."

For the next twenty years until the Clintons left the White House in 2001, a line between his Arkansas friends who predated Hillary and all the others was increasingly apparent. When bad things happened to one or both of them, many in the old Arkansas crowd attributed the problems to Hillary—to aspects of her character rather than this. Those who had not known Clinton in his youth in his home state were inclined to more complex and probing explanations of the difficulties.

During Bill's first term as governor, rumors of his alleged affairs with a multitude of women were persistent. Though he was now married, he was also now the governor, and women gravitated toward Clinton as never before. He loved the attention. Being on the road was always fun, because Hillary wasn't around and he could freely flirt, not that he was too reticent sometimes when she *was* around.

It may be that, as in his White House years, Clinton was trying to restrain himself, with difficulty. One of the ironies of the Lewinsky circus was that their "relationship" began during a period when he'd tried to put the brakes on his libido, in his first term in the White House. In his initial term as governor, "Bill was like a kid with a new toy," said an acquaintance. "The perks, the mansion, having the most powerful people in the state paying court to you. And he always had a weakness for bleached blondes with big jewelry, in short skirts, their figures shown off to best advantage." Rudy Moore, Bill's campaign manager, had fired a travel aide for bragging about taking the candidate to nightclubs. But Moore thought "appearances were more than what was going on," which was often the result of Clinton's bad judgment about being in the wrong place at the wrong time. Randy White, another aide who traveled with Clinton, said that he never saw any evidence of Clinton having an affair during that first term. Inevitably, though, rumors reached Hillary, who, in the pattern of their marriage for years to come, became suspicious, incensed at Bill, and then seemed—to those around them—to experience "a quiet humiliation," in the words of one observer. But she was determined to stay married to him.

CHELSEA CLINTON, from the moment of her difficult conception through the dysfunction and difficulties, personal and political intertwining, of the first family's life in the White House, was an enormous factor in keeping her parents together.

After Chelsea's birth, far more complicated considerations were at work than the simple nostrum of parents who "stay together for the sake of the children." But Hillary's and Bill's devotion to their daughter, an only child, was in its unconventional way (given the chaos and tension they generated) absolute and unconditional. Whatever the distractions, the family unit, when isolated from the outside world, functioned reasonably well. Bill and Hillary were both good at being hands-on parents. Given the time-devouring nature of their public lives, they found a remarkable amount of time to be with their daughter: discussions at the dinner table, driving her to school, cheering from the soccer sidelines, Scrabble games, and enjoying movies—including her favorite, *Snow White*, and his, *High Noon*—and then taking them apart. There was a genuine naturalness to it all.

For Bill Clinton, being a constant, loving father was, to his mind, the real test of his manhood: creating what he had never had, ensuring the wholeness of a real family. For Hillary, having a child was an equally consuming desire and drive: "I don't think I could ever be a woman without having a child," she told a friend during her pregnancy. Hillary had married for love, to have children, and to create her idea of a model family life—such as had been denied her mother, twice, in childhood and marriage. She felt she could figure out how to make the political part of her life work, but unless she could be a mother with a loving husband who was father to their children, life's fulfillment would elude her. Thus the prospect that she could not bear a child, which seemed increasingly likely in the first two years of her marriage—and which she had probably feared even earlier—could have been as frightening to her as anything she might conjure about her husband and other women.

Since very early in their marriage (or, as he said, "for some time"), Hillary and Bill had been trying to have a child. Unsuccessful, they decided in the summer of 1979 to see a fertility specialist in San Francisco, and scheduled an appointment for shortly after their return from a brief vacation in Bermuda.

Hillary suffered from a condition called endometriosis, which often makes conception difficult, can cause infertility, and frequently results in extreme pain during and after intercourse. In Fayetteville, before moving to Little Rock, she had told two friends (both women) that she feared the condition might prevent her from conceiving a child. Some doctors believed endometriosis could cause miscarriage. It is not clear whether the condition preceded her marriage—which seems possible, given when she mentioned it to the women—and at what point Bill first learned of it. Bill, with his desire to learn everything there was to know about any subject crossing his horizon, upon hearing the news would have logically sought to learn all its implications. According to standard medical literature, "between 30 percent to 40 percent of women with endometriosis are infertile, making it one of the top three causes of female infertility." Many women don't learn they have the malady until they experience difficulty getting pregnant.*

There is little question that Hillary's difficulty getting pregnant— and all the extraordinary measures and frustrations that attend such a situation—added strain to the early years of their marriage. But within days of their return from Bermuda in July 1979, and before they were to leave for their doctor's appointment in San Francisco, Hillary learned she was pregnant. Diane Kincaid and Jim Blair were among the first to be told. Hillary and Bill radiated excitement, and relief.

She and Bill took Lamaze classes together, in preparation for natural childbirth. Other expectant parents with whom they attended seemed, after some initial curiosity, to take it in stride that the governor and first lady of the state were practicing deep-breathing exercises with them. They read parenting handbooks (Dr. T. Berry Brazelton, the author of one of the most famous, would lend support and expertise to Hillary's health care task force); sought advice from their friends; asked questions about doctors, nurses, and midwives; and received plenty of unsolicited suggestions ("Think of a baby like a football, and hold it tight," advised an ex–football player).

In January, late in her pregnancy, Hillary flew to New York with board members from the Arkansas Children's Hospital, for which she did pro bono legal work, to make a presentation to underwriters who would determine the hospital's bond ratings. That would be her last trip before Chelsea was born. She developed problems (of a nature neither she nor Bill publicly described) late in her pregnancy, and was instructed by her doctor to cease traveling. The doctor's orders were both worrisome and disappointing. At the end of February, she and Bill had planned to attend the annual Washington meeting of the National Governors Association and dinner at the White House with President and Mrs. Carter. By now they were on the "extended list" of guests for state dinners and other official functions; both Hillary and Bill—not always by virtue of being a couple, but also through the particular qualifications of one or the other—were asked frequently to participate in conferences under either White House auspices or convened by the Democratic

---

*The condition occurs when endometrial tissue, the tissue that lines the uterus and is shed during menstruation, grows outside of the uterus—on the ovaries, fallopian tubes, ligaments supporting the uterus, and other areas in the pelvic cavity.

Party. In the last week of February, Bill attended the governors meeting, accompanied at the closing White House dinner by Carolyn Huber, who had left the Rose Law Firm to manage the governor's mansion for Hillary and Bill. Every few hours he phoned home.

Fifteen minutes after his return to the mansion on the night of February 27, three weeks before Hillary's due date, her water broke. Frenzied preparations for the trip to the hospital ensued. Consulting his list of instructions from Lamaze class, Bill shouted to the troopers to get the car ready and to bring a bag of ice cubes for Hillary to suck on during labor. Meanwhile, he threw together other items on the list for Hillary's hospital stay. As Hillary got unsteadily into the car, one of the troopers arrived with a huge garbage bag filled with ice—enough for a whole Lamaze class of mothers in labor—which got heaved into the trunk of the sedan. The drive took only minutes, and upon immediate examination, doctors told Hillary and Bill that the baby was in breech, upside down—the kind of last-minute surprise that expectant parents most dread. Hillary had never before been hospitalized. Now she would have to undergo cesarean section to deliver her baby, and she was terribly frightened, trying not to panic. Normal procedures forbade fathers in the delivery room when surgery was ordered, but Bill appealed to the hospital's administrator, saying that Hillary needed him, and promised "that they could cut Hillary open from head to toe and I wouldn't get sick or faint." The administrator gave his approval, either because Bill was the governor or simply because he had been his usual enormously persuasive self, or both.

Throughout the surgery, in which a local anesthetic was administered, Bill held Hillary's hand. He could see what was happening over a screen that blocked her own "view of the cutting and bleeding," Bill recalled. At 11:24 P.M. he watched the doctor lift out the baby, a girl, healthy. She weighed six pounds, one and three-quarter ounces. Bill professed later, "It was the happiest moment of my life, one my father never knew." And perhaps just as tellingly, "At last I was a father." A few minutes after the umbilical cord was cut, their newborn was cleaned up and handed to Hillary and then Bill to hold.

Like most parents whose child has been born healthy after last-minute complications—plus in this case Hillary's extreme difficulty conceiving—their daughter's birth seemed to Hillary and Bill to be even more special. They frequently referred to Chelsea as their "miracle child."

On a Christmas vacation in London in 1978, they had chosen her name, after hearing Judy Collins's version of the song "Chelsea Morning," an evocative Joni Mitchell (who also recorded it) piece of quasi-poetry of the day, set in London. Bill had said to Hillary that, if they ever had a daughter, they should name her Chelsea, where they had been walking when they heard the song. During the Clintons' years in the White House, Judy Collins would entertain or be a guest there on several occasions, invariably singing "Chelsea Morning."

That night, while Hillary was in the recovery room, Bill carried their daughter to be seen by Virginia, members of his staff, and friends he'd summoned. He "talked to her . . . sang to her," and, he later wrote, "I never wanted that night to end." Hillary, too, noted that Bill was, from the beginning, a doting dad.

Hillary has described herself as the "designated worrier" in the Clinton family (others have more frequently identified her as the designated warrior) and said that, for months after Chelsea was born, she worried incessantly. Years later, she wrote of praying that she would be a good enough mother for her baby. Some aspects of motherhood did not come easily, including breastfeeding. Hillary at times seemed "mystified" (her word) by Chelsea's arrival, noting how disconsolate Chelsea was at times despite the most gentle treatment. To calm them both, Hillary came up with a motherly mantra: "Chelsea, this is new for both of us. . . . We're just going to have to help each other do the best we can."

Hillary had no shortage of motherly help in the mansion. Eliza Ashley, the cook, was a pampering presence from the beginning, and Carolyn Huber became Chelsea's adoring surrogate aunt. Dorothy and Hugh arrived from Park Ridge to coddle their first grandchild. Few settings could be more advantageous to a mother and her baby. And Bill was constantly holding her, playing with her, singing to her, nuzzling her. Later, when she reached nursery school age and thereafter in Little Rock, he drove her to school himself, as often as possible, putting her on his lap in the car.

Hillary was determined—and, to a remarkable degree succeeded, from the time of Chelsea's birth through college graduation—in keeping the press away from their daughter. More than a week passed before the governor's press office consented to giving Arkansas's newspapers a picture of the new first family. Not surprisingly, Hillary was later almost totally unsuccessful (despite trying) in shutting down journalistic exploration of the Clintons' marital history. But both she and Bill went to extraordinary lengths to see that Chelsea's childhood be as normal under the circumstances as possible (a difficult concept in the case of someone raised almost exclusively in a governor's mansion and the White House).

Hillary took four months off from her job at the Rose Law Firm after Chelsea was born but continued to travel for board meetings and other responsibilities outside the state. She was sensitive to any criticism that she skimped as a mother. Carolyn Yeldell Staley, who had gone to high school with Bill, had had a very brief romantic interlude with him when he was at Georgetown, and maintained a genuine friendship afterward in which they corresponded, came to visit shortly after Hillary and Chelsea had come home from the hospital. Carolyn, an opera singer, and her husband had moved back to Little Rock from Indiana so she could work for the Arkansas Arts Council. She had written a song about Chelsea, which she sang for mother, daughter, and father, to her own piano accompaniment. The song was written from the point of view of the baby's parents, and was partly about humility and the awe of bringing a child into the world. One line was: "We may not be worthy, but we'll try to be wise." When Carolyn had finished singing her offering, Hillary seemed to bristle at the notion she was unworthy.

Six weeks after giving birth, Hillary went to Memphis and left Chelsea with Peach Pietrafesa, a friend from Wellesley days whose husband had gone to work in Bill's office. "The feminist I considered myself to be did not think a child of six weeks old should be left with anyone else," Pietrefesa said. "Especially to go to some second-rate junko regional bar association meeting. This was her denial of emotional circumstances—by getting out there to fight what she had decided was going to be a terrific fight, it was a way to make what she was doing heroic." This was the kind of damned-if-you-do, damned-if-you-don't critique that Hillary was constantly subjected to (and not just on motherhood), especially by former employees in the governor's office or White House who had left under disagreeable circumstances. It became part of the constant and increasingly vocal dialogue about her.

Whispering had started at the Rose firm among female employees and partners both about whether Hillary might resign after Chelsea's birth despite the fact that she had been made a partner in 1979. Some partners "had assumed she would quit 'when her husband got a real job,'" Webb Hubbell said. "They assumed she would quit 'when Bill became governor.' *Surely* she would quit 'when she had a baby.'"

It was then, Hubbell said, that Hillary began to believe that the partners wouldn't acknowledge her work as much as that of her male colleagues. (Some of the partners simply believed her work was not up to par.) "Hillary began—subconsciously at first, I think—taking her show on the road," he said. "She looked for causes, board memberships, other ways she could expand her career as a lawyer and her persona as an independent person. But she was also feeling the pressure of Bill's problems in the state—especially when it became clear that some of the criticism of him was due to her."

Indeed, her desk at Rose—after she went back—was increasingly a platform from which she could reach out to the world beyond Little Rock, and concentrate less on cases assigned by the firm; that was for the most part tedious, routine work that somebody in every law office had to do. She was far more interested in her pro bono activities on behalf of Arkansas Advocates for Children and Families, which she had helped found. It worked closely with the Children's Defense Fund in Washington. Her work on the Governor's Commission on Early Childhood was important to her. But the office at Rose was still a place where she could find camaraderie with her Two Amigos—and a strong shoulder and confidant in Vince Foster when there were bumps in the road.

Friends of the Clintons were aware of her disappointment at not being able to have a second child. Even during their early years in the White House, she and Bill talked seriously about adopting, and discussed with friends in California who had adopted how they might go about the process themselves. In Hillary's forty-ninth year, she raised the subject bizarrely in an interview with a *Time* magazine reporter. "I must say, we're hoping to have another child," Hillary said. When the stunned journalist asked if she meant by natural birth, she added: "I have to tell you I would be surprised but not disappointed. My friends would be appalled, I'm sure." Having another child had been a recurring discussion in the Clinton marriage. "I think we're talking about it more now," Hillary said. "We'd obviously wait to get serious about it until after the [1996] election." This was before she'd heard the name Monica Lewinsky.

BILL CLINTON had become governor of Arkansas in 1981 with enormous goodwill toward him in his state. He was the youngest governor in the nation; he had shinnied higher and faster up the greasy pole of American politics than any member of his generation; his wife was recognized as a first-rate political organizer and a highly principled advocate for people in need; he was a model of the new Southern politician but transcended regional appeal; and he (and his wife) held the loyalty, affection, and awe of an army of well-placed young men and women who had been saying for years that he would someday be president and were prepared to help make that happen. Bill possessed a voracious intellectual capacity and curiosity that could be harnessed to practical politics in the best sense, on behalf of ideas, many of them bold, new, and with a real chance of making the lives of citizens of his state and his country better.

He was also capable of self-absorption, self-defeating distraction, juvenile outbursts, a debilitating weakness for women, and a tendency to throw it all away when he was on the edge of greatness. This was particularly true—and would become more so—when left to his own devices, without the constant help, guidance, and encouragement of his wife.

During the first eighteen months of his two-year term as governor there had been some solid achievements—creating a new economic development department and making incremental progress on reforming rural health care, for instance. But Bill's record fell far from meeting his or Hillary's hopes and expectations, and was hardly triumphant. He had encountered serious, unexpected obstacles, not the least of which was that his wife hadn't turned into the available political asset and invaluable adviser that, under different circumstances, she might have been. Instead, with his encouragement, she had gone off to pursue her own career, under her own name, for which he was being made to pay in loss of political support from too many Arkansans reluctant to accept a first lady with such nontraditional ideas. Moreover, parenthood, as much as it was welcomed, was not necessarily consistent with immediate political needs. Hillary had been understandably preoccupied by her pregnancy and then the care of their baby, born two months into his governorship, when he could have greatly benefited from her help.

Hillary felt certain that Bill had the brains, the manner, the analytical skills, the energy, and the rhetorical ability to overcome any serious difficulties. And, at home, there were sublime moments with their baby daughter.

As his campaign for reelection was reaching critical mass, the perception of Clinton as champion of ordinary citizens was taking a beating. He was losing the support of too many people who worked hard for their money and were left with little, who resented the power and wealth of the oligarchs and industries that had run roughshod in Arkansas for years and were showing few signs of losing influence. After all, he had been elected largely on the strength of his promises to make the lives of its working people better, to take the state in a new direction in which his smarts and contacts would yield tangible results: improved schools, lower utility rates, new roads, extended health care, benefits in jobs and aid dollars that would flow from his closeness with the folks in Washington, most importantly from the new Democratic president for whom he had campaigned and helped deliver Arkansas's electoral votes. Clinton had said he could do more than his opponents and predecessors, but the results were hard to see—which was one of the problems of a two-year term: you were running for reelection before you could convincingly show why you should be reelected. Moreover, the whole country seemed to be in an unusual slump, economic and psychological. There were hostages in Iran, race riots in Miami, the Russians had invaded Afghanistan, and the states—

including his own—were not getting their expected share of revenue from Washington because the economy had gone into serious decline. Cars were lined up at gas pumps. Ronald Reagan was leading a conservative crusade for the presidency that looked as if it might swamp Carter. Castro had permitted 100,000 Cubans, many of them criminals and mental patients, released from jail, to leave for Florida in the so-called Mariel boatlift, overwhelming the state's capacity to deal with them.

One of Clinton's objectives for his inaugural term as governor was to put to bed once and for all the idea still held by some Arkansans, particularly those in rural areas, that he wasn't really one of them, that his time as a Rhodes Scholar and Yale Law graduate and his four years at Georgetown and bringing his wife down from—wherever it was she was from—had defined him more than his roots. With polling help from Dick Morris, even before he'd been sworn in, Bill decided that road-building was both the answer politically and a way to drag the state toward modernity in at least one basic way. It would be his signature issue. Arkansas's roads were a disaster, undermining the economic future of the state, which was heavily dependent on trucking. But to fund $3.3 billion in highway and road improvements, he unwisely gave lobbyists for the trucking and poultry industries a dominant hand in devising a formula for additional taxes on car license fees. The fees would be based on weight, not value, of a registered passenger vehicle. Thus, in a state full of old pickups and junkers, the less-well-off generally paid higher tax fees to get their license tags than the swells who drove around in faster, newer, lighter, costlier cars. Meanwhile, the trucking and poultry companies got off easy, too.

"I could sign the bill into law and have a good road program paid for in an unfair way, or veto it and have no road program at all," Clinton said years later. "I signed the bill. It was the single dumbest mistake I ever made in politics until 1994, when I agreed to ask for a special prosecutor in the Whitewater case when there was not a shred of evidence to justify one." He had alienated rural Arkansans and blue-collar urbanites as well. People waiting in DMV lines to pay higher car taxes were fuming all over the state.

Hillary, a rationalist as always, was unhappy about the uproar, but not yet overly worried. People would surely understand that Bill had tried to do the right thing. Then a turkey farmer named Monroe Schwarzlose, who had challenged Bill in the Democratic primary, received 31 percent of the vote (he'd gotten 1 percent in the same primary in 1978) by attacking Bill on the car tag issue. This was the kind of demagoguery that made Hillary uncomfortable with electoral politics. Bill's Republican opponent in the general election, Frank White, was also making headway on the issue. But increasingly, the focus of his assault on Bill became Hillary's decision to remain Hillary Rodham.

Usually, she introduced herself as "Hillary—Governor Clinton's wife," but formal invitations to dinner at the governor's mansion were in the name of "Governor Bill Clinton and Hillary Rodham." The Republican nominee took to introducing his own wife as "Mrs. Frank White" at campaign stops. But perhaps most disturbing to those who tended to be disturbed by such matters—and most advantageous to White—was Chelsea's birth announcement, which gave the names of her parents as Hillary Rodham and Governor William Jefferson Clinton.

Hillary maintained that keeping her maiden name had been a show of self-esteem and independence, and would mitigate any conflict of interest allegations, an odd assumption. But Hillary's discussions with friends made clear that she regarded it as anything but a small gesture. "It showed that I was still me," she said. And, as Jim Blair noted: "She still had that same child-of-the-1960s aura."

Bill, meanwhile, looked younger than his thirty-two years and, as his political troubles worsened, editorial cartoonists took to depicting him as a child, often on a tricycle, and calling him "Baby."

The most staggering blow was especially painful for Hillary and Bill because it was administered, inexplicably, by Jimmy Carter, to whom they had been unceasingly loyal. Carter had been challenged for the 1980 presidential nomination by Senator Edward M. Kennedy. Most of the liberal wing of the Democratic Party supported Kennedy, including many friends who had been with Hillary and Bill since the McGovern days in Texas. But Hillary was steadfast in her support for Carter, admonishing them, saying, "You have to look at who can get elected and what he can accomplish." (Her argument against Kennedy was the same one that many Democrats would use to oppose her own candidacy for president a quarter-century later.)

When 100,000 Cuban refugees arrived in Florida in the Mariel boatlift, Carter had dispatched them to four military camps, including 18,000 to Fort Chaffee, in northwest Arkansas. On June 1, more than 1,000 rioted and breached their quarters at the Chaffee resettlement camp. Bill's performance under pressure as governor was cool and impressive, including his justifiable assignment of responsibility for the incident to Army personnel who had failed to maintain order at the facility. ("Well shit, General, who left the wire cutters in the stockade if none of this was the military's fault?" he challenged the commanding general in a private conversation.) Only the intervention of state police had quieted the situation, after hundreds of the Cubans had run down a highway carrying sticks and bottles. But it was inevitable that Bill would pay politically for the riot, because of his and Hillary's close identification with Carter. Frank White used pictures and film footage of the rioting—showing only black rioters—to great effect in his ads, associating Bill with an aura of anarchy. And then it got even worse: Carter broke a promise to Clinton that no more prisoners would be sent to Fort Chaffee. On August 1, he sent word to the governor's office that all remaining Mariel refugees from resettlement camps in Florida, Wisconsin, and Pennsylvania would be shipped to Fort Chaffee, and that a single holding facility would be established there for the whole boatlift operation. "You're fucking me," Bill yelled over the phone to a presidential aide, but it was too late.

Hillary saw ominous signs before Bill did. By October she told Bill her feeling that polls with him in the lead were wrong, and that he "might actually lose." She also made a mental note that would inform the conduct of all future Clinton campaigns: the negative ads of Bill's opponent trumped not just the news broadcasts but the reality and complexity of what had happened at Fort Chaffee.

Just eight days before election day, Hillary called Dick Morris in an effort to save the Clinton campaign. Morris had been fired shortly after Bill was elected because so many people on the governor's staff disliked working with him, and Bill himself was ambivalent. To him, Morris combined the powers of a savant with a snake. But he had warned Bill about the potential negative political consequences of raising the car tag fee, and Hillary's practical instincts weren't wrong in asking him to help save the campaign.

Hillary's phone call to Morris initiated her new role in managing Bill and his campaigns. A basic dynamic in the Rodham-Clinton marital and political relationship was undergoing a momentous shift. "She believed very much in him but felt that he needed someone to protect him, someone more maternal or lawyerly more than anything else," Morris said. "You know, This guy's so nice he'll sign anything and [I've] got to read the contract first. That kind of stuff."

Morris, in Florida working on a Republican campaign, told Hillary that it was probably too late to salvage a win for Bill, but he went to Arkansas anyway. As was often the case when Hillary considered electoral politics, she was appalled at its unfairness and illogic. Bill's ideas and ideals towered above not just Frank White's, but (to her mind) the whole political class in America. That fact had been on prominent display at the Democratic convention in New York in midsummer. Bill had been a Carter floor whip, and was chosen by the Democratic governors to deliver a prime-time speech as their representative. His speech was enlightened. The time had come to find "more creative and realistic" solutions than the old Democratic coalition had been recycling for two generations, he said.

We were brought up to believe, uncritically, without thinking about it, that our system broke down in the Great Depression, was reconstructed by Franklin Roosevelt through the New Deal and World War II, and would never break again. And that all we had to do was try to reach out and extend the benefits of America to those who had been dispossessed: minorities and women, the elderly, the handicapped and children in need. But the hard truth is that for ten long years through Democratic and Republican administrations alike, this economic system has been breaking down. We have seen high inflation, high unemployment, large government deficits, the loss of our competitive edge. In response to these developments, a dangerous and growing number of people are simply opting out of our system. Another dangerous and growing number are opting for special interest and single interest group politics, which threatens to take every last drop of blood out of our political system.

That synthesis would be the foundation of the "New Democrat" movement in politics that Bill Clinton would come to symbolize over the next ten years. But it was also a synthesis, to some extent, of his and Hillary's ideas. She had labored over preparation of the speech with him, and when she felt his message was becoming too contrarian, too critical of the well-worn path of traditional liberalism, and perhaps intended too much for Republicans tuning in to a Democratic convention in prime time, she moved it back toward basic principles.

But basic principles were of little help in undoing the damage Bill had caused himself, with help from Jimmy Carter and Frank White, in Arkansas. Shortly after Morris's arrival, he brought Hillary and Bill his latest poll, which showed Clinton with less than 50 percent of the likely vote. With Hillary's consent the Clinton campaign bought radio and television time for one last—negative—ad against White.

On election night, Hillary and Bill received the early returns at the governor's mansion, not campaign headquarters, a few blocks away. The first results showed him carrying Texarkana, to the encouragement of his supporters. But Bill told Hillary it was over. Nobody could read election returns better than he could. His immediate reaction was anger—at himself, the press, Carter, the Republicans, his staff. He was calm when he and Hillary arrived at campaign headquarters, but she was trembling, trying to appear composed.

He had lost 52 percent to 48 percent, and in Hillary's words, he "was devastated." He felt he wouldn't be able to make a proper concession speech and face supporters and reporters. Instead, he sent out Hillary, who thanked them all and invited them to the mansion the next morning for a gathering she later described as being like a wake.

Vince Foster and Webb Hubbell were among the first to arrive. "Bill's eyes were puffy and his voice was hoarse," Hubbell remembered. "Hillary had dark circles under her eyes. Both of them looked more fragile than I'd ever seen them." Hillary and Bill never made the same mistakes again. "From then on," Hubbell noted, "they ran their campaigns themselves, going on their gut instincts, and they never again failed to hit back fast when the situation demanded it."

That afternoon Hillary and Bill went to lunch with Jim and Diane Blair. An indelible image of Bill remained with Diane: "He was half-laughing, half-crying over the country song on the café jukebox, 'I Feel So Bad I Don't Know Whether to Kill Myself or Go Bowling.' "

BILL'S COLLAPSE after his loss was psychologically and emotionally absolute. He was utterly undone, wounded so critically that Hillary feared he might never recover. "He couldn't face people," said Deborah Sale. "It was unbelievably devastating. He just thought it was the end of his life."

Hillary recognized that she was the only person who could nurse him back to health. "She basically had to take care of him," said Sale. "She is very strong. She felt there had to be some way to shore him up. She felt that recovering politically was absolutely essential to his recovering emotionally. They had to have some sense of hope that there might be a political future for him because he really saw that as a way, as his path in life."

If she failed, the path she had chosen in life—with Bill, and their grand future as a couple destined to do great things—would be inaccessible. Whether he could regain his emotional and political strength was an open question. Hillary knew the only way to do it was to regain office in two years.

Her instincts for political survival dictated her first major decision toward that end—to call Morris again, only days after Bill's defeat. She wanted Morris to start putting together, with her, the pieces for another campaign.

Meanwhile she seethed at the press for allowing Frank White to make her name part of his campaign. "People said, Oh, you know, she didn't even change her name. This was a terrible thing. But, in fact, this was just an excuse," said Sale. "They really didn't like [Bill]. They didn't like the way he was conducting himself at the time." Hillary vented about Jimmy Carter, too—and she has never been one to let go of grudges. Twelve years later, as Bill Clinton ascended to the White House she decreed that members of Carter's inner circle could not serve in a Clinton presidency.

But in Little Rock in November 1980, Hillary was one of very few people who believed that Bill Clinton might still be able to reach the White House.

While she was firm, determined, and encouraging in dealing with Bill, it was difficult for her to keep her emotions under control. First, there were enormous practical considerations. Ann Henry could see how hard Hillary was struggling: "They now have to move out and find another place to live. They have a baby. Living in the governor's mansion you have a lot of things taken care of. Now it's all on you. So she's still going to work. They have this baby. Bill is depressed. No troopers, no maids, no cook, no nothing."

At Hillary's behest, less than ten days after the election, Bill phoned Betsey Wright in Washington and asked her to come to Little Rock to shut down his office and to put his records and files in order. He told Wright he needed "a trainer to get back on the track." She arrived to find the staff demoralized and worried about where they were going to find jobs, and Bill deeply depressed and shocked. "It was like going to somebody's house when somebody that you love dies, and you talk about the life that had been lived, and the things that were good, and where you screwed up. I felt like I went to a permanent wake but without the Irish jubilation."

Betsey moved into the guest cottage on the mansion grounds, and when other friends arrived, the mansion basement. She had brought only a suitcase. She left Little Rock eleven years later.

In effect she was forming a partnership with Hillary to put Bill's political career back together. Along with Joan Roberts, Bill's press secretary, they would come to be referred to by reporters clandestinely as "the Valkyries."

The files that Hillary and Betsey were so concerned about were not routine official records related to Bill's governorship, but rather the working papers of his life in politics: contacts, phone numbers, addresses, notes made to himself, old calendars, and, absolutely essential, the voluminous collection of note cards listing, in his hand, his campaign contributors and political contacts. Each card was a diary of Bill's interaction with an individual who figured in some way, no matter how small, in Bill's political development: each contribution, each meeting, each letter sent

and received. Computers were not yet common, but Betsey found a program that could catalogue the cards—perhaps ten thousand of them.

While Bill wallowed in self-pity, calling friends, asking constituents
how he had done them wrong, flagellating himself for bad decisions, and
seeking guidance from preachers, Hillary made plans for their move from
the mansion to a house in the same Hillcrest neighborhood they had left
only two years before. The new house was even smaller than the last.
They created a nursery for Chelsea—eleven months old when they
moved in January—in a converted attic. Hillary and Bill combed thrift
shops and secondhand stores for traditional furniture and a few near-
antiques of the sort she seemed to favor. When Virginia looked around
their new quarters, she asked why they liked such stuff, remarking that
she had spent her entire life trying to get away from old furniture and
houses. Then she gave them a Victorian "courting" couch that had been
sitting in her garage. The household they managed to cobble together
was a depressing display of their slide from life in the mansion. Dick Morris described the decor as a testament to Hillary's lack of domesticity. The
furniture, Victorian style in red velvet, looked like "the lobby of a hotel in
an old Western movie." Bill had picked out some of the pieces, heavy
German sideboards and chairs, and bric-a-brac that inclined toward the
garish and the curlicued. The kitchen had a college dorm feel, said Morris. "The glasses and plates looked like they came from a gas station or
supermarket—mismatched, in clashing sizes and designs."

Bill found a job of sorts at the law firm of Wright, Lindsey & Jennings, little more than a pit stop for Bill with a desk and telephone. Often
he was out and about trying to reestablish himself with voters. Politics,
he told a class of Diane Blair's at Fayetteville, was "the only track I
wanted to run on." "Political leaders," he said, "were usually a combination of darkness and light. The darkness of insecurity, depression, family
disorder. In great leaders, the light overcame the darkness."

Hillary had also ever so briefly considered a job offer—as president
of Hendrix College, which was affiliated with the United Methodist
Church—and then set about rebuilding her life and Bill's. She joined the
First United Methodist Church in Little Rock, became a member of its
board, and did pro bono legal work on its behalf. Her renewed emphasis
on spiritual life led her to give a series of talks around the state on why
she was a Methodist, including a visit to a Baptist church across the
Arkansas River in North Little Rock where her topic was "Women
armed with the Christian sword—to build an army for the Lord."

Friends from around the country came to see how she and Bill were
doing. There were good days and bad. The good ones tended to involve
Chelsea. The bad ones tended to involve screaming and tension and,

once again, Bill's penchant for other women. Friends surmised that Hillary believed Bill had lost the election in part because, as governor, he had let himself become distracted by the women who always seemed to be throwing themselves at him. "As I look back," said Rudy Moore, "it is more evident that Bill Clinton was not the same person psychologically in 1980 that he had been before. It must have been something personal, perhaps with his relationship with Hillary, but he was ambivalent and preoccupied. His reelection campaign reflected it." Later Gennifer Flowers, the nightclub chanteuse with whom Bill had an affair, said their relationship began in 1977 and that Arkansas newspaper reporters were making inquiries about it toward the end of his first term as governor.

To journalist Max Brantley, Bill seemed to be in a period of mourning—for his political career. "Bill obsessed on the subject. He was in a funk for months afterward, and he just couldn't leave it alone. You'd catch him in the grocery store, he was at loose ends, particularly right after he left office, and he'd go on obsessively about the factors that had caused it and what had gone wrong, and was just feeling sorry for himself." "He really felt like sackcloth and ashes, and that people should be flogging him with whips or something," Betsey Wright said.

To help ease their transition, Hillary had taken a brief leave from the Rose Law Firm. Now she returned to find a chilly reception. It was clear the partners had expected her to be a rainmaker, bringing in business from the contacts she and Bill had established over the years. "The apolitical firm I'd joined seven years earlier was no more," Webb Hubbell said. " 'You need to talk to Hillary, Webb,' was the mantra. The message to her boiled down to this: Either leave . . . or start billing to make up for the liability you create. They wanted Vince and me to talk her into leaving." Neither of them talked to Hillary about leaving.

More than ever, in fact, the Rose Law Firm—and Vince Foster—were a refuge. Colleagues began to notice subtle differences in her relationship with each of the Amigos.

Bill Clinton and Vince Foster were as different in most aspects of their character as Hillary could have imagined. But she and Vince were, in many regards, a natural fit. "Vince was just born middle-aged," an acquaintance had observed. Hillary could identify. As Bill once said, "I was born at sixteen and I'll always feel I am sixteen. And Hillary was born at age forty."

Vince had comparatively little interest in politics, exuded integrity, was meticulous in habit and dress, studied fine wines, was conversant in every nuance of politesse, and spoke ill of almost no one. In the firm, he was regarded as the soul of discretion, and it stood to reason that if ever Hillary would choose a confidant outside her marriage it would be someone of his mien and judgment. He and his wife, Lisa, gave frequent formal dinner parties in their home, at which the social elite of Little Rock felt comfortable.

Hillary found it easy to let her guard down with Vince. "I don't think there was anyone closer to Hillary for twenty years," said Hubbell. "But I don't think it was sexual. I think it was, Here are two people with like brilliance who enjoyed the same things, enjoyed each other's company and had extreme confidence in each other. I mean, you love a friend more than you love a lover." At office retreats, Hillary and Vince often remained together while the others went off to play golf or tennis. They would stroll, talk earnestly over a glass of wine, and laugh uproariously.

Those who knew them best doubted that they had had an affair. One friend wasn't sure: "He loved Hillary. I hoped they had an affair. I think they both deserved it. They both had complicated spouses, complicated marriages. I think all marriages go through periods where the partners aren't very close." Vince and Hillary "found comfort that was unique and special for them," said a friend of Foster's—who knew Hillary, Bill, and Vince well. As for the Three Amigos, "They did everything together, and Vince and Webb covered her back and handled her business."

But no matter how contentious her marriage, Hillary rarely, if ever, seemed to doubt how deeply she was in love with her husband, no matter how flagrant his provocations. In early March 1981, she and Bill were in Los Angeles because Nancy Bekavac persuaded Bill to be the speaker at her law firm's Monday partners lunch. During the question period, as he talked of his experience as governor of Arkansas, someone rushed in and shouted, "Reagan's been shot!" All hurried to an anteroom to watch the events on television. Bill looked grave, the color draining from his face. "I looked around," said Nancy, "and didn't see Hillary. She was back in the corner with her arms crossed, and a hand on each shoulder, cradling herself, all hunched over in the corner. And I went over and said, 'Hillary . . .' and she said, 'Bill gets death threats.' I said, 'What are you talking about?' She said, 'When he left the governorship one of the last things he did was to commute a bunch of death penalties to life sentences. And he's gotten death threats [from opponents, crime victims, and death penalty proponents] ever since.' " Nancy sat down next to her, put her arm around her, and realized that, for Hillary, this was not just about Ronald Reagan. "It was so immediate," Nancy said. "It was so physical."

BY OCTOBER 1981, Hillary, Betsey, and Dick Morris were ready to set the campaign express back on the tracks. Morris had been traveling to

Little Rock to meet with the Clintons and Betsey for a few days each month. He and Betsey could see that Hillary was battle-ready for this campaign, and would be far more involved than in the previous one. She would be the chief adviser and strategist. Working closely with Betsey and Dick, she would persuade Bill to adopt more pragmatic political positions. She seemed to grasp intuitively what needed to be done, and how Bill should do it. First, he would have to apologize to the people of Arkansas, an acknowledgment of what had gone wrong. Bill was hesitant. Hillary was insistent. As Morris remembered it, she said, "Bill, they didn't want to throw you out—they just wanted to make sure you knew how they felt. Put aside your damned pride and show them that you get it." Morris's polls confirmed her interpretation.

Morris proposed to Hillary, Bill, and Wright that they buy television time for an ad in which Clinton apologized for his mistakes, most notably the car tag increase. This led to an advertising campaign with the theme, "My Daddy Never Had to Whip Me Twice." Given another opportunity by Arkansas citizens, said Bill, he would pay them heed and not make the same mistakes again. The ads aired in early February, but Bill would not officially announce his candidacy until Chelsea's second birthday, February 27, 1982. At that press conference, Hillary gave Bill a framed picture of the three of them, with the engraving, "Chelsea's second birthday, Bill's second chance."

The 1982 campaign became the model for their political future, with Hillary assuming a far more direct, hands-on role in terms of policy, strategy, scheduling, and hiring staff for the campaign. She wasn't the campaign chairman in name, but she was the campaign director in fact. After 1982, she and Bill were always in effect their own campaign chairmen. "She was out in front, on the campaign trail, and in charge. She had an opinion on everything. I mean everything. Issues. People. Where Bill was going to speak. I mean everything," said Woody Bassett, who had been their law student and worked in every campaign. "Hillary was never bashful about telling you when she thought you made a mistake, or when she thought you could have done something better, or if she didn't think enough people were at an event. Bill Clinton would never tell you that, though he might think it. He was the good guy. Hillary was the one that laid the law down and she was the one that made it known if they weren't happy about something." Successful campaigns usually have a backbone of discipline and Hillary was the one to provide it.

THEN HILLARY RODHAM became Hillary Clinton, as she had vowed never to do. Changing her name, which seemed to signal to voters that she was changing her attitude, was as essential to Bill Clinton's future as apologizing for the car tag fiasco. Or, as Jim Blair said about the name change, Hillary "would sacrifice some of her principles to keep political expediency." Hillary talked to Hubbell about why she now thought changing her name was important. "We had a long conversation that day, and I understood a lot more about her afterward," he said. "There was the notion of retaining her own identity, which she had submerged in coming to Arkansas, and the conflict of interest sensitivity she felt as a lawyer. And there was something closer to the bone. It hurt her that people would think she didn't love her husband. It hurt her when people asked what Chelsea's last name would be. It hurt her that people in Arkansas didn't try to understand her as much as they wanted her to understand them. But the name had become an issue, and she was prepared to change it to help her husband."

On the day Bill announced his candidacy, Hillary wore a conservative suit, permed her hair, and said: "I don't have to change my name. I've been Mrs. Bill Clinton. I kept the professional name Hillary Rodham in my law practice, but now I'm going to be taking a leave of absence from the law firm to campaign full-time for Bill and I'll be Mrs. Bill Clinton. I suspect people will be getting tired of hearing from Mrs. Bill Clinton." But the personal sacrifice was real. "I teared up. I had a lump in my throat," said Betsey Wright, who knew how hard the decision had been. Hillary had worked her way into it on her own. Bill had never asked her to do it, as she confirmed in a 1994 interview. He had initially resisted the change. "She understood that it was part of a picture that we had painted for the voters that had made them feel alienated from us," he said. "And she said to me—I will never forget . . . I respected her so much for this, because she came in to see me, and she said, 'We've got to talk about this name deal.' She said, 'I couldn't bear it—if we're going to do this, let's try to win. I couldn't bear it if this cost you the election. It's just not that big a deal to me anymore.' "

The fact that her physical appearance was a campaign consideration also hurt her personally. Though she had resisted her parents' frugality as a child, she had come to respect and even appreciate their rather inconstant ascetic ethic. Her mother, who did not need a Cadillac or fancy clothes, had taught her not to concern herself with frivolousness. Hillary said with great earnestness she had been raised to look for "the inner qualities of people," rather than what they wore.

She was, in Dick Morris's words, "really taking his career in hand. In meetings typically I would urge a fairly aggressive strategy. Clinton would demur and then Hillary would say, Bill, you've got to do this. This is what you've got to do. And she was always very much the person who would ram home the need to run negative ads, to be aggressive. For the most part, Hillary, Betsey, and I always saw eye-to-eye, and it was Bill who was sort of the odd man out as kind of the naive do-gooder who would come along eventually. She became his campaign manager, and sometimes the candidate was strong, and sometimes he was weak, but she was the manager. And her mental attitude at that point was, This guy is too nice to manage his own life. He doesn't understand how venal people can be. He's not tough enough. I've got to move in and take this over."

That characterization, of course, ignored a crucial part of the equation: Bill Clinton was perhaps already the best political campaigner in America. No politician better synthesized ideas or knew how to work a crowd, or how to think fast on his feet, or how to analyze the political landscape ahead. Hillary knew how to harness that.

She also became a campaigner. She showed up at a parade where the incumbent Frank White spoke and when he attacked Bill, "she jumped all over me, said I wasn't being truthful about her husband and his record," White recalled. "This was a new thing in Arkansas politics. She comes in and lays waste to the opponents and you know it's kind of difficult to get up there and let a woman have it." When White refused to debate Bill she taunted him in absentia: "Frank White would probably try to avoid being in the same room as Chelsea. Chelsea could debate him and win." The press took note of her transformation. "Mrs. Clinton is almost certainly the best speaker among politicians' wives," reported the *Arkansas Gazette*. "She is an Illinois native, perhaps a little brisker, a little more outspoken than the traditional Southern Governors' lady. . . . The name change indicates she's working at softening her image a bit . . . and succeeding apparently. She has become a good hand-shaking campaigner in the traditional Arkansas style . . . her spirit shows when she speaks on her husband's behalf."

She was also motivated: if Bill lost this election, his political career—theirs—was finished.

Bill, and Hillary, won reelection, 55 percent to 45 percent. No other governor of Arkansas had ever lost and come back to be reelected.

It is inconceivable that Bill Clinton would have become governor in January 1983 without his wife's having taken charge. Now in office, at her urging he decided that education would be the single issue to define his administration, and that he would put the person he most trusted, his wife, in charge of reforming the state's education system. Before taking the oath of office, however, he had learned that his task would be especially difficult—he was inheriting a $30 million budget shortfall from his predecessor.

The same pattern would repeat itself a decade later. Hillary would be the key to managing his presidential campaign, he would inherit a potentially ruinous budget shortfall, and he would put Hillary in charge of the signature issue of his presidency, health care. The future of his presidency, like his governorship, and perhaps the prospects for his reelection, would depend on her performance.

Bill far surpassed Hillary, or arguably almost everybody else in politics, both in seeing the long-term danger ahead for his state or his country from antiquated thinking and outdated policy, and developing nuanced ideas and substantial plans for dealing with the peril. By the time his family had moved their clothes back into the governor's mansion, he had a sense that the state was facing imminent disaster, just as he perceived in January 1993, when he assumed office knowing George H. W. Bush's people had fiddled with the budget numbers to obscure a huge deficit.

He recognized that his state was not prepared to enter the modern economic age, in which success and competition would no longer be measured in the old manufacturing, mining, and agricultural sectors, but by education-dependent fields such as information services, engineering, and technology. As much as any of the other states, Arkansas was living in the economic dark ages, kept dim by an outdated education system that had left its children far behind the rest of the country in opportunity and achievement.

Clinton had plenty of ideas about how to deal with these problems. He'd read everything he could get his hands on about political economy. Distinguished work in the field had been conducted by friends and classmates, including Bob Reich, now teaching at Harvard. But he'd also learned, from his experience with car tag taxes and Jimmy Carter's transshipment of human cargo, that it didn't matter how good the ideas were if somebody like Frank White could come along and tar your hide with negative ads. To be successful at governing—which was different from being successful at running and winning election—you had to find a way to preempt the critics. Hillary and Dick Morris believed that you had to make somebody else the villain before you got fatally tarred yourself.

This strategy of villainizing became a dominant leitmotif of Clintonian governance, a strategy meant to allow Bill's big ideas and grand goals—and Hillary's tempered idealism and experience—to flourish. The villains were real most of the time, though their views did not always represent a simple black or white choice vis-à-vis the Clintons'. Not all teachers and health insurance executives were bad—but they were all made to seem like part of systemic problems and failures, in which the state legislature or the U.S. Congress were complicit as well. Hillary had learned something about this with her rural health care initiative in Bill's first term, and it didn't hurt to have the local medical association taking her to court.

The Clintons' villains of choice in 1983 were the utility companies, which Bill had campaigned against in the election with considerable success. But too many legal technicalities and constraints could get in the way of successfully villainizing them from the governor's office, though there was no question that the companies were usurious and that their influence needed to be curtailed. So dealing with the utilities would have to be a secondary priority.

The Arkansas State Teachers Association would become the leading villain instead for the rest of Hillary and Bill's hold on the governor's mansion. This was in spite of the fact that there was no difference of opinion between the ASTA and the Clintons about the need for a massive infusion of funds from the legislature to give Arkansas kids an equal chance to compete with kids in other states, even next door in Mississippi. The ASTA was not exactly the antichrist, and in fact had done some pretty good things in a state where the legislature had typically accorded more attention to protecting the rights of poultry farmers to saturate half of Arkansas's topsoil with chicken feces than providing its children with a decent education. The little money that teachers earned (Arkansas teachers were the poorest paid in the nation), what little serious attention in the state was paid to the condition of schools and classrooms, was often at the behest of the teachers association.

But Arkansas's moribund education system represented an enormous opportunity for its governor. The system was about to get picked apart by the Arkansas Supreme Court for good reason: a lower court had ruled that the state's system of funding public education was unconstitutional because it discriminated against students in poor school districts. During Clinton's upcoming term, it was virtually certain that the Supreme Court would uphold the lower court, and toss the matter back at the governor and the legislature to solve. Better that Clinton get in front of the issue and use the case to his advantage.

While he was reading Reich and others on political economy, Bill was also engaged in a nonstop strategic dialogue with Hillary and Dick Morris about how to attain lofty goals through the messy process of ground-and-gut-level politics. The education problem had to be solved on a practical, political level, combined with the best ideas for helping the students and the state—a synthesis of means and ends. The education agenda occupied the three of them during the transition between Bill's election and inauguration, just as the health care agenda would occupy much of the transition period from election day 1992 to the start of the Clinton presidency.

The most facile solution would be to raise taxes—the riskiest thing a governor (or a president) could do, as he had learned with the relatively simple matter of car tags. Another solution—combining some school districts and eliminating others, taking from the rich school districts and giving to the poor ones—was an invitation to racial and class warfare, and to ugly reminders of Orval Faubus; it also wouldn't get to the basic problem, the state's failure to spend sufficient money on education.

The most perceptive of Clinton's biographers, David Maraniss, would write about a strategy, managed largely by Hillary and Morris, to do whatever it took to get elected and use the same philosophy to govern. He called it the Permanent Campaign. The concept was derived from Morris, who had observed that Clinton, after learning his hard lesson on the high road in 1974 and being defeated for Congress, had become compliant enough to do almost anything not to get beat in an election. But once in office, he had continued to ignore a dangerous consequence of governance. "When you lead in an idealistic direction, the most important thing to do is to be highly pragmatic about it. And when necessity forces upon you a problem of great pragmatism, you need to use the idealism to find your way out of the thicket," wrote Maraniss. Maraniss defined this as a basic tenet of the Permanent Campaign—interweaving ends and means, pragmatism and idealism, lofty goals and getting there. The supporting elements were a determination to use paid media in the form of TV and radio commercials and mailings to reach voters, rather than expect print and broadcast journalists, "free media," to deliver a political message, and constant polling to see what voters were responding to at a given moment, what they would accept and what they would reject. It was a system that played to Hillary's strengths as a strategist, disciplinarian, and motivational force, and offset Clinton's sometimes lackadaisical optimism.

So at Hillary's urging, and trusting his own instincts and Morris's polling as a litmus test, education was made the signature issue of his administration. Hillary would coordinate a great effort at reform, and, instead of focusing public attention on its financing by tax increases, she and Bill would promote it as an idealistic cause that Arkansans should be proud to support. They would also make sure that those who got in the way of the crusade were identified and stigmatized.

Ten years later, they would do almost the same thing with health care. In both instances, there were solid reasons for choosing the crusade they did. The results were not the same.

In May 1983, the Arkansas Supreme Court ruled that the state's system of funding public education was inequitable and therefore unconstitutional. Hillary took another leave of absence from the Rose Law Firm and, as had been planned months earlier, became chairwoman of the governor's Education Standards Committee.

"We [Hillary and Bill] were sitting around talking about it," Bill told a reporter, "and I said, 'This could be the most important thing we'll ever do. Who should I name the chairman of the Standards Committee? The chairman is the key.' Either the first or second day we talked about this—we talk about a lot of things like this—she said, 'I think I'd like to be it. Maybe I'll do it.' " When he reminded her that she'd just taken eight months off from her law practice to help him get reelected, she responded, "Yeah, but this may be the most important thing you ever do, and you have to do it right." Hillary's memory was different: she wrote in *Living History* that it was his idea and that he was insistent about it when she protested.

That Hillary was a woman didn't hurt either. Most schoolteachers, most educators, were women; helping in this traditionally feminine area of endeavor was acceptable to the same Arkansans who had been upset about Hillary's keeping her maiden name.

In announcing to his staff and the state's citizens that he was naming Hillary to head his task force on education reform, Bill said, "This guarantees that I will have a person who is closer to me than anyone else overseeing a project that is more important to me than anything else"— words almost identical to those he would use in announcing that Hillary would become head of his health care task force in 1993.

That summer and fall in Arkansas, the Education Standards Committee took public testimony across the state, held seventy-five meetings, and formulated a program of reforms, which had been largely predetermined by Hillary and experts with whom she was working. The reforms were overdue and addressed debilitating shortcomings in a public education system that had been built on inequality: 200 high schools in poor areas that taught no foreign languages or music, no physics curriculum at 150, no math beyond algebra at 135. Because of such conditions, the percentage of Arkansas students who failed standardized achievement tests was the highest of any state in the nation. Arkansas ranked last in the percentage of high school students who went on to college.

Hillary's preparation for her assignment (as in Washington with health care) was exhaustive, her expertise made almost as sharp as that of professionals with years of experience. She researched the curriculum of every Arkansas school district and traveled the state to attend public hearings. Hillary said she kept hearing stories about grossly incompetent teachers who could hardly read or spell.

Ultimately Hillary would prevail in the political battle for education reform. It would be her greatest achievement in public life until she was elected to the U.S. Senate, though the substantive results fell short of the grand expectations of her plans. And the methodology she employed to win the battle, and the lessons she and Bill took away from the experience, would haunt the Clinton presidency and doom health care reform from the start.

In addition to teacher-testing, the plan that Hillary and her task force eventually formulated required that all local school districts adopt uniform, state-imposed standards for curriculum and classroom size—devised by educational experts who were consultants to her commission. Any basic philosophical disagreements about those standards had been resolved before she traveled the state holding public hearings to solicit ideas. In June 1983, Hillary spoke at the statehouse before a joint House-Senate legislative committee and outlined her recommendations, including compulsory testing of students before they could matriculate to the next grade, a 20-to-1 student-teacher ratio, adding more math and science courses, and mandatory all-day kindergarten. At the end of the ninety-minute presentation, Representative Lloyd George remarked, "Well, fellas, it looks like we might have elected the wrong Clinton!" (After her first trip to Capitol Hill to sell the Congress her ideas on health care, she received almost exactly the same encomium.)

The Arkansas Department of Education estimated that $200 million would be needed to execute the plan adopted by Hillary's task force; it would require 3,781 more teachers, administrators, nurses, counselors, and librarians, and two thousand new classrooms. The initiative would be financed by increasing the state sales tax for the first time in twenty-six years.

Morris did the polling: 50 percent of voters would support the tax increase as a means to fund education; but if teacher-testing were a requirement in the reform package, which Hillary was secretly considering, the number went up to 85 percent.

Early in their discussions of an education agenda, Hillary enthusiastically embraced the idea of competence tests for teachers, as did Bill. But she decided not to make her opinion public, even to members of her own task force. When Hillary announced the plan to the state legislature that fall, she called teacher-testing "the real heart" of the reform package.

It was clear that the state's teachers would therefore oppose it. The National Education Association, the most powerful lobby and union in the field of education, had long held that competence tests were an affront to the profession. The Arkansas Education Association was one of its affiliates.

"She made it very clear that there had to be a bad guy in this," said Richard Herget, Bill's campaign chairman. "Anytime you're going to turn an institution upside down, there's going to be a good guy and a bad guy. The Clintons painted themselves as the good guys. The bad guys were the schoolteachers." The day before Hillary's plan was announced publicly, Bill told the head of the Arkansas Education Association that teacher-testing would be part of the reform package. The official was, predictably, furious.

Exactly how Hillary decided that teacher-testing might be the smoothest road to education reform is unclear. Former governor White, among others, eventually took credit, and indeed Republicans had long advocated competence-testing for teacher certification; Democrats, especially liberal Democrats, were generally opposed to the idea. More than expediency was certainly involved. Hillary's basic statements about education sometimes sounded as if they could have been written by Dorothy or Hugh Rodham, and had taken firm hold long before her assignment. She was sure that testing teachers' competence and holding them to minimum standards would help the schools educate. Frequently Hillary and Bill would talk about one teacher who, reading from a textbook, reportedly referred to World War II as "World War Eleven." But Hillary also knew her words would appeal to Republicans and conservative Democrats: "The first purpose of school is to educate, not to provide entertainment or opportunities to socialize. Discipline holds no mystery. When it is firm, clearly understood, fairly administered and perceived to be so, it works. When it isn't, it doesn't."

Bill, in presenting his budget plan to a special session of the legislature, called mandatory teacher tests "a small price to pay for the biggest tax increase for education in the history of the state and to restore the teaching profession to the position of public esteem that I think it deserves." The teachers called it an outrage, racist. They accused the Clintons of calling the entire teaching profession incompetent. Civil rights organizations condemned the testing provision.

It genuinely pained Hillary and Bill that they were accused of appealing to racist sensibilities, just as they would be attacked for "playing the race card" to achieve welfare reform a decade and a half later. But it was also true that if a specific group of individuals were to suffer disproportionately in the process of reform it would be black teachers (and later black welfare recipients).

The union pursued its case in court—Hillary's task force and the state were the defendants—for eight years. Most of the teachers' wrath was trained on Hillary. Diane Blair remembered "walking through a crowd with her at a school, and you could hear teachers hissing at her. She just shook her head and said, 'I get this all over the state. It's heartbreaking. It's hard. But someday they'll understand.' " In fact, Hillary didn't seem to mind too much. At times she wore the teachers' enmity as a badge of honor, and for almost a decade used the example of their villainy as a basic component of the Permanent Campaign in Arkansas. When it came time for health care, there would be another villain—the medical establishment—but it was richer and better organized than the teachers, who did not prevail.

Her substantive legacy in Arkansas was real, though the teachers association tried through two elections to defeat Bill Clinton at the polls and to repeal the teacher tests. As Dick Morris had predicted, the more the teachers heaped scorn on the Clintons, the more popular they became.

Education reform became the model on which Hillary Clinton would one day build her teetering health care initiative. In Arkansas, though, her achievement was less about the specifics of what worked and what didn't than the fact that she and Bill were able to focus the state for the first time on its educational needs. Their approach was almost holistic. Its aim was to convince Arkansans that, in their desire for better education and willingness to accept controversial action to get it, the state's children were already better off than any statistics could measure. They deserved better than they had been offered in the past. What they had lacked was opportunity. Now Hillary had provided it.

In Arkansas, a generation later, citizens and teachers would still be debating the extent to which Hillary's reforms worked. The record would appear mostly positive: the percentage of high school graduates who went on to college increased within four years from 38 percent to 50 percent; all of the state's school districts complied with the dicta of her commission to reduce class size and offer standard course offerings. In every school district, pupils could take classes in foreign languages, advanced math, and science. However, the Winthrop Rockefeller Foundation (named after one of Bill's predecessors as governor of Arkansas) found in a survey of parents, teachers, and administrators that "thus far, the Arkansas school reform effort has bypassed teachers. From their perspective, it has had a heavy, top-down regulatory quality. The result is a serious, large demoralization of the teaching force. They feel constrained by what they perceive to be a stranglehold of mandates, needless paperwork and limited encouragement."

SINCE BILL AND HILLARY'S triumph in initiating and funding serious educational reform in Arkansas, Bill was leading a charmed and, on the issues, extremely intelligent political life. Hillary's choice of education as their signature achievement was brilliant politics that had bought him time to think, govern, and put his stamp on Arkansas, and push his ideas onto the national stage. It had also made him virtually unbeatable for reelection, as long as he averted self-inflicted disaster. The educational standards that Hillary had championed were not scheduled to take full effect until 1987, making effective criticism of them virtually impossible until the next decade. The whole education financing package, tied as it was to teacher-testing, was an issue that won Bill Republican and independent votes and gave him a sturdy platform he could run on in 1984 and, by virtue of a change in the Arkansas constitution, for a four-year term in 1986. And it guided his move to the center, away from the shibboleths of traditional Democratic liberalism, giving an intellectual and political framework to his ideas for welfare reform, neighborhood-business tax relief, and other concepts fashioned in the New Democrat mold of his and Hillary's education experiment in Arkansas.

Meanwhile, his politics and profile were getting national attention in the Reagan years. They were seen as a means to energize a moribund Democratic Party. He wanted to run for president in 1988, though Hillary expressed doubts that the Reagan Revolution had run its course. She thought Vice President George Bush would be hard to beat. And if Senator Dale Bumpers of Arkansas decided to seek the Democratic nomination—a very real possibility, and they both believed he could run a good race—it was obviously out of the question that Bill would oppose him.

IN 1982, Hillary had installed Betsey Wright as Bill's chief of staff, with an office just outside his own, an announcement of Hillary's determination that her husband would never again drift on the job with unchecked ease—whether toward women or ennui, as she believed he had in his first term as governor. Bill easily accessed all the indexed political information Betsey had computerized as he began making exploratory calls in late 1986 and early 1987, the same kind of calls he'd made when getting ready to run again for governor. Some were to raise seed money, some to seek opinions from his old friends and political colleagues as to whether he could win, assuming Bumpers didn't run. When Bumpers announced in late March that he wouldn't be a candidate, Betsey, a first-rate political operator of great repute at every level of Democratic Party politics, dispatched scouts to New Hampshire and Iowa to report back on how quickly campaign organizations could be established in the two early primary and caucus states and who might be available to run Bill's campaign there if he declared for president.

In April, Bill went to New Hampshire for a speech to the state Democratic Party and to do the ritual "testing of the waters." He had returned to Little Rock enthused, and Betsey then sent teams out to the Southern states that were going to cast ballots in the Super Tuesday primaries. She had already arranged to take a leave of absence to work on an exploratory Clinton presidential campaign, and a substitute chief of staff had moved into the governor's office. Much later, Hillary and Bill both said—not convincingly—that she had preferred he stay out. She persuaded Bill to set a deadline for his decision and said she was prepared to enthusiastically support whatever course he chose. He picked July 15 and reserved the ballroom of the Excelsior Hotel to make his announcement, "whatever it might be," as Hillary put it. Betsey was certain Hillary wanted him to make the race. Dorothy and Hugh Rodham had bought a condominium in Little Rock and were expecting to move to the mansion to be with Chelsea while her parents were campaigning.

Hillary also called on Geoff Shields, her old boyfriend from the Wellesley years, who had become a Chicago lawyer and power in the Democratic Party there, and Bernie Nussbaum, whom she went to see in New York. "Don't commit [to a candidate] until we talk," she'd said over the phone to Nussbaum in the late spring, and they arranged soon afterward to meet for dinner in midtown Manhattan. Fourteen years had passed since they'd last had a serious face-to-face talk, though he'd occasionally steered some legal work her way at the Rose Law Firm. They spent the better part of three hours catching up. Nussbaum, who had gone on to become a powerhouse New York lawyer and important figure in the state Democratic Party, found Hillary more accessible emotionally and more fun than when they'd worked together in Washington.

Hillary talked at length about Chelsea and how the birth of their daughter had changed the focus of her life. She seemed softer, less querulous. Only as they were finishing dinner did Hillary raise the subject of the upcoming presidential campaign. Remembering their difficult conversation fourteen summers earlier, Nussbaum said, "Hillary, I know you told me he'd be president, and I acted badly. But isn't this a little early?" Bill Clinton was now forty years old.

Meanwhile, she continued making similar calls, in person and by phone, to a formidable network of old Rodham and Clinton associates and friends who could be assets in a presidential campaign.

ON MAY 7, 1987, Senator Gary Hart of Colorado, who had recruited Bill to work in Texas during the 1972 McGovern campaign, grudgingly withdrew his candidacy for the Democratic presidential nomination after details of his extramarital sex life became a media sensation. Bill was both the immediate beneficiary of Hart's withdrawal, and, understandably, its victim as well. As Webb Hubbell noted, "The rumors about Bill had been rampant for years—he was a man with an appetite, people said. He couldn't pass up a pretty face."

When reporters in Washington had asked Hart about rumors that he was seeing women other than his wife, he had denied it, and invited the press to follow him if they had any doubts. Predictably, they took up the challenge, and within days the *Miami Herald* had published a story about Hart spending a night on a sailboat with a young woman, Donna Rice, followed by pictures in a supermarket tabloid of Hart and Rice on the boat, named *Monkey Business.*

The coverage by the mainstream press of Hart's extramarital life was a departure from journalistic tradition, which had allowed presidents and leading politicians considerable running room in keeping their affairs private, out of the papers and off the air. In Arkansas, no stories had appeared in print about the Clintons' marital problems, despite the familiarity of every statehouse reporter with the rumors and some of the reality. However, a new standard was taking hold based on the Hart experience. If a politician's sex life, particularly indiscriminate sex, could be seen to cast doubt on matters of judgment and stability, it might well be considered legitimate news. In the *Washington Post*, David Broder, *eminencia* of the capital's political reporters and columnists, offered his blessing of the *Herald*'s decision to run the Hart story: "What was at issue was Hart's truthfulness, his self-discipline, his sense of responsibility to other people— indeed his willingness to face hard choices and realities. . . . The fundamental character questions raised by Hart's actions in this incident remain unchanged, and if they are not vital in judging a potential President, I don't know what would be." Broder was as well aware as any journalist in America of Bill Clinton's awesome political potential and talents and the rumors that hounded him. His words in the *Post* that day could not have brought comfort to Bill, who read the newspapers, or Hillary, who didn't.

Hart's withdrawal had put more pressure on Bill to run, and to quickly wrap up the support of many of Hart's backers. Among the Democrats seriously under consideration, Hart and Clinton most inhabited similar ideological territory. In Washington, a foreign policy briefing for Bill was convened by friends from Yale and from Hart's campaign staff. More significant, the nature of some of Bill's inquiries to friends and associates began changing. He sought Dick Morris's advice about how to confront the "infidelity issue," expressing "a tremendous terror of the race . . . which led him to a feeling that this was a terribly inhospitable environment upon which to tread," according to Morris.

To some friends, he asked whether an expression of "causing pain in my marriage" would be sufficient to keep the press at bay. At a school softball game in which Chelsea was playing, he approached Max Brantley, whose wife, Ellen, Hillary's classmate at Wellesley, had been on Bill's staff in the attorney general's office. "He was using Hart's withdrawal as a sounding board, asking, You know, do you ever outlive your past mistakes? Are they ever forgotten? Are they ever forgiven? Or do you carry them all your life? And is there a point beyond which a politician can expect to be left alone? Is there a time period when you can say, No, that's in my past? Or are you not forgiven for it? Everybody makes mistakes, and it's not right that they should have to pay for them forever and ever and ever. It was pretty clear what this discussion was all about."

Betsey Wright could see the uncharacteristic doubt and fear gnawing at him. In the post-Hart atmosphere, the rumors about Hillary and Bill's marriage, and Bill's sexual activities, were becoming thunderous, especially when it was learned that he had booked the Excelsior for an announcement.

For five years, Betsey had watched and listened as Bill made arrangements for assignations and slipped out of the office for meetings with various women. Sometimes the troopers gave her sly heads-ups. She had no doubt that a few of them were soliciting women for him.

Wright also recognized that "Hillary had long ago made some peace with his womanizing and the trade-offs. And that what she wanted out of the relationship was worth putting up with some of that. . . . She was as aware as I was that those women were not people that he wanted any deep relationship with. They weren't the kind of women that he shared a passion with intellectually or for politics or certainly not for Chelsea, who was a huge bond with them."

But Gary Hart's defrocking had terrified Wright. On several occasions, she tried to tell Bill how vulnerable she thought he was, but he kept evading the issue. The question raised by Hart's withdrawal, he said, should not be about a candidate's sexual life but whether he could be a good president. Betsey doubted that Hillary would have been as tolerant as Lee Hart, Gary's wife, had been. And Bill could be finished politically by a similar humiliation. There had been "huge schisms" in the Clinton marriage since Wright had arrived in Little Rock to help rescue Bill at his lowest ebb, "when Hillary did really drastic things" (which Betsey has never spelled out). But Betsey thought no situation between Hillary and Bill was as fraught—and dangerous to Chelsea—as the one they would face if Bill now sought the presidency.

Two days before his scheduled announcement at the Excelsior, Betsey asked to see Bill privately in the mansion. She arrived with another person, whose name she has never disclosed. "I just thought he had to confront the issue," she said later. She did not want Bill to be able to deny that the conversation had taken place—as he had done after previous confrontations with her about women, including Gennifer Flowers. Contrary to later media accounts, Betsey did not bring to the mansion a "list" of women she knew Bill had been with, though investigators would later try to subpoena such a document from her. Rather, there was a serious conversation about the implications of Hart's withdrawal in which she insisted that Bill recount for her and the other person present "all of the women he had been with, when and how often." She explained much later, "This was a conversation. Specifically what I said was, 'Let's walk through all of the women who might decide that they had a bone to pick with you who might emerge in the middle of the campaign.' And of course I was horrified because I thought I knew everybody. And he came up with these people I didn't know about." When they had reviewed the names a second time to evaluate which women were most likely to seek out the press, or be tracked down by reporters, she told him it would be disastrous to declare his candidacy, devastating to Chelsea and his marriage.

Friends from around the country were already flying into Little Rock for the declaration they expected Bill to make; many had been waiting since college for such a moment. After his meeting with Betsey, he took several of them aside and, with each, shared his growing sense of doubt. A few of them said later they had been quite dramatic in describing their own concerns about how a presidential race would affect Chelsea. Mickey Kantor, a California lawyer who served on the Legal Services board with Hillary, said that Chelsea had approached Bill and himself while they were talking and asked her father about a family vacation planned for the summer. When Bill said he might be running for president and not able to go, Kantor said Chelsea responded, "Then Mom and I will go without you." Carl Wagner, who went back fifteen years with Bill and Hillary, to the McGovern campaign, and was staying at the mansion, said that as the Clintons were about to walk upstairs to their bedroom, he told Bill: "When you reach the top of the steps, walk into your daughter's bedroom, look at her, and understand that if you do this, your relationship will never be the same. I'm not sure if it will be worse or better, but it will never be the same."

Hillary wrote many years afterward that Bill was still undecided the day before his announcement. The next day, at the Excelsior, with Hillary next to him and wiping tears away, Bill announced he would not be a candidate in the 1988 presidential election.

"If people had told me five years ago that I would ever have a serious chance to run for president and not take it, I would have told them they were crazy," he said. "I hope I will have another opportunity to seek the presidency when I can do it and be faithful to my family, my state, and my sense of what is right." Later in the afternoon, his office issued a statement in his name:

> I need some family time: I need some personal time. Politicians are people too. I think sometimes we forget it, but they really are. The only thing I or any other candidate has to offer in running for President is what's inside. That's what sets people on fire and gets their confidence and their votes, whether they live in Wisconsin or Montana or New York. That part of my life needs renewal. The other, even more important reason for my decision is the certain impact that this campaign would have had on our daughter. The only way I could have won, getting in this late, after others had been working up to two years, would be to go on the road full time from now until the end, and to have Hillary do the same thing. . . . I've seen a lot of kids grow up under these pressures and a long, long time ago I made a promise to myself that if I was ever lucky enough to have a child, she would never grow up wondering who her father was.

Hillary seemed relieved on one level and angry on another. There was no way of knowing when there would be another clear opportunity to gain the White House. Whatever her indignation at the new journalistic environment, she knew that Bill's own irresponsibility was the reason for his decision, and an abdication of more than just his marriage vows. The good news was that Bill would have four more years to build his national base of support, and he would still be only forty-five years old, or forty-nine if the Democrats won in 1988. Meanwhile, they could work on their relationship.

BILL WOULD LATER say of the decision, "Finally I felt as though the weight of the world had been lifted from my shoulders. I was free to be a father, husband, and governor, and to work and speak on national issues unencumbered by immediate ambitions."

Most of his closest friends and associates, however, believed he immediately went into another deep depression of the sort he'd suffered after losing the governorship in 1980. Whatever the case, it is certain that over the next three years the Clinton marriage teetered, as his actions became increasingly compulsive, even bizarre, and deeply hurtful to Hillary.

While he was considering running for president in 1987, Bill had been operating at full throttle, doing what he always did best—campaigning, planning, formulating ideas, creating contacts, working the phones. But when he decided not to run, Betsey Wright noted, "there was an adrenaline cutoff immediately, and the funk after that. I mean, he just thought his life was over. There was nothing else for him to do. And he was nutty . . . reckless. I couldn't get his attention in the office of the governor. He was tired and burned out on being governor. There wasn't anything to capture his interest in the job. He really got careless with fooling around."

Still, the affairs of state in Arkansas continued to get attended to in a somewhat decent fashion, good works were performed by the first lady and her husband, important speeches were made about globalization and the interdependence of economies, preschool programs based on an Israeli model that Hillary had learned about were instituted, and at her instigation a successful development bank modeled on one in Bangladesh was established for poor families in Little Rock. But, as so often happened with the Clintons, their relationship began to affect the rotation of the wobbly wheels of state.

There was another brief rush of adrenaline preceding the Democratic presidential convention in July, in Atlanta. Bill was scheduled to give the nominating speech for Governor Michael Dukakis of Massachusetts, who had emerged from the group of candidates condescendingly called the "Seven Dwarfs" by some reporters after Clinton and Hart had withdrawn from consideration. In fact, it was a reasonably strong Democratic field, including Senator Al Gore and Dukakis, who remained ahead of Bush in the polls coming out of the Democratic convention.

From the time the Clintons arrived at the convention arena, things began to go wrong. First, the house lights weren't kept dimmed, a customary technique ensuring that delegates would calm down to listen to the nominating speeches. Meanwhile, Bill was cued to begin delivery of his address while demonstrations were continuing on the floor. Betsey ran to find Anne Wexler, who was directing the program, to turn down the house lights to no avail. Dukakis floor whips continued to lead parts of the crowd in chants after Bill's speech was well under way.

Bill then droned on for thirty-two minutes in prime time while the delegates in the hall, even the network TV anchors, grew increasingly restive. Tom Shales, writing in the next day's *Washington Post*, would call it the night of "The Numb and the Restless." When Bill finally said, "In closing," the hall erupted enthusiastically in rowdy relief. The late-night TV comics would have a ball with their monologues the next night. Not for one minute had Clinton commanded the audience's attention.

Hillary, pinned in her seat as television cameras and news photographers documented her misery, was already thinking about how to publicly accuse the Dukakis people, and explain how what had happened was their fault, according to the Little Rock aides she spoke with afterward. The fury at the Dukakis people was more than justified. The speech had gone through nine drafts—she had never seen Bill work so hard on a text—because the nominee and his aides kept adding suggestions. Still, it timed out at sixteen minutes, four less than the allotted twenty, which should have been just enough to accommodate the pauses for applause and demonstrations of enthusiasm on the floor. On their way to the convention hall, Hillary, Bill, and Betsey had stopped in the nominee's suite to give Dukakis one last look at the text, partly because of Bill's concern that the speech was too long and, in Betsey's words, "overburdened" with ideas and a tone not his own. "Great speech," Dukakis had said. "That's what I want. Give it."

Leaving the hall, Hillary had wanted to go back to the hotel with Bill, who was only beginning to sense how terribly things had gone wrong, though he knew it was bad. "She was going to take care of Bill, and she felt that they just needed to get out of there," recalled Betsey. But Betsey, who knew many of Bill's rhythms as well or better than Hillary, felt "he had to talk it out." He proceeded that night to "talk to anybody he knew that he ran into. And we did that until about two o'clock in the morning. And Hillary stayed with us, but we weren't hanging on to Bill. He was moving around the restaurants and bars," trying on the one hand to get a read on how bad it was, and, on the other, looking for reassurance that it wasn't as bad as he thought.

IN THE IMMEDIATE AFTERMATH of the 1988 Democratic convention, Harry Thomason, a television producer friend of the Clintons whose brother as a boy had sung next to Bill in the church choir in Hot Springs, called from Hollywood with the suggestion that Bill go on the Johnny Carson *Tonight Show* and make fun of the speech he delivered to the convention. Bill agreed, and Thomason arranged it. And Bill's self-deprecating interaction with Carson, who told the audience not to worry, "because we've got plenty of coffee and cots in the lobby," and then placed an hourglass on his desk as he introduced Bill, was triumphant.

Here was an essential difference between Hillary and Bill: he was far more capable of genuine irony than she, able to salvage a difficult situation by mocking himself. Self-deprecation is not her forte; her attempts are stiff and come off rehearsed usually, though with close friends she can sometimes mock the most obvious, and usually superficial, aspects of her countenance, like problems with her hair and headbands.

What had he been trying to do in Atlanta? Carson asked. Bill said he'd been trying to make Dukakis—never known for rhetorical splendor—look good. "I succeeded beyond my wildest imagination," said Bill, adding that Dukakis was so fond of the speech that he wanted him to go to the Republican convention to nominate George Bush, too. The audience howled.

The redemption didn't last long.

MARILYN JO JENKINS was Hillary's worst nightmare: an attractive, accomplished, rich antagonist with whom Bill believed himself to be in love. He wanted to end his marriage. Hillary refused. She would fight to keep her marriage and her family together, she told Betsey Wright. She had put too much of her own heart and mind and soul into her partnership with Bill to abandon it. She had invested too much.

In 1992, after the affair had played itself out, Hillary answered an interviewer's question for *Glamour* magazine with words that may have shed unintended light on at least some of her thinking during the "Jenkins period" of their lives.

No marriage is perfect, but just because it isn't perfect doesn't mean the only solution is to walk off and leave it. My strong feelings about divorce and its effects on children have caused me to bite my tongue more than a few times during my own marriage. . . . One of the many difficulties with divorce is that it becomes a public matter. It goes to court. Painful child custody decisions must be made. Regardless of individual feelings, everyone involved in the process, especially a parent, has an obligation to temper the pain children will inevitably experience.

Betsey Wright had concluded toward the end of 1988 that Bill was "having a severe midlife crisis." She told him, "Bill, you're crazy if you think everybody in this office is oblivious to the fact that you're having an affair. You're acting like an idiot. We're all seeing the way you giggle, the way you shut the door, you know, this is just dumb. Too many people on this staff know about it." The troopers knew about it, she said. Hillary and Bill were screaming at each other in the mansion. Plus, Wright could see "he was playing some games with some of the women I had on staff, and I had been able to keep all of that under control. Heavy flirting.

They would amazingly have to run errands out to the mansion when Hillary wasn't there, and stuff that was just driving me crazy. He wasn't doing his job. He wasn't paying attention. He was resisting trying to make his appointments. And he was having this affair." Wright did not at the time know the woman's name, or particularly want to.

"I was switching the people I always sent with him on the road," said Betsey. "So it would just be the ones that I thought would keep him out of trouble the best. It was just a very dangerous era of time." Bill began a series of assignations, she was convinced, that were increasingly heedless even by his standards. "And I really did eventually become quite depressed over all of this. And I'm sure I was driving him crazy then, too. And I mean he came to really resent that I always knew when he was screwing up. By the time the whole thing came to a head he just went crazy in '89. He nearly burned his relationship with Hillary. He burned it with me. Then he decides he wants to fix them both. He can't. That's when I resigned and left the governor's office, because I knew he couldn't fix both relationships at the same time.

"I talked to Hillary several times during that period by phone, and we were pulling our hair about him. He was a mess. During one of the conversations she said, 'There are worse things than infidelity,'" and gradually—in pieces from her and Bill—the story came out that Bill had told Hillary he wanted to leave the marriage. Hillary had not been very specific, but she was clear enough. According to Wright, "Hillary [also] said, 'What you have to remember, Betsey, is that he is an adult and he is the governor, and we have to let him be responsible for his actions.' And I said, 'Hillary, you've always been so much better about standing back and doing that. I always feel like I've got so much invested in this, and it hurts when he acts like an idiot.' And I was never able to stop beating him over the head. . . . She would pull back. I used to be in awe of her ability to do that. And I don't think she ever stopped doing that. . . . But this Jenkins was different."

Marilyn Jo Jenkins was about the same age as Hillary, a Southerner, a beauty, a mother of two young children, a businesswoman with an MBA from Western New England College in Springfield, Massachusetts. She had grown up in Crossett, Arkansas, and had attended Henderson State College in Arkadelphia, where she'd met the man she would later marry, Norman Jenkins III, a military man. Her sister had married into one of the wealthiest families in Arkansas, the Blands, who made their fortune in soda-pop franchising. After fifteen years of marriage, Jenkins divorced her husband in 1984. She then began work as a customer service representative for Entergy Arkansas. When she and Bill began seeing each other, probably in 1988, she was a marketing manager there.

Around this time, Bill was also asking some fellow governors whose marriages had deteriorated how they had dealt with the political consequences of divorce. He was clearly suggesting that he might be in a similar situation.

"He would wait me out," Hillary had observed about the period of time when she was considering whether to marry Bill. Now she would wait him out.

When Wright confronted him on the subject in the spring or early summer of 1989, Bill confirmed he had fallen in love with another woman, but now he wanted to fix his marriage to Hillary. He also confirmed to her, Betsey said, that Hillary had refused to give him a pass out of the marriage. "And that he had thought he was really in love with this woman, but he had also decided he wanted—he'd rather save the marriage with Hillary."

Wright told Hillary that she was ready to quit her job, and "explained why I had decided to go ahead and leave, that I had a voluntary contract with him and, in a lot of ways, she didn't. Because the minute Chelsea was born, hers wasn't. And that he seemed pretty determined to fix his relationship with her, and I knew he couldn't fix it with both of us at the same time, and that I was leaving." However, Betsey continued to work closely with both Hillary and Bill and Dick Morris over the next four years, though not as Bill's chief of staff.*

Meanwhile, "in trying to calm our relationship and feeling depressed," Betsey made arrangements for Bill and herself to see a therapist together. She and Bill were extremely voluble characters, each prone to outbursts, each with responsibilities to the other, and each with responsibilities to Hillary. Two years earlier, they had consulted with a psychologist who specialized in "business dynamics, office management kinds of things. He had done some work with the staff, and he was a friend of the Clintons,"

---

*Part of Wright's workload was assumed by Bill's scheduler, Nancy Hernreich, who, in the White House, became his administrative chief of operations with an office just outside the Oval Office. In the second year of Bill's presidency, when Wright, back in Arkansas, began hearing from the Clinton inner circle that there were "troubles" developing again with Bill, she called Nancy:

"I said, 'Nancy, there are just too many rumors coming to me about what's going on in the Oval Office. I trust you're not letting him in there by himself with hardly anybody, much less some female, as all the rumors are.' And she said, 'We promised him that he would never live under an iron thumb like yours again.' "

Senior members of Bill's White House staff confirmed that Nancy Hernreich, and others working around her, were indeed operating under just such an understanding; now that Wright no longer sat outside Bill's door, it was felt that the inhibiting and suffocating aura that had come to permeate the governor's office would not be reestablished in the White House.

according to Wright. But she concluded after several sessions that, although Bill "liked him [the therapist] a lot, the problem with him was that he was far more interested in social invitations to the governor's mansion than he was in being a psychologist trying to help us with a problem."

In July 1989, said Wright, she and Bill had two more counseling sessions, this time with Karen Ballard, the psychologist who had worked with Virginia, Bill, and Roger Clinton after the latter's arrest and imprisonment for dealing cocaine during Bill's second term as governor. Hillary had seemed positive about the results of the Clinton family's counseling; Bill learned much about the long-term consequences on his mother, Roger, and himself of his father's alcoholism and violence—and the secrecy it engendered in the family.

Bill's evaluation was less effusive: he talked only about the insight he gained on Roger's problems.

Betsey Wright did not find Ballard useful in dealing with the relationship between herself and Bill, and never told Hillary of the consultations (or those with the previous counselor). The sessions with Ballard were at Betsey's house. But they were discontinued within a month or so on Betsey's initiative, "because she kept telling me I had to . . . confront the alcoholism in my family. But there was no alcoholism in my family." According to Betsey, Ballard was a specialist in the fields of alcoholism and co-dependency. "I was perfectly willing to believe I was into a co-dependency [with Bill]," she said. "I don't think we accomplished a thing. So I just went and found somebody else on my own, just for me." One thing was certain: the theory of co-dependency, that particular specialty of New Age psychology being the realm of expertise of Betsey's and Bill's psychologist, definitely figured in, though who was co-dependent on whom, and how many people could be co-dependent in a single governor's mansion, was something not clearly delineated.

Dick Morris had concluded that Hillary and Bill's relationship was not co-dependent, because "I don't think he's in any way addicted to her. I think that he uses her to help enable him. To do good things and bad things, but to enable him. He sees the world in very functional terms. In regard to affection and relationships and conversation, and rewards, punishments and coldness and warmth and praise and thanks and blame and yelling and all those things, these are tools he uses to get people to do what he wants them to do. And his goal is to get everybody to do what he wants them to do. I don't think he draws a whole lot of a distinction among people. . . . Some people he just feels are more important to him than others. It's a largely functional relationship: I've always said it's a shorthand that she loves Bill and Bill loves Bill, so they have something in common."

· · ·

HILLARY WENT to visit Diane and Jim Blair in Fayetteville. "We were doing our usual long walk and she was very concerned," said Diane. "She was thinking that they had not made much money. Chelsea was there now. What if she were on her own? She didn't own a house. She was concerned that if she were to become a single parent, how would she make it work in a way that would be good for Chelsea. Hillary never went into details—absolutely never. And I doubt she did with anyone." The possible exception might have been Vince Foster. "I knew at times that she was pessimistic about their marriage when Bill was governor, but again, I wasn't taking notes back then," Diane said many years later. She noted that, along with her Methodism, Hillary's zealously guarded zone of privacy is essential to understanding her. "No doubt about it. The fact that nobody has ever wanted their privacy more and had it more excruciatingly violated is still just staggering to me."

In 1989 and 1990, Hillary joined half a dozen corporate boards, bringing in annual fees in excess of $200,000. Her billing at the Rose Law Firm increased as well. And, as she did in 1999 after Bill's impeachment for lying under oath about Monica Lewinsky, Hillary began talking seriously to friends about running for public office—in this case, for Bill's job as governor, if he didn't run, of course. She had never before explored the possibility of elective office.

With his and Hillary's life in turmoil, Bill had to decide whether to seek another term as governor in the election of November 1990. He had little time to make a decision, and Hillary had shown no inclination to consent to divorce. He continued to surreptitiously see Marilyn Jo Jenkins, and professed to at least one person to be in love with both his wife and Jenkins. To Dick Morris, with whom he discussed the possibility that he might seek a divorce, he seemed "dithering and depressed." Since the announcement in July 1987 that he would not seek the presidency, his performance as governor overall was inattentive, almost negligent at times, his energies obsessively focused on his relationship with Marilyn Jo and then his attempt to deal with the future and fate of his marriage. If he wanted to become president, whether in 1992 or later, it must have seemed a far reach on his own, without Hillary, with the weight of an ugly separation dragging on him, and his relationship with Chelsea altered perhaps irrevocably.

The first decision, the one that affected all the others, was what he chose to do about his marriage to Hillary. Jim Blair had heard the rumors about Bill's relationship with Jenkins, but he was certain that Bill would never leave the marriage, even with a pass from Hillary. Among other things, it would mean Bill could never run for president, in all likelihood. Bill never suggested to Jim he was considering leaving, and Blair never asked. "I just don't believe that," he said. "Would it be a woman he might like to spend ninety days on a Caribbean island with? Yeah." Other friends said Hillary had either demanded or suggested that Bill go into counseling for his "problem."

Hillary and Bill decided they would work at saving their marriage, whatever was required, presumably including some kind of counseling that Bill would undergo; it was a commitment, and Bill understood his obligations not to be unfaithful. (One can only speculate as to exactly what led to the decision. Betsey Wright's interpretation was that there was a "negotiation," after which "Bill had to be a puppy dog and do everything she wanted him to do. . . . I watched the same thing play out after Lewinsky. She would take it [abuse], but she was going to get something out of it, too. So she ran for the Senate.")

As it happened, Bill and Marilyn Jo Jenkins continued to remain close and see each other on a number of occasions until Bill and Hillary reached the White House. Clinton had called either her office or home fifty-nine times between 1989 and 1991, according to the phone records introduced into the various investigations to which the Clintons were subjected.

AT FIRST, after their reconciliation, Bill decided tentatively not to run for reelection as governor, and to focus on his relationship with his family. It might also be advantageous not to be burdened with the governorship if he decided to seek the presidency in 1992. If he ran for governor and lost—a possibility, since Dick Morris's preliminary polls were showing that 50 percent of Arkansas voters would prefer a new governor—the presidency might never be attainable.

He and Hillary discussed the possibility of her running to become his successor. Morris conducted two polls to assess her chances. "The conclusion that I came to in those polls was that she had not developed her image, and that she was seen as Mrs. Clinton. She was not seen as Hillary. Which is hard to imagine, but it's true. And people felt that if she were going to run for governor, it would be him putting her in as a placeholder to control Arkansas while he ran for president. And, in fact, I called it in my briefing to her—an unfortunate choice of phrase which she was angry at—the Lurleen Wallace* phenomenon. . . . People saw

---

*Lurleen Wallace, wife of George, ran for and won the governorship of Alabama in 1966 when her husband was prevented by state law from serving consecutive terms. She and her husband acknowledged from the outset that he would continue to make the administrative policies and decisions.

that, and she was very angry about it, very annoyed. And Bill, more so than she, in defending her, saying . . . 'Did you tell them that she was on the board of the Children's Defense Fund? Did you tell them that she was head of Legal Services Corporation? Did you tell them about what she did for education reform?' And so on. But it was very clear that she had not established her own identity." Morris and others could see that Bill was being extremely solicitous of Hillary in the aftermath of their decision to remain together, as well as affectionate, appreciative, and far less stressed.

Bill declared his candidacy for another term as governor. Soon he was regaining his form, energized by being on the road again, traveling the state, talking about its future, what he and Hillary had done for its people. Four weeks before election day, Larry Nichols, an ex-employee of the Arkansas Development Finance Authority, who had been fired for making almost 150 private phone calls to the Nicaragua contra leadership, announced to the press that he had filed suit against Clinton, accusing him of using a "slush fund" as governor to conduct concealed affairs with five or more women. One was Gennifer Flowers.

The suit was an obvious attempt to damage Clinton not just in Arkansas, but in any future race for president. (Nichols was a surrogate for Clinton's opponent and longtime antagonist in the governor's race, Shef Nelson.) As such, it was particularly dangerous in both the long and short term to Bill and Hillary, as she recognized.

At the behest of Betsey Wright and Hillary, Webb Hubbell and Vince Foster were then hired, by or through the campaign, to represent the women and obtain from the women their signed statements that they had never had sex with Bill Clinton. Some of the women were brought into an interview room to be questioned by Vince, Webb, and, on one occasion, Hillary. Two of the five women were prominent friends of Hillary and Bill—both black—and almost no one familiar with the case believes they were anything more than friends. But a line had been crossed, in appearance if nothing else: Hillary, or her law firm, or both were now acting as counsel to the women with whom her husband was accused of having illicit affairs. Acting through another lawyer, Betsey Wright was able to get Gennifer Flowers to sign a statement that she had never had a sexual relationship with Bill.

There could be no question that Hillary was Bill's fiercest defender in preventing his other women from causing trouble. Always. It was as if she, much more than he, better understood the danger—to him, to her, to Bill's future, and to their dream. She never doubted that if the women, and the enemies who used them, succeeded or became too visible and credible, the whole edifice could come down, including their marriage.

· · ·

IN NOVEMBER, Bill Clinton was reelected governor in a landslide, 57 percent to 43 percent. He had carried Sebastian County, which was still hard-core Republican territory, as it had been when he lost by six thousand votes in the congressional election of 1974. At a stop in Fort Smith during this final campaign for governor, Bill had promised that if he won Sebastian County he would dance down Garrison Avenue, the town's main street. Two days after the election, he and Hillary and a couple of hundred others danced away in the rain and cold in celebration.

Happy days were here again.

5

The Prize

While Bill talked about social change, I embodied it. I had my own opinions, interests and profession. . . . I was outspoken. I represented a fundamental change in the way women functioned in our society.

—*Living History*

S INCE JOHN F. KENNEDY'S election in 1960, a particular style of political journalism had established how presidential campaigns were historically regarded. This genre, known as "tick-tock," was perfected by Theodore H. White in *The Making of a President* and established the myth of Camelot. White and many of his successors recorded every sort of scene-setting and minutiae, with dramatic emphasis added by piling detail upon detail from the point of view of a fly on the wall. But flies are not very discriminating, and the standardization of this technique over the next decade for the most part did little to reveal the real stories of presidential campaigns. This was especially true in 1972 when White wrote the final book in his *Making of the President* series, which in its first edition canonized the geniuses of Richard Nixon's presidential campaign. In the Clinton campaign twenty years later, journalists covering it—and others who wrote books after its conclusion—faced a unique problem: the real story, of course, was the relationship between Bill and Hillary, their partnership and how it largely determined the philosophy, strategy, offenses, defenses, sound bites, ideas, attacks, and general health of the Clinton campaign. This was a new phenomenon in Washington: a campaign that emanated from the collaboration of the candidate and his wife. The essential dialogue was the one between them, and few aides or friends—if any—ever learned the couple's exact conversations when they were alone. The principal deputies of the campaign did know that she sometimes spoke for him, and that his words were often hers, and that she always proved to be the elephant in the room.

Bill was intellectually and politically deft enough to throw George H. W. Bush off-guard and challenge the menacing machine at his command, a battlefield army of brilliant young political savages directed by Lee Atwater and his disciple Karl Rove. Moreover, Bill and Hillary had real ideas and programs to address the real problems of the country in a thoughtful, nonideological way and with a generally positive message— no matter how hard the Bush people tried to taint them pejoratively with the label "liberal." The easy part for the Clinton campaign was setting out what the candidate believed. The tough part was getting the press and the voters to turn down the noise that Bill and Hillary believed was extraneous: about his sex life and escape from military service, and the public's perception of her as ambitious and power-hungry. They needed to find ways to engage voters with the campaign's ideas and to present themselves convincingly as an appealing new force in American politics—not Machiavellian monsters or opportunists, as the Republican campaign would have it, but a young, smart Kennedyesque couple attempting to send George Bush and his white-haired wife packing.

Bill's tendency to be his own worst enemy didn't help. The sensationalistic rumors, accusations, and revelations about him lent themselves to journalistic hyperbole. Partly because his political life was so intertwined with Hillary's it was difficult to know precisely the reality and context of her life. Remarkably for so public a figure, especially one whose husband had been reelected governor four times and was running for president, the book on Hillary was awfully thin, suspiciously repetitive, and contextually lacking, whether the media narrative in question was admiring, hostile, or an honest attempt to separate the real Hillary from the myth generated by Clinton campaigns past and present. She wanted it that way, through their years in the White House and after.

Meanwhile, of singular significance in the campaign and later in the White House, he often needed to be managed, pushed, reassured, guided, or scolded, depending on the moment, to perform at the level of which he was capable. This was the key to his effectiveness, almost like tuning an instrument. The person who knew best how to do that was his wife, partly because he would listen to her.

HILLARY BELIEVED, before Bill did, that he could win in 1992—even when President George Bush's popularity registered near 90 percent. "That's one where her instinct was right, and I didn't feel that way for the longest time," Clinton said years later. "She thought that in '88 we still had a reasonably good economy and that the adverse consequences of Reaganomics were not fully apparent to most voters; and that by 1992 they would be. And she always believed that. And she never changed her opinion. . . . It was quite amazing."

Through the spring and summer of 1991, Hillary and Bill had been discussing between themselves, and to a limited extent with others, the pros and cons of Bill running. George Bush towered over the political landscape after America's victory in the Gulf War, so much so that only a single Democrat, an ex-senator—Paul Tsongas of Massachusetts—had thus far come forward to challenge him. But the most important consideration for Bill and Hillary was not Bush's stature. Rather, it was the same question that ended Bill's flirtation with running in 1988, and consumed the candidacy of Gary Hart.

Hillary quoted Bill as telling her in the early summer of 1991 that he didn't know if he wanted to run. He *knew* how vulnerable he was to insinuation and revelation from the Republicans about his women; Hillary did not know how sordid some of the facts were. But she clearly knew enough to recognize that if the lid were pried open more than slightly, his candidacy would, in all likelihood, be finished. She talked to him about withstanding the kind of take-no-prisoners campaign the Republicans would wage. They were both aware a presidential race would be brutal on their family. In the gubernatorial campaign of 1986, Hillary and Bill said years afterward, they had staged mock debates at the family dinner table in which one of them played the role of Bill's opponent and said mean things about Chelsea's dad (not about sex). Chelsea was now four years older and would understand far more.

In late August 1991, shortly before the school term was to begin, Hillary pressed the case one morning, she said, just as they were getting out of bed, in the guest cottage on the mansion grounds, because their own bedroom was being painted. She had supplied the dialogue to journalists years later.

Her: "I think you have to do it."
Him: "Do you really?"
Her: "Yeah."
Him: "Why do you believe that?"
Her: "I think you are absolutely the right person to make these
    arguments."

They had been discussing "the arguments" all summer, she said: restoring strength to the economy; pursuing racial justice; reversing the sleazy ethical climate of the Reagan-Bush years; moving the Democratic

Party to the center without compromising its fundamental principles. Bill was the right age. The country was ready for its first president born after World War II.

She said she thought he would win, and that he should run only if he was ready for what winning would require.

In one subsequent account—a book written by *Newsweek* reporters about the 1992 campaign—there was a slight variation in the details ("The sudden movement wakened Hillary. She could guess what was on her husband's mind.") and the dialogue she supplied:

> Her: "We have to do this, don't we?"
> Him: "We don't have to do anything we don't want to do."
> Her: "But if we don't what will our excuse be?"

Through the fall, Bill sought advice from numerous friends about running for president. Most of them believed that he and Hillary had already made up their minds, and that these exploratory conversations were more for self-assurance, going through the motions rather than genuinely seeking counsel. Many had been with Bill since Georgetown and Oxford, and with Hillary since Wellesley, and with both of them ever since. They had been waiting most of their adult lives for a Clinton presidential candidacy.

HILLARY AND BILL together devised a plan to test whether it was possible to acknowledge the problems of their marriage in a general enough way that "serious" journalists would pry no further, or perhaps halfheartedly, or that would at least give the Clintons a dignified means of refusing to answer any more questions about their conjugal life—and beyond—without being untruthful. If all hell broke loose, Bill could withdraw before he had formally declared his candidacy. But they had no plans to do that. There was no question how badly Hillary and Bill both wanted 1992 to be their year.

The optimal venue at which to float their plan was a Washington institution where trial balloons were often released, the so-called Sperling Breakfast, at the Capital Hilton Hotel. Many scenes from the movie *Mr. Smith Goes to Washington*, with Jimmy Stewart as the hayseed hero who brings honor back to politics in Washington, were filmed in the hotel. At the Sperling Breakfast, members of the national press corps broke bread with politicians over sausages, eggs, grits, and coffee.

The breakfast of September 16, 1991, was notable almost as much for its lack of spontaneity as the news that ensued, which was exactly what

Hillary and Bill had hoped for. They had rehearsed for days with advisers and aides how they would comport themselves, trying out different versions of the same message: that there had been problems in their marriage in the past, that the problems were behind them, and that Bill and Hillary were a strong and committed couple.

Bill was reluctant to say even that much. In one meeting leading up to the breakfast, he told Hillary and the others present that he was inclined to draw a clear line and state plainly that he wouldn't answer personal questions about his marriage or private life. Period. But Hillary understood the need for preemptive measures. "We've got to put a stop to this," she told two aides, Stan Greenberg and Frank Greer, who would spend the most harrowing hours of the campaign in consultation with her about how to respond to personal attacks on Bill and herself. For the Sperling Breakfast, they all agreed, as Hillary had urged, that Bill should acknowledge that there had been problems in their marriage, but he would not get into the details because those were private matters only for his family to discuss. He was committed to Hillary and to Chelsea, and that's what mattered. End of story—they hoped. They were well aware that the beginning of the end of Gary Hart's campaign had come in a meeting with members of the Washington press corps, when a reporter from a reputable newspaper, not a supermarket tabloid, had asked the candidate if he had ever committed adultery.

Since then, however, there had been some second thoughts within the mainstream press establishment about the zeal involved in helping instigate Hart's collapse, and the tone of coverage.

To Hillary's and Bill's surprise, by the time the dishes were being cleared at the Sperling Breakfast, none of the reporters had asked any questions about their marriage or private lives. Instead, Bill had been at his best at what he was best at: talking policy, evangelizing, fulfilling the kind of expectations that had led one aide to call him "Propeller-Head," revving at thousands of RPMs about the meaning of New Democratic politics and his commitment to tax cuts for the middle class and an improved health care system. At last, on his own initiative, he brought up the premeditated matter they were actually there to discuss. "All of you are nice not to bring it up," he said, "but I know all of you are concerned . . . ," and one of the reporters picked up from there, gingerly.

Bill's answer was exactly what had been rehearsed: Hillary was seated next to him. "Like nearly anybody who has been together for twenty years, our relationship has not been perfect or free from difficulties, but we feel good about where we are and we believe in our obligation to each other, and we intend to be together thirty or forty years from now, whether I run for president or not."

Godfrey Sperling, the breakfast's founding eminence, wrote later in *The Christian Science Monitor*:

> Mr. Clinton received a "boffo" rating in the articles written by the 40-plus journalists there that day. The test very specifically included the need to find out whether the widely circulated rumors about Clinton's infidelity would be too much baggage for him to carry out a winning campaign. Clinton received an especially understanding and sympathetic response from the journalists when he said that, like so many married people, he and Hillary had had personal problems between them to work out—and they had done so. . . . Mrs. Clinton nodded emphatically.

Two weeks later, at 2:30 A.M. on October 3, Bill was poring over his announcement speech, making the final revisions. In preparation for his address, he had watched tapes of John F. Kennedy, hoping he would be able to suggest JFK's gestures. All that was left was to consult Hillary one more time. Soon he would be standing in front of the Old State House to declare his candidacy for president.

As Bill finally stepped to the podium, he could see among the crowd of two thousand many of the same friends who had come to Little Rock in July 1987 expecting him to announce his candidacy. Diane Blair, looking at Hillary next to him, remembered later that she was thinking about how, when they had first met, her friend had looked more like a hippie than a first lady. Bob Reich, who had flown in that morning, thought to himself, "God, I hope they know what they're getting into."

SOON AFTER THE ANNOUNCEMENT, Diane Blair, who had written a well-regarded political science textbook, decided she would write a book about the Clinton campaign of 1992. She was certain Hillary and Bill were going to the White House. As preparation, she asked campaign workers at every level to make extensive notes through the whole campaign. After the election, she interviewed them—126 members of the campaign staff in all. The answers to her questions, verbatim, with their firsthand reports of everything from advance team preparations to the most important strategy decisions of the campaign, filled four enormous binders. Her book was never written. She died of cancer in 2000, at age sixty-one, and the binders were locked in storage.

In the aggregate, the single-spaced contents of the binders, kneehigh, provide a developing portrait of Hillary as she became the chief strategist and sounding board of her husband's presidential campaign, and contemplated the kind of first lady she intended to be. Her over-reaching is recorded, on the one hand, and on the other, her incomparable ability to channel the best of Bill Clinton into action. And she is seen at her fiercest and most determined, grabbing the reins of the campaign when it appeared the Clinton candidacy would be buried in allegations—in the same week—that he had dodged the draft and had a long sexual affair with Gennifer Flowers.

At Hillary's direction, a special "defense team" was established to deal with allegations about Bill's history with the Selective Service System, women claiming to have had affairs with him, and other personal aspects of the Clintons' lives. Betsey Wright was dispatched to Little Rock from Washington to research the underlying facts—including and beyond Gennifer Flowers—about women in Bill's past, and to find any old records relating to his draft status; James M. Lyons, a Denver lawyer and friend of the Clintons, was summoned from Colorado to assist her—including hiring detectives to check the backgrounds of the women—and to handle questions about the Clintons' finances; and Kevin O'Keefe of Chicago, a friend of Hillary's for many years, dealt specifically with the draft issues. Part of the problem was that the campaign had been unprepared and lacked documentation and relevant information that it should have had on hand in anticipation of the inevitable questions.

Among the questions Diane asked each of her interviewees was, "This campaign is now being described as the most effective presidential campaign in recent American history. What, from your perspective, made it so effective?" Their answers, because of their trust in Hillary's closest friend, tend to be very revealing.

"Probably Hillary. Honestly," Nancy Hernreich, Bill's scheduling secretary, answered. Many others came to the same conclusion. "She just has a way of cutting through to the core of something," noted Hernreich, who would become Bill's secretary in the White House. "She can see what the problem is and she can make a decision and find the right people to come in . . . Bill listens to Hillary. He's obviously very bright and creative." Undoubtedly, when the campaign was in deep trouble that could have buried Bill's future, Hillary stepped in decisively to dig it out.

There had been hints of how vicious the attacks on the Clintons would be, said Hillary, especially in a telephone call to Bill from an aide in the Bush White House, Roger Porter, while the Clintons were still trying to reach a final decision on whether Bill should run. Porter, whose White House portfolio included education, had worked with Clinton and other governors on an education project. According to Bill, they were having a serious phone conversation for about five or ten minutes when Porter's tone changed abruptly, and he startled him with the words, "Cut the crap, Governor." Porter allegedly said the Bush high command feared Bill's candidacy and therefore they would have "to destroy" him.

"Roger said he was calling as my friend to give me fair warning," Clinton wrote in his autobiography. "If I waited until 1996, I could win the presidency. If I ran in 1992, they would destroy me and my political career would be over." Some journalists who covered the Clinton campaign thought the story was exaggerated.

Still, the slash-and-burn attack through the campaign was unceasing: constant assertions about Bill as a sexual predator, as a sybarite (orgies with black hookers), about ethical lapses in Arkansas, the fact that Bill had dodged the draft, a supposed murder that Clinton had covered up as governor to protect cocaine and arms trafficking out of Arkansas's Mena airport, Hillary's feminist advocacy, her supposed lesbianism, his and her (especially) histories as supposed left-wing ideologues (Bill, one rumor had it, had "disappeared" in Russia while dodging the draft). Sometimes it was difficult to separate the lunatic from the half-true, the outright lies from fact in the heat of a campaign, particularly in the new media config-uration in which the gap between the standards of the *New York Post* and the *Star* tabloid (later bought by the *Post*'s owner, Rupurt Murdoch) was often a narrow one, and the lead-time between trash television and CNN could be very short. There was certainly insufficient time to try to estab-lish the relationships, or lack of them, between the official Bush cam-paign apparatus and the armies of right-wing and religious-inspired Clinton-haters, which served as an echo chamber for every charge and accusation, no matter how outlandish.

By the time of the New Hampshire primary in March 1992, Hillary's view of the vast right-wing conspiracy was taking more precise shape, for good reason.

The contents of Diane Blair's notebooks document Hillary's increas-ing skill at managing the response to the attacks, and the acuity of her judgment that George Bush would be reelected unless the Clinton cam-paign could find a way to rapidly and effectively repel them—and keep the attack machine silenced long enough to effectively trumpet the Clin-tons' own substantive message (the platform of Putting People First: health care, middle-class tax cuts, job creation, the whole panoply of ideas that had, in fact, been Bill Clinton's political lifework, and to an extent hers, too). Getting the public to listen carefully to anything Bill said would be especially difficult, Hillary believed, because of what the press—as posse—had become. Long before the Gary Hart episode, she saw the press as out of control, hell-bent on personal destruction and manufactured controversy—while ignoring serious issues, whether at the local level or in Washington. In 1977, she told a Rotary Club audience, "One of our problems is trying to control a press that is far out of line because of Watergate."

The big story of the campaign, she feared, was going to be Bill's private life and hers, and a grotesque distortion of the record of the Arkansas years. The famous mantra inside the Clinton campaign was "It's the economy, stupid." But it's apparent in interview after interview in Diane's binders that the real guiding premise was: Keep them away from us and our private lives. Turn the attacks on us into our issue.

Hillary's ability to manage Bill—sensing his moods, knowing how to schedule him so he got adequate rest, all the things she had done in Arkansas to help him be effective—were of little help in the new situation she faced in 1992. Now she had to handle her own staff, her own campaign, her own schedule, the focus on her by the national press—without any clear guidelines from the central campaign. Instead of an integrated campaign structure, it had been decided with her approval that Hillary would have her own aides, who reported to her. Communication between the two layers of assistants and policy aides and schedulers was cumbersome. Even maintaining regular contact with a designated aide to Bill on his plane became difficult. The same problems would plague the Clinton presidency, because Hillary's operation seemed an alien culture to the presidential staff in the West Wing, and vice versa. "I think that Hillary got very mixed signals from the campaign about what they wanted her to do," said Jody Franklin, Hillary's chief of staff, as quoted in one of the binders. Not until very late in the campaign were adjustments made.

Inevitably, the contents of the binders picture Hillary as the campaign's crisis manager. But that was too simple a reading, as one of her aides noted:

> She doesn't look at her life as a series of crises but rather a series of battles. I think of her viewing herself in more heroic terms, an epic character like in *The Iliad*, fighting battle after battle. Yes, she succumbs to victimization sometimes, in that when the truth becomes too painful, when she is faced with the repercussions of her own mistakes or flaws, she falls into victimhood. But that's a last resort and when she does allow the wallowing it's only in the warm glow of martyrdom—as a laudable victim—a martyr in the tradition of Joan of Arc, a martyr in the religious sense. She would much

rather play the woman warrior—whether it's against the bimbos, the press, the other party, the other candidate, the right-wing. She's happiest when she's fighting, when she has identified the enemy and goes into attack mode. . . . That's what she thrives on more than anything—the battle.

The crucial test of the Clinton campaign came in New Hampshire on January 23, with a call from Bill to Hillary: the *Star* tabloid was about to run a story that Gennifer Flowers, one of the women who had sworn in an affidavit in 1990 that she had not had sex with Bill Clinton, now was claiming she, in fact, had had a twelve-year affair with him. Bill denied it.

Hillary set the tone of the campaign's response at a rally in Bedford two nights later. "From my perspective," she said, "our marriage is a strong marriage. We love each other, we support each other, and we have had a lot of strong and important experiences together that have meant a lot to us." Yes, there had been "issues," as she called them, in the marriage. But that was between them, and they deserved a "realm of protection. . . . Is anything about our marriage as important to the people of New Hampshire as whether or not they will have a chance to keep their own families together?" The cheers of the crowd made it impossible to hear the rest of her answer.

A week later, Flowers, a not-so-talented lounge singer, was back, in the *Star* again, this time under the headline, "They Made Love All Over Her Apartment." Flowers claimed she had tapes of telephone conversations with the governor. Hillary now recognized that a tabloid story had become a huge national media sensation, and she was prepared to go to the mat. Mandy Grunwald, a media consultant hired in part so a woman could defend Clinton in an instance just such as this, was dispatched to appear on *Nightline* with Ted Koppel. "If we don't turn this into a positive, we're going down," said Paul Begala, one of the campaign's principal consultants, who, like his business partner, James Carville, had won the trust of both Hillary and Bill.

Hillary did not disagree. Her initial impulse, after getting the call about Flowers from Bill a week earlier, had been to "just go for it. Tell them the truth and get this off our backs," according to people on his staff. They had the old affidavit that Flowers had signed. Now that strategy did not seem viable, given what else Flowers was saying: that Bill had frequently jogged over to her house for quickie sex, had once asked her to have sex in the men's room of the mansion while Hillary was on the premises, and that he had told her he was considering leaving Hillary for her but couldn't because a divorce would finish his career as a politician. And Flowers said she had tape recordings.

Harry Thomason, Paul Begala, Mickey Kantor, and George Stephanopoulos devised a media strategy to save Clinton's candidacy: a joint appearance by Bill and Hillary on *60 Minutes* immediately following the Super Bowl. "It took a lot of convincing that such exposure was worth the risks, loss of privacy and potential impact on our families, especially on Chelsea," said Hillary. But without such an extraordinary response, she became convinced Bill's candidacy would be finished.

Before the *60 Minutes* taping, Hillary and Bill met with a small group of aides to prepare. Both were adamant that he would not utter the word *adultery*. They would not go into specifics. It was nobody else's business. Hillary, others could see, was still worried that she might cry on television.

Then they went downstairs to a room where the television cameras were set up. They were ready—Hillary in a turquoise suit with her arm fastened around her husband. They sat next to each other on a white couch. "She steeled herself," said Bob Reich, who had gone to Boston to offer moral support. "When she steels herself, you know, she knows that she's going into a kind of combat position. . . . And she is ready for that."

Who was Gennifer Flowers? correspondent Steve Kroft asked. How would you describe your relationship? (Very limited, said Bill.) He and Hillary talked on-camera about how they loved each other, how deeply they cared about Chelsea, how they had stayed together through the kinds of "problems" that married couples often encountered.

Don Hewitt, the show's producer, whispering off-camera, urged for a second time that Clinton simply confess to adultery. It didn't happen.*

A few days later, in a packed press conference, Flowers was asked if Clinton had used a condom. She played tapes, scratchy, their audio quality not unlike Nixon's tapes that Hillary had heard eighteen years before, but this time it was her husband's voice, bragging to Flowers about how he had "shoved it up Larry Nichols's ass" when, after Nichols had named five women in his suit against Clinton, all the women had signed affidavits denying they had had sex with Clinton.

Richard Nixon, meanwhile, had been asked to comment about the Clinton campaign in an interview during a rare visit he had made to Washington. "If the wife comes through as being too strong and too intelligent," he remarked, "it makes the husband look like a wimp." Nixon said voters tended to agree with the assessment of Cardinal Richelieu: "Intellect in a woman is unbecoming."

---

*"He beckoned the producer to him at one point as he paced and asked as a personal favor that he not be on camera if he happened to be mopping sweat from his face," Theodore H. White had written of Richard Nixon in the original *The Making of the President*. The "producer" of the Kennedy-Nixon debates was Don Hewitt.

. . .

I T WAS HILLARY that night, after *60 Minutes*, who rallied the campaign staff. A message to the troops was clearly called for, and she had good news. A conference call was arranged. The polls were showing that Bill was still leading in New Hampshire, despite Flowers's press conference, despite the tapes. Eighty percent of Americans thought Bill should stay in the race.

"She was her husband's ultimate character reference," said Brooke Shearer, a friend who traveled with Hillary during much of the campaign and was interviewed by Diane Blair. That role would be Bill's salvation.

The next day Hillary telephoned Tammy Wynette. On *60 Minutes*, Hillary had said, "You know, I'm not sitting here, some little woman standing by my man like Tammy Wynette. I'm sitting here because I love him and I respect him and I honor what he's been through and what we've been through together. And you know, if that's not enough for people, then heck, don't vote for him."

Wynette was not pleased. She had publicly demanded that Hillary apologize for . . . well, it wasn't quite clear what for, but it appeared that she was offended that Hillary hadn't distinguished between her and her famous song, "Stand by Your Man."

"I didn't mean to hurt Tammy Wynette as a person," Hillary said. "I happen to be a country-Western fan. If she feels like I've hurt her feelings, I'm sorry about that." Hillary's attempt did not go over well with the singer, and the following day Hillary again called Wynette at her home in Nashville to apologize personally, and told her she would try to bring up the issue on her scheduled taping of *Primetime Live* with Sam Donaldson that night. After the call, Wynette said, "She seemed like a very nice lady and she seemed genuinely sorry." The apology didn't exactly fix the problem. "The undercurrent we couldn't eradicate was the notion that their partnership was less a marriage fired by love than an arrangement based on ambition," said George Stephanopoulos.

Nonetheless, Hillary's appearance on *60 Minutes* was a triumph, and probably had saved Bill's candidacy—because she had indeed stood by her man, as she would do again on the *Today* show when Monica Lewinsky became (like Gennifer Flowers) a household name. Bill finished second in the New Hampshire primary—a near-miracle, given what they had been through. His campaign, and Hillary, were not about to go down.

STAN GREENBERG, the campaign's chief polling consultant, was in awe of Hillary's talents, her intellect, and especially her tough-mindedness. In

1990, the Clintons came out of a difficult gubernatorial primary nervous about the general election ahead. They invited Greenberg to Little Rock to help manage the rest of the campaign. The candidate's brain trust became Hillary, Dick Morris, Greenberg, and Gloria King, who had replaced Betsey Wright as the governor's chief of staff. "I came in to try to figure out a rationale for why you would give him another term," Greenberg said years later. Clinton's opponent was attacking him relentlessly on both his record and his character. The overwhelming strategic question, discussed immediately upon Greenberg's arrival, was: "How aggressive to go in attacking the opponent and when to do it. And I can tell you she came down on the side of aggressive, and all on her own. She had a strong point of view . . . she was a fighter."

Greenberg, a slight man with wire-rimmed glasses, far more bookish in his appearance than in his muscular approach to campaigning, pronounced all this in a tone of unbridled admiration for both Clintons, and the ability of each to play to his or her respective strengths. Bill "was listening" and took a while to agree. "It was a very spirited discussion. Once we decided what the attack was, and we had his agreement, she wanted to do it strong, and she wanted to do it early. Which was exactly what occurred." Her political instincts, her urge to defend her man (and herself) and, once attacked, to go for the jugular won Greenberg over almost immediately. And it was no negative in his eyes that she also counseled aggressive handling of the press.

In fact, Greenberg and Hillary looked at politics through the same lens. From the late 1960s on, Democrats had developed a reputation for being soft. Like her, Greenberg believed that Jimmy Carter, who lost his presidency to Ronald Reagan in 1980, typified that weakness. "I don't mean just soft on policy terms, on crime, or soft on foreign policy. The Democrats were soft in campaigns. They didn't fight. They didn't show what they were made of, and people couldn't trust them to govern. And I think that Hillary was of that point of view that you were not going to have people's confidence unless you could show that you're strong and tough against your opponents. Your opponents need to know that you're not going to be passive, you're not going to be a punching bag, that you're not going to get pushed . . . that you're going to take control over your destiny." The Republicans had learned the lesson long before.

Greenberg was with Hillary when she made her first statement defending her husband just after the Gennifer Flowers story broke. "Her attitude was that people will do anything" to derail her husband's candidacy, "and she said it as forcefully as anything she'd ever said in her life. This did not come out of any kind of campaign discussion. She just got up there and said, 'People have been saying these things about my husband for years.' This was her, and what she believed. The press were stunned by it. It was not a planned moment. She took it to a new level [and] set the tone for everything that followed on that issue. We were in a crisis. And she continually set the tone. Her position was defiant— defiant that this was a political conspiracy, that this was being done by the people who were trying to bring down Bill Clinton, using this issue, playing it out to the tabloid press, and our response had to be defiant. This was politically motivated. People had an agenda, the people that hated Bill Clinton, and that they were using Gennifer Flowers, putting her up to it. Bill Clinton certainly agreed with Hillary's analysis."

As they moved from the Arkansas scene to the national scene, they carried with them enemies from Arkansas. Those enemies tried their best to take them down in New Hampshire, and the same people played a role later on in future scandals.

"You know, sometimes even paranoids have enemies," said Greenberg. "I think they have been seared by the experience. I don't view her as an angry person because I've seen her laugh. . . . I don't see a simmering kind of anger. But she does believe that there are forces out there that aren't right, that are determined to take him down, and I think she views herself as the strong, defiant force that deals with them."

Nothing demonstrated this more than the revelation, implicitly confirmed in Diane Blair's notebooks, that Hillary pushed after the Gennifer Flowers incident to publicize allegations that Bill's opponent, Vice President Bush, had also had a history of affairs during his marriage. The binders—and other conversations with campaign aides—confirm that she was furious that the mainstream press and even the tabloids had not gone after the supposed story of Bush's private life. Several of Bill's aides took it upon themselves to calm Hillary on the subject and convince her that, if such information were traced back to the campaign, it would be disastrous.

ON MARCH 8, the *New York Times* published a story on its front page headlined, "Clintons Joined S&L Operator in an Ozark Real Estate Venture." The Clintons had known for at least a month that reporter Jeff Gerth had been looking into their 1978 land deal with Susan and James McDougal, a fifty-fifty partnership in which the two couples had bought land along the White River in Arkansas in hopes of dividing it into forty-two lots and selling them for vacation homes. Bill and Hillary had resigned themselves to seeing the land deal as an unfortunate venture in which they had lost money. The *Times* saw something sinister: conflicts of interest and insider deals to line Hillary's and Bill's pockets. Susan

Thomases—officially in charge of the campaign's scheduling but, in fact, Hillary's political deputy and troubleshooter—and the campaign's counsel had met with Gerth the week before Super Tuesday, desperately trying to persuade him to run the story after the primaries that day. Thomases told Gerth that there were documents that would vindicate the Clintons—but, for the moment at least, they were missing. This added to the brew of suspicion, and rather than delay publication, the suggestion that records may have been removed was now part of the story. Gerth's story reported that the Rose Law Firm had performed legal work for McDougal's savings and loan company while Bill was attorney general and governor—but the *Times* failed to note that McDougal was not yet in the S&L business when the Clintons bought the land.

Bimbos, draft-dodging, and now corruption. In Arkansas, Hillary had become accustomed to being attacked—for not taking her husband's name, for being overly tough, for her *way* of doing things. But the *Times* story represented the first time she was being put on a plane of malfeasance such as Bill was all too familiar with. He asked Paul Begala what he should say at a previously scheduled press conference that day. Defend her, Begala said.

Meanwhile, the investigative engines of the *Washington Post* began turning. During Bill's preparation for a major debate on March 15, among all the Democratic candidates, George Stephanopoulos had advised him, "The minute you hear the word 'Hillary,' rip his head off. Don't let him finish the sentence." Toward the end of that debate, the candidates were asked whether they thought Clinton could be elected given his "recent problems." Paul Tsongas sidestepped the question. Former governor Jerry Brown of California did not. "I think he's got a big electability problem," he said. "It was right on the front page of the *Washington Post* today. He is funneling money to his wife's law firm for state business." Clinton's face turned red and then he tore into Brown. "Let me tell you something, Jerry," he said. "I don't care what you say about me . . . but you ought to be ashamed of yourself for jumping on my wife. You're not worth being on the same platform with my wife. Jerry comes in with his family wealth and his $1,500 suits and makes a lying accusation about my wife."

Brown asked whether the *Washington Post* was lying. Clinton answered firmly, "I'm saying I never funneled any money to my wife's law firm. Never."

The next morning, Hillary and Bill were at the Busy Bee Coffee Shop in Chicago, working the breakfast crowd, when a group of reporters walked in. They began asking him about Hillary's job at the Rose Law

Firm—whether there were inherent conflicts of interest in being a partner of a law firm that did business with the state. Hillary was behind him, drinking coffee from a Styrofoam cup. When one of the journalists asked if it was okay to speak directly to her, Bill said, "Sure. Ask her anything you want." NBC News correspondent Andrea Mitchell asked the first lady of Arkansas whether it was ethical for a governor's wife to work in a law firm whose clients did business with state agencies. Hillary had been waiting for such a question. "I suppose I could have stayed home, baked cookies, and had teas," she said memorably. Later, that quotation often stood alone in the press, seemingly indicating only her contempt for housewives, absent her words that followed: "The work that I've done as a professional, as a public advocate, has been aimed in part to assure that women can make the choices that they should make—whether it's a full-time career, full-time motherhood, some combination, depending on what stage of life they are at—and I think that is still difficult for people to understand right now, that it is a generational change."

The abbreviated version, in sound bite form, permeated TV and radio news for days, and columnists cited her remarks as evidence of radical feminist disdain for traditional values. William Safire wrote in the *New York Times* that Bill had a "Hillary problem," and called her words the "second outbreak of foot-in-mouth disease," the first one being her Tammy Wynette remark.

Hillary went on television again to explain her position, but it was too late. "Cookies and tea" would continue to plague the campaign for months to come. Gloria Cabe, manager of the campaign's Washington office, said they "were inundated with calls from professional women who felt it had insulted them, who made the decision to take a few years off, and many of them talked about baking cookies. And of course lots of cookies were mailed to us. . . . And the trouble was, I felt like we could overcome the traditionalists, the women who were suspicious anyway of who Bill was and who Hillary was, but when I realized it was eating into our core support, that's when I really got worried."

HILLARY HAD BEGUN the campaign as her husband's full political partner. He had boasted famously that by voting for him, you could "buy one, get one free," a slogan he had first used campaigning in the New Hampshire primary (with emphasis on his wife's two decades of work on education and children's issues).

The cookie quotation, her defense of her work as a lawyer, and her aggressive, explicit direction of the campaign to discredit Gennifer Flowers had put her stage-front. That had not adversely affected the New Hampshire primary election, but it was the first of a long season of primaries, and her assertiveness in public suddenly loomed as a liability as she found herself becoming a moving target for the Republican right— "The Lady Macbeth of Arkansas," the "Yuppie Wife from Hell." A *New York Post* cartoon pictured Bill Clinton as a marionette, with a fierce-looking Hillary pulling the strings.

Delicately, the campaign's strategists and worried pollsters urged the candidate to trim his wife's billowing sails. Hillary, her back up, got the message, though neither the tabloid headlines ("Bill Clinton Love Tapes," "Gennifer & Bill Romped in Our Apartment") nor the criticism abated. "Hillary Clinton in an apron is Michael Dukakis in a tank," declared Roger Ailes, the Bush campaign's designated hit man, soon to be head of the new Fox News channel.

The savaging of Hillary as a doctrinaire leftist and/or "Feminazi" who would encourage the dismemberment of the American family soon became a catechism of the Bush campaign, echoed and intensified in the right-wing press. Bill Clinton's record in Arkansas was, of course, hardly that of a leftist, but even before he took the oath of office it became commonplace to attack him through her, and so locate his politics on the outer fringes of the "liberal left," based on the presumed ideological bent of his wife.

Such attacks on her were exploiting what the Clinton campaign was learning to its own dismay from polls, namely that many voters were coming to believe that Hillary was in the race "for herself" and "going for the power." These were, in fact, phrases from a strategy memorandum that proposed she assume a low political profile for the rest of the campaign, and that "press opportunities" be contrived to show the Clintons acting more affectionately toward each other, and Hillary as a more traditional, maternal figure. "More than Nancy Reagan, she is seen as 'running the show,'" the memo said. "The absence of affection, children and family and the preoccupation with career and power only reinforces the political problem evident from the beginning." Recommended were "joint appearances with her friends where Hillary can laugh [and] do her mimicry." The Clintons, the memo suggested, should take a family vacation in Disneyland, and the campaign should create "events where Bill and Hillary can go on dates with the American people."

The more she was vilified by adversaries as a radical feminist, the softer and fuzzier she allowed herself to be portrayed. Encouraged by the campaign's press attachés, a new story line began to take hold in the media about a more feminine Hillary. *W,* the glossy fashion and celebrity magazine, was typically fed tidbits about how the Hollywood production company run by Hillary's friend Linda Bloodworth-Thomason had lent three stylists—one each for hair, makeup, and wardrobe—to give Hillary "a softer, natural, honey-blonde look." Dozens of reporters on the campaign trail advised their readers or viewers that she was no longer wearing her trademark headbands (too "brainy-looking"); that she had "zipped her lip" and now gazed lovingly and silently at her husband from a wifely vantage point. A few cynics intimated in print that she had undergone a personality transplant, "allowing handlers to substitute the heart of Martha Stewart for her own," as *Time* magazine put it. But this missed a larger point about Martha Stewart. Divorced, independent, and later to become a close friend of Hillary, she was a powerful, driven, ambitious woman who had established herself near the top of the very male worlds of publishing and communications thanks to the way she wielded the most feminine of arts and crafts.

Hillary would be forced into semi-exile, though less severely than when perceptions of her became overwhelmingly negative after the health care debacle in 1994. Diane Blair's campaign binders reveal that the schedule was contrived to keep her away from the national press and covered more flatteringly by local reporters.

The anti-Hillary rhetoric reached a crescendo at the Republican convention on August 17, where Pat Buchanan, in a prime-time attack, painted Hillary as a radical feminist. " 'Elect me and you get two for the price of one,' Mr. Clinton says of his lawyer spouse," Buchanan ranted. "And what does Hillary believe?" That children "have a right to sue their parents," he answered, and a view that marriage is an institution comparable to slavery. "Well, speak for yourself, Hillary. Friends, this is radical feminism." (Buchanan's assertion was rooted in an article on children's legal rights—"Children Under the Law"—that Hillary had written for the *Harvard Educational Review* in 1974, in which she advocated such lawsuits by minors only in extreme cases of abuse and neglect.)

But the strategy backfired on the Republicans in that it made Hillary a sympathetic character and a political victim of the right, something the Clinton campaign never could have done on its own. Until then, Jody Franklin was quoted in the Blair binders, "it was hard for people to see her as a sympathetic figure because she was too strong, she was too independent, she knew what she believed in, and I think people didn't want to see a warm side to her. Or couldn't feel sympathy. Or connect with her. But then once she was in a position where she was attacked, people could then connect with her. So I think that's really what turned things around." It wouldn't be the last time.

By the end of the 1992 campaign, Hillary was doing a lot of what presidential candidates' wives had traditionally done: sit demurely onstage through the drone of their husbands' speeches, applaud at the appropriate moments, and wave to the cheering crowds at oratory's end. She had even taken to holding an umbrella over Bill's head when he spoke in the rain.

The final weekend before election day, a cartoon showed Bill saying to a human-sized box with air holes, "Only a few days more, Hillary."

She and Bill spent the last twenty-four hours in a tempest of campaigning: Philadelphia, Cleveland, Detroit, St. Louis, Paducah, Fort Worth, Albuquerque, Denver, then back to Little Rock to cast their votes. Hillary was expecting victory, but took nothing for granted.

Within hours, she and Bill were discussing who should be in the cabinet.

6

A Transitional Woman

*[I]t wasn't clear to either of us how this partnership would fit into the
new Clinton Administration. . . . When it came to political spouses, we
certainly didn't expect the nation's capital to be more conservative than
Arkansas.*

—Living History

S EVERAL DAYS AFTER the election, Dick Morris and Hillary talked
by telephone about what her formal role should be in the new
administration. Morris had, contrary to myth, always been closer to
Hillary than to Bill. He had, in fact, often found that the only effective
way of influencing the governor was through his wife, and so he was well
aware of the degree to which the two were a single, intertwined governing and marital power. He had regularly operated through Hillary to get
political schemes and projects reconsidered that he'd first proposed
unsuccessfully to the governor.

Others in the governor's office tended to view Morris as a kind of
Rasputin to the Clintons (the fact that he appeared no taller than Hillary
contributed to the image), and labels like "mercenary" or "evil force"
seeped into Little Rock political discussions about him. Among the characteristics that Clinton partisans found distasteful was his equal enthusiasm for working on behalf of Republicans and Democrats; he also had a
reputation for engaging in almost any kind of subterfuge or negative
campaigning to gain political advantage. Morris correctly perceived that
Bill Clinton himself had begun to think of him as "something dirty that
he didn't want to touch without gloves," so it was increasingly Hillary
who had sounded the alarm when her husband needed help, Hillary who
booked Morris's services, Hillary who strategized and plotted with him

on Bill's behalf. That pattern had been established on the eve of Clinton's 1980 defeat for reelection.

Now Dick and Hillary were on the phone again, mapping out the future on the grandest stage of all. In her first post-victory conversation with him, Hillary noted that *Time* magazine had suggested she would make a good White House chief of staff—a job held in previous administrations by such skilled political operatives as James Baker, the Bush family consigliere; Howard Baker, the former senator and Reagan white knight from Tennessee (who had famously asked, as vice chairman of the Senate Watergate Committee: "What did the president know and when did he know it?"); and H. R. Haldeman, who ran Nixon's White House (and knew the answer).

Morris said it was a terrible idea because a chief of staff, among other things, was the person who had to take the heat for the commander-in-chief. It was important that the president be able to fire his chief of staff. "I said it's like a baseball owner being able to fire the manager," Morris remembered. "Something may not be the manager's fault, but you have to be able to fire somebody at some point. And Clinton couldn't fire her."

Hillary seemed to accept the logic of this, according to Morris, and then raised the possibility that, with her legal background, she might instead make a good attorney general, just as Bobby Kennedy had in his brother's administration; or that, with her experience in the fields of child and family welfare work and education reform, she might make a reasonable secretary of education.

Morris, who talked in staccato bursts with a nasally infused New York accent, responded that secretary of education might be a good idea, "but the better thing would be for her to assume a specific task, become the head of a task force that would deal with a discrete issue, which would be her issue, and develop her credibility like that. And she said, 'And then maybe in the second term I could become secretary of education?' And, I said, 'I think something like that might work out well.' "

He was one of several people with whom Hillary discussed the question of being chief of staff or, alternatively, her husband's principal deputy for domestic policy, in title and in fact. That idea, too, was opposed by Morris and by almost everyone else with whom she consulted.

In the end Hillary chose Morris's single-issue approach and settled on an issue of vital interest to the Clintons and America. She would oversee and shepherd through Congress what she hoped would be the single greatest change in domestic social policy since the New Deal, something that had been the unattainable goal of Democrats for decades. The lack of universal health care, or anything resembling it, was a defining failing that set the United States apart from other advanced democracies, and both Clintons were certain that an overwhelming majority of Americans favored universal coverage, even yearned for it. The promise to provide meaningful, affordable, guaranteed health care services to all Americans had been the most resonant pledge of the Clinton campaign, and polls showed that it was perhaps the biggest factor—apart from negative perceptions of President George H. W. Bush, and the third party candidacy of Ross Perot—in Bill Clinton's victory.

Health care was also, in the judgment of both Hillary and Bill, the ideal issue for her to focus her talents and energy upon. Though she had spent most of her professional career as a lawyer representing corporate clients, her more satisfying work (as opposed to remunerative) had been in the field of children's advocacy; and she'd had extensive experience in other aspects of social policy dealing with families and children and health care. The notion that she might be able to bring to the most vulnerable and embattled of American citizens what she and Bill believed ought to be a national right—decent medical care—was beyond enticing. It felt right.

And there was also an obvious political component to the equation, as she would remark to members of the White House staff before the Clinton administration was yet ten days old: fulfilling the campaign's health care promise could ensure the reelection of Bill Clinton in 1996, and a *real* mandate from the voters. With the Clintons' youth, Bill's charisma, her expertise, and the demand by so many Americans that medical costs be contained, how could they not sell such a program to the public and Congress, and at the same time launch the country toward a new era of responsible social policy?

As THE MEN and women picked by Bill and Hillary to guide his transition from candidate to president gathered in Little Rock, any doubts that she would be the new president's closest adviser and indispensable deputy—an entirely new kind of first lady—were quickly dispelled. She meant to be involved in the essential decisions of the transition, even to the occlusion at times of the vice president–elect: interviewing candidates for the cabinet (at the kitchen table of the governor's mansion, on occasion), presiding over the selection of White House staff, deciding how to follow through on the major themes of the campaign. Her primacy was abetted of course by proximity: she was with the president-elect after the others involved in the transition had gone back to their hotels, and in the morning before official meetings were convened. Of course, he could trust her judgment, but more than that, Hillary Clinton, her husband had said more than once, possessed the best mind he knew.

If the process seemed a little jarring to the transition's eminences—Vice President–elect Gore, former deputy secretary of state Warren Christopher, and the Clintons' good friend and transition co-chairman (with Christopher) Vernon Jordan—it was familiar to those who had lived through the Clintons' ride through Arkansas politics. Ernie Dumas, one of the state's preeminent political reporters, described the frustration of the governor's first chief of staff, Bobby Roberts, who "would talk about things [with Clinton], get them decided, and then . . . the governor would talk to Hillary and everything would be turned upside down." Deborah Sale noted, "He talks to her about everything, and thinks that no one else will listen to him as carefully and challenge his ideas as constructively." The process was not always pretty. "They don't do anything that isn't *strongly*," said Betsey Wright. "Whether it's agree or disagree, it's strongly. They are two of the most passionate people I ever met. They love passionately, they argue passionately, they parent passionately, they read passionately, they play passionately."

The Clinton transition occupied several floors of offices in Little Rock, as well as dozens of office cubicles in Washington. In both places, the chaotic pace of the campaign persisted, as members of myriad task forces rushed to produce hundreds upon hundreds of three-ring binders filled with more information than the intended recipients—the president-elect, his wife, and their advisers—could possibly digest. There were reams of data about virtually every issue the new administration would face—foreign, domestic, political. "Message teams" were assessing the new Congress and how best to approach it; "constituency teams" were analyzing the special concerns of and favors owed to labor unions, women, blacks, gays, blue-collar workers, mayors, and municipalities.

The selection of the cabinet, subcabinet, and senior White House staff was being made, and the new administration's agenda and priorities decided at the governor's mansion. The Clintons were joined Monday through Friday by the others directly involved at a round six-foot-wide table in the family room, just off the formal dining room. The atmosphere was somewhat less harried, though the time pressure was enormous: Bill had promised publicly, if needlessly, to announce his cabinet by Christmas Eve (almost a month before inauguration day), after which Hillary and her close friend Susan Thomases would proceed to staff the White House, with the president signing off on their choices—a process to be kept from the public.

To complicate matters, Bill was visibly exhausted, and confessed to being "bone-tired" after thirteen months of virtually nonstop campaigning. Hillary, fatigued but focused as ever, concentrated her attention on the areas of domestic policy that most concerned her: education, health care, jobs, child care—the issues of Putting People First that had dominated the Clinton campaign. She and the president-elect had agreed on the importance of selecting a diverse cabinet—one that "looks like America," he had pledged that spring at San Francisco's Cinco de Mayo celebration. ("I will give you an administration that looks like America. The people here will be involved—women and men, Latinos, African-Americans, Asian-Americans." Soon after, he said, "I would be astonished if my cabinet and my administration and my staff . . . is not the most fully integrated this country has ever seen.")

As the slots were filled, and responsibilities defined, the question of Hillary's formal position came to be more and more the focus of attention. Late in November, lawyers examining the question for the Clintons advised that the president's wife could indeed be his chief of staff or his domestic policy adviser, or could serve in any other position that did not require confirmation by the Senate. But she was prohibited from being in the cabinet under an anti-nepotism law enacted during the Nixon administration, a belated response to the appointment of Robert Kennedy as his brother's attorney general.

It did not augur well that such elemental information had not been evident or available immediately. Soon thereafter, Dick Morris expanded on his advice that Hillary head an issue task force. He suggested to her that she take charge of something akin to the Hoover Commission, which had been appointed to study government reorganization by President Harry Truman in 1947 and, two years later, had produced its transforming recommendations. Morris, however, never mentioned health care; it was Hillary who brought up the idea with him, noting that Bill was drawn to the idea of her being responsible for implementation of the campaign's key domestic promise.

Apart from selecting a secretary of the treasury and the other principals of the president's economic team, designating who would oversee the health care initiative was the major decision affecting the new administration's domestic agenda. Al Gore had indicated to the president-elect that this was the job he might most like to take on, drawing on his legislative skills from his years in the Senate and lending it the prestige of his new office. Clinton was intrigued by the idea, but he worried that the job would demand too much, perhaps almost all, of the vice president's time. Hillary had a different objection: she felt Gore, not she, would dominate domestic policy if responsible for health care. Clinton had also been thinking about Senator John D. "Jay" Rockefeller of West Virginia for the health care portfolio. As Democratic governors—Rockefeller had been governor from 1977 to 1985—they had grown close, and Rockefeller had studied the issue extensively. But the Democratic majority leader, George Mitchell, advised against putting a senator in charge of an executive branch task force.

A third, less politically charged name under consideration was that of Ira Magaziner, a mercurial Oxford classmate of Clinton's. The year before, at the high-toned, spiritually infused Renaissance Weekend attended by the Clintons almost every Christmas season, Magaziner had spoken passionately about his role in establishing a public health care system in Rhode Island. Afterward, Hillary and Bill had asked him to contribute ideas on the subject for the campaign, and Magaziner had responded with a series of briefing papers and memoranda that had impressed both of them.

Another Oxford classmate—and close friend—Robert Reich, had been chosen by the Clintons to oversee the assembly of the new administration's economic team. In the period between election day and the inauguration, the Clintons and Reich often convened privately in the cozy kitchen of the governor's mansion, away from the full presidential transition team, to discuss policy and personnel questions. These talks had an almost familial quality, which was hardly surprising: Bob and his wife, Clare (she, like Hillary, was a lawyer with great interest in the rights of children and poor families), had known Bill and Hillary since college.

Early in the transition, Hillary asked Reich if he thought Magaziner was the right person for the health care job. Reich emphatically said no. "If you really want him to do it," he warned her, "just get somebody to look over his shoulder all the time who's very politically cunning, because he has a tin ear when it comes to politics." Almost no one, least of all Reich, imagined that on this issue Hillary, with all her years backstage in politics, might have a tin ear as well.

NEAR THE END OF THE YEAR, only weeks before Bill Clinton was to take office, the nature of his presidency took an irrevocable, unexpected turn: the Bush administration's outgoing budget director, Richard Darman, revealed that the federal deficit was far more substantial than the White House had acknowledged during the campaign. While President George H. W. Bush and his aides had been claiming that the deficit was "only" $250 billion or so, it was in fact $387 billion. The resulting shortfall clouded Bill and Hillary's optimism about sweeping into Washington and expeditiously achieving the panoply of domestic programs and reforms promised in the campaign's platform. The whole complexion of the presidency-to-be was altered by what he—but not she—recognized almost immediately as economic necessity: postponing so many of their promises to the voters and instead cutting the federal deficit close to the bone, to the point even of producing a balanced budget. Health care would be the most important program threatened by the new numbers.

Clinton had never been comfortable in the campaign with any health care proposition that was put to him. It was not a lack of knowledge, necessarily; it was an uncertainty about what the solutions might be. After absorbing the shock of the deficit news, "He didn't think that he either had the time or the ability to figure health care out, given the circumstances," said a close friend, with whom both Clintons often spoke frankly.

Magaziner had always seemed to Bill cavalier about how large a portion of the federal budget might be consumed in any serious attempt to solve the health care dilemma. (Medical costs in the United States already absorbed 14 percent of GNP, the highest in the world.) Suddenly, he found himself beginning to regard health care as a monster, not just his administration's greatest domestic opportunity. It was in that context that he finally decided that Hillary was the right person to fill the job. And, of course, she wanted it.

In the Clintons' years together, there had evolved an intuitive methodology in which each deferred to the other in what they considered their respective areas of expertise and greater experience, though they often argued passionately about each other's views. "Economics and trade were the issues that he'd really been engaged with for a very, very long time, and [felt] he knew—he has a philosophy, and he had a plan, and he knew where he wanted to go," said Sale. The same could be said of Hillary in terms of health, education, and welfare issues, especially those most affecting families and children. But confronting the health care quandary—forty million adult Americans had no health insurance whatsoever—would require great skill and expertise both in social policy and economics.

Working within the structure of the Clintons' marriage—instead of the traditional bureaucratic structure of the executive branch—to forge solutions appealed not just to Hillary, but also to her husband. If she were in charge of the issue, the Clintons could maintain an uninterrupted dialogue about its shifting political dynamics and make rapid adjustments in ways no bureaucracy could—as they had done in Arkansas, when he had entrusted her to solve the volatile question of education reform. Moreover, putting her in charge of health care—a specific project, with specific responsibilities, albeit great visibility—seemed to address the question (already of tantalizing interest to the press and to political opponents) of granting the president's wife too overarching or ambitious a formal title, say, assistant to the president for domestic affairs. And it would avoid the appearance of a "co-presidency," an idea from which he had been forced to flee publicly since the blithe introduction of the campaign slogan, "Buy One, Get One Free."

MUCH LATER, when seeing was easy, more than a few of the administration's principals concluded that those first weeks after the election were when Hillary "made most of her big mistakes," as a senior presidential aide put it. Many of her miscalculations were a result of "overrating the win"—which had come with considerably less than a majority of voters in the three-way race.

During the transition, said one of Bill's principal deputies in the campaign and White House, her combative posture often seemed to announce: "This is the victory for us, and our party, and our generation. And, so that means I'm going to get the job I want. I'm going to have that office in the West Wing. We're going to show the press who's in charge. All our friends are going to get jobs. And, it's not just friends, it's our ideological compatriots who are going to get jobs. This is our chance to do it all the way. And we've got to seize it."

The Clinton plurality seemed forgotten. "I mean, that was a fault we all had," said the deputy. "We all fell into it. But she had it pretty deep." Some friends who knew her well and newcomers to the Clinton entourage sensed in Hillary (though this was by no means a universally held view) an attitude of entitlement: that because of the rightness or even righteousness of what the Clintons were trying to do, Bill and Hillary could ignore some of the natural laws of politics, or the more reasonable protocols and traditions indigenous to Washington. As they came to feel ever more besieged in the White House, this aspect of her character seemed increasingly pronounced, to her great detriment.

Sometimes it appeared inseparable from an attitude of elitism sensed by her co-workers. A high official who worked closely for years with both the president and his wife said, "It's as if she thinks that there are some unpleasant compromises one makes when given the responsibility— perhaps by God—of leading the lesser lights to the Promised Land. . . . She thinks she should be telling the 'little people' how to live. Some people react so strongly to her because they sense it about her. Even in the way she gives a speech. She talks sometimes as if she's explaining something to a third grade class."

To their total surprise and consternation, among the jolts the Clintons endured in the flush of their victory was serious resistance to putting Hillary in charge of health care from the most experienced members of the incoming domestic and economic policy team: Senator Lloyd Bentsen of Texas, the treasury secretary–designate; Congressman Leon Panetta, to be the new director of the Office of Budget and Management; Alice Rivlin, formerly director of the Congressional Budget Office and the newly designated deputy OMB director; and Donna Shalala, chancellor of the University of Wisconsin, who had been handpicked by Hillary to be secretary of health and human services. Even a decade and a half after Hillary's health care debacle, it remained secret that the president's senior-most appointees had seen trouble coming from the beginning and opposed her for the job. "Mostly, [these] people thought the idea—the whole system Hillary was setting up—was crazy," said Shalala, a good friend of the Clintons who had been assistant secretary of housing and urban development in the Carter administration.

The foremost concern was that Hillary's ideas for solving the health care problem, already reflected in the Putting People First agenda, were too ambitious. There was also fear she would become a lightning rod for anti-Clinton sentiment in the Congress and the country. Her internal critics felt that, almost single-handedly, because of her outsized influence with the president, she could set the whole American economy off-course. Hillary discounted and, according to Shalala, even resented the advice of the naysayers. To accept their judgment would have meant to controvert her most basic notion about herself: that given the responsibility and the power, she could solve virtually any problem she applied herself to by dint of sheer force of will, intellect, study, and hard work.

Bill seemed troubled by the internal opposition, however. He kept delaying his announcement of his wife's appointment. It would be five days after his inauguration when he finally made it.

"I suspect that there was a level at which he knew it was a really dangerous idea," said a presidential deputy who was in and out of Little Rock during the transition. "He was president in no small measure because she stood by him in the Gennifer Flowers mess. And he had to pay her back. This is what she wanted, and he couldn't figure out how not to give it to her. And so he hoped for the best, and jumped over the side with her."

Even before she settled on the health care job, Hillary was insistent on having an office not in the "social" East Wing of the White House, where other first ladies had traditionally claimed space, but in the West Wing, the demonstrable seat of power. The most influential, and foreboding, voice opposed to giving her a West Wing office was that of their closest Washington friend, Vernon Jordan, who in early December turned down

Bill's pleas to serve as attorney general. Because of Jordan's bona fides with both Bill and Hillary, and his savvy in the ways of the capital, it was impossible to ignore his arguments. His view had nothing to do with self-interest or ulterior motive, nor did it reflect disapproval of Hillary, to whom he and (even more so) his wife felt especially close. Jordan—handsome, imposing, the former president of the National Urban League, and as well connected an operator as there was in Washington—believed that the press, Republicans in Congress, and the Clintons' ideologically driven enemies, already gathering, would pounce on any evidence (or even suggestion) of an unelected co-presidency; and they would feast on an announcement that Hillary was to have an office a few feet down the hall from the president's.

Other senior aides also warned that an overt demonstration of Hillary's primacy—whether in the form of a West Wing office or the health care portfolio—would divert public attention from the administration's agenda, and rekindle tales of Hillary as the evil power behind the throne.

Through her surrogates—which was often her preferred mode of battle—Hillary fought back. During the transition, a discerning eye or ear could pick up subtle indications of essential ways in which the politics and personalities of the two Clintons differed. His instinctive tendency, for instance, to accomplish his goals through compromise and accommodation was set against her reflexive urge to stand her ground on principle and fight, even more so after the experience of the campaign. He was always looking for a way to win over opponents before taking up arms. Her approach was more frontal and confrontational, which sometimes undermined the larger plan of battle—but she could also be deadly and on the mark. This difference would have dire consequences for his presidency and her role in it.

Susan Thomases, the woman she and Bill had chosen to organize the staffing of the White House, and Margaret "Maggie" Williams, Hillary's formidable chief of staff–designate, argued strenuously to Jordan and others that the symbolic importance of a West Wing office for the first lady would send an essential signal about the values and priorities of the new administration.

To the surprise of no one who knew Bill and Hillary well, he sided with his wife. If it were up to him, the president-elect told the press later, he might knock down a wall in the Oval Office and have adjoining his-and-hers offices. "I don't know that anybody's office has been fixed except mine," he said. "That's true. We're keeping looking at that. I wish—the office structure in the White House is not the best. We're trying to figure out what to do about that. They won't let us knock down any walls."

· · ·

DURING THE TRANSITION period in Little Rock, others directly involved in the process of selecting the cabinet and the senior White House staff were Al Gore; Gore's designated chief of staff, Roy Neel; Bill's closest personal aide and offstage facilitator, Bruce Lindsey; Mack McLarty, who had known the president-elect since they'd been in kindergarten together in Hope; and the transition panel's co-chairmen, Vernon Jordan and Warren Christopher. As a group, they could not help but be impressed by Hillary's knowledge of policy issues, which often exceeded their own. Her enthusiasm for what lay ahead was palpable. If she felt any fear or trepidation, she did not betray it. She was well prepared for the topics of the day, her questions revealing familiarity with even the most arcane matters of governance, as when she conducted an interrogation of candidates for secretary of commerce and asked about policies in one of the Commerce Department's least understood bureaus, the U.S. Patent Office.

Usually she was tactful at the table when it came to demonstrating her power. But even before the Clintons had moved into the White House, new members of the administration had caught glimpses of her tendency to overreach through surrogates—more often than not Susan Thomases—without revealing her own hand if things got sticky. In Little Rock, Thomases was said to be talking up a future Hillary Clinton presidential campaign, and some newer members of the Clinton entourage, among them Neel, came to regard her as meddlesome, stubborn, and politically tone-deaf. She was also extremely able, had a quick and easy wit, and was one of the best campaign schedulers in the business, drawing on skills refined in the presidential campaigns of Eugene McCarthy, Walter Mondale, Bill Bradley, and Ted Kennedy.

In December, Thomases went to Washington to tour the White House and obtain floor plans of the West Wing and the Executive Office Building. Upon her return, according to Neel, she announced that Hillary might occupy the suite of offices in the West Wing that, in previous administrations, had been used by the vice president and his staff.

"I told Susan that under no circumstances would that happen, and if she didn't like it she could take it up in person with the president-elect and the vice president–elect," Neel recalled. Thomases said Neel's memory was mistaken and that she and Hillary were simply seeking any space in the always overcrowded, surprisingly tiny West Wing. But the new vice president, and others who had worked less closely with the Clintons, regarded Thomases's involvement as an example of how Hillary's methodology could insulate her from actions bound to rile the sensibilities of presidential aides and outsiders alike. The incident registered negatively with Gore, who began to regard Hillary with more than a soupçon of suspicion and distrust.

In announcing his senior cabinet choices just before Christmas, Bill Clinton made little effort to play down the role of his wife—a lawyer with more Washington experience than he. Fourteen of twenty cabinet-level appointees were lawyers, despite Clinton's campaign pledge to select "a cabinet that looks like America." He did not, however, reveal the offstage process that preceded their selection: interviews first with members of the transition team, then with the president-elect (and sometimes Gore, if he hadn't already been present for the initial session), and finally one-on-one in the kitchen of the governor's mansion with Hillary. He made no bones about her role. He was properly proud of her. "She advised me on these decisions, as she has on every other decision I've made in the last twenty years," he said. However, he did not yet want to publicly discuss in detail how Hillary would define her tasks as first lady, and what job she might take. Even with his staff he remained coy about it. "I'm not prepared to define her role in the White House yet," he said, "but I will before long." He did express his hope that she would attend cabinet meetings, observing, "She knows more about a lot of this stuff than most of us do."

ONE THING WAS CERTAIN: Hillary Clinton, in many respects a very private person, intended to keep it that way. That didn't mean she was shy. She had rarely been reticent about her political views or what she saw as matters of right and wrong—her values, she would say. However, she zealously protected herself (and her family) from almost any invasive inquiry that might reveal something of her emotional life, her deeper ambitions, or her machinations, especially after her marriage had become an issue during her husband's presidential campaign.

Her closest friends, professional colleagues, and staff members were fiercely loyal and reflexively protective, and would become more so once the Clintons were in the White House. Over the years, she had become extremely careful about what she revealed and to whom on matters that might be of interest to the press. Like many people in public life, the more that was written or rumored about her (inevitably, she believed, bound to be wrong or miscast) the harder she, her entourage, and her husband's handlers tried to control her public image. The book on her husband was voluminous, of course. For every month of his life, it seemed, there was some sort of documentation (including the famous photo of sixteen-year-old Bill shaking hands with John Kennedy), and there always appeared to be a friend, relative, classmate, or acolyte around to offer testimony. In fact, too much was known about Bill Clinton for his own good, down to the fact that (as he had revealed on television during the campaign) he wore boxer shorts, not briefs. Winston Churchill had once said that all great men have an air of mystery, and though the modern media had sorely tested the point, such an air had eluded Bill Clinton long before he reached the White House. Ronald Reagan possessed more mystery after eight years as president than when he was elected. Hillary wanted to maintain that aura of mystery. The Hillary narrative she wished to maintain, from the vantage points of the press and a celebrity-hungry public, was that of a powerful, perhaps transforming figure in the new presidency.

The most vocal internal opponent of putting Hillary in charge of health care was Donna Shalala, who (like Vernon Jordan) knew Hillary far better than most new members of the president's team, and so felt freer about speaking out. Shalala continued to warn both Clintons that Hillary would become a magnet for every kind of criticism, however unrelated to the merits of their health care proposals. If the health care effort failed in Congress, he and Hillary would be personally blamed— and he would not be able to distance himself from the ensuing firestorm of criticism and political fallout. Moreover, she was the only person he couldn't fire. Better, suggested Shalala, that the first lady work behind the scenes in conceiving the Clinton health care plan and campaign vigorously for its implementation.

Shalala, four feet eleven inches tall, of Lebanese descent, an ardent feminist with both academic experience and sharp political skills, had known Hillary almost twenty years, since they'd first served together on the board of the Children's Defense Fund. And though she and the new first lady were friends, Shalala was certain that Hillary was ill-prepared for the job. There was too much mythology about Hillary that stretched the facts, she felt. Shalala had always been made uncomfortable by hyperbolic statements from friends and acolytes of Hillary, as well as leaders in the women's movement who didn't know her personally, who put forth the notion that had she pursued her own political career and not deferred to Bill Clinton's, she would have been a governor or senator in her own right by 1992. "They assume that [just] being smart is enough," Shalala said. "And it's not enough. It's judgment. It's experience. It's being strategic at the right points." Hillary had never run a large enterprise. Shalala believed that Hillary often tried to do too many things at once—and later, as her personal and legal troubles accumulated, became distracted. "She's also someone who doesn't do things in depth. Because Hillary's so smart and well educated, I think people missed the fact [that] she has essentially been his supporter, and his support partner. . . . She hadn't really fully developed an identity until she came up here [to Washington]. She also had a job, but it wasn't with one of the New York law firms with big, high-profile cases. She's clearly smart, and clearly could have been a partner in a New York firm, had she chosen that path."

Shalala also noted that, in Little Rock, the Clintons "had always been big fish in a little pond." Until they got to Washington in 1993, they "had never actually banged up against people as smart as they were. They'd spent all of their adult lives in which they were the smartest people in the room. These were two extremely able people who had not really been tested before. So they really had to learn their way."

Panetta, Rivlin, and Bentsen, as relative strangers to the Clintons, though no less troubled, had to be more concerned about offending the new first lady. Gently, they took their worries directly to the president-elect. It became clear to them that Bill didn't want to disappoint his wife on an issue that obviously meant so much to her. Nonetheless, they all made known their belief that it was a mistake for the president to appoint his wife to run his most important initiative (which was also likely to be the most costly domestic program in the history of the republic), one on which so much of his presidency would be riding.

"That was the argument that everybody gave him when he decided to do it. But Bill and Hillary had already made up their minds," Shalala said. "I basically said to the president that we had to have a process that was open and participatory. And he said, 'We will. Ira [Magaziner]'s going to run it day to day.' I said, 'You can't run a major policy like this out of the White House. You've got to have some insulation from it, in case it falls on its face.' "

The opposition that gave Clinton the most pause was that of Lloyd Bentsen. Bill had an almost filial respect for Bentsen, a tall, patrician Texan who had served in the Senate for twenty-two years, had chaired its Finance Committee, and had run for vice president in 1988 on the ticket with Michael Dukakis. Bentsen, a conservative Democrat who commanded unusual admiration in the capital from both parties, had a keen political sense and, at age seventy-one, no ambitions beyond being secretary of the treasury.

Like Bob Reich, Shalala was particularly concerned as well about the Clintons' general disdain for old Washington hands, and by their decision to include few of them in the new administration. Reich kept telling them that they would need more Washington experience in the White House and prodded them to consider D.C. insiders who might move into senior positions and help them negotiate the tricky culture of the capital. But more than Bill, it was Hillary, reinforced by Susan Thomases, who adamantly insisted that as many senior positions as possible be bestowed on friends and aides who had been with them through the Arkansas years, as well as loyalists from the campaign. Only as a last resort would such posts be offered to members of Congress or other Washington insiders who had not been actively in their corner, particularly if they had been close to Jimmy Carter. The Clintons had never forgiven Carter for overwhelming Fort Chaffee with Fidel Castro's outcasts.

In choosing a White House chief of staff, Hillary, Bill, and Thomases all wanted not a Washington eminence (who could conceivably create a separate base of power within the administration), but someone with whom the new president and first lady would find almost familial comfort. Their choice was Thomas F. "Mack" McLarty, CEO and chairman of the board of the Arkla natural gas company, Bill's childhood friend from Hope. McLarty was more than sufficiently close to Hillary to ensure an easy line of communication with the new first lady and her staff. Later, Bill observed, "I spent so much time on [selecting] the cabinet that I hardly spent any time on the White House staff. . . . The real problem with the staff was that most of them came out of the campaign or Arkansas, and had no experience in working in the White House or dealing with Washington's political culture."

BUT THE CLINTONS' desire to do things differently in Washington was also born of many good intentions and some sound reasoning. Whatever their shortcomings, Hillary and Bill understood that the culture of the capital was often inhospitable to serious political ideas in ways it had never been in the days of Roosevelt, Kennedy, or even Nixon. Washington had changed radically. It had become a money town, a power town, a town where appearance routinely eclipsed substance, and idealism was considered weakness. "Washington is largely indifferent to truth," wrote *New York Times* columnist Leslie Gelb before escaping the capital to head the Council of Foreign Relations in 1993, in Manhattan. "Truth has been reduced to a conflict of press releases and a contest of handlers. Truth is judged not by evidence, but by theatrical performances. Truth is fear, fear of opinion polls, fear of special interests, fear of judging others for fear of being judged, fear of losing power and prestige. Truth has become the acceptance of untruths." During the campaign, the Clintons had seemed to understand this, or at least that the voters apprehended this. The new president and his wife had therefore pledged that the Clinton administration, in addition to promoting serious policies, would be the most open and ethical in history, and that they would restore honesty and candor to the political process. In her campaign speeches, Hillary had stressed the point repeatedly, heaping scorn upon the ethics that dominated during the Reagan-Bush years.

Since the days of her work on Watergate, a whole new city had grown up along K Street north of Pennsylvania Avenue, stretching from fashionable Georgetown to political downtown—gleaming office buildings that housed more than 100,000 lobbyists, regulatory lawyers, public policy advocates, and their attendant pollsters, PR people, and legions of so-called grassroots guys who were paid millions of dollars by corporations and trade associations and unions to "spontaneously" organize the folks back home so that their congressmen wouldn't be tempted to controvert the will of their biggest contributors. Part of this lobbying boom had been fueled by loopholes in campaign finance reform laws passed in the wake of Watergate, which had allowed hundreds of millions of dollars in campaign contributions to be spread around the Congress, mostly by corporations. In Franklin Roosevelt's time there were only a dozen lobbyists in town; when Ronald Reagan was inaugurated there were still fewer than one thousand. Capitol Hill, by the time of Clinton's election, danced enthusiastically to the tune of the ten thousand lobbyists clustered around K Street, a gigue that owed almost nothing to either tradition, protocol, or decent government. The coarseness had its effect on debate in the House and Senate, which often sounded more like talk radio than deliberative government.

"The concept of service has little political currency in Washington," wrote political journalist Sidney Blumenthal in *The New Yorker* as the Clintons were getting ready to settle in. "Everybody is fair game, simply for being on the other side. Humiliating one's prey, not merely defeating one's foes, is central to the process. The press is hardly an impartial referee; rather, it is often caught up in a blundered game of chase."

Whatever Blumenthal lacked in irony he was on the money about much of the Washington press corps and the culture of the city they covered. His was a message that Hillary could embrace, along with its author, who would decamp soon enough from the magazine to become her amanuensis.

HILLARY AND HER MENTOR on the Nixon impeachment staff, Bernie Nussbaum, had stayed in touch since 1974, as her young husband moved up the political ladder. Nussbaum had become a leading New York City lawyer specializing in corporate takeovers. In 1988, she had asked him to get ready to raise funds in New York for a presidential race. When her husband had finally made the run four years later, Nussbaum had helped organize some fund-raisers among lawyers in Manhattan. During the transition he had presided over a team of attorneys dealing with Justice Department policies.

Less than two weeks before the inauguration, Susan Thomases phoned Nussbaum in Puerto Rico, where he was vacationing. She asked if, given a choice, would he rather be counsel to the president or deputy attorney general.

Counsel to the president, he said without hesitation.

Thomases told him to be in Little Rock the next morning, January 8, to meet with the Clintons. Upon his arrival, Nussbaum met with Thomases and Harold Ickes. The job was his. They immediately introduced him to the man who had already been named deputy counsel to the president, Vince Foster. It was clear to Nussbaum that the choice of a deputy was being imposed on him, and that in a sense Foster was looking him over, vetting *him*. Then he went to see Hillary.

Watergate had been the crucible of Nussbaum's experience in government, and over the next fifteen years, he had watched, somewhat bewildered, as each of Nixon's successors became debilitated by legal difficulties: Carter in the Bert Lance affair; Reagan in Iran-contra, which then went on to taint Bush; even Ford in Nixon's pardon.

Now Nussbaum cautioned Hillary that since Watergate a new culture had taken hold in Washington, a culture of investigation, suspicion, and exposure that drove the media, but also the congressional opposition. The culture of the town had turned mean, and nobody was immune. FDR, Ike, JFK, Johnson—they'd all have been easy prey in today's atmosphere in which every aspect of a president's private or public life was fair game. Any legal problem, no matter how small, had to be dealt with quickly and effectively, before it did the kind of irreparable damage that Clinton's immediate predecessors had suffered.

Nussbaum was convinced that the counsel must be the president's boldest and most determined advocate, serving him only. The counsel had to use every legal means to contain the small problems that could balloon into the kinds of scandals that had undermined Carter and Bush, and brought even the most popular president since Ike, Ronald Reagan, to the brink of impeachment. The independent counsel was still investigating Reagan after he was back on his ranch in California, and Bush's role in Iran-contra was part of the investigation, too.

"I'm looking for you to keep me out of trouble," Clinton told Nussbaum—any kind of trouble, wherever it was coming from. The president's counsel was his early warning system, his first line of defense.

Clinton also asked Nussbaum what his impressions were of his deputy-to-be, Vince Foster.

Nussbaum said he'd liked him and could see how serious and professional he was.

"He's a great guy," said Clinton.

Nussbaum liked the idea that Foster was a close friend of both Bill and Hillary. He regarded Foster as his partner in a new law firm. Foster concurred. "We'll build a great little law firm," he said. From the outset, it was clear that Nussbaum would report directly to the president, and that Foster saw his primary job as being Hillary's lawyer, representing her private and public concerns.

Given the investigative atmosphere of which he had warned, Nussbaum suggested that he and Foster examine each other's potential vulnerabilities.

"What's the worst thing they can say about you?" asked Nussbaum.

"Some people claim I had an affair with Hillary," replied Foster.

"Is it true?"

"No, it's not true," said Foster.

Several days later, Bill called Webb Hubbell and asked him to help prepare the new administration's takeover of the Justice Department. Zoë Baird, a Warren Christopher protégée, the woman Hillary and Thomases had agreed should be the new attorney general ("the last woman standing," joked other members of the transition team), needed help in organizing the department, Bill said. He wasn't sure yet exactly what job Hubbell would eventually get at Justice, but there was no hesitation on Hubbell's part about joining the team.

Before leaving for Washington, he wanted to remove several cardboard file boxes from his office at the Rose Law Firm. They contained records he and Foster had put together on Whitewater—including the law firm's files relating to the land deal—and other materials assembled by Betsey Wright and Diane Blair. Hubbell later said he assumed the papers, which were left behind when he went to Washington, would go to the Clintons' personal attorney, once that person was designated.

Hillary, Vince, and Webb—the Three Amigos—were to be reunited in Washington.

7

Inauguration

There is no training manual for First Ladies.

—*Living History*

I T I S R E M A R K A B L E how many of the contradictions of the Clinton presidency and its two principals were on display at the new administration's difficult birthing: the faultless intentions, the reckless fund-raising, the seriousness, the infatuation with Hollywood, the idealism, the physical exhaustion, the sensitivity to matters of race, the boomer sensibility, the surprising naïveté, the intense religiosity of the new president and first lady, their folksy grandiosity, her disregard for the rituals of Washington and disdain for the press, the rivalry between Hillary and Al Gore, her sense of entitlement and the shading of the truth, her protective instincts toward her husband, her confusing relationship to feminism, her occasional tin ear, her lack of sophistication, her misreading of the voters' health care mandate, the propensity of their enemies to hammer them for conduct that other presidents and their wives had gotten away with routinely. Less visible was the first fraying of the disintegrating and doomed relationship between Vince Foster and Hillary.

The inauguration week was almost as much Hillary's show as her husband's—in conception, too—and marked her debut as story editor of the Clinton presidency. She and Bill had settled on five days of nonstop festivities, beginning with their arrival in the capital with the Gores by bus caravan. But it was Hillary, Susan Thomases, and Harry Thomason and Linda Bloodworth-Thomason who had perfected the neopopulist motifs and fine-tuned the symbolic references into a coherent tale of national redemption and renewed civic purpose. The last, triumphant stage of their long journey to governance resonated profoundly for Hillary—

from Monticello, Thomas Jefferson's plantation home overlooking the Shenandoah Valley, through rural Virginia, in exact reverse order of the route she had followed southward in August 1974 when she had left Washington upon Richard Nixon's resignation to join twenty-nine-year-old Bill Clinton in Arkansas. The final miles to the crowds awaiting them in the city took the procession down Lee Highway, lined on both sides by citizens who seemed more prayerful and hopeful than exuberant. Bundled against the January chill, many held signs blessing the new president and first lady and wishing them Godspeed. The Clintons, through the windows of their bus, could glimpse the icy Potomac stretching below the Arlington Heights. The cherry trees on the riverbank were bare as the motorcade crossed Memorial Bridge to Lincoln's temple, where tens of thousands of cheering, exultant supporters were waiting to proclaim the end of the Reagan-Bush era and the reclamation of the presidency by enlightened Democrats of a new generation.

Every public inaugural appearance thereafter swathed Hillary and Bill in the symbolism of their heroes and shone a light on the new first lady as his full partner. The week's events were choreographed to fix the attention of the American people on the historical legacy the Clintons saw their presidency as reviving and carrying forward into a new millennial age—Jefferson's (the great Democrat and libertarian), Lincoln's (hence the trip from Monticello to Lincoln's marbled Memorial on the Mall), John F. Kennedy's (hence Hillary and Bill's visit to his simple gravesite at Arlington National Cemetery the evening before the inauguration), and Martin Luther King's (whose birthday Clinton observed with an eloquent speech at Howard University).

Every opportunity was exploited to contrast the egalitarian values and youth of the Clintons with the privileged era of Reagan and Bush, a plutocratic epoch that Hillary, more than Bill, believed was now in final retreat; and to proclaim a transparency in government that would extinguish all vestiges of Nixonian secrecy and paranoia in the White House.

The tab for the week of celebration was fit for a pasha, running to more than $25 million, a record unsurpassed until George W. Bush's $40 million extravaganza in 2000. Most of it was financed by the same kind of special interest and corporate back-scratching that had long paid the bills for Republican presidential campaigns and inaugurations. The new Democratic president seemed to justify it because of the "new direction" of his leadership. The explanation, with its attendant sense of entitlement, sounded positively Hillaryesque.

Hillary thought the price in dollars was justified by the all-embracing message of every theme tent on the Mall, including Native American heritage, gay rights, country music, clog dancers, wood choppers, and unionized stevedores. In a sports arena in suburban Maryland, there was a star-suffused salute to the Clintons on inaugural eve. The gala, watched on television by a huge national audience, projected precisely how the Clintons wished to be perceived—as a brilliant, appealing, informal young president and his equally impressive, attractive wife, who was essential to the package, the two secure in marriage and unswerving purpose after a long and difficult journey in which their principled vision for the country never wavered. They sat onstage in two high-backed chairs through the whole production, smiling and interacting with a cast and script such that Washington had rarely seen. Barbra Streisand looked the new president in the eye and dedicated her signature song "Evergreen" to "You and Mrs. Clinton," adding: "We must put children first and we are so fortunate to have a first lady who has fought for and will continue to fight for the rights of children." The arena erupted. Fleetwood Mac, reunited for the occasion, flogged the chorale of the Clinton campaign, "Don't Stop (Thinking About Tomorrow)."

Observing events from high in the rafters, a reporter who had attended more than a few quadrennial rituals of presidential assumption jotted in his notebook, "remembering Kennedy Inaugural, a snowy day when America was mesmerized by another young President's wife.... This time the priority won't be redecorating WH or bringing Pablo Casals to play in the East Room. HRC wants to tend to affairs of state with husband, change the country, not just hairstyles, bring the values of women—liberated women?—to the national weal; this time, Yo-Yo Ma and Stevie Nicks in the East Room."

Meanwhile, Jack Nicholson recited the words of Abraham Lincoln. Aretha Franklin, swathed from neck to toe in furs, sang from *Les Misérables* about single motherhood. Bob Dylan mumbled, "We gazed upon the chimes of freedom flashing." Chuck Berry rang out "Reelin' and Rockin' " with "Set my watch and it was quarter to eight/You know Bill's gonna get the country straight." LL Cool J rapped, "Ninety-three! U-ni-tee!/Time to par-tee with Big Bill and Hillaree." Judy Collins sang "Amazing Grace." Yo-Yo Ma played Bach. Michael Jackson appeared in formal Jackson moonwalk military dress and white gloves, his eyes hidden behind dark glasses, and his pet monkey perched on gold epaulets. Inevitably, he led the house in singing "We Are the World."

The gala was produced by Harry Thomason and Linda Bloodworth-Thomason. Whatever the program's considerable excesses (Warren Beatty, just married, recited poetry about marriage and honeymoons, political and otherwise), there was also a sense of unstilted fun to the evening, a quality in almost constant decline in official Washington for many years.

Much of the week's focus was on Hillary, who remained reticent when questions were raised by reporters about the costs of all the partying in her and her husband's honor. A few days before the gala, she had been forced to instruct her brothers, Tony and Hughie, to cancel a series of self-aggrandizing parties they had dreamed up with help from delighted lobbyists to honor campaign aides and relatives of the Rodhams and the Clintons. The brothers had obtained $10,000 pledges from major corporations, always on the prowl for influence, to underwrite the events, the grandest of which was to have been a dinner-dance for one thousand guests, with ballroom-view tables on a balcony reserved for sponsors who could gaze upon the hoi polloi below. Ron Brown, the outgoing chairman of the Democratic Party and new secretary of commerce, was likewise compelled to scrap a dinner-dance in honor of himself that was to be financed by $10,000 donations from corporate invitees. The cancellations occurred only after the prospective sources of funding were disclosed in the press.

Tony and Hughie, said Lisa Caputo, Hillary's press secretary, had simply "made a mistake. . . . They didn't tell Hillary. They didn't tell the governor. They just didn't know any better" than to solicit corporate financing for a presidential-family party.

Hillary was fiercely protective of her younger brothers, who within months would be known throughout the West Wing as "the Monsters" for their embarrassing scrapes, strange attempts at policy intervention, and ethical imbroglios. Hughie and (more so) Tony represented a certain ironic yet harmonious continuity of the legacy of underachieving presidential brothers from Richard Nixon's to Jimmy Carter's: they were but presidential *brothers-in-law*, and yet, along with Bill's brother, Roger, filled their stereotypical Washington roles with typecast fealty.

"We're now dealing with appearance problems, and they [Tony and Hughie] didn't know the way it would appear," Hillary's incoming chief of staff, Maggie Williams, elaborated. "They didn't think they were doing anything more than trying to get a reception paid for. . . . They now understand that this was not the right way of going about it, and it's stopped."

The explanation was more forthright than the awkward attempts to explain how Hillary had come into possession of the beaded $14,000 designer gown that she was planning to wear to one of the inaugural balls. Asked who was paying the tab, Caputo initially described the dress as "a labor of love" by its creator, who considered it "a contribution to the Clinton-Gore efforts." However, after press accounts noted that this was news to the couturier, Caputo backtracked. "There had been a miscommunication about the gown," she said, adding that Hillary had intended to pay for it all along. A "check has already been cut." The first lady "has also returned, or will be returning, any clothes that were sent to her which she did not decide to wear" for inaugural week, Caputo added pre-emptively. The new administration hadn't yet reached the White House, and already Hillary, the first avowedly feminist first lady, found herself in the sort of situation, whether silly or symbolic depending on the judge, for which Nancy Reagan had had her wrists slapped by the press and Democrats.

THE CLINTONS ARRIVED back at Blair House from the gala at 2 A.M., January 20, ten hours before Bill was to take the oath of office. His inaugural address was still rambling to the point that his aides were as worried about its length as its substance. With Hillary, Chelsea, and Al Gore seated on folding chairs in a small reception room, Bill stood in front of a TelePrompTer and began reading. Hillary, as usual, was his most important audience and critic. She had been discussing with him the themes of his address for weeks, since he'd started writing it back in Little Rock. The tone it set for the new administration had to be just right, and the example of JFK's stirring edict to another generation—the last time a president in his forties had been inaugurated—was never far from mind.

When a film of Kennedy's inaugural address had been shown during the festivities on the Mall, the television cameras cut away to Clinton miming the words, "Ask not what your country can do for you, but what you can do for your country." Kennedy was forty-three when he became president; Jackie Kennedy was thirty-one. Clinton, at forty-six, was the second youngest in history; Hillary was forty-five.

"We must care for one another," Bill enunciated at one point in the rehearsal, ignoring the TelePrompTer and looking directly at his wife and daughter. Then he paused. "Or do I say, 'We must love one another'?" Hillary grimaced—which Chelsea imitated to everyone's amusement. "Too soft," Hillary told him. "It will remind people of Carter." Despite its still overlong duration, the speech as rehearsed with his family and aides between 2 and 5 A.M. was specific in its goals and ambitious in its sweep, its most resonant promises focusing on delivery of decent health care to all Americans; a reordering of economic priorities to jump-start the country's productive momentum; programs to restore economic fairness and increase opportunities for middle-class Americans; and a momentous change in Washington's political climate.

He recited—and, with Hillary, reworked slightly—an unequivocal pledge that the Clinton administration would be the most open and ethical in history, restoring honesty and candor to the political process.

The words on the TelePrompTer also pledged to initiate a new dawn of compassion—his term—to the presidency. Hillary nodded emphatically as he read the passage in its final form.

One of their most effective and heartfelt promises during the campaign had been to end the cronyism, favoritism, illegal fund-raising, frequent mendacity, and deliberate obfuscation of the Reagan-Bush years, exemplified in the waning days of George Bush's presidency by his Christmas pardon of former Secretary of Defense Caspar Weinberger for lying to Congress—and of five other officials implicated in the Iran-contra scandal. For more than a year, Bush and his lawyers had resisted demands of a special prosecutor to hand over the outgoing president's contemporaneous notes about Iran-contra. His pardon of the scandal's accused felons mooted the matter, rendering Bush's notes legally irrelevant and historically inaccessible, because there were no defendants left in the case to put on trial. Many Democrats and some Republican officials in the Justice Department believed it a case of the president, in effect, pardoning himself from possible prosecution, because Weinberger's indictment charged, in part, that he'd lied about the knowledge and active role of then Vice President Bush in Iran-contra.

Later, the Clintons, seared and scarred by the press and opposition party for their own ethical lapses, complained bitterly that from their first days in office they had been singled out and judged by harsher standards than any of their predecessors, and victimized by a consortium of enemies and an overzealous press. There is little question that they were treated more harshly, and often pursued with different standards and more relentlessly—during virtually the whole of their occupancy of the White House—than any president and his wife of the twentieth century. Moreover, the underlying assumptions of some of the basic charges and assertions that fueled the unceasing investigation—most notably those related to the so-called Whitewater matter, beginning with a series of stories in the *New York Times* and others covering similar ground in the *Washington Post*—were often contextually misleading, exaggerated in significance, and sometimes factually off-base.

Yet there also can be no question that the Clintons had invited unusual scrutiny by their impassioned promises of probity to voters in the campaign of 1992, and an unwavering inaugural theme—which would begin to tatter even before the festivities were finished—that stressed the ethical reform they said they were bringing to Washington. There was something of an implicit challenge in their manner, almost a calculated recklessness (it would seem in retrospect), not altogether unlike Gary Hart's challenge to reporters to learn for themselves if his claims to fidelity in his marriage were truthful.

Hillary and Bill had had plenty of foretastes—in their years in Arkansas and during the presidential campaign, of the vitriol and determination of their enemies. Certainly there was no indication by inauguration day of any surcease or disarmament by an embittered Republican army that, fearful of what was already being called Clintonism, and emboldened by allies from the religious right, was remobilizing for a holy war. And who should have known better than the new president's wife that Nixon's excesses and resignation had incubated a new investigative era, in both Congress and the press that, compared with the 1970s, seemed unrestrained and oblivious to contextual considerations? The 1992 presidential campaign had made clear that Hillary, as much as her husband, was a moving target for legions who wished them ill. At first glance, it would appear almost unfathomable that the Clintons did not better anticipate and inoculate themselves and their administration against such obvious dangers. To a large degree, any explanation for the disasters that befell them in Washington has to be considered not just in the virulence and cleverness of their enemies, but in the complex relationship between them and the need each perceived, for separate reasons, to protect their secrets.

FROM THE CLINTONS' point of view, the first public event of inauguration day, an 8 A.M. prayer service at the Metropolitan African Methodist Episcopal Zion Church, the capital's most prominent black congregation, was a matter of great importance, symbolic and literal. Among other factors, wall-to-wall television coverage of the inaugural would begin at the church, and video from the service would be rerun throughout the day. Black America had helped Bill Clinton win the election, turning out for him decisively at the polls. Since childhood his empathy for, understanding of, and easy camaraderie with blacks had been essential to his character, and these marked his identity as a politician and a human being. He and Hillary came to their commitment to racial equality from different backgrounds and environments, but intellectually, personally, and socially they had achieved an extraordinary comfort and ease with black people (and vice versa), all the more notable in an era when so many white professionals and politicians were finding it increasingly difficult to maintain close personal relationships with blacks, no matter how firm their commitment to racial justice.

Vernon Jordan, their closest counselor in Washington, was black. Of Hillary's closest friends, almost as many were black as white. Her mentor, Marian Wright Edelman, was black. The woman she had chosen to be her chief of staff, Maggie Williams, was black. Some of the most important jobs in the new administration were held by black men and women who had marched with Martin Luther King and participated in the great civil rights campaigns of the 1960s and 1970s.

King "was the most eloquent voice for freedom and justice in my lifetime," Clinton had said at Howard University the day before becoming president, to more than one thousand African-American officeholders specially invited to the inauguration. If any more contrast with his predecessors was needed, this gesture, unthinkable in the era just ending, provided it. When Clinton finished speaking, he clasped hands with the mayor of the District of Columbia and Hillary, and led the singing of "We Shall Overcome."

The themes of religion and justice were woven into the program of the interfaith prayer service. The red-brick church, dating from the 1860s, was located two blocks west of 14th Street NW, the main corridor of the capital that had burned in the week of rioting that began the night of Dr. King's murder.

TRADITION HOLDS that the new president and first lady be received on inauguration morning at the White House by the outgoing president and first lady, and that the two presidents ride together to the Capitol, a protocol that has made for difficult presidential changeovers, most notoriously the argumentative, shared limousine journey of Harry Truman and the successor he despised, Dwight Eisenhower. The Clintons arrived at the White House from Metropolitan AME Zion Church twenty-seven minutes behind schedule, accompanied by Harry Thomason and Linda Bloodworth-Thomason and Ron Brown. The Thomasons wanted an advance peek inside the Lincoln Bedroom, where they had been invited by the Clintons to spend the night.

Despite the harsh words and feelings of the campaign, the Bushes could not have been more gracious on this day. "Welcome to your new house," the defeated president told twelve-year-old Chelsea, who petted outgoing First Dog Millie, the putative author of a best-selling book that would pave the way for a best-seller by the incoming presidential pet, Socks, the Clinton family cat. "Good to see you; good luck," Bush told his successor, for whom he'd left a more personal note in the Oval Office wishing him well.

After coffee, the outgoing first lady led Hillary to the South Lawn, where dozens of photographers and reporters had been waiting. On November 19, during a White House tour arranged for the Clintons' post-victory trip to Washington, Hillary and Barbara Bush were swarmed by journalists. "Avoid this crowd like the plague. And if they quote you, make damn sure they heard you," advised Mrs. Bush.

"That's right, I know that feeling already," said Hillary, whose hostility toward the press needed no encouragement and, even at the hour of her husband's swearing-in, would get the new administration off to a horrific start with the men and women who would be covering the White House for the next four years.

The Clintons' belongings arrived at the White House in a moving van with Arkansas license tags that pulled into the East Driveway on Pennsylvania Avenue a few minutes before noon, as a procession of much larger trailers containing the Bushes' possessions was leaving through the West Gate. Like the Reagans before them, the Bushes had accumulated a glut of gifts while in the White House, and kept literally tons—a practice the Clintons would continue and for which they, far more than either of their two predecessor occupants, would be roundly criticized upon their leave-taking. Shortly before departing Arkansas, still in their kitchen in the governor's mansion, Hillary and Bill had indulged in a moment of giddy elation that was also, perhaps, a commentary: most of their belongings, she told Robert Reich, who was staying with them at the time, were already packed in boxes. The movers, she pointed out with a certain glee, would haul away the Bushes' possessions on inauguration morning. George and Barbara, she giggled, were moving out to make room for them. Hopefully, chimed in Bill, the Bushes would leave the chandeliers.

THE LINCOLN BEDROOM had been occupied the previous night by the Reverend Billy Graham, who, as the formal inaugural ceremonies got under way at the Capitol, prayed for the nation, its president, president-elect, and vice president–elect as well as their wives, whom he said "would share so much of the responsibility and burdens." Shortly after noon, Hillary stepped forward from her place in the front row to stand between her husband and the chief justice of the United States, William H. Rehnquist.

The view from the West Front of the Capitol atop Jenkins Hill is, on any day, arguably the most spectacular in all of Washington, an awesome testament of the nation's struggle to realize its ideals and achieve union and preserve freedom—with the Mall and Reflecting Pool stretching below to the Lincoln Memorial, and across the Potomac, the Iwo Jima Memorial and the aligned rows of graves at Arlington Cemetery and the cream-colored Palladian mansion of Robert E. Lee. Now that Hillary was standing at the parapet of the Capitol's West Terrace, she could see the immensity of the crowd below, more than a quarter of a million people jammed together on the Mall, and another 800,000 lining both sides of Pennsylvania Avenue between the Capitol and the White House, along the route of their inaugural parade.

Al Gore, the son of a senator, had been sworn in as vice president moments earlier by Justice Byron R. White, a last-minute replacement for the ailing Thurgood Marshall, the Supreme Court's first black justice, a hero to both Hillary and Bill. Custom dictated that the chief justice administer the oath of office to the president of the United States, but this chief justice in the view of the new president and his wife had done untold damage to the United States and to the Constitution that Clinton was about to swear to uphold and defend. When Marshall had argued before the Supreme Court on behalf of Negro schoolchildren in the case of *Brown v. Board of Education* in 1952, Rehnquist had been a law clerk to Justice Robert Jackson, and as Hillary and Bill were aware, wrote a legal memorandum urging the justice to uphold the legality of school segregation, which was finally outlawed in the Court's decision in the case in 1954. Rehnquist had also been head of "ballot security" for Republican presidential campaigns of the 1960s (which Hillary knew, from her work at the Watergate committee, was a euphemism for aggressive efforts to challenge black voter registration, as well as prevent voting fraud such as had occurred in her native Illinois in the 1960 election). Thurgood Marshall had struggled mightily to hold on to his seat on the Court past the inaugural of Bill Clinton, so that another justice in his image—not Rehnquist's or the justices appointed by Nixon and his Republican successors—could be appointed in his stead. He died four days later.

The Clintons intended to reshape the whole federal judiciary after a generation of Republican presidents had packed the courts with conservative judges. The new administration's assistant attorney general, in charge of picking and vetting judicial nominees, was Hillary's Wellesley classmate Eldie Acheson. Acheson had clerked for a federal district judge in Maine, and distinguished herself in private practice in Boston for nineteen years as a litigator in state and federal courts.

Now, as Rehnquist delivered the presidential oath of office, Hillary's right hand remained rock-steady as she held the Clinton family Bible beneath her husband's left hand and heard Bill respond to the chief justice in a strong, clear voice that he would "preserve, protect and defend the Constitution of the United States." Then an immense cheer resounded against the marble front of the Capitol, echoing again and again in waves. As the sound was still reverberating against the facade, Bill kissed Hillary on the cheek, then Chelsea, who had stood on the other side of her father during the oath, and scooped them up in a family hug, whispering, "I love you." Next, he hugged his own mother, dressed in white and black that matched the distinctive color scheme of her hair; hugged Gore and his wife, Tipper, then hugged mezzo-soprano Marilyn Horne and poet Maya Angelou, who had taken part in the ceremonies.

Hillary returned to her seat, still carrying the Bible handed down from Virginia's mother. During the oath, it had been opened to the passage, "For he that soweth to his flesh shall of the flesh reap corruption; but he that soweth to the Spirit shall of the Spirit reap life everlasting." Exactly how the Clintons arrived at this choice of scripture from Galatians to mark the inaugural moment is unknown, though it seems they intended the day's "lesson" to be focused on "corruption," not on "the flesh."

In his address, the new president declared, "This beautiful capital, like every capital since the dawn of civilization, is often a place of intrigue and calculation. Powerful people maneuver for position and worry endlessly about who is in and who is out, who is up and who is down, forgetting those people whose toil and sweat sends us here. . . . Let us resolve to reform our politics, so that power and privilege no longer should drown the voice of the people."

When the reverberations of the cheering and applause had at last abated, Bill and Hillary escorted George and Barbara Bush down the Capitol steps to the presidential helicopter, Marine One, which was waiting to whisk them away to an unexpectedly early retirement in Houston, and waved them goodbye.

Not in their worst nightmares could Hillary or Bill have imagined that in eight years, instead of being hailed for their service to the nation, they would be pilloried for what was being carted away in their moving vans at the other end of Pennsylvania Avenue; or, even more astounding, be sharing that same inaugural platform again with George and Barbara Bush—at the swearing-in of their son George W., who, having won the presidency by promising a new dawn of compassion and a higher standard of ethical behavior in Washington following the impeachment of Bill Clinton, would escort the Clintons off that same platform.

Perhaps most astonishing of all, as George W. nudged Bill Clinton off the platform on January 20, 2001, Hillary went inside the Capitol to join her fellow ninety-nine U.S. senators for lunch in the Senate Dining Room.

No INCOMING FIRST LADY since Jackie Kennedy had received the kind of frenzied attention Hillary was getting from the press and public.

The affection of the crowds along the inaugural parade route for her, as well as her husband, was palpable. Shrieks of "Hilllllarry!" and "We Want Hillary" grew louder as she waved from behind the bulletproof glass of the presidential limousine. Soon the chant became "Walk! Walk!" and, she, Chelsea, and the new president stepped from the limousine to walk the last two and a half blocks of the parade route. Hillary in this moment "seemed very much and most impressively her own woman, striding the parade route at her own pace, several yards out of the shadow of a husband who had to stretch to cling to her hand if there was hand-holding to be done," wrote a *Washington Post* reporter. Despite the chill of a crystal-clear winter afternoon, in a Kennedyesque gesture she left her coat behind in the limousine. But she chose not to remove the enormous cadet-blue hat that had caused consternation among the commentating classes all day—"a blue unidentified flying object that landed on Hillary Clinton's head," in the words of a newspaper fashion critic, who also confessed bafflement at "the tan tourniquet applied to her neck" (a cashmere turtleneck). All week, her longish blond hair loosely tousled, she had uncharacteristically put on a fashion show, seemingly with ease. Featuring outfits by American designers, she had changed clothes three or four times a day, often wearing dramatically flowing coats and scarves over brightly colored suits and dresses. Many of the outfits, including the one she chose for the swearing-in at the Capitol, were designed not by famous couturiers but by her fashion designer friend from Little Rock, Connie Fails.

If you look again at the tapes of that week, it is readily apparent how down-to-earth and unsophisticated this young first lady seems in contrast to the more familiar post-millennium Hillary, and how much more spontaneous her words and reactions appeared to be in January 1993. After what feels like a lifetime of the Clintons' lease on the national consciousness, it is also hard to recall the excitement and expectations surrounding her arrival—the first unretired working woman to be first lady, the first of modern feminism's sisters to live in the White House, the first presidential wife to be given an official portfolio. Though she and her husband had already acquired a formidable list of enemies, and though there was unquestionably something about Hillary that agitated the psyches of men and women disinclined to share her professed values, Americans were fascinated, and many captivated (a word fewer would use today) by this brainy, attractive, articulate woman who was very much of her time. Like Eleanor Roosevelt, her heroine who had also been marked by the vitriol of her enemies, she was determined to use every bit of her unprecedented dominion for the public good. That was the motivating fact of all she and her husband had struggled for. Of this she (and, for that matter he) had no doubt. Eleanor had been a woman ahead of her time, a time that harshly circumscribed her potential and her ability to act. Hillary was determined to locate and assert the remote reaches of her own potential. It would have been unthinkable in the first half of the twentieth century—Eleanor's time—that a first lady select members of the president's staff and cabinet, occupy an office in the West Wing of the White House, participate in her husband's policy meetings, or take charge of the planning of the most costly domestic policy initiative in history. Even in the last decade of the century, these were still daring assertions of authority for a first lady, and soon enough she would become an icon to millions and a hated target for millions of others because of it. Every major poll suggested that Hillary was entering the White House with considerable goodwill, though inauguration eve polls tend to reflect the rosy glow of the event itself. "Does she represent the values that you find important?" the *Los Angeles Times* had asked respondents across the country a few days before the swearing-in. Fifty percent had answered affirmatively. One-fourth said no, and one-fourth responded that they "didn't know." Meanwhile, 58 percent of those polled claimed to have formed a "favorable" impression of the new first lady, 19 percent held an "unfavorable" opinion of her, and 23 percent answered "don't know." And though most of those in the same survey expected Hillary to play a larger role in national affairs than other first ladies, their wariness also registered clearly:

Do you think the new First Lady should sit in on the President's Cabinet meetings?

> Should sit in: 24%
> Should not: 68%
> Don't know: 8%

Other polls by major news organizations recorded similar results, and one in *U.S. News & World Report* concluded that "most Americans object to Mrs. Clinton's plans to carve out an unprecedented role for herself." In every survey, health care reform remained at or near the top of the public's expectations for the Clinton years. Hillary and the president had decided to announce her portfolio a few days after the inauguration.

After their arrival at the heated reviewing stand in front of the White House, the Clintons proceeded to watch the inaugural parade for more than two hours, until dusk, laughing, clapping, waving, and giving thumbs-up signs to the marchers. With more than ten thousand participants, the parade was both a display of traditional pomp and celebration, and a preview of the values the Clintons hoped to inculcate in their America. It was meant to be a tribute to the diversity of the nation, and a tip of the hat, blue or otherwise, to those who had been ignored in previous inaugurals. There was a marching band whose members were all physically disabled; there were 120 men and women carrying an oversized section of the AIDS memorial quilt; there was a float celebrating American family life that included a lesbian couple and two gay men; another featured an Elvis impersonator (and members of the King's original band). As the twenty-two-unit Lesbian and Gay Bands of America passed the reviewing stand, the new president and vice president each held up three fingers—a sign-language salute to the marchers meaning "I love you." The Hope (Arkansas) High School Superband saluted their hometown president, and for Hillary, there was the Maine South High School Marching Band, from her alma mater in Park Ridge.

In the reviewing stand, with the Clintons, the Rodhams, and the Gores, were senior members of the incoming administration, including two who were already becoming nagging problems for a presidency not yet six hours old: attorney general–designate Zoë Baird, the highest-ranking woman ever named to a president's cabinet, whose nomination was in jeopardy because she had hired an illegal immigrant couple to work in her household; and General Colin L. Powell, chairman of the Joint Chiefs of Staff. Powell, a genuine national hero since presiding over the successful war in Iraq, who had served notice that he was adamantly opposed to his new commander-in-chief's plan to allow known homosexuals to serve in the military. Already Hillary and Bill were second-guessing their decision not to appoint Powell secretary of state, as Vernon Jordan had urged.

But such matters were for the future. It was time to relish the moment. Shortly after 6 p.m., holding hands and smiling, Bill and Hillary—accompanied by Chelsea, Virginia, and Roger, and members of the Rodham family—entered the White House for the first time as president and first lady. As they walked up the stairs to the North Portico and into the Grand Foyer, some one hundred members of the permanent White House staff, standing at the ready, were there to greet them.

The dream had come true.

Inside the White House, one of the first photographs the new president and first lady had passed on their way upstairs showed a young Jackie Kennedy, attired in her inaugural gown, adjusting the bow tie of her husband's tuxedo. On this evening, thirty-two years later, a White House photographer would snap a similar shot of Hillary adjusting Bill's tie, the picture soon to hang prominently in a hallway leading to the Solarium, with an inscription from Bill to Hillary, telling her how beautiful she looked. That night, the Clintons attended a dozen raucous inaugural balls, at which they were cheered by some seven thousand celebrants. "Does Hillary look great tonight or what?" Clinton asked, as the crowd at the New England ball shouted its approval. Dressed in a beaded blue-violet gown with sweeping over-skirt, she looked enraptured as she danced with her husband to the tune "You're the Biggest Part of Me." The most glamorous of the inaugural balls, in terms of invitational cachet, was the one sponsored by MTV. Packed with hundreds of celebrities of all ages from Macaulay Culkin to Jack Palance, it was a peculiarly Clintonian event: simultaneously unpretentious and over-the-top. At the Arkansas ball, jammed with twelve thousand people, rhythm 'n bluesman Ben E. King handed the president a tenor sax. Clinton wailed a couple of choruses of "Your Mama Don't Dance," while his own Mama (as *Ebony* put it) joined him onstage, and Hillary picked up a tambourine and banged along, though her lack of rhythm and inability to carry a tune were Rodham family lore. What struck many of those present was how fixated on each other Hillary and Bill seemed onstage.

Meanwhile, Chelsea and eight of her friends went on a history-heavy scavenger hunt that the curators and staff had organized at the White House, providing clues like "the painting with the yellow bird" (in the Red Room) and "where it is sometimes said a ghost has been seen" (the Lincoln Bedroom).

IT WAS AFTER 2 A.M. when they returned to the White House. The retinue there for the inauguration included Hillary's parents and brothers, Bill's mother and her husband, and his brother, Roger; Chelsea's friends from Arkansas; Harry Thomason and Linda Bloodworth-Thomason; and Jim and Diane Blair. Hillary and Bill had visited the second-floor living quarters before, as guests, but now, as president and first lady, they explored the premises with their friends. Bill said later he "was too excited to go to bed." The bulk of their belongings from Arkansas were books—more than there were available shelves for in the White House; bookshelves would have to be built—and Chelsea's things. The Clintons owned only a few pieces of furniture. The high ceilings and elegantly comfortable antique furnishings were nothing like what they had left behind in the governor's mansion. Patterned panels of fine Chinese silk wallpaper covered their new bedroom. Hillary decided that its sumptuous anteroom would become her sitting room. Like the living room and bedroom, it faced south, with a view of the manicured lawn and its century-old elm trees and Southern magnolia, still softly lit on this inaugural night, and beyond, the Ellipse and Washington Monument. A more inspiring sight would have been hard to come by. Abraham Lincoln had had his office at the far end of the hall, where the Thomasons were staying, and one of his handwritten copies of the Gettysburg Address lay on his desk.

It was almost three o'clock when Hillary and Bill finally got to bed. At 5:30 A.M., a presidential butler dressed in a tuxedo arrived carrying breakfast on a silver tray—to the total surprise of the Clintons. The Bushes had begun their day with breakfast in their bedroom at 5:30, but this was not the Clinton way. Bill, startled, sent the intruder on his way, according to Hillary.

In fact, this was the Clintons' first serious encounter with the so-called permanent staff of the White House—the ushers, chefs, phone operators, valets, butlers, and maids who serve from administration to administration, and whose loyalty, as the Clintons would discover to their chagrin, was often more affixed to their predecessors.

8

Settling In

I cared about the food I served our guests, and I also wanted to improve the delivery of health care.

—*Living History*

IT WOULD BE DIFFICULT to overstate the chaos of the first one hundred days of the Clinton presidency or the shock to the established political order that the Clintons and their exhausted retinue brought to Washington after a quarter-century in which Republican occupancy of the White House was a constant of capital life, interrupted only by Jimmy Carter's Watergate-driven interregnum from 1977 to 1981. Many of the mistakes of the hundred days had, unknowingly, been set in motion during the transition between election day and the inaugural, a result of preventing experienced Washington figures from joining the team and helping the Arkansans navigate the difficult terrain and culture of political and social Washington. The absence of enough seasoned native guides in crucial positions on the White House staff was, from the start, crippling, no matter how well intentioned.

Hillary, far more than Bill, brought an attitude of distrust and antipathy to the incestuous anthropology of political and social Washington, based in part on her perceptive recognition of its stultifying effects on governmental accomplishment for a generation. Democrats had controlled Congress through the Ford, Carter, Reagan, and Bush administrations, yet by almost any measure, four presidential terms had passed in which infrastructure, education, poverty programs, health policy, and natural resources had been allowed to stagnate. Meanwhile, a new class of powerful lobbyists held sway over the legislative process to the point where special interest legislation, tax breaks, subsidies, and set-asides overwhelmed the possibility of coherent lawmaking or effective funding to meet national needs.

From Hillary's perspective, Washington journalism was part of the problem, much too often a product of cozy, corrupting relationships between reporters or editors and many of the people they covered. The media seemed almost unwilling to deal seriously with ideas beyond the narrow agendas of powerful factions in the capital—partisan, ideological, or paid—and appeared at times more interested in generating controversy for its own sake than illuminating the serious business of governing. Reporters, she believed, were far more fixated and enthralled by turf fights and sensation than substantive debate. Her belief that the principal power players in media and politics wined and dined together to the detriment of thoughtful policy and new ideas was hardly off-base.

But the Clintons also brought with them to Washington a self-defeating chip on their shoulders, evident from the beginning. Carter's entourage had done something of the same thing, but in the Clintons' case it was far more extreme. Both presidents, of course, had been outsiders.

In these early days, Hillary ignored three essential truths: The first, long ago expressed to a young reporter by one of the capital's most articulate sages, held that "Washington is an easy lay—for power." This should have worked to the Clintons' great advantage. The second was a maxim from the business world that applied equally to the strange folkways of the nation's capital: it was a bad idea to take over another company without keeping some people on the payroll who really knew how the place worked, and bringing them into management. The third was that the capital had some first-rate minds and experienced professionals who were iconoclastic and tough enough to buck the system, especially if entrusted with important opportunities on the White House staff, or elsewhere in the administration. Such exceptional people could be found in the press, too, which was hardly the monolithic juggernaut the Clintons seemed to imagine.

"I wouldn't have gotten elected if it was up to Washington," Bill Clinton became fond of saying, and Hillary parroted the slogan. "So they sniffed and they decided the press was against them," said one capital insider, "that Washington was against them, and almost set out to alienate the two groups. More than anything, it was stupid, and she had it worse than he did." The assessment was correct.

Katharine Graham, publisher of the *Washington Post* and doyenne of social Washington, gave a dinner for the Clintons in December 1992 at which she and much of the capital's A-list—Republicans, Democrats, lobbyists, journalists, lawyers, diplomats—were captivated by Hillary and Bill. Other movers and shakers followed in Graham's wake. But the Clintons never extended a genuinely friendly hand afterward. They seemed determined to cultivate their "outsider" status, despite the fact that Bill represented the mainstream centrist element of his party, and Hillary brought more professional Washington experience to the White House than any first lady in history.

The president's facile one-liner about Washington was the kind of political cliché he usually rose above. Democrats in Congress represented official Washington as much as anybody else. As for the Washington press corps, and the reporters traveling with the candidates during the campaign, an overwhelming majority probably favored Clinton's election. Moreover, they were drawn to his personality, and Hillary's, too. Reporters craved good stories, and the best story of all, from the point of view of most, would have been the excitement of a Clinton presidency. This seemed to be a president with great potential. But the characters— and secrecy—of the Clintons were inseparable from the larger story.

As THE NEW ADMINISTRATION tried to get its footing, unusually green presidential staff in the White House immediately confronted a calamity of Hillary's making. On her orders, the corridor that for the past quarter-century had given reporters access to the West Wing was closed off, effectively locking the world's most important (and self-important) press corps in the White House cellar. Hillary had left to George Stephanopoulos, now the administration's communications director, the impossible assignment of explaining the new arrangements to some two hundred reporters accustomed to unfettered access to the press secretary's office—his office—on the first floor. And Stephanopoulos was to keep the origins of the new arrangements to himself. In neither task was he successful. Stephanopoulos regarded Hillary's plan as downright disastrous, with no upside. He knew that the longer they were confined the more dangerous they would become. As diplomatically as he could, he tried to get the president to abandon the scheme. On his first full day in office, Clinton asked Stephanopoulos—for the second time—why they had sealed off the corridor. Stephanopoulos said uncomfortably that the idea was Hillary's. "She says you wanted to be free to walk around without reporters looking over your shoulder." Clinton remained silent. Many years later, he described the plan as a terrible mistake, without mentioning that Hillary had formulated it.

Barring the door was only part of a larger blueprint devised by Hillary and by Susan Thomases, who was even more contemptuous of Washington folkways than her liege. Without difficulty, they had sold the idea to Mack McLarty, the already timorous chief of staff. Of all the men to hold the job since the presidency of Gerald Ford, McLarty, an immensely likable and well-intentioned corporate executive with virtually no Washington experience, may well have been the least equipped for the position. He regarded his assignment as enabling the unfettered implementation of the ideas and orders of the president and first lady—not to challenge Bill or Hillary, or postpone their directives for further consideration by others or, as some of his predecessors had done, wait for the boss to cool off and let a dumb idea die a natural death.

Stephanopoulos was certain McLarty would have put a stop to the counterproductive intrigue with the press had anyone other than Hillary introduced it. But in fact she had grander plans. Inspired by Barbara Bush's advice to show reporters who was boss from the outset, Hillary was planning to have them moved out of the White House altogether, as quickly as possible, relocating the press room in the Old Executive Office Building across the street. That would keep the press away from potentially talkative aides to the president. The secondary benefit of such a step was that the White House swimming pool (built for FDR, to help relieve the effects of his polio, and over which the current press room had been installed during the Nixon administration) could be reopened for the first family's use. Hillary had apparently forgotten Dick Morris's advice the last time she decided she and her family needed a swimming facility paid for with public funds, in the first days after the Clintons had moved to the governor's mansion in Little Rock. He'd told her to forget about it.

It would have been difficult to dream up a scheme that would more rapidly raise journalistic suspicion or alienate reporters covering the White House. In the next hundred days the Clinton presidency would be hammered in print and on TV as none of its modern predecessors had been, during what traditionally has been considered a honeymoon period between a new administration and the press.

Some of the reporting certainly accurately reflected the unprecedented disarray of the early Clinton presidency, but it also represented the peevishness and shallowness of some reporters assigned to the White House, many of whom went far beyond the facts. Perhaps a less antagonistic greeting from the new administration might have inclined reporters to treat the early stumbles more fairly and in context, including recognition in their coverage that a radical, historic overhaul of economic policy was under way.

One of the Clintons' senior-most aides described with blunt acuity how Hillary and Bill regarded the press in general, and reporters in particular: "Her ground zero assumption is that you're an asshole. His ground zero assumption is that you're an asshole, but he can charm you." For the next eight years, that pretty much summed up the approach of each. Their contempt for the press had been telegraphed at the inaugural gala, in a film segment produced by Linda Bloodworth-Thomason. In a series of quick clips, half a dozen of the country's most prominent reporters—including journalists from the *New York Times, Washington Post,* and *Los Angeles Times*—were held up to ridicule as, on the campaign trail, they minimized Bill Clinton's chances of ever being elected president. Years later, Harold Ickes, in many regards Hillary's most important adviser during the whole of her eight years in the White House, said:

> They really saw themselves as the White Knight and the White Queen coming in to do good, trying to put the economy back on track, trying to deal with people's fears, and economic circumstances. From their point of view, the press wanted to focus on— for lack of a better word—these "character" issues as manifested by "Gennifer," "I didn't inhale," the draft, and then subsequently into "Troopergate," Paula Jones, commodities, et cetera. It was just a continuum. They came in very sour and felt the press had really mistreated them. . . . But instead of reaching a hand out to the press, which they should have, and saying, Okay, we had a rough time in '92, we're here. We're going to be here for at least four years. You guys are going to be here. Let's make a truce, and at least have a decent working relationship—that olive branch was never extended [and] the press . . . continued to carp and they continued to get their backs up. Once they got to the White House, they thought there might be a surcease, and that the press would know that the gamesmanship of the campaign was over, the horse race was over, that the so-called legitimate press would then get down to the business of looking at the main issues of the day. That, they felt, never came to fruition, with rare exception. And they just finally gave up on it, and said, "Fuck 'em. They're out of here."

On her first morning after awakening in the White House, Hillary walked the short distance from the family quarters to her new office in the West Wing. Like all the working space of the presidential staff, it was cramped and incommodious, in this case even more so than most, low-ceilinged with barely room for a desk, some file cabinets, and a cubbyhole for her principal deputy. Symbolically, though, it loomed monumental.

Across West Executive Avenue, the little alleyway running between the White House and the Executive Office Building, the remainder of her staff—some twenty policy aides, press attachés, schedulers, secretaries, and personal assistants—set up shop in an imposing suite of rooms occupying a whole corridor of the ornate pile built in 1871 to house the state, war, and navy departments, long since departed from the building beloved by Washingtonians for its wedding-cake excess, and universally called The EOB. Within weeks, the first lady's EOB operation would be referred to by all in the administration's top ranks, including her own aides, as "Hillaryland," the same sobriquet that had attended her narrower dominion in the campaign.

Asked why the first lady was getting an office in the West Wing, Dee Dee Myers, the presidential press secretary, said, "Because the president wanted her to be there to work. She'll be working on a variety of domestic policy issues. She'll be there with other domestic policy advisers." Stephanopoulos had elaborated: she would supervise the drafting of a proposal to revamp the nation's health care system. That was the first hint to the public of her eventual responsibility for the entire initiative. Her own press secretary, noting that the first lady had ordered herself announced at the inaugural ceremonies as Hillary *Rodham* Clinton—as opposed to "Hillary Clinton" during the campaign—said the change would be permanent. Her new role, whatever it was ("breaking decades of tradition"), was the off-lead story in the next day's *New York Times*, and on front pages across America.

Hillary's transfiguration from campaign Svengali to cookie-baking mom, to the president's most trusted adviser, billeted in the West Wing, a few steps from the Oval Office, was moving apace.

THE OFFICIAL SCHEDULE for the Clintons' first full day in the White House, Thursday, January 21, was dominated by a chaotic open house to the public that, at times, threatened to spill out of control. The idea had been borrowed from Andrew Jackson's famous precedent of throwing open the doors of the Executive Mansion to the people on inauguration day. Now, four thousand Americans of almost every station—one thousand more people than expected—trooped through the Diplomatic Reception Room, where they offered the president and first lady handshakes, hugs, trinkets, and advice. They presented the Clintons with business cards, commemorative coins, personal artwork, and hometown souvenirs. They lingered in the Rose Garden. They strolled the lawns.

At about 1 P.M., Clinton abruptly left the reception to preside over his first meeting in the Oval Office. A few minutes after his arrival, Hillary joined him. Both looked exceedingly frazzled to the others present: Stephanopoulos, Nussbaum, and Howard Paster, the new administration's liaison to the Congress. Neither Bill nor Hillary had had a vacation in thirteen months, since the beginning of the campaign, and it showed. Clinton was seated behind what was probably the best known of presidential desks, brought from storage on his order, its top still bare. It had been used by Franklin Delano Roosevelt for his fireside chats, and become iconic in a famous *Life* magazine photo of John F. Kennedy Jr., age one, crawling out from underneath it while his father worked.

"So where are we with Zoë?" Clinton asked. Hillary, obviously the principal adviser in the room, stood to the side of the desk with a severe look on her face. At that very moment, at the other end of Pennsylvania Avenue, the attorney general–designate, Zoë Baird—selected by default, in haste, vetted more by Hillary than by him, though he'd certainly gone along with the choice—was being submitted to punishing questions from the members of the Senate Judiciary Committee, Democrats as well as Republicans, who almost uniformly professed themselves aghast that Baird could have been nominated in the first place since she had clearly broken the law.

Congressional grandstanding (always unattractive) aside, this was not an altogether unreasonable position, given the attorney general's role as the nation's chief law enforcement officer. Worse, before Baird was selected, she had told the chairman of the Clinton transition team, Warren Christopher, her mentor and godfather, that she had hired illegal immigrants, a Peruvian couple, as household help, and failed to pay Social Security taxes for them. She intended to testify, truthfully, that the president had also been informed. Hillary, too, had also learned of the potential problem.

Originally, Baird had been selected to be counsel to the president, a position not requiring Senate confirmation and in which she might have survived scrutiny. But with time pressures building during the transition, she had emerged as the only woman under serious consideration, after two others had turned down the opportunity to be attorney general, and another two (including Susan Thomases) were passed over. Baird, the forty-year-old counsel of Aetna Life and Casualty, the insurance giant, had been interviewed by both the president-elect and Hillary in Little Rock, impressing both, and brought with her impeccable recommendations from Christopher and a certified Washington wise man, Lloyd Cutler. Though other cabinet-level jobs had gone to women, there had never been a woman secretary of the oldest and most prestigious departments—Treasury, State, Justice, and Defense (formerly called War). And

Hillary had insisted that, with Lloyd Bentsen, Les Aspin, and Christopher getting the other three, the attorney general would be a woman.

The Clintons seemed shocked, even noncomprehending at first, by the rapid congressional furor and gathering public storm over the fact that, having pledged to end business as usual and restore ethical standards in Washington, they had chosen as attorney general a $500,000-a-year corporate lawyer who had evaded her taxes and broken the immigration laws. Howard Paster, formerly head of the giant Hill & Knowlton public relations and lobbying firm, had more Washington experience than anyone else in the room; he told them that the heart of Baird's testimony— that she was informed in Little Rock that her hiring practices were nothing to worry about—had ensured her defeat and was bleeding the new president barely after he had taken charge. He urged a quick withdrawal of her nomination.

Bernie Nussbaum had been explicitly chosen as counsel to the president by Hillary and Susan Thomases to aggressively protect Bill and Hillary from the capricious investigative climate of Washington. Nussbaum wanted the president to fight, arguing that capitulation would send Congress an unseemly signal of weakness on the administration's first full day in office.

"No, he can't do that," Hillary shot back. She didn't want Baird's continuing problems to become the administration's problems; she wanted no diversions from their agenda, particularly health care; better Zoë go quickly into the night, which was exactly what happened. At 1:30 that morning, Baird, recognizing that the tide was going against her and that neither Bill nor Hillary would try to save her, withdrew her name from nomination. But first she released a statement that she had been "forthright [with the president] about the circumstances surrounding my child care from the beginning." The new presidency was off to a rickety start.

The furor had initially been generated by Rush Limbaugh and other right-wing radio broadcast hosts who jumped on the Baird nomination, with justification. That Sunday on *Meet the Press*, the conservative columnist Robert Novak blamed the first lady for setting the debacle in motion. He contended that she had been more interested in finding a woman attorney general than appointing a legal scholar or a capable, qualified candidate whom her husband could trust. This, he insisted, reflected "the hidden hand of Hillary Clinton trying to play Bobby Kennedy at the Justice Department, but unable to get the job on a de jure basis because of the anti-nepotism law." The comparison to Kennedy was more apt than Novak might have imagined. Bobby was JFK's most trusted confidant, the person with whom he shared private information and expressed unvarnished views that others were not privy to. If there was a good cop/bad cop routine in the Clinton White House, Hillary, like RFK, most often emerged as the bad cop. Now, in the first week of the Clinton presidency, she had already been singled out as a target by malevolent (in her view) forces.

Nonetheless, Hillary retained the right of approval over the choice of attorney general. The process would assume farcical proportions by the time Janet Reno was finally nominated twenty days later. It was not lost on experienced Washington hands that the Clintons, both graduates of Yale Law School, whose closest friendships were with lawyers, were unable to find among them someone they could put forth as a qualified attorney general. Reno's name came to Bill's attention via an unsigned note left on his desk by Hillary, after she had spoken with her brother Hughie, a public defender in Dade County, Florida: What about Janet Reno, Florida D.A., for A.G.?, it suggested. The Clintons, anxious to fill the job, settled on Reno, someone they knew virtually nothing about, a state prosecutor who, it was condescendingly implied by Novak and others, had slithered up from Alligator Alley. In fact, Reno was a by-the-book prosecutor whose resistance to political pressure would seriously injure the Clintons.

Nussbaum was urging that, to take up the slack pending formal nomination and Senate confirmation of an attorney general, Webb Hubbell be appointed associate attorney general, the third-ranking job at Justice, and directed to oversee all but the Criminal Division, which reported to Philip B. Heyman, the highly regarded deputy attorney general. This, he felt, would give a sense of leadership to the department's career staff while the process of finding and confirming their boss went on—and would keep the department firmly under White House observation. Hubbell was already installed at Justice, and operating as a de facto chief. However, appointment as associate attorney general would require confirmation by the Senate.

Vince Foster was opposed to subjecting Hubbell to Senate confirmation. Already *The Wall Street Journal* had pronounced Hubbell a political hack, a "Clinton crony," who should either be "out of the corridors of justice [or] . . . in the light of day through nomination for a confirmable post."

Was there anything damaging in Hubbell's background or the Rose firm? Nussbaum asked Foster.

No, said Foster. Rather he feared "people will take shots at Webb to get at Hillary."

That possibility didn't disturb Nussbaum. "If there's nothing there, then he should be confirmed. Why not?" he asked.

Foster vaguely repeated his fear that the confirmation process would hurt Hillary. He seemed to know something that Nussbaum didn't.

AFTER THEIR FIRST full day in the White House, Bill and Hillary gathered with Chelsea, Virginia, and the Rodhams in the Solarium on the third floor for their first dinner in the Executive Mansion. Also at the table were Hugh Jr.'s wife, Maria, and Nicole Boxer, who had just begun dating, and in sixteen months would marry, Tony. Nicole, the daughter of Senator Barbara Boxer of California, was having dinner with the Clintons for the first of many times. Over the years she would become a reliable observer of the Clintons during their domestic downtime.

There was no talk at dinner that evening about the next four years, or matters of policy, or the Zoë Baird nomination. Hillary in all seriousness addressed her husband as Mr. President. They were beaming at each other, the depth of their affection for, and their pride in, each other obvious. The warm family atmosphere liberated the conversation. Away from the ceremony, protocol, and travail of the previous thirty hours, the Clintons, with the Rodhams, allowed themselves at last to celebrate: *This is really happening! Can you believe we are here?*

THE PROJECTED BUDGET deficit inherited from the Bush presidency was staggering, and projected to grow by a ruinous $68 billion more by 1997. Like it or not, Bill Clinton now felt a commitment to the kind of fiscal policies out of which Republican presidents had made rhetorical hay for two generations, while presidents of both parties allowed mountains of debt to pile up. This would contribute to the chaos that ensued.

Most of the platform that had been the foundation for Clinton's victory, which featured a full menu of social programs and reforms ("investments," in Clinton parlance, such as health care and a significant tax cut for the country's middle class), was instantly endangered. Ironically, in those first one hundred days, while the bottom sometimes seemed to be falling out of the new presidency, the course was actually set for a historic economic recovery and sustained boom.

The Clinton administration hardly did this alone. The end of the Cold War meant that, for at least a few years, defense expenditures would not continue to rise in double-digit percentages annually. Nor could the president or anyone else have predicted the extent of economic luck that would be bestowed upon the country during his tenure. Alan Greenspan, the chairman of the Federal Reserve Board, inherited by Clinton from the Bush administration, regulated interest rates with uncanny effect.

But Clinton alone among contemporary presidents grasped the powerful possibilities of the global economy, and what the explosive power of America's technical invention and new industries could do for the domestic economy, as evidenced in the technology-driven boom that marked his tenure. He had been preaching the message for years. In his first interview after the election, Clinton had told Ted Koppel of ABC that he was going to "focus like a laser beam on this economy," and he made good his promise. He became the first modern president to actually exercise, as opposed to merely talk about, the fiscal discipline necessary to cut, and even balance, the federal budget, though not altogether by choice.

He was constantly frustrated by the process and hampered by fiscal constraints unimagined during the campaign. He and Hillary had expected to preside immediately over an ambitious, modernized expansion of federal programs in almost every area of domestic policy, reversing the trend of the Reagan-Bush years. The Clinton model, as envisaged during the campaign, called for more government spending on domestic priorities but with far greater oversight and performance requirements than the so-called big government programs of the 1960s and 1970s. But the new deficit numbers meant forestalling almost all such reforms— except health care, and even that was endangered unless the nation's fiscal well-being could be restored. Both Bill and Hillary fumed and lashed out during meetings about the financial straitjacket restraining their plans. But deficit reduction, the president felt, was essential.

"I compare it to the importance of education in Arkansas," Hillary told Joe Klein* of *The New Yorker* in the waning days of the Clinton presidency. "He knew that deficit reduction was the predicate, that we couldn't have a credible activist government unless we could get the budget under control."

Contrary to the impression left by her remarks to Klein, Hillary's acceptance of her husband's economic program was forced and grudging at almost every step. She sensed, quite correctly, that it could endanger their planned initiatives, including her health care mandate, whose preeminence as the cornerstone of Clintonism would be diminished. She also feared that fiscal reform might eliminate whatever appetite Congress had for health care. "We didn't come here to spend all our time cutting

---

*Perhaps better than any other journalist, Klein managed to capture—in fiction— the appetites and contradictions of the Clintonian character, male and female, in his prescient novel *Primary Colors*, a thinly veiled account of the Clinton ascendancy, ending on election day 1992.

deficits created by Republicans," she would complain in one variant or another during White House meetings in the first months of her husband's presidency. She had to be convinced over and over again.

THOUGH HILLARY EVENTUALLY had to accede to the demands of her husband's budgetary decisions, her slowness in adapting carried some benefits: she served as a positive reference point, reminding him and others in the White House of the basic beliefs and principles she and Bill had held and honed since college; that there was a danger in straying too far, of forgetting or giving up as unattainable those programs that had propelled their pursuit of the presidency in the first place.

Clinton's economic team, unlike almost every other corner of the administration, could be regarded as Washington-seasoned and Wall Street establishment. Bill, with Hillary's assent, had asked Texas senator Lloyd Bentsen to be secretary of the Treasury and Leon Panetta, of California, the former chairman of the House Budget Committee, to be director of the Office of Management and Budget. Robert Rubin, who had stepped down as chairman of the investment banking giant Goldman Sachs to head Clinton's newly created National Economic Council, took it upon himself to tutor Hillary, with the president's obvious gratitude.

Rubin was taking the long view: he hoped that under his tutelage, she would show the same kind of political flexibility as her husband and, eventually, bend sufficiently to scale down her grand vision of health care to more manageable dimensions. He figured wrong.

"Rubin was terrified that she was going to drive the country over the cliff. He worried about it," said a top aide to Clinton. "Rubin figured out pretty early that he needed to be engaged in it [Hillary's management of the health care portfolio], and that whatever problems there were he would try to fix it with the people like Lloyd Bentsen, who also thought the same thing."

Not long after absorbing the implications of the alarming deficit numbers he had inherited, the president was told by Senator Bob Dole, the Republican majority leader who already aspired to oppose Clinton for the presidency in 1996, that not a single Republican in the Senate would support the budget and economic plan the president was developing. Thus the stage was already set for a partisan struggle that would absorb most of the policy energies of the Clinton presidency for almost a year, and—combined with relentless pursuit of the Clintons through investigations by Congress and the special prosecutor—would further poison Washington's political atmosphere for the rest of the century.

The question of how to deal with the deficit and with Hillary's health care initiative produced an enervating and sometimes bitter internal struggle, as most of Clinton's senior campaign strategists—James Carville, Paul Begala, Mandy Grunwald, and Gene Sperling, as well as Bob Reich—challenged the fiscal orthodoxy of the so-called deficit hawks on the economic team, and continued to push for a tax cut for the middle class, and for expedited consideration of most "investments" promised in Putting People First. No matter how Hillary parsed the numbers, they seemed to add up only to an abdication of what she and her husband had promised the people who'd put them in the White House. She couldn't shake that feeling.

Because she was the president's most influential adviser, her reservations ate at her husband's trust in his course. But his choice held firm. He told his aides he had to deal with budget deficits first, to get the economy going. Once he did that, he was confident the administration's underlying priorities could successfully be attended to.

But in the chaos of the administration's first days, neither the deficit discipline that would come, nor the economic successes that would follow, were yet tangible. And other, politically dubious priorities established by the new administration in its earliest days caused controversy both within the White House and outside, and captured the attention of the press.

ON THE FOURTH DAY of the Clinton presidency, January 23, the twentieth anniversary of *Roe v. Wade*, the Supreme Court decision that established a woman's constitutional right to choose abortion, Bill Clinton signed, in a televised Oval Office ceremony, a series of executive orders undoing the draconian policies of the Reagan-Bush era relating to abortion, contraception, and family planning. Until almost the eleventh hour, the Clintons' senior pollster from the campaign, Stan Greenberg, had tried to persuade the president to postpone the measures until much later in his tenure. Greenberg was extremely close to Hillary, who had pushed unequivocally for the orders, but she was dead wrong on the timing of such a hot-button issue, he had argued. He believed that by acting on abortion policy as one of the administration's first pieces of business, the president and, worse, Hillary would be perceived as governing from the left, moving away from the New Democrat identity of the campaign and endangering reelection to a second term in office. But Hillary regarded the prohibitions in question as a powerful symbol of Reagan-era policies, and an opportunity to declare boldly that the Clinton era had begun. There was an additional appeal: it was fiscally neutral, monetarily cost-free, and not subject to a drawn-out legislative process.

The policies to be undone were symbolically enormous and carefully designed by Clinton's predecessors for maximum effectiveness: Reagan, and then Bush, had ordered an absolute prohibition on abortion counseling at federally financed health clinics; outlawed the use of U.S. funds for international population programs that advocated abortion (including those of the United Nations) or for family planning clinics in the United States or abroad promoting contraception; forbidden American military hospitals abroad to perform privately funded abortions; and constrained the federal government from considering importation of the French abortion pill RU-486.

The Clintons believed the comprehensive prohibitions, especially in the case of George H. W. Bush, a onetime proponent of choice on abortion matters, had been promulgated more to offer political red meat to the right-wing Republican base and to entice Catholic voters than out of principled, personal opposition. The policies were sufficiently extreme that organizations like Planned Parenthood (of which Barbara Bush had once been a member) could not promote the use of condoms to fight the spread of AIDS in Africa unless all federal funds and tax breaks were rejected.

The milestone anniversary of *Roe v. Wade*, in Hillary's view, was the perfect opportunity to move the new presidency on course unambiguously in terms of women's rights, signal the religious right that its decade of dominance in regard to such personal questions was over, as was the uninterrupted ascendancy of the conservative movement. Once again, Hillary's misreading of the election's results, in which almost 60 percent of voters had cast ballots for a candidate other than Bill Clinton, would be eventful.

Yet Hillary's personal views of sexuality and the exercise of women's reproductive rights were far more complicated—and conservative—than perceived at the time. While some of her friends from Wellesley, Yale, and Arkansas had undergone abortions, and (in the era of sex, drugs, and rock and roll) had been promiscuous, she had not. The idea of choosing to abort a child she had conceived, except under the most extraordinary of circumstances, would have been totally out of character and at odds with her own values. One of the fortunate facts of her life was that she was of the generation whose sexuality was fashioned in large measure by the pill and its easy availability and efficacy. Her own difficulty in conceiving a child had only intensified her deeply held belief that abortion, for anyone, was a personal choice that should be made with the greatest reluctance.

Politically, the timing of the executive orders was fraught. Greenberg, a principal architect of the Clinton campaign in whom both Hillary and

Bill had great confidence, was distressed about the damage already incurred from the gathering controversy over gays in the military. Greenberg correctly perceived that congressional Republicans, especially Bob Dole—an honored World War II veteran with the use of only one arm as a result of battle injuries—were all too happy to mine the controversy. Dole was making loud noises (pandering ones, in Bill and Hillary's view) about removing the president's authority to act on the issue.

In the campaign, Bill had been attacked, near fatally, as a draft-dodger. Now he was instructing his secretary of defense to develop a plan that honored the campaign's promise to permit openly gay men and women to serve in the armed forces. On January 25, the outraged Joint Chiefs of Staff, led by their chairman, General Colin Powell, sought an "urgent meeting" with the president to discuss their objections, and in a remarkable show of disrespect for their new commander-in-chief, shared their "request" with the press. Senator Sam Nunn of Georgia, another powerful Southern Democrat, who was chairman of the Armed Services Committee and bitter at not being named secretary of defense by Clinton, intended to announce his adamant opposition to gays serving in the military.

Instead of demonstrating the White House's focus on the ailing economy and on health care, the Clintons were, by their fifth day in the White House, swamped in controversy over homosexuality, abortion, Hillary's hidden hand, situational ethics, and a perception that, now that they were in the White House, they were ready to reward a coalition from the party's left that had worked so hard for Bill Clinton's election and New Democrats be damned.

No office-holding politician had done more than Governor Bill Clinton to advance the intellectual and political agenda of the so-called New Democrats, and both Hillary and Bill had embraced the movement as a symbol of their independence from down-the-line, old Democratic Party views (especially in Congress) that they believed had kept the White House largely in Republican hands since 1968. The New Democrats' political philosophy had been nurtured in the 1980s by Clinton and others who embraced the traditional, compassionate themes and programs of perennial Democratic liberalism, but also accepted some unorthodox (for Democrats) notions: far more cooperation and partnership between government and business; rigorous fiscal oversight and restraint; welfare prevention and reform; fewer restrictions from Washington on how federal funds could be spent at local and state levels; acceptance and encouragement of an interdependent global economy. In 1990, Clinton had accepted the chairmanship of the Democratic Leadership Council, the dominant engine, philosophically and electorally, of New Democrat principles and strategies.

The Clinton presidential campaign was committed to building a centrist Democratic majority, to counteract the rightward shift and congressional gridlock of the past quarter century. The goal of the Clintons' politics and the New Democrats' was to reach out not just to the liberal base that had been the Democratic Party's intellectual and ideological foundation since FDR, but to more conservative "Reagan Democrats"— blue-collar workers and middle-class suburbanites, many of them Catholics, who had begun to abandon the Democrats in the Nixon years and had significantly helped put both Reagan and Bush in the White House.

But the Clintons' political ideologies and methodologies were actually far more complex than "New Democrat" or any other label could encompass. It was not always easy to grasp them.

"He's a hell of a lot more liberal than people understand," said one Democratic friend during the 1992–1993 transition. "But he's guileful and he moves crablike, with certain kinds of conservative cover. Part of [the Clintons'] initial attraction [to each other] was that they are both very political people, and there's not a terrific ideological difference between them."

"She is much harder-edged on issues, and he's much more accommodating on issues," Harold Ickes had concluded early in the Clinton presidency. "To her, the issue itself is more important, but getting it adopted either legislatively, and/or implemented, is also important, and he's always got a weather-eye over the shoulder about how it's playing politically. Principles with a Big P are probably more important to her than him. . . . He's taking other factors into account, and she won't necessarily." Hillary, he added, brought "a collective sort of hewing back to 'Why are we here? Why are we doing this?' " The same considerations led Bob Reich to put "a little bit more trust in her values. She held them [more] dear."

"My politics are a real mixture," Hillary told an interviewer early in 1993. "An amalgam. And I get so amused when these people try to characterize me: 'She is "this," therefore she believes the following twenty-five things.' Nobody's ever stopped to ask me or try to figure out the new sense of politics that Bill and a lot of us are trying to create. The labels are irrelevant. And yet, the political system and the reporting of it keep trying to force us back into the boxes because the boxes are so much easier to talk about. You don't have to think. You can just fall back on the old, discredited Republican versus Democrat, liberal versus conservative mind-sets." By the time she mounted her run for the presidency (with Bill Clinton and Ickes as her strategists), it would be harder than ever to discern some of her principles, especially in regard to the gravest issue of the era: the war in Iraq.

Diane Blair was struck when she first met Hillary by how traditional her personal values were. Virtually everyone in her circle eventually recognizes that. From this, Blair and many others deduced that her politics were no more liberal than her husband's. But an equal number of friends and associates became convinced that her politics hewed closer than his to the perennial theology of Democratic Party liberalism. Blair disagreed: "It's not true that she is the liberal one. She came from that family where—with her father, especially—the idea was that you work for everything. She believes in personal responsibility."

In the Arkansas years, Dick Morris had regarded her as "a very practical, hard, down-to-earth, tough person. At the time, I had no sense either of warmth or of ideologies. I became very surprised in subsequent years when she began to become a liberal, because in the 1980s she wasn't. I would be sure she would be to the right of him. She would always be against raising taxes. . . . She was very tough. Bill Clinton was really a Southern moderate-conservative. And Hillary was nonideological, just pragmatic. That all changed in 1993."

There was another formative factor in the Clintons' politics: for more than a decade, Bill served as a governor and she as a governor's wife. Governors (and their wives) generally understood on-the-ground realities, needs, and problems of ordinary citizens better than politicians who had moved on to Washington. Voters seem to perceive that, as evidenced by the fact that only Warren Harding and John F. Kennedy had gone directly to the presidency from the Senate.

The Clintons had run the 1992 campaign with their experience in Arkansas very much in mind. It was a conservative Southern state in most regards, and they understood how to appeal to Reagan Democrats. So it came as a shock to many in Washington, in and out of the media, when the first substantive acts of their presidency, most of them principled, some of them even brave, seemed to signal that the new administration's priorities were actually listing heavily toward what the Clintons' opponents insisted was a "leftist-liberal" agenda.

DEEPER PROBLEMS were eating away at the Clintons' patina of political astuteness with the administration less than a week old. There was still no nominee for attorney general, and the president and his wife had seemed ethically at sea and legally clueless in the Zoë Baird fiasco. Meanwhile,

Hillary's decision to ban reporters from the West Wing had members of the White House press corps seething. ("Well, I want to tell you that I've been here since Kennedy, and those steps have never been blocked to us, and the press secretary's office has never been off-limits. Ever," Helen Thomas, the dean of the press corps, lectured Stephanopoulos.) The deficit numbers the Bush administration had dumped in their budgetary lap had sent the economic team back to square one, and word was out, accurately, that the new president would probably have to abandon his pledge of a middle-class tax cut, and was even considering—columnists were already writing about it—a new energy tax that would hit the middle class hardest. The latter idea was Al Gore's.

The nascent perception of ineptitude was heightened by an unauthorized, anonymous quote in *Time* magazine that put the White House on shaky ground with Senator Daniel Patrick Moynihan, the august Democratic chairman of the Senate Finance Committee. Unfortunately, Moynihan was the senator upon whom the Clinton agenda—and Hillary—was most dependent, since health care, welfare reform, and the budget were all handled by his committee and, on all three issues, his colleagues accorded him a level of deference usually reserved for a potentate. "He's not one of us," said an unnamed "top administration official" quoted by *Time.* "We'll roll right over him if we have to." Unbeknownst to the president or Hillary, the official was Lloyd Bentsen, trying to tell his former Senate colleague, "one gray hair to another," to lay off the young president. In fact, it sounded like something Hillary would say, and some members of her staff were suspect at the time.

The president, furious at the leak, was on the phone to Moynihan posthaste Monday, January 25, the day the item appeared. "If I find out who did this, they'll be gone, I promise you that," he told the senator. (He ordered Stephanopoulos to find out who leaked and fire him.) "Well, if you're upset, I'm not," Moynihan responded, but the affront rankled him (and Moynihan's wife as well, who came to particularly distrust Hillary). The senator would make life difficult for the Clintons for years.

The buzz around town was becoming a question: how could this most surefooted of politicians and his astute staff, including his wife, be stumbling so quickly and so badly? Inside the White House, the cacophony from Congress and the Pentagon, amplified by the press, sounded deafening—especially when Sam Nunn had thrown in his lot with the Joint Chiefs in opposing gays in the military. Nunn purposefully had made his announcement in Norfolk, Virginia, aboard a submarine, to demonstrate the close quarters of military life in which gay sailors would be forced to cohabit. No other controversy could have so underscored Bill Clinton's inexperience with the military (which may have led Sena-

tor Hillary Clinton as a freshman to successfully seek a seat on the
Armed Services Committee). The timing of Nunn's declaration was
itself a declaration of war: it eclipsed Clinton's announcement the same
day, January 25, that Hillary would be formally appointed head of his
task force on health care, and that Ira Magaziner would be her deputy.

The president had assembled his senior cabinet officers and members
of the White House staff (including the first lady's) in the Roosevelt
Room to inform them of her appointment. He decreed that Hillary was
to be treated like anyone else—an impossibility, of course. He urged
those in the room to be as frank and challenging with her as they'd be
with any other cabinet member. He intended to submit a health care
package to Congress within one hundred days, he told them, a totally
unrealistic pledge that he and Hillary had agreed on, and which he
repeated before the cameras that afternoon. Asked if the deadline was
"hard and fast," he added, "If it were 101 days, I wouldn't have a heart
attack." But the accelerated timetable was now part of the agenda, and
many of those in the Roosevelt Room were aghast as a result. Hillary
professed confidence she could meet the deadline.

Hillary, however, was livid that a profusion of official statements and
headlines about deficit reduction were already obscuring the broader
goals and purpose of the Clinton presidency. She ascribed some of the
blame to the same individuals who were expressing, even in these first
days, private doubts about the viability of the sort of colossal health care
plan she and Magaziner were planning to announce to the president's cabinet. Though she felt collegial toward Panetta, Rivlin, Shalala, Bentsen,
and Rubin, she worried they did not understand her husband's priorities
or his style of operating; true, they were all on the same side, and everyone
was just getting to know one another, but Hillary wasn't wrong about the
developing attitude of the deficit hawks.

"Bentsen, Rubin, Panetta—we sat around meetings just looking at
each other," recalled Shalala. "Most of the people sitting around the table
had been here before. We had never seen anything quite like it. . . . This
was not Franklin Roosevelt in the middle of the Depression, in which
you had to design these huge programs."

HILLARY WENT TO New York during that first week, both to receive a
humanitarian award and demonstrate her concern for children by visiting a school, and to visit Jacqueline Kennedy Onassis. The two women
shared more traits than might have been apparent, and were predisposed
to liking each other. Both had a public reserve that masked a wicked sense
of humor and private irreverence. (Among friends, Hillary was famed as

a mimic—especially of pompous politicians.) And both were mesmerized by men of credentials, accomplishment, and wealth. Then there was the obvious: both were married to presidents who, long before they reached the White House, had established reputations as womanizers.

They had met several times before, most recently the previous May. Jackie and her son, John F. Kennedy Jr., had been among the first contributors to Bill Clinton's presidential campaign, even before he had formally announced his candidacy, while he, Hillary, and Betsey Wright were raising money through an exploratory committee. In May 1992, while Hillary was still recovering from the Gennifer Flowers ugliness, Jackie had invited Hillary to lunch at her apartment on Fifth Avenue. Much of their conversation was about how to keep Chelsea shielded from the press; Jackie had been remarkably successful in protecting her own children in New York through their teenage years.

Later, Jackie told friends that of all her successors as first lady, she was most fond of Hillary. Caroline Kennedy Schlossberg said her mother was immediately struck by Hillary's intelligence, her interest in issues related to the well-being of children, and her appreciation of the arts and culture. When Hillary said she liked the ballet, "that sealed it forever," said Caroline.

On this visit to Jackie's apartment, the conversation turned to the White House, its history, and the strange, undefined nature of being a president's wife. Jackie's refurbishment of the White House had been an oddly defining event of the Kennedy presidency, contributing to the mythology of Camelot and of the dashing, cultured young couple who held court there. Hillary was determined to make her own imprint on the mansion as well. She was discussing the matter with Kaki Hockersmith of Little Rock, who had helped with the decoration of the governor's mansion and stayed on after the inauguration to take the measure of the Clintons' new quarters. Hillary, at Bill's behest, was determined to get rid of the silken "bird wallpaper"—a rare Chinese print, actually—that Nancy Reagan had installed in the presidential bedroom. He said it reminded him of Alfred Hitchcock's movie *The Birds*. Hillary had a great enthusiasm and appreciation for art, music, and ballet, but she was definitely not an aesthete in the sense that Jackie was.

Hillary had spent considerable time researching and reading about the lives of the nation's first ladies, a practice that would continue over several years. To her surprise, she had found Pat Nixon one of the most thoughtful and sympathetic of her predecessors, whose trials as the wife of the disgraced president touched her. As first lady, Pat had gone on the record as pro-choice, before *Roe v. Wade*; she had favored the Equal Rights Amendment; she had taught poor Mexican children in California before marrying. In the White House, she had revivified the Preservation Office, dormant since the Kennedy years. Pat Nixon had abhorred being a political wife, but she adored her two daughters and was a hands-on mother, who was revered by her children. Her younger daughter, Julie, in fact, had written a well-regarded memoir about her mother, whose qualities she felt had been ignored or maligned in the period of her father's investigation and exile.

Hillary, however, identified most with Eleanor Roosevelt, increasingly so as she came under attack for her political beliefs and actions. But in some ways, her situation would more resemble that of Pat Nixon.

Motherhood had been exceedingly difficult for Roosevelt, and the six children she bore had all experienced disorienting and troubled lives. She later expressed regret in putting "too much belief in discipline when my children were young. . . . I was so concerned with bringing up my children properly that I was not wise enough to just love them."

Nothing was more important to Hillary than ensuring that Chelsea have as normal an adolescence as possible, despite the extraordinary circumstances of being the president's daughter. Chelsea had gone to a public school in Little Rock. "She was a normal kid, she did everything every other kid did, and by any definition was not suffering any," noted Melanne Verveer, one of Hillary's principal aides. "So Hillary went up to talk to Jackie about how do you have normal kids when you live in a fishbowl." Chelsea, for her part, was hardly thrilled at the prospect of leaving Little Rock and her friends for a new life that required twenty-four-hour Secret Service protection. As the governor's daughter, she could come and go almost like any other child. That would be impossible in the White House. Socks, the family cat, would help represent continuity for Chelsea, but no longer could he roam free either. Because the White House fence was wide enough for him to escape the grounds, he had to be kept on a leash whenever he was outside—a metaphor the whole family could identify with.

As in Little Rock, both Hillary and Bill tried to arrange their schedules to fit Chelsea's, to have dinner together in the family kitchen, which they planned to enlarge. One of Hillary's first acts upon arriving at the White House was to instruct her staff that afternoons and early evenings be left as free as possible so she could spend time with Chelsea. "I don't go out unless I absolutely have to," she said shortly after they had settled into the White House. "I try to be home when she's home in the afternoon, or at least talk to her, have dinner with her, help her with her homework. It's been a difficult move for her, too." As in Little Rock, Hillary directed her daughter's concentration toward school, church, ballet, and family.

In her relationship with her daughter, it was possible to see all the attributes, intensified, that Hillary's close friends recognized in her but that remained largely hidden from public view. "With Chelsea, she is warm and tender—and provocative, too," observed Bruce Lindsey, the president's chief personal aide.

In Arkansas, Chelsea Clinton had attended a racially integrated public school not far from the governor's mansion. With Hillary's education portfolio for the state, it would have been unthinkable that she attend private school there. Though the Clintons explored the possibility of Chelsea enrolling in a public school in Washington—as Rosalynn and Jimmy Carter's daughter, Amy, had done—the city's hopelessly inadequate public education system as well as 1990s security realities made that almost impossible. Instead Chelsea was enrolled at Sidwell Friends School in upper Northwest Washington, which Tricia and Julie Nixon had attended while their father was vice president. By 1993 co-ed Sidwell was considered the most "progressive" and racially integrated of the capital's elite prep schools, chosen by the Clintons over the somewhat tonier National (Episcopal) Cathedral schools, which had been attended by Al Gore and the daughters of President Lyndon Johnson.

Hillary's childhood had been marked by the stringent discipline of her father and the nurturance of her mother. Bill's childhood, in Hillary's view, had been adversely influenced by Virginia's willingness to let her older son do anything he wanted. Hillary was determined not to do the same with their daughter.

Bill was a doting father, eager to please their only child, enthralling her with his conversation, his stories, and his knowledge. The structure and discipline were left to Hillary. On one occasion, after Chelsea and several other girls watched a movie in the White House theater, Hillary made them get down on their knees to pick up every kernel of popcorn they had spilled on the carpet. It wasn't like pecking for toothpaste caps in the snow in Park Ridge, but the idea was the same.

9

Portrait of a First Lady

[Dick] Morris's presence helped in unexpected ways.

—Living History

OVER THE NEXT YEAR, Hillary and Jacqueline Kennedy Onassis periodically phoned each other and enjoyed an occasional lunch. Jackie's White House staff had always been struck by how in control she was, how fastidious about details, and just how involved she was in shaping her image, as evidenced by a paper trail of memos she left behind. Hillary, in her eight years in the White House, left no paper trail of any sort. But her attempts at image-building, and her attempts to remain in control of many things she had never expected to elude her, can be documented just the same.

Early Saturday morning, the tenth day of the Clinton presidency, the Clintons boarded Marine One, the presidential helicopter, for their first trip to Camp David. Despite their obvious need for rest and relaxation, the weekend had been set aside for a working retreat (the idea had originally been Al Gore's) at which the president's cabinet, staff, and campaign consultants would better get to know one another and set "personal goals" for the next four years. It was just the sort of New Age touchy-feely gathering—with two "facilitators" equipped with Magic Markers and metal easels, whom Gore had procured to inspire bonding and brainstorming—that too often lent Clintonia the aura of a boomer romper room. By lunchtime Saturday, however, it was apparent to the campers that Hillary intended to transform the occasion into a war council, to fire up one more time the furnace of the Permanent Campaign and get her husband's presidency back on the rails.

The term "Permanent Campaign" had always denoted a tactical continuity in campaigning for election and governing. In the 1992 presidential race, during which Hillary and James Carville had presided over the creation and operation of the so-called War Room at campaign head-quarters in Little Rock, the attitude of the Permanent Campaign came to be symbolized by her bunker and the overwhelming barrage of rapid-response return fire that issued from it, overpowering or outmaneuver-ing almost every incoming threat. By activating the strategy so soon into the Clinton presidency, she risked eroding the magisterial, mythic, even mysterious advantages that went with occupying presidential territory, commanding the high ground of the White House.

For many of those present, the weekend was a dizzying and discon-certing introduction to the wild personal and political psychology of the Clinton presidential enterprise, and not without its unintended humor. At one session, the president discussed his childhood trauma of being a fat boy ridiculed by other children, and of being knocked down as a tod-dler by a wild boar and picking himself up. (Hillary, characteristically, gave away no guarded memories.) Camp David, the rustic hideaway in Maryland's Catoctin Mountains named by Dwight Eisenhower for his grandson (now long married to Julie Nixon), was first used as a presiden-tial lodge by FDR, who called the place Shangri-la. Most of the forty aides of the new president and first lady were there for the first time, and, given the cachet of the place, were expecting something much grander than its mildewed, motel-sized cabins. "The sheets are damp," Bob Reich remarked. George Stephanopoulos was reminded of a low-rent resort in the Poconos.

Before the session, the president had summoned Stan Greenberg and, without mentioning Hillary, conveyed her view, which he shared, that they were governing and being perceived as if they had forgotten the principles and priorities that had been the basis of the Clinton campaign. The necessary fiscal sacrifices being considered by the economic team could not be permitted to undermine the very reasons behind his presi-dency. The weekend retreat, the president hoped, would help the new economic team and veterans of the campaign to better understand one another.

The managers of the Permanent Campaign from 1980 to 1990 had been Hillary and Dick Morris, their unusual bond sealed by a mutually aggressive approach to the political process. It was also based on a pro-found understanding of Bill Clinton, his strengths and his weaknesses. "We were the enzymes that helped him digest his thinking . . . literally sort of his insulin," Morris said. Clinton sometimes had trouble pro-cessing ideas in an orderly fashion and prioritizing them; he needed "someone to help him with that digestive function. Almost like a dialysis machine, or something." Hillary had often performed that role; Morris said he did as well. Hillary gave a bravura demonstration of the role at Camp David, and also of taking the fight to the enemy.

At the noontime session, as the senior-most members of the new administration watched and listened—awed, admiring, uncomfortable—Hillary delivered a lecture that was to be a defining moment of the Clinton presidency. It was about the Journey, the Story, Enemies, and Villains. No first lady had ever addressed a president's cabinet and staff with such unvarnished political candor (though in the Reagan White House Nancy Reagan had demonstrated a sophisticated understanding of her husband's priorities, and operated discreetly through Reagan's assistant Michael Deaver to manage his time and influence his agenda), or flaunted her obvious primacy in the conduct of her husband's presidency.* She would lead them in writing what she called "a narrative" for America in the Clinton years, so the country could understand—almost as if being provided a roadmap—where this administration was taking it.

Hillary's evaluation of the initial week of the Clinton presidency, and the damage caused in the combustible environment of Washington and beyond, was on the money. The newspapers were full of inside stories about an economic plan the administration was developing that would stress harsh budget-cutting, deficit reduction, and program-slashing, and would forgo the middle-class tax cuts that the Clinton campaign had promised. What the accounts did not say, because the new administration had not gotten their message out effectively, was that the president and his advisers were developing an economic *recovery* plan to put the country *back on course;* that cutting the budget somewhat and reducing the deficit in a reasonable way were necessary to *recover* from the Republicans' *mismanagement* of the economy that had been so much a part of Bill Clinton's victory in the first place. They were working to deliver what they had promised, not welsh on their commitment to investment or compromise basic principles. Hillary said the belt-tightening that had been forced on them was a necessary first step if they were to deliver jobs, health care, welfare reform, and improved education. What needed to be conveyed to the public, she said, was that the Bush White House had lied about the economic peril the Republicans had put the country in. As in Arkansas, this was a tale of the Clintons' own idealism and the dark forces arrayed against them.

She began by comparing the situation they had inherited in Washing-

---

*Hillary's primacy was a different sort than that of Edith Wilson, second wife of Woodrow Wilson, who became known as the "Secret President" for the role she played when her husband suffered a prolonged and disabling illness.

ton to what she and Bill had faced after rebounding from his defeat in 1980 to win a second term as governor in 1982. Her manner was tutorial. She was unaided by either Magic Markers or notes as she addressed the men and women who would now have to perfect the Story of the Clinton presidency and its aspirations through what would be required of them. His presidency could not succeed, she told them, unless voters came to understand, as the citizens of Arkansas eventually had, that Bill was going to lead them on a long "journey" (and the way she said the word instantly gave it a capital J). Without communicating a Vision, which was another term for the Story (and it seemed by now that she was speaking in all capital letters), he'd walled himself off from the folks who had put him in office, tried to do too many things in his first term, and as a result he was beaten.

But going into the second gubernatorial term they'd captivated the citizens with the tale of good and evil. The villain of the piece had been the Arkansas teachers union, which until then had steadfastly supported Clinton. You show people what you're willing to fight for, Hillary said, when you fight your friends—by which, in this context, she clearly meant, *When you make them your enemy.* Not surprisingly, some of those who heard her words were deeply discomfited.

Right now, the Story was confusing and being written by outsiders in the press and political opposition. That had to change. The Story needed some villains, some wicked enemies. Hillary's colleagues shouldn't hesitate to identify them as Clinton's opponents in Congress, or in the media. They, like the Republicans' fat-cat campaign contributors who were already lining up to oppose health care, were intending to thwart the public will. What better way than to convey the righteousness of the Story? Moreover, said Hillary, health care reform would be the key to Bill's reelection in 1996.

After Hillary's remarks, the president offered an even more demanding list of goals for the administration's first year: the immediate creation of jobs and opportunity through enactment of an economic stimulus plan, in addition to his comprehensive economic plan of deficit reduction and investment; welfare reform; a campaign finance and lobbying reform bill; and a bill mandating national service for young Americans. To this list, he added incremental policies to encourage free trade; environmental protection; reading programs for all those in the workforce in need of them; a reduction in the homeless population; and the creation of more apprenticeship programs in government and the private sector. When Clinton had completed his list, Secretary of State Warren Christopher questioned whether the goals were too ambitious, given how difficult each task would be to accomplish. He suggested eliminating some of the president's priorities.

Hillary challenged Christopher sharply. The secretary's experience in the executive branch was extensive. With Bentsen, Christopher was the member of the cabinet with the most high-level Washington experience. He had served in the Johnson administration as deputy attorney general and in the Carter administration as deputy secretary of state—and that added some heft to the Clinton team. Increasingly, though, Hillary came to view him pejoratively as part of the Washington establishment, though he had made his professional mark as a lawyer in Los Angeles. She now delivered a point-by-point sermonette advocating the antithesis of what Christopher had suggested. She was ignoring lessons learned in Arkansas, and was contradicting her own point of half an hour before, when she said in Bill's first term he had tried to do too much. And he was defeated for reelection.

Immediately after the session adjourned, Hillary instructed Paul Begala and Mandy Grunwald, two of the campaign consultants most opposed to the message of the deficit hawks, to rush back to the White House and prepare a written version of the Story: with heroes, enemies, and villains.

Al Gore's staff had expected the meeting to be his show. But what those present saw was the president telling them they were in danger of losing their way, and then turning over the agenda to his wife to plot their course. She had told them exactly what was expected of them to get back on track. The weekend announced to the senior members of the administration that this presidency was intended to function as a joint venture.

Moreover, they had now seen Hillary in a battle zone, operating with ease, intelligence, and calm. She had taken the measure of the situation, dictated an order of march, and positioned the artillery pieces. She seemed to thrive under the conditions of siege, trouble, crisis, and combat. After less than two weeks in the White House, Hillary had assumed her command as America's first warrior first lady.

IN EARLY DECEMBER, Dick Morris had flown to Little Rock and met with the president-elect and Hillary in the governor's mansion. "Bill said, 'Stay in touch with me, and why don't you do it through Hillary?' " according to Morris. "And, I said to Hillary, 'I'll be your political consultant.' " During the first two years of the Clinton presidency, Morris claimed, he spoke to her at length every two weeks or so. "So, in '93 and in '94," he said, "I was constantly calling her with advice. And, the calls would always have two parts to them. My advice for her and my advice for him. She was frequently restless during the parts where I was talking about him, but always attentive during the parts when I was talking about her. And, it was very clear to me that she very much felt in business for herself in '93 and '94. She very much felt that she had a task, that she had a goal. Health care was her thing. 'Talk to me about my image,' she'd say. I would give her advice; for example, at one point very early I remember saying, 'There's an East Wing and a West Wing to the White House. And they're like barbells that you hold as you walk across a tightrope. And they need to be evenly balanced when you walk the tightrope. Whenever you get a little bit too West Wing, which is substantive, hold a dinner party and get more East Wing, which is social. And whenever you get too much talking about health care policy, you talk about what you like to cook at a state dinner."

Which was exactly the subject of Hillary's first White House interview with the press, held two days after she'd met with Jackie Kennedy Onassis in Manhattan.

To the outrage of the same White House reporters whom she'd already confined to the basement, Hillary spent several hours talking with Marian Burros, the food editor of the *New York Times*, in a cozy sit-down with unusual ground rules negotiated by her press secretary, Lisa Caputo: there would be no substantive discussion about the likes of health care, or the sputtering one-week-old presidency; only questions about food, entertaining, decorating, and other "first lady" things. It was further stipulated that the interview would be published two days after the Clintons' first formal White House dinner, in honor of the nation's governors, to be held the evening the Clintons returned from Camp David.

Hillary, Caputo, and Ann Stock, the new White House social secretary, had carefully rehearsed the points and attitude they wanted to convey (a softer, gentler Hillary than the newly appointed health care czarina). Hillary enthused to Burros about how she'd loved every minute of preparing for the governors dinner, from selecting the menu and china to making a last-minute change in the flowers and the color of the tablecloths.

The story ran on page one, next to a photo of the new first lady wearing a bare-shoulder, black Donna Karan evening dress (very un–Barbara Bush). Hillary expressed surprise to Burros at the attention accorded her dual roles—traditional first lady, hostess-in-chief; and head of the President's Task Force on National Health Care Reform, comparing herself to "every woman who gets up in the morning and gets breakfast for her family and goes off to a job of any sort where she assumes a different role for the hours she's at work, who runs out at lunch to buy material for a costume for her daughter or to buy invitations for a party that she's going to have and after work goes and picks up her children and then maybe goes out with her husband: our lives *are* a mixture of these different roles. I'm still always a little bit amazed at how big an issue this is for people because if they will just stop and think, this is what women do," she said. "Eventually, I expect, it won't be a subject for a lot of comment. It's still in transition."

The "news," such as it was, was that there would be far more American food served at family meals and state dinners than the Frenchified fare of previous administrations, a decision that sent Pierre Chambrin, the French-born White House executive chef of the Bush years, into a *frisson* and toward the door (though this was not mentioned in the *Times* interview). To Chambrin's surprise, Ann Stock had consulted with three restaurant chefs, celebrated for their American cooking, to come up with the menu for the governors.

"We're trying to get a kitchen cabinet, so to speak, of people who will advise us about new menus, new ideas," Hillary said. "It will keep us up to date about what a lot of American chefs are doing around the country. Asking people for their advice, whether it's about policy or food, is a way to give even more people a feeling of inclusion. And you get good ideas."

This was just the type of straight-faced earnestness—inclusive food—that (among other things) tended to drive Hillary's detractors around the bend. Not to mention the chef. "I can't say I'm very pleased," said Chambrin. At Hillary's instigation, some thirty cookbooks stressing low-fat, nouvelle American cuisine were delivered to Chambrin's kitchen. In the chef's estimation, the Bushes had been perfect clients, undemanding and sophisticated ("they had lived all over the world"). The obvious implication was that the Clintons were hayseeds.

The changes in the kitchen were in fact perfectly understandable. The Clintons' desire to show foreign guests, among others, the best of indigenous American culture fit their image in the best sense. In December, a group of American chefs led by Alice Waters, the renowned owner of Chez Panisse in Berkeley, California, had sent a letter to the Clintons urging the appointment of a White House chef who would promote American cooking, emphasizing local ingredients and organic food. Hillary told Burros she agreed with many of Waters's ideas. "I think she's been a breakthrough figure in American cuisine, in the kind of food she's prepared and in the kind of positions she's taken. I think what she says makes a lot of sense." The handwriting was on the wall, or at least on the front page of the *Times:* Chambrin was on his way out.

All of this, in retrospect, might have seemed trivial, but in the capital, a one-industry town, it was part of a congealing judgment among the grandees of the Washington social-political circuit, the chattering commentators, and the permanent White House staff that the Clintons did not mind clearing house and changing local customs at the same time. After less than two weeks in the White House, an impression was already taking hold among those inclined to cause trouble for the Clintons that they were sweeping into town like a band of hillbillies with no respect for tradition or what passed in Washington for good breeding or pedigree, whatever that was.

One of Hillary's most querulous attributes, perfected over decades in public life, was to set herself up as a kind of straw woman—responding to criticism, whether real or imagined, with a claim of being confused about why her actions might be subject to question or even analysis in the first place, when the answers were so obvious (to her at least). With regard to the Burros story, she said people who wanted her to fit in a "certain box, traditionalist or feminist," were going to be disappointed. She could handle a big job and domestic functions, too. But her dubious premise remained "that people could perceive me only as one thing or the other."

Hillary chose the *Times* interview to announce her decision to impose a total ban on smoking in the White House ("because of the atmosphere here, and the age of the house, the furnishings"). She had done the same in Little Rock. "It took some people some adjusting," she said. "We tried not to be too harsh about it. The big issue about health is so paramount to me that I don't think we should permit smoking." At his desk in the Oval Office, the president was often encountered with an unlit cigar in his mouth.

PERHAPS NO PERSON aside from the Clintons knows as much about their political designs, development, ideals, and methodology—together and singly—in the years between 1978 and 1996 as Dick Morris. Only Betsey Wright and Diane Blair had the proximity to be as knowledgeable about the gubernatorial years, with their advantage of friendship and total trust. (Vince Foster, always discreet, was extraordinarily close to Hillary but less so to Bill.) Morris, a firsthand witness through the first three and a half White House years, is brilliant, insightful, prejudiced, megalomaniacal, disloyal, as narcissistic as the president he served, and a Clinton-hating convert of the first order by virtue of his being left no choice than to resign or be fired by Bill and Hillary during the 1996 Democratic convention upon publication of a tabloid report of his affair with a prostitute. His testimony must be judged through the filter of his animus. But he is also a Clinton-hater with a difference: Morris knew both Clintons intimately, and the origin of his bias is not ideological or partisan, though, after his firing, his politics moved far rightward in keeping with his new life as a Fox commentator and Murdoch columnist.

His portrait of the Clintons, drawn meticulously with many shades of light and dark, took form in a series of interviews in the fall of 1999, before he had invented a career for himself as a Clinton-basher. After Hillary's election to the Senate (he didn't think she would run), Morris would publish furlongs of newspaper columns and four books about the Clintons and Hillary in particular, with conclusions and assertions often at odds with his interviews of 1999, when his opinions were far less jaundiced.

Morris began by talking of her "aggression," her satisfaction in "taking the fight to the enemy," and her inability to see her own role in harming others ("When she does worry about the payload of the missile, it's kind of like somebody else is delivering it").

Yet Morris quickly made it clear she could manifest the opposite side as well: "Unlike him she's a normal human being, with emotions. She is capable of love and affection and caring and compassion and warmth and empathy in a way that he is simply not. When he's with other people, he absorbs their emotion and their energy, and gives it back to them with a tremendous radiance that *passes for emotion*. It's nothing phony, it's heartfelt at the moment, but it's *your* feeling coming back to you. When he's alone, he's incapable really of feeling much of anything. He's an emotional albino."

"Her spiritual mysticism," in Morris's view, is an essential characteristic: "She doesn't feel all the bumps in the road because she does have a faith. . . . It's not 'Let Go, Let God,' because she tries to manipulate the outcome. But I think that she has a peace with herself over the outcome . . . that in times of threats that loom in her life, or have loomed and still loom, they are such that if she took all of them very seriously she'd be a wreck. I think that there's a kind of detachment that probably has a spiritual sense."

Surprisingly, Morris almost demeaned her intellect. He called it ordinary. Many colleagues of the Clintons had concluded that Hillary was not as intrinsically bright as her husband (whom they regarded as off the charts). Her intelligence was of a different, more practical order, and few would compare her intellectual curiosity or breadth of knowledge to Bill's.

"He works in a different way than Hillary," said another of the Clintons' most important aides. "Because his is a more creative intelligence. He can take in the world, and put it together in new ways. She takes in the world, and can at times make good decisions, and can see the fault lines and where the fights are. But she can't necessarily create something new out of it, or create a solution where one doesn't necessarily exist, or have the patience to let the decision present itself. She's much more apt to, when she hits a wall, bang her head into it. He'll figure out a way to get around it or to jump over it."

"She's not a creative thinker," Morris said. "She's not a heavily substantive person. She's not a heavy-duty intellectual. He's much brighter than she is. She's bright, but she's not *very* bright. She doesn't spend her time like he does worrying about every problem facing the world, and trying to come up with a solution. She's a lawyer. . . . She has a certain genre of intelligence, which is that of a very effective advocate."

He said Bill's intelligence was of a completely different order: "He's always talking about books that he either just read or something he read in college. And he'll talk about Thomas Aquinas in the conversation. He'll talk about Erasmus. And he'll talk about Paul Kennedy. Or he'll talk about the latest op-ed piece by E. J. Dionne. It will be a mélange, a mosaic. . . . With her, there are never footprints of anything she's read beyond immediate preparation for her work."

Others find her bookish. Morris preferred the term "substantive." Morris said, "She is not supple, flexible, or terribly skillful politically. She's brittle, rigid, the fragility of iron that cracks when you drop it as opposed to steel, which doesn't." This might reasonably apply to the first few years of the Clinton presidency, but by the end of the second term, she seemed to have learned some important lessons. And certainly, since running for the Senate, she has readily demonstrated a sophisticated political acumen.

In 1999, Morris said she had been "playing the part of Eleanor Roosevelt. There's a conscious, overt mimicry that's going on. It's Eleanor being the dominant person—but others, too. She's almost more like Reagan in the sense that she's sort of playing . . . the role of activist and socially involved, socially conscious, hard-fighting, aggressive, strong first lady played by Hillary Rodham Clinton. It's a role that she consciously adopted and consciously pursued."

Like Nixon, said Morris, "she definitely has a streak of ruthlessness and paranoia in her political style, in her personal style. She has enemies. She has an Enemies List. She has people who she talks to, and people she does not talk to. When she's mad at you she doesn't talk to you for months and months and months. She has a very long shit list. And, she believes always in taking the fight to the other side. In every campaign strategy meeting I've ever been in with her, she always wants to run negative ads. She always wants to go on the attack."

The efforts "to savage women who have been alleged to have had sex with Clinton, or subsequently said that they had sex with Clinton," always originated with Hillary, Morris said. (If so, she had a handmaiden in Betsey Wright.) "In a real sense she is his human face, not just his advocate. . . . She's a real person. I think the big frustration of their marriage is that she's married to the most elusive, withholding, anal-retentive man you can imagine. He uses denial of affection as his method of getting people to do what he wants them to do—the ones he's close to—rather than to praise or give affection. It's the strangers he showers everything on. . . . If he feels that his relationship with you is set, there's nothing to lose. . . . As he does with her.

"I believe that it's a relationship in which she is . . . addicted to him. And she adores him. She's the best thing that ever happened to him. But he's very elusive and very remote. And when he requires rescue she gets more attention, more affection, more love, more of the caring that I believe she craves from him, and also more power than she otherwise would get."

Morris's timeline of the power shifts in the Clinton marriage is compelling. "In terms of getting more power, Hillary's best year at the White House was 1998," the year of Lewinsky, he asserted. "Her next best year in [power terms] in the White House was 1993, after Gennifer Flowers. . . . I believe that it's a relationship based on mutual enabling. Because she likes what happens when she rescues him. . . . I think to the extent that he's capable of loving anybody, he loves her. But it's a very limited capability in the first place. I think that he sometimes resents her and shakes under her domination. Sometimes he welcomes her and needs her, because he requires her rescuing. And, other times he doesn't think a whole lot about her at all. . . .

"I think if she left him it would be a big blow to him, not in the sense that he'd miss her, but in the sense that he would find unacceptable the image of himself that he'd see in the mirror: the man that Hillary left. But he'd get over it, and he would go on."

IO

A Downhill Path

We . . . had to isolate the attacks and focus on the reality of our lives.

—*Living History*

THE CLINTONS, from their first days after the inauguration, felt they were living in a bell jar. Most of the previous decade they had lived in a governor's mansion modest in comparison with almost all the other forty-nine, a reasonably private family home. The household staff was small. A few state troopers (all personally vetted for their assignment by Hillary and Bill) remained in a separate wing from the living quarters and were available for errands, appearing only when summoned or for receptions. Mornings, Hillary had driven to work in her Oldsmobile, and Bill had driven Chelsea to school. Their lives were minimally affected by security concerns, or (so they thought) the presence of the troopers.

With their move to the White House, the Clintons inherited a grand personal service staff of dozens—maids, butlers, housekeepers, telephone operators, cooks, ushers, stewards—and were under the constant supervision of the Secret Service. Most members of the White House personal staff had been enamored of the Bushes, whose WASPish, Junior League formality was an easy fit. During the eight years when George and Barbara Bush had lived in the vice presidential mansion on Massachusetts Avenue, they had adjusted readily to the heavy Secret Service presence, and acclimatized themselves contentedly to the privileges of morning-to-night silver-tray service.

Clinton style and Bush style could hardly have been more different. George and Barbara Bush were far more formal, and their daily regime more predictable: they had stuck to a schedule every day, almost rigidly, making it easy for both the Secret Service and the household staff to serve them efficiently. Bush's aides were decorous and orderly, as had been President Reagan's. The permanent staff identified personally with both families, regarding the twelve-year Republican epoch almost as a single, uninterrupted regency, subject to their guardianship and service. Increasingly, many also came to identify with its political philosophy.

The Clintons weren't imagining a lack of appreciation for their Arkansas-influenced ways, following the Hollywood royalty style of the Reagans, and the *noblesse oblige* of the buttoned-down Bushes. The Clintons liked to kick back. They were used to a thoroughly relaxed atmosphere, even with the troopers, to casual Fridays and late nights out with friends, while the troopers hung back or stayed in the car. The White House Secret Service agents were ever present, trained never to speak casually to the president or first lady, only to respond or lead the way, and they seemed almost hostile in comparison with law enforcement officials assigned to the governor's detail in Arkansas.

Presidents Reagan and Bush, when they left office, were age seventy-seven and sixty-eight, respectively, with wives who had long before seen sixty. The Clintons were young and informal. Twelve-year-old Chelsea was the first young child living in the White House in twelve years, and only the second preteenager since the Kennedy clan had run roughshod on the lawn. But what really distinguished the Clintons was the chaotic atmosphere they and their rather ragged retinue of aides (in comparison with the departing Republicans) introduced.

The many twenty-somethings and thirty-year-olds in Clinton's administration raced around what they called "the campus," the young men often tieless, the women sometimes in slacks. This youthful cadre, now installed in offices in the West Wing and the Executive Office Building, shared their president's round-the-clock work habits and energy. George Stephanopoulos, the communications director, was thirty-two; Dee Dee Myers, the press secretary, was thirty-one; and Mark Gearan, the deputy chief of staff, was thirty-six.

The White House of January 1993 was surprisingly lacking in high-tech toys like laptops and cell phones. It operated at the mercy of a manual telephone switchboard system that could be maddeningly slow and through which half a dozen presidents had placed and received their routine calls. Bill Clinton, zealous of his privacy and suspicious of a switchboard's capacity for abuse, insisted within weeks of his arrival that he be able to dial out directly, and that operators be incapable of listening to his calls once routed to him. His aides slammed down phones and complained loudly that they needed more lines, fax capability, and portable communications. Some members of the holdover office staff were horrified at what they considered the shockingly unprofessional manner of

An early picture of Hugh, Hillary, Hughie, and Dorothy Rodham

Hillary with three high school classmates
(AP Wide World Images)

At Wellesley
(Brooks Kraft/Corbis)

With Bill on the Yale campus
(William J. Clinton Presidential Center)

Below: Hillary and Bill on their wedding day, October 11, 1975
(William J. Clinton Presidential Center)

Right: In the governor's mansion with newborn Chelsea, February 1980
(William J. Clinton Presidential Center)

Greeting well-wishers on the Mall during inaugural week, 1993
(William J. Clinton Presidential Center)

On Pennsylvania Avenue during the inaugural parade
(William J. Clinton Presidential Center)

Chief Justice Rehnquist administers the presidential oath.
(AP Wide World Images)

At one of the inaugural balls
(Getty Images)

The new first lady
with schoolchildren in
Washington, D.C.
*(William J. Clinton
Presidential Center)*

Dancing in the
White House
*(William J. Clinton
Presidential Center)*

At Chelsea's high school graduation
in Washington, June 6, 1997
(William J. Clinton Presidential Center)

With Chelsea and Jordan's Queen
Noor after a visit to the grave site
of her husband, King Hussein
(*AP Wide World Images/Enric Marti*)

With American peacekeeping
troops in Kosovo
(*William J. Clinton Presidential
Center*)

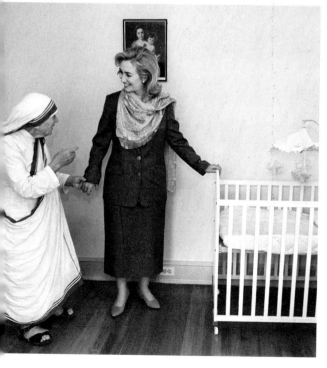

With Mother Teresa
at her orphanage
in India
(*William J. Clinton
Presidential Center*)

With Chelsea at the Western Wall in Jerusalem
(*AP Wide World Images*)

Right: Hillary's chief of staff Maggie Williams being sworn in to testify at congressional Whitewater hearings
(*AP Wide World Images*)

Hillary on *The Tonight Show with Jay Leno* during her first Senate term
(© *Reuters/Corbis*)

the twenty-somethings who sometimes chewed gum as they talked, answered telephones like they were in their dorm rooms, and let unanswered messages pile up for days. Soon, the offended holdovers were on the phones to departed colleagues relating anecdotes both fabulous and fact-based about the lack of decorum in the White House. The stories were repeated in newsrooms, at dinner parties, everywhere.

Permanent staff members generally preferred Hillary to the president, whom some of the help judged inconsiderate, rude, and un-presidential. He stayed up until 2 or 3 A.M. (often discussing policy, playing cards, chewing a cigar, and working crossword puzzles all at once). He allowed junior aides to wander unannounced into the Oval Office. Upstairs, in the family quarters, the ushers and Secret Service agents could not finish their shifts until he was in bed. Only after he retired could they turn off the lights and reduce the number of agents at work. The Bushes and the Reagans, or someone acting on their behalf, had always sent word what time they expected to turn in, so the agents and ushers could plan appropriately. But with the Clintons, particularly given Bill's habits, there was often no word of when this might be. Morning plans were similarly indefinite. He kept in shape by jogging, but whether he felt like a pre-breakfast run depended on the previous night's sleep; hence two teams of Secret Service agents stood ready in the morning, one dressed for running and the other attired in business suits.

Bill found the copious procedures, particularly the requirements of the Secret Service, suffocating. He half-joked about the White House being a high-class "penitentiary." Though his mother had coddled him, he was uncomfortable with all the personal attention. When he was ready to get dressed in the morning, one of two Navy stewards arrived to put out his clothes, brush them, and make sure everything was in order. When he decided it was time to go to the Oval Office, downstairs, the Secret Service detail that hovered overnight in the bedroom hallway accompanied him to the small elevator. A valet accompanied him with his papers, and four agents covered him front and rear as he made his way— less than 150 feet—under the colonnaded walk by the Rose Garden to the Oval. (It was never the Oval Office with the handlers—just the Oval, and his codename was "Eagle.") One night, he and a group of aides working in the Oval Office decided to order pizzas. As the president opened his mouth to take a bite, he was tapped on his shoulder by an agent who told him to put the pizza down. The slice had not gone through screening procedures. A steward brought Clinton cookies—screened—to munch on instead. "Why can't I do what I want?" he had once shouted, after being told that his sudden decision to drop in on a friend's book party downtown could not be accommodated by the Secret Service.

The tensions between the Clintons and some members of the household staff and security details were obvious. One usher had never removed the "Re-elect Bush" bumper sticker from his car. Hillary and Bill, not unreasonably, questioned the loyalty of at least a few aides. Hillary complained to Vince Foster that some of the agents seemed abrupt and unfriendly. Their constant presence was intrusive. She became especially concerned about the number of functionaries who hung by doorways, and the agents who were always stationed in the long living area that stretched east–west on the second floor, within listening distance of conversations. Four Secret Service agents were assigned to be inside the Oval Office or just outside when the president was there. The potential mischief from conversations overheard was too obvious to ignore. This seemed particularly true after Harry Thomason, who with his wife, Linda, was living part-time in the White House during early 1993, came back one night from a dinner attended by some reporters. He told the Clintons that particulars about the first family's personal life in the White House were being leaked to the press by some of the agents. He urged replacement of the whole White House Secret Service detail. The problem was deemed serious enough for Hillary to tell Foster to solve it, and that she wanted new agents assigned who were more inclined to be sympathetic, perhaps who had worked with them in the campaign.

Among the things Hillary valued most about Foster's judgment were his caution and calm, his ability to look beyond the immediate, to see the big picture. He worried that precipitous replacement of the White House Secret Service contingent, or even a few agents, would inevitably leak to the press—especially if Thomason's information had been correct—and would produce a professional and public backlash. He met with David Watkins, another Hope native who was assistant to the president for management and administration (Watkins, Foster, and Mack McLarty had all been student-body presidents at Hope Senior High School), and Mark Gearan. It was agreed that they should watch the situation carefully, but do nothing for the moment.

On February 19, vivid evidence of the problem showed up in a *Chicago Sun-Times* column by Bill Zwecker: "Seems First Lady Hillary Rodham Clinton has a temper to match her hubby's." Zwecker reported, without attribution, that Hillary had smashed a lamp during a fierce argument with Bill in the family quarters. "Just in case you care," he added, "Bill and Hillary sleep in separate bedrooms"—which, in fact, was not the case. Other mainstream media outlets picked up the story, some embellishing it: Hillary, it was said, had thrown a vase or a Bible at her husband. In one version, a Secret Service agent supposedly had to break up the dispute, telling Hillary, "We've got to protect him, including from you."

That Hillary had a temper and that she had directed it toward Bill (and vice versa) was hardly news to people who had been close to the Clintons in Arkansas. They had scrapped and screamed at each other since their courtship. None of their friends or aides is known to have given credence to the *Sun-Times* story. Still, it raced through the capital as no other bit of Clintonian gossip had since their arrival.

Hillary was livid about the story and about the Secret Service. When the Service failed to issue a formal denial, she became even angrier. (Later, Zwecker said that one of two sources for his column had been someone involved in "White House security.") When *Newsweek* picked up the item, she declared the magazine *escrit non grata* and said she would never allow its correspondents to interview her.

She was also harsh in her response to Foster. If she had ever previously had a really cross word with him, no one had ever heard about it, including Webb Hubbell. The relationship between Hillary and Vince had always reflected a solicitous mutual caring, and a deep understanding of the vulnerabilities beneath the surface of each. In this instance, she seemed to draw no distinction between Watkins and Foster, reprimanding them at the same time. Both were subordinates who had failed to take action when she had expressed her urgent concerns. The two of them were "too naive and too nice, being from Arkansas," Hillary said, making a strange connection.

Watkins seemed to take her rebuke in stride, but Vince was clearly devastated. Thereafter, he referred to Hillary as "the client."

Vince had come to Washington a week before the inauguration, excited at the prospect, filled with high hopes. He was not a political animal, and never had been. His allegiance was personal—to the president, but even more so to Hillary. His wife, Lisa, had told him, when he was asked to join the administration, "I'm afraid if you don't do it you'll always be sorry." But now he was beginning to have doubts, according to many of his fellow Arkansans who also made the trip.

While Bernie Nussbaum had temporarily moved into the $300-a-night Jefferson Hotel, Vince felt he couldn't afford such extravagance. He had a family back home to support. The price of living in Washington was generally shocking to him. Real estate, food, going to the movies—he could see that he would not be able to live nearly as well as he had in Little Rock, no matter how exalted his position. He moved into the Northwest Washington house of his sister, Sheila, who was married to a former congressman from Arkansas, Beryl Anthony.

Lisa had been expecting to enjoy living in the capital—her husband was deputy counsel to the president; there would be state dinners at the White House, congressmen and senators to rub shoulders with, the Kennedy Center honors. But Vince had insisted that she and their children stay behind until their youngest son had finished the high school year in Little Rock. She was not pleased with his decision. She and their children came to Washington for the inauguration, but Vince had no time for them. As soon as the ceremony at the Capitol was over, he had hurried to the White House because of the trouble with the Zoë Baird nomination. Lisa and the children were left behind on the Capitol grounds, in a strange city with little idea of how they would get back to Sheila's house. She was so angry that she refused to go to the inaugural ball that evening. In fact, she said later, "I was angry at Vince about 90 percent of the time. I wasn't angry at him for going [to Washington]. I was just angry at him for ignoring us and leaving us behind, and making me have to deal with everything, all the decisions, and he was getting all the so-called glory."

Immediately Vince was thrown into the maelstrom of the administration's difficult first days, almost everything in which Hillary was involved. Though he was deputy counsel to the president in title, he was, in fact, her counselor, all the more so as she became preoccupied with her health care mandate, and left more and more details of other matters to him. "This is gold," he told Webb Hubbell, referring to his White House pass. "I could never go back." In the White House, Vince and Hillary "were the team he had always imagined they would be," Hubbell said. The glow did not last long.

Foster appeared to internalize the blame for the item in the *Sun-Times*, as if he had failed to protect her and the president. She was right, he told Nussbaum. He had not been forceful enough. Nussbaum thought Foster's initial instincts—that dismissing members of the presidential Secret Service detail would leak to the press and cause a backlash—were probably correct, but by now, Vince and Watkins had no doubt that action was in order, if for no other reason than to calm the first lady.

Foster and Watkins met with the Secret Service official in charge of the presidential detail, John McGaw, and expressed the displeasure of Hillary and the president over both the *Sun-Times* story and the attitude of agents in the residence.

McGaw defended his men and women—the fact that the agents were taciturn didn't mean they were hostile, he said. They were going by the book. He expressed certainty the leak had not come from them.

His days heading the presidential security office were soon over. Through the intercession of Foster and Watkins, he was "promoted" to director of the Bureau of Alcohol, Tobacco, and Firearms. As Hillary had demanded, many of the resident Secret Service agents were now given jobs outside the White House, and replaced by others who had not served directly with the Bushes or Reagans. The number of agents assigned to the residence was reduced, as was the size of the detail hovering around the Oval Office. Upstairs, the agents now stayed out of the living area—and Hillary's way.

I I

Health Care

I didn't fully realize the magnitude of what we were undertaking.

—*Living History*

THE CLINTONS CAME to Washington to accomplish great things. The greatest of their goals was to establish a system of universal health care in which every American would be insured against catastrophic illness and guaranteed adequate, paid lifelong medical care. Such an undertaking would be the biggest public works project in the nation's history, and was perhaps the most necessary since the advent of Social Security. "If I don't get health care done, I'll wish I didn't run for president," Bill told his aides in February.

Both the Clintons were, by nature, optimists, but also realists. They understood the inevitability of political combat. But they had not expected to come to Washington and immediately find themselves under constant attack and suspicion, or forced to change their course abruptly because their predecessors had sailed recklessly into a fiscal storm and couldn't find, or did not try to find, their way out in an election year. But those were the realities.

As in Arkansas with her education portfolio, by the time Hillary had begun consulting with experts, she already knew where she wanted to go. Hillary wanted to combine government controls and the will of the competitive marketplace, taking the best elements of both to restrain health care costs. The government (rather than private insurance companies) would dictate a set of basic medical benefits that would be available to all patients, and require private insurers to offer all of these benefits in their policies. A competitive bidding process in each state would determine the price of insurance policies, so that state officials could bargain with insurance companies for the lowest premium rates for their citizens.

Most American companies would be required to pay for 80 percent of their employees' health insurance; the government would partially subsidize the cost to smaller businesses, and buy insurance for the unemployed poor.

Hillary's plan was an impressive demonstration of her intellect, dedication, and ability to grasp the entirety of a huge policy debate. But it was tangled from the start with political missteps that could have been avoided. Her demonstrable sense of entitlement, the idea that the goal was so worthy that extraordinary procedures could be justified to achieve it, hence her insistence from the start on secrecy that appeared almost conspiratorial, made her task far more contentious than necessary, and almost immediately jeopardized her cause.

From the beginning, Hillary and Ira Magaziner were confronted by an inherent conflict with the budgetary realities the president was trying to deal with. But they insisted that the health care model they were proposing would be more efficient and less costly than the existing Medicare and Medicaid systems it would replace. By their calculations, they could bring about substantial savings that would cover the costs of insuring the millions of Americans currently uninsured, and eventually reduce the federal deficit further to help the president. It was almost a magic bullet, they felt.

Unfortunately, most of Bill Clinton's economic advisers thought Hillary and Magaziner's numbers were wishful thinking.

To develop the specifics of her proposal, Hillary established what was formally known as the President's Task Force on National Health Care Reform, comprising five hundred consultant-experts in various aspects of medical and health care policy. The consultants were drawn from congressional staffs, federal agencies, academia, corporations, and professionals in the medical community. Under Hillary's watch, Magaziner divided the task force participants into thirty-four "working groups," designated by specialty. They were expected to debate the issues in their purview, present a set of recommendations, and then defend their conclusions. Group assignments ranged from how to serve the particular medical needs of Native Americans to deciding whether prescription drugs and mental health counseling should be included in the basic benefits the government would guarantee.

As conceived, the duties of the task force seemed overly complex—not to mention impossible to complete within the hundred-day deadline set by the president. Magaziner distributed a rigorous—some said outlandish—schedule that called for each of the thirty-four working groups to develop recommendations on seven different topics, and present their suggestions to a huge formal assembly at seven different meetings. He explained to doubters, "People work best when they work for deadlines. It forces discipline." Many of the task force members were working six- and seven-day weeks, often for eighteen hours a day.

The scene inside the Executive Office Building, where the five hundred consultants met, always seemed on the brink of chaos. Task force members were crammed into makeshift meeting rooms that lacked sufficient desks and chairs or adequate light.

The conclusory presentation meetings of the individual groups were held in the Indian Treaty Room, an ornate, inadequate space that had once been the Navy Department Library and Reception Room. About two hundred people would attend, usually including either Magaziner or Hillary; Shalala or an analyst from her Department of Health and Human Services; and representatives of various cabinet departments. The last to arrive—excepting senior officials—had to sit outside in the hall. The sessions often went late into the night, without reaching conclusions about the matters under discussion, as Hillary, Magaziner, and others tried to pay attention.

Hillary spent hundreds of hours in such meetings, taking notes on every issue, and trying to absorb the numbing detail. Whether she was in the White House or traveling on airplanes, she always seemed to be studying. But for all of that, she was floundering.

The White House, meanwhile, refused inquiries from the press and interested organizations to identify her five hundred consultants, or provide any details of what they were working on. This made practical sense. There was no precedent for presidential administrations drafting legislation in public and, even in secret, the process was disorderly. Advance release of partially developed ideas might encourage premature debate, divert energy from formulating final recommendations, and hamper the work generally.

But health care reform was one of the most charged public policy issues of the day. Republicans, ideological opponents of government controls, and important segments of the health care industry that stood to lose money in a revamped system complained immediately that they had been cut out of the process. For the most part, they had.

The first week in February, William F. Clinger Jr., the ranking Republican member on the House Government Operations Committee, charged that the process was illegal, and demanded that the General Accounting Office investigate whether Hillary was authorized to conduct such proceedings in private. He cited the 1972 Federal Advisory Committee Act, which mandated public meetings unless all task force members were federal employees. Clinger danced around direct criticism of the first lady, but his target was unmistakable. His accusation of illegal and abnormal secrecy was devastating. It resonated both with Hillary's potential opponents—legislators and bureaucrats committed to existing standards and structures of the health care system, lobbyists with narrow agendas, and Republican partisans—and also with those who could have been her natural allies: journalists who covered the medical field, associations of professionals in medicine and health care, Democratic politicians, and the president's principal economic and domestic program advisers, including Bentsen, Rubin, Panetta, and Shalala.

Clinger's charges made Hillary appear to be something of a paranoid. It was now made to seem that she and Magaziner were running their operation with a military-like secrecy unprecedented for a peacetime domestic program. (That was pretty much true.) They had devised a security system in which it was forbidden to photocopy drafts of documents under discussion or even to bring writing instruments into many meetings. Room monitors were assigned to keep track of who reviewed certain papers. All meetings were closed not only to the press, but to all outsiders. "They would take documents away from us and look for leaks. They didn't trust us. You'd think you were in the FBI," said former Minnesota health commissioner Mary Jo O'Brien, who served as a task force member. "The funny thing was, these were not new ideas. I expected it would be stuff that could be patented, but there was nothing new, just discussions of policy. It was handled very poorly. It became a military operation."

Many blamed Magaziner for the secrecy requirements, but it was Hillary who wanted them, as Magaziner confirmed later.

Hillary wasn't open to any substantive compromise with her vision of health care reform. She ignored the possibility that instituting a system of gradually phased-in improvements to the existing health care system, leading eventually to her larger goals, might be helpful both to the Clintons' political allies, up for reelection in 1994, and to her husband's own political future. As Stephanopoulos said, "Compromise didn't come naturally to Hillary."

Hillary also tended to view anyone who criticized her plan, even constructively, as an enemy. Michael Bromberg, head of a lobbying organization for private hospitals, had tried to explain to Hillary that compromise was the biggest lesson he'd learned from working with Congress. "Any bill that passes Congress will be a credit to you," Bromberg told her. "But if you say, 'This must be in there,'" and the provision fails on Capitol Hill, "then it will be perceived as a loss." Hillary replied, "Bill and I didn't come to Washington to play the game as usual." Hillary drew a line in the sand: she said that she and the president would make the midterm congressional elections in 1994 a vote about her health care plan, and would use the public's support for her approach to attack those who opposed her. "We know how to run a populist campaign," she said, reviving the warrior woman theme of Camp David.

Her husband's top deputies were beginning to worry that she was both politically tone-deaf and strategically inept, especially within the toxic Washington environment. Hillary had convinced her own aides and a few important members of the president's domestic policy staff that the administration could pass health care legislation without any Republican votes. A senior White House official later explained, "Among Clintonites, it was widely thought that the Republicans had engaged in so much malign neglect over the years that the public would rally to Democratic nostrums." Lawrence O'Donnell, the principal aide to Senator Moynihan, concluded that "Hillary believed . . . this is so clearly a moral good that no one can stand up and say, 'I'm going to stop it.' "

Hillary was more than three months into the job before she started soliciting suggestions from Republicans and conservative Democrats. She visited dozens of congressmen in their offices, asked about their families, complimented their work, and dutifully followed up with a thank-you note. But many lawmakers believed her attempts were mainly for show. In fact, Republicans were totally frozen out of the process. As Senator Dave Durenberger, a Republican from Minnesota, said, "We may have been consulted, but we weren't involved."

By then, Hillary had established her health care war room, staffed by young aides who, around the clock, monitored threats and attacks against her still secret plan. Her message was unambiguous: she did not want negotiations that would end in compromise. She was looking for unconditional surrender. Health care had now become part of the Permanent Campaign, too.

"There's just nothing stupider in government than, You're with me or against me," said O'Donnell, reflecting the Washington experience Hillary lacked at that point. "Campaigning is: You beat the other guy, you leave him for dead in New Hampshire, that's the end—you don't care what happens to him. But you never, ever, ever beat Dole. He's there the next day in the Senate. And he's there for the next vote, which you desperately need."

Shalala and the president's other senior economic experts expressed modest objections to Hillary and Magaziner's tactics. But a dangerous dynamic was developing: the president's aides and advisers felt increasingly uncomfortable confronting the first lady. Even Stephanopoulos and Greenberg did not make known to Hillary their deep reservations about her plan. McLarty remained silent, too, though he believed Hillary was moving in the wrong direction. Bentsen and Rubin became so diplomatic and circumlocutous in their criticism that at times Hillary and Magaziner didn't comprehend the extent of their concern. Laura Tyson, chairwoman of the Council of Economic Advisers, Shalala, and Deputy OMB Director Alice Rivlin were less inhibited. But they were no more successful in persuading Hillary to change what they perceived as flaws in the plan or her methodology.

Magaziner said that such concerns—particularly the sensitivity to offending conservative Democrats and Republicans—would be addressed as the legislation moved through Congress. His strategy was to get liberals on board first to ensure their support later in the process. Inevitably, he said, the bill would have to be modified during congressional negotiations but, he hoped, to the least extent possible. Shalala warned that reaching out to one group first, instead of building initial support across the political spectrum, would unite opponents against the administration's plans. Hillary ignored the warning.

Many of Bill Clinton's top aides felt that Hillary was impatient when listening to their criticisms or condescending, as if even Bentsen and Rubin could not be trusted. Magaziner exacerbated problems with his dismissive manner. "The president has already decided that," he would say, or, "It hasn't been decided yet." Hillary frequently interrupted the president's advisers. "You're right." "You're wrong." "No, that's not right," she would say. Meanwhile, Magaziner infuriated the president's aides when they learned he was meeting privately with the Clintons in the White House residence and urging them to make important decisions without consulting either the task force or the economic team. Hillary's stature with Bentsen and even her old friend Shalala was deteriorating.

The president seemed caught between his wife and his advisers. More often than not, he would mediate disputes between them by saying, "Let's revisit this." In fact, a new dynamic in the Clinton partnership was developing: for the first time, he seemed inclined to placate Hillary, and make decisions he strongly believed were against his better instincts. That was a mistake.

SOON AFTER BILL appointed her, Hillary had begun lobbying to have her plan included as part of the president's budget. Clinton was already proposing a relatively drastic budget that would increase taxes and make large cuts to government programs. His economic advisers and congressional liaison staff had predicted it was going to be a very hard sell without the added burden of incorporating health care.

Since progress on virtually all other administration bills would be delayed until Congress acted on the overall economic plan, Bill's political and economic advisers wanted to push a budget bill through Congress as quickly as possible. Health care would not only slow it down, it might also increase spending so significantly that it could erase the deficit reduction central to the president's plan to get the economy back on track.

Hillary realized that the budget bill was going to be so contentious that debate about it on Capitol Hill would suck air out of her health care initiative. Unless her plan was included in the budget bill, she feared it would be impossible to enact health care reform before the midterm elections. As a matter of tactics, she argued that health care belonged in the budget because of its impact on spending, taxes, and entitlement programs.

House Majority Leader Dick Gephardt had urged Hillary to incorporate her health plan in the budget proposal. The reality of gridlocked Washington was that any bill passed in the Senate required more than a simple fifty-one-vote majority. At least sixty votes were needed to counter the opposing party's inevitable attempt to stop passage with a filibuster—sixty votes cast to end debate and consider the legislation on its merits—and Gephardt had no doubt that Hillary's health care proposal on its own would head straight into a filibuster. Budget resolutions, however, required only a majority vote to be considered under Senate rules.

Persuaded of Gephardt's position, Hillary arranged a meeting with Bill and the House leader. The president found the case for adding health care to the budget a compelling one and told Hillary and Magaziner to approach Senate Majority Leader George Mitchell. He was also supportive, telling Hillary that if the administration were to introduce a health care plan as a separate bill, it would decrease its chance of passage. As midterm elections neared, "the rules in the Senate are such that you dramatically enhance the leverage of the opposition," he explained.

It was significant as well that not having a separate bill would take jurisdiction of the health care plan out of the realm of Senate Finance Committee Chairman Pat Moynihan, whose influence on both houses of Congress was enormous and who was skeptical of wholesale, ungraduated, health care reform. He had urged the Clintons to tackle the issue of welfare reform first.

The president, however, continued to be noncommittal about whether to include Hillary's proposal in his budget to Congress. Frustrated, Hillary believed she needed to win over Bill's advisers. She was in the odd position of needing their support in what she believed should be solvable in a marital discussion.

Hillary and Magaziner invited the whole economic team to a meeting in the EOB during the first week of February. The president's advisers pointed out that details of her reform plan could not be fully enough developed in time for the president's joint address to Congress on February 17, when he was scheduled to introduce his budget plan. Bentsen, Rubin, Shalala, and Tyson all reiterated their doubts about including health care in the president's budget, suggesting that it might keep the budget from passing. "George Mitchell and Dick Gephardt don't think it's [a] crazy [idea]," Hillary said.

One of the president's principal deputies, who was present for many of the meetings at which Hillary tried to persuade her husband's advisers, could see her frustration growing, "because the budget [uncertainty] was preventing him from preparing for health care." This official concluded that Hillary's real interest in deficit reduction was virtually nonexistent. "The Rubins and Bentsens of the world were also the ones who were most skeptical about the health care plan. They saw it as big government—that it wouldn't be respected by the markets. She was feeling hemmed in—her attitude was, 'The same people that are making us give up our dreams on the economy are trying to do it to health care too.' So you could sense her bristling. Rubin was careful. He certainly believed in universal coverage. But he had specific questions—doubts—about the way Ira and Hillary were doing it. The numbers. The mechanism. That it wasn't thought through enough."

IN A BRILLIANT STROKE, the president had invited Alan Greenspan, the chairman of the Federal Reserve Board, to sit next to Hillary in the gallery for his speech to Congress of February 17, thus demonstrating implicit support for his economic plan and Hillary's ambitions for health care. Though the chairmanship of the Fed was considered a nonpartisan position, and Greenspan had been appointed by George Bush, the president's request that he sit next to the first lady made it all but impossible for Greenspan to decline. Moreover, he was pleased with the direction in which Clinton was proceeding on the budget.

Though the budget Clinton described in his speech did not include funding for universal health care, Hillary received meaningful consolation in a few lines in which he reaffirmed his commitment to her plans. "All of our efforts to strengthen the economy will fail unless we also take this year—not next year, not five years from now, but this year—bold steps to reform our health care system," the president said. "Reducing health care costs can liberate literally hundreds of billions of dollars for new investment and growth and jobs, reducing not only our deficit but expanding investment in America." It was the biggest applause line of the night, and the television cameras were trained on Hillary, beaming, with Greenspan beside her, as Clinton had known they would be.

But the opponents of the health care reform envisioned by the Clintons now knew they had the means to effectively attack her plan, and perhaps sink it. The country's medical establishment, represented by the American Medical Association, had been successful since the Truman administration in killing all attempts at health care reform. On February 25, the equally establishment Association of American Physicians and Surgeons and new organizations formed specifically to fight Hillary's health care plan filed a lawsuit in federal court demanding that the secret deliberations of the health care task force be outlawed; that its meetings be ordered open to press and public; and that the names of the five hundred consulting experts be released. "That would be like opening the White House at every staff meeting we have," the president said. It would be impossible to "get anything done." Health care would be fully and fairly debated, he promised, and every interest group would be able to voice its opinions, once the bill made it to Congress.

Hillary fully understood what had happened. She charged that her opponents had used an "obscure law" to undermine the orderly process of developing her plan. It had been a deft political ploy to create an exaggerated impression of secrecy.

She told Vince Foster to fix it.

THE RELATIONSHIP BETWEEN Hillary and Foster, said Webb Hubbell, "was no longer co-equals. He was working for her. Originally she had worked for him [at the Rose Law Firm]. At first he was thrilled to be working at the White House. But the relationship was shifting. . . . As opposed to, Let's talk this out, it was, Let's get this fixed."

In effect, Hillary burdened Foster with much of the weight of her hopes for health care. The high stakes of the lawsuit were clear. If they lost in court, she feared something akin to Humpty Dumpty's fate— Hillary was not sure her health care initiative could ever be put back together again.

"I think the beginning of Vince's downturn was when the health care task force was sued," said Hubbell, whom Foster immediately enlisted to help him. Vince said he would need all the available resources of the Justice Department. Every relevant related case needed to be researched, as well as the legislative intent of Congress in regard to government boards. Was there a way to get an immediate dismissal of the suit on jurisdictional grounds? Did the plaintiffs have standing? And speed was essential.

Within several days, more than one hundred Justice Department lawyers were working under their supervision on health care matters, several from every department. Then 150 were working. Hillary was constantly on the phone asking questions, following up.

"Instead of a team working together toward a glorious goal, [Vince and Hillary] were suddenly attorney and client," said Hubbell. "His legal advice was now front-page news. And with the pressure Hillary was under to get a health care bill passed in the administration's One Hundred Days, she became a very demanding client indeed."

Vince's office was only a few feet from Hillary's, across a reception area in the West Wing. Hubbell was seven blocks away at the Justice Department. Vince told him, "Webb, I told Hillary you're in charge of this at Justice. And that you and I are talking, and talking constantly. This is the most important thing we can do—make sure that we get this thing through, win this litigation." Hubbell had always known Foster to be cool, methodical, imperturbable. Not now. Reporters were constantly calling him. " 'Fix it, Vince!' he said she had hissed. It hurt him deeply. The stress was getting to us all. . . . She was the boss. And when she says, 'Win the litigation,' you're feeling pressure from the boss. Not only the boss, but a very good friend, who's under a lot of stress, and taking a lot of heat for this. . . . He was feeling the pressure, and it was a different relationship."

The efforts of Foster, Nussbaum, Hubbell, and an army of Justice Department lawyers came to virtually naught. On March 10, U.S. District Judge Royce Lamberth, a Reagan appointee, ruled that Hillary should be treated like an "outsider" working for the White House, and thus the health care task force would have to meet in public when gathering facts.

Technically, the decision was not a total loss: the judge ruled that staff-level working groups could still meet behind closed doors and that the task force could meet privately when creating policy proposals for the president or giving him advice. Practically, the White House would merely have to comply with legal requirements for crafting a task force charter and publish meeting notices in the *Federal Register.* But it would have to list its consultants, whom reporters would immediately seek out.

Perception was the most important consideration of all, and it was clear that the judge had delivered a stinging rebuke to the first lady and the president. He had armed the Clintons' opponents with exactly the weapon they needed: opprobrium.

Hillary had put enormous pressure on Foster and he had failed.

· · ·

NEARLY A MONTH AFTER Bill's speech to the joint session of Congress, he still had not made a decision about whether to include health care in the budget. But he was feeling Hillary's unrelenting pressure.

On March 11, he placed a phone call to Senator Robert Byrd of West Virginia, chairman of the Senate Appropriations Committee, the senior Democrat in the Senate, whose support was essential to the legislative success of health care reform. The senator was famously known for his "Byrd rule," prohibiting the introduction of "extraneous" matters into the supposedly pure budget process: incorporation of health care in the budget would put its consideration on a fast track and exempt it from much of the scrutiny required of other bills, and keep it insulated from threats of filibuster. Majority Leader Mitchell, Senator Jay Rockefeller (also of West Virginia), and the president all pushed the chairman to forgo his rule and allow the incorporation of Hillary's health care plan in the budget. Byrd refused.

Thereafter, Gephardt and Mitchell, the senior leaders of the president's party in Congress, warned Hillary that it would be impossible to pass both the budget and health care legislation before the 1994 congressional elections. The Clintons would pay a great price for ignoring the two leaders and not delaying. Later, Bill recognized his mistake in not taking a longer view.

Hillary now hurried to meet with congressmen and senators to agree on a bill they could give Congress to vote on. Only later, with the benefit of her Senate experience, did she realize that to ignore Byrd's opposition was a grave error. Her desperation to present a good health plan to the American people, to keep her promise, in her eyes, had forced her to act imprudently. Later, while a member of the Senate herself, she came to appreciate Byrd's position.

At the time, however, Hillary's outrage was concentrated as much on the Democratic political establishment as the Republican opposition. "She was furious with the Democrats because they didn't rise up and stand with her in what she tried to do," her friend Sara Ehrman said.

There had been no "due deference" paid by the Democratic leadership to her and her husband, the president, Hillary said.

12

The Politics of Meaning . . . and Family

[I]f I hadn't believed in prayer before 1992, life in the White House would have persuaded me.

—*Living History*

A T THE TIME of his son-in-law's inauguration, Hugh Rodham was eighty-one years old, in frail health and more foul-tempered than ever. "When he turned eighty," said his son Tony, "he figured out that he could say just about anything he wanted. Who's going to stop him?" His health had been in decline since he had suffered a heart attack during Bill's gubernatorial inaugural speech to the Arkansas legislature in 1983, after which he'd undergone a coronary bypass. Several strokes followed in the next decade, during which his wife became his caretaker. At the White House, often confined to a wheelchair, Hugh was regarded by many members of the staff and Secret Service as rude and nasty. "He was mean, mean, mean," said one aide to the president.

On March 19, Hillary and some twenty staff members had decided to celebrate the House passage of Bill's economic stimulus package with lunch in the White House mess. It was one of the rare moments when Hillary let down her guard. It was then that Carolyn Huber whispered to her that her father had had a stroke. She traveled immediately to Little Rock to be by her father's bedside. While she was in Arkansas, Vince Foster would file an appeal to the court's decision regarding the health care task force, and Donna Shalala and Tipper Gore would take over Hillary's responsibilities at previously scheduled health care forums and tours around the country.

Hillary's days in the hospital were a painful yet transforming experience. While the press waited outside for news, Hillary talked to other family members of patients who were sick and dying, and to hospital personnel. She wrote in *Living History* that she learned of doctors distressed because their patients couldn't afford to have prescriptions filled, as well as people who had to make prescriptions last by riskily skipping doses. She said all of this buttressed her notion of how vital health care reform was.

While Hillary was away, the American Medical Association bused hundreds of doctors from every state to Capitol Hill to visit their elected representatives with a central message: universalize health insurance, stop the rise in health costs, but do not freeze physician fees as Hillary wished to do. In a closed meeting, Magaziner told about thirty House Democrats that the administration was "leaning toward requiring" that individuals pay the percentage of health insurance that their employers did not cover, or, if they were self-employed, buy their own policy. Meanwhile, under a court order, the White House released the names of the 511 federal employees, congressional aides, and outside consultants who were participating in the health care task force.

IN THEIR FIRST months in the White House, both Bill and Hillary were force-fed the unpalatable truth that, contrary to their expectations, the capital was not to be easily commanded in the same way they had dominated the politics of a small Southern state. Bill matured politically during his eight years as president, learning to achieve many of his objectives piecemeal in the face of adamant Republican opposition. But in terms of his character, he remained basically unchanged: ambitious, narcissistic, charming, brilliant, roguish, undisciplined, incredibly able— and often personally disappointing. The engine of Hillary's evolution and of her enormous capacity for change seemed sturdily bolted under the hood of her religious convictions, a set of beliefs that to some bordered on a messiah-like self-perception, to others a license to do whatever she pleased in the name of God, and to others a touchstone of spirituality that infused her notions of love, caring, and service.

Since mid-century, with the exception of the Carter years, the White House had been largely the spiritual province of such establishmentarian preachers, priests, and evangelists as the Reverend Norman Vincent Peale, Francis Cardinal Spellman, and Dr. Billy Graham. Their eminent visitations had lent an imprimatur of white Christian approval to the works of Democrats and Republicans alike. The Clinton White House, however, from the earliest days of the administration, became a welcoming beacon for a procession of less exalted reverends and rabbis, theologians and gurus, New Age spiritualists and sages, from serious to (arguably) charlatan. Eventually, Graham's role of unelected spiritual adviser to the president would be inherited by the Reverend Jesse Jackson, a comfortable and—especially during the Lewinsky affair—politically useful presence whose own sins of the flesh were of a nature quite familiar to the first couple.

Part of the changed religious dynamic of the Clinton White House was an openness to new ideas and spiritual paths plowed since the 1960s and 1970s, particularly offshoots of the movements inspired by the Reverend Martin Luther King Jr. and the black church, and the psychospiritual pseudosciences derived from twelve-step philosophy and theories of co-dependence. But most of the change was attributable to the simple fact that Bill and Hillary were both genuinely religious. Bill would say that one of the two most impressive world figures he'd met during his presidency was Pope John Paul II (the other was Yitzhak Rabin), notwithstanding the Clintons' profound disagreement with the pope's views about women's rights, abortion, and birth control.

The ambitious nature of Hillary's vision could be glimpsed vaguely through the inarticulate haze of her extemporaneous commencement remarks at Wellesley. A decade later, as a woman in her thirties, she had preached a series of Sunday school and church sermons in Arkansas (never unearthed by the national press) which were clearer evidence that she was evolving a politics that borrowed heavily from her spiritual notions. Before the presidential campaign, she had done occasional lay preaching and taught adult Bible classes. During the campaign, she had carried with her everywhere a tiny Bible.

Perhaps the most revealing interview she gave between her husband's election and inauguration was with the United Methodist News Service, though it received scant attention in the mainstream press. A single paragraph encapsulated much of what her friends found so appealing about her, and her enemies were most enraged by: her seeming moral certainty.

Methodism's "emphasis on personal salvation combined with active applied Christianity," she said, was what she believed in. "As a Christian, part of my obligation is to take action to alleviate suffering. Explicit recognition of that in the Methodist tradition is one reason I'm comfortable in this church."

Though Hillary had often spoken from the pulpit, never had she allowed herself so public an epiphany, or preached so grandly, as at the University of Texas Field House in Austin on April 6, 1993, with fourteen thousand congregants in attendance, while her father lay dying not far away in Little Rock. The occasion was the annual Liz Carpenter Lecture, named for Lady Bird Johnson's White House press secretary, a woman who had commanded a degree of influence, respect, and affection in Washington that few of Hillary's aides, sadly, would ever attain. Both Lady Bird Johnson and Liz Carpenter were seated on the stage with Hillary.

It had been her intent, and that of the White House political staff, to use the occasion—on the seventy-fifth day of the Clinton presidency—for her first major speech on health care reform. Instead, as she flew from Washington to Austin on Executive One that morning, she began scribbling notes that reflected both the intense internal turmoil, personal and political, of the past weeks, and the calm, purpose, and steadiness she found in scripture and religion. The stroke her father suffered eighteen days earlier had left him in extremely critical condition and the family with an imminent decision about discontinuing life support. She had rarely left his bedside for more than a day since. Newspaper photos of Hillary during the previous two weeks, taken between hospital and car, "showed the toll of universal truths about what it means to lose a loved one," a *Washington Post* reporter wrote.

The themes of the speech she delivered in Austin, though obviously rendered more immediate and profound by the fact of her father's illness ("When does life begin?" she asked at one point, then lowering her voice, "When does it end?"), had been developing in her mind for months, maybe even years, some of her aides said later. The speech—a sermon, really—was as audacious a public address in memory by a first lady, ample evidence of how far (or not, some critics later decided) Hillary had traveled as a thoughtful human being and as a speaker since Wellesley. Instead of searching for words at the podium, as she had at her commencement, they now flowed almost perfectly, in full, often elegant sentences delivered from her handwritten notes jotted on the plane, extemporaneous bursts, and (to a much lesser extent) from an earlier draft of a health care speech she had worked on with the White House speechwriters. Yet, as she'd struggled to do since Wellesley, she was still determined to solve the mind-conservative, heart-liberal, dilemma.

Her message was as presumptuous as it was direct. The United States, she declared, was undergoing nothing less than a grave national "crisis of meaning and spirituality," which she further diagnosed as "a sleeping sickness of the soul." The latter phrase was that of Albert Schweitzer, she noted, who had discovered in colonial central Africa that more than the body could be ravaged by sleeping sickness.

To support her sweeping assertion of sea-to-sea affliction, she shrewdly invoked the repentant deathbed remarks of Lee Atwater, the young architect of the slash-and-burn Republican politics of the Reagan-

Bush era, who when he was "struck down with cancer . . . said something . . . which I cut out and carry with me in a little book I have of sayings and scriptures that I find important and that replenish me from time to time." Her tack, brilliantly executed, sought (not incidentally) to reclaim from the Republican right its corner on issues of so-called family values. In the twelve years since the defeat of Jimmy Carter by Ronald Reagan, the male moguls of the Democratic Party had eschewed prominent mention of God or of the old verities and virtues, which by 1992 seemed to have become an exercise of Republican divine right. Hillary meant to change that.

"Much of the energy animating the responsible fundamentalist right," she said in an interview a few days after her Austin sermon, "has come from their sense of life getting away from us—of meaning being lost and people being turned into kind of amoral decision-makers because there weren't any overriding values that they related to. And I have a lot of sympathy with that. The search for meaning should cut across all kinds of religious and ideological boundaries. That's what we should be struggling with—not whether you have a corner on God."

Her witness was Atwater. "He said the following," she proclaimed to her audience in Austin: " 'Long before I was struck with cancer, I felt something stirring in American society. It was a sense among the people of the country, Republicans and Democrats alike, that something was missing from their lives—something crucial. I was trying to position the Republican Party to take advantage of it. But I wasn't exactly sure what it was. My illness helped me to see that what was missing in society is what was missing in me. A little heart, a lot of brotherhood.

" 'The eighties were about acquiring—acquiring wealth, power, prestige. I know. I acquired more wealth, power, and prestige than most. But you can acquire all you want and still feel empty. What power wouldn't I trade for a little more time with my family? What price wouldn't I pay for an evening with friends? It took a deadly illness to put me eye-to-eye with that truth, but it is a truth that the country, caught up in its ruthless ambitions and moral decay, can learn on my dime.

" 'I don't know who will lead us through the nineties, but they must be made to speak to this spiritual vacuum at the heart of American society—this tumor of the soul.' " In fact, Hillary regarded the result of the 1992 presidential election as a cleansing of the national soul, a spiritual and political verdict.

"That, to me, will be Lee Atwater's real lasting legacy, not the elections that he helped to win," declared Hillary Rodham Clinton, the first Democratic first lady since Lee Atwater had enunciated the postmodern

Republican gospel and written the ballad of Willie Horton.* And there came from the crowd filling the arena in Austin shouts of "Amen" and "Yes, yes," and cheering, followed by the kind of fervent murmur that, appropriately, usually attends a religious rally, not a political speech.

"[T]he debate over family values," she declared, was "off point" and "devised for political purposes. There is no—or should be no—debate that our family structure is in trouble. There should be no debate that children need the stability, the predictability of a family. But there should be debate over how we best make sure that children and families flourish. And once that debate is carried out on honest terms, then we have to recognize that either the old idea that only parental influence and parental values matter, or the nearly as old idea that only state programmatic intervention matters, are both equally fallacious.

"Instead we ought to recognize what should be a common-sense truth—that children are the result of both the values of their parents and the values of the society in which they live. . . . That's the kind of approach that has to get beyond the dogma of right or left, conservative or liberal."

Balancing the conservative-mind, liberal-heart equation, addressing "this tumor of the soul," filling the "spiritual vacuum" that Lee Atwater had discovered on his deathbed, these notions, she suggested, would inform the Clintonian principles of governance.

"*We need a new politics of meaning.* We need a new ethos of individual responsibility and caring. We need a new definition of civil society which answers the unanswerable questions posed by both the market forces and the governmental ones, as to how we can have a society that fills us up again and makes us feel that we are part of something bigger than ourselves."

On this day, Hillary appeared intent on articulating for herself, her husband, and their presidency an overarching, benevolent, even deistic governmental philosophy that embraced both traditional notions of family and individual responsibility, as well as belief in compassionate government programs to help those less able to help themselves. The Clinton presidency would be the calm spiritual harbor in the ugly political storm. By choosing her husband as president of the United States, the electorate had shown it was intent on "remolding society." It had now embarked on fundamental change, including the recognition of a proper

*Horton, a convicted felon serving a life sentence in Massachusetts for murder, was released as part of a weekend furlough program supported by Governor Michael Dukakis, the 1988 Democratic presidential nominee. On furlough, Horton, a black man, raped and robbed a white woman, and the Bush campaign effectively used the incident in its ads against Dukakis, a classic example of negative campaigning (with clear racist overtones).

spiritual realm in government policy; and the faithful at last had a path to follow. To Lee Atwater's question, she responded:

"Who will lead us out of this spiritual vacuum? The answer is, All of us. Because remolding society does not depend on just changing government, on just reinventing our institutions to be more in tune with present realities. It requires each of us to play our part in redefining what our lives are and what they should be . . . seizing the opportunities that you are given, and of making the very best choices you can. That is what this administration, this President, and those of us who are hoping for these changes are attempting to do." It sounded a little like a presidential partnership with God.

A few weeks earlier, Hillary had been visited in the White House by Michael Lerner, the editor and publisher of *Tikkun*, a bimonthly secular Jewish journal that was an amalgam of liberal cultural and political commentary, post-Marxist dialectic, Talmudic principle, and New Age jargon.

In Hillary's office, as he had in his magazine, Lerner had propounded his Politics of Meaning, a vision of spiritually infused public life that very much fit Hillary's perception of the raison d'être of government service. Lerner's underlying assumption held that government had satisfactorily addressed the basic question of political rights, if not the economic needs, of the people; "but for the majority of Americans, there's another set of needs, totally ignored: The need to be part of an ethically based spiritual community that links us to a higher purpose. Many of us are involved in social change movements like the women's movement, the environmental movement, the movement for economic justice, the civil rights movement, the gay rights movement, the labor movement," Lerner had written. "And yet, we believe that these movements have tended to underplay or even deny a very important dimension of human life—the spiritual dimension."

In Austin, Hillary borrowed from her discussion with Lerner, asserting that "We are, I think, in a crisis of meaning. Why is it in a country as economically wealthy as we are . . . there is this undercurrent of discontent—this sense that somehow economic growth and prosperity, political democracy and freedom are not enough? That we lack, at some core level, meaning in our individual lives and meaning collectively—that sense that our lives are part of some greater effort, that we are connected to one another, that community means that we have a place where we belong no matter who we are?"

Her father's dying was obviously weighing on her, and when she did briefly discuss the need to "provide decent, affordable health care to every American" the words sounded almost tortured. "We have to ask hard questions about every aspect of our health care system. Why do doctors do what they do? Why are nurses not permitted to do more than they do? Why are patients put in the position they're in? When does life start; when does life end? Who makes those decisions? . . . [These] are issues that we have to summon up what we believe is morally and ethically and spiritually correct and do the best we can with God's guidance.

"How do we create a system that gets rid of the micro-management, the regulation and the bureaucracy, and substitutes instead human caring, concern and love? And that is our real challenge in redesigning a health care system."

By the end of her sermon, Hillary seemed to be lapsing back into the same kind of banal generalities ("We must make change our friend, not our enemy"—the same words that her husband had used in his peroration at Camp David, just before introducing her) that had punctuated her Wellesley commencement remarks. Her answer to most of what ailed the nation—indeed humanity—might be construed as a spiritual malaise that had settled over the planet, and enervated its elites from journalists to politicians.

"What do our governmental institutions mean? What does it mean to be educated? What does it mean to be a journalist? What does it mean in today's world to pursue not only vocations, to be part of institutions, but to be human? And, certainly, coming off the last year when the ethos of selfishness and greed were given places of honor never before accorded, it is certainly timely to ask ourselves these questions."

Such generalities, both in her remarks at Austin and in Michael Lerner's annunciations in *Tikkun*, led *The New Republic* magazine to comment, "It is good to hear the First Lady is also pro-meaning, but before we sign on, one question:

"What on earth are these people talking about?"

The end of her sermon, about the necessity to reject cynicism, was especially striking for a woman who, only weeks earlier, had sent her minions from the Camp David mountaintop down to the White House swamp to write a story about "villains" and, in her next major appearance after Austin, would advise the Senate Democrats that the time had come to "demonize" those who would slow down the health care train for some important roadwork. "To fill that spiritual vacuum that Lee Atwater talked about," she said in Austin, would require "most profoundly and importantly . . . millions and millions of changes that take place on the individual level as people reject cynicism . . . as they truly begin to try to see other people as they wish to be seen and to treat them as they wish to be treated."

. . .

ONLY HOURS BEFORE her father died, Hillary returned to Washington from Little Rock. She had been at his bedside there, along with Chelsea, for two weeks as the family awaited his death.

Upon her return, Hillary found the White House in disarray. She had always been the one person able to keep her husband focused, so her short absence was noticeable. She blamed Bill's staff for making bad judgment calls, for not planning and executing well enough. The health care initiative was in trouble. She was frustrated, sad, and drained.

To make matters worse, Hillary learned that while she had been tending to her father on his deathbed Bill had taken Barbra Streisand—who had gone to the White House to give the president a preview of her new album—and his mother to the annual Gridiron Club dinner (a Washington institution at which the Washington press corps salutes itself and the president). Streisand had boasted about sleeping in the Lincoln Bedroom. Soon after, Hillary reportedly ordered Streisand banned from the White House (on the ground that, being unmarried, it would be unseemly for her and her then-fiancé to stay together in the presidential mansion). Members of the press accompanying Clinton on his jog the following morning noticed that he had a deep scratch along his jaw. Dee Dee Myers explained to reporters that Clinton had cut himself shaving. But she, like many of the reporters, came to believe the wound had been inflicted by Hillary in her anger over the Streisand invitation at a time when her father was dying.

Two days later, the president eulogized his "tough and gruff" father-in-law in a simple funeral service at the Scranton church where Hillary, her father, and her brothers had been baptized. Hillary's relationship with her father had been rocky and tense at times, but she felt a heavy weight of grief at his loss. Bill recalled so many years before when Hugh drove to Arkansas to help in that first campaign in 1974. "He never told a living soul I was in love with his daughter, just went up to people and said, 'I know you're a Republican and so am I. I think Democrats are just one step short of communism, but this kid's all right.' "

As the church bells pealed, naval pallbearers had carried the coffin, draped in an American flag, into the brick-and-stone church. Looking toward his wife and the Rodham family in the front pew, Clinton said, "Lord, they loved to argue. Each one tried to rewrite history to put the proper spin on it. It was a wonderful preparation for politics."

AT THE END of the month, on the weekend of April 23–25, Bill and Hillary attended a political retreat for Senate Democrats at the Kingsmill Conference Center in Williamsburg, Virginia, that was closed to the press. Hillary updated those in attendance about the progress of the health care reform task force and the upcoming reform bill.

Hillary's Golden Rule could be a sometime thing. Her remarks now were received with disgust and distrust by two senators in particular, Bill Bradley and Pat Moynihan, who were among the most thoughtful and highly regarded men in Congress and who should have been natural allies of the Clintons. Instead, they became deeply alienated from both. Bradley and Moynihan later said they were flabbergasted at Hillary's words and attitude that afternoon, but each came to believe that the incident was indicative of something more revealing about her character.

Hillary understood—has always understood—that words count, and on this occasion she was asked by Bradley whether the Clintons' failure to meet their promise of submitting health care legislation to Congress in one hundred days—by then only a few days ahead—would make it more difficult to win passage as the administration's plan became competitive with other legislative goals on the calendar. Perhaps some substantive changes might be required in the interest of realism, Bradley suggested.

No, Hillary responded icily, there would be no changes because delay or not, the White House would "demonize" members of Congress and the medical establishment who would use the interim to alter the administration's plan or otherwise stand in its way.

"That was it for me in terms of Hillary Clinton," Bradley said many years later. "You don't tell members of the Senate you are going to demonize them. It was obviously so basic to who she is. The arrogance. The assumption that people with questions are enemies. The disdain. The hypocrisy."

Lawrence O'Donnell explained the depth of Moynihan's disappointment with the woman who would eventually succeed him in the Senate. The senator "didn't hold grudges, didn't personalize such matters," said O'Donnell. "But the 'demonizing' colored his perception of Hillary, and how she operated, for the rest of his life."

APRIL WAS a particularly difficult month. Hillary had to grieve her father's death while trying to pick up the pieces of health care reform, something she believed would be the most important aspect of her husband's presidency and her legacy. She was angry that other things were taking precedence over her portfolio.

Bill and Hillary recognized they had not been able to make progress on nearly as many things as fast as they had hoped. To mitigate some of the criticism the administration was expecting, Bill held a press conference on April 23, a week shy of the first hundred days. "In this first hundred days we have already fundamentally changed the direction of an American government," he said. It was a bold statement for a president who couldn't deliver a health care plan within the timeframe he had promised, and whose basic economic stimulus package—the first element of his larger fiscal plan—had failed to pass in the Senate.

On April 30, every member of the White House staff upstairs and downstairs was given a long-stemmed pink rose, and a notecard. It read: "I want to thank you for all the work you've done since the inauguration. We have an historic opportunity to make great things happen in our nation. Thanks for being part of the first 100 days." Each was signed, "Bill" and "Hillary."

13

The Cruel Season

[T]o achieve our overall goals for the economy, we had to sacrifice some specific promises.

—Living History

HILLARY'S ANGER at her husband's aides, the Democrats in Congress, and the Republican opposition was heightened by the toxic culture of Washington itself, manifested, as she saw it, in the unchecked power of the press, and personified by a permanent political and social elite more covetous of its personal prerogatives and perks than zealous of the commonweal.

She had arrived in January displaying supreme self-confidence. No first lady had come to the White House with as much substantive experience in government and politics. Yet, somehow, this bright, orderly, and supposedly most logical and disciplined of women failed either to comprehend or appreciate the degree to which the town's political, social, and media cultures were inextricably linked, and required careful tending.

There were Freudian, Machiavellian, even Darwinian theories about her self-destructive disdain for the ways and means of Washington (prior to her election to the U.S. Senate), and her inability to convert an inbred, parochial, local culture to her own uses—as she had in Arkansas, a place that would seem at first glance far less amenable to her charms than the nation's capital. It was all the more confounding because she was now positioned to "do all the good you can" as perhaps no woman in American history before her.

But something essential had changed since the Clintons had left Little Rock. In Arkansas, her hand had always been firmly on the wheel with his, and on the infrequent occasions when their enterprise had been forced to take an unexpected sharp turn, they were accustomed to steering it together. The exception had been after his decision not to seek the presidency in 1988, when his recklessness had almost destroyed any chance of fulfilling their dreams.

In their first months in the White House, a new and unfamiliar political dynamic was in play, owing largely to the hard economic realities they faced. Bill had surrounded himself with a coterie of strangers to deal with the economy, actuaries, Wall Street bond traders, and Washington insiders (however distinguished) whose instincts were almost exactly the opposite of Hillary's. Lloyd Bentsen seemed to have cast a spell over him. Worse, from her point of view, they all seemed to be steering Bill in the wrong direction, pulling against her, oblivious to her guidance and ignoring her navigational skill, heedless of what she and Bill stood for or how he had successfully operated in the past.

In Arkansas, almost no major policy decisions had been made in contravention of Hillary's views, and if they were, she had been present at the creation. Betsey Wright had an inviolate rule: that Hillary, Bill, and Dick Morris, convened by Wright, were always fully involved in consequential discussions and decisions. Since the Clintons had come to Washington, Hillary had to fight both for time on the president's calendar to deal with health care and, incredibly, given their history, for dominant influence over policy and process. The situation increasingly exasperated her, diminished her stature inside the administration, and chipped away at her mystique. Whatever indignities she may have suffered because of her husband's sexual adventuring, she had never before experienced a diminution of her primacy in policy matters.

Bill now seemed to be occasionally avoiding or ignoring her advice, acquiescing even to her exclusion from some meetings that had significant implications for her health care plans. "You keep telling us we have to put off these meetings [to discuss health care] because it's going to hurt the economic plan," she complained to her husband and his advisers en masse. Others implied in her stead—since it was not the kind of thing she would say—that the situation was *humiliating* to her. He had appointed her to develop the signature policy initiative of the Clinton presidency, yet he and she seemed at times to be operating at cross-purposes to achieve it.

"You could see her feeling hemmed in," said a senior aide to the president. She believed the administration should ride health care as its lead vehicle, clearing the way for other achievements and reelection in 1996. "Her attitude was, The same people who are making us give up our dreams on the economy are trying to do it to health care, too."

In Little Rock during the transition, she had put in place, with Bill's approval, a structure to ensure her oversight of all domestic policy. She and Susan Thomases had staffed the White House so that her influence and, if necessary, intervention would almost always prevail. Maggie Williams attended the daily meeting of senior presidential aides chaired by Mack McLarty, whom Hillary had personally favored to keep the trains rolling smoothly. The cabinet and the president's economic advisers had been vetted personally by Hillary, to ensure Bill's comfort and hers, and guard against surprises. She had located her own office in the West Wing, where little of consequence was likely to escape her attention, and others could not fail to notice her big foot. She had intended and expected that the clear goals and priorities she and Bill had evolved over a lifetime would guide administration policy. Those goals were methodically catalogued in a presidential campaign platform she had helped draft, and that hadn't been meant to be discarded the minute the new president was inaugurated, as was the custom.

Fundamental economic decisions, in her expectation, were to be driven by the Clintons' larger goals, not vice versa. But the enormity of the budget deficit had, of course, caught everyone by surprise, and had utterly upset the priorities and planned methodology of governance in the first hundred days, and from there forward. The new economic realities gave the economic advisers, notably the deficit hawks, a sovereignty in social policy that had never been intended—certainly not by Hillary.

By June, she believed *their* agenda was on the verge of overpowering basic principles and programs she and Bill stood for. Bentsen, Rubin, Shalala, Panetta, and Rivlin kept chipping away at her health care design before she could even see the whole picture in sufficient detail herself.

The orthodox litany of the hawks pierced her ears and was unceasing: "It won't be respected by the markets." "Wall Street won't accept Big Government." "We must keep down costs." "If there are price controls, there will be a negative reaction by the markets." Sometimes Bill seemed to follow his economic aides like a dog on a leash, other times he'd strain and bark and lash out, but in the end he—and, increasingly, she and her health care mission—was restrained by their superior strength. Hillary felt she was losing the fight for the soul of the Clinton presidency.

Bentsen, especially, felt Hillary approached her work with a holier-than-thou attitude that left little room for criticism of any kind. She appeared at times to be uncharacteristically bewildered, driven too often by frustration and increasingly by wrath, instead of her usual methodical ways. Through the summer, the conflict between Hillary and the economic advisers expanded and became both superheated and personalized. Bentsen and his deputies believed Hillary was extracting her own directives about health care in private from the president, and that further advice wasn't welcome. In fact, "we did give the right kind of advice," Shalala insisted later. "She just didn't take it. The first month, Alice Rivlin gave the president an idea: simply go to the Hill with a set of policy ideas, and then draft the legislation with the Hill, so [members of Congress] would be co-opted. In the end, we co-opted no one."

The advisers worried that Hillary's plan, as developing, was bloated with overregulation, too ambitious in concept, and too difficult to maneuver politically. Part of the problem was that they could not get a handle on what it was she and Magaziner were proposing exactly, because they both spoke in generalities and promised forthcoming details that rarely materialized with meaningful specificity. To fully realize the "grandiose" (as some of them called it behind her back) kind of reforms Hillary was envisioning might take a decade or longer. It was difficult to get Hillary to focus on the substantive aspects of decisions being made that mutually affected health care and the overall economic plan. "It was hard to get her attention on thinking through the implications of the decisions or anything else," Shalala recalled. "But that was my experience with Hillary. She was doing twelve things at once, especially after her father's death and the disarray in the White House in her absence."

Concerned that the president's economic advisers weren't included enough in the health care reform process, Rubin suggested in May that two teams debate how extensive the proposal should be. More than thirty top advisers gathered with Hillary and Bill in the Roosevelt Room to hear the arguments in behalf of two approaches: The first was less costly but essentially covered only catastrophic or serious health problems. The second was much more comprehensive, Bill and Hillary's preferred plan according to those who observed their reactions that day. But, inexplicably, the health care task force hadn't come up with hard numbers about the actual savings over the existing system the plan would produce. The stakes of that were enormous: if the promised savings did not materialize, Clinton's advisers feared he'd have to raise taxes radically. Some of the people in the room were even worried that the plan might cause enough small businesses to go bankrupt and trigger a recession. In private, many members of the economic team were terrified by how Hillary was going about health care reform. At the debate, however, officials who were already wary of criticizing the first lady in front of the president were loath to poke holes in her plan in front of a group. Instead, they pronounced the more comprehensive plan commendable but added phrases like "if the numbers work out" or "so long as it doesn't divert resources from other things we want to do."

At the close of the three-hour meeting, Hillary warned those present not to talk to the press. Still, accounts reached the *New York Times* and the *Washington Post* in a matter of days, with headlines declaring a dispute between Hillary and Bill's economic advisers. The first lady was enraged, and she took her frustrations out on her husband. "Are these people part of the administration or not?" she demanded. "What side are they on? These guys are going to derail you." The American people hadn't put him in office to reduce the deficit, she snapped. "You didn't get elected to do Wall Street economics." Worried about future leaks, Bill decided that health care meetings would no longer be so inclusive.

BILL CLINTON, no matter how fiercely embattled or frustrated in those first six months of his presidency, woke up every day thrilled and enthusiastic about the task ahead. He'd had his sights set on this job since he was a teenager. "I love this stuff," he often said. An optimist by nature, he had confidence in his vision and his ability to move past the obstacles. His anger and ill-humor in those early months rarely lasted long. The pattern had been established many years before: he blew up, used and sometimes abused people around him who became accustomed to his outbursts (though he seemed oblivious to his own excess), but he was invariably invigorated by the challenges. "The difference between their temperaments is very simple as far as I'm concerned," said Bob Boorstin, Hillary's deputy for press and communications on the health care task force. "He gets angry, and he gets over it. She gets angry, and she remembers it forever."

A White House aide who saw Hillary almost daily observed, "Some mornings she would wake up pissed off, and some mornings it would be okay. Sometimes it would be a glorious day. She has the capacity for epiphanous, spiritual awakenings." Unfortunately, those days on which the spiritual equation was wrong-sided could be brutal for others. "The person on the receiving end never gets over it," her longtime aide and family retainer Carolyn Huber had observed of Hillary's ire in the last year Bill served as governor.

One of the most senior White House officials, who was often at her (and her husband's) side during the many critical events of the 1992 presidential campaign and the White House years, raised in a conversation toward the end of the Clinton presidency the question of whether Hillary had ever been by nature a genuinely happy or even contented person. This deputy maintained that perhaps the most essential thing to understand about Hillary was that (from what he had learned and observed) she must have been an unhappy person for most of her adult life. And a very angry one at that, in his view, often in a state of agitated discontent in the years he worked with her, sometimes icy cold and embittered, though obviously capable of fun and laughter and warm friendship (though rarely of irony). Not everyone agreed, especially in Hillaryland. And it's important to note that much of the anger and unhappiness seemed to dissipate following her election to the Senate. Thereafter, for the first time since her wedding day, she began to eclipse and succeed in the public consciousness—and Democratic Party—the dominating presence of her husband. It was her turn, and that might have liberated her.

The deputy believed that Hillary's deepest anger was toward her husband, perhaps the source of most of it, unless it came from her childhood and had been aggravated by Bill and the compromises she'd allowed herself to make in their marriage. But the deputy was also aware of the enormous strength of the bond the Clintons had forged, their own obvious belief (most of the time) in the love between them, their shared commitment to certain important values and ideals, to Chelsea, and, within weeks of their arrival in Washington, their growing sense that they couldn't catch a break.

One friend who knew the Clintons quite well thought they were caged in a marriage that they both deeply resented; the ultimate prize, the presidency, was so alluring, however, that it was worth suffering. It might even be redeeming. Such an observation was not terribly original, but was dismissed by most of their close acquaintances.

But the high-ranking deputy agreed there were aspects of the relationship that trapped the two of them in ways that only increased their anger at and resentment of each other. It was obvious that Bill and Hillary could never have achieved what they had without each other, yet it had come at the cost of some great periods of unhappiness.

"Does he need her?" the deputy asked rhetorically. "Yes. Does he like her? Yes. And there are times when he's almost embarrassingly affectionate toward her. But the ambivalence is there on both sides: Because he's trapped in the marriage. He has no way out . . . it just pops out in ways he can't control. He acts out by fucking around. She's unhappy, and angry a lot of the time, and lashes out at people. . . . Punishing him, with maybe being remote, going out on her own, establishing her own identity, fighting even harder against his enemies." The deputy could see Hillary's increasing frustration with Bill in their first year in the White House.

Betsey Wright believed there was an altogether different source and timeline of Hillary's deep anger, locating its beginnings in the 1992 campaign, when Hillary's integrity first came under heavy attack, and intensifying thereafter. In Wright's view, and the view of many of Hillary's close female friends, the political facts of life in the nation's capital and the White House, not her past domestic life with her husband, were the source of her anger, and her resentment was transitory.

"Bill's women problems were not the core," said Wright. "The core was [the attack on] her integrity, her law practice, her board memberships, her income, the Whitewater development. That was the anger. The White House staff probably knew her only as an angry person because she was being besieged. . . . The real question is, Is she still an angry person now, or was that just part of what she had to do to survive? That's not always the way she was." Despite the ups and downs, until taking up residence in the White House, Hillary appeared to have absorbed Dorothy Rodham's lesson with the leveling bubble inside the ruler: stay steady.

But that would have required virtually superhuman restraint during the White House years for any first lady subjected to what Hillary had to deal with, no matter how much might have been of her own making. During her time as first lady, Hillary was being judged constantly—in a sense, penalized—not for what she saw herself as actually doing and believing, but rather as a cartoonish misrepresentation of other people's speculation, envy, anger, and even hatred. Or so she explained it to others. It is certain, though, that Hillary was tested as few public citizens have been.

More than her husband, Hillary thrived on predictability and order. Since inauguration day, the rhythm of her life had changed radically, in ways and to an extent she probably could not have anticipated, despite the baptism of a presidential campaign. Bill was not the only Clinton locked in a golden cage after January 20, 1993. To an even greater extent perhaps, Hillary was finding herself a prisoner of the presidency. For the first time since she and Bill were married, she had no independent life, no identity to pursue separate from his, no outside job, no agenda of her own, no escape. She had little outlet except for her time with Chelsea, no opportunity to shoot the breeze with Webb or enjoy the closeness of her friendship with Vince, who was now her vassal and employee, and who was increasingly troubled and distant. In Little Rock, she had been able to go about her business largely under the radar. Now there was no getting away from the intrusive presence of cameras and reporters and Secret Service agents. Since January her every move and word had been scrutinized. She had no privacy. She had to whisper in the corridors of the White House lest she be overheard by servants or security people. More than ever before, she was a captive of her marriage. She no longer had the option of leaving even if things became intolerable.

"Once that impeachment and the investigation and all that stuff was shut down is when I think she came out of her anger," Betsey Wright said. "And part of coming out of the anger was what she worked out with Bill. And I think what she worked out with him was: I'm going now. . . . It's my turn."

· · ·

HILLARY WAS THROWN more off-balance than the president in the first months of the administration. Her attention lurched without apparent method from one problem or issue to another. Her seeming disorientation was not without cause. More than Bill, she seemed to recognize early on the seriousness—even intractability—of some of the problems they were already up against, and the interconnectedness of so many seemingly disparate factors that would determine the administration's success or failure. She comprehended, beyond the budget mess and health care, that lethal dangers lay ahead (partly because she had superior knowledge of some of the troubling matters lurking in the past, aside from his womanizing). She recognized earlier that they were under attack from very powerful forces who would use that past to undermine the Clinton presidency.

According to Webb Hubbell, both he and Vince Foster formed the impression by early spring that Hillary feared her health care agenda could become an unintended casualty. Though she felt blindsided by her own economic team, the opposition from Republicans, outside lobbying interests, and a nasty chorus on talk radio felt to her not like criticism on a single issue, but a first strike against "Clintonism."

After five months in the White House, she was under constant strain, still grappling with the death of her father, unable to get the time or space to grieve in private. More than Bill, she was physically exhausted; she lacked his stamina and was losing weight. A newspaper story noted archly that Hillary "looks thinner than ever, even though she confesses that her exercise regimen has gone the way of the middle-class tax cut since she moved into the White House." On trips to the Hill, her aides noticed how she would perform perfectly during an appointment, then immediately afterward begin yawning and then collapse in the car on the way back to the White House. Bill would stay up to two or three in the morning, looking at the pictures in the halls, or reading, especially about the presidency, playing cards, picking up the phone at any hour to discuss some matter of strategy. She spent tiring hours each afternoon and evening trying to help Chelsea with her own difficult adjustment, and the extraordinary attention accorded the daughter of a president.

Not surprisingly to those who knew her best, and without calling any public attention to it, Hillary turned to prayer under duress.

On February 24, three weeks before her father suffered his stroke, Hillary and Tipper Gore had been invited to a luncheon of a Christian women's prayer group at the Cedars, a grand estate on the Potomac maintained by the Fellowship, sponsor of the National Prayer Breakfast movement and hundreds of prayer groups under its auspices. They were a surprising group, among them Susan Baker, the wife of James Baker, the Bush family's grand retainer and former secretary of state; Joanne Kemp, wife of former Republican congressman Jack Kemp, who would run for vice president in 1996; Grace Nelson, wife of Democratic senator Bill Nelson of Florida; and Holly Leachman, wife of Washington Redskins chaplain Jerry Leachman and herself a lay minister at the McLean Bible Church in Virginia, where many prominent Republican senators and conservative luminaries worshipped, including Kenneth Starr. Each of Hillary's "prayer partners," with whom she tried to meet each week when she was in town, promised to pray for Hillary regularly and presented her with a handmade book of biblical passages, personal messages, and spiritual quotations to help sustain her during her time in Washington. Susan Baker later visited Hillary and showed her great compassion about the death of Hugh Rodham and Hillary's personal political difficulties. Holly Leachman came to the White House to pray with Hillary or just to cheer her up throughout the Clinton presidency.

Hillary would later be accused of cynically becoming religious and adopting more traditional values for the purpose of political advancement after her election to the Senate. That's hard to imagine given that knowledge of her affiliation with the prayer group during the White House years was kept to a few in her inner circle.

DESPITE DICK MORRIS'S advice to Hillary about "balancing" the opposing sides of her job, there was little evidence throughout 1993 of the first lady as hostess to the nation, the world, and Georgetown. Hillary's initial approach to entertaining was highly politicized and personalized, reflecting her embattled posture, thus accelerating the Clintons' estrangement from a permanent Washington establishment that was, in many quarters, prepared to welcome them warmly.

No new president and first lady could have done much worse with the locals, or more directly set a presidency on a collision course with the inbred values of the place. In retrospect, especially given the secrets Hillary was trying to keep—embarrassments, more than outright lies—the collision was probably inevitable.

Hillary was not wrong that there were certain institutions and people in the capital, important people, who were vehemently opposed to the Clintons and their ideas, who valued sensational stories or a particular political ideology more than honest, measurable results or sincere attempts at constructive governance. Given the chance, they would derail her. But the Clintons didn't help themselves.

The first lady's social secretary was flabbergasted by Hillary's initial unwillingness to engage in the usual protocols of White House entertaining. The problem soon became so acute that members of the secretary's staff had their own term for it, borrowed from the name of one of the capital's social elite: it was called the Buffy Cafritz problem. (She had for years been a member of the Kennedy Center board and leader of many of the city's charities.)

Part of the Clintons' frustration with Washington was their comprehension of the hypocrisy of the place. The city's dominant ethic seemed too often premised on vicious, interpersonal warfare and ideological combat by day, yet treating the most hateful of combatants as honored colleagues during off-hours, even smiling at and flattering one another across the dinner table.

Instead of the basic business and conversation of the town focusing on the substance of governance (as it once did), the emphasis—conversational and journalistic—now was increasingly on who was up and who was down, and the minutiae of political horse-trading. In a quarter-century of political life in the capital since the passage of the Civil Rights Act and Voting Rights Act, perhaps two or three historic pieces of legislation had become law. Since the bipartisan consensus on Watergate and impeachment, far more energy had been expended on political and cultural warfare than on constructive civic engagement.

In choosing a social secretary who understood the anthropology of the capital, Hillary had made what seemed an inspired choice: Ann Stock, vice president of public relations for Bloomingdale's department store in New York. Stock had established a winning rapport with reporters in the Carter White House as Vice President Walter Mondale's deputy press secretary, and had since divided her time between Washington and Manhattan.

She had considerable knowledge of the contrasting power structures and players in each town: New York, a worldly meritocracy; the smaller federal district, a baronial outcropping still clinging to a peculiarly American version of primogeniture—the seniority system prevailed in Congress and was felt in the lobbying precincts of K Street beyond. This imperative was abetted by a press corps that rarely questioned the effect of such feudal arrangements, in which former members of Congress, ex-cabinet secretaries, and retired presidential aides eventually made the easy (or sleazy) transition from Capitol Hill and the White House to the high-rises of K Street.

Stock was a professional, not a socialite, unlike many of her predecessors, which should have added to Hillary's comfort with her. Her selection came as a shock to the doyennes of Washington society. ("Do I know her?" typically asked one, Polly Kraft Cutler, the widow of columnist Joseph Kraft and wife of one of the town's most eminent lawyers, Lloyd Cutler, who would later become White House counsel for Hillary's husband during the relentless advance of the special prosecutor.)

Hillary came to like and respect Stock, and to rely on her. Unfortunately, for almost a year, the first lady routinely resisted Stock's advice to mollify so-called Permanent Washington, including those who identified themselves as Democrats and were anticipating with considerable ardor a restoration at court after twelve ignominious years of the Reagan-Bush era.

Just as Bob Rubin had undertaken the higher education of Hillary Clinton in Wall Street economics, Stock attempted to tutor her in the equally arcane pseudoscience of Washington protocol. Stock was fascinated and captivated by the woman who had hired her, especially intrigued by some of Hillary's intertwined qualities that might have at first seemed incompatible. "Who would ever have expected her to go to Susan Baker's prayer group, for one? I was surprised by this incredibly together, smart, talented, determined, human, funny woman. I was blown away by her. And that consistent, first view never changed."

Stock understood how to navigate the tricky political and social shoals of Washington. She soon felt the Clintons were governing as if they didn't really grasp that they had won the election. As a result, Stock's office and the Executive Mansion itself became adjuncts of the permanent campaign, used to entertain and court constituencies and key members of Congress and pay off old debts and entertain old friends. But it was not being used as an institution of state. Instead of honoring the grandeur and cachet of the home of America's presidents, the Clintons' retinue "treated the White House as if it were a campaign venue," said Stock. "They didn't really understand the significance of the president's house." Many people in important administration positions were young and had had no previous experience in Washington.

After Hillary's much heralded (and supposedly hands-on) dinner for the nation's governors on the tenth day of the Clinton presidency, there were no more official state banquets for the next ten months. Instead, there were more than three hundred political teas and receptions at the White House, almost one every day. Most were ad hoc affairs in support of the Clintons' various policy objectives or friendly political constituencies. Meanwhile the so-called Georgetown set, leading members of Congress from both parties, the city's permanent political class—lobbyists, political consultants, influential representatives of the press—and high-level officials lured by the Clintons to Washington for important policy jobs were ignored, often studiously. One undersecretary of a government department, personally recruited by the president and Hillary, was never invited to a White House function during his three years in office except for a Christmas party to which he finagled an invitation. "They don't care about people," said the official, who had taken a huge pay cut to become a government servant.

Regularly, the Clintons' personal friends, many from Arkansas, showed up on short notice for supper at the White House. So did visiting royalty from Hollywood and the entertainment industry, who were invited to stay the night, usually in the Lincoln Bedroom. Bill, more than Hillary, enjoyed meeting celebrities, and Stock's staff was enlisted to peruse the newspapers and hotel VIP lists to see who was in town. If the star was somebody the president or Hillary wanted to meet, they were invited over.

"I think where she missed the boat and he missed the boat was at the beginning when they underestimated what it was going to be like dealing with this town and the Congress," Stock said. "And I really think they thought they were in Arkansas and didn't realize that many things are just different here."

Part of the slighting of the Washington crowd was consistent with the way the Clintons saw their jobs: "He understands why he got elected," said one of Bill's friends. "The country wanted action. He's going to give it to them. Coming down the stairs to a state dinner isn't about action." Hillary made clear that her priorities were policy, not protocol, and she intended to keep it that way. "I'm more interested in being part of helping to change our country, which is what I care about."

Terry McAuliffe, the Clintons' good friend and fund-raising savant, had a way of trying to explain their attitude, which only highlighted the problem of perception: "You have to understand these people are busier than most presidents and first ladies," he said. "I mean, they don't just go out to someone's house for dinner. I mean you've seen the guy's schedule. . . . Listen, they're into issues. They like to socialize, but they believe that's secondary to the reason they're here today." In fact, they often went to dinner at a local restaurant or the home of friends.

Those invited to the White House were not the usual guest list. As Stock noted, "It was a very issue-oriented crowd, and events were issues-oriented, built around whatever issue of the day they were trying to push." Guest lists came out of the Office of the Public Liaison, the political outreach operation, not the protocol or social office.

For almost a year, "they ran it from a campaign war room," Stock said of the "social" side of the White House.

"The mentality of the first year was more [that] of a campaign staff than a White House staff. . . . The first six months we probably did 110 to 120 events, of which we sent out only four written invitations, because we never got everything together more than twenty-four to forty-eight hours ahead of time. So, I would have my people picking up the phone and saying, 'Hi, we're having an event day after tomorrow—the president would like you to be here.' People would go, 'Excuse me, I've got to call you back. I'm getting an invitation from the White House and it's less than forty-eight hours ahead of time? . . .'

"In social Washington, even the out-of-office party still usually gets invited to the White House. But very few of the 'Washington establishment,' if you will, were invited to our White House. And, when they were, it was last-minute."

Stock, one of the few experienced Washington hands in the White House, had been assigned a principal aide who was an Arkansan, Ann McCoy, formerly the Clintons' events coordinator in Little Rock. McCoy would tell Stock, "We've got to have these FOBs [Friends of Bill] over for supper," which usually meant an informal get-together with a buffet table and then a movie in the White House theater, or popcorn and a basketball game on the big-screen television. When Stock would propose that maybe Bill and Buffy Cafritz and others on the more traditional Washington social circuit be included, McCoy would put her foot down.

"I mean, Bill and Buffy Cafritz only walked through the White House door the first couple of years for the Kennedy Center Honors reception," said Stock. "By virtue of what she does, she is an important player. There are lots of people like that in Washington. But that's the group that Hillary did not want to deal with right off the bat. And, you know, my point to her was neutralize them," by inviting them to informal gatherings at the White House and lending the first lady's name to a few selected local charity events of importance to both Washington's ordinary citizens and wealthier organizers. Hillary would respond, "I don't have time. I don't want to do this. I don't need them." Stock tried to explain to both Hillary and Bill, "It's really good for you to do some of these things. You need buzz to go around town about the good, wonderful things that you do."

Such considerations and sensitivities might appear trivial or relatively insignificant compared with weightier affairs of state, but part of what tripped up the Clintons, especially Hillary, were matters that in saner times and less overheated and polarized circumstances would have been judged in a far less significant context. For better or worse, effecting change in the capital, and thus changing the country, was an intricate process that involved a certain amount of bowing and scraping, and the first lady was no exception from the requirement. It was something of a local tradition for the first lady to attach her name as sponsor for any number of local events: the National Symphony ball; a designated disease event; the Veterinary Society dinner dance. Hillary refused. No work would have been required for the first lady, just an endorsement. ("When the president and the first lady put their name on an invitation, they don't do anything," a member of Stock's staff noted.)

Hillary told her aides (and, in less offensive terms, the press), "I'm not doing that. I've never put my name on anything where I've never worked in my life. I only lend my name to what I actually do." The local ladies perked up their ears and noticed. "That's part of how this town runs," said a member of Stock's staff. "Make them feel like they're part of the presidency. . . . I don't know that they care about issues. They care about charities."

Stock felt that if the Clintons' Arkansas friends and political supporters were coming to the White House for supper and a movie anyway, including half a dozen socially prominent Washingtonians would scarcely be a hardship. "They want to be able to say tomorrow, 'I spent Saturday night in the White House movie theater watching a movie that's not out.' That's what that game is. . . . Your whole informal buzz about what the president and first lady are doing comes through things like that. Nancy Reagan was the master of it. Barbara Bush was the master of it. The Clintons are now the master of it"—she noted in the final year of the Clinton presidency.

"It was somewhat a wasted [first] year in that it could have been easy for them to help lay the groundwork for health care and the rest of their legislative agenda," said Stock, "had they skillfully entertained. Oh my God! The people you could have had over there for a movie. And you neutralize your yip-yappers. You take a Sally Quinn . . ."

EVEN BEFORE Bill Clinton had taken the presidential oath, a marker for Hillary's conduct had been laid down by Sally Quinn, who, like Hillary, was a powerful woman in Washington who owed much of her position and influence to a husband who was one of his era's most dazzling and accomplished citizens, Benjamin C. Bradlee, the former editor of the *Washington Post*.

There were intriguing similarities between Quinn and Hillary. Both had made life far better for men of brilliant accomplishment and ability. Both of these women were resented and feared by many of the people who nonetheless courted them and desired a seat at their table; most of the courtiers, both men and women, were far more drawn to their husbands than to them.

Quinn, the daughter of an Army general, had gone to Smith College, another of the Seven Sisters schools, down the road from Wellesley. Hillary, the daughter of a martinet with none of the general's avuncular skills with people, shared with Quinn a propensity for long-held grudges. Both had experienced professional shocks—Hillary with her failure to pass the bar exam, Quinn with a hugely public embarrassment as a failed television anchor, for *CBS Morning News*—and almost immediately after had decided to throw the dice with men famously unreliable with women. Both women could be acerbic, were admirably curious, and not as sure of themselves as they liked others to think. They were also capable of wonderful friendships. Each had one child and was an unusually devoted mother.

Each was determined to be known for her own work—in Quinn's case as the author of long, penetrating profiles in the Style section of the *Washington Post*. As an employee of her husband (until his resignation as editor), she had a unique status in a uniquely powerful institution, a situation somewhat similar to Hillary's. Neither would have been commended for an ability to see herself as others did, except that Quinn knew she was better at decorating houses than almost any professional in the game, and, with her husband, she kept buying them and decorating them. Both women had a playful side that few people outside their immediate circle knew. Hillary held strong opinions that were a logical consequence of her politics and her own struggles. Quinn took surveys.

Almost any discussion of the Clintons' estrangement from the Washington establishment began with reference to a 2,200-word piece Quinn had written in *Newsweek*, which is owned by the Washington Post Company, on December 28, 1992, entitled, "Beware of Washington." Quinn's piece was prescient, presumptuous, nasty, and showed a reptilian understanding of the Washington terrain. She predicted that, "For Hillary Clinton it will be worse than it has ever been for any other first lady because she is charting new ground. Her advisers and friends are warning her of all the problems she is likely to encounter. But it is important that she be prepared for how tough, how complicated and how uncharitable the atmosphere in Washington can be when the stakes are so high."

Perhaps the first suggestion of just how uncharitable had been Quinn's *Post* attack, six weeks earlier, headlined, "Making Capital Gains: Welcome to Washington, but Play by Our Rules." By way of telling the president-elect that he was going to spend the next four years in a jungle, she wrote: "Think of it this way: Your plane has crash-landed in the middle of Brazil and you found yourself surrounded by a curious and possibly hostile tribe. Instead of giving them beads and eating the monkey tongues they offer you, you decide that you don't need their help. Fine, but don't be surprised if you end up with poison darts in your backside. Like any other culture, Washington has its own totems and taboos. It would serve the newcomers well to learn them and abide by them."

In her *Newsweek* piece Quinn offered for Hillary's consideration some thoughts about how Hillary could maneuver her way through the treacherous Washington terrain. "She must know her constituency," Quinn proclaimed. "Hillary Clinton was not elected president. At a Washington dinner recently she was heard to talk about the budget. She was impressive and knowledgeable. But her conversation was peppered with 'we': 'We got our first look at the budget.' Those who've known Hillary for years say that she has always used 'we,' that the Clintons have always operated as a team. But Little Rock is not Washington. 'We' is the kiss of death in Washington."

"She should not attend her husband's meetings," Quinn also wrote. "Hillary's attendance at the meeting in Little Rock with congressional leaders was considered by many professional Washington women to be a mistake. 'I don't go to my husband's meetings; he doesn't go to mine,' said one high-powered woman journalist."

She should not allow herself to become a scapegoat. . . . If the First Lady is wielding power, if she sits in on staff and cabinet meetings, if she makes policy—and people know it—two power centers will automatically develop, his and hers. The infighting, gossip and backbiting will be unmanageable. All of that would be distracting and damaging to the president. For Hillary Clinton, having Mack McLarty as chief of staff may seem like a perfect choice. He's someone who is reputed to be conciliatory and easygoing. He could allow her to function virtually as chief of staff. But that could be a trap for Hillary Clinton if she plans to involve herself in running the government. She won't have anyone in that job who can act as buffer. She shouldn't make Bill Clinton look like a wimp. Washington wants the president to be the president. If the perception is that his wife is telling him what to do, it will only make him look weak. If he looks weak he will not be nearly as effective as he could be. Power is what Washington is all about. If it looks like the president isn't powerful, people in this town can smell it a mile away. Symbols, appearances and perceptions are sometimes more important than reality.

The new president and the Arkansans who had come to work in the new administration were livid at both the tone and substance of the piece. "[Bill] was a little ranting. About the disdain," said presidential deputy Rahm Emanuel. "He said it to Carville and me. But James and I had the same take on it, which was, 'God bless Sally for being honest.' She was fucking honest."

Quinn now represented for Hillary the epitome of the Washington press establishment. That was ironic, because Quinn herself was ridiculed by some of the town's best reporters, though she could write a singular kind of Washington piece which arrived at certain truths that eluded more conventional journalists. And Quinn did play a kind of intriguing and visible role in the Washington social scene.

IT IS UNDERSTANDABLE that, feeling isolated and alienated in the town to which they had moved to serve the country, the Arkansans would build a substructure in which they could connect to their common past and place. "We were in a new, more unforgiving league," said Webb Hubbell. "But we Arkansans felt a need for companionship, for connection. Never mind that the Washington attitude was that if that's what you yearned for, perhaps you were in the wrong place." From this evolved Arkansas Nights, "conceived as a port in the storm," said Hubbell, in which Razorback victories could be celebrated, old stories swapped, and friendships maintained now that the Arkansans were spread across the Washington bureaucracy, many with their families back home, in jobs that kept them at their desks fifteen hours a day and in many instances living in hotels, or friends' houses, and seeing their spouses and children only on occasional weekends.

The first Arkansas Night, on a Tuesday at a Capitol Hill restaurant called Two Quail, was attended by fewer than a dozen: among them Vince Foster and his sister Sheila Anthony; Hubbell; Bruce Lindsey; Mack McLarty; Ann McCoy; Betsey Wright; Deb Coyle, an assistant to Lindsey who had worked at the Rose Law Firm and later in the governor's office; Nancy Hernreich (the president's secretary); and Marsha Scott, a bright, politically savvy former girlfriend of Clinton who became chief of staff in the personnel office. Within a month, Arkansas Nights had become institutionalized and reserved for Tuesdays. The regular crowd swelled to a couple dozen Arkansans and a select group of out-of-staters in the administration who were declared honorary Arkansans, among them Kevin O'Keefe, a Chicago lawyer and politician who had known Hillary since college; Bernie Nussbaum; trade negotiator Mickey Kantor; and Vernon and Ann Jordan. "The real test of being invited to

Arkansas Night was loyalty to Bill and Hillary," Hubbell said, "not where you came from. No one in this group would ever be a source of leaks or gossip about our friends." Movie and ball game nights in the White House theater with the president and Hillary—and often Chelsea— became an extension of Arkansas Nights.

This socializing was ridiculed by some as evidence of the cronyism and Dogpatch mentality of the new administration. The theme of the supposed small-state insularity of Hillary, the president, Hubbell, Foster, and others fascinated no one more than the editors of *The Wall Street Journal* editorial page, where it inspired irrational vitriol and contempt. Despite Foster's warning that he feared hearings on Hubbell's confirmation as assistant attorney general could lead to problems rooted in the Arkansas past, the process on Capitol Hill had been relatively painless. But not on the *Journal's* editorial page. "Who is Webb Hubbell?" the *Journal* first asked on March 2, 1993, the first of six such "Who is . . . ?" editorials about Hubbell between his nomination as assistant attorney general and his sentencing in January 1995 to a jail term of twenty-one months for embezzling funds at the Rose Law Firm. The "Who is . . . ?" formulation began on March 12, 1992, with the first of three "Who is Bill Clinton?" bombardments. The sitting ducks for the *Journal's* editorial writers included Harold Ickes, Janet Reno, Susan McDougal, Lindsey, Hillary, Patsy Thomasson (who worked under David Watkins), deputy counselors William Kennedy and Jack Quinn, and, most famously, Vince Foster.

By mid-spring, many of those present at the Arkansas Nights were concerned about Foster. He was no longer an elegant, self-assured leader. He was obviously preoccupied, a troubled and tired functionary who was having great difficulty making the adjustment.

THERE IS a photograph taken by one of the White House photographers in mid-May 1993 and never publicly released that speaks volumes. Hillary, Foster, and Bill Clinton could look no glummer. "The Travel Office is spinning out of control. They're already acting like the presidency is over," said one of their assistants in the room with them, aware of his own hyperbole. "But that's how she was taking it in '93. 'Why can't you people bring this under control? Why are we being treated like this? Why are these stories continuing? Why are these stories dominating the news? Why can't we stop them? Why are we getting totally beat up and made to look like . . .' "

Hillary was primarily addressing the lawyers in the room: Foster, Nussbaum, Lindsey, and one of Nussbaum's deputies.

The most distressed-looking person in the picture is Hillary. Foster is gaunt, sad, empty. Bill looks like he just doesn't want to be there.

The question of what exactly transpired in regard to the firings of seven employees of the White House Travel Office preoccupied the special prosecutor for more than seven years, despite its relative insignificance. As with Whitewater, a huge amount of investigative resources—judicial (but hardly judicious), journalistic, congressional—were expended. However, the "Travel Office problem" came to acquire huge symbolic importance, not least because of what George Stephanopoulos came to describe to some of his colleagues as Hillary's "Jesuitical lying."

The Travel Office difficulties for the Clintons could be traced to Bill's authorization of their friend Harry Thomason to be given a White House pass, an office in the East Wing, and a vague charter, known as the "White House Project," to continue shaping the public images of the president and first lady and the new administration. With two assistants working on the project, Thomason came up with a plan to hire the "best and brightest" directors in Hollywood to film presidential and White House events and "get the most appealing visuals"; design a new presidential seal that would project the "image of the new generation of leadership"; and use the White House as the backdrop of a lavish sixty-fifth birthday party for Mickey Mouse.

Harry and his wife, Linda Bloodworth-Thomason, had long been the Clintons' devoted friends, invaluable in the campaign and in helping plan the inaugural. As befit Hollywood producers, they were extremely skilled at packaging, and their focus had largely been matters of cosmetology and showmanship: Linda's with Hillary's appearance—clothes, makeup, hair; and Harry's with marketing the candidate and making him more appealing to the voters. He had helped coordinate and sat at the Clintons' side on the 60 Minutes set. After being billeted in the Lincoln Bedroom during the inaugural week, Linda went back to Hollywood, but Harry stayed on to pursue his White House Project and advise Hillary and Bill in private. And it was he who had first suspected Secret Service and White House domestic staff leaks.

On February 17, the day the president presented his economic plan to Congress, Bill also took a moment to peruse a note from one Darnell Martens, a business partner of Thomason. It suggested that the aviation business in which the two were partners, TRM, be awarded a government consulting contract to review government use of nonmilitary aircraft. During the campaign, TRM had been paid commissions for arranging air charters for the candidate and his entourage, usually aboard the airplane referred to by the press as "Air Elvis." Now that Clinton was president, Martens had also suggested to Thomason that they change the name of TRM to Harry Thomason and Associates, to "capitalize on 'Thomason' name recognition."

"These guys are sharp," the president wrote to Mack McLarty on a note accompanying Martens's proposal. "Should discuss with Panetta, [Philip] Lader," the director and assistant director, respectively, of the Office of Management and Budget. More important than the note was Thomason's insistent pushing of a related matter. He and other Arkansans in the White House claimed that the Travel Office, which handled the multimillion-dollar business of arranging flights and hotel accommodations for members of the press accompanying the president, first lady, and other White House officials, was haphazardly managed and more than likely a semilegitimate operation in which fraud or embezzlement might be occurring.

In late April or early May, Thomason discussed the matter of the Travel Office with both Bill and Hillary. She was receptive. "Harry was more the instigator," said a White House aide. "It was as if someone put a lever under the boulder and it started down the hill and hit the village at the bottom of the hill."

Because the Travel Office served the press corps directly, Hillary—inspired by Thomason's assurance, according to her aides—became convinced that a spate of favorable stories would result from the disclosure that the Travel Office was being operated dishonestly, its employees fired, and new procedures and people put in place on orders of senior White House officials. One of the president's pledges in tandem with his economic plan for reduced spending throughout the government included a pledge to trim, by as much as 25 percent, the number of employees in the White House. Reconstituting the Travel Office as a lean, well-run entity would add legitimacy and seriousness to the claim.

"Stay ahead" of the problem, Hillary had told Thomason in early May, agreeing that weeding out corruption would make a "good [press] story."

The first lady's intervention compelled senior staff members to resolve the Travel Office situation with alacrity. McLarty later explained, "the fact that the first lady, one of the principals, had raised this issue, that adds an element of priority to any matter, and it did to this one."

Thomason relayed to Watkins that the first lady was "very interested." On May 12, Cornelius reported back to Thomason, Watkins, Foster, and William Kennedy (Foster's deputy in the counsel's office) that Billy Dale, director of the Travel Office for thirty years, and his Travel Office employees were careless in their accounting and recordkeeping. It was true that for many years, the Travel Office had laid out large amounts of cash for tips and unanticipated expenses on press trips, and afterward charged each media organization for its estimated share without providing an itemized breakdown. However, Cornelius exaggerated the facts. She claimed that the checks written for large amounts of cash without corresponding records were financing "lavish lifestyles" for employees of the office; she had learned, actually, of only one employee's boat and another's vacation home.

To further demonstrate likely criminality, Kennedy prevailed on friendly FBI agents who worked with him on vetting presidential nominees to open a formal investigation. He told them the matter was of interest at the "highest levels" of the White House. With this suggestion Kennedy had acted inappropriately. He had either been unaware of, or ignored, a rigid protocol initiated after Watergate that required all White House officers to inform the head of the Justice Department before contacting the FBI. This protocol, when ignored, could lead to real trouble: one of the articles of impeachment against Richard Nixon was for impeding the FBI's investigation.

Hillary increased the pressure to take action on the Travel Office situation the next day. "Are you aware that there are potentially very serious problems in the Travel Office?" she asked McLarty when they met privately at her request. He said he was.

"Oh, well, good," she said. "Then if you're aware of it, I know you're looking into it."

McLarty alerted Watkins and Foster about his conversation with Hillary.

She also talked to Foster directly about the Travel Office twice that day. "HRC generally appeared less than satisfied with timeliness of decision-making, i.e., cloture," Foster jotted in his notes.

The next day, Friday, May 14, Foster asked Watkins to call Hillary. An audit of Travel Office records by the Peat Marwick accounting firm had found a serious lack of organization and numerous inconsistent financial practices, especially in the handling of petty cash on press trips, Watkins reported to her.

"Harry says his people can run things better," Hillary replied, according to Watkins. And with the staff cuts, "we need those people out—we need our people in. We need the slots."

Since the transition, a twenty-five-year-old cousin of Bill's, Catherine Cornelius of Little Rock, who had supervised travel arrangements for the Clinton campaign, had been agitating for her own appointment as director of the Travel Office, and urged that its career employees be fired and a new staff of Clinton loyalists be named to work under her. She was assigned in April to work in the Travel Office and report to another Arkansan, David Watkins, White House director of management and administration.

Watkins called Thomason later that evening to tell him about his conversation with Hillary and the progress of the audit.

On Sunday night, May 16, Hillary spoke with McLarty before a dinner party in the White House residence. McLarty told her that Peat Marwick already found "mismanagement and possible misconduct." Hillary seemed unsurprised.

"Well, this is a serious matter," she said. "Let's be sure we make a decision on this. Let's stay after it."

On May 17, Watkins told McLarty and Foster that he had decided to fire the Travel Office employees, citing his phone call with Hillary. He planned to hire a Little Rock company to take over, and put Cornelius in charge.

"Well, I had dinner with the president and Mrs. Clinton last night, and it was certainly on her antennae," McLarty agreed.

Watkins had his assistant prepare a memo detailing the plan for the firings, and he sent a copy to Hillary.

In urging these changes, Hillary had failed to take into account the close relationship between Dale, the Travel Office employees, and members of the press who traveled with the president. The Travel Office performed numerous favors for reporters, including making it easy for them to clear customs, get around in foreign cities, and ship gifts back home. With the reporters already deeply distrustful of the administration—by now Stephanopoulos was considered by many of the same journalists who had liked him during the campaign to be an unreliable source of information who had failed his duty to carry through on the Clintons' promises of an open, truth-committed administration—the Travel Office affair was an easy mark to establish the dissembling of its top officials, including the first lady.

On May 19, without any opportunity for Travel Office employees to defend themselves, all seven holdover members of its staff were fired and told to clean out their desks. There had been moments when some officials—Watkins and, perhaps, Foster—had wondered whether Hillary wasn't moving too fast. But they had felt her ire when they had expressed caution about getting rid of longtime Secret Service agents and White House domestic staff, and they were disinclined to be reprimanded by her again.

Neither Hillary nor Bill, who had less intimate knowledge of what was happening with the Travel Office, was prepared for the firestorm of press fury that now struck the White House. In fact they had expected to be congratulated for shutting down an operation that ostensibly was cheating the taxpayers. Instead, many reporters concluded that the firings were a cover-up for the Clintons' cronyism, especially after the White House confirmed that the beneficiaries of the firings might include Harry Thomason and a young cousin of the president.

Only three weeks earlier, the Clintons had brought their staff to Camp David to discuss how their story should be told to the American people. Reporters now discovered that Watkins had improperly ordered an FBI investigation, and that Stephanopoulos had asked an FBI agent to modify the bureau's public statement in a manner that would strengthen the case for firing the employees. Janet Reno, the new attorney general, complained publicly that the FBI had been contacted by the White House without her authorization. When the White House claimed belatedly that the Travel Office problems had, in fact, been discussed as part of the vice president's "Reinventing Government" assignment, Gore's office denied it.

The same day that the Travel Office dismissals were announced, newspaper front pages and the morning television broadcasts were already trumpeting the dissonant tale of Air Force One burning fuel on the tarmac at Los Angeles International Airport for forty-five minutes while the president had his hair cut by Christophe of Beverly Hills, whose fee was usually $200 a clip for nonpresidents. Though the White House press office denied heatedly that the tarmac trim had resulted in flight delays of other planes, the Federal Aviation Administration made clear that numerous aircraft were held up because two of the airport's four runways had to be closed for more than an hour. (To make matters worse, a press plane had waited behind Air Force One while Christophe administered his haircut.)

For the press, the confluence of these events was something straight out of *The Beverly Hillbillies*. Linda Bloodworth-Thomason gave the critics more ammunition by appearing on *Good Morning America* to defend her husband, who she said would never have thought, "Ooh, I'm going to like take my six-figure salary a week and fly off to Washington and see if I can't get those seven little guys out of that Travel Office in the White House. It's sort of the equivalent of taking over a lemonade stand."

Later, Hillary and Bill noted wanly that the Travel Office—even in the final view of the special prosecutor, as it turned out—was hardly a professionally run operation, and was worthy of scrutiny. But for weeks after the firings, the White House response, much of it fashioned through the counsel's office and Vince Foster, was to backtrack under duress while going to great lengths to keep Hillary's role obscured. Each unappealing detail that revealed her and the Arkansas "cronies' " involvement excited the investigative instincts of the press. This was confirmation, as many had always maintained, that Hillary manipulated her husband, and that, as always, she had something to hide.

For the Clintons, a state of warfare now existed. The White House became the Clintons' bunker, and stonewalling often seemed to be the safest defense. Dee Dee Myers confirmed under harsh questioning that Catherine Cornelius was, indeed, related to the president, but no nepotism was involved because she was "a distant cousin."

Six days after the firings, the administration totally distracted, the White House announced that five of the seven Travel Office employees would receive new government jobs. "Travelgate" rolled on, though, as editorial pages expressed outrage. Now Hillary argued against further apologies or backtracking.

In fact, there was wholesale mismanagement and financial chicanery in the Travel Office. The Peat Marwick report established that records for press receipts were not meticulously kept.*

On May 26, Bill ordered an "internal investigation" of the firings, to be led by a senior presidential deputy, John Podesta, and his aide Todd Stern. Throughout the inquiry, McLarty, Thomason, Foster, and Watkins all downplayed Hillary's role to the point of nonparticipation. Foster pressured Watkins to protect Hillary by preventing disclosure that she'd suggested cleaning house to get "our people" in the Travel Office.

Podesta faced a dilemma in whether to fully investigate Hillary's role. As Stern described in his notes, "We need to think seriously about whether or not it won't be better to come clean. In sense of saying, even to point of conceding, that HRC . . . had some interest." In their initial interviews with Podesta and Stern, neither Foster nor Watkins had mentioned Hillary.

What Hillary did and did not do in the Travel Office matter, the circumstances, and who else was involved, were described in a memorandum written by Watkins six months later but not revealed until it was turned over to the special prosecutor's office under a subpoena. It stated:

> At the time the Travel Office situation began to receive our attention . . . we had not had a victory or any press success since the February address to the Joint Session of Congress on the Economic Plan, and the perception was that a big success was

*After the auditor declared $18,000 of petty cash unaccounted for, Dale came up with $2,800 that he said he found in a drawer (he had also retrieved $2,500 from a personal account the same day). Charged with embezzlement, he attempted to fashion a plea bargain for himself by agreeing to admit to "inadvertent" wrongdoing and by giving $69,000 back to the government. After the prosecutor refused his offer, he was acquitted of embezzlement at trial. The legal verdict, however, did not address the indisputable fact of reckless management of the Travel Office and of the hundreds of thousands of dollars that regularly passed through it.

needed. This was apparent to all at the White House, but especially to the First Lady whose Health-Care Task Force was being delayed and extended beyond its May deadline.

Harry [Thomason] sold the First Lady on his plan and vision of this as a good story, and he got her excited about it. Her enthusiasm for the issue and story likewise got Harry more excited and more committed to the project. Then, Vince Foster became involved, and Vince conveyed his, Harry's and the First Lady's excitement to me via regular visits and discussions. . . . The First Lady, in particular, was tired of delays on Health Care and other fronts; she wanted us to just do it—we are in control.

In late May, the Clinton administration seemed to many outsiders to resemble a car barreling downhill with failing brakes. There appeared to be no one in the White House capable of preventing a fatal wreck. The question of whether the Travel Office machinations represented a "Gate," a "fiasco," a "conspiracy," or a "criminal enterprise by the president's cronies and his wife" seemed to overshadow everything else. The perception was not altogether fair. The economic plan was moving forward. But Hillary was right that they weren't getting their message out, though she saw herself as blameless. Reports of fights between Democratic members of Congress and the White House on the economy and the budget were still overshadowing her health care reform agenda. To her horror, the leaked item in the *Chicago Tribune* (about her supposed lamp-throwing tirade) had revived—in the press and among Washington gossips—questions about the emotional state of the Clinton marriage, just when she'd thought the subject might be retired.*

Throughout May, Hillary showed up on the cover of one magazine after another, the result of a public relations blitz originally intended by the White House to correspond with the release of the health care bill, which didn't exist. *People* magazine's "Hillary Clinton—Mom, Wife, Policy Wonk" showed her trying to balance her work with her role as a nurturing mother. *Time's* cover read, "Hillary Rodham Clinton is the most powerful First Lady in history. Does anybody have a problem with that?"

---

*In Arkansas, the local newspapers had never addressed intimate questions about their marriage until Bill had declared for the presidency in 1992. In fact, their quarrels there were louder and more frequent than in Washington, according to aides. As Hillary told Bill's old friend Carolyn Staley one afternoon during his governorship, she enjoyed some of the back-and-forth, particularly if the arguments had an intellectual component. "I wonder how history is going to note our marriage," Staley quoted her as saying. Hillary said she could never have married someone as deferential and quiet as Staley's own husband.

Another *Time* cover that month pronounced him "The Incredible Shrinking President." By the end of May, his poll ratings had slipped twenty points to below 40 percent, the lowest approval rating any president had received so quickly. The controversies and lack of focus of the first hundred days had taken their toll.

When he wasn't angry he seemed dejected. Clinton was disgusted with Republicans and the press for refusing him a honeymoon. He saw himself responsibly adapting his presidency to the new fiscal and political realities, but critics were still branding him as a tax-and-spend liberal. He was so down that his appointments director, Nancy Hernreich, constantly readjusted his pace to accommodate his swinging moods. At one point, Bob Rubin asked another cabinet officer going into a meeting with Clinton to find some way to cheer the president up.

When called for, Hillary had always acted like a supra-chief of staff, protecting her husband and holding his staff accountable. Now, as she had in the past, she called her husband's aides to bawl them out. In the White House, she addressed her frustrations in larger staff meetings. Her anger sometimes seemed to be an indirect criticism of her husband, as if his staff's missteps were a reflection of his own inadequacies. Describing one of her outbursts at the White House, a top administration official said, "Her words were about the staff, but it was clear the president was her target."

On another occasion, aboard Air Force One en route to meet the pope, Hillary intervened in a discussion between her husband and his trip director, Wendy Smith, about whether the president should leave his briefcase on the plane upon arrival in St. Louis. "You don't need it. Leave it here. You always do that. Leave it. We have maybe five minutes of downtime. Just leave it," Hillary told him. But when Clinton's entourage reached its destination, they learned the pope would be three hours late. And the president was without his briefcase. "You know, your staff always does that," Hillary was heard to whisper to her husband. "They don't serve you well. They never ever serve you well." The president ordered the entire party back to the plane, which required a forty-minute drive. The Clintons' rage intensified on the way back. "Everybody [was] just in a pissy mood," a member of the staff said. "Everything [was] building. The pressure. . . . She [had] been screaming at him for forty minutes by car about how shitty his staff is." When they reached Air Force One, the president exploded at his trip director in front of the press.

During this period, Hillary went to see a prominent Democratic elder—not an elected official, but one of the capital's most powerful insiders—for advice. "She was very nervous about the press," he said. She told him that Washington was very different than she expected it to be.

People were vicious. They would try to stab you in the back. She said she was particularly unnerved by the coverage—news stories, editorials, columns—of the *New York Times* and the *Washington Post*. They seemed to object to her having opinions, she said, playing a role in the administration, her health care portfolio. They always wanted to project the idea that she was usurping the powers of the president.

"I said [in response] there's never been a first lady who's really been an acting policy adviser, and been given a major policy role by the president," recalled the Washington elder. "And that I didn't know if it was a role that anybody could possibly succeed at." Learning to deal with the press was essential to getting anything done in Washington, however, and probably as difficult a trial as any presidency had to undergo.

Gently, he suggested that there were not enough people on the president's staff or her own who had sufficient experience in Washington. At night, especially, when the president would have people over and summon friends for conversation, except for Vernon Jordan, he was hearing too much from "the outside," not the inside.

She responded that they wanted to have "a national staff—not an Arkansas or a Washington staff." The Washingtonian noted that Magaziner and Nussbaum seemed to be running into particular troubles; he was sensitive to the fact that her months in the White House were "probably the first time she really had been consistently criticized for her policy judgments."

Aware that members of the city's establishment felt she was snubbing them, Hillary said she didn't "mind doing all the things a first lady is supposed to do." Throughout, she referred to Bill as "the president," and proceeded to talk about "We" in terms of plans for the administration.

BILL ASKED Mack McLarty to engage Washington veteran David Gergen in conversation about the administration's troubles. Gergen had been writing critical editorials in *U.S. News & World Report*, making suggestions about what the president ought to do. After their initial conversation, Gergen suggested McLarty hire someone like Stu Eizenstat, who had worked in the Carter administration. A few nights later, the two talked again, but this time McLarty said the president wanted him for the post and invited him to dinner. Gergen could solve several serious problems. His Republican credentials would help Clinton appear more centrist, his age (fifty) and experience would lend comparative seniority to the White House team, and his knowledge about the inner workings of Washington would help the president improve relations with the city's press, politicos, and socialites.

The next night, after the two ate a lamb dinner at McLarty's home, the president called around midnight. "Bill Clinton can be highly persuasive one-on-one, and over the next thirty minutes, he made a convincing appeal," Gergen recalled. "How deep a hole he was in. How my experience and judgment could help him out. How I could serve as a bridge to the press, to Republicans, and to people I respected in Washington. How much it mattered to the country. Would I please consider it?"

The position was billed as counsel to the president, which would put Gergen in the inner circle with Hillary, Al Gore, and McLarty. Gergen understood the most important dynamic of the Clinton presidency, so before agreeing to sign on, he wanted to meet with the first lady. He wanted to know if she was the hard-core liberal pulling her husband to the left that the press was painting her as.

"I didn't want to be there for decoration. So I had to talk to her. I also had to know this wasn't being done against her will."

Gergen met Hillary on the third floor of the residence while they waited for Bill to return to the White House from a speech in Philadelphia. Hillary was already sold on Gergen, whom she knew fairly well from several Renaissance Weekends. She started in right away about why she thought Gergen was the right choice to help the Clintons. The staff had never established a satisfactory daily routine to make the White House run smoothly. The president was not conveying a single, coherent message, and he didn't have any Washington veterans on staff to help him avoid amateurish mistakes. "She was very positive," Gergen said. "She said, 'You've got to help us,' and you know, 'We really need somebody to help [us] understand Washington.'" Gergen was blunt. *Why did she hate the press so much? Why hadn't she made an effort to court the Washington elite?* Hillary sidestepped. The press had been brutal, she said, but she genuinely wanted to improve the relationship. Sure, she would reopen the press corridor if he thought it would help. And she was planning social events—dinners to court the Washington establishment and a barbecue for the press. Gergen was just as concerned with Hillary's ideology. "If he's asking me to come in and help him get back to the center, I don't want to get in a fight with you about getting back to the center," Gergen said to her. "I mean, I've got to know where you're coming from. And she said, 'No, you have to understand I'm much more traditional,' going back to the Goldwater Girl stuff, and you know . . . 'I want traditional values, and I really think we can do it in a bipartisan way,' and so forth and so on. She gave me all the stuff that is very reassuring about why someone of my background and interests would feel comfortable."

The internal mess Gergen found when he arrived was greater than he had anticipated. It had been caused to some degree by parallel power structures that had been allowed to form in the White House. "In the new world, the first lady and the vice president maintained sizable staffs of their own whose primary loyalty ran to them, not to the president," Gergen said. Gergen and his deputy were "tagged as 'Bill people' when we arrived and everyone assumed he was our liege, which he was, in effect. But we soon found there were 'Hillary people' and 'Gore people' who were less interested in the president than in the person they served. Some crossed barriers. The president, for example, had faith in the political judgment of Maggie Williams . . . and Maggie managed to serve both principals well. But she was a rarity."

Hillary's criticism of Bill's staff could be caustic, and she made no secret of her view that the staff of the first lady was better and more efficient. "One felt that even though people were on the White House staff, some belonged to her and some belonged to him in their first loyalty," Gergen said.

Dick Morris said Hillary thought Bill's staff members were too independent: "She'd say, 'That staff in the White House. They're so screwed up. They just talk to each other. They don't talk to anybody else. They don't care what I think. They don't care what Bill thinks. They just go ahead and do things. And they screw it up every time.'" Said Roy Neel, the vice president's majordomo, "She was very frustrated in having senior staff have a kind of misplaced deference to her, and I think she found it insulting that they wouldn't [engage] with her. It was kind of patronizing, and I think there were people who were frightened of her as well . . . unclear how they were supposed to relate to her."

Hillaryland had quickly morphed from an offhand remark in the campaign to a full-blown culture in which Hillary surrounded herself with people who were loyal to her cause and would do her bidding. When the stress of the office got to be too much for the first lady, Hillaryland became a place of comfort that she might not otherwise have had. It was a protective recovery zone. In *Living History* she wrote about their "own little subculture." She said leaks came from the president's people, not hers, who were discreet and loyal. She spoke of their "camaraderie."

"She probably has the least amount of staff turnover and the most loyal staff of anybody in Washington," said James Carville. But the loyalty, some believed, could be blind, and came at a price. A senior aide to the president said the only people Hillary could get close to her on the staff were "Kool-Aid drinkers." In *Talk* magazine, Hillary's deputy chief of staff, Melanne Verveer, had asserted that the staff didn't hesitate to stand up to Hillary. But others said that meant nothing: the only criticism of their boss had to do with trivial things. "They think because they can say to her, 'Oh my God, that [outfit] looks ridiculous,' that they have a really honest relationship with her. But I'll tell you one thing. There's not one of them that, when she comes off of an interview, they say, 'You know, Mrs. Clinton, you fucked up,' or 'Mrs. Clinton, I mean, what were you thinking?' It doesn't happen," said the presidential aide.

Tinkering with the levers and personnel changes, however, were just that: tinkering. In the last year of the Clinton presidency, a member of the White House legal team, Mark Fabiani, succinctly and devastatingly explained many of the difficulties of the early days of the administration: "Based on everything that anybody ever found out about that period, she was the one that was directing. During the campaign, they went out and got Jim Lyons, the lawyer in Denver, to write the so-called Lyons Report to justify their investment in Whitewater. She was the general. She said, 'You know, these people are coming after us. Here's what we're going to do.' And no one ever disputed that. When the *New York Times* threatened to run a front-page story saying that she lied about having released all the Whitewater records, there wasn't even a thought about saying, 'Well, she wasn't in charge of releasing the records.' Because she was in charge of it. She was the one that made the decision. And as far as I can tell it was that way from then on. . . .

"But it was always very ad hoc. It would be event-driven: scramble, marshal what people you could drag together. Drag John Podesta in. Drag Susan Thomases in. You know, get people in a room. Decide what to do and then, you sort of handle it as part of your other duties. Which never really worked for anybody. The Travel Office was a very similar thing. . . . No matter what you believe about what she said or didn't say, she was at the center of that whole effort to review the Travel Office. People updated her about it. People talked to her about it. And, you know, she's in the middle of these things, because she wants to be in the middle of these things. And she's concerned about this stuff.

"When there was an [internal] investigation of the Travel Office, she was not under oath. But the counsel's office basically wrote an answer that purported to be her. 'Mrs. Clinton does not believe . . . Mrs. Clinton did not do this, or that . . . Mrs. Clinton did not instigate. . . .'

"Basically, the response was to say, she did not order the firing of these people and wasn't involved in it. And, again, it's the type of situation where the aftermath is much worse than the original action.

"And there was a pattern. . . . I mean it happened every time. It happened with Whitewater in '92. It happened with the Travel Office. It happened when Foster killed himself. You know, she was the one who got people together and figured out, you know, 'How are we going to handle this? How are we going to deal with it?' "

FOR THE LAST MONTH of Vince Foster's life, Hillary spoke with him at most once—and then for hardly a second. Foster's position in the White House was unique. He was deputy counsel to the president, technically the deputy to Bernard Nussbaum, but his knowledge of what was going on in the White House, upstairs and downstairs, was far greater than Nussbaum's owing to his lifelong friendship with the president and, even more important, his relationship with Hillary. In fact, his overriding knowledge of the intricacies of White House business, private and public, exceeded that of the chief of staff, McLarty, or anyone else in the administration.

No one has ever presented convincing evidence that Vince and Hillary were lovers. But they had been, in some ways, closer than lovers, absent the rancor and messy business that usually attends a love affair. By all accounts, Hillary was totally unguarded in his presence, and, until they got to Washington, he in hers, at least as far as his restrained self would permit.

Perhaps even more than Bill Clinton, Vince understood Hillary's good intentions in everything he had ever seen her do. And because he knew her so well, he understood her gray areas, the shadings, complexions, and context that would never be nearly so apparent to someone else.

In four months in Washington, Foster had come to understand the harshness of the place. Unfortunately, he found little to enjoy, not even the physical beauty of the city. The political combat that had come to define the capital and demean the practice of governance was something far removed from anything he'd observed in Arkansas, or from his far-away view of Washington from Little Rock. He had been completely unprepared for the sheer brutality of the place, and he was out of his league.

A first-rate litigator, a wise counselor, a gentle soul, his rapid immersion into the Washington cauldron, feet first, was far different than that experienced by, say, a congressman, who gradually got used to the place without the whole country watching his every move.

Foster came to Washington to personally serve the president and the first lady; by extension, he was there to help them serve the country. His interests were theirs. Let Bernie Nussbaum worry about the institutional sanctity of the White House (Nussbaum actually spent little time doing so, and saw himself as a zealous, pugnacious defender of this president and his presidency).

Only Betsey Wright had ever had as clear a view of what transpired between Bill and Hillary in public and private, and her view was from the perspective of the governor's office; her interaction with Hillary was based on the mutual interest they shared in keeping Bill functioning at his best. Vince's perspective was almost exactly the opposite of Betsey's: though he had first known Bill when they were children in Hope, he had become a presence in his life again only after Hillary came to work at the Rose Law Firm in 1976. He knew more about Bill from Hillary than from Bill. Vince had become a shoulder for her to lean on. Though insouciance was not the first word that many acquaintances would use to describe Hillary, Vince saw that in her and loved it. He shared a side of himself with her as she shared a piece of her life that she could not with Bill. There was nothing threatening to Bill about their closeness, nothing illicit, and he, too, had great appreciation for Vince's qualities of discretion, wisdom, legal skill, and—something Bill often lacked—decorum.

Foster was particularly stressed about the internal investigation of the Travel Office firings. He had brought Bill Kennedy in to work on the audit and FBI investigation, and now he felt responsible. He told Webb Hubbell he was thinking of hiring a lawyer, though Hubbell didn't know if that was for Foster or his deputy. Foster was also worried that there would be hearings on Capitol Hill, and that he would be part of the investigation. The stress was taking a physical toll on him. His face became drawn and gray, and he appeared perpetually exhausted. His wife and children had recently arrived to take up residence. "At the time, we laughed about the fact that Bruce, Vince, and I were all losing weight," Hubbell recalled. "We called it being on the Stress Diet."

Particularly grating to Foster was the series of destructive editorials in *The Wall Street Journal* criticizing the president's aides. When one day the newspaper asked him for a photograph of himself, he stalled because he knew the *Journal's* intentions weren't good and because he wanted no part of the political spotlight. Lawyers should do their work in private, he told a friend.

Foster eventually sent in his headshot, but on June 17, the paper printed a column entitled "Who Is Vince Foster?" with a large question mark where the photo normally would have gone. The editorial argued that the Clinton White House tended toward "carelessness about following the law," and pointed to the example of Foster's refusal to provide the newspaper with a photograph of himself, the *Journal's* Freedom of Information Act request to obtain one, and how Foster and the White House had not responded within a ten-day period as law required. "No doubt Mr. Foster and company consider us mischievous (at best)," the *Journal's* editors wrote. "Does the law mean one thing for critics and another for friends? Will we, in the end, have to go to court to get a reply, or will even that work? Does it take a $50,000-a-day fine to get this mule's attention?"

On June 24, another *Journal* column, "Vincent Foster's Victory," attacked Foster's partially successful appeal defending the procedures of Hillary's health care task force, in the physicians and surgeons lawsuit. "We suspect that Vincent Foster and Ollie North might hit it off," the editors wrote.

Barely anyone in Washington outside of the political right paid attention to the paper's editorial page, which was overtly biased in contrast to the rest of the paper's journalism. But Foster knew that members of Arkansas's professional community read the *Journal,* and its editorials, religiously. He believed the *Journal's* editors were trying to force an Arkansan to leave the White House. Foster also worried that its reporters or someone else's would again allege that he and Hillary had had an affair. Foster's sister, Sheila Anthony, and his colleagues at the White House tried to convince Foster that the editorials were "par for the course" in Washington politics.

THE WHITE HOUSE released the internal Travel Office Management Review's findings on July 2. Watkins, Kennedy, Cornelius, and Jeff Eller, director of media affairs in the White House, received formal reprimands. Harry Thomason, Myers, Stephanopoulos, and the counsel's office were also criticized.

Podesta and Stern had allowed Maggie Williams to review a draft of the report before it was released, and, in the final version, barely mentioned Hillary's participation and the effect her interest had on the staff. Still, Hillary was furious at Podesta for dragging her through the investigation. She would hold a grudge and blacklist him the following November when he was considered for deputy chief of staff.

As the White House had hoped, the report lost some of its sting in the dead news cycle over the long July 4 weekend. Still the *New York Times* asked, "Why was notice sent to Hillary Rodham Clinton and not her husband the president?"

Back in May, Senators Bob Dole and Arlen Specter had called for a congressional investigation, but the Democrats who controlled the majority rejected hearings on the firings. On July 14, Dole made a speech from the Senate floor asking Attorney General Reno to appoint a special counsel. This was the first moment in the Clinton presidency when Republicans made a strong case for a criminal investigation of the

Clintons and the people around them. A line was crossed psychologically for Hillary, and even more so for her chosen protector, Vince Foster.

Foster was beside himself. He believed that he had personally failed Hillary and the president on the Travel Office matter. He spoke to his wife about resigning. Foster told Hubbell he feared his office phone was being bugged by the Secret Service or Republican loyalists at the White House. Foster's wife suggested he put his frustrations on paper as a kind of therapy. "I made mistakes from ignorance, inexperience, and over-work," he wrote. "I was not meant for the job or the spotlight of public life in Washington. Here ruining people is considered sport." He wrote of the *Journal* editorials, "The WSJ editors lie without consequence." The Travel Office fiasco appeared to be the greatest source of his anxiety. He wrote, "No one in the White House, to my knowledge, violated any law or standard of conduct, including any action in the Travel Office. There was no intent to benefit any individual or specific group."

He urgently asked Susan Thomases to meet with him. He told her he feared Hillary would be blamed for the Travel Office firings and dragged through the mud. He also confided to Thomases that he was exhausted and that his marriage was strained. He and his wife were fighting about whether to go back to Arkansas. "I'm sure he wanted to go, but felt he couldn't," Hubbell explained. "He also wanted to stay in Washington, but felt he couldn't. He couldn't do either because of that thing inside him that demanded he not fail—that he always march proudly forward toward excellence and never turn back in defeat."

At the same time, it was increasingly hard for Foster to keep fighting tooth and nail for Hillary's interests when their relationship had degener-ated, said Hubbell. "Vince had her heart, he did," said a close friend of Foster. "In the end, I think they both were brokenhearted. He couldn't serve her, he couldn't do enough for her, once she became the first lady. And, she couldn't allow him to be her real friend, like he'd been, because she wasn't herself." When he had left Arkansas for Washington, he had expected the relationship with Hillary to remain as deep as ever. The last thing he had expected is that it would turn upside down. Some days he was a flunky, some days he was a legal counselor, other days he was a fixer, but no longer was her intimate. "He was completely out of his game, and the work kept piling up," Foster's friend recalled. "And Hillary does not like things not happening when she wants them to happen. And trails were leading back toward her."

Each day he came back to his drab office. He had no pictures on the walls, just a few in a bookcase. There were still boxes everywhere. He couldn't really confide in his friends about much more than the work-load. Still he got together once or twice a week for dinner with his old friends from Arkansas—Hubbell, Marsha Scott, Nancy Hernreich, Deb Coyle. They would go to Two Quail or other places open late. They wouldn't leave work until after 10 P.M. The Arkansas crowd knew he was struggling, but they did not suspect the severity of the depression he was experiencing.

On July 16, Foster went to the White House medical unit to have his blood pressure taken. He called his sister and told her that he was depressed. She recommended three Washington psychiatrists.

The Wall Street Journal tied Foster and Hillary to the Travel Office firings in yet another editorial on Monday, July 19. "The mores on display from the Rose alumni are far from confidence-building," the editorial chided. "So the gang that pulled the great Travel Office caper is now hell-bent on firing the [outgoing] head of the FBI. . . . Mr. Hubbell and Mr. Kennedy are alumni of Little Rock's Rose Law Firm, as are Mrs. Clinton and Deputy White House Counsel Vincent Foster, both of whom were also involved in the travel-office affair."

The president was concerned about how Foster would react to the editorial, and called to invite him to a White House movie screening of *In the Line of Fire* (strangely, about a would-be presidential assassin and a heroic Secret Service agent) that night. Foster declined, saying that he was already home for the night and wanted to spend some time with his wife. Clinton tried to help him forget about the *Journal's* criticism, telling him the editorials had no influence except with conservatives already hostile to the administration, Clinton recalled many years later. Foster remained upset. As Clinton wrote in his memoir, he felt like "everyone had read the negative things about him and believed them." Foster agreed to come see the president two days later.

Foster had received a prescription for antidepressants from his family doctor in Arkansas. That night, he took his first dose.

On Tuesday, July 20, Foster left the office around 1 P.M. Five hours later, the United States Park Police found him shot dead at Fort Marcy Park in northern Virginia. A bullet had been fired into his mouth. A revolver was in his hand.

Hillary got the news from Mack McLarty, who called her between 8 and 9 that night. Hillary was stunned silent. She had taken the call in her mother's kitchen in Little Rock. She and Chelsea had flown there to visit her mother and some friends. From across the room, she appeared so stricken that Lisa Caputo worried that something had happened to the president.

"I can't believe it's true," Hillary said. "It just can't be true." She started to cry.

"Let's hope and pray that this is some terrible mistake," McLarty said, giving her some of the details of how the body was discovered. "What about Bill, does he know?" she asked.

McLarty said he hadn't yet told the president, who was in the middle of being interviewed live by Larry King on CNN. He promised to call her back when there was more information.

McLarty entered the White House Library, where the president was being interviewed. The appearance was going so well that Clinton had agreed to continue for an extra thirty minutes. But McLarty told the producers the president could not stay, and he led Clinton out during a commercial break. They went upstairs to the residence, and McLarty relayed what had happened.

Does Hillary know? the president asked, his eyes filling with tears.

Clinton and McLarty went to Foster's house to comfort the family, where they were joined by Webb Hubbell and his wife, Suzy, Marsha Scott, David Gergen, Vernon Jordan, and other friends.

Hillary stayed up all night calling friends and crying. "I'm okay," she told Hubbell over the phone. "How are you holding up?" They agreed to talk more in person when Hubbell came to Arkansas for Vince's funeral. "Take care of Lisa and the kids, Webb," she said. "But hurry home."

Hillary had already had the experience of her uncle's self-destructive death and the suicide of Bill's close friend Frank Aller, in 1971, the first year of the courtship, but she said she could never have made the assumption that Foster had hit his breaking point. "Of a thousand people, of those who *might* commit suicide, I would never pick Vince," she said. She asked Nussbaum, How could he have done this? Why didn't he tell us? We could have helped him. We could have known. We should have known, she said.

The president gathered his staff the day after Foster's death to urge them to spend time away from the office with their loved ones. He eulogized Foster's "extraordinary sense of propriety and loyalty, and I hope that when we remember him and this, we'll be a little more anxious to talk to each other and a little less anxious to talk outside of our family." Hillary had already consulted with Tipper Gore, who had suffered from depression, about bringing in grief counselors. She told her staff to take some time for themselves, to go on vacation.

When Clinton addressed reporters in the Rose Garden, he unintentionally made it sound—to those who wanted to listen for it—like he had something to cover up. "As I tried to explain, especially to the young people on the staff, there is really no way to know why these things happen," Clinton had said, referring rather to the theory that the motivations for suicide were difficult to understand. Some right-wing groups and press immediately intimated that the president, the first lady, or surrogates had ordered Foster killed. It would become a familiar refrain.

Such outrageous accusations aside, there were eventually legitimate questions raised about whether the first lady and Nussbaum improperly interfered with the police and FBI investigations into Foster's death and the disposition of documents in Foster's office about the Clintons' personal finances and Hillary's work at the Rose Law Firm that she might have wanted suppressed.

Almost immediately after McLarty had conveyed news of Foster's death to Hillary, she called Maggie Williams in Washington, and then Harry Thomason in California. Later, Hillary and those who talked with her testified she called to share her grief.

The next day, Tuesday, July 21, Nussbaum prevented the Park Police from searching Foster's office, and told them to come back the following morning at ten. Just before eight on Wednesday morning, Hillary spoke over the phone with Susan Thomases, who was staying at a Washington hotel. Thomases promptly phoned Nussbaum. When the Park Police officers, FBI agents, and Justice Department lawyers arrived, Nussbaum again prevented a hands-on search. He told the investigators they could sit several feet away and watch as he sorted documents and other items from Foster's office into three piles. The first pile, he said, was for items that weren't subject to any privilege and could be examined. He designated the second pile for personal papers to be turned over to Foster's lawyers, who were also in the room. The third pile, he said, was for privileged material belonging to the White House and the Clintons, and was to be taken to the residence and then given to the Clintons' personal lawyers at the firm of Williams & Connolly. The disposition of matter in that third pile, including billing records of Hillary's work at the Rose Law Firm, would haunt the Clintons for years to come.

Hubbell went to see Hillary at her mother's house as soon as he got to Arkansas. They hugged and went to the bedroom Hillary was staying in.

"Webb, did you have any idea he was that depressed?" she asked, dabbing her tears. Hubbell answered no. He shared with Hillary some of his recent conversations with Foster.

"With health care and my dad's death, I didn't have time to see him on a personal basis as much as I should have," Hillary told him.

Hubbell didn't tell her that Foster had complained to him about that.

Hillary asked about Foster's family, and about the group who had gone to be with them the night he died. She also asked if his face "was messed up" by the bullet.

"We shouldn't have asked him to come to Washington, Webb," she said.

"It would've destroyed him if you *hadn't* asked," Hubbell consoled her. He told her about how he and Foster had agreed that they would both go together to Washington if the Clintons asked them. He shared with Hillary how excited and proud Foster had been to be a part of the administration and how proud he was of her.

Hillary then changed the subject to ask Hubbell for some help regarding a rumor she had heard that before his death Foster had been investigating a group of assassins who worked for the Navy and made their victims look as though they'd committed suicide. She said that the president had already been approached by a reporter about it. Hubbell said he'd talk to the reporter if he called.

As they hugged goodbye, Hillary told him, "I know you're being a rock for everybody else right now. But don't hold it all in forever."

"I could offer you the same advice," Hubbell replied.

Hillary smiled sadly at him, promised to talk with him again in a few days.

The last time Hillary had seen or talked to Vince in person, according to Hubbell, was on June 17, the same day the *Journal* had published its "Who Is Vincent Foster?" editorial. His fury and hurt had been evident.

Hubbell was at the White House that day for the announcement of Ruth Bader Ginsburg's nomination to the Supreme Court, which Vince had helped speed through the vetting process. Foster and Hubbell celebrated—then Vince said how concerned he was about the internal review of the Travel Office difficulties and other matters.

"Hillary saw us and came over," Hubbell recalled. "She linked arms with both of us, the way we had . . . so long ago."

"When are we going out, guys?" she said. "Let's go eat Italian."

Hubbell and his wife, Suzy, had finally moved in to their house in Spring Valley, a well-to-do neighborhood of large brick homes just inside the D.C.-Maryland line. Everyone should come by for drinks on Saturday, he said, and then they'd go eat Italian in the neighborhood. Bill, Hillary, Vince, Lisa. "Hillary said that would be great, and Vince and I gave her a hug. He seemed genuinely excited now, almost the polar opposite of the way he had been just moments before."

The Secret Service arrived Saturday morning to check out Hubbell's house and the surrounding area for the arrival of the president and first lady. That evening, Vince and Lisa arrived, expectant. Webb showed them around, and they then sat down for drinks in the living room. The phone rang. The White House operator put Hillary through. She said

Parade magazine intended to report the next day, Father's Day, that Bill had a half-brother he'd neither met nor heard of. The *Washington Post's* Style section was on to the story. One of a dozen or so boxes of sensitive files that Betsey Wright had turned over to Hubbell after the campaign contained records relating to Bill's birth father. "Hillary asked if I knew where that file was, and I told her I guessed it was downstairs," said Hubbell. "I said I would go look and call her back. . . . Vince and I went to the basement to search through the boxes." They couldn't find the file, and called Hillary back to tell her. Webb told her he'd look again and call her back; she suggested the next day would be fine.

"Webb, you all go on to the restaurant. I'll still try and meet you. Bill is a little stressed out and I doubt if he'll be coming," she said. The president had to reach his mother to tell her there was a story that would reveal that the father recorded on his birth certificate, William Blythe, had had at least two other marriages before he'd met her.

The Fosters and Hubbells left for the restaurant. Hillary called soon after their arrival, said Hubbell, and told him she couldn't make it. In her memoir, which is consistent with what she later told investigators, Hillary said she remembered it differently. She wrote that Vince had picked up the phone at Webb's house.

" 'Oh, I'm sorry,' " Hillary quoted Vince as saying to her, disappointed that she and Bill wouldn't be at dinner.

" 'So am I. You know, I'm just so sick of this [the sensational stories about their lives].' That's the last time I remember talking to Vince."

At the restaurant, Vince went into what Suzy called a "sulk" and said barely anything through the rest of the evening. He had pulled his chair from the table, and was turned away from the others. "It was so uncharacteristic of him," she said. Hubbell described him as resembling "a child who had been promised quality time with a parent, only to have the parent renege when business had called him away."

When Hubbell called to talk the next day, he recounted, Vince "opened up some about what was bothering him"—Hillary. "It's just not the same, Hub," he said, and, for the second time, told him how she'd say, "Fix it, Vince!" or "Handle it, Vince!" He was unhappy they could never talk. To Hubbell it sounded "in the nature of a lament," rather than anger.

Foster's funeral was in Little Rock at St. Andrew's Catholic Cathedral. The Washington contingent was mixed in among the many people Foster had known since kindergarten and grade school. Clinton gave the eulogy about Foster's honor, friendship, and service to the country. He quoted from Leon Russell's "A Song for You": "I love you in a place where there's no space or time. I love you for my life you are a friend of mine."

Hillary was crying at the church. She spontaneously hugged a mutual friend of hers and Foster's, whom Hillary herself had never treated with great warmth. The friend thought that perhaps Hillary was literally trying to grasp on to her closeness with Foster.

HILLARY WAS BACK in Washington when, on July 26, an associate White House counsel found in Foster's briefcase what appeared to be the scraps of a torn-up suicide note. They apparently hadn't been noticed in the initial search of Foster's office, and in fact were the remnants of the list Foster had written at his wife's behest to describe his frustrations.

"I can't deal with this thing. Bernie, you deal with it," Nussbaum later said Hillary told him when he tried to show her the scraps of the note.

Later that day, Hillary walked into the counsel's suite while Nussbaum and others were piecing together the scraps of paper, but quickly left after she realized what they were doing.

With Hillary's knowledge and—investigators suggested—possibly at her command, the White House held on to what they believed was a suicide note for thirty hours before handing it over to the authorities. While they were deciding whether to turn it over at all, Hillary insisted that the president not be told about the note. She summoned Susan Thomases back to Washington.

The Justice Department and Park Police released the text of Foster's note two weeks later, as part of their report declaring his death a suicide. There would eventually be four additional inquiries that came to the same conclusion.

Foster's suicide, the president told friends and aides, had "destroyed" Hillary. "I think she just bled deep inside," a close friend of Foster observed. "I don't think she ever really quite recovered from that." "She was so far down," David Gergen said, "you just sort of felt like you wanted to reach out, and say, 'It's okay. You'll be okay.' Because she opens herself up then, and it's a very real woman with vulnerability. And there's nothing false about it. It's just there."

She would be haunted "that the actions and reactions concerning the travel office helped drive Vince Foster to take his own life," Hillary would later write.

In *Living History*, Hillary described going on "automatic pilot" for the six months following Foster's death, feeling a "private" pain and getting by on "sheer willpower."

Hillary had always had a tendency to look at people and events with almost biblical judgment. "She often weighed matters in terms of good and evil," noted an old friend in Fayetteville, architect Dick Atkinson.

After Vince's death, she "found more to judge as evil," Atkinson could see. "There seemed to be something basic that was reinforcing her view of good and evil, an element of embitterment there, and the notion of conspiracy. There was no reason to have that so early in her life. But it existed." Yet Atkinson also believed she was forming "a dangerous attitude—not just with Republicans and enemies, but even toward people like [George] Stephanopoulos: 'Are you with us or are you against us?' And that led to more demonizing, more judgment of evil around her. It seemed more potent because of self-justification fueled by these Old Testament judgments of good and evil."

IN MID-AUGUST, with health care now finally put on the calendar—there would be congressional hearings in the fall, though there still was no plan—Hillary and Bill took their first real vacation in four years. They spent eleven days on Martha's Vineyard. Clinton read, jogged, golfed, and took Chelsea horseback riding. Hillary used the vacation as an opportunity to talk to Bill about her health care plans—without his economic advisers present.

Ira Magaziner and his aides were well along in drafting the legislation, and he and Hillary had told the president that he had to make some final choices about the bill's content so it could arrive on Capitol Hill when Congress returned after the Labor Day recess. Before leaving, the president had been besieged by Rubin, Bentsen, Rivlin, and Shalala, who continued to warn that the deficit would be in danger of exploding if he listened to Hillary. They saw the plan she was developing as too big and too costly. The Clinton presidency would historically succeed, they advised, only if he would scale back his wife's grandiose ideas about reform and settle on a more manageable and incremental approach. In frustration, Clinton had said he would reach a final decision after his vacation at Martha's Vineyard.

The Clinton family made the social rounds as well. Since the inaugural they had become increasingly attracted to the glitterati, and being on the Vineyard presented many opportunities to further their courtship. The Clintons dined at the homes of Carly Simon and Vernon Jordan, and they sailed around the nearby islands with Jacqueline Kennedy Onassis, her friend Maurice Tempelsman, Caroline Kennedy, and Senator Ted Kennedy and his wife. Aboard Tempelsman's $1 million yacht, Hillary continued her dialogue with Jackie about how to raise a child under the White House spotlight.

The Clintons could reflect on the fact that Bill's job approval rating was still below 50 percent, as it had been since May. Polls showed that even after the historic passage of Clinton's economic plan by one vote, Al Gore's, on August 6, 1993, 48 percent of the country disapproved of the bill. The collective mood of the country was bleak. Seven out of ten people, according to the polls, agreed that the country was "pretty seriously off on the wrong track." A majority didn't trust their leaders in government, and thought their tax dollars were being wasted. The Clintons' mood was nearly as sour. They were exhausted and frustrated with the way the administration's agenda was moving, even given the economic plan's approval by Congress. And the dark cloud of Vince Foster's death had not lifted.

Hillary now urged her husband to look at the big picture: to consider what to convey to the nation about the deeper goals of his presidency and the legacy he hoped to leave. She told him that he had been elected to steer the car, not to fix everything under the hood.

The fact that novelist William Styron and his wife, Rose, owned a summer home on the Vineyard may have influenced the Clintons' choice of vacation spot (the Clintons had originally considered going to Wyoming). Styron had written about his own suicidal depression in his book *Darkness Visible*, and Hillary had read it after Vince Foster's suicide. As Hillary and Styron hiked the woods, Styron said he "got the impression the book had helped her understand what [Foster] must have been going through.

"I recall telling her that I felt it need not have happened, that he got the wrong advice . . . he was steered in the wrong direction, had he sought counsel, therapy of some sort, he probably wouldn't have ended up the way he did. . . .

"Hillary was not teary. . . . It was nothing as dramatic as that. . . . She was upset. . . . It hung over her. . . . I had the feeling that she just felt grieved by the whole thing. . . . I was only able to offer my best wisdom as to what had taken place with him. . . .

"She absorbed what I was saying; I don't recall her saying anything specific about Washington; but even then she was beginning to be aware of what [later] became evident in large sense, of an unbelievable amount of hostility against them by those people she later accused rightly of being a vast right-wing conspiracy. . . .

"They were absolutely taken aback by the ferocity of the kind of hostility that was looming around them. . . . She seemed to be constantly aware of this menace, of what was turning out to be this war against the White House."

14

Not a Crook, Not a Degenerate

It was too much. I wondered if what Bill was trying to do for the country was worth the pain and humiliation.

—Living History

FOR ALMOST TWO DECADES, Hillary, aided by Betsey Wright, lawyers, other friends, and aggressive private detectives, had struggled to keep Bill's sexual compulsions from contaminating his political viability. Upon the Clintons' arrival at the White House, both seemed confident that the ugliness was behind them. The notion that their failed $200,000 investment in an old real estate deal would lead to the president's impeachment for lying about his sexual conduct was inconceivable.

After their return from Martha's Vineyard, their administration would become a series of crises, uninterrupted and overlapping, pervaded by a leering special prosecutor and by their past in Arkansas. These crises would define the Clinton presidency and shape Hillary's character and future even more than her husband's. The Clintons would be blindsided at times, but they absolutely refused to surrender—even when others pronounced them dead politically, or, when it was clear they would survive, condemned them as incapable of rehabilitation.

The word "Whitewater" came to assume many meanings during Bill Clinton's two terms as president. First and foremost, if for only a short while, it referred to the details of a once obscure land transaction that the Clintons had consummated in the third year of their marriage, and that, after scarcely a year of the Clinton presidency, launched an unbound inquiry by a special federal prosecutor into every aspect of their lives, galvanized their enemies, and convinced editors and reporters at the nation's three best newspapers—the *New York Times*, the *Washington Post*, and *The Wall Street Journal*—that Hillary and Bill were neck-deep in corruption.

In truth, the "Whitewater story" became overblown almost from the moment the *New York Times* first wrote about it, during the campaign, in a series of articles and editorials that were increasingly long on innuendo, short on context, and in some important ways unfair to the Clintons. The Clintons' response was not straightforward, and served only to create more suspicion. The initial *Times* story was a model of restraint compared with the coverage of "Whitewater" that followed in the press free-for-all during the next eight years.

Mark Fabiani, the presidential lawyer entrusted by Hillary with the rapid press-response capability for the White House in 1995 and 1996, understood the entire nature of Whitewater as well as anyone in the administration. Fabiani said he was told by Jeff Gerth, the *Times* reporter who wrote the first Whitewater story, that Gerth believed it was a good "campaign story" that "never deserved to be the subject of years of long independent counsel work."

Fabiani's view was that, the Clintons' protestations to the contrary, it was a reasonable issue to explore in a presidential campaign: "[The] governor of a state who had regulatory authority over a savings and loan was in business with the owner of the savings and loan. . . . And the owner of the savings and loan was probably carrying more than his share of the costs of the business, the piece of land owned jointly with the Clintons."

It was also obvious, almost from the beginning, that Hillary, as a lawyer representing the looted savings and loan while her husband was governor, had engaged in the kind of conflict of interest that she should have steered clear of, even though that kind of incestuous relationship was common practice in Little Rock and, increasingly in the 1980s and 1990s, Washington. But in retrospect, it's shocking how much was made out of that mistake. Their joint partnership with the savings and loan owner and his wife in a piece of land never worth its purchase price grew into a federal case that was not resolved until after the Clinton presidency had ended and the office of the special prosecutor had been forced to acknowledge—after six years of investigation, $52 million, and the Senate trial of a president—that there had been no violation of law by either Hillary or Bill surrounding the land transaction (or in the Travel Office affair for that matter). The allegation that stuck was that Bill Clinton lied about sex.

As Hillary angrily predicted to her husband when he acceded to demands from the press, important Democratic leaders and Republican opponents, that a special Whitewater prosecutor be appointed, the investigation triggered by Whitewater consumed their lives and the Clinton presidency, perhaps even more than she could have imagined.

It is obvious that the Clintons, especially Hillary, had sought to obscure some of the facts, withhold information, and keep investigators away from other matters, many of them sexual, some financial, and all of which seemed hardly criminal. Far more than the numbing details of tax deductions and interest payments on a piece of land in the small town of Flippin, these other matters—including Hillary and Bill's remarkable clumsiness in playing fast and loose with the facts—would provide grist for their enemies and fuel for the press.

New ground was being broken: the actions of a sitting president—actually his wife's, more than his—while governor overshadowed his actions as president (at least until the investigation led to the discovery of the Lewinsky relationship). Had Lyndon Johnson, or either of the George Bushes for that matter, been similarly investigated *in office* about their pre-presidential past, it is interesting to contemplate what the results, and precedent, would have been.

Six years after the initial mention of Whitewater in Gerth's *Times* report, when the president was impeached there was not one word in the charges about Whitewater.

THE GREATEST POWER of the presidency, and the essential tool put to use by modern American presidents, was the ability to set the national agenda, to maintain it, and to adapt it to changing circumstances.

The joint Clinton presidency lost the ability to set the national agenda perhaps as no other modern presidency had, even Nixon's. Whenever Clinton was able to regain control of the agenda, he was almost always successful: the economic plan, NAFTA, welfare reform, and a series of orders and actions toward the end of his administration that made higher education available to almost any American who sought it. His craft and skill and perseverance in winning the major achievements of his presidency were extraordinary.

But from its very outset, and certainly after Vince Foster's death, until Clinton's acquittal in the Senate trial, the terms of national debate were more often set by the press, the Clintons' enemies, the Republican opposition, and the special prosecutor than by the president. The best efforts of the Clintons, their top aides, and an army of lawyers were spent in response to endless investigations and the maintenance of secrets: secrets that, at any moment, could have made matters even worse, if revealed.

The Clinton presidency was sapped of its almost limitless potential, including ironically its aim of ending partisanship. The Clintons had to fight for the levers of power constantly.

In displaying her least-appealing traits—the demand for absolute loyalty, the first-strike mentality, the truth-trimming—Hillary was in fact doing what she had always done, clearing a way for her husband to do what he did best: to think and act in terms of policy and implementation of their goals and ideas arrived at over a lifetime. Her method brought both success and failure. It also brought more pain. And then it brought a circuitous restoration of dignity and stature.

All of this was again on the table, in Hillary's view, because of the press. For the first time since Vince Foster's death, Whitewater had reappeared in the news in a major way on October 31 in the form of a story by *Washington Post* reporter Susan Schmidt. The front-page story said that Resolution Trust Corporation, a Treasury Department agency created to liquidate the assets of failed savings and loans, had asked federal prosecutors to look into whether funds from Madison Guaranty—the S&L mismanaged by Jim McDougal—had been illegally used to finance political campaigns in Arkansas in the 1980s, including one of Governor Clinton's. The referral included specific questions about whether checks written on Madison accounts wound up in Clinton's reelection campaign fund and whether such money was paid either from overdrawn accounts or from loans made ostensibly for other purposes and directed to the governor's campaign.

The Clintons' Whitewater land deal and their relationship with Jim and Susan McDougal were nothing new. But the referral for criminal investigation was more than sufficient to resurrect—rather sensationally, of course, now that the Clintons were in the White House—questions about the business dealings and associations in their Arkansas past. Adding to the journalistic combustion, just days after the *Post* story ran, David Hale, a former judge in Arkansas who was trying to broker a better deal with federal prosecutors regarding his own fraud indictment, complained to newspaper reporters that the Justice Department wasn't taking serious note of his allegations that then Governor Clinton had pressured him to lend $300,000 to a phony marketing firm owned by Susan McDougal. Hale claimed he was told by Jim McDougal that the money would "help conceal earlier favors for the governor," but investigators found no evidence to corroborate the assertion.

Schmidt's initial story (as opposed to some of her later ones, based uncritically on leaks from the office of Independent Counsel Ken Starr) was real news. Both Hillary and Bill had been listed in the RTC referral as witnesses. Meanwhile, Bernard Nussbaum began making phone calls to monitor whatever investigations were underway in the Treasury Department and in the criminal division of the Justice Department.

Bill and Hillary had no choice but to hire an outside attorney. After interviewing three other candidates, Nussbaum and his deputy, William Kennedy, recommended David Kendall, of Williams & Connolly, the same firm as Bob Barnett, the Clintons' lawyer on other personal business affairs. Hillary, who took more care in weighing the matter, and Bill felt comfortable with Kendall's selection. The arrangement would make for smooth communication and counsel across the board.

Years later, Hillary remarked that when she read Schmidt's story on Halloween, she realized that what happened in Arkansas would continue to haunt their lives, but nothing would come of the ghostly allegations, she predicted.

"From [the Clintons'] point of view, they're convinced they did nothing wrong," Harold Ickes said not long after Whitewater and its ramifications had become the staple of presidential news. "This was a twenty-year-old land deal in Arkansas that had nothing to do with current events. And they were just absolutely taken aback. . . . I think mystified is the best word, initially mystified by the focus that was [being] given to Whitewater, commodities trading, to the conspiratorial theories that were being cooked up about Vince's death. They came here to do good. They thought they were on the right track. And they were just completely befuddled and mystified by the energy and the focus that was put on what they considered raggedy-ass and trivial issues, especially in contrast to some of what some other presidents had reportedly done. So, that in turn gave way to a real bitterness toward the press. They were already very unhappy with the press when they came here, and this just solidified it."

Yet as a lawyer, Hillary must have recognized at least the appearance of her own conflict of interest, no matter how benignly she viewed her motivations. In 1985, after the Federal Home Loan Bank Board had released a report about bad loans and other practices that had led to Madison's insolvency, the Rose Law Firm was hired by McDougal to represent the S&L in presenting its recapitalization plan to the Arkansas Securities Department. That same year, McDougal held a fund-raiser to help Governor Clinton pay off his campaign debt from the previous year. And as part of the Rose firm's representation, Hillary wrote a letter to Beverly Bassett Schaffer, who recently had been appointed state securities commissioner by Bill, seeking permission for Madison to try two new approaches to raise funds and stay in business. Schaffer, the sister of Woody Bassett, the Clintons' former law student and aide to Bill in all his Arkansas campaigns, obliged the request, but the money was never raised, and by 1986 federal regulators insisted McDougal be removed and the government took over the S&L.*

According to Betsey Wright, the Clintons had a soft spot for Jim McDougal. "He was this pathetic, [psychologically] sick person who they had loved and didn't want to disavow and somehow or other were trying to keep him from surprising them with stuff like not paying the taxes.[†] I mean, he was a problem always. Always. And they felt a certain sense of responsibility to take care of him."

Bill Clinton met McDougal in 1968 when McDougal was working for Senator J. William Fulbright, and Bill interned in Fulbright's office. The two became friends. When, in 1978, Jim suggested that Bill and Hillary join them in an investment deal, they jumped at the chance. The two couples created Whitewater Development Corporation when Bill was governor in 1979, and then borrowed $200,000 to invest in 230 acres of land along the White River. The idea was to subdivide the property and sell it to older couples who were retiring in northwest Arkansas. Clinton had invested a few thousand dollars on another McDougal deal and had made a profit, so the Clintons thought, Why not?, according to their later explanations.

"He was working for Fulbright, and he bought some hill of land for a hundred dollars an acre or some ridiculous price and cut it up into smaller tracts and sold it and made money," Jim Blair said of McDougal. "And he thought he had discovered the Holy Grail, and so he did this three or four times. . . . Really all he was looking for was a finance vehicle, and he got to thinking he was a developer. Well, he was never a developer. Anyhow, he had made a few of these and I think in some casual

---

*Jeff Gerth's original Whitewater story in the *New York Times*, on March 8, 1992, had raised the obvious conflict of interest questions, including whether the governor should have been a partner in a land deal with someone whose business was regulated by the state—though in fact McDougal had not been in the S&L business when the Whitewater partnership was formed—and whether it was proper for Hillary to have been paid legal fees for the work she did for Madison Guaranty. The story also said that the Clintons had "improperly" deducted about $5,000 on their personal tax returns in 1984 and 1985 "for interest paid on a portion of at least $30,000 in bank loan payments" that had actually been paid from a business account in the name of their Whitewater partnership with the McDougals. It was the kind of accounting error often made innocently, and sometimes not. The deductions saved the Clintons perhaps $1,000 in taxes, but since the error had occurred more than three years before the story ran, "Internal Revenue Service regulations [did] not require the Clintons to pay."

Meanwhile, the Clinton campaign had been able to challenge the perception that Bill and Hillary had done something wrong in relation to their Whitewater investment by releasing an independent audit that showed they had ultimately lost about $69,000 on the deal.

[†]McDougal suffered from manic depression.

conversation with the Clintons one time when he was making money he said, Why don't you do this and we'll make all this money? And they agreed to this Whitewater deal. . . . He just never, ever separated in his mind his investments and his partners'. It was all his. It was all his idea. He moved money around anytime he wanted. He wrote checks. He did all kinds of crap. They had no idea. At the end of the day, if you take the literal deal that they were full partners and then full shareholders once they incorporated, did he steal from them? Yes. Did he embezzle from them? Yes."

Though McDougal talked up the idea that the investment would earn a nice nest egg for the Clintons' retirement, interest rates in the late 1970s skyrocketed, and retirees became less interested in buying homes, so they all lost money on the venture.

Wright and other Clinton friends insisted that Whitewater was a bad real estate deal that the Clintons were constantly trying to get out of. "And at one time they thought they were out of it. It came up every year with me in filing the disclosure forms, getting them prepared for filing. And I just very well remember the year I had to go back and amend it because they thought they were out of it, and then found out that they weren't," said Wright.

Though hurt and angry at her treatment by the Clintons after they left Arkansas, Wright steadfastly defended their motivations and actions in the Whitewater deal. Hillary and Bill were thirty and thirty-two years old, respectively, when they made their investment. "It was a mess from the beginning. This was a case of trying to be landowners by typical do-gooders who didn't know anything about setting up a business. And they thought Jim [McDougal] did. That's why it was a mess. They didn't worry about it. . . . It's a big step when you buy your first investment. . . . They were idealistic kids when they did this."

By the time a special prosecutor had been appointed to investigate their investment, they were a long way from being idealistic kids.

AFTER SCHMIDT'S Halloween story ran in the *Washington Post*, she and the paper's editors began an insistent effort to get the White House to provide them with the underlying documents—especially tax returns—mentioned in the Resolution Trust Corporation's criminal referral, and which the Clintons insisted would exonerate them.

Later, it became almost a parlor game in Washington to speculate on what would have happened had the Clintons agreed to give the material to the *Post* and make public their tax returns and the related documents. After all, went one line of reasoning, Bill and Hillary's decision to refuse release of the materials—against the urging of some of their senior political advisers—and insist on their privacy led indirectly but almost inevitably to the appointment of a special prosecutor, which in turn led to Ken Starr's obdurate investigation, which in turn brought the Paula Jones civil case into Starr's line of questioning, which in turn led to Monica Lewinsky, and eventually the impeachment. And it appeared to be true that, in the tax returns, there was no evidence that the Clintons had done anything illegal, only the extremely embarrassing revelation that Hillary had made a $100,000 killing on cattle futures, which led to her subsequent feeble attempts to explain her supposed expertise on the subject.

But with the White House creating an indelible impression that it was trying to stonewall, suspicion grew. The media seized on it and powerful and ordinary citizens alike who were predisposed to dislike the Clintons smelled blood. Less than two weeks after Schmidt's story, on November 11, Andrea Mitchell reported on *NBC Nightly News* that there was a "connection" between Vince Foster's death and the Clintons' involvement in Whitewater. "Before his death in July, former White House lawyer Vince Foster also got involved, helping the Clintons sell their share of the land company," she said on the air. "He also discovered a tax mess; the partnership had not filed federal or state returns for three years. Now questions are being raised about a possible link between the growing Arkansas investigations and Foster's death."

The White House could no longer effectively manage the story (if it ever could), or control the damage. "Whitewater became the catch-all term for any allegation of unseemliness or impropriety against anyone anywhere near the Clintons or the White House—and it stuck," George Stephanopoulos recalled. Meanwhile, the Clinton legislative agenda, including health care, was stalled and the president's popularity was plummeting, he noted.

In November and December, the *Washington Post* sought to obtain the Whitewater documents through an unusual set of negotiations. "The *Post* was convinced we were hiding something sinister," Stephanopoulos said. "Executive Editor Leonard Downie made a series of extraordinary personal requests for the documents," and White House correspondent Ann Devroy "warned me that the paper would go on the warpath unless we answered their questions and released the documents." The requests set in motion a series of meetings to debate the issue within the Clinton administration. Hillary set the tone for the White House's response. She was joined by Nussbaum, Lindsey, and a cadre of lawyers who were implacably opposed to providing the records—especially the tax returns—to the *Post* or releasing them elsewhere publicly. Stephanopoulos, Gergen, McLarty, and Nussbaum's deputy Joel Klein, on the other hand, argued that the facts would come out eventually so the administration might as well turn over the records and get it over with. "I don't want them poring over our personal lives," Hillary told Nussbaum. He needed no convincing. "You're entitled to your privacy," he told her. "If you turn them over . . . [e]very document will be a news story. It will go on and on." Gergen had been hired specifically to deal with just this kind of problem with the press. The *Post* had submitted a list of questions in the first week of December about Whitewater. Gergen told Bruce Lindsey, "We can't just sit here and stiff them. You're just inviting a tough response. My strong recommendation is to see what they want and then see what should be in the public domain and release it." Lindsey and Gergen sought the advice of Betsey Wright. She, too, was opposed to cooperating with the *Post*. "They have managed to twist every piece of information out of context. . . . I wouldn't give them anything."

By December 10, Hillary said, she and Bill were especially angry that Gergen had gone to the *Post* newsroom to meet with the paper's editors, and had seemed almost to promise that the newspaper would get the documents; the Clintons had not authorized him to hold out such a promise. The next day Gergen and Stephanopoulos made a final plea to the president after his radio address. Clinton sat between the two men drinking a cup of coffee. He listened intently. "I don't have a big problem with giving them what we have," he told them. "But Hillary . . ." She was not about to consent to reporters sifting through the documentary remnants of their past, looking at records of their investments, their tax returns, her legal work at the Rose Law Firm.

"Saying her name flipped a switch in his head," Stephanopoulos said. "Suddenly his eyes lit up, and two years' worth of venom spewed from his mouth." Stephanopoulos could usually tell when the president was making Hillary's argument: "even if he was yelling, his voice had a flat quality, as if he were a high school debater speeding through a series of memorized facts." Now Bill began a tirade about the press. "No, you're wrong. The questions won't stop. At the Sperling Breakfast I answered more questions about my private life than any candidate *ever* and what did *that* get me? They'll *always* want more. No president has ever been treated like I've been treated."

Gergen and Stephanopoulos continued to argue that it would be better to release the documents while the American public was focused on the upcoming Christmas holidays. "On this issue, Clinton wasn't commander-in-chief, just a husband beholden to his wife," Stephanopoulos realized. Hillary had steadfastly defended him against allegations about "bimbos." Now it was his turn to defend her. Gergen and I didn't know what was in the Whitewater documents, but whatever it was, Hillary didn't want it out—and she had a veto."

Hillary, indeed, had the greatest influence over her husband's final decision. A high-ranking aide knew how the first lady's anger could often transfer to Bill and color his response to situations. "She would get him all riled up in a way that wasn't exactly his nature. He has this terrible self-pitying anger inside of him, but it's a slightly different thing when she would get her hand into it. This was an example of where he hadn't thought the choice was so clear-cut; he could see the political benefit of both sides, including giving up the documents and telling everything he knew to the *Post*."

The decision came down to two points, the aide said. "There was a principle which was, If we give this up, we give up everything, we'll never be able to claim privacy again. And they were right. They'd put themselves into a precedent-setting situation. They didn't know how it would come out. There was also this fear that the questions would never end. Because that's what she kept saying."

Hillary never wavered. "These are my papers. They belong to me. I could throw them all in the Potomac River if I wanted to."

Some White House aides later speculated privately that Hillary feared continued attention on the Whitewater land deal and the Clintons' partnership with the McDougals might reveal an affair between Bill and Susan McDougal in the 1970s or 1980s, as gossip in Arkansas had long had it. If the purported motif of Watergate had been "Follow the Money," Whitewater's was plausibly "Follow the Women." In the end, that was really where public, press, and prosecutorial interest seemed to redound most fervently.

Hillary's influence in regard to the Whitewater documents was determinate, and further discussion was ruled out. A hand-delivered letter from Lindsey to Downie was sent on December 10:

> As you know, in March, 1992, the Clinton Campaign released a report by an independent accounting firm which established that the Clintons lost at least $68,900 on Whitewater Development Corporation. They received no gain of any kind on their investment. The Clintons were not involved in the management or operation of the company, nor did they keep its records. We see no need to supplement the March, 1992 CPA report or to provide further documentation.

Now, handed their sheet music by the White House, a Republican chorus on Capitol Hill enthusiastically chanted the familiar stanzas of the oratorio of Slick Willy and His Wife, and thunderously demanded intervention from the prosecutorial gods.

HILLARY SAID she was hosting a Christmas party in the White House a week later when she took an urgent call from David Kendall, who told her that *The American Spectator*, a far-right monthly of particular vitriol on the subject of the Clintons, planned to publish a story about Bill's supposed sexual encounters with a multitude of women while he was governor, based on testimony from state troopers who claimed they had helped facilitate their rendezvous.* Kendall's advice to the White House was to issue no comment; it would only attract more attention to the story. Its author, David Brock, claimed to have spent more than thirty hours interviewing Arkansas state troopers. He said the troopers also told him that Betsey Wright and George Stephanopoulos had "strong-armed" other sources into keeping their mouths shut.

Two of the troopers, Larry Patterson and Roger Perry, described on the record the ways in which they allegedly facilitated Bill's affairs. The troopers said the governor asked them to drive him to hotels where he'd visit the women. Or they'd stay on "Hillary Watch" while he was away from the mansion. On one occasion, Clinton instructed a trooper to approach a woman named Paula, who was standing in the lobby of the Excelsior Hotel in Little Rock, and ask her to meet with the governor in a room upstairs. Brock's editors had inadvertently failed to eliminate her name from the story. Eventually, Paula's identity and her purported encounter with Clinton would be excruciatingly detailed.

The general allegations weren't exactly new. But seeing them in print was. Betsey Wright and other aides had been able to contain similar stories during the presidential campaign, and even before. What was unquestionably new this time was that four troopers, two of them on the record, went into detail about whom the former governor met, how, and when.

Once again, Wright had been dispatched—to Little Rock, by Mack McLarty—to pour water on the fire, before *The American Spectator* reached the newsstands, but her effort was to little avail. "Basically I think there was a lot of hope that I could get the troopers who weren't quoted in the article to make public statements that this wasn't the

*Hillary, contrary to the impression created in *Living History* that Kendall's call was the first time she'd heard about the *Spectator* story, already knew through Betsey Wright that the troopers were talking to reporters.

truth," Wright said. "That wasn't possible, and I knew that wasn't going to be possible. But I did get from Danny Ferguson, who was quoted in the article, an affidavit. That took some real doing. It was most specifically about Paula Jones because . . . he was supposed to be the trooper who was with Bill when they went back to the hotel."

In essence, the affidavit alleged that Jones was a stalker, the same claim (which in its abbreviated form was not untrue) that Bill made to Hillary and to his aides about Monica Lewinsky when it was first alleged that she had boasted of a sexual relationship with him: According to Wright, Paula Jones "was on a major stalking campaign and anytime a trooper would come in and out [of the governor's office] she would befriend them and talk about when she could get with him. . . . This was after the so-called incident [at the Excelsior Hotel]. Absolutely. The pursuit was hot and heavy after the incident. People on the staff didn't know what to do, how to get rid of this woman, who is stalking him. They didn't know what she was going to end up saying later."

Wright believed that some of the troopers told the truth and others didn't. "They were all bitter," she said. "They all felt unappreciated, that they had been through a lot of tough times with [Bill], and he just left [Arkansas] and told Buddy Young [his chief of security] to sort of take care of them. He had talked to a number of them about coming to D.C. with him and there was never any follow-up. And so it got to be more and more poison. And I'd get calls from a couple who liked Bill the most. They were saying, You know, we can take care of this, we can head this off if he'll just come down and have a picnic with them or something, you know, a barbecue, anything just to convey to them that he really appreciates them."

Wright said she called Bruce Lindsey a couple of times to relay the message, but nothing ever came of it. "Bruce was not a dialogue person with me. I never got answers." There was no question, Wright said, that troopers had pulled women out of crowds for the governor at Bill's direction (and for themselves), but that the situation was more volatile than she had realized. "Bill had told me before he announced [for president] that any indiscretions he ever engaged in were in the presence of only two troopers that he knew he could trust . . . and that nobody else would have ever been around so there wasn't anything to say. Well, that was a flat-out lie. I was a little taken aback by it at the time he told me because it was completely unlike him to have that much foresight and care in the situation."

Another story (the day after the *Spectator*'s appeared) ran in the *Los Angeles Times*—whose reporters had been pursuing the same line of inquiry for weeks—saying that Clinton had recently called the troopers and dangled the possibility of federal jobs in return for their silence.

The *Spectator* story and its fallout in the mainstream press represented the convergence of all the avenues of pursuit of the Clintons by a press corps already frustrated with Hillary's refusal to be forthcoming about the family finances and increasingly convinced of her lack of truthfulness; by their avowed enemies back in Arkansas; by Republicans in Congress and far-right-wing allies, especially on talk radio; and, eventually, by the law, as represented by a special prosecutor who seemed more than willing to feed and be fed by all of those parties.

Bob Barnett, the Clintons' personal lawyer upon entering the White House and, to this day, one of their most trusted friends and counselors—especially Hillary's—attempted to comfort her, and, judging from Hillary's own comments later, keep her anger from exploding, whether at Bill or the press. She pointed out that Bill had been elected, not her, and admitted to feeling "very much alone," something she almost never said, and which signaled she was at her lowest ebb. And Bill, clearly, could be of no comfort.

Hardly a year had passed since Bill's election. Her attitude now—frustrated, angry, weary—announced, "I thought we were through with this; and now, here it comes again," said McLarty. She told him, "It's going to distort everything that we do."

As aides to Hillary and Bill considered how to respond publicly, they were understandably self-conscious about discussing such matters around the president and first lady. Hillary seemed to have absorbed the full force of the story by the time she and Bill attended another Christmas party at the White House, for family and close friends, the next night. Her press secretary, Lisa Caputo, took her aside to tell her that the troopers were now telling their tale on CNN. "My first thoughts were of Chelsea and for my mother and Virginia, who had already been through too much," said Hillary. The plausibility of at least some of what the troopers were claiming was exacerbating matters.

It was obvious to White House aides that Hillary was deeply humiliated by the stories, and that Bill "was deep in her doghouse," in Gergen's words—"like a bouncy golden retriever who has pooped on the living room rug, he curled up and looked baleful for days." But Hillary and Bill tried to project a lawyerlike detachment, and when they did explode, their anger was always triggered by some detail of the story they said was wrong, or misinterpreted, and they conveyed a sense that there were higher principles at work here, rarely their own lives. Bill insisted that the troopers were vengeful because they'd wanted jobs in Washington and he hadn't offered them; Hillary was certain the stories had been carefully timed to sabotage the Clinton agenda.

The policy implications of what was occurring were of course clear to Hillary, and as distressing as the private hurt. Now, the familiar dynamic of the Clinton marriage in extremis was again in play, but for the first time on the Washington stage. Hillary held the upper hand; Bill would not risk her further ire. He would challenge her on nothing remotely in her purview. As the first anniversary of the Clinton presidency approached, they were moving into the crucial period of the health care struggle. "I cannot recall him publicly confronting her on any health care issue after that," said Gergen. Her continuing refusal thereafter to compromise with either leaders on Capitol Hill or her husband's economic team was a major factor in the failure of the Clinton initiative for health care reform.

THE DETAILS that emerged from the troopers' stories put the White House in an impossible bind in terms of fashioning a public response. Two of the troopers had been excruciatingly precise in laying out the nature of Bill's sexual activities. They also alleged that he had offered a third trooper, Danny Ferguson, a bribe, in essence—in the form of a federal job—for keeping silent. It is a violation of federal law to solicit something of value in exchange for promising a government job—in this case a position as regional director of the Federal Emergency Management Agency or U.S. marshal in Little Rock, according to the troopers. Buddy Young, himself a FEMA regional manager in Texas by then, had been a go-between, talking to the president and the troopers about possible jobs. As a state trooper in Arkansas, Young had earned the maximum salary accorded after five years of service, $25,600; at FEMA, he was earning $98,000. Bruce Lindsey, too, had been in frequent touch with Young in the preceding weeks.

The initial statement issued by the White House, on Sunday night, December 19, in Lindsey's name, was anything but a convincing denial: "The allegations are ridiculous. Similar allegations were made, investigated, and responded to during the campaign, and there is nothing here that would dignify a further response." The statement said that no offers of jobs had been made to any of the troopers, but that the president "has had conversations about the fact that false stories were being spread about him."

Dee Dee Myers and Lindsey were left to deal with the public response while the president stayed mum. Myers announced that the press briefings for Monday and Tuesday, September 20 and 21, were canceled. Hillary had been scheduled to do interviews Tuesday on ABC, CBS, and NBC, for broadcast during Christmas week. All three network news organizations canceled after Caputo informed them they could only inquire about the observance of Christmas at the White House— "about the crafts and the ornaments and the kind of entertainment the Clintons were having."

However, Hillary went ahead with an interview with the Associated Press. Her remarks seemed carefully fashioned to convey outrage and were totally in character. Her heartfelt words—seasonal references notwithstanding—became the leitmotif of her refrain through many of the troubles of the next six years:

> I find it not an accident that every time he is on the verge of fulfilling his commitment to the American people and they respond . . . out comes yet a new round of these outrageous, terrible stories that people plant for political and financial reasons. . . . It's pretty sad that we're still subjected to these kinds of attacks for political and financial gain from people, and that it is sad that—especially here in the Christmas season—people for their own purposes would be attacking my family. . . . I think everybody forgets that, even if public figures don't have any protection from these kinds of attacks, you still have feelings.

Hillary's conspiratorial notions about the origins of the trooper story, beyond whatever Bill and the troopers might actually have done, were not far-fetched. This, too, should have been a subject of great interest to the Washington reporters covering the Clinton presidency. But it would be years until such reporting was undertaken by major news organizations. The genesis of the *American Spectator* account was remarkably close to the circumstances she had outlined in her discussions with William Styron.

The author of the *Spectator* story, David Brock,* in 2001 publicly apologized to the Clintons and chronicled his life—with emphasis on his right-to-left conversion—in a memoir entitled *Blinded by the Right.* Brock said in the book that while he was on the payroll of *The American Specta-*

---

*Brock's career as an ideological scourge had taken off during *Spectator* coverage of the Senate confirmation hearings on the nomination of Clarence Thomas to the Supreme Court. Brock had then written a book about Thomas's accuser, *The Real Anita Hill*, in 1993, and became something of a hero in right-wing circles for both his investigative skill and nastiness of phrase. (He'd dismissed Hill as "a little bit nutty and a little bit slutty.") In a *New York Times* column in 1994, Frank Rich criticized Brock as a "smear artist" whose "motives are at least as twisted as his facts."

tor; he was also receiving money from Chicago financier Peter Smith, who was a major fund-raiser for Representative Newt Gingrich and, in preparation for the 1996 presidential campaign, bankrolled investigations into a college trip Clinton had made to Russia.* Smith had also helped spread rumors—definitively squelched during investigations by the House Banking Committee and the office of the CIA Inspector General—that Clinton, while governor, had ordered state law enforcement officials to ignore a cocaine-smuggling ring.

Pittsburgh billionaire Richard Mellon Scaife, a major source of funding for far-right-wing activities and causes, was particularly impressed and energized by Brock's article on the troopers, and undertook to finance more such pieces thereafter through a secret operation known as the "Arkansas Project." Scaife was a pivotal element of Hillary's "vast right-wing conspiracy"—and on the flow charts of her deputy, Sidney Blumenthal, who monitored it—for good reason: Scaife spent more than $2.4 million gathering intelligence and funding anti-Clinton articles based on it.

Brock's much anticipated 1996 book, *The Seduction of Hillary Rodham,* was a shocking disappointment to his old ideological comrades who were expecting an explosive, vicious attack on Hillary. Some parts were surprisingly sympathetic to its subject, not that the book could be interpreted as friendly. Rather, it was the product of some impressive fact-digging, its narrative swathed in a historical dialectic that emphasized the long ideological struggle of left and right in the Cold War years in America, and tried too hard to place many of Hillary's actions in a context of leftist radicalism. As Brock continued to move leftward himself, he wrote another apologia in 1997 for *Esquire* entitled "I Was a Conservative Hit-Man," in which he criticized his own reporting in *The American Spectator* and said his stories about Hillary and others were deliberately distorted for ideological purposes.

His conversion seemed complete in 2000, when he received funding from a Clinton friend and major contributor—Steve Bing, who had inherited a real estate fortune and who also financed good government initiatives on the California ballot—for a Web site called Media Matters, dedicated to finding and correcting examples of right-wing media bias. By 2007, as the season of presidential campaigning approached, Media

---

*In the 1992 presidential campaign, President George Bush had made suggestions that Clinton had acted unpatriotically during his Russian trip, and suggested he should disclose to voters "how many demonstrations he led against his own country from a foreign soil." Clinton was a Rhodes Scholar at Oxford during the time he'd made the trip, and no evidence has ever developed that he led any demonstrations abroad or did anything of an anti-American nature during his Soviet visit.

Matters had more than fifty employees, and expended a disproportionate part of its effort to correcting stories about Hillary: so much so that the favor with which it treated her suggested it was almost an outlet for her ambitions.

Later, Elizabeth Drew, the unusually perceptive Washington journalist who wrote for *The New York Review of Books*, would describe December 20—the day *The American Spectator*'s story about the troopers appeared on newsstands—as "the most bizarre day thus far in this and perhaps any other administration." An air of crisis had seized the White House, and men and women who had joined the administration expecting an enlightened battle of ideas were now wrestling in the gutter. Paul Begala walked into the office of George Stephanopoulos and said, "I think I'm going to throw up." That morning the conservative *Washington Times* published a front-page story that combined suspicions about Whitewater and the death of Vince Foster to sinister and synergistic effect. The banner headline read: "Clinton Papers Lifted After Aide's Suicide." The subhead was equally suggestive: "Foster's office was secretly searched hours after his body was found." To ideologues and Clinton enemies who already were proposing the idea that Foster had been murdered (in a government safe house, in some of the versions favored on the far right), the convolution of skepticism about Whitewater and Foster's death was the ultimate gift. Nonetheless, the basic facts reported in the story were solid.

Documents related to the Whitewater land deal had been taken from Foster's office during two searches following his death, the story reported; the first sweep, less than three hours after he was found dead, was conducted by Patsy Thomasson, Maggie Williams, and Bernie Nussbaum. The second, by Nussbaum, was the one that had led the Park Police to complain to the Justice Department that the White House counsel had impeded their investigation. Even before elaborating the most damaging details about the removal of records pertaining to Whitewater, the article noted darkly that Thomasson's previous employment had been as executive director of an Arkansas investment firm run by "a man who had done a lot of bond business with the state of Arkansas and who was convicted of distributing cocaine (including to the president's brother, Roger)." The story said it was unclear exactly what the files contained but that they had been turned over to Foster's attorney, James Hamilton, not federal investigators.

Now the conditions for a perfect conspiratorial storm were gathering in the hothouse atmosphere of Washington. In place of "land deal," the term "cover-up" was becoming a common appellation for Whitewater. On Capitol Hill, Republicans including Senate and House leaders Bob Dole and Newt Gingrich rushed to microphones to demand the release of the pilfered Whitewater documents and the appointment of a special prosecutor.

Hillary and Nussbaum, from the first mention of a special Whitewater prosecutor, drew a Maginot Line. In the White House she made clear her view that the Clinton presidency would be effectively rendered powerless if that line were crossed. The White House had wiggle room. The 1978 Ethics in Government Act had expired—though Clinton had pledged to renew it in 1994—including its provision for court-appointed independent counsels. So the only procedure available would be for Attorney General Janet Reno, who was confident in the abilities of her own prosecutors, to appoint a special counsel–prosecutor whose powers and independence would be similar to those guaranteed under the expired law. Hillary and Nussbaum wanted no part of that. They understood—from their experience in Watergate, and then watching a special prosecutor in the Iran-contra affair abuse that legacy with a seven-year investigation—all the dangers. A special prosecutor had only one case to focus on, and no time limit. Ambition could figure prominently. No, especially in the current atmosphere, they were certain that was the worst possible road to take.

Two days before Christmas, on the defensive again, the White House agreed to release to the Department of Justice, but not to the press, the Clintons' tax returns and specific papers related to the Whitewater purchase. Kendall had prevailed on Justice officials to secretly subpoena the documents so they would no longer be subject to the Freedom of Information Act, and therefore not available to the press or to Congress. A statement for the press released by the White House concerning the handover of the papers made no mention of the subpoena. This was just the kind of fancy footwork that always seemed to trip up the Clintons, and when it was revealed a few days later, Bill and Hillary were wounded again.

HILLARY WAS NOT wrong that old enemies in Arkansas, in conjunction with organized right-wing groups and the mega-wattage of talk radio, were hard at work. The unprecedented campaign against a sitting president and first lady, well organized and increasingly effective, continued. The roles of Sheffield Nelson, who in the 1990 gubernatorial campaign had pushed to publicly identify some of Bill's women—and misidentify some who were not—and Cliff Jackson, an Arkansas lawyer who had befriended Clinton at Oxford, in disseminating venomous tales of Clinton's past were indisputable. Some were based in truth, others in fantasy. Jackson's own political ambitions in Arkansas—as a Republican—once had been similar to Bill's, but went nowhere. At Oxford, Jackson had counseled Clinton on avoiding the draft, and he was eager to disclose the details (and did) when Clinton sought the presidency; and it was Jackson who led the state troopers to David Brock. Nelson, Jackson, and others with old axes to grind were in close touch with newer ideological enemies, who viewed "Clintonism" as a plague to be eradicated. Across the Potomac, in northern Virginia, David Bossie and Floyd Brown (he had produced the Willie Horton ad during the 1988 presidential campaign of George Bush) had set up shop as Citizens United, an organization that existed largely to fight the pestilence (and geared up again in 2007 for Hillary's presidential campaign). They issued a constant stream of lies, half-truths, devilish gospels, and conspiratorial epistles that told a tale of perdition and evil, and were peddled by the pair to mainstream news organizations, Republican offices on Capitol Hill, and right-wing talk show hosts especially. The distance from Citizens United to Rush Limbaugh and televangelist Jerry Falwell could sometimes be measured in milliseconds.

But however accurate Hillary's perception of an organized threat against the Clintons, she seemed unable, or unwilling, to grasp the desire of less antagonistic citizens, members of Congress, and the press to be given straightforward, timely responses to legitimate questions being raised by the stories, whatever the origins of the information and of the motivation of those promoting them.

Bill believed his own White House staff had failed to develop and execute an aggressive but reasoned public defense months before, when problems had so obviously been building and would have been more manageable. But largely at Hillary's insistence, he had decided consistently against taking actions that might have won them some favor by reasonably full and prompt disclosure. Instead, they had chosen a narrow, legalistic approach that relied on containment, and had entrusted much of the response largely to Bruce Lindsey instead of encouraging a broader process of internal discussion and coherent planning.

In mid-December Deputy Chief of Staff Harold Ickes took on the assignment of forming a Whitewater response team, which began meeting twice a day as the problems seemed to career further out of control, regardless of any order Ickes or anyone else could impose. The biggest obstacle, in the view of many of those deeply involved, was Hillary's continued objection to asking for a special prosecutor, and the failure to release information publicly on a timely basis. "It was Hillary who made the decision [to keep resisting]," said Lindsey's wife, Bev, herself an aide to the president. "She is the practicing lawyer in the family. Bill is the theoretical lawyer. . . . And I think they both felt that they could tell people there was nothing there and people would believe it. The staff realized it wasn't working. So all they could do was keep bringing it up . . . but that angers her and each time they brought it back to her, there was more tension." Something similar would happen during the year of Monica Lewinsky denial. But for now, the backing of Kendall and Nussbaum, neither of whom was particularly astute about recognizing the relative revulsion of ordinary citizens to slick lawyering, only seemed to reinforce her certainty.

The first few days of the New Year were consumed with divisive internal debate about whether to appoint a special prosecutor. Hillary was unyielding in her opposition, as were Lindsey, Nussbaum, and Kendall. She argued that permitting a high-profile investigation by a special prosecutor would further distract attention from health care reform and other legislation that she and Bill wanted to push forward. An independent counsel would also cost the Clintons a lot of money, and such an investigation could be endless.

"Sadly, the Whitewater affair is exploding into a press frenzy," Deputy Treasury Secretary Roger Altman wrote in his diary on January 3, 1994. "It's mostly a testimony to the press mania and the crazed world of Washington." Two days later he wrote: "This Whitewater situation is one big mess. Administration perceived as stonewalling; 'There must be something to hide.' Big issue is independent prosecutor. Lots of speculation that HRC is the one who handled this in Arkansas. . . . White House seems engulfed in this and is mishandling it."

It was hardly lost on those arguing about a special prosecutor that Hillary, along with the president, would be the subject of any special prosecutor's inquiry. Maggie Williams had told Altman, "On Whitewater, HRC was paralyzed by it," according to another note he made. Then Williams had added: "HRC 'doesn't want [an independent counsel] poking into 20 years of public life in Arkansas.' " Unless the Clintons' Whitewater problems were "defused," health care reform would die, Williams warned.

In the first days of 1994, while Hillary was absorbing new revelations about Bill's sexual past, Betsey Wright was rummaging through some gubernatorial records in Arkansas at the behest of Hillary and the Clintons' lawyers. She came upon a series of canceled checks written on the account of the Whitewater Development Corporation. Adjacent to the checks was a carbon copy of an urgent telephone message to the governor from Jim McDougal, the Clintons' Whitewater partner, urging him to appoint Beverly Bassett Schaffer as commissioner of the Arkansas Securities Department, the state regulatory body that oversees the savings and loan business. Schaffer was appointed by Clinton shortly thereafter, and then assumed jurisdiction over McDougal's attempts to keep his failing S&L from being closed down.

Wright had been searching for campaign finance materials that might be necessary to answer questions by investigators, to segregate them from other gubernatorial papers being archived in Arkansas. In the process, she said, "I accidentally found some Whitewater documents. They were not what I was looking for at all." As soon as she found the message from McDougal, she phoned Hillary at the White House.

"I told her that I found the phone message about Jim McDougal calling to support Beverly Bassett Schaffer for securities commissioner," Wright related. "And [Hillary] said, 'Oh, I'm sorry you found that.'

"And I said, 'Well, you know, they're carbons or copies, you know, it doesn't matter.' "

Hillary then told her, "There's going to be an investigator, a [special] counsel or something. . . . You've got to get a lawyer."

Discussing the matter many years later, Wright explained: "Well, I mean, okay. I mean who am I to argue with a lawyer [Hillary] about when I need a lawyer?"

Hillary's advice to get a lawyer was not specifically a response to finding the checks or discovering the message from McDougal, Wright believed. Rather, Hillary appeared to be advising her that it was likely that a special prosecutor would be appointed, and that they would therefore *all* need their own private legal counsel. Wright was unaware of the furious debate underway in the White House about whether to accede to demands that a special prosecutor be appointed. Hillary was adamantly against it, of course, but given what she told Wright, she must have sensed already that she was going to lose the argument.

Following her conversation with Hillary, Wright also told the president's top personal aide, Bruce Lindsey, himself a lawyer, about finding the checks and the telephone message, and that, in addition to engaging her own lawyer, she intended to turn the material over to the Clintons' personal attorney, David Kendall.

At a meeting in McLarty's office later that first week of January, Stephanopoulos made the case for an independent counsel to Hillary. "Assuming we did nothing wrong," he said it would be advantageous for a special prosecutor to confirm it. If they didn't ask the attorney general to appoint one now, it seemed inevitable that Congress would pass the Independent Counsel Act and the Court of Appeals would impose its choice of a counsel. The White House, by resisting, appeared to be hiding something.

Hillary lashed back at Stephanopoulos, accusing him of never believing in the Clintons in the first place. She began to cry. Shocked at her reaction, the room was quiet. Hillary soon regained her composure and barked out her expectations: she wanted them to mount a campaign and fight back.

Whitewater overshadowed everything. A subsequent meeting was convened by Ickes to discuss whether Hillary's opposition could be contravened. Ickes wondered if Secretary of State Warren Christopher or Bob Barnett should be enlisted to talk to her. But most people felt it would be impossible for anyone to get her to change her position—not even Bill. Nor was it clear that Barnett would disagree with her. Another White House document marked "Confidential: Second Draft, Summary of Arguments Re: Whitewater" listed reasons to oppose appointment of a special prosecutor, including that it "may result in focus on friends and associates of the president, begin to squeeze them and may make some subject to indictment." Notes from the meeting that Ickes convened show that Nussbaum, who had spoken to Betsey Wright in the previous weeks about how to defuse the situation, was predicting that "Indictments will be Betsey Wright."

HILLARY AND BILL were asleep when the phone rang in the early morning hours of January 6. Dick Kelley, Virginia's fourth husband, was on the line to tell the president his mother had died in her sleep at their home, on the outskirts of Hot Springs. She had been fighting breast cancer since 1990, and had surgery that year to remove a lump in her right breast but the cancer spread. Later she had undergone a mastectomy, chemotherapy, and frequent blood transfusions once the cancer had invaded her bloodstream.

The Clintons started making phone calls to family members and close friends, and brought Chelsea into their bedroom to break the news. Chelsea had lost her grandfather, Hillary's father, six months before.

Virginia had been the great influence on Bill's life. She had persevered through hard knocks, inculcated in him her optimism and drive. She loved placing her two-dollar bets at Oaklawn racetrack, and the attention of men. She had buried three husbands, two of whom had drank and abused her. Her home was filled with mementos of Bill's high school years and his accomplishments in Boys Nation. She had worked long hours and paid most of Bill's tuition to Georgetown. "I got my stamina from my mother," Clinton once said. Her last conversation with her son had been two nights before she died: "Mother called me at the White House," Bill recalled. She had just returned home from a trip to Las Vegas, her favorite city. She had been thoroughly enjoying herself and told him she had loved Barbra Streisand's concert, during which the singer had dedicated a song to her and had introduced her to the audience. Virginia had seemed strong and "was in high spirits" on the phone. "She just wanted to check in and tell me she loved me." He knew the end was near, but he "wasn't ready to let her go."

Clinton's gregariousness, his fun-loving nature, his glad-handing, his hugging, his empathy, his ability to focus on whomever he was talking to—all those were traits he'd shared with his mother. In high school, he had "showed more affection toward his mom than any of us showed toward our moms," said a childhood friend. "You could tell they were close and drew on each other."

Hillary believed that Bill and Virginia shared great optimism, along with a tendency to repress unpleasant thoughts or memories. He had nearly photographic recall, yet for decades he had blocked out painful scenes involving his abusive stepfather, Roger Clinton, as had Virginia.

The next morning, January 7, Bob Dole appeared on *CBS This Morning* and attacked Bill's conduct in handling the Whitewater matter, arguing for the appointment of a special prosecutor. "I hate to even discuss these things today, but I think it's fair to say that it appears, from what we know this morning, that the White House worked with the Justice Department on the subpoena," Dole said. "These [tax returns and other documents] weren't turned over voluntarily. They worked out a subpoena in an effort to protect the privacy of the records. It's almost unbelievable that the White House would work with the Justice Department in a matter of this kind. . . . I think it cries out more than ever now for an independent counsel, and it seems to me that Attorney General Reno must move at this point. You know, they've known since December 24 or 25 that the subpoena was going to be issued. We were told by White House sources, not the president, they were being turned over voluntarily, and I just believe it's gotten out of hand now."

Though Bill and Hillary said they didn't normally watch the morning talk shows, their bedroom television was on that morning—for "background noise" in the residence. When they heard Dole, Bill became "utterly stricken," Hillary said; he was being hit when he was down and that violated his personal canon. A few years later, when Dole learned how hurt Bill had been, Dole wrote him an apologetic note, which Clinton deeply appreciated.

As the Clintons prepared to travel to Virginia's funeral in Arkansas, Dole's office made public a letter he had written to Reno, pushing for a special prosecutor. "It is in the president's interest for you to stop hiding behind the fact that the Independent Counsel Act has not been reauthorized," Dole wrote, though he had voted against reauthorizing the act when the Senate considered it in November.

White House aides and Democrats on Capitol Hill hastened to criticize Dole and other Republicans, including Gingrich, for the inappropriate timing of their attacks. "I just have to tell you . . . as the president goes home to bury his mother, to have the political opposition on the warpath, hammering away, raises all sorts of questions about what has happened in this town," Gergen said on NBC's *Today* show. Senator David Pryor of Arkansas appeared genuinely stunned: the Senate was a collegial place, where members rarely criticized each other personally. "You know, I've never seen anything like this," he told CNN. "In the name of human decency, it would appear to me that Robert Dole and his friends would allow the president of the United States and their family to bury his mother."

Gergen had tapped into a central truth about the way war was fought in Washington. There were no days off from battle.

Dole's office now issued a statement criticizing Al Gore for using Virginia's death to stifle criticism of the conduct of the White House and the Clintons.

Of Hillary, Gergen noted later:

Clearly, she had internalized her anger over the years, resolving that she should put her energies into working even harder for their joint success. When she saw mistakes made by his team or by him, she couldn't hold back any longer. Her emotions boiled to the surface. She was also a sensitive, vulnerable woman, as I found. Weeks after our blowup over *The Washington Post* request for Whitewater documents, I agreed to defend the Clintons on NBC's *Today* show. I was trying to show I was a team player. Before going on live that morning, I had a call from Hillary. She and her husband were leaving that morning for his mother's funeral in Arkansas. I expressed sympathy for all she had gone through in recent months. As we talked, she started crying. "You can tell your friends at *The Post*," she said, "that we've learned our lesson. We came here to do good things, and we just didn't understand so many things about this town. It's been so hard." I murmured a few things and finally said, "I wish I could come over and give you a hug. I would give a lot to cheer you up." . . . Looking back, I wish it had all turned out differently. They did come to Washington to do good things. They were not simply grasping for power. If their relationship had evolved in a different way over the years—or if he had been elected later in life—perhaps it would have been more settled and would not have spilled over into his presidency. They would never have attempted a co-presidency. As it was, they each paid a dreadful price in those days I saw them together. And there was worse still to come.

Kendall was due to arrive in Little Rock that evening for the funeral of the president's mother, on January 8. Wright said that she went to the Little Rock airport to meet his plane. "Kendall would not take the box of documents I had found from me. . . . I do not know [why]. To this day I don't know." Not long after, however, the documents were air-expressed to Kendall by Betsey and stored with other records of the Clintons' at Williams & Connolly.

Eventually, Wright's legal fees, unrecompensed by the Clintons, ran to $650,000.

Meanwhile, with the question of a special prosecutor still up in the air, Hillary's opposition to allowing such an appointment hardened to the point of intransigence.

BILL AND HILLARY had thought that his tour of Central Europe and the former Soviet Union, beginning on Sunday, January 9, his first to the region as president, would produce many favorable foreign policy stories, pushing domestic scandals aside. They were wrong. Senator Pat Moynihan went on *Meet the Press* that Sunday and said Reno should appoint a special prosecutor. He urged the president to give up all papers related to Whitewater. "Turn over the papers. I don't care what your lawyer says. Turn them over. If there are things that are embarrassing, turn them over faster. . . . Presidents can't be seen to have any hesitation about any matter that concerns their propriety. And this is an honorable man. We have a fine president. He has nothing to hide."

No defection from the ranks of Democrats could have been more damaging. Soon, eight other senators joined Moynihan's call, including Bill Bradley. Gergen, who was on the presidential trip—Hillary was in Washington—told reporters, "If it comes to a special counsel, then he'll be very cooperative," Gergen said. "We've been cooperating with the Justice Department, and if there is a different investigative body, we'll cooperate with that—whatever the investigative body is." The White House finally seemed to be softening its position.

Clinton stopped briefly in Kiev to meet with Ukrainian president Leonid Kravchuk in preparation for an agreement the United States, Russia, and Ukraine would sign the following week that would eliminate intercontinental ballistic missiles and nuclear warheads directed from Ukraine at the United States. At a press conference later in the day, reporters demonstrated almost no interest in the agreement or the foreign policy aspects of the trip. They wanted Clinton to answer questions about Whitewater, Moynihan, and Dole. "I have nothing to say about that on this trip," Clinton told them. When NBC's Pentagon reporter—on the trip because of its arms control implications—asked the president about Whitewater in a one-on-one interview, Clinton got up from his chair, turned off his microphone, and snapped, "You had your two questions. I'm sorry you're not interested in the trip."

Clinton had had enough. On January 11, the Whitewater response team met in the Oval Office with Hillary and Kendall. Bill was on speakerphone from Prague. Years later, Hillary said, the scene had reminded her of a cartoon in which a man stood in front of two doors, one with a sign saying "Damned if you do," the other saying "Damned if you don't." It was obvious to Hillary that Bill was tired and still grieving over the loss of his mother. It was the just before dawn in Central Europe.

Ickes moderated, instructing Stephanopoulos to argue for a special prosecutor and Nussbaum to argue against. Stephanopoulos recalled years later that it was the only time he could remember being in the Oval Office without Clinton present. Before the meeting, he'd researched the work of a dozen previous independent counsels. He now pointed out to Clinton and the assembled group that few of the special prosecutors had brought indictments. He cited the investigation of President Carter and his brother regarding their ownership of a peanut warehouse, which concluded within six months and produced no indictments. "You've done nothing wrong," Stephanopoulos said to the president. "This will all be over in six months. Health care is coming. Let's get this behind us."

When Stephanopoulos finished, Nussbaum said he was still against turning over documents to the press, and he was still against asking Reno to appoint a special prosecutor. "I've lived with this institution," he said. "It is an evil institution. The world has changed since Carter. Iran-contra lasted seven years. You will create a roving spotlight which will examine your friends and everyone you've ever had contact with." When aides in the meeting argued that the inquiry could be limited to the Whitewater dealings in Arkansas, Nussbaum got agitated. "Mr. President, one year from now Bruce Lindsey will be under investigation. Your friends, your family will be chased to the ends of the earth." At that moment it sounded to many in the room like hyperbole. In fact, Nussbaum was prescient.

Frustrated and exhausted, Clinton demanded an alternative. Nussbaum suggested the Clintons turn over every document to Congress and announce that they'd testify on Capitol Hill to get their side of the story out within a month. Stephanopoulos thought the idea was crazy and said so. Nussbaum countered, "If you create a special counsel, it will last as long as your presidency and beyond." The debate was passionate and emotional, as aides, only too aware of the high stakes, interrupted each other and tried to get their points in. The president wanted to know what Hillary thought. She said that asking for the prosecutor would set a "terrible precedent," capitulating to a media frenzy instead of holding to legal principle. But it remained his decision to make, she said. The president then asked to speak to Hillary and David Kendall alone. Bill told them he thought there was no other choice than to appoint a special prosecutor. He and Hillary had done nothing wrong, he said, and if they didn't it would completely smother their agenda. Hillary asked him to give it more thought. Bill said he had made up his mind.

Hillary went to Nussbaum's office the next morning to break the news to him. She hugged him and told him he had acquitted himself well. Nussbaum was obviously upset and disappointed by the decision. "This is a great tragedy," he said. "Why are you going to put your head in that noose?"

Nussbaum drafted a letter to Attorney General Janet Reno saying that the president had asked him to request a special counsel to investigate the Whitewater matter. Its tone made clear he opposed the decision. Stephanopoulos went to the White House briefing room to explain the decision to reporters.

Reno, too, was disappointed. She believed that if Congress wanted an independent counsel to investigate, it should first reauthorize the lapsed statute; then a three-judge panel would choose a special prosecutor. Now she was charged with finding one. Quickly the name of Robert Bishop Fiske Jr. rose to the top of her list. He was known for his integrity, toughness, and, above all, his reputation for sifting through and evaluating the facts of a complicated case. Appointed a United States attorney for New York, he'd made a name for himself as an aggressive prosecutor. At sixty-three years of age, he was now a senior partner in the old-line Wall Street firm of Davis, Polk & Wardwell. Most important, he was a Republican.

Fiske flew to Washington on January 19, where he wrote his own charter for the job, outlining a broad jurisdiction that included the freedom to investigate any activity even tangentially related to Whitewater. It stated that the investigation would look into "whether any individuals or entities committed a violation of any federal criminal law relating in any way" to Bill and Hillary's relationship to Whitewater, Madison Guaranty Savings & Loan, or Capital Management Services, a small investment firm owned by David Hale, the Arkansas judge indicted for fraud, that was created to help struggling businesses. The statement would allow Fiske to investigate anything that happened in the 1980s or during the presidency related to those companies, including the actions of White House aides who took Whitewater files from Vince Foster's office after his death. The investigation could now begin. "I want you to be completely independent," Reno told him. "I don't expect to talk to you again until this is all over."

On January 20, Reno announced his appointment and introduced him to the press. It was the first anniversary of the Clinton administration.

15

Truth or Consequences

"You know, they're not going to let up. They're just going to keep on coming."

—*Living History*

WITH THE APPOINTMENT of the special prosecutor, the Clinton administration really consisted of two White House enterprises: the one struggling to be a presidency, and the other a law firm and public relations office struggling to protect its clients and minimize the damage. When the two branches came together, the legal thicket intruded inexorably on governance. When Bill met in Washington in early March with Eduard Shevardnadze, the president of Georgia, to sign an arms control agreement, he was confronted by reporters with question after question about his wife's morality—not about foreign policy. It took all his self-control not to explode on-camera. "I'm telling you, the American people can worry about something else," he told the press. "Her moral compass is as strong as anybody's in this country, and they will see that."

Meanwhile, Peter Jennings devoted eighteen of twenty-two commercial-free minutes of his ABC *World News Tonight* broadcast to Whitewater, to "try and explain in one fell swoop the . . . jam that Bill and Hillary Clinton seem unable to get themselves out of."

The first two sacrificial post-Foster casualties of Whitewater were Bernard Nussbaum and the undersecretary of the treasury Roger Altman. Both had tried to monitor the Resolution Trust Corporation "referrals" in which the Clintons were listed as potential "witnesses" in possible criminal action involving Madison Guaranty. Their object had been to protect Hillary and Bill by gaining knowledge about what the investigators were doing and thinking. Such oversight of a criminal investigation through executive branch back channels was hardly regular procedure, but did not violate the law, the prosecutor later affirmed. Nussbaum resisted resignation vigorously, but the president reluctantly concluded that fighting to save him would only make things worse. Altman was perhaps the brightest star in the Clinton entourage. Tall, telegenic, a fabulously successful investment banker and Clinton fundraiser, he'd shepherded the passage of NAFTA and the economic plan on Capitol Hill, and had been expected to succeed Lloyd Bentsen as treasury secretary in the not-too-distant future. Instead, on Capitol Hill, Senator Alfonse D'Amato, the senior Republican on the Banking Committee, was gearing up for public hearings at which Altman would be the star witness. D'Amato made little secret of his desire to clean the Clintons' collective clock. Maggie Williams had been instrumental in urging Altman to reverse his original decision to recuse himself from the RTC matter. She, Lisa Caputo, and Mark Gearan had already been summoned to appear before Fiske's grand jury.

In an interview with *Elle* magazine that had been scheduled for months, Hillary was asked, "How do you counter the constant attacks?"

"You don't," she said. "Since I know, in the end, nothing bad happened—and that's what everybody's going to know eventually, because they have yet to come forward with anything other than the wildest kind of paranoid conspiracies—you just don't pay much attention to it. . . . I'm not interested in spending my days falling into the trap that the fomenters of all this want us to, which is to become isolated and on the defensive and diverted. I'm not going to let that happen. Unfortunately, in today's climate, anyone can say anything about a person in public life, and it will get printed."

"Are you really able to blow it off?" Hillary was asked.

"I blow most of it off. I get angry. I get confused about why people are doing what they do. I don't get up every day thinking destructively about others. I don't spend my hours plotting for somebody else's downfall. My feeling is, gosh there's more work that can be done, everybody ought to get out there and improve the health care system, and reform welfare and get guns out of the hands of teenagers."

That Hillary, who had come to the White House expecting to be the president's biggest political asset, was becoming an albatross was evident at the Democratic National Committee's spring meeting on March 11. Those in attendance wore buttons that read "Don't Pillory Hillary" but, sotto voce, there were suggestions by influential leaders of the party that Hillary could help with damage control by explaining more forthrightly her role in Whitewater. "Her integrity and effectiveness are at stake," said Lynn Cutler, then vice chairwoman of the DNC. "They are peeling away her ability to be what she is, which is our leader on the health care reform issue."

Each day Ickes's special response team prepared a summary of its deliberations, which was sent to the first lady. Nussbaum's replacement as counsel to the president, Lloyd Cutler (no relation to Lynn), seventy-four years old and a pillar of the Washington legal establishment, recruited for the job by Vernon Jordan, wanted Hillary to turn over as many documents as possible. But she and Kendall wanted to make the special prosecutor wear himself out trying to get them, subpoenaing them one at a time to prevent him from establishing a daisy chain of witnesses.

For the first time, Republicans could see the first lady clearly in their sights. Senator D'Amato, who was scheduling some forty witnesses to appear at his banking committee hearings, suggested that Hillary owed a detailed explanation of her actions to the American public, and Bob Dole said he intended to force a vote in the Senate about whether more open-ended hearings should be held in Whitewater and other matters. Dole had something far grander in mind than the Banking Committee hearings: he was thinking along the lines of the Senate's investigation of Watergate.

Under this intensifying pressure, Hillary decided to sit for interviews with the three weekly news magazines and appeared, on March 13, 1994, on the three Sunday morning talk shows. Again she tried to make short shrift of the furor enveloping her. The appointment of the special prosecutor would lead to "people spending millions and millions of dollars [to] conclude we made a bad land investment."

Her timing was dismal. Jeff Gerth had now discovered her commodities trades, and realized that the refusal of the Clintons to release their 1978–1979 tax returns must have been because they would show her $100,000 windfall—on her $1,000 investment with Red Bone. The *Times*'s editor, Joseph Lelyveld, had called all the paper's investigative reporters to a meeting in January and set them loose on "the Clinton story."

Almost no revelation that fell short of demonstrating an overtly criminal act could have been more damaging to Hillary than the *Times* front-page lead of March 18: "Top Arkansas Lawyer Helped Hillary Clinton Turn Big Profit; Commodities Trading in '70s Yielded $100,000." Not for the first or last time, the White House response compounded the damage. Lisa Caputo was the unfortunate aide called upon by Hillary to provide background for the story. She was asked how Hillary, as a newcomer to the tricky commodities market, had managed to turn a huge profit (in unborn cows, no less) and knew when to quit. Caputo argued that Hillary had read *The Wall Street Journal* and had sought advice from "numerous people." Gerth had mentioned one, Jim Blair. "There was no impropriety," the White House insisted. "The only appearance [of it] is being created by *The New York Times*."

HILLARY'S COMMODITIES windfall dominated news coverage and gleeful Washington gossip for the next three weeks. The open wound was worsened by Webb Hubbell's abrupt resignation from the Justice Department the same week—it was guilt by association, but suggestive nonetheless. Newspaper accounts said that the Rose Law Firm planned to file a complaint with the Arkansas Bar Association because Hubbell allegedly overbilled clients and padded his expense account in excess of $500,000. That matter, too, had become part of Fiske's investigation. Hubbell gave her a plausible—to her at the time—explanation for his actions, and said the "misunderstanding" would blow over. She was inclined to believe her friend. But the events furthered the perception that the Clintons and their entourage had come up to the capital from a Southern cesspool. The stench hovered.

At a Democratic Party fund-raiser the night of Hubbell's resignation, Bill's temper flared and he put aside his planned remarks about creating jobs. Red-faced, his voice rising, he attributed the investigatory climate to the Republicans, who were "committed to a politics of personal destruction" and would rather criticize Hillary than develop their own health care plan.

Shortly thereafter, Bill scheduled a prime-time, full-scale news conference, hoping to calm the atmosphere.

"Have you taken any lessons from this ordeal, whether it's about the presidency, about the process, about the city, or anything?" he was asked.

"I think there is a level of suspicion here that is greater than that which I have been used to in the past. And I don't complain about it, but I've learned a lot about it. And that my job is to try to answer whatever questions are out there so I can get on with the business of the country. And I think I've learned a lot about how to handle that.

"I've also learned here that there may or may not be a different standard than I had seen in the past, [though] not of right and wrong."

The press conference didn't work.

Hillary and her advisers decided it was essential for her to have her own press conference, at which she would answer all questions thrown at her. Her $100,000 profit-taking now public knowledge, Bill had agreed to release their tax returns for 1978–1979. The day before her press conference, the latest *Los Angeles Times* poll showed her approval rating had declined from 56 percent to 44 percent in the three months since January. Bill's had remained steady at 54 percent.

"I don't think she really wanted to do it at the beginning," said a senior member of her staff, "but it was collectively decided between everybody—the West Wing and the East Wing—that she needed to face the charges. And so we went through this whole thing about trying to put together a press conference, and basically did it in the State Dining Room under the portrait of Lincoln, and she had on this pink suit. That's why we call it the Pink Press Conference. . . . And she basically stayed until almost every single last question was answered." Thirty-four reporters asked questions and follow-ups. All the networks overrode their regular programming to provide live coverage.

Her answer to the first question about the commodities trading—was it hypocritical to condemn the 1980s as the decade of greed while she was milking cattle futures and investing in speculative land?—was classic Hillary-under-pressure: obsequious, well rehearsed, not quite right. There was a faint echo of Richard Nixon in his famous Checkers speech. Hugh Rodham had read his young daughter the stock tables from the *Chicago Tribune*, she said, and now Hillary carried on the tradition by studying the finance pages with Chelsea. "You know, I was raised to believe that every person had an obligation to take care of themselves and their family," she said, preternaturally calm. She continued: "I don't think you'll ever find anything that my husband or I said that in any way condemns the importance of making good investments and saving or that in any way undermines what is the heart and soul of the American economy, which is risk-taking and investing in the future. What I think we were saying is that, like anything else, that can be taken to excess—when companies are leveraged into debt, when loans are not repaid, when pension funds are raided. You know, all of the things that marked the excess of the 1980s are things which we spoke out against. I think it's a pretty long stretch to say that the decisions that we made to try to create some financial security for our family and make some investments come anywhere near there. . . . We obviously wanted enough financial security to send our daughter to college and put money away for our old age and help our parents when we could."

Later, she claimed to have been grateful for the questions, so she could put everything out in the open. She was asked if she believed that withholding information had "helped to create any impression that you were trying to hide something."

"Yes, I do," she answered. "And I think that is one of the things that I regret most, and one of the reasons why I wanted to do this. . . . I think if my father or mother said anything to me more than a million times, it was: 'Don't listen to what other people say. Don't be guided by other people's opinions. You know, you have to live with yourself.' And I think that's good advice. But I do think that that advice and my belief in it, combined with my sense of privacy . . . led me to perhaps be less understanding than I needed to [be] of both the press and the public's interest, as well as [their] right to know things about my husband and me."

Did she and Bill "ever look in the mirror and wish that you just never got into this?"—meaning the presidency.

"No, never, never. This is really a result of our inexperience in Washington," she insisted. "I really did not fully understand everything that I wish now I had known"—including the need to keep the people informed by answering questions from reporters. ("I'm certainly going to try to be more sensitive to what you all need and what we need to give you.") In terms of the difficulties of Whitewater, "I feel very confident about how this will all turn out. This is not a long-term problem or issue in any way."

The final question was eerie. Richard Nixon, eighty-one, was in a deep coma after suffering a stroke three days earlier. "Considering what you've been through, do you have any greater appreciation of what Richard Nixon might have been going through?"

For the first time since she had entered the State Dining Room in her pink outfit, she seemed to be genuinely emotional. Her tears were visible on television, and her voice broke. "What I think we ought to be doing is praying for President Nixon," she said. "And from my perspective, you know, it was a year ago April that my father died at the age of eighty-one, and so, you know, I'm just mostly thinking about his daughters right now."

It would be the last such full-scale press conference she allowed as first lady. After that, noted Roger Altman, "she essentially reverted to a Reagan approach to the press and benefited every day of the week from doing so." Reagan had cupped his hand to his ear when he was asked a question by a reporter, and declined to answer on grounds of deafness (he was deaf in one ear). "She started off with one approach of being accessible, or at least fairly accessible," said Altman. "It's just too bad. . . . If they ever ask me again, 'How should you play the media?' I'd say, 'Just follow Ronald Reagan's playlist, follow it A to Z.' So, Hillary, I think, changed her mode in that regard, and much to her benefit. I don't know how many times she was actually accessible to the press after her famous Pink Press Conference. But in terms of the definition of accessible that I would use, not too often."

It had been a bravura performance. She *had* looked pretty in pink, and watching the press poke, probe, and pile on for sixty-eight minutes made her a much more sympathetic figure. Afterward, David Kendall proclaimed that "Whitewater is evaporating." Bill told the *Los Angeles Times* that he had simply banned the topic and would permit "no discussion of this in my household, no discussion of this in my office."

At dinner that night, Bob Reich sat next to Hillary. "She felt good about the press conference. She had been very effective. That was the word we heard from everyone, all of the pollsters, all the political people, my little free-floating focus group—my wife and sons and friends. Everybody thought she had done very well. She was obviously relieved that that particular press conference was over, but she was also hurt and bewildered, and I think quite pained by Whitewater. It was worse than a distraction. It really seemed to her to be some sort of almost retribution, political retribution. She didn't understand why, but there was anger directed at her."

And there was *her* anger to consider—at Democrats in Congress, especially. She expressed as much in a conversation with Sara Ehrman. Couldn't people see that the onslaught against her and Bill was intended to kill health care and undermine Bill's reelection, to tar both her and her husband to the point where they would be considered pariahs? She couldn't fathom why Democrats weren't taking an aggressive stance and attacking the opposition for such patently obvious political and personal persecution. There was no deference to the presidency, not even by their own party. This was beyond acceptable politics to her, yet the Democrats on the Hill, especially the leadership, always seemed to be on the defensive. Even Dick Gephardt, the Democratic leader of the House, sometimes seemed more concerned about his relations with the opposition in the House than with the president. Why weren't they out there defending the presidency and the Democratic agenda?

She had even less kind words for the local establishment, the people in Washington who thought that the "politics of personal destruction"— the phrase was Bill's*—were perfectly acceptable and even amusing fodder for dinner table conversation.

THROUGH THE SPRING and summer of 1994, as Hillary tried to focus and get the country to focus on the merits of reforming the country's health care system, the Whitewater "madness" continued to do damage. "They are peeling away her ability to be what she is, which is our leader on the health care reform issue," said David Wilhelm, chairman of the

---

*She would use it effectively, too, in her presidential campaign.

Democratic National Committee. He accused Senators D'Amato, Dole, and Phil Gramm, another senator seeking the Republican presidential nomination, of overlooking their own ethics problems, adding that "they can't stand her success, and that's why they're on the attack." Fortunately for the Clintons, special prosecutor Fiske prevailed on Republican leaders to postpone any latitudinous Senate inquiries until he had finished his own investigation.

Hillary and David Kendall drew increasingly close. She spent far more time with him discussing strategy and specifics about Whitewater and its spawn than did her husband. She trusted Kendall totally, and there were many things she would share with him that she would not share with the other lawyers, some of whom believed that Kendall carefully parsed out his knowledge to the rest of the legal team, which had expanded as Hillary's and Bill's troubles grew deeper. Kendall and Nussbaum had seen eye-to-eye on most questions, so Nussbaum had had a fair (but hardly complete, he later concluded) view of the legal chessboard. But that could not be said of the new White House counsel, Lloyd Cutler, or (even more so) the next heavy-hitter brought into the mix, Robert Bennett. Bennett was at first recruited by Cutler "to have a seat at the table on all Whitewater issues," said one of the lawyers. "There was considerable discontent at the way Kendall was handling things. David viewed the problems as 80 percent law and 20 percent politics. Ickes, Harry Thomason, and others felt the reverse."

Kendall, Barnett, and other lawyers at Williams & Connolly working on matters involving the Clintons were not pleased with Cutler's choice of Bennett, an experienced Washington litigator and former prosecutor renowned for his tenacity in the courtroom. Cutler intended that Bennett would bring both toughness and some public relations skills to the table, in part to compensate for what many in the West Wing believed was Kendall's inability to make a sympathetic case for his clients on television. Kendall came off as unforthcoming, argumentative, and prissy.

The three-year statute of limitations to file a lawsuit in the Paula Jones matter was running out on May 8, 1994, around the time Bennett was brought on board, and Cutler wanted it settled posthaste. There was no percentage in letting that sideshow go on, even if Bill Clinton were to "win" through the courts. He could be ruined in wide-ranging depositions. Cutler overrode the objection of Kendall, who wanted to handle the matter himself. Before signing on—at $475 an hour—Bennett met with Hillary, then with Bill, who told him, "I swear to God, it didn't happen." The president also told Bennett, according to those familiar with the circumstances of his hiring, not to discuss the Jones case specifically with his wife. Bennett had already heard from others that Hillary did not want to settle the case; after all, if nothing had happened with this woman, why should Bill settle? She wanted the matter to be made to disappear.

At the same time, Clinton was being urged to settle with Jones by Jim Blair, Vernon Jordan, and Bruce Lindsey.

"I begged him and begged him to settle the Paula Jones case and by the time I got him around to my way of thinking it was too late," Jim Blair recalled. "Had he settled it when I asked him to none of this [Clinton's lying under oath, in a deposition for Jones's lawsuit, about Monica Lewinsky] would have ever happened. . . . Hillary did not want it. . . . I think he felt like if he did it [settle], he was . . . telling Hillary something that he didn't want to tell her."

Bennett had reached the same conclusion. He had personally favored settling, even under conditions that would have been more ambiguous than the president seemed to be willing to accept. The risk of a lawsuit proceeding, he felt, was too great. At crucial moments during the negotiation, Clinton had seemed ambivalent, unsure of what to do.

The Jones matter had been simmering since February, when she showed up at the annual meeting of the Conservative Political Action Conference. The event had less to do with a genuine conservative political agenda than with Clinton-baiting and -bashing. David Brock, as yet unreconstructed, was the hero of the hour. Mobbed by autograph hounds, he posed for pictures and, with the state troopers he had interviewed, was canonized by speakers on the program. "Impeach Hillary" T-shirts were hawked throughout the event, as were provocative photographs and postcards doctored to show the first lady mostly nude or in full dominatrix dress. Other first ladies had had detractors, and even enemies. But this was not the kind of thing that Eleanor Roosevelt, Nancy Reagan, or Jackie Kennedy had been subjected to. More than one hundred reporters were in attendance, many of them drawn by the promise of a press conference by Jones, who was in the company of her husband, as well as Clinton's old nemesis Cliff Jackson.

"The whole scene screamed 'setup job,' " said George Stephanopoulos. He and others in the West Wing regarded the matter as another "cash for trash" holdup, not unlike the Gennifer Flowers threat. Jones was seeking book and movie deals, he claimed. To the disappointment of the reporters hoping for more, Jones declined at her press conference to describe in detail the "sexual encounter" she'd allegedly had with Clinton, except to say, "It's wrong that a woman can be harassed by a figure that high. It's humiliating what he did to me." And when Dee Dee Myers responded, "It's just not true" that Clinton had met with her, and Stephanopoulos referred to her press conference as "a cheap political fund-raising trick," she proceeded to go on the Jerry Falwell–Pat Robertson Christian television circuit to tell her story, and thereafter make the tabloid TV rounds. "Only after Mr. Clinton and his staff denied that these events had ever happened, and called me 'pathetic,' and in effect a liar, did I decide to seek legal relief," she said, and threatened to file a civil suit against the sitting president alleging sexual harassment and defamation.

In fact, Hillary had perceived the danger from Jones at the outset and, through Betsey Wright, tried to bury Jones's story before a lawsuit could be filed. She had phoned, and "she was begging me to stop it," said Wright. A few weeks before her call, Wright said she had asked Hillary, " 'Do you want me to go down there and try to stop this?' I was in D.C." Not long after, Hillary called her back, and Wright began making inquiries.

Bob Bennett, entrusted with the task of heading such a lawsuit off, entered into negotiations with Jones's attorneys, who said they wanted nothing more than an admission from Bill that he had been in a hotel room with her and that she had not engaged in any kind of "immoral conduct." Bennett agreed. But Clinton insisted that Jones, who had been twenty-three years old at the time of the alleged incident, say likewise that he had made no sexual advances or otherwise acted improperly. Meanwhile, having learned from Betsey Wright's contacts that a former boyfriend had some nude photographs of Jones, and might be willing to attest that she had had many sexual partners, Bennett dispatched a team of attorneys to Little Rock to get a notarized statement from him. In the interim, he told her lawyers that he knew there were nude photos of her.

This was what lawyering for the president of the United States and his wife had come down to. On May 5, with the deadline for filing a lawsuit imminent, Bennett moved operations into Stephanopoulos's office, and shuttled between the telephone and the president next door, in the Oval Office, who was calling members of Congress to win support for a cliff-hanger vote on an assault weapons ban.

Jones's lawyer had told Bennett there could be no deal unless Clinton *personally* made the statement she was demanding—not the White House press office or his lawyers. Clinton would not agree. Jones's attorneys were seeking a so-called tolling agreement that would invalidate the statute of limitations for filing a sexual harassment suit under certain conditions—a trap for re-opening the matter as the reelection campaign drew close, the White House believed.

In this instance, Clinton, through Bennett, had already been informed that such a suit could allege that Governor Clinton had taken down his pants and asked her to perform oral sex, and accordingly, she could identify "distinguishing characteristics" on his penis.

This kind of thing was Hillary's nightmare—the humiliating details, the three-ring Clintonian circus. It was the reason she had asked Betsey Wright to try to prevent it. It wasn't only a question of whether the allegations were true. And, in fact, those who knew Hillary best thought she was disinclined to believe such things. In this case, she wanted to believe that Jones was a stalker, as Wright had maintained all along, and sought affidavits to that effect; that was preferable to believing that anything had actually transpired. But since hearing some of what was on the Gennifer Flowers tapes, and learning what was in the *Spectator* article, it must have been harder for Hillary to keep denying the plausibility of such an encounter. And she was powerless to work this out in the confines of her marriage. She was hardly the first wife (or husband) to be dragged through a searingly humiliating experience by a spouse. But her predicament was painfully unique on many levels. It was no wonder that her acolytes in Hillaryland marveled at her ability to get up every day and go to work without breaking down.

The assault weapons ban, despite vigorous opposition from the National Rifle Association, passed by the narrowest of margins, a triumph for the Clinton presidency. The next day, exactly three years after the alleged incident at the Excelsior Hotel, catty-corner to the governor's mansion, Paula Jones filed suit seeking $700,000 in civil damages, alleging violation of her civil rights and defamation. "This complaint is tabloid trash with a legal caption on it," Bennett said at a press conference in response. It was "really about trying to rewrite the election results." By now it was evident that Jones had joined forces with the Clintons' political enemies, who saw her case as a means to greater triumphs beyond the courtroom.

Almost immediately, Bennett, the president, Cutler, and Hillary decided to try to delay all proceedings in the suit past the 1996 presidential election by filing motions to prevent Jones and her attorneys from seeking additional information through discovery in depositions; and, as coincidentally a matter of genuine constitutional principle, they filed a motion asserting that the president was immune from civil damage suits during his time in office. Such a motion was filed in Federal District Court in Little Rock on June 27. After the inauguration of Bill's successor, Jones would be free to file her lawsuit, the motion argued.

FISKE CAME TO the White House on June 12, to question Bill and Hillary. Reluctantly, Kendall had acceded to the special counsel's insistence that they be examined under oath.

Whatever else the Whitewater investigations might have been, they were certainly an assault on a married couple by four agencies of the federal government: the Treasury Department's Resolution Trust Corporation, the FBI, the Justice Department, and the Office of the Special Prosecutor (and both houses of Congress ready to conduct additional hearings).

During Watergate, Richard Nixon, who declared famously, "I am not a crook," was never questioned by a special prosecutor or a grand jury, even though he was a constitutional criminal, and the cover-up had been about concealing his constitutional offenses. If there was anything that Bill Clinton was not it was a constitutional criminal, or a president who would deliberately accede to constitutional criminality. Nor would his wife. Her reverence of the Constitution was unshakable. But the Clinton presidency was being eclipsed (as they saw it) by the petty past—especially by his wife's handling of the family finances, and their private life. She stood accused of being a crook, and he, increasingly, of being a degenerate.

Each of them, after twenty years of marriage, knew better. Whatever the failings of the other, there was a deep understanding of the goodness of each. To see his wife portrayed as a crook and a harridan outraged and hurt Bill, even more than to see himself depicted as a degenerate. He, at least, knew the truth of his own sexual excesses, and, whatever the pathology, he didn't consider it anybody's damn business but his own and Hillary's. Her view was no different: whatever had happened in their marriage was between them, not subject to the salacious excesses of the political process; she had spent years trying to keep their difficulties from affecting his enormous talent, good heart, and humane and brilliant politics, and, not incidentally, her own. For her sake and that of their marriage, she chose not to look too closely at the specific facts of her husband's libidinous inclinations. She had managed relative success at all those tasks in Arkansas, but in Washington all her ingenuity and craft had failed her. It was a terrible irony that the man she had depended on to protect her as Bill could not, Vince Foster, had, in committing suicide, opened up a Pandora's box that seemed to have no bottom. Now she had only hired guns like David Kendall and Bob Barnett and a slew of lawyers and spinmeisters to protect them and their marriage.

Fiske's questioning of the Clintons at the White House was a courtesy—a respectful gesture to the office of the presidency. In lieu of a traditional appearance before a grand jury, he would take Bill's and Hillary's testimony and then have it read to the grand jurors who were considering evidence under his auspices. This was serious business. Say the wrong thing with intent to deceive, and you could be indicted for perjury or obstruction of justice. At least that was true of Hillary. The Nixon precedent held that a sitting president could not be indicted, though Nixon had been named an unindicted co-conspirator in the Watergate cover-up. Impeachment was the only legal sanction for a president who had violated the law, or abused the Constitution.

Fiske's intent—as explained to Kendall, Cutler, and the Clintons—was to question Hillary and Bill about Vince's suicide, about the disposition and handling of documents, files, and papers in his office; and the monitoring of Treasury's RTC referrals to the Justice Department. Fiske had another grand jury at work in Little Rock, with twenty-five FBI agents assisting his legal staff, handling the Arkansas end of the Whitewater investigation. Fiske wanted to wrap up the "presidential" end of the investigation, in Washington, so that Congress, if it chose, could proceed with its own inquiries. He also wanted to make his own personal judgment about the Clintons, to get a feel for who the Clintons were, some notion of their intent, and how it fueled whatever actions they had taken.

Bill answered each question put to him, some of which were repeated when, as frequently occurred, he said he wasn't sure of the answer or that he couldn't recall something. Both he and Hillary of course were lawyers themselves, and Kendall and Cutler had formally prepared and rehearsed them for their depositions as potentially vulnerable parties. They were advised to answer Fiske's inquiries as concisely, clearly, and convincingly as possible, without extraneous verbiage. Bill, particularly, was a master of excess verbiage, which usually served him well, and he was true to form. His answers tended to meander, though not in a detrimental manner. He hadn't realized how depressed Vince Foster had been, he said. He'd instructed Nussbaum and the lawyers to cooperate fully with investigators and turn over whatever papers from Vince's office they were entitled to; but that was about the extent of his own knowledge. He said he really knew nothing about how the RTC referrals had been monitored by the White House or Altman and other Treasury officials. He came across to Fiske as gregarious, likable, and sometimes genuinely bewildered by the investigations his administration was trying to deal with.

Hillary said she was so shocked and grief-stricken when Vince committed suicide that she couldn't remember much of what she had done in the immediate aftermath of his death, except to cry and await the arrival of Webb and Bill. There must have been dozens of calls during the trauma. Who had phoned whom, and when, was a blur. As for the document search of Vince's office, she had been in Little Rock and remained removed from the process—or at least she couldn't remember the specifics of who said what to whom, except to see that Vince's family got whatever personal effects he had in the office. Fiske found her personable, at ease, and well spoken in a way that was neither particularly forthcoming nor suggested being surreptitious. What she knew about the RTC contacts was what the lawyers had told her, which was only that the referrals to the Justice Department had been made and that they were confident it would all come out okay, because there had been nothing untoward in any of her dealings.

Kendall and Cutler were relatively pleased with the way the afternoon went, and formed the impression that Fiske was getting ready to complete the Washington phase of his investigation. There was nothing that had been said by Hillary or Bill, or implied in Fiske's questions or demeanor, that suggested big problems.

On the last day of June, Fiske issued two reports. The first found that Vince Foster had, in fact, committed suicide and that his death was not an attempt to conceal facts related to Whitewater. With regard to the Madison Guaranty matter, Fiske wrote in his second report: "After a review of all the evidence, we have concluded that the evidence is insufficient to establish that anyone within the White House or the Department of Treasury acted with the intent to corruptly influence an RTC investigation."

A third investigation, which would determine whether anyone should be charged with obstruction of justice related to the removal of files from Foster's office, was not yet complete. Fiske said in a statement that it would be completed within ten days.

White House officials praised the report as vindication of Hillary's and Bill's conduct. Republicans furiously criticized Fiske and accused him of not being truly independent. Representative Jim Leach, the ranking Republican on the House Banking Committee, said the findings were "essentially those expected from this extremely narrow aspect of the probe." Leach was one of the few House Republicans who carried influence with Democratic members, due to his reputation as an old-school "moderate."

That same day, Bill very reluctantly signed the reauthorization of the Independent Counsel Act, fulfilling a promise he had made during the campaign, when he and Hillary had made the malfeasance and misfeasance of their predecessors in the White House such a front-and-center issue. The White House issued a statement in Bill's name that described the concept of an independent counsel as "a foundational stone for the trust between government and our citizens. It ensures that no matter what party controls the Congress or the executive branch, an independent nonpartisan process will be in place to guarantee the integrity of public officials and ensure that no one is above the law. This is a good bill that I signed into law today." He didn't believe it.

But with some rare good luck, it was hoped, Fiske would—logically—be appointed to the new position and wrap up his investigation expeditiously. Perhaps there really was light at the end of the tunnel. The Clintons' enemies, however, did not intend to go gentle into the night.

BILL CLINTON'S first eighteen months as president had hardly been what he'd wanted, or prepared for. He believed his economic advisers had narrowed his options to the point where he couldn't pursue even his most basic goals; his own staff was so ill-equipped that they didn't know how to help him function; the Democrats in Congress weren't allowing him to effectively exercise the constitutional and political powers of the presidency because they were too weak to stand up to the Republican opposition; the journalistic impressionism practiced by reporters was undercutting everything he was trying to do. Add all of this together and, it was clear to him, this was an unprecedented season in the modern presidency, an investigatory witch hunt by Congress, the press, and the judiciary. The president felt it was in the country's interest—not just his own and Hillary's—to bring the wretched excess to an end. He felt Fiske's report, and the suggestion that he would finish his investigation without bringing any high-level indictments, was the first step to terminating this spell of witchery.

When Bill had signed the legislation reactivating the Office of the Independent Counsel, he had asked Leon Panetta, the budget director and a former congressman whose legislative expertise was without peer in the administration, whether there was any way to resist its enactment. Panetta said no, that there was no alternative to keeping his campaign pledge, especially in the midst of an investigation.

Hillary had vehemently argued against the reauthorization—unless the act was amended to provide for grandfathering Fiske's appointment. This would guarantee continuation of his supervision of the investigation, with no possibility of his replacement by someone more partisan. Even before Fiske had issued his report, she had listened to the drums banging at the other end of Pennsylvania Avenue and had not mistaken their enemies' intentions. The drumming became louder and more frenzied as consideration by Congress of health care, and the midterm elections, approached. Their opponents' persistence in believing that Vince Foster had been murdered, perhaps on orders from Hillary and Bill, proved they were "really fucking crazy," Hillary said. The fact that Fiske's report had emphasized, like the FBI and the Park Police reports, that Vince had been depressed and committed suicide did nothing to dispel the conspiracy theories.

Hillary's fears were so extreme that she believed Chief Justice William Rehnquist and others in the judiciary would manage to oust Fiske and replace him with a conservative idealogue. Some officials in the White House regarded her as paranoid. But she knew Rehnquist's history, from her work on the Watergate investigation, and she did not believe that Rehnquist's elevation to chief justice had changed his character or his politics.

Hillary would have found a ready ally in Bernie Nussbaum had he still been counsel to the president. Like Hillary, Nussbaum had no doubts about the viciousness and perseverance of their enemies, and he had no reverence for Rehnquist. But when Nussbaum had come to Hillary and asked her to intervene with Bill to stop his own forced resignation, she had let him be cut loose. She knew he had done nothing unethical, she told him, but the press wouldn't be satisfied until he was gone. Nussbaum had been almost disbelieving of his shabby treatment by the president and, even more so, his former protégée, Hillary. Everybody seemed expendable to them, he had concluded, even those who defended them most vigorously.

She had expressed her unalloyed anxiety about renewal of the Independent Counsel Act to Lloyd Cutler. Hillary regarded him as a wise owl in the Washington forest, but she thought he had spent perhaps too much time in the trees to tangle with the likes of what they were up against. She told him her explicit concern that "the Republicans and their allies in the judiciary, led by [the] Chief Justice" would screw them. This was especially likely now that Fiske's report had been released. Hadn't Cutler been paying attention to the fury of Republicans in Congress and conservative commentators who were fulminating about the so-called Fiske cover-up? They had dredged up Fiske's membership, seven years earlier, on an American Bar Association committee that had opposed the nomination of Judge Robert Bork to the Supreme Court. They saw Fiske as a pawn in the culture wars. Senator Lauch Faircloth of North Carolina had already called for him to be relieved of his duties and replaced once the new Independent Counsel law took effect.

Cutler dismissed Hillary's concerns. More courtly than confrontational in his approach to lawyering and to being counsel to the president, he expected the same from his colleagues at the bar and on the bench, including the Supreme Court. He told Hillary he would "eat his hat" if he was wrong and Fiske was replaced.

Under the terms of the law signed by Bill on June 30, the independent counsel was to be chosen by a three-judge panel—known as the "Special

Division"—appointed by the chief justice. Rehnquist named Judge David Sentelle of North Carolina, a Republican protégé of his state's ultraconservative U.S. senators, Jesse Helms and Faircloth, to head the Special Division, whose other members were Judges John D. Butzner of Richmond and Peter Fay of Miami.

The day after Clinton signed the law, Reno asked Sentelle and his two colleagues to appoint Fiske as an independent counsel under the newly reauthorized Independent Counsel Act so he could continue his investigation. Republicans, led by Faircloth, intensified the attack. Faircloth said Fiske was too close to former officials in Clinton's administration, including Nussbaum. He said the three-judge panel should "appoint a new, truly independent counsel." He added: "Given both the appearance of lack of independence . . . and the relationship between Mr. Fiske and the Clinton administration, Mr. Fiske should not be appointed. His appointment as independent counsel would guarantee that the current cloud of doubt and suspicion hanging over his appointment would remain."

On August 5, the panel announced that Kenneth Starr, a former U.S. Court of Appeals judge who left the bench to become U.S. solicitor general in the Bush administration, would replace Fiske. "It is not our intent to impugn the integrity of the attorney general's appointee but rather to reflect the intent of the act that the actor [sic] be protected against perceptions of conflict," the judges wrote in a four-page order. Bill and Hillary were distraught. Others in the White House were outraged. It would likely mean months and months more of prying into their private lives. Clinton was suspicious of Starr immediately; he wondered why the Democrats hadn't fought off the appointment. Hadn't anybody looked at his record? There had hardly been a peep.

A strategy meeting was convened in Panetta's office. Cutler said Starr's reputation was not that of an ideological jurist—he had written a landmark libel decision in favor of the *Washington Post* and freedom of the press, and he had been a reasonably decent solicitor general in the Bush administration. Yes, he was a staunch conservative, a Republican, but that didn't make him less respectful of the legal precepts of fairness. Meanwhile, Hillary despaired, especially when Cutler confirmed that Starr would probably reexamine everything Fiske had done in his investigation, including Vince's work and suicide, and the disposition of the files in his office. She and James Carville favored a campaign to attack the nomination of Starr as partisan and unjudicial, then to get Starr to refuse the position if sufficient wrath could be aroused among Democrats in Congress and even in the press. Bill thought they were right, but he worried that a campaign obviously inspired by the White House could, as

Cutler warned, backfire if Starr took the job and came after them. Kendall was horrified at the prospects of a Starr appointment.

Perhaps the most portentous piece of information had appeared in the *Washington Post* on August 12. It reported that Judge Sentelle had joined two senators from his home state, Helms and Faircloth, for lunch in the Senate dining room a month earlier. No senators had been more savage in expressing their enmity to the Clintons and their politics, or about Whitewater. All three men denied that the subject of Whitewater or replacing Fiske was under discussion; their dissembling was regarded as laughable even by many Republicans on the Hill: Helms said they had talked of "Western wear, old friends, and prostate problems." There was additional cause for demoralization and objection to Starr's appointment: his law firm, Kirkland & Ellis, had filed a brief in support of Paula Jones's argument that the president wasn't immune from a civil lawsuit. This alone should have been cause for Starr to recuse himself.

It was decided that Bob Bennett would appear on the Sunday-morning television news shows to attack the sacking of Fiske and subsequent choice of Starr. But when no groundswell of support for Bennett's position materialized, Lloyd Cutler disavowed any opposition by Bennett or the White House. Bennett was speaking for himself, said Cutler, not for the president or first lady.

Despite continued quarreling among Clinton's aides about whether to attack the appointment, Bill capitulated a few days later. "Everybody else has talked about that," he said. "I'll cooperate with whoever's picked. I just want to get it done."

Hillary asked Cutler what kind of hat he was going to eat.

THE STARR appointment, so soon after the hopeful news in Fiske's report, plunged both Hillary and Bill into gloom. Both were edgy, dark, and frustrated. Moreover, for the first time, aides could see that Hillary was frightened. Bill was usually the more optimistic, but the price he was paying for putting Hillary in charge of health care was becoming clear. He recognized that the investigative focus on her and Whitewater, especially the ridicule and derision heaped on her because of the commodities trading episode, was making success at her assignment almost impossible. Her prominence in his administration was untenable in the eyes of his economic aides and many allies on Capitol Hill, he now recognized. He also blamed himself for not accepting the advice of Pat Moynihan and others to wait until after the 1994 election to push for health care, and only after the enactment of welfare reform. Both he and Hillary could tell by summer that the Democrats were heading toward electoral difficulty, even disaster, if they could not slow down the investigative train and somehow rev the engine of health care reform. Neither possibility seemed likely.

When he had appointed Hillary to head the Task Force on National Health Care Reform, Bill had not only promised to submit a comprehensive reform bill to Congress in one hundred days, but he had also pledged that health care would stand as the fundamental achievement of the Clinton presidency. In one of the most memorable moments of his presidency, after the Clintons' return from Martha's Vineyard in the summer of 1993, he'd stood in front of the cameras and explained the relationship between health care, his economic plan, and deficit reduction: "Our competitiveness, our whole economy, the integrity of the way the government works, and, ultimately, our living standards, depend upon our ability to achieve savings without harming the quality of health care." He'd taken from his pocket a blue plastic card the size of a credit card. Under the plan Hillary was developing, "Every American would receive a health care security card that will guarantee a comprehensive package of benefits over the course of an entire lifetime, roughly comparable to the benefit package offered by most Fortune 500 companies," he promised.

For a night at least, tens of millions of Americans thought that the country was finally going to get universal health care. That it never happened was largely Hillary's doing, though it is impossible to separate that failure from the siege of the Clinton White House enabled by Whitewater.

Still, she was largely to blame for the political failure. "I find her to be among the most self-righteous people I've ever known in my life," declared Bob Boorstin, a former reporter for the *New York Times* who joined the Clinton campaign as a writer and became Hillary's deputy for media relations on the task force. "And, it's her great flaw, it's what killed health care, in addition to their joint stupid decision to give it to Ira Magaziner, and to keep it within their friends, and timing, and all sorts of other things, but generally speaking I think you can say at the core of it was her self-righteousness."

THE HIGH POINT of Hillary's health care accomplishment had been her appearance before committees of the House and Senate in September 1993, upon the Clintons' return from Martha's Vineyard. For a week, Hillary awed lawmakers on Capitol Hill. Over the three days, she appeared before Dan Rostenkowski's House Ways and Means Committee, John Dingell's House Energy and Commerce Committee, Ted Kennedy's Senate Labor and Human Resources Committee, William Ford's House Education and Labor Committee, and Pat Moynihan's Senate Finance Committee. Even Moynihan was impressed, though he remained skeptical. After she finished her session with Rostenkowski's committee, the congressman kissed her and said, "In the very near future, the president will be known as your husband." On day two, Hillary's plan won its first Republican endorsement. "I am pleased to be the first. I am absolutely confident I will not be the last," said Jim Jeffords of Vermont.

It was Hillary's beatification. In each hearing room she sat perfectly poised at a witness table before the committee members, few of whom had reputations for self-effacement. They were seated in a semicircle on a riser, as if to make witnesses before them smaller. Her manner was persuasive, confident, and calm. "I'm here as a mother, a wife, a daughter, a sister, a woman," she told the House Ways and Means Committee. "I'm here as an American citizen concerned about the health of her family and the health of her nation." She sat forward in her chair and answered more than 150 questions from the members, never consulting notes or the aides sitting behind her. Her preparation was textbook perfect. Her humor, and even a brief willingness to roll with the punches, was on display.

The only House member who had challenged her seriously was Republican representative Dick Armey of Texas, who referred to her health care plan as a "Kevorkian prescription for the jobs of American men and women."* Armey, a deputy to the Republican whip, Newt Gingrich, had also said of the first lady, "Her thoughts sound a lot like Karl Marx. She hangs around with a lot of Marxists. All her friends are Marxists." In the hearing room, Armey began his cross-examination of Hillary with a promise to make the health care debate "as exciting as possible."

"I'm sure you will do that, Mr. Armey," Hillary said. Laughter filled the hearing room.

"We'll do the best we can," said Armey.

"You and Dr. Kevorkian."

"I have been told about your charm and wit," Armey replied when the laughter subsided, "and let me say, the reports of your charm are overstated and the reports on your wit are understated."

The week may have been the pinnacle of her career as first lady. Hillary was making history, and there were comparisons on the floor of Congress to Martha Washington, Eleanor Roosevelt, and, in one particularly tortured leap of logic, Abraham Lincoln. Freshman con-

---

*Dr. Jack Kevorkian was a leading proponent of legalizing assisted suicide.

gresswoman Lynn Schenk of California described her own mother's admiration for Hillary. "Not since Eleanor Roosevelt has she so admired a woman in public life—and my mother is not a woman who admires easily." "I hope my mother is listening," Hillary replied, grinning.

The *New York Times* editorialized on Sunday, "Hillary Rodham Clinton dazzled five Congressional committees last week, advocating health care legislation in the most impressive testimony on as complete a program as anyone could remember, and raising hopes that an issue that had stymied Congress for fifty years was now near solution." Mary McGrory of the *Washington Post* wrote, "It's a long way to Tipperary on getting health care through Congress. But Mrs. Clinton has made a brilliant beginning. She is a superstar." She was forty-six years old. Maureen Dowd wrote in the *Times*, "It was, in a way, the official end of the era in which presidential wives pretended to know less than they did and to be advising less than they were." Newt Gingrich was on the mark as well when he said, "If Ira Magaziner had tried to defend that same plan, he would have been destroyed."

Hillary's critics had long complained of her tendency to be too clever by half. Nothing demonstrated the point better than her decision soon after to send a copy of the bill she and Magaziner were developing to a friendly California congressman, knowing it would be leaked to the press. The bill was purported to reduce the deficit by $91 billion, a preposterous assertion given the huge dimensions of the program they had devised.

Representatives of Congress, especially Democrats, were incredulous at having been kept out of the loop and then reading about her proposal in the *Washington Post*, before they had been properly informed and briefed themselves. "My colleagues who have taken the time to go look at [the leaked proposal] are kind of appalled by the complexity of it all. It's magic. It is a house-of-cards kind of financing that is going to fall apart when people start to poke at it," said Democratic representative Jim McDermott of Washington. Even more damaging, Pat Moynihan, who carried more weight on this issue than anyone in Congress, called the calculations "fantasy" numbers. Institutional and ideological opponents seized the opportunity handed them by Hillary and Magaziner. Republicans were content to sit on the sidelines and laugh.

Bob Dole took easy advantage of the situation on *Meet the Press*. "I can't believe they're having hearings on a plan that nobody has seen and we may not see for another thirty days. . . . I think it's unprecedented."

Lloyd Bentsen felt compelled to tell the *Post* on background that he was postponing his testimony "until the legislation is complete" and the numbers were available to him. He reached Hillary directly and insisted that Treasury Department experts have the opportunity to verify the economic and cost assumptions of the package the administration would submit to Congress. Leon Panetta also directed that the Office of Management and Budget review the figures. Others could see that the bottom was falling out of Hillary's health care boat; not her.

She had publicly promised during her brief ascendancy to submit a finished bill by mid-October. Now she was restrained by the requirement of input from Treasury, OMB, and other cabinet members. Seeing that a deadline would once again be missed, she stalled. The delay produced one of the more outlandish episodes of modern congressional history, in a curiously ostentatious ceremony at Statuary Hall on October 27. The occasion had been intended to mark the delivery of her health care bill to Congress. The president stood at the lectern and pounded his fist, expressing his desire to provide universal health care to all Americans. But there was no bill.

"I don't remember if it was four weeks, eight weeks, or ten weeks, but it became obvious pretty soon that the opponents had successfully characterized the plan as the government taking over health care," Roger Altman recalled. "And once that became clear, you knew that the plan, more or less as proposed, was not going to happen."

Instead of being the new administration's strongest suit, health care reform—desired by an overwhelming majority of Americans, according to virtually every poll on the subject—had become a rallying cry for all the Clintons' opponents and enemies, providing a single issue that mainstream Republicans, the far right, and conspiracy-minded anti-Clinton zealots could agree on. It also gave more self-interested enemies of universal, government-supervised health care—many doctors, insurance companies, owners of small businesses, and individual constituents—a chance to mobilize. Hillary and Magaziner had attempted to woo interest groups—medical, professional, small business—early in the process, but once these constituencies got a look at what was going to be included in the bill, they withdrew.

WHEN REPUBLICAN senator John Chafee and Democratic representative Jim Cooper introduced their own separate alternative proposals, the Clintons overlooked what may have been their best opportunity to compromise on a health care plan. Chafee, a liberal Republican with no animus toward the Clintons or their politics, introduced his plan with twenty Republicans already pledged to support it in the Senate. House Republicans pitched a similar bill on the same day. And when Cooper and his principal House co-sponsor, Iowa Republican Fred Grandy, came forth with their bill, they were already endorsed by forty-six other

Democratic and Republican co-sponsors. Both Chafee's and Cooper's proposals would have given huge numbers of Americans adequate health care coverage for the first time—about 85 percent as many as the Hillary-Magaziner proposal—and had enough support to make passage in the House and Senate likely.

At such a pivotal juncture, Hillary could have thrown her support behind either bill. Later, Bill Clinton said perhaps he should have intervened. Hillary would eventually write that she knew the Republicans would spare no effort to defeat any bill that she favored, because if she were perceived as victorious her husband's second term would be assured.

The Republican alternative proposed by Chafee would come close to attaining the administration's primary goal of universal coverage but would not impose price controls on insurance premiums or mandate that employers buy their workers' care. Hillary had initially hoped that Chafee, whom she regarded as a real champion of health care reform, would work with her to draft a bill. But when she suggested a joint proposal months earlier, the senator had told her that Republicans were intent on creating their own alternative and that it would be better for "you to get your bill, and we will get ours. Then we will sit down." Chafee, true to his promise to Hillary, spoke only positively about the broad outlines of her plan as it developed. "It's certainly possible that serious discussions could bring us closer to agreement on those issues that we have in common," he told reporters. Meanwhile, the first lady continued to keep lines of communication open to Chafee and publicly complimented his health care record.

As the process dragged on, the dedicated, determined opponents of reform seized the debate with news conferences, television ads, jaded public opinion polls, and successful fund-raising appeals. They enlisted grassroots support to target key members of Congress in their home states. Lobbyists began calling Hillary "Big Sister," and when events took a turn for the worse, "Shillary."

The most damaging attack in the war on the Clintons' plan came from Harry and Louise, a couple invented by lobbyists and ad agencies that together represented 270 small and midsized insurance companies. The commercials, which cost $30 million to produce and air, used the Everyman characters to vocalize and provoke many Americans' fears about the Clintons' health care proposal. In one ad, the married couple sat at their kitchen table fretting over whether Hillary's health insurance would cover them as sufficiently as their present health plan. A voice-of-God announcer warned, "The Government may force us to pick from a few health plans designed by government bureaucrats." Then Louise chimed in: "Having choices we don't like is no choice at all." Another ad noted that there would be spending limits on policies: "The Government caps how much the country can spend on all health care and says, 'That's it!' " Harry asks Louise, "So what if our health plan runs out of money?" Louise ponders, "There has got to be a better way."

The White House had been offered an opportunity to stop these ads, early in the debate. The day after Bill had held up his blue card in front of the cameras, the HIAA—the Health Insurance Association of America— offered to cancel the Harry and Louise campaign if Magaziner and Hillary would reopen negotiations with the organization. They did not respond.

At the White House, polls showed the opponents' ads were killing off support for Hillary's plan. Hillary commanded the lieutenants in her war room in the Executive Office Building to work overtime to answer the attacks. The Democratic National Committee escalated its offensive with harmful, self-defeating language that tarred important segments of the insurance industry and medical community. Hillary had earlier showed some willingness to compromise with Chafee, but when push came to shove, her unwillingness to compromise further undermined any chance of implementing real reform.

By the time Hillary and Magaziner had provided the White House a formal bill to be submitted to Congress—on the last day of the 1993 session—it had grown to 1,324 pages and was so large and complex that even Hillary's closest allies on the Hill could not fathom its contents. The president's own advisers were still flummoxed about how it could be paid for.

Hillary believed the size of the bill was used against her unfairly. Other bills ran to that length, she wrote, and her bill would have replaced "thousands of pages" of regulations, which was true. But Republicans had turned an asset into a vulnerability, she acknowledged.

Once the Clintons had submitted their bill, William Kristol, a leading Republican strategist and conservative voice who had served as former Vice President Dan Quayle's chief of staff, sent a memo to all Republican members of the House and Senate. Compromise in any form, Kristol warned, was a mistake if Republicans were to succeed in the upcoming midterm elections. He wrote perceptively, if cynically, that the passage of health care reform "will re-legitimize middle-class dependence for 'security' on government spending and regulation. It will revive the reputation of the party that spends and regulates, the Democrats, as the generous protector of middle-class interests. And it will at the same time strike a punishing blow against Republican claims to defend the middle class by restraining government." Republican congressman Lamar Smith of Texas also circulated a letter to the Republican offices on the House side, laying out a strategy in which "Whitewater and health care" would be the sole themes of a week of speeches and media concentration by his GOP colleagues. Smith's letter provided several pages of suggested talking points and harsh sound bites. Shockingly, even at this late juncture, the White House had failed to set in motion even a rudimentary constituency campaign in support of health care reform.

By late spring of 1994, Bill understood that health care—and the Democratic majority on Capitol Hill—was in trouble. Stan Greenberg told him that the Democrats might have difficulty retaining the Senate. In a memo for the president and Hillary's eyes only, Greenberg wrote, "The administration, the Democrats in Congress and the party face a disaster in November unless we move urgently to change the mood of the country." Greenberg's research with a focus group led him to conclude, "The voters believe Bill Clinton is struggling to handle the presidency and guide the country." Their perception held that he was "over his head," "indecisive," "immature. . . . This is about being young and inexperienced, from a small, backward state, and failing to master the bad forces at work in Washington."

WHEN, AT LAST, Hillary and her health care brain trust threw overdue resources and energy into recovering the initiative during the summer of 1994, the Whitewater effect had spread its stain. The young first lady who had come to the White House with such high expectations and, the polls had indicated, the wind at her back, was now a weight on her husband's presidency, with persistent enemies.

The decision to emulate the Freedom Rides in the American South of the 1960s with a bus caravan of Reform Riders trying to create a national movement in 1994 to pressure Congress for health care reform was well intended. But a send-off rally in Portland, Oregon, was sabotaged immediately by an angry anti-Clinton mob who blocked the way with their own dilapidated bus covered symbolically in red tape and dragged by a tow truck with a sign that read, "This Is Clinton Health Care." A low-flying light plane pulled a banner that said, "Beware the Phony Express." The pro–health care, cross-country bus trek had been named the "Health Security Express."

By the time the caravan reached Seattle, the threat of violence was constant. All week, talk radio hosts, both in the Northwest and on national broadcasts, implored listeners to confront the Reform Riders, to "show Hillary" their feelings about her. This "call to arms," as she described it, attracted menacing hordes, many of whom identified themselves as militia members, tax resisters, and anti-abortion militants. She estimated that at least half of the 4,500 people in the audience of her Seattle speech were protesters. She agreed for the first time to wear a bulletproof vest. Rarely had she felt endangered, but this was different. During her speech, the catcalls, screaming, and heckling drowned out much of her remarks. When she left the stage and got into a limousine, hundreds of protesters surrounded the car. They were rabid with hatred. Several arrests were made by the Secret Service, which impounded two guns and a knife.

Though Hillary had returned to Washington, the buses were confronted at each major stop by angry demonstrators. They shouted that Hillary and Bill intended to destroy their way of life, "ban guns, extend abortion rights, protect gays, socialize medicine." The protests were vocal, virulent, menacing, and well organized by a previously unknown organization called Citizens for a Sound Economy (CSE). Its agents were secretly working with Newt Gingrich's staff on Capitol Hill and with Republican senators and their aides, reporters later discovered. The funding for CES was provided by Richard Mellon Scaife, who was simultaneously providing hundreds of thousands of dollars for the Arkansas Project.

There had been four caravan routes publicized by the Health Care Express riders. Each became "an expedition into enemy territory . . . with better-armed, better-prepared, better-mobilized anti-Clinton protesters at each stop along the way," wrote David Broder and Haynes Johnson, in their study of Hillary's health care failure. The implicit threats of violence caused many stops to be canceled and the buses rerouted.

The same week, Gingrich announced that House Republicans were now united against health care reform and hoped "to use the issue as a springboard to win Republican control of the House." He predicted the Republicans would win an additional thirty-four House seats in November, and that enough Democrats, perhaps as many as six, would switch parties to give the Republicans control of the House. His prediction, though mentioned in the *New York Times*, received little media notice.

For months, Bob Dole had been toying with trying to work out a compromise on health care. "Is it time yet for the Moynihan-Dole bill?" he asked in a note slipped to the New York senator. There had been speculation that the two senators would quietly put together a deal that would provide a more limited health reform package than Hillary's. Meanwhile, Dole was coming under pressure from his party's right, including a letter signed by Richard Viguerie (the direct-mail maven of the conservative movement), Phyllis Schlafly (of anti-abortion crusades), and L. Brent Bozell (who had campaigned against "liberal bias" in the media for decades before the term became a buzzword) cautioning that signs of "willingness to compromise on behalf of Big Government" would mean that Dole—and Gingrich, who received the same letter—would "be denied conservative grassroots support in 1996." Dole soon said he opposed any compromise.

By the time the Health Security Express reached the White House on August 3, its six hundred exhausted Reform Riders welcomed in the Rose Garden by Hillary and Bill, health care reform was on life support. Majority Leader George Mitchell submitted a "rescue" package in the Senate and Dick Gephardt a corresponding bill in the House. Both pieces of legislation were much scaled down versions of the original Magaziner-Hillary plan, less bureaucratic and less government-driven in the extreme. Two weeks later, at a congressional Democratic leadership luncheon at which the compromise was discussed, Senators Ted Kennedy and Bob Kerrey got into a loud argument about strategy. When word of the bitterness got out, it contributed to the image of a Democratic Party splintering on the Clintons' watch.

By the time Mitchell pulled the plug on health care reform on September 26, 1994, it was an idea whose time had come and, tragically, gone.

WHEN POLLSTER Greenberg had first told Bill Clinton in the spring that Democrats might have trouble retaining the Senate, Greenberg also advised the president to attack the Republicans for obstructing health care reform, withdraw its consideration until after the 1996 election, and then, in its place, introduce a welfare reform bill. The administration at the time was already on the verge of passing a crime bill. If they could win passage of both a crime bill and welfare reform—a key enticement to independent and swing voters—they would have a strong record on which Democrats could run in the November congressional elections. Health care, meanwhile, could be postponed until after the voters had gone to the polls.

Clinton had asked Greenberg to discuss the matter with House Speaker Tom Foley. "Foley said absolutely not," Greenberg reported. "He said the liberals would be totally opposed to welfare reform, and there was still the hope that health care could be pushed through."

In the West Wing, by fall, the criticism of Hillary by some of the president's aides was hard to ignore. Bill seemed disconsolate. He was obviously feeling isolated and withdrawn even from some of his closest associates. He was angry, yet at times he appeared almost bereft. They had never seen him in this state before. Stephanopoulos, Myers, and a few other deputies familiar with his habits surmised that such melancholia was occasioned not only by the harsh political realities and attacks, but from isolation and tension building between him and Hillary as well.

Since Vince Foster's death, Bill had been trying to move gently in one direction, and Hillary in another, their aides said later. Often, it wasn't even that stark, and Bill was probably trying to moderate her aversion to compromise and hadn't been very successful. This applied to health care, the investigations of Whitewater and its fallout, the press, and the Washington establishment. He didn't like drawing lines in the sand, at least until there was no room left to maneuver. Some aides talked about a "schizophrenic" co-presidency and implied that his negligence had let Hillary run away from his own instincts, and right off the cliff. He didn't agree, but it was undeniable that Hillary, for all her immense strengths, her love and protection, had left them vulnerable, no matter how much her actions had been intended to advance a policy vision they shared completely, and to bury the difficulties of their Arkansas past.

Hillary had definitely upset his centrist compass at times, and rejected his attempts at getting her to compromise in the health care dilemma. On the other hand, he had made fundamental decisions against her wishes to pursue an economic plan and policy priorities in such a way that had made her health care assignment much more difficult. She obviously had difficulty accepting that.

In all their years together, this was the first time they had had an extended practical disagreement—not merely hypothetical or vaguely philosophical—about what political course to follow. And the consequences of their dilemma, at once deeply personal and intensely political, had roiled and complicated both their own relationship and the most important matters of national policy. Perhaps if they had been dealing only with such issues, the fabric of their marriage would have remained intact. But that fabric had been weakened by Whitewater, an eighteen-month-long nightmare for both of them in which they had been forced—with a national audience looking on—to reexamine every crevice of their past, and absorb the suicide of a beloved friend devoted to them. And now, as it was becoming clear that the midterm elections could cost them congressional control and further empower a prosecutor obviously hostile to them, the Clinton partnership was fraying.

With the death of her health care effort, the major vocational and political undertaking of her life, Hillary could see the situation crumbling around her. Fourteen years earlier, at another moment when the walls of their personal and political lives seemed to be collapsing, she had called Dick Morris in desperation. It had been too late to prevent Bill losing his governorship, but Morris had worked with her and Betsey Wright through the following two years to resurrect his career, and thus their life together. Bill had never lost a campaign since in which Morris had signed on at the start. Clinton's senior advisers insisted that Bill not use Morris in the 1992 presidential campaign. But Hillary had stayed in close contact with Morris through the transition and spoke on the phone with him frequently in the first eighteen months of the presidency, though she apparently told no one else, except occasionally Bill, about their dialogue.

In October 1994, after the burial of her health care ambitions, she called Morris. The implications of the coming November congressional elections were profound. They needed his ability, Hillary told him, as "a creative pollster and a brilliant strategist." She knew Morris was unhappy that he had lost his place to Greenberg and that he was still resentful at the way Bill had treated him. But Newt Gingrich had just aggressively unveiled his "Contract with America," a document that in its specifics was a reassertion of conservative, post–Rockefeller Republican orthodoxy—tax cuts, welfare reform, increased defense spending, restricted appropriations for the United Nations. It was threatening. Later Hillary said she summoned Morris because few other people seemed to sense the onrushing problem.

This ignored the fact that Greenberg had been telling the Clintons since the spring that the Democrats were in trouble. He had specifically warned her in his May memo of a coming "disaster." Hillary was calling Morris simply because she believed he was better at devising a winning strategy and taking whatever steps necessary than Greenberg, whose approach to politics was premised on a consistent base of underlying political values and principles that identified him as a Democrat.

Morris reiterated that he was upset by the way he had been treated. But, Hillary wrote, he was unable to refuse the offer.

Morris was convinced the Democrats were going to experience huge losses, not just in the Congress, but also in the statehouses and governors' mansions. The only way he saw for them to cut their losses, perhaps enough to hold on to the House, was for the Clintons to virtually disappear from the debate and, in Bill's case, to do no campaigning on behalf of Democratic candidates.

He conducted a poll to try to gauge sentiment about Hillary and Bill and "how the Clintons could best defend themselves." "I found that very few Americans believed Clinton when he said he had cut the budget deficit or created a lot of jobs," Morris said. "But they did give him credit for some small advances: AmeriCorps, his volunteer plan; the Family and Medical Leave Act; pro-choice judicial appointments; the Brady gun control bill; and the assault rifle ban. If they could be reminded effectively of these accomplishments, my poll suggested that enough voters might come back to the Democrats and avert defeat."

Meanwhile, word began to circulate through the administration that Morris was back on the scene. Robert Reich was one of the first to hear and called Hillary to complain. "This guy is terrible," he said. "He doesn't stand for anything we stand for. . . . He's a disaster. I've talked to him several times, and he just makes my skin crawl."

Hillary said he shouldn't be concerned. Reich, knowing that "she had been the one to bring him in in '80," had deduced that it was Hillary who brought him back this time as well. For the first time, Reich feared that Hillary, perhaps more than Bill, was willing to compromise basic beliefs to win.

The results of Morris's poll angered the president. During a conference call with Hillary and Morris, he had thundered, "I cut the deficit by one third. I've created millions of jobs. *I've done big things.*" Morris judged it "a throwback to the arrogance of 1980 and his refusal to admit his license-tax mistake in Arkansas."

The president thought Morris's advice to stay away from the congressional races was overkill. Democrats had controlled the House since the Eisenhower administration. He was about to leave with Hillary for a four-day trip to the Middle East where he would be a signatory to a Middle East peace agreement between Israel and Jordan, which had resulted from direct talks he had encouraged between King Hussein of Jordan and Israeli prime minister Yitzhak Rabin. No American president before him had been invited to address the Jordanian parliament in Amman. His speech to the Israeli Knesset and the Clintons' visit with King Hussein and Queen Noor (who became one of Hillary's close friends thereafter) were covered by the American press as a milestone in post–Cold War achievement. His personal poll numbers were up a tick, and upon his return, he was looking forward to getting out and campaigning, rescuing his party and his own agenda. He knew how good he was at campaigning and, if he couldn't push through his policies in the Congress (a reference to the failure of health care), he could at least go out and do what he did best—appeal to the voters directly. Hillary was opposed to the idea. She thought Morris was right that the anti-Democratic tide was too nasty to be reversed by personal charm.

Almost immediately upon the Clintons' return from Andrews Air Force Base by helicopter on October 29, they spoke with Morris. Hillary and Bill were in her cozy study-office attached to their bedroom. They listened together on a speakerphone to his report: the Democrats were on the way to losing control of both houses of Congress.

Hillary said later his assessment "confirmed" her sense of things, but neither she nor her husband were expecting how overwhelming the wave would be. Bill told Morris he was determined to go out and campaign even harder. More was at stake than the legislative agenda of one party or the other. The Clintons' opponents had already served notice that, should they win control of Congress, they would drag Hillary and Bill through the Whitewater rapids with subpoenas.

NEWT GINGRICH was a once obscure party whip and former junior college professor who was riding an ideological bandwagon that gained camp followers each time he attacked the Clintons for their morality and political values. Things were so bad that during the summer Greenberg had distributed a strategy memorandum to Democratic candidates that recommended they virtually divorce themselves from Hillary's expiring health care campaign and even the Clinton presidency itself. They should campaign as local candidates "fighting to get things done for" their districts, "not . . . advancing some national agenda."

Election day 1994 was indeed a disaster for the Democrats—and Hillary and Bill. Republicans would now control both houses, claiming their first Senate majority in eight years and their first House majority since 1954. The Democrats lost an astounding fifty-two seats in the House, and eight in the Senate.

There had been historic losses by the president's party in other elections—Ike had lost sixty-one Republican seats in the midterm elections of 1958. But this was a different kind of repudiation in that it was tied to the president and his wife. Only four times since the Civil War had there been such a rout. It was the worst midterm rejection of a president's policies and persona since Truman's in 1946, which proclaimed unequivocally that the New Deal was over. In 1938 Roosevelt had lost eighty-one House and eight Senate seats after his failed attempt to pack the Supreme Court.

The list of distinguished Democrats who had lost was disheartening for the Clintons. Tom Foley became the first speaker of the house to lose his seat since 1862. Governor Mario Cuomo lost in New York. In Texas Hillary's great friend and feminist icon Ann Richards lost the governorship to George W. Bush.

The Clintons could see that the country, not just Washington, was on the verge of a new political age, much of it informed by antagonism to *them*. For the first time, the Southern states—once the "Solid South" of the Democrats—sent more Republicans to Congress than "D's," as they were called in the capital. Equally important, these were deeply conservative (by their own definition) Republicans, far to the right of those who had come to power, say, in the previous Republican wave of 1980. In nine of the most populous ten states Republicans won governorships.

Perhaps the worst news from the Democrats' point of view was that every Republican up for reelection in the country—for the House, Senate, and governorships—won.

Bill knew what had gone wrong, and he recognized the practical implications of the loss: the Republican control of Congress would not only threaten to scupper the Clintons' agenda, but it would also embolden the Clintons' enemies—including the new chairmen of several important House and Senate committees with jurisdiction to investigate Whitewater, the death of Vince Foster, or any aspect of the presidency, or his and Hillary's past.

Hillary wrote in *Living History* that at this point she was "deflated and disappointed." She knew she had mishandled her portfolio, and had inspired anger, and that both had helped bring Democrats down. Some soul-searching was in order.

"My view is Hillary Clinton destroyed the Democratic Party," said Lawrence O'Donnell, Pat Moynihan's aide. His perspective of the constitutional order of things was Moynihan's as well: "It is more important to me in my definition of what America is," said O'Donnell, "that the Democrats control the Congress than the White House. . . . Hillary was a disaster for what we were trying to do in government . . . this person who, with just a couple of tweaks, could have been great, it always seemed to me." Her most prominent difficulty, he judged, was arrogance: "You simply had to have modesty instead of arrogance. Not any loss of idealism or loss of ambition. But modesty in the face of a guy named Bob Dole, who I knew could beat me when [he] wanted to, when he had to. So going up against that kind of force and saying, 'I can beat it,' was a recklessness of arrogance that ended up destroying the party's control of government. And that, to me, is unforgivable."

Though Hillary's method and attitude were really no less offensive than what would be practiced by Republicans for the next dozen years, her critics were far less accepting of it. "When your purpose is to pass legislation," said O'Donnell, "you don't set up war rooms and you don't believe that you are going to vanquish the opposition." Such "campaign-think" had dominated the Clintons' governance, but it was native more to Hillary than to Bill. The Clintons had declared war on the Arkansas teachers and had prevailed. But that was far different from Hillary being in a permanent state of warfare with Congress, including members of their own party—and especially different from demonizing powerful senators.

Bill blamed himself for delaying health care, passing up the opportunity to enact meaningful welfare reform, and for including a gas tax and a levy on upper-income Social Security recipients in the economic plan. He did not blame Hillary in any overt way, but her exile had already begun.

HILLARY'S EMOTIONAL state was now as fragile as it had ever been. The cumulative effect of her father's death, Vince's suicide, Whitewater, the failed health care program, and now a repudiation by the voters was devastating. She was overwhelmed. "I don't know whether she was seeing a doctor or not"—she wasn't, as far as is known—"but she was depressed," said David Gergen. "Deeply depressed. I just felt she went into a downward spiral." This was a near universal view in the White House.

Bill's state, in the short run, was equally bad.

"I was profoundly distressed by the election, far more than I ever let on in public," he said later.

Gergen thought it took about two or three months for Bill to come out of his depression. But for Hillary, "it was a matter of many [more] months. I think she still must be scarred by that," he said several years later, before she had decided to seek election to the Senate. "What was clear was not only her policy advice had failed, but she was politically at fault. . . . Bill no longer asked her for political guidance after that."

As the president and first lady sank into a fog of depression, one of the strangest episodes of modern American governance proceeded from it: the ascendancy of Dick Morris as presidential regent. For the next several months he virtually took over the White House. And for the period from 1994 to 1996, he was the real power in the Clinton administration after the president. Hillary had choked on her opportunity. Now it was Morris's turn (again), and the circumstances were ideal for his machinations. In the next two years, there would be two primary objectives: survive Kenneth Starr and the inevitable investigations led by Republicans in Congress, and win reelection. Morris could do relatively little about the former. But in terms of molding new policies and preparing for the next presidential campaign, Morris was the ideal fixer.

"We weren't moving after that election," said Donna Shalala. "It was three or four months before we regrouped." She said the president was "almost incoherent."

"My friends [closest to the Oval Office] kept telling me that he was extremely distracted," said Gergen, "and he would lash out, but then he would pull back. He just sort of seemed lost. . . . Leon [Panetta, the new chief of staff] was sort of running the day-to-day, and then Morris came in. . . . The fact is, for whatever else you think about Dick Morris, he helped to save the president."

Hillary's instinct had been right in this instance. "I think she saw him as just . . . the person you turn to when you're in real trouble," Gergen said. "She saw how much trouble they were in politically. I mean, it was a comeback all over again. It was the two-year problem that they had in Arkansas. And he'd rescued them once before, and performed as an anchor.

"Morris replaced [Hillary] as consigliere—though that may be a little simplistic. But there was a real passage of power away from her and to Morris. And to some degree, the president felt he was also liberated afterward from having to be deferential to Hillary. He took health care as a defeat, but because it was her defeat, it was okay. . . . He still needed her emotional support, but there had been a time in which he felt that he had to be very deferential." No longer.

Though Bill did not criticize her openly, he was less hesitant about making his displeasure—and, for a while, real anger—known with those whose advice he thought, in retrospect, had been just plain bad. They—Magaziner, Stan Greenberg, Mandy Grunwald among them— were all widely regarded as "Hillary people," though that, too, was an oversimplification. Stephanopoulos was also hung out to dry.

Morris was unambiguous about Clinton's attitude toward his wife at this point: in terms of the co-presidency, it was over—"he pushed her aside. It's very clear to me that in 1995 and even 1996 he did not speak to Hillary very much about anything, because I would know. I mean, she never attended strategy meetings, and I never saw her gravitational pull in his thinking. He and I would talk on Monday. We'd talk on Tuesday. We'd talk on Wednesday. And we'd talk on Thursday. And, on Friday, he'd take an action. And over the five-day period, I couldn't see any of Hillary's fingerprints on anything." (Unfortunately, her fingerprints would show up—literally—on the White House billing records, at the most inopportune of moments.)

After the election, said Harold Ickes, "she literally withdrew. I mean, you just didn't even see her. She would come over to her West Wing office from time to time. I would talk to her on the phone. But even I, who was as close to her as anybody on the president's staff, hardly saw her at all. And I don't know what she was doing. I don't know what she was thinking. It must have been a stinging time. . . . She wears a stiff upper lip, as we know. . . . But she no longer participated. . . . She didn't talk to the White House staff."

SHE RETREATED at first into the relative comfort of Hillaryland. "She didn't trust" most of the president's staff, said Ickes. "She didn't like a lot of them, and thought many of them were young, self-serving assholes who should have been fired a long time ago. And her staff was extremely loyal. There had been almost no turnover in her staff, which really puts the lie to the fact that she's a wicked witch."

In the early weeks after the election, Hillary frequently turned to Morris in her frustration. "I had a conversation with her in November where she said, 'You know, I'm so confused. I just don't know what works anymore. I mean everything we're trying is screwed up. I just don't know how to do it, what we ought to be doing,' " Morris recalled. Despite her confident manner, Hillary could "lose her bearings when things didn't go right. Her strong and resolute leadership has a brittle quality to it; when her basic assumptions are proven wrong, they undermine her resolve. Hillary has less flexibility, less give than Bill. When her way works, she does very well. But when it doesn't—as in 1994—it can paralyze her."

Meanwhile, Morris, newly empowered, set up shop. Stephanopoulos watched it all happening:

[A]s Clinton withdrew from those of us on staff, the clues were silent but still visible, like the boldly inked crib sheets the president slipped out of his folder during meetings. Or the anonymous calls announced by Betty Currie that Clinton would take in the privacy of his study. Or the yellow Post-it notes left by his phone, reminding him that "Charlie called."

"Charlie" was Dick's code name. The president had engaged him to run a covert operation against his own White House—a commander's coup against the colonels. The two of them plotted in secret—at night, on the phone, by fax. From December 1994 through August 1996, Leon Panetta managed the official White House staff, the Joint Chiefs commanded the military, the cabinet administered the government, but no single person more influenced the president of the United States than Dick Morris.

Twenty-four months earlier, in triumph, Hillary had demanded an office in the West Wing. Now she was a drag on the White House. It was time to decamp for long periods at a time, withdraw from the working White House altogether, to rethink and to travel. She had never been given to introspection, but she had also never failed on such a scale before. She knew that a midcourse correction of historic magnitude would be required if she and Bill were to remain in the White House a full eight years.

Hillary was well aware that many of her husband's advisers blamed her for the situation now confronting them. She was bound emotionally, professionally, parentally, and publicly to her husband, but she'd have to step aside as a visible policy presence.

Hillary appears to have kept to herself her deepest feelings about the wreckage of the twenty months between inauguration day and election day. And to whatever extent she shared those feelings with her husband is known only to the two of them. Except for conveying her general despondency she did not even discuss with her close friends like Diane Blair, Sara Ehrman, or Linda Bloodworth-Thomason her role in the debacle. As always, there was prayer, and the support of those in her prayer group, who included the wives of some of the men who had led the assault on the Clintons' presidency.

Hillary did not need to be pushed into exile. She was ready to go. Her stunning withdrawal from the inner sanctum of power was encouraged by Morris. Bill was having difficulty enough regaining his own composure and was hardly going to object to her disengagement. But given her dominant position in the White House for almost two years, her leave-taking represented the passing of a huge presence.

First she made sure Morris was installed. If she had to go, it was essential that Bill have a handmaiden who could take her place, engage him, and help him lead. Over the next weeks, she would remind Morris of the little things that she knew Bill liked and needed, as if she wanted to be sure he'd continue to have the fullness of his presidential life.

"To help get to the bottom of the Clintons' loss," Morris devised a series of surveys in November and December. Shortly after the new year, he reported the results to Bill. "I told the depressed president [he later wrote] one third of the people feel you are immoral and one third think you are weak." Such brutal candor at a delicate time was just the kind of thing Morris reveled in. He defined the president's "perceived moral failings" as his "draft avoidance, the Gennifer Flowers scandal, Travelgate, Whitewater, or the innumerable scrapes to which the First Family seemed forever prone"—the latter referring, apparently, to the occasional stumbles of Roger Clinton and Hillary's two brothers.

There was nothing we could do about his perceived moral failings. But as I examined the reasons that people gave explaining why they thought that the president was weak [wrote Morris] one concern kept coming up over and over again: Hillary. "She's the power," the respondents complained. "She wears the pants." "She thinks she's president." "I voted for him, but she's in charge now." I read them to Clinton, one after another, letting their cumulative effect wash over him.

Morris suggested that, rather than nourish the perception that Hillary was continuing to manipulate events behind the scenes, she should do something in which "her outspokenness before audiences can be an antidote to the perception of hidden power. The voters know she's not sitting there doing nothing. The more they read about her public role, the less they will speculate about her private doings."

A week later, said Morris, Bill asked him to "start sending Hillary memos suggesting new directions for her public advocacy, always making sure to send him copies." Soon, said Morris, "she withdrew from *all* White House strategy meetings. For a year she didn't even send a representative. She totally cut herself off from overinvolvement in White House strategizing. She was less involved in decision-making than she had been at any point since the early two-career-couple days of the late 1970s."

THE BOOK *It Takes a Village*, conceived at her post-electoral ebb, was intended to define Hillary Clinton as she saw herself and wanted to be seen, and to establish a public persona based on thoughtfulness, seriousness, and traditional family values.

For nine Christmas seasons before Bill's election as president, Hillary, Bill, and Chelsea together had attended Renaissance Weekends with the families of other prominent Americans. Scientists, journalists, educators, business executives, and political figures were afforded a chance at these gatherings to participate in off-the-record panel discussions and workshops that focused as much on individual empowerment and public service as policy. In contrast to Washington political discussions, the Renaissance meetings tended to include a spiritual or religious dimension, from mainstream Protestantism to New Age.

Of all the New Age thinkers the Clintons had gotten to know from these weekends, few had intrigued Hillary (and millions of other Americans) more than Texas-born Marianne Williamson. Like many New Age authors and circuit-riders, Williamson's résumé was a mix of the serious (infusing politics with spiritual principles), the celebritized (presiding over Elizabeth Taylor's eighth wedding), and the silly (promoting a version of solitaire with a fifty-card "miracle deck"). She was five years younger than Hillary, and her "underlying message," according to one reviewer, "encourag[ed] women to seek and find God via the love inside themselves and to reinforce their sense of self-esteem."

In December, when Hillary seemed near the point of emotional collapse, with Bill deeply depressed and dysfunctional and their political future imperiled, Hillary reached out to Williamson. New Age thought borrowed heavily from traditional theology, especially its message of going deep within and finding personal strength in adversity. No one had preached this message more effectively, or profitably, than Williamson, who took the initiative to suggest that Hillary and Bill consider getting together with her and a group of people far removed from the political establishment to discuss alternative ways of looking at the next two years of the presidency, and the difficulties of the previous two.

Hillary was receptive, and the weekend of December 30 and 31 was set aside at Camp David. Williamson, with Hillary's approval, picked the other participants, including Anthony (Tony) Robbins, the motivational infomercial king and author of *Awaken the Giant Within*, and Stephen Covey, author of *The 7 Habits of Highly Effective People* and its successor best-sellers. The titles were suggestive both of the participants' approach and Hillary's sense of what might have been missing in their first two years.

Since Don Jones's counsel to Hillary during her depression at Wellesley, she had been receptive to a pep talk that advised digging down into yourself to call on your inner resources, while maintaining belief in some sort of higher power. Though she had come to see herself since the inauguration as a victim, she was not one to collapse in a heap of self-pity. Even her decision to retreat from the front lines of the administration—regarded by many acolytes and opponents alike as a kind of abdication (when her withdrawal became more obvious)—represented this precept of taking action.

For the Camp David weekend, Williamson had also engaged two lesser-known women on the seminar and lecture circuit whom she thought Hillary would take comfort in talking to in her current state: Mary Catherine Bateson and Jean Houston, who often worked in tandem.

Bateson, the daughter of renowned anthropologists Margaret Mead and Gregory Bateson, was a highly regarded cultural anthropologist, specializing in the burgeoning field of gender studies. Hillary had read and recommended to friends Bateson's 1989 book, *Composing a Life*, which concerned itself with choices women in the post-feminist era could make in balancing and constructing their lives. Jean Houston, with her husband, Dr. Robert E. L. Masters, was co-director of the Foundation for Mind Research, in Pomona, New York, best known for research into psychedelic drugs, hypnosis, sexual behavior, and "humanistic psychology."

She was also founder and principal teacher of "the Mystery School," a bicoastal seminar ($2,995 per student) of "cross-cultural, mythic and spiritual studies, dedicated to teaching history, philosophy, the New

Physics, psychology, anthropology, myth and the many dimensions of human potential." She described herself as a "scholar, philosopher and researcher in Human Capacities."

More than anything else, the weekend at Camp David was tacit acknowledgment that Hillary's hard-edge approach to governance had failed. The direction she was now inclined to test didn't leave much room for hard edges. The concept of trying to love one's opponents and enemies was, of course, a cornerstone of Christ's teachings, and Williamson eagerly applied it to politics in her work. She did not, however, recite at Camp David her published prayer, "For the Healing of America," in which she had written: "God loves Bill Clinton and Rush Limbaugh both, and He loves them equally." Yet, in some way, that was one of the main points the healers (Houston's term) seemed intent on making: there was only one way to overwhelm Limbaugh's prejudices and politics, which was through one's own good works, and to turn the rest over to God.

If there was one thing the New Agers were not, it was demonizers. Williamson, Bateson, and Houston (by the second day of the retreat Robbins had to make an unscheduled return to his Aspen headquarters) all had a healthy dislike for the Gingrich crowd, but they had earned their livelihoods preaching harmony. Over the next year, Bateson and, especially, Houston—who would form an unusually close relationship with Hillary—struggled to get the first lady onto a new, more "positive" track and off her "negative" woman-warrior path.

There were hardly any staff members present for the weekend, partly to keep the sessions, with their obvious potential for ridicule, from leaking. In summoning the participants, Williamson had told them that Hillary was at a "low point" and wanted to discuss, among other things, how to better communicate the administration's message in the next two years. Houston "did the major guiding" (as she later put it), which evolved into a discussion of "the communication of visions"—which, of course, harked back to the Camp David staff meeting of April 1993 in which Hillary had been so adamant both about communicating the new presidency's "vision" and concomitantly demonizing the Clintons' enemies and Democratic skeptics alike.

Chelsea, fourteen now, listened in fascination, pausing from her work at a large table on a three-dimensional jigsaw puzzle of the White House. Periodically the adults would join her, trying to fit pieces together.

At first, Hillary remained almost silent as Houston, at Williamson's direction, encouraged a dialogue about personal goals and strengths. Bill, however, from the beginning of the weekend, seemed much more willing to open up. Though Houston had studied psychology extensively, she rejected the term "psychologist" for herself, preferring to say she was "a midwife of human capacity, an evocator, a lifelong student of development in its various stages and types." Once Bill got going for Houston on what he and Hillary and the administration were trying to do, and the problems they were up against, Hillary gradually became more engaged. She spent a good deal of time walking and talking with Mary Catherine and Jean, away from the others. Later, she remarked on the contrasts between the two women, comparing Bateson's soft-spokenness and plain dress to the flamboyant manner of Houston, who draped herself in multicolored shawls and capes, and tended to dominate a room physically and in conversation—quoting from literature, reciting snippets of poetry, citing historical and scientific detail, and displaying an outsized sense of humor. Hillary was becoming increasingly convinced that these two women could help her find a way toward better communicating her vision: they were "experts in two subjects of immediate importance to me": writing books and traveling through South Asia and Africa, where Hillary was scheduled to visit in a few months.

At one point, Houston asked Bill what his vision for the country was, and how it fit with the best aspects of his character.

He responded that he wanted to do everything he could for the country and its citizens—that was the goal of his plan for economic recovery, combined with programs to improve health and educational services, and equal opportunities for all Americans. But he was frustrated. The election results had left him feeling both rejected and trapped. He'd gotten beat up by the Republicans, who had done a better job at getting their message right. At the moment, he seemed fixated on Gingrich. "He respected him and worried what Gingrich was doing in his orchestration of all those young Republicans" who had been elected in November. Gingrich was his biggest obstacle, he said; he also talked about Ken Starr, though far less extensively or meaningfully. Houston said she told him, "I think you have the wrong focus. Starr is much more the problem than Gingrich."

Both Bateson and Houston were shocked at how fragile and confused Hillary seemed: "battered . . . tormented" (noted Houston), lacking her customary confidence in herself, clearly exhausted—reaching out for some help, and settling on a course of making things better through prayer, travel, and writing. When Houston asked Hillary some of the same questions she had asked Bill, the first lady had hardly responded.

Later Hillary would write about summoning the strong voices inside oneself of parents, mentors, and teachers whose messages of encouragement and care helped children grow into confident, capable adults able to weather the inevitable storms of a lifetime. But at this juncture Hillary seemed depleted even of those voices.

The one voice she seemed to identify with was Eleanor Roosevelt's. Eleanor had gone through some of the same trials and experiences— including the kind of opprobrium Hillary had been subjected to, said the first lady. She was intrigued that Houston, who was ten years older than herself, had known Eleanor. Houston's father, Jack, a gag writer for George Burns, Bob Hope, and Henny Youngman among others, had supplied occasional jokes for FDR's speeches, and, on half a dozen occasions as a teenager, she'd been to Eleanor's house on the Upper East Side of Manhattan; during her tenure as U.S. ambassador to the United Nations under President Truman, Eleanor brought together young people, including Houston, to talk about their interests in international affairs.

Hillary, in her fourth week in the White House, had spoken at a dinner in Manhattan to raise funds for a statue of Eleanor Roosevelt, to be erected nearby at the entrance of Riverside Park. "I thought about all the conversations I've had in my head with Mrs. Roosevelt this year, one of the saving graces that I have hung on to for dear life," said Hillary in her remarks. In these "conversations," she looked to Eleanor for guidance, encouragement, and insight. Among the questions she had sought Eleanor's answers to were, "How did you put up with this?" and "How did you go on day to day, with all the attacks and criticisms that would be hurled your way?"

Houston told Hillary that, like Eleanor, she was being made to suffer for functioning as a woman in a métier that was too associated with men for her to be accepted without savage criticism and resistance. It was as if she were carrying the history of womankind on her back. But now Hillary was on the cusp of almost biblical opportunity, far greater than Eleanor's because this was an era in which a lone figure like Hillary could break through on behalf of all women. But first she needed to find her voice, to promote her powerful message that transcended mere politics: a woman's voice, speaking about children and families and principles and policies that would make the world a better place. And on this Jean and Mary Catherine promised they could help her, by shaping the book Hillary said she was about to begin writing. "I was essentially an editor; I'd written a whole lot of books," Houston said. "My whole life has been devoted to pushing the membrane of the possible, to push the boundaries of human capacity." Those books included *The Varieties of Psychedelic Experience: The Classic Guide to the Effects of LSD on the Human Psyche*, written with her husband; *The Passion of Isis and Osiris*, which used Egyptian myth as a modern "design for the marriage of body and soul, life and death, the tangible and the hidden"; and *Godseed: The Journey of Christ*, in which, through "mythology, Jungian psychology, mysticism, anthropology, new science, and just plain creativity," Houston suggested ways to "experience the Christ life."

This was not exactly what Hillary had in mind for the book that came to be *It Takes a Village*—or Simon & Schuster, the publishing house that her representative, Bob Barnett, was already negotiating with—but there were many elements of Houston's and Bateson's experience and counsel that fit well with her objectives. Above all else, she was very comfortable in their presence. Here was another difference between Hillary and Bill: he encouraged people with different ideas than his own to challenge his perceptions; he did not want to be surrounded by sycophants. Hillary, however, was not comfortable being challenged, especially when she was going through a difficult period. She preferred massage, from familiar hands. The few people she trusted enough to seek advice from—and almost never advice of a personal nature—were almost all either worshipful of her or in essential agreement with her.

Whatever Houston and Bateson could contribute to the book, what they felt was most important was to encourage her to "act as if" all the attacks, reproof, and disparagement were not something she absorbed and bought into (as Jean had put it), to not let it erode her own belief in herself. Her faith in her own competence and abilities had been deeply shaken, they believed. Her defenses were so weak that "hostile messages" were taking root in her being. It was important that Hillary not believe she had become the person her critics claimed she was.

Within two weeks, the press was on to the Camp David weekend, gleefully tweaking details about the first family's "convention of New Age guru authors." The *Washington Post* took special note that "personal growth guru" Jean Houston "specialized in walking on hot coals as a demonstration of the power of positive thinking," though not on this particular weekend. Bill Clinton was not amused. His press secretary repeatedly denied that he "lacks a sense of who he is as president and where he wants to go." The same story in the *Post* noted that New Age guru-ism is mostly alien to Washington's practical political culture. None of the stories, however, covered what was discussed. Nor were the reporters who wrote them cognizant of how vulnerable and desperate for answers Hillary was.

Dick Morris had told Hillary, just after the elections in November 1994, that she needed to tell her own story and define her own values in formats that, as she later put it, "could be evaluated directly by people without being distorted or mischaracterized." In December, she had written a retort in *Newsweek* to Newt Gingrich on the subject of child care, after he had advocated the "Dickensian" solution of building orphanages for children whose mothers could not take care of them, rather than placing them in foster homes.

Morris suggested Hillary take another page from Eleanor Roosevelt's book—by writing a newspaper column in which she could present her opinions. Hillary needed redefining, but not another makeover by the Thomasons.

In February 1995 Hillary interviewed and approved the hiring of the person recommended by Simon & Schuster to "help prepare the manuscript" for her book project: Barbara Feinman, a Georgetown University professor of journalism who had previously written a political memoir with Congresswoman Marjorie Margolies-Mezvinsky, and done research for books written by Bob Woodward, Ben Bradlee, and this author. Feinman saw the initial part of her job as drawing out of Hillary material suitably dramatic and revealing to hold a reader's interest. For the next eight months, when the first lady was in Washington, Hillary and Feinman worked most days side by side in the first lady's office in the residence, usually a few hours a day. The process started with Feinman interviewing her and Hillary jotting her ideas on yellow legal pads. The book's title was suggested by Feinman; Hillary had once used it in a speech. It came from a well-known African proverb, "It takes a village to raise a child."

Hillary's desk was neat, though not compulsively so, and she tended not to chitchat while she worked. Rather, she would come prepared with a book about policy or history that she would use to make a point. There was no doubting, as all those on the project would see in the next years, that Hillary was deeply affected by the plight of the poor generally, and poor children particularly, to the point that her eyes would tear up when she would talk about what she had seen in Africa or India, South Side Chicago or Appalachia.

Eventually there would be several circles of facilitators involved in processing the notes and the full pages that Hillary drafted: Feinman and Hillary's Simon & Schuster editor, Rebecca Saletan; members of the Hillaryland staff, including speechwriters and her closest personal aides;* Bill, whom Hillary frequently consulted for anecdotes and family history (and whose opinion of the book she seemed to hold the most important during its writing); and, increasingly, Marianne Williamson and the New Age women.

---

*They tended to do the work at home, on their own time. By now Hillary feared that if it became known she was using her aides for a private project, she would be publicly savaged.

. . .

IN FEBRUARY 1995, Hillary gave an interview to *U.S. News & World Report* that announced—if an announcement was necessary—that she was moving to the back seat. Her primary job, she said, was to be a help-mate, to assist her husband so that his administration would succeed. "My first responsibility, I think, is to do whatever my husband would want me to do that he thinks would be helpful to him," she said. "It may be something of great moment, but more likely it's just to kick back, have a conversation or even play a game of cards and just listen to him rumi-nate. I mean, whatever it takes to kind of be there for him, I think is the most important thing I have to do." By her own implication she had gone from presidential partner to pinochle player.

Bill announced soon after that Hillary would make a five-nation trip to South Asia as an expression of American interest in the region and to improve the United States' relationship with India and Pakistan. It was Hillary's first extended trip overseas without Bill. It was not, she said, an attempt to improve her image after the debacle of her failed health care initiative and the election. "I wished I was so clever to think that up," she said. "But actually, I was asked more than a year ago to go to that part of the world by the State Department." Hillary was looking forward to meeting women from other cultures. Almost anything at this point would have been preferable to Washington, but the opportunity to high-light women's and children's issues in another region of the world was the timeliest and most welcome of respites. It was also an opportunity for Hillary to take a trip with Chelsea, now fifteen; they needed concen-trated time together, to share "some of the last adventures of her child-hood," as Hillary put it.

Hillary rarely commences an undertaking without some idea of the destination, and members of her entourage sensed that she was already trying to find a new role for herself by going abroad and communing with other women. A few weeks earlier she had represented the United States at the United Nations World Summit for Social Development, in Copenhagen. Her address to the conference emphasized "my conviction that individuals and communities around the world are already more connected and interdependent than at any time in human history, and that Americans will be affected by the poverty, disease and development of people halfway around the globe."

The words sounded rote at first, but there was more than the seed of an idea there.

On the first stop on her twelve-day South Asia tour, in Islamabad, she met the wife of Pakistan's president, Nasreen Leghari, who lived in purdah, or isolation, so that men outside her immediate family would never see her. Hillary spent more time with the country's elected leader, Prime Minister Benazir Bhutto.

Hillary, who had always been concerned with human rights and feminist struggles, was now thrust into a world where equality between the sexes was part of a larger cultural struggle, where men were often expected to make life-changing decisions on behalf of their wives. Going from the private visit with Leghari, where only female Secret Service agents could enter, to a luncheon with Bhutto, where invited guests included women who were bankers, academics, and other accomplished professionals, felt to Hillary like "being rocketed forward several centuries in time." While Leghari's wife lived in isolation, Bhutto had attended Harvard. Hillary was concerned with the fate of newborn girls in the region. She took note of the elemental contradictions: Pakistan, India, Bangladesh, and Sri Lanka all had had governments headed by women, yet women are held in such disregard in their cultures that newborn girls are sometimes killed or abandoned.

Chelsea and Hillary visited rural villages in Pakistan and celebrated at more formal state parties and dinners. Mother and daughter had consulted State Department officials about proper attire, and tried out local forms of dress. Hillary brought along plenty of scarves to cover her head in case they went to a mosque or into an area governed by religious tradition. She wanted to be respectful but she also bridled at how women's lives were limited by stifling traditions and religious strictures. Pictures of the Clinton women in exotic plumage, on the backs of elephants, in palaces as well as in squalid villages and in small gatherings at schools, were integral to news coverage of the trip. In India, Chelsea swaddled babies at Mother Teresa's orphanage, many of whom had been abandoned on the streets because they were female. Hillary said she was impressed by the determination of those struggling to support human rights. In Nepal, Muslim women were willing to come to a Hindu village where she was speaking in spite of personal risk. Hillary also wanted to hear what they had to say.

Amazing to her, she got on better with the press. Photographers and reporters on the journey saw her at ease, as a mother, as a woman among women, an emissary, and they took note of how the people she was visiting responded to her, and vice versa. Enormous respect and some emotion appeared to course in both directions. She was at once a revered celebrity, a powerful woman who came to listen to the plight of women in primitive and misogynist societies who would take that message back to America; but she also gave something back, an earnestness and a promise that this was not just another first lady going through the motions.

Women, children, and men waited on dusty rural roads to catch a glimpse of her, to hear her give a speech—even as she was sorting out in her own mind what she would like to accomplish.

While Hillary and Chelsea were in South Asia, Bill addressed the annual dinner of the Gridiron Club, at which the elite of the Washington press corps celebrated themselves and the people they covered, in skits and roasts. "The first lady is sorry she can't be here tonight. If you believe that, I've got some land in Arkansas I'd like to sell you," he said. Before Hillary left for her trip, she had recorded a five-minute satirical take on the movie *Forrest Gump*. At the touch of the play button, there sat Hillary on a park bench in front of the White House with a box of chocolates balanced on her lap. "My mama always told me the White House is like a box of chocolates," she said. "It's pretty on the outside, but inside there's lots of nuts." Later that night when Hillary and Chelsea called the president, he told them that the taped segment had received a standing ovation.

BY WAY OF forewarning, Gingrich had declared, "Washington just can't imagine a world in which Republicans have subpoena power." Now they had it. Hillary and Bill had no illusions that in the next two years leading up to the 1996 presidential election they faced open-ended investigation by congressional committees, chaired by the hungry opposition, in which their Arkansas past and the Clinton White House would be chewed over mercilessly. These investigations, in turn, would feed the inquiry of the new independent counsel, Kenneth Starr, whose long arm was already reaching into the White House for documents and information. Gingrich had said as many as twenty congressional subcommittees or special task forces might be mobilized to get at the "corruption" the Clintons had brought to Washington.

The Clintons felt all of this imposed a threat to Chelsea. As an adolescent it had been possible to keep her shielded from the devastating specificity of what was being said about her parents and their marriage, their morals, and their sexuality. At age fifteen, uncommonly bright, attending school with Washington's most privileged children in a media-centric capital, her insulation was at an end.

Lloyd Cutler had left the White House, as planned, after six months and a brief transition, coincidentally, with Starr's appointment. The new White House counsel was Abner Mikva, a former congressman from Illinois who had resigned his seat on the U.S. Court of Appeals bench—on which Ken Starr had also sat—to replace Cutler. He was not a street fighter, but more important, he knew Starr, and they could get along. Harold Ickes would be responsible for the wider strategy and daily mechanics of meeting the assault they were fully expecting on the White House through the 1996 election season.

Before leaving, Cutler had recommended to Ickes that he hire as his deputy Jane Sherburne, a skilled, tough investigations specialist from his law firm, Wilmer, Cutler, & Pickering. She had worked on Cutler's staff at the White House and knew the territory and the players. She would have just the combination of savvy and skill to put together a rapid-response team. The fact that Sherburne, forty-three, was a woman was not incidental, though nobody said aloud that it was a major factor in the choice. But dealing with Hillary and her staff might be better handled than in the past if there was a legal emissary who was not another white male. And Sherburne had the advantage of already knowing Hillary and Maggie Williams.

Not long before Hillary had left for Asia and Africa in March 1997, Sherburne met with Hillary and Maggie in the West Wing office, now seldom used, of the first lady. As much as anything else, what registered with her was Hillary's weariness, both generally and in terms of the specific subject under discussion: trying to make the Clintons' case more sympathetically in public and still resist Starr's intrusions and the Republicans' determination to smear them. Sherburne said she wanted to stay in front of the facts. She wanted to put together a team of six or eight people who would handle specific assignments for congressional investigations and relations, Starr, media, subpoenas, and political outreach strategy related to all the inquiries, including reporters. Sherburne would hire these people herself and run the unit as a tight ship. Kendall had already approved and was accepting of the approach, and Sherburne's leadership. Part of the plan was to appear as forthcoming as possible and not unnecessarily antagonize Starr or the committee chairmen on the Hill. Hillary remained skeptical that yet another new approach was going to make anything better.

Sherburne had already listed some forty avenues of likely investigation, beginning with the obvious: Whitewater (the land deal), Madison Guaranty, Vince Foster, Paula Jones, and problems specific to Hillary's earlier statements. Hillary said she wanted to be kept well informed.

She was not expecting to get her information from the source of the Clintons' first post-electoral crisis, however—a biography of Bill, *First in His Class*, written by David Maraniss of the *Washington Post*. As was too often the case, the information tore into the domestic fabric, not just the public perception, of Hillary's world. And it sent Bill and his new hand-maiden, Morris, into cover-up mode.

Maraniss's book, which the White House obtained in galley form in early February before publication, was a masterful work, a broad character study of Bill Clinton before he won the White House, focusing on the forces that shaped him from his boyhood in Arkansas to his decision to enter the 1992 race—where the book ended.

Its biggest revelation was of the meeting between Bill and Betsey Wright in which they discussed the names of women who might come forward if he decided to seek the presidency in 1988, and Wright's forceful suggestion that he not run. Maraniss's brief description of the meeting noted that Bill and Wright discussed the fact that the state troopers who chauffeured and guarded Clinton were witnesses to many of his assignations.

Upon reading the offending passages in the galleys of the book, Bill was especially upset because he had never told Hillary about his discussion with Betsey. When she learned of it as the White House was debating how to respond to Maraniss's book, she was devastated and enraged—at both Betsey and Bill. The three years before he decided to run in 1992 had been among the worst in her life, and had strained their marriage to the breaking point. Now, yet more humiliation was about to be heaped on her, with Maraniss's confirmation that the troopers quoted in the *Spectator* article were believable. Moreover, she now had for the first time a clear understanding of why Bill did not run in 1988. She felt betrayed, Wright was sure.

Wright had come to Washington after the 1994 election to join the staff of Anne Wexler, the lobbyist and close friend of the Clintons since the Connecticut senatorial campaign of her husband, Joe Duffey, during the semester at Yale when Hillary and Bill had first met. Wright was on local jury duty in the municipal courthouse in downtown D.C. when Wexler's driver came into the jury holding room and handed her a cell phone, saying, "You're supposed to call the White House, and the president asked that we make sure you're connected by regular [landline] phone. But don't call him on this phone. This is just so that they can get you if they need you." Wright made her way to a pay phone and was connected through the White House switchboard to Bill. "And he starts in on me about the Maraniss book," Wright recalled. " 'Why would Maraniss say that you had met with me?' "

"Presumably because I told him we did," Wright responded.

"But that didn't happen," Clinton insisted, according to Wright.

"And I said, 'Sure it did, Bill.' I mean I reminded him who else was there, and there was just this silence."

Wright did not believe Clinton was deliberately lying, but rather exhibiting a family trait: "He and his mother both have a fabulous ability to lock stuff away . . . to genuinely forget things." This tendency was exactly the reason Wright had brought another person to the meeting with Bill in 1987—to have a witness to remind him.* She was convinced that the president was not coaching her to disavow something truthful. But she knew from what he was saying that Maraniss's book posed massive problems for him with Hillary, and for his lawyers as well.

"I never talked to Hillary about womanizing," Wright explained years after the courthouse phone conversation. "Never, never, never! And it's something I feel very guilty about. That by calling her my friend I couldn't warn her before stuff hit her. I didn't. And it was a confusion between her as a friend, and the fact that I worked for him. There was no point in telling her about all of it. . . . I clearly took on a role of protecting her from him in his philandering, which certainly was an inappropriate role for a staff person. But I don't think I would have ever viewed it as inappropriate. It was what I was going to do. Period. . . . I guess my expectations to some degree differ between them because I worked for Bill at that point."

As he read the galleys, Clinton wrote in the margins, apparently in preparation for meeting with his lawyers and members of the White House staff who would have to deal publicly with the book's revelations. "In his handwriting, it said: 'This never happened.' Or, 'I don't know why she makes this stuff up,' " recalled Wright, who was shown the materials in one of the numerous legal depositions at which she testified over the next five years. But in that first conversation, she held her ground.

Clinton, meanwhile, had summoned Dick Morris.

"Why did you talk to Maraniss? Can't I trust you anymore? Can't I trust *anybody* anymore?"

Morris was dumbfounded. Clinton was railing at him for telling Maraniss that they had worked together on negative campaign ads attacking Jim Guy Tucker. "That was in 1978," he told the president.

"But he's now the governor!" Bill shouted.

"What the fuck do you care?"

"He controls the state police!"

That was the other legal problem the lawyers had identified. They feared that some of the troopers might testify that Clinton, as president,

*The witness was an old friend who had come to Little Rock for the expected announcement of Bill's candidacy, said Wright. She would not further identify the individual.

had held out the possibility of getting them federal jobs if they either didn't cooperate with or disavowed their conversations with Brock and other reporters. Serious questions of federal law were involved. It was possible that some of the troopers, who still worked for the incumbent governor of Arkansas, might seek Tucker's advice.

The pages of Maraniss's book became the urtext that lawyers, prosecutors, reporters, and presidential aides spent hours and hours parsing and studying, poring over the brief passages that dealt with the troopers, and Betsey's meeting with Clinton. It was pregnant with the possibility of ruinous assertion, testimony, and lines of inquiry: Clinton had correctly identified the biggest problems in his angry conversation with Morris— about the state police, i.e., the troopers, who could talk about alleged offers of federal jobs whether true or not, and the meeting with Paula Jones in such a way that would give her claim a measure of legal (not just gossipy) credence.

Wright could see there was broad agreement among Clinton, Morris, and at least one of Clinton's lawyers, Bob Bennett, that it was necessary to immediately challenge Maraniss's version of the facts. But Wright insisted to them that "David Maraniss is one of the most careful researchers I have ever met in my life. . . . He may have misunderstood me, which is easy to do, but it wouldn't have been because of sloppy research or writing." At the time Maraniss had interviewed her, said Wright, "I was in such deep clinical depression that . . . all the time I talked to him, all I remember was that I was crying all the time. . . . And I remember nothing I said to him. But I know he didn't make anything up."

Bill, Morris, and Bennett, according to Wright, persuaded her to deny the key element of Maraniss's account: that the Arkansas troopers attached to the governor's office had solicited women for Bill—despite the fact that, as Maraniss reported, part of the conversation between Wright and Clinton in July 1987 directly touched on the question of women procured by the troopers, according to Betsey.

"Well, there was one thing that they [the president and his lawyers] really didn't like in [the Maraniss biography] about the role the troopers played in the procuring. . . . Bill said, 'That plays right into the Paula Jones lawsuit. What are you talking about?' " Clinton was screaming at her, trying to get her to disavow it, Wright said. On the other end of the phone she could hear Dick Morris and the president "talking to each other, Dick being there in the room with Bill, I could hear him saying, 'Tell her this. Tell her that.' "

Wright did not have Maraniss's book with her. Morris and Clinton were reading to her from a text, she said. "I felt I was at a real disadvantage. I wasn't seeing what they were talking to me about and screaming at me about. . . . Bill was screaming. . . . 'Why did you say this to him?' "

She got off the phone and called Maraniss—immediately after the president had screamed at her. She was upset. Why had Maraniss written about their meeting and what she'd said to him about the troopers? she asked.

"Are they coming down on you?" she said Maraniss asked.

"Yep, they are," she told him.

"Bill Bennett, Bill, Bob, one of those Bennett boys—Bill's lawyer Bennett—was very concerned about" what she'd said to Bill's biographer.*

Under this pressure "I ended up issuing a statement saying that David Maraniss must have misunderstood me" about the troopers' alleged role in procuring women. Following her disavowal, "David [Maraniss] has never spoken to me since," said Wright.

Later, Morris described the event this way: "I was with Clinton in the residence—in the Treaty Room—and we were talking to Betsey on the phone, both of us: we were negotiating a statement in which she would deny what she obviously had said to Maraniss, and which was true, about the state troopers and getting women. Bill was getting unbelievable grief from Hillary about the Paula Jones business and he had told me that, for the first time, Chelsea was mad at him over this and that he was very upset at Betsey for talking to Maraniss. He'd said 'I don't care what she knows, I'm finished with Betsey.'

"I said, 'I think you should be careful about that because she knows everything' . . . I was saying don't alienate her totally because she could do you a lot of damage; earlier she had told me she had all the files on all his women; and when I'd cautioned her to move them to a safe deposit box, she said a warehouse would be more like it.

"So in this [telephone] conversation in the White House, with Bill, I was urging Betsey, trying to negotiate a statement she would make in which she would deny saying what she actually said. Clinton was very focused on it, and [Bob] Bennett was involved. I worked with Bennett on it, and Bill was talking to Betsey and to Bennett by phone, working out what Betsey was going to say. While we were working on the statement with Betsey, it went back and forth for several drafts; she was very upset,

---

*Like many people in Washington, Wright sometimes mixed up Bob Bennett with his brother Bill, the former Reagan administration secretary of education and conservative ethical philosopher who was also a secret gambler (with blackjack losses in the millions in surreptitious trips to Las Vegas), and author of a book called *The Book of Virtues*.

and so was Clinton; it was a hard situation to handle, Clinton on one hand, Betsey on the other."

The statement that Wright issued under duress later that afternoon, February 4, 1995, said:

> I think that David Maraniss may have misunderstood what I told him about the troopers. What I believe is that some of them solicited women for themselves, exploiting the fact that they worked for the governor. I do not believe that they ever solicited women for the governor, certainly not with his knowledge. My recommendation [that Clinton not run for president in 1988] was based on my fear that in the climate of Gary Hart that liars and gold diggers would come out of the woodwork. What I learned from my conversation with the governor was that the rumors were nothing in reality. My concern was for the impact the rumors would have on Chelsea and Hillary.
>
> My fears were borne out in the 1992 campaign when liars and gold diggers did emerge, and I proudly and truthfully defended Governor Clinton against them. My admiration was strong for his determination to keep his marriage intact, and I became upset that his public acknowledgment of troubles in his marriage then made him more vulnerable to lies. Any so-called cover-up for Bill Clinton was the usual staff role in explaining why he was late for a meeting or couldn't see someone or couldn't agree with them.

Maraniss was flabbergasted, and issued his own statement, which accurately described what had happened and the dynamic so obviously involved: "I interviewed Betsey Wright several times for my book and based my account of her dealings with Bill Clinton directly on what she told me during those interviews." Maraniss said, "Before the book's release, I met with her and read to her the sections related to her. Her response at the time was that I had fairly and accurately reported what she had said. During the two years I spent working on this biography, I came to understand the complicated love-hate relationship between Betsey Wright and Bill Clinton, which seems to be in evidence again."

Meanwhile, the Maraniss book caused Hillary to stop talking to Dick Morris, for months, by his account. "She was mad at me because of my telling Maraniss about the swimming pool she wanted to build at the Little Rock mansion," he said. "She was pissed that I talked about this, and she stopped talking to me. She also, I think, basically stopped talking to Bill because she was mad about Betsey Wright saying to Maraniss that state troopers were used to get women, and also about the list of women in connection with the 1988 race."

During the first twenty months of the Clinton presidency, Morris had usually communicated with Bill through Hillary, since Bill did not want to be seen or heard speaking to him; nor did the president particularly like talking with Morris. Now, according to Morris, things changed. Hillary wouldn't speak to him.

"I would talk to Bill constantly about the advice that I'd give Hillary and he would pass it on," said Morris. "And, I would periodically say to him, 'Listen, I've known you guys for twenty years. Relationships with you don't work if your wife doesn't want them to work. And I'm nervous that I don't get to talk to Hillary.' And he said, 'Well, I pass on your advice.' Or he'd say things like, 'Well, you know it's a tough situation for everybody. I mean I'm having problems, too. She's very mad at both of us for the Maraniss book.' And then after a few months into it . . . I complained again about the lack of access and he said, 'Well, she takes your advice.' And she did. I had recommended she do a newspaper column, and she was doing that. And I recommended that she talk about the Gulf War disease and she was doing that. And mammograms . . . I called them soft-core health care issues. I said, 'We'll carry forward the image [of concern about adequate medical care], but it won't have the same hard social engineering component.' And she would do everything that . . . I would advise. And, Bill said, 'She's following your advice.' And I had a line, which was perhaps a little too unequivocal, I'd said, 'Yeah, we put out the dog food at night, and in the morning the dish is empty.' "

16

Truth or Consequences (2)

Anger is not the best state of mind in which to prepare for a grand jury appearance.

—*Living History*

THOUGH HILLARY had withdrawn from the West Wing and a visible policymaking role, she tightly held the legal reins, consulting and instructing her lawyers almost daily over the next two years.

Shortly before leaving for Asia, Hillary met with Mark Fabiani, the Harvard-educated lawyer and former counsel and deputy mayor of Los Angeles, whom Ickes and Jane Sherburne had recruited. Fabiani was chosen because he had successfully coordinated legal and media strategy for Mayor Tom Bradley during city and federal investigations of his personal and family finances.

Having watched the Clintons' problems unfold from afar, Fabiani wanted to meet with his prospective clients before signing on. Immediately it became clear to Fabiani that Ickes was recruiting a legal team for Hillary, "not for anyone else." Ickes had told him, "You should come in and meet the president and first lady." But "when I came in," said Fabiani, "the person I met was the first lady, not the president. Hillary had set this [mechanism] up. And Harold was her surrogate in sort of setting it up and then running it."

In *Living History*, Hillary described the Whitewater response team in terms suggesting that it had little to do with her: Mack McLarty and Maggie Williams as well as other senior staff had recommended its establishment, she said, to "centralize" all discussion of Whitewater.

"Hillary was clearly orchestrating it from the beginning. . . . She was the conductor of it—the damage control operation," which meant the legal operation, said Fabiani, "and had been going back to 1992 and the first Whitewater revelation . . . directing Susan Thomases, directing Webb Hubbell, Vince Foster, to try to structure the Whitewater defense. And she'd been doing it ever since"—to the Clintons' great disadvantage, in the view of a number of her lawyers. Hubbell confirmed that Hillary had, from the start, taken over the defense. Ickes's operation, said Mark Fabiani, "was another iteration of her damage control, and it never changed." In his initial meeting with Hillary, and in a subsequent discussion the same day with Williams on the veranda of her office, "we talked about what this all meant, and how to fix it."

Hillary's personal instrument was David Kendall. Over the next two years, Fabiani came to "like him very much," but "he's a soul mate of hers in terms of his instinct, in terms of his carefulness about saying anything publicly, in terms of his attitude toward the press. He is very much someone that she's comfortable with, because he reinforced everything she thought, and she reinforced everything he thought. You never heard them disagree in a meeting."

Several members of Sherburne's team, said one, came to believe that Hillary's "instincts are horrible in terms of politics, in terms of managing a crisis like this, like the one that she was in, like the one [Bill] got in with Monica. . . . We had a joke that all we had to do was ask her, What would you do? And then do just the opposite, without even thinking about it . . . because almost always her instincts were wrong, backwards. . . . And she never surrounded herself with people who would stand up to her, who were of a different mind."

Until the special prosecutor caught Monica Lewinsky in his sights, Kendall rarely dealt with the president, only Hillary, said Fabiani. "The president wasn't the client, except in name only, and except when there were a few flare-ups that involved him. But those were rare and . . . he was easy to deal with compared to her." In two years at the White House, Fabiani never met with Bill and Hillary together.

It is impossible to know how much Hillary told Bill about her lawyering back in Arkansas on behalf of McDougal and their Whitewater investment, and in defending herself when she came under investigation by reporters, prosecutors, and the Congress. Just as he never told her about his assignations with other women, it seems reasonable from what we know that she never fully told him just how legally exposed her actions might have made her.

"She is so tortured by the way she's been treated that she would do anything to get out of the situation," Fabiani realized time and again over the next two years of trying to defend her. "And if that involved not being fully forthcoming [in releasing documents and other materials], she herself would say, 'I have a reason for not being forthcoming.' " Her reasoning, said Fabiani, followed a linear path: "If we do this [she would say], they're going to do this to me. If we say this, then they're going to say this. You know, fuck 'em, let's just not do that." Meanwhile, she would "wake up in the morning . . . saying, What are they going to do to me today? Where are they coming at me today? What do I need to do today." Eventually Fabiani, Sherburne, Ickes, and the other lawyers on the team came to be known in the West Wing as "The Masters of Disaster."

The president, said Fabiani, "never seemed to be too concerned about her legal vulnerability. There was never any detectable concern. His concern was, What do I say about it? if an event had occurred that he was going to be asked about." Bill's general attitude toward the legal situation was "keep your eye on the ball, get good people who can handle it for you, deal with them only as necessary, and keep trying to move the administration forward."

Until the president personally became enmeshed in the Lewinsky scandal, Fabiani saw Bill explode only once—"very late in the [investigations] over the treatment of Susan McDougal," when television broadcasts showed her being taken to prison, shackled, in an orange jumpsuit.

Fabiani underwent a trial by fire. In early May 1995, the Senate had formally authorized, by a vote of ninety-six to three, a resolution creating the Special Committee to Investigate Whitewater Development Corporation and Related Matters, under the auspices of Alfonse D'Amato's Banking Committee. Democrats, still reeling from the election results of November and many of them now mistrustful of the Clintons' assurances that Whitewater was a dry hole, had little choice but to go along. Because Democrats were the minority party now, D'Amato and other implacable opponents of the Clintons would control the investigations and—especially moving toward a presidential election year—try to use them as a means of denying him a second term.

D'Amato focused on Vince Foster's death for maximum publicity; investigating his death would grab more headlines and attention than the minutiae of Arkansas real estate and banking practices. The most probing questions of the investigation would be about Hillary, Foster's friend and enabler, not the president. From the outset, the rhetoric of D'Amato and his fellow Republicans made clear these would be viciously partisan hearings. The first batch of subpoenas issued by D'Amato's committee was for information related to the Travel Office, Foster's death, his duties, and the documents removed from his office—which, D'Amato implied, could lead to the president and his wife.

Fabiani and Sherburne, determined to make an end run around D'Amato, appealed to Hillary to allow leaking to the press—prior to the scheduled start of the hearings on July 18—the relevant documents sought by the committee. These included thirty "personal" files removed from Foster's office after his death, about one hundred pages of which dealt with his work on Whitewater for the Clintons. Kendall opposed the idea, on grounds that such disclosures might give the committee a roadmap to new leads and an opportunity to contradict old statements by the Clintons. Hillary said the press would, as usual, report the material negatively (some of the contents *was* embarrassing, but not criminal), but she left the matter in Kendall's hands.

In this instance, Kendall met with unusually vigorous opposition from the new counsel to the president, Abner Mikva, and virtually the whole legal defense apparatus outside of Williams & Connolly (where many of the records were held in a secured area). Kendall relented. It was decided to let the press present a coherent account, based on the documents, of what had happened both in Whitewater back in Arkansas and on the night Foster died—before D'Amato offered his skewed and selective interpretation. The material was carefully parceled out to reporters, the biggest cache going to *Newsweek's* Michael Isikoff, who was known to be very tough on Whitewater matters and the Clintons in general. Isikoff produced a long account titled "The Night Foster Died," in which he concluded that there was no evidence of a connection between Foster's death and Whitewater, "no document, memo, note or scrap of paper suggesting that Foster, the Clintons or anyone else was orchestrating a cover-up," before or after Foster's death. Foster's colleagues—who were also his friends, in shock, grieving—had tended to make a jumble out of the materials in his office, but that was all.

But it wasn't.

Kendall had withheld important documents from the White House lawyers, some of which related to Whitewater tax matters. D'Amato had obtained copies of that material and triumphantly accused the White House of yet another cover-up. The records that Fabiani and Sherburne now demanded from Kendall showed that the Clintons' claim, during the 1992 campaign, of a $68,900 tax loss from their Whitewater investment had been wrong. Foster had calculated the real loss was only $5,800. The IRS was undertaking an audit of the matter. More ominously, Foster had written in his notes held back by Kendall that Whitewater was "a can of worms you shouldn't open."

That quotation was in the next day's headlines and read aloud portentously in D'Amato's nasal Long Island accent on the evening television news broadcasts.

Among the first witnesses called by the committee were Susan Thomases, Maggie Williams, and Betsey Wright, all of whom expressed degrees of reluctance, forgetfulness, and exasperation as they were savaged by the chairman, the committee's counsel, Michael Chertoff,* and its Republican members. In Thomases's case, the situation seemed particularly cruel; she was becoming debilitated by multiple sclerosis, and her difficulty in providing quick responses to the questions shouted at her by D'Amato (who called her a liar) was perhaps more a result of her physical condition than anything else.

The basic methodology of the hearings was Chertoff's, who implied—through his questions and the introduction of White House phone logs showing a series of back-to-back phone calls between Hillary, Thomases, Williams, and Bernie Nussbaum—that Hillary had attempted to delay and prevent investigators from going through Foster's office before damning evidence could be stashed away or removed.

Wright was on the stand for eight consecutive hours, "bobbing and weaving with Chertoff in her sarcastic and colorful fashion," as the *Washington Post* reported. "Go ahead and talk," she told him at one point, when he tried to frame an unusually elaborate and convoluted question. "And then sometime next week I'll come back and answer." As she neared the end of her testimony that day, after providing answers to "nigh on a jillion questions," as she put it, D'Amato inquired about how she was holding up. "I'm tired and I'm bored," she said with a sigh.

Williams testified on July 28, during the second week of the hearings. A Secret Service uniformed guard, Henry P. O'Neill Jr., an eighteen-year veteran of the White House detail, had testified that he'd witnessed Williams taking a stack of files from Foster's office the night of Foster's death. She denied it, and had undergone two lie detector tests to buttress her account. But her lawyer released the results of only one. She was near tears finally, after being hammered on the stand by D'Amato, whose presenatorial reputation as a local politician with deep conflict-of-interest problems of his own, including the prosecution of his brother for mail fraud,† was well known. She said she had visited Foster's office that night only because she had seen a light on and had a momentary "irrational

---

*Chertoff, later President George W. Bush's secretary of homeland security, had been a prosecutor and trial lawyer in New Jersey before becoming D'Amato's alter ego and committee counsel. His objective in the hearing was to build a circumstantial case against Hillary, in particular, the people around her, and by extension the president, and to show "how they withheld information and documents or claimed to forget things in a coordinated effort at damage control." His tactics were opposed at every turn by the special committee's counsel, Richard Ben-Veniste, who had been one of the Watergate prosecutors.

†Armand P. D'Amato was convicted of mail fraud in 1993, though the conviction was later overturned, according to the *New York Times*.

hope that I would walk in and find Vince Foster there." She had spoken to Hillary perhaps three times in the forty-eight hours after Foster's death, she said, phone conversations in which they discussed Vince's apparent torment, the question of where the Clintons' "personal files" in his office should go, and how to deal with a distraught White House staff, including sending in grief counselors. She'd spoken to Thomases only once, about Foster's insurance policy, she testified. Aggressively challenged by Senator Connie Mack, a Florida Republican, who said phone records demonstrated that Thomases had called her nine times in forty-eight hours, and that her account made "very little sense," Williams responded that the records showed only that Thomases phoned the office of the first lady, not that she had reached Williams. "Everything that happened is not some big plot."

For instance, two days after Foster's death, she said, she had some of the Clintons' personal records transferred from Foster's office to a locked closet in the first family's personal residence, only because she was too tired to wait for a messenger from the office of the Clintons' lawyers to pick them up—not (as the Republicans on the committee were intimating) for nefarious reasons. Bernard Nussbaum had asked her to send those records to the attorneys.

Her voice choked up, and she wiped her eyes, when she recalled Hillary's phone call informing her of Vince's death. Evelyn Lieberman, Williams's deputy and later White House deputy chief of staff, was seated at the witness table next to her, and put her arm around Williams to console her.

The Secret Service agent, O'Neill, stuck to his story despite a pounding by Democrats who kept him at the microphone for nearly four hours. He said he told no one about Williams taking the files until he was interviewed by FBI agents in April 1994, in connection with one of the investigations of Foster's death.

At 10:30 that night, he said, he was on his regular tour accompanying a cleaning crew from office to office in the West Wing. His duties included locking and unlocking offices for the cleaners, and securing sensitive "burn bag" documents for disposal.

O'Neill said his first stop was the White House counsel's suite, where Foster and Nussbaum had their private offices and aides worked in a common open area with several desks. Around the time he entered the suite, he said, Nussbaum arrived and entered his office. O'Neill and the cleaning crew then left the suite, and in the hallway outside he encountered Howard Paster, the White House liaison to Congress, who told him Vince Foster's body had been discovered, apparently a suicide. O'Neill then walked back to the counsel's suite and encountered Williams's aide Lieberman standing outside the door; she asked him to make sure the counsel's office was locked properly.

When he returned to the suite a short while afterward, Patsy Thomasson, the White House deputy administrative director who sometimes reported to Foster, was sitting at Foster's desk, looking down, apparently reading something. O'Neill thought she might be Foster's wife, so he left. When he again returned to lock up, Lieberman was just coming out, as was Nussbaum. Then, "after a few more seconds, Maggie Williams came out, walked by me carrying what I would describe as folders." By way of explanation, Lieberman told him, "That's Maggie Williams, the first lady's chief of staff."

O'Neill said Williams walked to her office nearby carrying a stack of folders, which he estimated to be three to five inches high, perhaps with a cardboard box on top. He locked the counsel's office at 11:41 P.M., and said that he, Williams, and Lieberman went down the elevator together.

WRIGHT'S LEGAL BILLS, in excess of $650,000, were probably the highest of all of Hillary's and Bill's aides forced to run a gauntlet between D'Amato's committee and Starr's grand jury. Williams's bills totaled about $150,000.

"I had assurance from both Lloyd Cutler and Bill Clinton directly that they would pay my bill because I was in effect custodian of his campaign papers, and they told me his legal defense fund was being structured in a way that it would be covered," said Wright. Later, she read an article in the *New York Times* saying only Hillary and Bill's fees would be paid by the fund. "I had approached the guy who was the keeper, and he told me he had never been given instructions to pay me; and when I asked him to go back to Bill, he told me that the president had never authorized the payment. That was a little embarrassing."

Meanwhile, Wright spent hundreds of hours searching through records in her lawyer's office and at Williams & Connolly that had been subpoenaed by the special prosecutor.

Joe Klein, the author of *Primary Colors* and a *Newsweek* columnist at the time, excoriated Hillary in print for failing to aid her beleaguered staff, especially Maggie, who was highly regarded by colleagues and reporters alike. Klein's column depicted Williams and other aides as the Clintons' victims, left to fend for themselves. Referring to Bill and Hillary as "the Tom and Daisy Buchanan of the Baby Boom Political Elite," he asked: "Why hasn't she come forward and said, 'Stop torturing my staff. This isn't about them. I'll testify. I'll make all the documents available. I'll sit here and answer your stupid, salacious questions until Inauguration Day, if need be.' " On the same day that Klein's column appeared, Webb Hubbell reported to the Federal Prison Camp in Cumberland, Maryland, where he was to serve twenty-one months for mail fraud and tax evasion.

Hillary, meanwhile, told Jane Sherburne that she wanted to testify, to go one-on-one with D'Amato and bury him. Her appearance would demonstrate that she was "a good person," and maybe once and for all put an end to the whole Whitewater outrage. Others were not sure if Hillary was serious or, more likely, that she knew the lawyers would never allow it. The lawyers were indeed unanimous in their opposition, and that was that.

In Hillary's first newspaper columns, appearing that month, she briefly deviated from her topic of families and children to reflect on her frustration, as first lady, without specifically citing the investigations by Starr or D'Amato's committee: "The truth is it is hard for me to recognize the Hillary Clinton that other people see."

Later, she wrote about her inability, for legal reasons, to talk with her friends about their mistreatment by investigators and prosecutors, and the "injustices" dealt them.

OF ALL the foreign policy dilemmas faced by the Clinton administration, the U.S. relationship with China was as vexing as any, a matter of delicate calibration based on the American adherence to the fundamental principles of human rights and China's status as a superpower.

For months, Hillary had been looking forward to going to China as honorary chairwoman of the U.S. delegation at the United Nations Fourth World Conference on Women, to be held in Beijing between September 4 and 15. The title understated her mission, which was to address, on behalf of the United States government, the most urgent questions of human rights abuses—particularly those of women—to the host Chinese regime and the rest of the world, while not causing a rift in the Sino-American relationship. Like her health care portfolio, this was not the kind of assignment normally entrusted to first ladies. The recent behavior of the Chinese complicated matters: imprisoning a Chinese-American human rights activist charged with espionage (and, on the eve of the conference, releasing him); selling M-11 missiles to Pakistan; and conducting provocative military exercises in the Taiwan Strait.

From Pearl Harbor, where Bill had spoken at the fiftieth anniversary observance of V-J Day, Hillary flew to Beijing, where her advance team was being badgered by the authorities, who wanted a prior look at what she was going to say in her address. Hillary was told that, while the Chinese government looked forward to her presence at the conference, it did not want to be embarrassed by her words, and hoped that she was appreciative of "China's hospitality." For most of the fourteen-hour flight across the Pacific she worked on her speech, consulting with the head of the American delegation, U.N. Ambassador Madeleine Albright, former ambassador to China Winston Lord, and Eric Schwartz, the National Security Council's expert on human rights in China. She was deciding how far she should go in condemning Chinese and other governments' and cultures' abuses. The bureaucrats found her draft tepid, despite her insistence that she wanted to "push the envelope" on behalf of women and girls. They recommended incorporating an affirmation of principles adopted at the recent World Council of Human Rights in Vienna.

Back home, Hillary's participation in the Beijing conference had already been attacked. Senators Jesse Helms and Phil Gramm complained that the meeting was "shaping up as an unsanctioned festival of anti-family, anti-American sentiment." Their view was reinforced by fellow Republicans disinclined to approve of any U.N.-sponsored event. They ignored that meetings such as this one were of great import to the worldwide human rights movement, women's rights advocates, and Third World governments, which were reluctant—for religious, cultural, or merely authoritarian reasons—to relax feudal policies regarding women and girls, in particular, and human rights in general. The U.S. delegation included Republican Tom Kean, the former governor of New Jersey (and a Catholic), nuns, and a vice chair of the Muslim Women's League.

Hillary had learned (or so she said later) from her health care experience that the tone and pitch of her voice often worked against her when she felt strongly about an issue. (She attributed this to women being subject to criticism if they showed too much feeling in public.) The Chinese, ultimately, blacked out her speech on official state radio and television, but her message was startlingly forceful and clear to her hosts:

> It is a violation of human rights when babies are denied food, or drowned, or suffocated, or their spines broken, simply because they are girls. It is a violation of human rights when women and girls are sold into the slavery of prostitution. It is a violation of human rights when women are doused with gasoline, set on fire and burned to death because their marriage dowries are deemed too small. It is a violation of human rights when individual women are raped in their own communities and when thousands of women are subjected to rape as a tactic or prize of war. It is a

violation of human rights when a leading cause of death worldwide among women ages fourteen to forty-four is the violence
they are subjected to in their own homes. It is a violation of human
rights when young girls are brutalized by the painful and degrad-
ing practice of genital mutilation. It is a violation of human rights
when women are denied the right to plan their own families, and
that includes being forced to have abortions or being sterilized
against their will.

Her twenty-one-minute-long oration ended with a plea that the delegates return to their countries and demand action to improve opportunities for women—in health, the law, politics, and education. Now there
was an agonizingly long delay before the translations were completed
(delegations from 189 countries were in attendance). Hillary anxiously
awaited the audience response. Suddenly there was something approaching pandemonium as hundreds in the hall leaped to their feet and began
a long-standing ovation for the first lady.

For the rest of her time in China, Hillary was mobbed by those who
had heard the speech, both in Beijing and at a huge meeting of non-
governmental organizations in Huarirou, whose conference—to coincide with the smaller official U.N. assembly in Beijing—had been moved
by the authorities to a distant city.

Her speech became front-page news around the world, noted (in
countries where its message was consistent with cultural and governmental principles) for its power and eloquence. In the United States, the *New
York Times* editorial page said the speech "may have been her finest
moment in public life."

"It kind of legitimized her as an ambassador for those issues," said her
speechwriter Lissa Muscatine, who had accompanied Hillary and worked
on the address. After two taxing years, and for the first time since her trip
to Capitol Hill when she had charmed the committees of Congress that
were to consider, and eventually help bury, health care reform, this was
the first widespread positive recognition she received.

The germ of an idea she had first planted in Africa and South Asia a
few months before was now firmly rooted. She could see that, no matter
how she was treated by politicians and the press back home, she had an
international platform from which to preach the ideas and concepts that
meant the most to her. Neither D'Amato's hearings nor Ken Starr's
investigation had paused during her trip to China, but with her own
powerful will and determination she had successfully been able to present an alternative Hillary. She—and others—could now see that she was
a figure of enormous respect around the world, regarded with fascination

and treated as a new kind of *statesperson*, a first lady who brought a compelling, important message, not just flowers to hand to a king or prime minister. She may have failed miserably at changing things at home, but she could sense her potential to effect change elsewhere. Her message had been skillfully presented in Beijing and would continue to be sharpened: to encourage democratic movements not by insisting on U.S.-style governance and constitutions in other cultures, but by promoting democratic and universal ideals of human freedom. For at least a moment, this felt like a return to her lifelong agenda.

A BATTERY OF White House lawyers and paralegals labored full-time to meet the demands for thousands of documents sought under subpoenas issued by D'Amato's Senate committee, a parallel investigating committee of the House of Representatives, and the office of Kenneth Starr. On December 29, one of Jane Sherburne's deputies, searching a batch of records carted from a federal warehouse in suburban Maryland, found David Watkins's memorandum with its damning detail about Hillary's "insisten[t]" role in the Travel Office firings instigated by Harry Thomason. "Foster regularly informed me that the first lady was concerned and desired action—the action desired was the firing of the travel office staff," Watkins had written.

If D'Amato were to wave this kind of memo in front of the cameras while reading its perditious words, the suggestion that Foster died because he knew the darkest secrets of the Clinton presidency would become more credible to some, whether his death was suicide or murder. It was already known that he had left a note expressing his worry that Hillary would be held responsible for the firings. It was well established that Foster had really been Hillary's in-house lawyer, not the president's. Foster's death had raised the Travel Office matter, which in any other administration might have been a minor blip for a few weeks, to a matter of national fascination and, with the newly discovered memo, potentially momentous political proportions. The Watkins memo was nine pages long, each making clear Hillary's centrality to the controversy. Worse, it was filled with the kind of language that D'Amato and others could have a field day with, given Hillary's persistent denials that she had anything to do with the Travel Office matter.

Inside the White House, the discovery of the memo sent the lawyers into another spasm of damage control, which lasted days before they finally turned it over to D'Amato. Hillary was set to begin her book tour for *It Takes a Village* on January 16, the triumphant event in her planned redemptive return to visibility at home. The publisher and author were looking forward to sales in the hundreds of thousands of copies as the first lady barnstormed the country delivering her message about the urgent needs of families and children in distress around the world. Watkins's memo made her sound neither first lady–ish, nor family-friendly.

Watkins had written that his memo was a "soul-cleansing . . . my first attempt to be sure the record is straight, something I have not done in previous conversations with investigators—where I have been as protective and vague as possible." That hardly improved the situation.

Watkins's memo was a classic "cover your ass" document that had not been intended for the White House files where a copy had been left behind (apparently accidentally), but rather was written for his lawyer in the event Watkins would ever be criminally investigated or charged in the matter. Watkins had been fired in 1994 for using a government helicopter to ferry him to a golf course, where he claimed he needed to play a round to scout a golf outing for the president. The helicopter ride had cost the government $13,000. Cronyism. Lady Macbeth. Hidden records. They were back to square one as the president was trying to cautiously approach the election season. The self-serving origins of the Watkins memo did not undermine its recitation of events, and its belated discovery, after months of denials, only underscored its capacity for damage. Hillary had said there would be "hell to pay" if Watkins didn't "take swift and decisive action in conformity with the first lady's wishes" to replace the Travel Office employees.

The congressional committees received the memo from the White House late in the day on January 3, four days after its discovery. William Clinger, the chairman of the House investigating committee, declared, "There was a cover-up here," requiring more hearings by his committee and further work by its investigators. Starr, in contrast to the lawyerly approach that his predecessor, Fiske, had adopted, publicly announced his "distress" at what had happened. "The White House had an obligation to turn this memorandum over to the Office of Independent Counsel as soon as it was discovered," he said, not several days later. D'Amato noted the "troubling pattern that keeps recurring involving Hillary Rodham Clinton."

The lead editorial in the next day's *Wall Street Journal* was "Who Is Hillary Clinton?," aping the headline of the *Journal*'s momentous attack on Vince Foster.

According to her aides, Hillary read the editorial. The *Journal* had devoted 1,600 words to its diatribe, three times the space ordinarily devoted to one of its editorials. The Watkins memo, said the *Journal*, confirmed D'Amato's contention that, in the first lady's case, there was a sinister pattern of denial and delayed discovery of information that contradicted earlier accounts claimed by her and the White House. The "related" matter of Whitewater was part of the pattern. As to whether Hillary had improperly sought state intervention on behalf of Jim and Susan McDougal's Madison Guaranty Savings & Loan, "The Rose Firm's billing records on the Madison account would, of course, clear up the issue, but the billing records have vanished," said the *Journal.* By the time Hillary read the editorial, the records had—disastrously, as it turned out for her—been found.

The disaster was less in what the billing records actually showed (lawyers, politicians, and bystanders alike would argue that question for years) than the impression of chicanery their discovery created; that eighteen months after their disappearance, with investigators pressing from all directions, the records suddenly appeared, in the office of Hillary's constant aide Carolyn Huber. The first lady's fingerprints were found on the records, specifically on a page that dealt with Madison Guaranty. Vince Foster's handwriting, in red pen, annotated numerous pages of the documents.

By any measure, this seemed to be damaging evidence.

They had been found, apparently on the morning of January 4, 1996, the day after public disclosure of the Watkins Travel Office memo, by Huber, who had managed the governor's mansion in Bill's first term, then served as the Rose Law Firm's administrator in the years Hillary was there, and now, ensconced in the White House, paid the Clintons' bills, maintained Hillary's and Bill's personal correspondence, and kept their financial records.

Huber said she had picked up the records—a half-inch sheaf of folded computer printouts—perhaps as much as ten months earlier, but most likely in the summer of 1995, from a small table in the Book Room, a kind of storage room, in which all manner of personal papers and gifts, including from foreign trips, were kept before being properly sorted. Space had to be created in the Book Room to accommodate Barbara Feinman's files for *It Takes a Village,* and things were being constantly moved around. She had not paid attention to what records she had taken; she simply put them into a box with some other items. They had languished in her own office since then, she said, even though subpoenas were issued ad infinitum and White House employees—including Huber—were ordered by the lawyers to search for them.

Some presidential aides in the White House—including critics of Hillary—found Huber's story plausible. Others deemed it absurd, particularly given her history as the Rose Law Firm's administrative manager and keeper of records. However, Huber was known in the White House

to be less than tidy and efficient at times, though one would expect someone with her job description to be well organized. Then again, the bulk
of records, papers, gifts, and books that kept accumulating from campaign to campaign and from Little Rock to Washington was enormous,
and kept being packed and unpacked and moved from one location to
another. As Huber told it, the box in which she found the records had
been sitting in her office on the second floor of the East Wing for
months; she just hadn't gotten to it yet. The box turned up (on January 4),
with several others, when she was disposing of some furniture in her
office, to make room for new bookshelves. They'd been under a big
table. She'd taken out the sheaf of papers—there was also a coat hanger
in the box—and that was when she saw that they were the billing records.

David Kendall and Jane Sherburne both said that Huber's hands were
shaking when she showed them the boxes and told them the story.

Kendall, apparently, had heard it once before. He said later that
Huber had called him that noontime, asked him to come to the White
House, showed him the records, and explained the circumstances. Then,
he said, sometime after 1 P.M., he'd gone to the National Gallery to see
the Vermeer show, for which he had a hard-to-get ticket. At 5 P.M., he
called Sherburne and told her he'd just had a call from Huber "and she
says she has found some documents that she thinks that I ought to look
at. And so I'm on my way over." He did not mention to Sherburne having seen the documents earlier in the day. "Well, let's go see what she's
got," he apparently told Sherburne when he got to her office in the West
Wing. The eleven-by-seventeen-inch pages were labeled "Madison
Guaranty: Client Billing & Payment History."

The lawyers were aware that, plausible as Huber's explanation might
have been to people who knew her and worked in the White House, it
would not fly smoothly in congressional and judicial Washington; with
the press, it would never get off the ground. Everything about the story
was strange, including Kendall's apparent withholding from Sherburne
that he had seen the records earlier in the afternoon—documents that
could cause enormous problems for Hillary—and then had sauntered off
to look at Vermeers. Why would one lawyer leave a fellow lawyer under
a false impression that he was hearing the story of the crucial witness for
the first time? (Kendall refused to discuss the matter with the author.)

Ken Starr would surely seize on what had happened with the billing
records as justification for trying to pin an obstruction of justice charge
on someone, and he would use the old prosecutorial tool of squeezing
one witness to get at another. And, in fact, as soon as Starr had the documents in his possession, he convened a staff meeting at which the prevailing view of his deputies was that all of Hillary's actions after Vince's death

seemed intended to conceal, and that she was a likely target for an obstruction of justice charge. The billing records were the most important circumstantial link to date. Starr wanted Hillary's testimony.

Sherburne urgently sought a meeting with the president to warn him of the obvious problems for Hillary. Clinton failed to see how the discovery of the billing records, or their contents, made Hillary or anyone else vulnerable: "Why would we be producing them now," she quoted him, "if we have been trying to hide them and obstruct. That doesn't make sense. Why would we have been hiding them if it was turning out that they're helpful or support what we have been saying all along?"

D'Amato, Chertoff, and Clinger would surely say these billing records were among the documents Maggie Williams surreptitiously removed from Foster's office, and which Officer O'Neill had seen her carrying.

Moreover, there was confusion and distrust among some of the lawyers themselves—more than a dozen were involved on behalf of the Clintons and the White House—once they had learned of the day's events. Some were less confident about what they were being told by their clients—Hillary and Bill—and the people acting on their behalf.

The records turned over to investigators by the White House later that day showed that in 1985–1986 Hillary billed about sixty hours for work on the Madison-McDougal account—"89 tasks, including 33 conferences or phone calls with Madison officials on 53 separate days." She had described her work as "very limited," and mostly supervisory. In two separate government investigations, she had denied working on a McDougal project, undertaken with Webb Hubbell's father-in-law, called Castle Grande. But the records showed that more than half the hours she billed were for that project. After that disclosure, she said she had known Castle Grande by a different name—IDC—and that her answer had been based on a semantic misunderstanding.

Kendall had recommended that the White House remain silent on all the questions raised by the discovery of the billing records. But at the insistence of the White House press secretary, Kendall made a statement from his office at Williams & Connolly. The records now turned over to Starr and Congress "confirm what we have said all along about the nature and amount of work done by the Rose Law Firm and Mrs. Clinton for Madison," said Kendall. "With the public release of these records, yet another set of baseless allegations can be laid to rest." But he had no explanation for why the billing records had disappeared in the first place.

Hillary's fear over the possibility of being indicted became palpable the day the billing records were found. It would become acute and terrifying for the next two years. "[It] could have been for obstruction," one of the lawyers said. "[It] could have been, These things were in your possession. You had a legal obligation to turn then over. . . . You didn't do it. The specter [of indictment] had already been raised by the discovery of this so-called Watkins memo just a week before the billing records."

Aides noticed a distinct change in Hillary's demeanor. She was angrier, and her anxiety about whether the lawyers were doing enough intensified. Before the discovery of the billing records, "everybody sort of thought our effort was successful because the D'Amato hearings didn't really get any traction, and nobody really cared about them," said the same attorney. "So everybody was sort of happy with the way things were going. But then, all of a sudden, Boom! . . . Everybody says, 'What are you people doing?' . . . I mean we had nobody defending us, for Sunday talk shows, which all of a sudden we needed. And we couldn't find anybody. And so she raised questions. 'What are you doing? Why don't we have surrogates? Why don't we have more people out there defending us?' And then she was . . . understandably concerned about what would happen. You know there was this specter of a search warrant being served on the White House. . . . But there were all sorts of possibilities, some of which didn't happen. And the grand jury is the first one that did. . . . She was subpoenaed to testify. So she was much more anxious, and who can blame her?"

Hillary asked aides why Democrats weren't coming to their defense. "People are nervous about taking a position that may not hold up," one of her aides reluctantly told her. "And, you know, we don't have answers for people. We can't tell them where these things [billing records] were. We can't tell them why it took two years to find them. So people don't want to go out there. And she would say, 'Yeah, but people should know that if I wanted to destroy these things I would have destroyed them. And they never would have been found. It's crazy to think that'—which is a decent argument."

PUBLICATION OF *It Takes a Village* had been scheduled for the first week of January, to be followed soon afterward by an eleven-city book author tour. Hillary's friend Jay Rockefeller described the book as "one of her ways of saying I'm still here" after her exile. "It was a campaign document," explained Neel Lattimore, her deputy press secretary, "but it was what she believed in, what she was all about. It was her writing something down for the first time. And it defined who she was in her commitment to children." It also attempted to explain to the world her commitment to her own daughter and family, including her husband, about whom she wrote in the book more thoughtfully and analytically than herself.

Perhaps the most painful aspect of the book for Hillary was that its elemental, truthful picture of herself as a wife and mother could be so at odds with what people saw on television news and read in their newspapers and magazines, that the perception of the public figure had become so negative that it overwhelmed even these basic truths about the private individual.

The promotional tour for the book—beginning with a Barbara Walters TV special—was largely for her personal redemption. But the tour became a schizoid marketing exercise, in which she would spend part of each day answering questions about the billing records, and the rest going to bookstores and signing autographs for the thousands of people who had lined up to buy the book. The profits were to go to children's hospitals and other charities—$1 million in the end.

Part of the money came from *Newsweek*, owned by the Washington Post Company, which had purchased the rights to excerpt the book and had intended to run a cover story on it the week of January 8. Instead, the cover line blared "Saint or Sinner?" above an unflattering picture of Hillary, and though the excerpts ran verbatim, inside, the cover story ("First Fighter") was more focused on Whitewater, the billing records, and general questions about the first lady's honesty than on the book. That same day, the influential *New York Times* columnist William Safire—an unscathed veteran of the Watergate-era Nixon White House—wrote a column calling Hillary a "congenital liar." Safire's epithet would become attached to the first lady for years. The president's press secretary, Mike McCurry, gave Safire's characterization enormous currency by declaring that if Bill Clinton weren't the president of the United States he would follow through with "a more forceful response to the bridge of Mr. Safire's nose," a statement that ensured its widest possible circulation.

The next day, in the Green Room of the White House, Hillary and Barbara Walters sat serenely bathed in flattering light, attended by makeup artists, for their long-scheduled interview. "Mrs. Clinton, instead of your new book being the issue, you have become the issue. How did you get into this mess, where your whole credibility is being questioned?" Walters began.

Hillary and Walters were friends. The first lady knew that the interview would have to address the matter, so she was prepared. "Oh, I ask myself that every day, Barbara," she said. "Because it's very surprising and confusing to me. But we've had questions raised for the last four years, and eventually they're answered and they go away and more questions come up and we'll just keep doing our best to answer them."

And the billing records?

"You know, a month ago people were jumping up and down because the billing records were lost and they thought somebody might have destroyed them. Now the records are found and they're jumping up and down. But I'm glad the records were found. I wish they had been found a year or two ago, because they verify what I've been saying from the very beginning. I worked about an hour a week for fifteen months [on the Madison account at Rose]. That was not a lot of work for me, certainly."

On January 15, when Diane Rehm, the host of a first-rate show broadcast over NPR from Washington, asked her about Whitewater, Hillary claimed she had consistently made public all the relevant documents—including "every document we had"—to the editors of the *New York Times* before its original Whitewater story ran in 1992.

Even her closest aides could not imagine what possessed her to say such a thing. It was simply not true, as Sherburne and the other lawyers—and the editors of the *Times*, who ran a page-one story about her latest twisting of the facts—recognized. Sherburne double-checked with Susan Thomases, the emissary who had tried to head off the original Jeff Gerth story in 1992. Told what Hillary had said, Thomases said, "Oh my God, we didn't," and explained how they had carefully cherry-picked documents accessed for the *Times*. The White House was forced—once again—to acknowledge the first lady had been "mistaken."

"All the work for the book, all the planning for the tour, it looked like it was going to be . . . the big thing to bring her back after '94. And now all of a sudden it was down the drain. Hillary was no longer depressed, per se . . . but was just resigned to perpetual beatings," said Mark Fabiani. "That hadn't stopped, and apparently was not likely to stop. And obviously [she had] some deep anxiety about being indicted. She was learning to live with the idea that she was going to be damaged goods."

It Takes a Village was not highly regarded by the critics. Because she is a sophisticated, knowledgeable advocate of children and families, it was hoped—as the *New York Times* noted in its review—that she would have produced "something deeper, sharper, and more tough-minded" than this "tepid and limited work." The book, however, sold well, and reached the top position on the *Times* best-seller list. The audio version, which she read herself, won a Grammy.

The book didn't reflect the serious political analysis or policy ideas of which Hillary was capable, or demonstrate any notable introspection. "There is no such thing as other people's children," Hillary had declared in interviews and speeches: this seemed to be the book's central thesis. With the breakdown of family structures and millions of children condemned to lives of poverty from Boston to Zimbabwe, all of society's institutions—not just government, but extended families, churches, charities, civic and business organizations—had to be enlisted to save them.

It Takes a Village is an extended Hillary-chat, the precursor of her "conversations" while running for president, delivered over the Internet from the warmth of a fireside hearth. She weaves personal anecdotes; vague, uncontroversial policy prescriptions; and pieties of the kind inscribed, in another era, on hand-sewn samplers. She describes her own and Bill's childhoods, with occasional emphasis on hardship; shows how their family members—particularly Virginia Kelley and Dorothy Rodham—persevered through difficulties and nourished their children with love; and expresses continual joy and wonderment at Chelsea and the experience she and Bill have shared as parents.

The chapter headings sound like bromides: "Security Takes More Than a Blanket," "Child Care Is Not a Spectator Sport," "Kids Don't Come with Instructions," "Children Are Citizens Too," "No Family Is an Island."

In these chapters, she enumerates the forces that corrode the village and family structure: video games, bad television, divorce, reckless globalization, inefficient health care, crime, bad schools, teenage sex.* There is nothing controversial enough for serious objection by any reasonable political caste. Her most vigorous advocacy is an honest reflection of her own "family values": prayer, religious study, churchgoing and affiliation; and working at marriage, through counseling if necessary, because divorce almost invariably leaves a scar on children, who need both mothers and fathers. For her detractors and political opponents who contend that Hillary's views on abortion, marriage, and adolescent sexual restraint have been tailored to fit her presidential ambitions, and represent some sudden and cynical move toward the political center, *It Takes a Village* contradicts that.

Her "strong feelings about divorce and its effects on children" caused her "to bite my tongue more than a few times" during her marriage and to think instead about what she could do "to be a better wife and partner." She and Bill had "worked hard at our marriage" with mutual respect and "deepening love for each other." Chelsea "enhances our commitment." Hillary acknowledges there are "reasons for divorce," citing the abuse and violence that Virginia Kelley experienced as something no parent or child ought to suffer. But with divorce "as easy as it is, and its consequences so hard," she urges parents to examine whether they have given a marriage "their best shot" and to seek more ways to make it work "before they call it quits."

---

*Sometimes Hillary sounded like the national nanny. She said she believed teenagers aren't ready for the unintended consequences of a sexual relationship, including pregnancy, venereal disease, or abortion. She said Americans should "do everything in our power to discourage sexual activity and encourage abstinence," adding that a good place to start is to encourage adolescents to value friendships first and to organize events in which young people can participate in supervised activities.

Mediating her reference to the difficulties of her own marriage are bons mots, lovingly delivered about the ironies and fun of sharing a house as a family—in this case a governor's mansion, and the White House. ("We're lucky that we 'live above the store,' the way a lot of families used to.") "One memorable night," she relates, Chelsea wanted her parents to buy her a coconut. The Clintons walked to the corner market, brought home a coconut, tried hammering it open, unsuccessfully. Finally mother, father, and child went out to the parking lot of the mansion, and took turns throwing the coconut onto the pavement until it cracked open. "The guards could not figure out what we were up to, and we laughed for hours afterward."

She tells homey stories of taking Chelsea to ballet class every Saturday and bringing her along for errands so they could spend more time together. It's as if the first lady's public stock had fallen so low that she felt compelled to prove that she is a loving mother.

The voice of *It Takes a Village* is unquestionably hers. Much of the book was composed on yellow legal pads, in longhand, after her collaborators and editors had tried to get her to dig deeper and beyond her penchant (even more evident in earlier drafts) for skimming the emotional surface with near-meaningless anecdotes.

Hillary's voice on the page was very similar to her public speaking voice. And her conversational voice, even with friends, could also mirror her public voice. Even in private, Hillary tends to articulate in whole paragraphs, rarely interrupting herself or needing to stop to struggle for the right word. This can be impressive in some settings, but other times it seems stilted, as if she is speaking from a set of sermons. Her private conversations are full of anecdotes, parables, vignettes that illustrate a point she is presenting. In both her talking and written voice there is a kind of grown-up Girl Scout–speak, full of concept words and phrases like "constructive citizenship," "civil society," "generational challenges." That kind of writing, combined with clichés, produced the sort of prose that made many reviewers cringe.

It Takes a Village is often banal: "Raising children, like most important work in our society, requires a constellation of skills and perspectives" and "Safety-minded parents keep household poisons, plastic bags, and matches out of reach." But the idea of community had always been vitally important to her, from her upbringing in Park Ridge, in her Arkansas years, in her earliest interpretation of American history—her high school papers and her college thesis about Saul Alinsky's community organizing in the impoverished neighborhoods of South Side Chicago. Hillary rightly sensed that, as America neared the twenty-first century, much of this sense of community, so essential to generations preceding her own, had been lost. She had rediscovered it initially in Africa, and later in other Third World societies, where people with little material wealth clung to their communal values as both a means of survival and cultural richness. In America, where families were disintegrating, she urged that old-fashioned resources of the village—churches, PTAs, neighborhood associations (of the kind her father had refused to join), community centers, and athletic leagues—serve as safety nets and sources for communal engagement for the family and for children. *Pitch in and help one another. Service is an obligation of citizenship.* An article of her faith had always been that families with some sort of institutional religious tie can weather storms better than families who don't. Washington, to her, was a "village" that had lost its soul.

Many of Hillary's aides thought the book was unvarnished, heroic Hillary: commonsensical, caring, concerned, feminine. But there were dissenters: "You know, turning a tuna casserole into a metaphor for community," said one disaffected aide who had seen too much of Hillary's other side. "Give me a break, when's the last time she took a casserole to a grieving friend?"

DESPITE HILLARY'S exile from the White House, working on the book had enabled her to discover and reconnect with aspects of her past and principles ameliorated in the years of attending disproportionately to Bill's career and worldview. The book—and the period of its preparation—turned out to be heavy on feminism, folklore, New Age concepts, human rights doctrine, traditional religion, psychology, and psychobabble. Conspicuously absent from the final text, though not from the book's original raison d'être, is realpolitik.

In some ways, *It Takes a Village* could be read as a logical extension of Hillary's Politics of Meaning speech, in which traditional values figured prominently. Yet in conception and execution, *It Takes a Village* also reflected Hillary's willingness to embrace New Age sensibilities, long an element of her spiritual quest but which in 1995 reached their ultimate expression.

The final draft reflected as never before the editorial help and thinking of Mary Catherine Bateson and Jean Houston. In November 1995, Houston had moved into the White House for weeks at a time to help Hillary on her book and offer general counsel and support. In the acknowledgments section of the book, Hillary didn't mention anyone by name, saying simply that "many people" had aided her and that she didn't want to mention individuals because she "might leave someone out."

When Hillary talked to her mother for the book, Dorothy, now that her husband was dead, seemed to open up more than in the past about her childhood and the abuse she suffered both as a child and an adult. "I don't think she [Hillary] knew the full extent" of her mother's abuse until she wrote the book, said Betsy Ebeling. Still, in the book, Hillary describes a "normal" family life, "straight out of the 1950s television sitcom *Father Knows Best*," and omits the true strains of her upbringing. Relatives were "a visible, daily part of the village," with grandparents, aunts, uncles, and cousins pitching in "if illness or some other misfortune strained the family." She does not mention such misfortunes as her father cutting his brother down from a noose. Rather, the examples of "pitching in" tend toward how, around the time she learned to walk, she grabbed a Coke bottle filled with turpentine, and started to drink it. "The adults around me reacted quickly to prevent serious consequences." From this primeval communal experience, she draws a lesson: "Parents should be willing to go toe-to-toe with their kids over taking certain precautions, like wearing helmets to bicycle, ride a motorcycle, skateboard or Rollerblade. . . . [W]earing helmets could prevent about forty thousand head injuries to children each year. Car safety seats, used properly, could help prevent another fifty-three thousand injuries in car accidents."

During the book tour, reporters were asking the White House whether, as rumor had it, Hillary's book had been "ghostwritten." To make clear it was *her* book, several reporters were invited to visit Hillary's private study to examine pages of the manuscript written on yellow legal pads in her hand. Soon, however, White House officials did acknowledge that Barbara Feinman had worked with Hillary for eight months. Feinman had worked with Hillary on the basic structure and content of about eight chapter drafts, which were rewritten after she left, aides said. Feinman had stayed overnight at the White House during 1995, and she accompanied the Clintons to Jay Rockefeller's Wyoming ranch for their vacation that summer to work on the book. In October, Feinman had taken a scheduled two-week break to go to Italy. Upon her return, she was informed that Hillary no longer required her services and that Simon & Schuster would withhold a quarter of Feinman's $120,000 fee. The White House told Feinman that Hillary had nothing to do with the fee being withheld, but privately, knowledgeable aides said otherwise.

> The actual writing experience of working on *It Takes a Village* with Mrs. Clinton was not extraordinary in any respect [Feinman wrote in *The Writer's Chronicle* in September 2002]. Together with our editor, we produced drafts in a round-robin style. We worked

well as a team and things went about as smoothly as can be expected when you're producing a high-profile book in eight months and one of you is married to the leader of the free world. The problem came when Mrs. Clinton decided, for reasons still a mystery to me, not to acknowledge my help, or that of anyone else by name. Because the White House had issued a press release early on in the process stating that I had been hired to "help prepare the manuscript," when it was finished and there was no mention of me in the acknowledgments, the anti-Clinton forces went to town— and began spreading the rumor the book was "ghostwritten."

When the "rumors" resulted in numerous news stories suggesting that Hillary had not treated Feinman well and that chapters were ghost-written, Simon & Schuster agreed to pay the full $120,000 fee.

HILLARY, in her interview with Barbara Walters, had recited a piece of childhood doggerel to describe her experience in the Whitewater con-tretemps:

> *As I was standing on the street,*
> *As quiet as could be*
> *A great big ugly man came up*
> *And tied his horse to me.*

On January 15, a few hours after Hillary appeared on Diane Rehm's show, Sherburne telephoned the first lady. She read her a statement in which the White House would concede Hillary's "mistake" in saying that all her Whitewater records were shown to the *New York Times* in 1992. Thus armed, the *Times* would run a front-page news story, in essence calling her a liar—a week after Safire had already called her that on its op-ed page. With the discovery of the billing records, the late-night television comedians were ridiculing her mercilessly.

Sherburne, now deadly serious, also informed Hillary that the independent counsel intended to subpoena her to testify before his grand jury. Hillary knew that Starr would be keen to have her perjure herself, and would be trying to establish grounds to indict her for obstruction of justice in the disappearance and belated discovery of the billing records. He would be asking her pointed questions about the Travel Office, and her denials to investigators of any involvement in the firings, and about what she had done in the hours and days after Vince Foster's death. Suddenly Hillary enumerated to Sherburne a litany of the indignities heaped on her over the past week:* "I can't take this anymore," she said. "How can I go on? How can I?"

Four days later, Hillary spoke at Wellesley College to promote her book, staying overnight on the shore of Lake Waban at the home of the president of the college. She awakened early and walked the wooded path that surrounds the lake. A quarter-century had passed since the afternoon of her commencement speech, after which she had gone back to her dorm, walked down to the lake, changed into her bathing suit, and gone for a swim to clear her head.

David Kendall reached her later in the morning, with news that Starr had formally subpoenaed her and was insisting that she testify in front of the grand jurors at the courthouse in downtown D.C., not be interviewed privately under oath at the White House, and a tape made for the jurors, as Fiske had permitted. Starr wanted her inside the jury room unaccompanied by her army of lawyers. This would be the first time in the country's history that a first lady had been summoned to testify in person before a grand jury. Hillary was traveling with Melanne Verveer, her deputy chief of staff. Though Verveer could see the first lady's agitation and distress, Hillary told her nothing specific about her conversation with Kendall. For months, Hillary had been reminded by the lawyers not to discuss anything relating to Whitewater with anybody but Bill and her attorneys; anyone she talked to who lacked a legal privilege was a potential witness against her.

Hillary returned to the White House "discouraged and embarrassed," worried that "whatever credibility I retained" was now being destroyed, and concerned about what her deteriorating reputation and legal situation were having on her husband's presidency. The presidential election was eleven months away, and she knew Starr would do everything in his power to find grounds for indicting her before then. In *Living History*, Hillary said Bill often expressed the wish he could do something to help. Chelsea, obviously concerned, kept close track of developments in the investigation and tried to comfort her mother. Hillary wrote she was unable to sleep and lost ten pounds in the week before her grand jury appearance, scheduled for January 26. She said she was angry, that she concentrated on preparing herself mentally and spiritually, focusing on her breathing (deep), and praying for God's help.

As she prepared with her lawyers for her appearance, they did not minimize the dangers she faced. Kendall, Sherburne, Ickes, and Fabiani

---

*The same day that Safire had called her a liar, the U.S. Court of Appeals in St. Louis ruled that Paula Jones could move ahead with her suit against the president.

all believed the odds were in favor of Starr seeking and probably obtaining an indictment. "When I say there was a serious fear that she would be indicted, I can't overstate that," said Fabiani.

The situation was aggravated by the fact that the lawyers could not come to agreement among themselves about what precisely had happened regarding the billing records. Huber's story kept changing in its details, particularly about when she had moved the billing records from the Book Room to her office. Hillary professed to know nothing about what had happened in regard to their disappearance or reappearance, but she obviously had been less than forthcoming in her past statements about the extent of her work on behalf of Madison and its subsidiaries, which had been recorded on the billing records, and which she had minimized in connection with the Resolution Trust investigation. It was not hard to see how a skilled and determined prosecutor could coax a compliant grand jury into bringing criminal charges—even against a first lady.

The senior attorneys on Ickes's team believed that she had gotten herself into a mess over next to nothing, that had she been forthcoming in the first place about events from Whitewater to the Travel Office, none of this would have come to pass. That kind of second-guessing was easy, they knew; it was also easy to see how the Jesuitical lying, evasion, and the stonewalling—about the Whitewater deal and its offshoots, at least— had begun during the first presidential campaign, after Jeff Gerth's story had appeared. Then matters had to be recast and explained again to loosely fit the version of events already shorn of the truth.

"Hillary had run everything" in the hours after Vince Foster's death, noted one of her lawyers. "Then she had denied it. You could see her . . . getting so intimately involved in . . . how you handle his office, and what are you going to do with the documents, and who's going to search the office. You can see her jumping into this." The discovery of the billing records, however, had changed everything.

"It was no longer just a political thing," no matter how serious. "We had seen the D'Amato hearings as a political matter," noted one of the lawyers. "This was a criminal matter." Once she had testified before the grand jury, Starr, with an army of FBI agents and federal prosecutors at his command, would spend months trying to tear her story apart, and searching for evidence of obstruction of justice and perjury. Kendall's holding on to the records for a day without notifying Starr had sharpened Starr's suspicions and appetite.

Several of the White House lawyers, including Sherburne, were skeptical of Huber's account. "Carolyn Huber [initially] called Kendall," said one. "When Kendall said, 'Where did you find these?' she didn't [immediately] go back to the summer and say, I remember seeing them on the table in the Book Room in the residence. Only later, when pressed by the FBI and then by the D'Amato committee, did she have a recollection of, I remember seeing these. It was sometime in . . . late July or early August, and I picked them up. I threw them in a box. The new year comes around, I'm cleaning out my office to where the box had been moved, and boom! I find them. I know they're important." The timing of their discovery did not inspire confidence, i.e., the day after the D'Amato committee's flagging investigation had been revived by David Watkins's memorandum about Hillary and the Travel Office.

Some of Hillary's lawyers believed that she had never wanted the billing records disclosed. Certainly that appeared true at the outset. She had had Foster make a copy of them in 1992, when Gerth had written his original story, apparently to see exactly what they showed—and then declined to give them to the *Times*. She had told the RTC that she had done virtually no work for Madison. She had always taken the position that as a lawyer she would never work for anybody who had pending business with the state. And, of course, the records turned out to show that she had, on behalf of Madison, the McDougals, and Webb Hubbell's father-in-law, Seth Ward.

Several of the lawyers kicked around theories about why Hillary acted as she had. Said one White House attorney, "This really goes to what you think of her . . . [and] the way she looks at herself, I think. Either she was embarrassed at having dealt with people like McDougal and was embarrassed by these business dealings and just didn't think they were the kind of thing that you would expect from a Yale Law graduate and one of the finest lawyers east of the Mississippi or west of the Mississippi or whatever in the world it was that people said about her, that it was just professionally embarrassing to be in that kind of a situation. And that it wasn't so much political damage control because, really, it was never going to be that much of an issue in the campaign. It wasn't going to be the kind of thing that was going to make people decide not to vote for [Bill Clinton] in a Democratic primary. Really it was personal embarrassment. . . . Maybe she just didn't want people to know that this is what her life was . . . small-time stuff, too. Her law practice, for example. The billing records are embarrassing, maybe for what they show about how she spent her time, which was not in any kind of high-minded or incredibly intellectual pursuit of the law, which is sort of her reputation, but [these were] small-potatoes deals. And a lot of people [on the White House legal team] believed that. I don't know what I believe about why she mishandled it, except that she was probably very suspicious then of the press and thought that you could gut it out and get through it, and it would go away and life would go on."

And then there was her promise when she went to work for the Rose Law Firm not to work for clients who had state business and the Bar Association's waiver Vince Foster had obtained for her, as the attorney general's wife, to join the firm. "The billing records are going to show that she did work for . . . a number of people that had connections: the McDougals. Seth Ward. So, in Foster's phrase, which he used later, it was a can of worms for her. That . . . once you let someone into your practice, maybe it turns out that you weren't quite as careful ethically, or maybe it just turns out that you don't want people to know that what you did on a daily basis was sort of . . . crude."

The evidence suggested Hillary might not have done some of the work for which clients were billed at her hourly rate, that in fact drafting attributed to her had been done by clerks and junior lawyers at the firm. This suggested to the same lawyer "that she was getting paid because she was the governor's wife. . . . The reason why that theory has some currency is she truly doesn't seem to know anything about [some] of the stuff that she supposedly worked on. Now, a cynical person would say . . . she's got a good memory and she remembers a lot of the stuff [but doesn't want to recall it]. The other answer is she never really did the work. . . . I think that she probably didn't do a lot of the work."

The D'Amato hearings, now reinvigorated, became the longest-running congressional investigation of a sitting president in history (though most of it had to do with his wife). C-SPAN broadcast them (seemingly endlessly). The ratings spiked briefly only when Vince Foster's death was on the agenda, and just after the billing records were found. Producers of the network evening news broadcasts thought their audience would be driven off by the accumulation of arcane detail.

"The biggest mistake D'Amato made in his hearings," said one of the White House lawyers, "upon the discovery of the billing records, he immediately, for some stupid reason, started to focus on what they said. I mean how many hours she did this. And how many hours she did that. And it's like wait a minute, Who cares about that? Instead of, Where were they [the records]? Who was keeping them secret? That's the interesting issue to people. But he immediately lost the focus of the whole thing by talking about how many hours she spent on this or that. We were more than happy to debate that with him because it was all impenetrable to people, and nobody really cared."*

---

*There was speculation by some presidential aides that "Foster had written a separation agreement for divorce papers and that's what was in there, and that's what was taken out of there that night after he killed himself," one of the lawyers said, and did not totally discount it. The existence of such a document was never confirmed.

Ken Starr did. He saw the billing records as a great tool for bringing an indictment against Hillary.

On January 26, rather than unobtrusively entering the U.S. District courthouse for the District of Columbia, she waded through the press mob and their cameras and microphones. Her intent—and effect—in testifying was to appear self-assured, nonconfrontational, and respectful of the jurors. Twenty-one were present, ten of them women, and perhaps 75 percent were African-American. Starr and eight of his deputy prosecutors—all white males who were Starr look-alikes, Hillary said—followed them into the grand jury room.

As her lawyers had expected and prepared her for, much of the questioning was about the perambulations of the billing records, not their substance. Starr, who seemed constitutionally unable not to exude sanctimony and piety, had on this occasion decided to let one of his deputies ask the questions. Under oath, Hillary testified that she, too, was "mystified" by the sudden appearance of the documents "after all these years." She might have seen them when they were generated in 1992, during the campaign, she said. How and why they had been taken to the residence from Vince Foster's office, and what stops they had made in various rooms upstairs she hadn't a clue, except what she'd been told by David Kendall when he informed her that Carolyn Huber had found the records in her office under a table, in a box.

Hillary was patient when questions were rephrased, over and over. She was a good witness, and that very skill had been the subject of a meeting in Maggie Williams's office two days earlier, in which the lawyers debated among themselves (Hillary was not present) whether she should also testify before the D'Amato committee, making a potentially beneficial preemptive strike.

"Some people made the argument that the only way that she could possibly rehabilitate herself in short order between now and the election would be to go to the Senate," said one aide. "Give testimony and be open and forthright." The idea's chief proponent was Bob Bennett, who saw it as a way—among other things—of overshadowing her sensational appearance as a prospective criminal defendant marching into a federal courthouse. The contrary argument was that Hillary would give D'Amato's committee credibility it didn't deserve, and lay down another set of sworn answers that could be used against her for a perjury indictment.

She marched out of the courthouse at 6 P.M. with her head held high. She stepped into a scene otherworldly even by Washington standards. On a winter's night, the courthouse plaza was enveloped in garish white light from the candlepower of hundreds of television crews, so bright that it was difficult to see without squinting. Helicopters hovered overhead, casting search beams downward for aerial shots for the networks and local news, the sky buzzing from their rotors and those of police and Secret Service helicopters.

Above the noise, Hillary's answer to the most obvious question was perfectly articulated: "I, like everyone else, would like to know the answer about how those documents showed up after all these years. I tried to be as helpful as I could in their [the grand jury's] investigation efforts."

Bill and Chelsea met her with hugs at the White House. Kendall and his colleagues were pleased with her testimony. Hillary, however, was "angry, agitated, worried," according to one of the lawyers, and ready to go on the attack.

"It was her against everybody," the attorney said. "Starr had forgotten about Bill Clinton basically." Hillary had now seen firsthand that she was fighting for her life.

"She became very upset that Starr was getting a free ride from the media," noted Mark Fabiani. She wanted an all-out offensive. Until Starr had ordered her to the courthouse, Kendall had thought it possible to work with him, and he had noted Starr's reputation for fairness, based on his record as a judge in cases decided in favor of newspapers. Hillary thought his First Amendment views explained why the press treated him with undue respect. Now, Kendall's objections disappeared.

"Starr wasn't the kind of guy you could chop down in a week or two," said Fabiani, who was asked to formulate a strategy. "I tried to make a case to her that the best thing to do is try to seed stories out there that were legitimate: Should Starr still be working for his law firm, making a million dollars a year? Shouldn't he be doing this [the independent counsel's job] full-time? Should he still be speaking around the country? Should he be representing the tobacco companies? And ultimately people started to write about those things. But she was very frustrated it was so slow. . . . She said, If we did the kind of things that Starr did, we'd be thrown out of here. Why don't people focus on that stuff?"

She initiated a morning conference call with lawyers and aides to review each day's events and develop assignments. One of the participants recalled, "Every morning at eight or 8:30 there would be a call where she would basically scream about what was in the paper in the morning [She was either reading them or getting summaries of what she needed to know for her own defense now.], and ask us what we were doing about it. She was religious about it. And she got very concerned that we weren't doing enough."

Until her grand jury appearance, only Kendall had Hillary's permission to deal with Arkansas, Whitewater, or Rose firm matters, with the exception of Bennett, who was handling the Paula Jones case. "The rest of us handled everything that had occurred after they [the Clintons] got to Washington. So, for example, we would do Vince Foster's suicide documents, but Kendall would do the Whitewater investigation," said a member of Sherburne's team. Once, Hillary exploded at Fabiani when he was quoted in a newspaper story about the Whitewater investment. "She just got furious. She said, 'This is Kendall's. You don't talk about that.'" Partly because Kendall disliked doing TV interviews and talking to the press, the arrangement was becoming untenable: "And Kendall was more than happy to let us talk about anything, as long as he was involved in deciding what to say." Meanwhile, Hillary would spray the lawyers with phone calls throughout the day about something that was being said on TV or a story brought to her attention.

"What she's very good at is sort of marshaling the forces," said one of them. "Get people ready to fight, get them together. Find the right people, find a Harold Ickes. And then have Harold go find people. But when it comes down to the tactics about, Now what do we do? What do we say? How do we handle this? That's where her instincts are just awful." An instance of that was her determination to systematically attack the *Washington Post*.

The idea of a campaign against the *Post* "went fairly far down the road before some of us succeeded in stopping it," said Fabiani. Hillary told her aides: "We have to figure out all the mistakes that the *Post* has made. We're going to document it, and then publicize it somehow or get a journalism review to write an article about it, or go to the *Post* editors and complain about Sue Schmidt with this evidence, this dramatic evidence in hand." She summoned a group to the residence: Kendall, Stephanopoulos, Sherburne, Fabiani, Maggie Williams. Fabiani said the first lady pointed at him, saying: "'You can take it over and meet with Len Downie [the editor of the *Post*] and . . . go through this, and then we can publicize it.' I said, 'Well, you know, I'm not sure that the content of it is going to be quite as dramatic as maybe you'd hoped for. A lot of the things that you're concerned about are matters of tone, and maybe a headline, or a placement in the paper, and that's not exactly the sort of stuff that's going to grab people.' And she said, 'No, if you look at it, I'm sure it's going to be true. Go ahead.'"

For the next ten days or so, a team worked to compile a dossier to be used against the *Post*. Finally, the virtually unanimous opposition of the lawyers and Stephanopoulos prevailed.

This reflected a new reality. "Mostly she was persuadable," said Fabiani. "But it took a lot of work, a lot of times it felt like she was going to eat you alive, or you weren't going to be there the next day. But, if people stood up to her, she listened. To her credit. When some of us stood up to her, she generally would back down. But the kind of people that were around her were yes people. She had never surrounded herself with people who could stand up to her, who were of a different mind. . . . I always thought that was a real tragedy in that if she had had different people around her [who would challenge her] earlier, that maybe some of the things that happened might not have happened."

Hillary was active and outspoken again, but hardly optimistic. "Well, okay, go ahead and do it, but it's not going to work," she would say. "We're never going to get a fair shake." Some problems were manageable, but for her, everything seemed doom and gloom, her lawyers could see. Much of the gloom no doubt reflected her fear of indictment. Kendall had told her at some point he believed her indictment was a strong possibility, that Starr would stop at nothing. Even if he failed, Maggie Williams had noted, the remainder of the term, the next year, would be dominated by the effort to criminalize and further stigmatize the first lady. The first three years had been dominated by Vince's suicide, the death of health care reform, the loss of the Congress . . . and now this. "We had all these great hopes, and they've come to nothing," said Williams.

As BILL and his aides developed a strategy for the 1996 presidential campaign, the phrase "damaged goods" was frequently used in the White House to describe Hillary's political utility and, sadly, more. She avoided planning meetings, preferring to give her opinions to her husband in private. "I would meet with her every two weeks from around July '95 until August of '96," said Dick Morris, "and I would have to brief her on what was going on. I would have to brief her on the ads that were running. I would have to brief her on the polling data. This was not stuff she knew. And while, allegedly, the agendas I prepared were given to her, and I'm sure that Bill did give them to her, she didn't seem to know it [the material] and wasn't terribly involved. And that was amazing to me. Her husband was running for reelection as president, and she really wasn't there."

Bill was enjoying the transition from entrapment in the White House to flat-out campaigning, and the opportunity to change some misperceptions.

There was no attempt, however, to rebuild Hillary's image before the election. "There was a deliberate calculation made that she was going to be damaged goods through the election," said one of the president's aides. On the occasions when she was scheduled to campaign on Bill's behalf, "it was understood that you would place her in with the hard-core [pro-Clinton] constituencies that weren't going to be affected by any of this [scandal talk]. She wasn't going to be able to go anyplace where there weren't true believers. . . . You weren't going to solve the credibility problems that she had unless you did something dramatic, and that carried huge risks. What if she were indicted? If she wasn't indicted, she was going to sort of limp along to the election. She was going to speak to women's groups and hard-core Democratic groups, and liberal groups, and raise money from those people. And her favorability rating was going to be what it was going to be. And over time it would get better, but you had to live with it."

Inside Hillaryland there was considerable consternation about the first lady being sacrificed. But the president had made a calculated decision. "Why didn't Bill defend his wife more vocally? Why didn't he sort of constantly buck her up? I mean he said the perfunctory things about her," a political aide noted, "but, you know, he was smart. He knew the less he said about this stuff, the better. The more he said, the more people would talk about it. . . . I mean that was our advice to him, and that was his instinct as well."

Bill Clinton's 1996 reelection strategy, especially before the Republicans had chosen their nominee, was to highlight the positive, incremental initiatives his administration had implemented, and the economy, which was stabilized and showing the first signs of explosive growth. The scandal-mongering, in Bill's view, had kept voters from the real story of what his presidency had accomplished under the most difficult circumstances: a minimum wage increase, changes in the Safe Drinking Water Act, acquisition of new lands for national parks, a crime-fighting bill, the Earned Income Tax Credit, an anti–teen smoking initiative, and serious educational reform, among other things. The Republicans had shut down the government during the previous November's budget battle, and he was happy to run against the opposition's irresponsibility.

Looking toward the Democratic convention, to be held in Chicago in August, Morris's polling indicated that the so-called scandals of Whitewater were having little effect on the voters—a conclusion that Bill found dubious, especially because Hillary's poll numbers had hit rock bottom. He seemed invested in holding the press and the Clintons' enemies responsible for stripping himself and Hillary of their dignity and political effectiveness. His tendency to self-pity was well established, but on this point his anger was understandable. Morris kept telling him, "None of this is having any effect as long as you don't make it an issue." Clinton formed the impression—probably correctly—that Morris believed that he and Hillary had been fast and loose both about the finances of their Whitewater investment and in their responses to the investigations that had marked them, thus making the president all the more angry.

. . .

ON FEBRUARY 27, Chelsea turned sixteen. Not long after, the president and first lady attended "college night" at Sidwell Friends School with Chelsea. She was a high school junior—motivated, self-possessed, bright, and remarkably unspoiled given the circumstances of her upbringing. On the way back to the White House, she surprised Hillary and Bill by saying she might like to go to Stanford University, in California. Her mother immediately responded that it was three time zones away and that, trapped in the White House, she and Bill would almost never get to see her. Bill told Chelsea she could go wherever she wanted. She had earned it.

A few weeks after her birthday, Chelsea traveled with her mother to Bosnia, now pacified, to meet with American peacekeeping troops there. Singer Sheryl Crow and comedian Sinbad were on the trip as well. The Dayton accords brokered by Clinton and his emissary, Deputy Secretary of State Richard Holbrooke, which ended the bloodletting among Croats, Serbs, and Muslims, was one of the great achievements of the administration, both morally and practically. (Yet neither the Clinton administration nor George W. Bush's administration—which never was willing to credit its immediate predecessors with success of any kind— sought to capitalize diplomatically from the fact that the United States, alone among the nations of the world, had sent troops to stop the genocide of Muslims.)

During Hillary's trip to Bosnia she spent many hours talking to individual soldiers about their view of the American commitment. That helped convince her that the United States military must continue to maintain secure borders and be engaged in some areas of historic conflict. Though it had been American policy since U.S. troops had stood between Israel and Egypt in the Sinai and the demilitarized zone between the two Koreas, Republicans (and some Democrats) were increasingly pursuing a more isolationist foreign policy in which European troops, not Americans, would be responsible for military commitments closer to home. Hillary's contrary view would figure later when she was a senatorial candidate and, more controversially, in regard to Iraq.

WITH THE DEATH of health care reform, Bill and his advisers considered it essential to follow through on his 1992 campaign pledge to "end welfare as we know it." Hillary shared his view that the existing system of welfare payments corroded the lives of millions of families who subsisted on them. This had become a poisonous subject of political debate, with most recipients subject to unfair characterizations such as "welfare queens"—people who supposedly lived the high life on their family's meager monthly payments. Contrary to what too many Americans believed, "welfare" went only to families with children at home—unlike unemployment payments for individuals who had lost or could not find jobs.

Since Republicans had won control of Congress at the midterm elections, conservatives had been trying to take over the welfare reform debate by introducing punishing modifications to the federal government's program, Aid to Families with Dependent Children, as welfare was known. Gingrich's "Contract with America" proposed a Personal Responsibility Act, which aimed to discourage teen pregnancy and illegitimate children by disallowing benefits to mothers who were minors and denying additional funding to those who had more children. Many of the Gingrich Republicans wanted to abolish the concept of welfare outright. Hillary and Bill both believed changes to the system should be much less harsh, and include funding for guaranteed job training and child care to help recipients as they went back to work.

Virtually all of the administration's experts on welfare and the organized "children's advocates" in Washington—including Marian Wright Edelman—opposed the kind of welfare reform that had been introduced in Congress late in the year. On November 3, 1995, Edelman wrote an open letter to the president in the *Washington Post* saying that it would be wrong for him to sign any legislation that would "push millions of already poor children and families deeper into poverty, as both the House and Senate welfare bills will do." She added: "Both the Senate and House welfare bills are morally and practically indefensible. Rather than solve widespread child deprivation, they simply shift the burden onto states and localities with far fewer federal resources, weakened state maintenance of effort and little or no state accountability."

Edelman's letter was intended as well for Hillary, who, given her professional history, had greater credibility on the issue than Bill and, despite her legal difficulties with Ken Starr, more specific political capital. Edelman knew that reporters covering the welfare debate would seize on her letter as putting Hillary under pressure from her close friend.

There was little danger that the president would sign the legislation under consideration by Congress, but Edelman—and Hillary—were less confident about what Bill might wish to do if squeezed in an election year. Hillary had never publicly opposed any legislation or policy of her husband's administration, but her views about welfare were strongly held and probably more complicated than his. She recognized the urgency of reform, she wrote, but her work as a child advocate had taught her that welfare was often required as a bridge of emergency support for impoverished families. She had seen the system exploited, but there were many instances in which it had rescued its beneficiaries. She told Bill and his deputies that she would make known her opposition to legislation that did not provide health care through Medicaid (to avoid cutoffs of welfare funds by the states), a federal guarantee for food stamps, and guaranteed child care assistance for recipients transitioning out of the welfare system. Bill vetoed the first welfare reform bill, which was part of a proposed Republican budget.

When Republicans passed a second bill in early January 1996 "with minimal changes," the president again vetoed it, and his action required little lobbying from Hillary.

In August, as the Democratic convention loomed and the prospect of an ugly election debate over welfare threatened, Bill had to decide whether to sign or veto a third welfare reform bill, largely shaped by the Republican majority and lacking many of the safeguards Hillary had specified. He feared, with good reason, that if he didn't sign the legislation, a great chance to enact serious welfare reform would be lost.

The latest bill required those who received welfare to work—plain and simple. It also instituted a lifetime benefit limit of five years, and reduced the federal welfare spending program by $54 billion over a six-year period. A particularly objectionable provision of the legislation was the elimination of benefits for most legal immigrants. Critics tried to persuade Hillary to talk the president out of signing the bill. Peter Edelman, who held the position of counselor to Health and Human Services Secretary Donna Shalala, urged that the bill be vetoed, as did Shalala. Hillary, Bill, and the Edelmans all had the same concerns—that the bill would throw millions of children into poverty, especially the children of immigrants.

Shalala's objections had troubled her particularly. Lynn Cutler, deputy assistant to the president for intergovernmental affairs, who discussed the matter with both Hillary and Shalala, noted that the first lady saw welfare reform first and foremost as a question that affected women and children. "Why should a huge number of women be condemned to a life on the [dole] instead of getting an education, getting the help, and having the self-respect of earning a living?" she said. "And I suspect at some level she [Hillary] absolutely believed in that. I think what might have concerned her, given her Children's Defense Fund background, was that the child care piece and the support pieces weren't there in quite the same way that they ought to."

Bill had always been inclined toward compromise to win a political fight, but as the death of health care reform had demonstrated, this had not been Hillary's way. But she had learned a punishing lesson about the perils of not compromising. In all likelihood, this would be the only chance she and Bill would have to accomplish something they had talked about for years. It *was* an imperfect bill, but Hillary was becoming inclined to support it. Later, many commentators speculated (and some reported as fact) that she had urged Bill not to sign the legislation and was angered when he did. In fact, she accepted the decision as inevitable.

Carl Sferrazza Anthony, author of a number of books and articles about first ladies, asked Hillary in 1999 whether she and her husband had disagreed on signing the bill. He said she told him, "I was in favor of welfare reform. I . . . just wanted to make certain that there was a safety net that . . . if the welfare-to-work didn't work in some cases, that families weren't out on the street."

On July 31, Bill and his cabinet members met for what George Stephanopoulos described as the "final decision meeting" about whether the president would sign the welfare legislation. Dick Morris vehemently told Clinton he would lose the election by 3 percentage points if he didn't sign the bill. Stephanopoulos believed that Hillary would rather Bill veto the reform, yet "after the failure of health care, and given the persistence of Whitewater, political prudence and the balance of power in their marriage weighed against a decisive Hillary intervention on welfare," he said. He sensed she was trying to gently note its flaws.

At a press conference later on August 22, Bill told reporters he would sign the bill, describing it as a timely, excellent chance to reform welfare. Hillary called it a "critical first step" to reforming welfare. She said she wanted Bill to sign it into law; though she was disconcerted by the five-year time limit, she felt importantly that it tried to foster independence rather than dependence.

In Hillary's autobiography, she described the bill as hardly perfect, and conceded that pragmatic politics had figured in her willingness to support the measure. She felt it was better to allow the bill to become law with a Democratic administration in charge of implementing it. She recognized that if Bill vetoed welfare reform a third time, he would be giving the Republicans an edge in November, risking not just his own reelection, but endangering other Democratic candidates as well. Eventually Hillary and Bill claimed great success for welfare reform.

The Clintons' decision came at a personal cost. Peter Edelman resigned in protest a few weeks after the legislation was signed by the president. For years the Edelmans shunned the Clintons; the breach was painful. Hillary went to great lengths in her memoir to recognize the sincerity and reasonableness of the Edelmans' opposition. But she said as well that there were times political realities required compromise, though never on "principles and values." As a senator and presidential candidate, many of her former supporters and other opponents felt she had done just that, especially in regard to the great issue of her time in the Senate: Iraq.

THE DEMOCRATIC CONVENTION in Chicago was something of a coronation for Bill. The Republicans, as he had expected, had nominated Bob Dole for president. The economy was finally showing evidence of a boom: ten million new jobs had been added to the workforce since Bill had taken office. The combined rate of unemployment and inflation was the lowest in twenty-eight years.

For years, Bill had been using the phrase "a bridge to the future" to describe his goals and policies. Now Dick Morris and Clinton made clear Dole was a link to the past, a Washington insider with thirty-five years in Congress. That was plenty of time to establish a voting record that could be picked apart for inconsistencies, particularly as his party had moved rightward and he had occasionally embraced the more extreme policies and views of the far right.

The only glitch in the convention script was Morris's mania, which had become a real problem, even as he had been of enormous help. He was responsible for "brilliant engineering of Clinton's comeback," said Stephanopoulos, in getting Bill back on his feet since the disasters of 1994. Morris, despite his professed dislike of personal publicity, was on the cover of *Time* magazine that week, telling how he had done it, and he was readily available to the reporters who lined up to interview him to tell them more. Meanwhile, he tried to scrap speeches carefully prepared by Al Gore and Hillary for prime-time delivery, and replace their themes with his own hastily composed thoughts, which meandered. "Dick's gone bad. Someone's gonna have to put him down," said Harry Thomason.

Ultimately, Morris did that to himself. On the evening of his great triumph, helping resurrect the presidency of Bill Clinton, he resigned. He had been hinting that something bad was coming, that he might be portrayed shabbily in a personal story the *Star* tabloid was threatening to run about him and a prostitute. The *Star* coverage was far worse: not only had he been photographed with the prostitute at a suite in the tony Jefferson Hotel in downtown Washington, he had allowed her to listen in on his phone calls with the president. She was quoted extensively in the piece, about her numerous meetings with Morris, who had bragged to her about writing the vice president's and first lady's convention speeches. Bill, meanwhile, seemed happy to see Morris go. He had done his job and was now expendable.

Hillary was concerned that Morris might commit suicide. Sensing how deeply troubled he was, she had issued a stern directive to the president's aides not to make any comment that might aggravate him or trip a circuit. This was a presidency that had already seen far too many deaths: in addition to Vince Foster, the naval chief of staff had recently committed suicide, following news reports that he had not earned the combat medals he wore; Secretary of Commerce Ron Brown, the former Democratic National Committee chairman who was close to both Hillary and Bill, had died with thirty-four others in a plane crash in Croatia in early April.

Hillary delivered her speech—which she had written herself, with some polishing by her aides—to thunderous applause by the twenty thousand conventioneers. Hillary's mother, brothers, Betsy Ebeling, and other hometown friends watched the speech from a suite high above the stage. Hillary had been taking lessons from Michael Sheehan, a media coach who was, among other things, trying to teach her how to use the TelePrompTer. She worried she might look "like a robot." She had also asked Bill to review her speech with her the previous day.

Hillary took her theme from Bob Dole, whose acceptance speech had attempted to bring her, unfavorably, back into the political spotlight. He had used her as the exemplar of those who would have the government intrude into every area of American life, including the family. He had implied that Hillary's book *It Takes a Village* used the village as a metaphor for the state—which it most certainly did not. "And after the virtual devastation of the American family, the rock upon which this country was founded," said Dole, "we are told that it takes a village, that is collective, and thus the state, to raise a child. . . . And with all due respect, I am here to tell you it does not take a village to raise a child. It takes a family to raise a child."

Hillary turned it around. She talked about "raising our daughter," and "that to raise a happy, healthy, and hopeful child, it takes a family. It takes teachers. It takes clergy. It takes businesspeople. It takes community leaders. . . . Yes, it takes a village.

"And it takes a president.

"It takes a president who believes not only in the potential of his own child, but of all children, who believes not only in the strength of his own family, but of the American family.

"It takes Bill Clinton."

FOR THE PRESIDENT the campaign was exhilarating. Though there seemed to be little doubt about the outcome, he was concerned that Starr might seek to indict Hillary before the election. This would be the ultimate "October Surprise," a term in the political lexicon that had come to mean a terrifying last-minute jolt or event that could knock a candidate off his horse. The Clinton campaign needed to raise more cash continually to match the spending of the Republicans. In the process, the campaign's managers were looking for money wherever they could find it—including the sale of nights to be spent in the Lincoln Bedroom and the Queen's Bedroom across the hall in the White House. The Clintons' fund-raising—Hillary was among those who picked paying guests for Lincoln's old room—provided fertile new ground for Starr's inquiry.

This led to renewed prosecutorial pressure on Webb Hubbell, who insisted he was being persecuted because of his association with the Clintons, and he had no more information to give the independent counsel about Bill and Hillary. Hubbell had been paid hundreds of thousands of dollars in consulting fees in the fifteen months between his guilty plea and entering prison, including by some of the Clinton campaign's biggest contributors, notably officials of a multinational firm known as the Lippo Group, with large operations in Indonesia. Starr and his deputies were determined to prove that Hubbell had performed no real work for this largesse. His Lippo employer, James Riady, had made a $200,000 contribution to the Clinton campaign after a limousine ride with Bill, and a big bundler of campaign cash who was associated with Lippo, John Huang, was appointed to a major position in the commerce department. Hubbell had known the Riady family since they had invested in an Arkansas bank in the 1980s with another Rose Firm partner. Millions of dollars had been raised for the campaign by Huang and his friends, much of it funneled through a maze of American subsidiaries of Asian firms.

Details were hard to follow, but any newspaper reader could tell that the whole mess reeked. But of what exactly, aside from the obvious desire—shared by thousands of big campaign contributors, Republican and Democrat—for influence and access? Johnny Chung, a Democratic fund-raiser who later pleaded guilty to funneling illegal contributions to the Clinton campaign, had shown up one day in Hillary's office with a check for $50,000 for the reelection committee. "You take, you take," he demanded of some startled Hillaryland aides. Maggie Williams was summoned, and she accepted the check, then sent it over to the DNC. Chung explained his methodology to an interviewer: the White House was "like a subway: You have to open the gates."

Bill, meanwhile, angrily asserted that "no one around here" knew of Hubbell's employment arrangements as a consultant to various enterprises. That was demonstrably false. Mack McLarty had made calls to help Hubbell get a job and testified (much later) that he'd told Hillary about it. Vernon Jordan and Erskine Bowles, the White House chief of staff, had also been enlisted—by Bruce Lindsey—to help.

FOR HILLARY, the conflict with Starr was almost a death struggle. She did not doubt that he wanted to destroy her and her husband. "You never felt you knew how Starr was going to impact the election," said Melanne Verveer. "You had weeks and weeks and months of imponderable horrors."

Hillary's orders to Fabiani and other aides to urge reporters to write about Starr's operation, and the prosecutor's acts of indisputable injudiciousness, were finally subjecting him to some degree of journalistic oversight. While an independent counsel, Starr had gone into federal appeals court to defend the nation's tobacco companies against a class action lawsuit brought on behalf of millions of Americans. The Clinton Justice Department, with numerous state attorneys general, had been the motivating force in finally bringing them to heel for medical costs associated with lung cancer. Starr's firm received $1 million a year from the tobacco industry. The president had initiated a ban on cigarette advertising aimed at teenagers and imposed other restrictions on the industry's advertising practices. How could an "independent" special prosecutor be investigating the president and first lady given this conflict of interest?

On September 23, in an interview with Jim Lehrer for his PBS *NewsHour*, Bill, for the first time in public, said what he really thought about Starr and his investigation. Lehrer noted that Susan McDougal had refused to testify (and been sentenced to jail for contempt) because, she said, it was obvious that Starr "was out to get the Clintons."

"There's a lot of evidence to support that," said the president.

Lehrer twice gave Clinton the opportunity to qualify the statement. He declined.

"But do you personally believe that's what this is all about, is to get you and Mrs. Clinton?"

"Isn't it obvious?" the president said.

Starr reacted furiously. The president had, unequivocally, accused him of unethical conduct, and he demanded, in a series of letters to the White House that went unanswered, a retraction. Privately, after Starr and his prosecutors had come to interview him at the White House that summer, Bill said, "They were the sleaziest, filthiest people you could imagine. I wanted to take a shower after it was over." At one point, apparently seeking a box they believed might have been removed from Foster's office and might contain something relating to the billing records, they had demanded a full household search of the White House living quarters, including Chelsea's room and Hillary's bedroom drawers. The search had, after much negotiation, been undertaken by Sherburne and witnessed by the head White House usher in lieu of a subpoena that would have required the FBI to conduct it. Nothing turned up.

The decision to fight Starr outside the grand jury room and beyond the reach of his subpoenas, vicious as the hand-to-hand combat was becoming, represented Hillary's thinking at its most clearheaded. She wasn't wrong that Starr would try to stretch the law and use his almost unlimited powers to indict her—or seek the impeachment of the president. But if he knew he was going to be more carefully scrutinized, and if more outrage among Democrats on Capitol Hill could be stirred by demonstrating his excesses, it might constrain him, especially in the midst of a presidential campaign when he could be credibly accused of partisanship if he brought an indictment against the first lady. Individual members of his prosecutorial staff maintained direct lines to Republicans on Capitol Hill; his office leaked constantly. (There were no leaks from the office of Leon Jaworski, the special prosecutor during the Nixon era.)

In September and October, when the press began reporting on the Riady organization's fund-raising and contributions to Bill's campaign—and its employment of Webb Hubbell in 1994—Starr and his deputies saw an opportunity to squeeze Hubbell and his wife. Surmising that the payment represented some kind of hush money, and that they had missed part of the big picture the first time around, they went back to Hubbell and questioned him again; as part of his plea bargain, he was obliged to answer prosecutors' questions. He produced no additional useful information. In fact, there is little reason to think that Hubbell possessed the kind of knowledge that Starr and his investigators were in search of.

Starr was looking for a grand conspiracy, and failing that, specific instances of when the president or, more likely, the first lady lied under oath. But he had little specific idea of wrongdoing beyond the first lady's obvious disingenuousness regarding the Travel Office, and some vague notions that the "Whitewater" finances were not what the Clintons and their aides had represented.

The president had dismissed any connection between meeting with the Riadys and doing them favors. He had seen an easy source of campaign money when he desperately needed it, meeting more than twenty times with Riady. Huang had visited the White House seventy-eight times while working as a DNC fund-raiser. Bruce Lindsey had been present at many of the meetings and told reporters they were "social meetings." That was untrue. Sherburne had found a memorandum that described some of Riady's objectives in one meeting, which were to lobby for Indonesia's participation, with observer status, at a G7 summit meeting; recognition of North Vietnam; and better relations with China. Sherburne and Fabiani, who had to explain the meetings to the press and the prosecutors, were deeply disturbed by Lindsey's continuing false characterization of the get-togethers and the seeming expectation that they would lie as well. They resolved to resign after the election—and did so.

In August, Hillary toured half a dozen New England colleges, including Wellesley, with Chelsea. Chelsea's eagerness to see Stanford, however, had not abated, and daughter and mother flew to California at the end of the month. They were met by the university's provost, Condoleezza Rice, who guided them around the campus. Chelsea was captivated by Stanford: its mission architecture, the Northern California weather, the surrounding hills—and perhaps the chance to put greater distance between herself and the bubble in which she had lived in Washington. She had an A– average at Sidwell, and there was no doubt she would gain admission.

BILL AND HILLARY made a last-minute campaign sweep on Air Force One, stopping in seven smaller states to support local Democratic candidates for Congress and governor in the final twenty-four hours before polls opened on November 6, 1996. In the early-morning hours of election day, the Clintons and their entourage of friends, aides, and reporters headed to Little Rock. While the press remained in the back of the plane, Hillary, Bill, Chelsea, and the Clintons' friends crowded into the conference room to break open the champagne. While the others clapped, Chelsea led her parents in an approximation of the macarena, that season's dance craze. The gathering turned nostalgic. A few of those aboard had been there in the first years of the journey. The stories flowed. Clinton was riding a wave of popularity and accomplishment. A week earlier he held a 51 to 35 percent lead in the polls. Throughout the campaign the crowds had been huge and almost deliriously enthusiastic. People waited all night on curbsides for him.

In the hotel, Melanne and Hillary stayed up talking. Maybe, with the election over, Hillary said, she and Bill could get back to why they had run in the first place. "Here we had made it to election day, and the worst did not happen," said Verveer. "I think for her it was a huge personal relief." At a lunch for the president and first lady attended by several hundred people, Senator David Pryor talked about Ken Starr's office across town, which remained as active as ever since FBI agents and prosecutors had set up shop two years before. "I think the biggest round of applause you could get in Arkansas is to say, 'Let's get this election over with and let Ken Starr go home,' " he said. The investigation had "ruined a lot of lives, broke a lot of people financially. . . . [I]t's time for them to let us go on." The voters had clearly agreed.

Later in the day, at Doe's Eat-Place, Hillary and a crowd of her friends ate greasy food at a long table covered with a paper tablecloth. They told stories from the road and about stupid hairdos, of which Hillary had had more than a few. Later, she described feeling an "unburdening" that day, "a real sense of liberation." From Doe's she went to visit her mother in the Hillcrest neighborhood, and prevailed on her Secret Service lead agent to let her drive. According to Hillary, it was her last time at the wheel. After midnight, following a gracious concession by Bob Dole, she and Bill held hands and, with the Gores, strode from the Old State House where Bill had announced his candidacy for the presidency on October 3, 1991. "I would not be anywhere else in the world tonight," Bill told the crowd of thousands on the lawn. "I thank you for staying with me for so long, for never giving up, for always knowing that we could do better."

They could finally get into the second term riding upward. Despite all the humiliation and the foreshadowing of doom, especially during the past two years, Bill had managed to govern with surprising effectiveness and accomplishment, given the obstacles. Beyond the strong economy that was now firmly established, the successful intervention in Bosnia, and bailing Mexico out of a currency crisis, much of what he had done was through executive order, a mechanism that had enabled him to bypass the Republican Congress and cobble together pieces of the social agenda he and Hillary had envisioned originally as attainable through legislation.

Bill won reelection with a plurality of 49 percent to Dole's 41 percent and Ross Perot's 8 percent. He had wanted a majority of the popular vote, so as to solidify his mandate, but the electoral vote count was overwhelming: 379 to 159. The Democrats had also done well in congressional races, picking up nine seats in the House and two in the Senate. Immediately, Bill began contemplating the changes he wanted to make in the cabinet and the White House staff. The most visible would be at the State Department: Warren Christopher was tired and ready to go home. The three candidates under serious consideration for secretary of state were George Mitchell, who was retiring from the Senate; Richard Holbrooke, the deputy secretary who had brokered the difficult settlement in Bosnia; and Madeleine Albright. Bill was inclined toward Mitchell. But Hillary would have the final word. She and Madeleine Albright—a 1959 Wellesley graduate, ten years before Hillary—had become good friends. Hillary urged Bill, persuasively, that Albright should be chosen. In her travels as first lady, she had seen women head governments and serve as foreign ministers. None had ever ascended that far in the United States. It was time.

HILLARY WAS ENTERING the second term with far more cynicism than she had brought with her to Washington. One of the blips during the campaign had been the revelation in June—based on a passage in Bob Woodward's book *The Choice*—that Jean Houston had led her in a "séance" in which she communed with the ghost of Eleanor Roosevelt. That had not quite been what the book said, but news stories interpreted it that way, and there had been a tape recording made of the session, so denying that a "conversation" had taken place was out of the question. The session had occurred in April 1995, when Hillary was near her lowest, and Houston, who specialized in such therapeutic techniques, thought it would be useful for the first lady to have an imaginary talk with her predecessor about the obstacles she was up against. In the ensuing "discussion," Hillary played both parts—Eleanor and Hillary—and the two of them went back and forth about the shock, enmity, and criticism that had attended the efforts of each first lady to find a meaningful role in her husband's presidency.*

Hillary's response to the news stories about the dialogue initiated by Houston was, after some initial defensiveness, self-mocking—which served her well. For the second term, Mike McCurry, among others, urged Hillary to let go of her disdain for the media and at least accept the reality of life in Washington as it was lived: lighten up, she was told, drop the defensiveness, build some bridges. In response, she reminded him that there had been attempts to do just that, and how they had failed.

Only a few months earlier, she and Bill had received a warning—as if another were needed—of what they were up against. It had come from Republican senator Alan Simpson of Wyoming, during a friendly chat with Bill in the Oval Office. Simpson was retiring after the election.

---

*None of those present—they included Mary Catherine Bateson, Barbara Feinman, Lissa Muscatine, Lisa Caputo, and one or two other aides—regarded the dialogue in the same over-the-top fashion as the press described it. Previously, Hillary had talked publicly about imaginary conversations she conducted with her predecessor about criticism and obstacles. This was before she had met Houston. The dialogue initiated by Houston was followed by a similar two-way "conversation" between Hillary and Mahatma Gandhi. Finally, when Houston had proposed that Hillary talk with Jesus, whose betrayal and martyrdom was a pillar of Hillary's belief, the first lady declined, saying it would be too personal.

"Now that I'm leaving office I can tell you something. You are going to suffer immeasurable difficulty, and this is payback [by Republicans] for Watergate. So expect the worst," Simpson had said.

The president had repeated the story to Bill and Rose Styron over dinner one night at the Styrons' house on the Vineyard.* Hillary had told Bill Styron that "this was the tip-off early on that she and her husband were going to continue to face a horrible struggle, which they did." Her apprehension about their enemies, coming into the second term, was barely diminished.

Hillary suggested to Bill that, tradition be damned, Chief Justice Rehnquist not be asked to administer the oath of office to the president at the second inauguration, noting Rehnquist "despised" the Clintons' politics. Either of Bill's two appointees to the Supreme Court, Justice Ruth Bader Ginsburg or Justice Stephen Breyer, would be more appropriate. By now, she was certain, Rehnquist was a partisan, ideological zealot, who was even willing to flaunt his relationships with "extreme conservatives" intent on undermining the Clinton presidency.

Bill considered the idea seriously, but finally bowed to tradition, and his instinct not to provoke Rehnquist and the Republicans any further.

A WEEK BEFORE the inauguration, Rehnquist had gaveled the justices of the court to order to hear the case of *Paula Jones v. Clinton*. Bill could tell from Bob Bennett's description of the justices' questions that it had not gone well. "Good luck," Rehnquist said to the president, and shook his hand after he had administered the oath on January 20. Clinton later said that he was certain Rehnquist had been hostile in the way it was stated, that he'd conveyed sarcasm when he spoke the words. At the congressional luncheon following the ceremony, Hillary was seated next to Newt Gingrich, while Chelsea—wearing a thigh-high miniskirt that she had concealed from her mother under a long coat until, leaving the White House, Hillary noticed but it was too late to turn back—was placed between House Republican whip Tom DeLay and Senator Strom Thurmond, the equally anti-Clinton ninety-year-old Republican from South Carolina who, in 1948, had bolted the regular Democratic Party and run for president as a segregationist "Dixiecrat" against Harry Truman. "You're nearly as pretty as your mama," Thurmond kept telling her

---

*Simpson, in a conversation with this author in 2006, confirmed the account of the conversation in the Oval Office in exactly the same way as Styron had related it. Though they were political opponents, Simpson and Clinton had a good relationship—Clinton wrote—"because of the friendship we had in common with his governor, Mike Sullivan."

through the meal, while explaining his secrets of longevity (at least some of them): one-armed push-ups, six small meals a day, and nothing on his plate bigger than an egg.

Gingrich seemed uncharacteristically glum, with reason: he had been under investigation for several months by the House Ethics Committee for setting up his own tax-exempt organizations to finance his public speaking, in violation of the tax laws and congressional rules. In addition to affirming those allegations, the Ethics Committee, which was under Republican control, had determined he'd deliberately tried to mislead its investigators throughout the inquiry. The day after the inauguration, the full House would consider his case, resulting in a reprimand and a $300,000 fine. His deputy Tom DeLay would complain the punishment was out of proportion to the offense. Others whose offenses were less grievous had been treated far more harshly, with Gingrich doing the flogging.*

Hillary believed the fact that Gingrich was to be punished would make him even angrier and more aggressive, more dangerous to herself and her husband. That supposition, and contemplating the chief justice while she held the Bible during the administering of the presidential oath of office, had left her spooked and "apprehensive" since the noon swearing-in ceremony, she suggested.

In the ten weeks since the election, she had been working with administration officials to find ways of saving vital government services and programs that Gingrich and the Republican majority were determined to eliminate in the new session of Congress. They included legal aid for the poor, educational assistance incentives, important Medicare and Medicaid benefits, pension protection, and the minimum wage. Her stated goal was to protect the so-called social safety net, especially for citizens most adversely affected by the disappearance of unskilled jobs due to globalization and technological innovation that benefited so many others. In the second term, she wanted to move further in this direction, to (in her interesting choice of words, so different from her attitude during the 1992 transition) "help shape" White House policies on issues most affecting women, children, and families, especially those at risk. She was reverting to what she had always done best, using her skills and her

---

*Gingrich, in 1989, had led the successful Republican effort to remove the Democratic speaker of the house, Jim Wright, because he'd sold thousands of copies of a privately published book of his speeches to political supporters as a way of circumventing House rules that forbade taking fees for speaking. Gingrich's conduct was thus particularly offensive to members of the House, even a few Republicans, who recognized he had tried to invent an even more elaborate dodge than Wright to make some money.

experience with great specificity, targeting individual programs to be saved, others to be improved, identifying the strong and weak points through diligent study and enterprise.

The judgment early in the presidency, by Stephanopoulos, Shalala, and others, of her difficulty conceptualizing original programs and promulgating breakthrough ideas (such as Bill seemed to do with ease) had been acute. Perhaps without articulating it to herself, she began to recognize it in her post–health care ambitions, at least until she decided to seek the presidency. She worked well with existing structures, building on them, finding their weaknesses if called for, studying the mechanics of a program, whether foster care (as she did through 1997 and 1998, leading to the Foster Care Independence Act of 1999) or women's health programs. She was good at it, and very, very bright, Dick Morris's judgment to the contrary. She was a powerful, effective advocate, as she was discovering in her expanding campaign for human rights. The Senate was a perfect place for such a mind, in fact, and until her presidential ambitions collided with this vision of herself, she excelled without the need for a lot of tutelage or advice, whether from Bill or her policy aides. This attitude and ability had been manifest in her younger years, but dormant later, notably in the first term of the Clinton presidency.

EARLY IN JANUARY, Hillary invited historian Doris Kearns Goodwin, who in 1994 had published *No Ordinary Time: Franklin and Eleanor Roosevelt: The Home Front in World War II*, to meet with her at the White House. She wanted advice on her second term as first lady, "about how she might focus her energies and her time in the next four years," said Goodwin. The meeting, which lasted several hours, included members of Hillary's staff, whom Goodwin was surprised to find "felt a certain sense of being embattled"—not just with outside forces like Ken Starr, but with the West Wing of the White House. "This was not her high point. Bill was over there, and he had won the election, and she hadn't played a big part in it. . . . They were complaining that she would go out and give a speech and nobody was following her around. And she'd say these important things and only when she went abroad [would] her speeches be well covered."

Hillary seemed unsteady. "She thought the special prosecutor's report was coming out sometime soon. And that she was going to take a hit, even though she didn't think she'd be indicted. But she might have to wait until that came out to do whatever this thing was she was going to do in the second term."

Goodwin said she noticed during her visit just how the Clintons' relationship had changed. She was astonished that, during a routine ceremony in which Bill presented a human rights award, Hillary's staff was elated when the president mentioned the first lady by name from the platform. "I thought, Oh, my God, this thing has really gotten out of balance in terms of how she had once been ascendant, up there or ahead of him, and now . . . I just remember being stunned at that."

Goodwin had concluded that there was a seesaw effect: "During the '92 campaign when Gennifer Flowers appears, and as Hillary pulls him up, she's way at the top and he's down. Then the health care failure occurs, and yet he's beginning to do well. He then wins election in '96 and she's down. And then she's down in '97 and he's going up until Monica. And then he falls down, and she goes up."

Hillary appeared unclear what her focus as first lady would be in the second term, said Goodwin. "She was talking about children. And she was going to have some children's conference. . . . She was looking for some way of giving a focus to various efforts." Goodwin tried to persuade Hillary that she should become the voice in the administration for "people who were being left out," reminding her of Eleanor Roosevelt's support for striking mineworkers. Since Hillary was already regarded as a "liberal lefty" by her opponents, "Why not get the benefits from it? Capitalize on that image," said Goodwin. Hillary did not act on the suggestion.

Goodwin also talked to Hillary about Eleanor Roosevelt's ability to deflect criticism. "If they made funny remarks about her, that it really wasn't personal. It was because the people out there who were criticizing her didn't like her liberal views. And as long as it was that, that was fine. Now it wasn't only that. Sometimes they'd actually be making fun of her, her hats, her curlers. But she didn't take it personally." Hillary said only that it was "great" that the former first lady was able to do that.

There was an essential difference between Hillary's situation and Eleanor's, said Goodwin. "Because Eleanor was so far ahead of her time, she didn't raise deep fears in men because she was going to somehow become a model. Men didn't worry that their wives were going to wake up in the morning and want to be Eleanor Roosevelt. Eleanor [was] so eccentric. . . . But Hillary is part of a whole movement of women becoming important in all sectors of life—and [thus is] unsettling life for many Americans. And I think to the extent that she got to be the symbol of that forward-looking, aggressive . . . sort of taking-control woman, then people did project onto her things that she hadn't even deserved."

ON FEBRUARY 17, 1997, Presidents Day, Starr announced he would resign as independent counsel to become dean of Pepperdine University

Law School in Malibu, California. Though not known publicly at the time, the position had been endowed for Starr by Richard Mellon Scaife, who had been the primary source of funding for the Arkansas Project and much of *The American Spectator*'s campaign against the Clintons. By then, as Kendall and the other lawyers had sensed of late, and especially given Starr's failure to bring an indictment against Hillary before the inauguration, his investigation gave the appearance of being low on fuel. Webb Hubbell had been Starr's last great hope of obtaining a lode of damaging information about Hillary. Now the White House was expecting a devastating literary exercise disguised as a legal report that would give microscopic attention to every inconsistency and embarrassment in a narrative of the Clintons' public and personal lives from Arkansas to Washington.

By the time of Starr's announcement, the Clintons had been subject to more than twenty expansive demands for thousands upon thousands of documents. Hillary and Bill had each testified three times under oath, and she had also been required to appear before the grand jury. The first term of the Clinton presidency had been consumed by the investigations undertaken by Starr, the Congress, and federal agencies. Yet with Starr's announcement that he was removing himself from Washington, the independent counsel found himself the object of scorn from every side—including congressional Republicans who asserted that he was guilty of judicial abandonment. "Your departure will have a very serious, if not devastating effect on the investigation," said Senator Arlen Specter of Pennsylvania, the Republican chairman of the Judiciary Committee and former federal prosecutor. "Deep down inside everybody knows he's a quitter now," said James Carville, the Clinton political consultant, who chose to ignore warnings from the White House hierarchy to avoid gloating. Rather, senior White House officials were quoted anonymously to the effect that Starr's ignominious departure was confirmation that he lacked a legal case, and that no indictments of Hillary or the president would ensue. Even Starr's own aides reacted with dismay and fury.

After four days of unceasing condemnation and ridicule, Starr did an about-face, observing, "As Fiorello La Guardia would say, 'When I make a mistake it's a beaut.' I try not to make mistakes. I do make mistakes." Specter's comments had been particularly effective, and Starr extended apologies to his staff for deciding to depart without consulting them.

Bill said later he didn't know whether to laugh or cry about Starr's departure plans and their abrupt cancellation. Hillary was traumatized. She looked ahead at a landscape still clouded with more agonizing uncertainty. On May 27, the Supreme Court announced its 9–0 decision that the Paula Jones case could go forward, ruling that there was no constitutional or practical reasons to prevent a private civil suit from moving through the court system against a sitting president. A few days later, Starr won a decision in the Circuit Court of Appeals that allowed him to subpoena Jane Sherburne's notes of her conversations with Hillary, which the White House had resisted vigorously. In June, Starr assembled his staff to review the evidence: Hickman Ewing, his deputy running the Arkansas end of the investigation, had drafted an indictment of the first lady for perjury. To the disappointment of Starr and his staff, Sherburne's notes had not been substantively helpful.

The review confirmed Starr's reluctant opinion that, though a circumstantial case could be argued, and might justify indictment, it would be a difficult case to prosecute successfully, even against an ordinary citizen. It would be political suicide—especially since the White House had begun landing some blows on Starr's operation—to bring forward an indictment under the circumstances. There were no witnesses to confirm chapter-and-verse that there was a pattern to Hillary's misstatements. To prove perjury is a difficult prosecutorial task if there are any ambiguities, and federal law requires demonstrable evidence of showing intent to lie. Hillary's Jesuitical distinctions would in the end probably protect her, no matter how misleading or evasive her statements might seem. Under the law, they were not perjurous.

Sam Dash, who had been counsel to the Senate Watergate committee, had acceded to Starr's wooing, and agreed to serve as the independent counsel's adviser on questions of prosecutorial conduct. He concurred that the evidence was insufficient, and urged Starr and his colleagues to start wrapping up their inquiry, absent some momentous finding against the president.

All the time Starr was desperately seeking records that might help him bring down the Clintons, fifteen boxes of potentially damaging material was sitting in a Washington, D.C., vault. Starr had been told about the boxes by Webb Hubbell, but had either failed to adequately grasp their significance or, much more likely, was able to obtain only a few of the files by subpoena, because of their zealous legal protection by David Kendall.

Much of the material was protected by the attorney-client privilege, the Clintons' lawyers maintained, and they were not about to offer Starr a laundry list of what the boxes specifically contained. Subpoenas would have to be extremely specific to obtain any of the material, so Starr was stymied.

If Starr—or reporters, for that matter—had been able to examine what was in that vault, it seems possible, given the political atmosphere at the time, that the Clinton presidency might not have survived.

The idea to collect this information came in March 1992, after the Gennifer Flowers scandal during the run-up to the New Hampshire primary, when it became evident to senior figures in the Clinton campaign, including Hillary, Diane Blair, Jim Lyons, Mickey Kantor, Kevin O'Keefe, and Bob Reich, that the campaign needed to be better prepared to immediately respond to any more questions about the pasts of the candidate and his wife. This was true especially in regard to Bill's other women, Whitewater, Madison Guaranty, Hillary's work at the Rose firm, the backgrounds of the Clinton and Rodham families, Hillary's commodities trading, aspects of Bill's record as governor (among them a lobbying reform bill), tax returns filed by the Clintons, and other financial records.

The obvious person to locate, segregate, and maintain such information in absolute secrecy was Betsey Wright. Only she had complete knowledge of the thousands of boxes of Clinton files in Arkansas. Wright was technically assigned to work for Lyons, who had helped her investigate some of the women who had claimed to have had affairs with Bill. The reports of a private detective Lyons had hired, Jack Palladino, were among the papers she had in the files she assembled. By working for Lyons, Betsey and her files could be protected by an attorney-client privilege, she said—formal custody of the files would actually be his, as a Clinton attorney. This was especially true of Whitewater and Madison Guaranty, since Lyons was responsible for an internal investigation the Clinton campaign had undertaken in response to Jeff Gerth's original *New York Times* stories. "Before I came, Lyons and Kevin O'Keefe were sort of in charge of the Defense of Bill Section," said Wright.

"The people who talked to me about doing this job in the first place were Mickey and Bob Reich, and I talked to Hillary before I started. And I didn't want to do it without talking to Bill because I could tell just from the news and the Flowers business that this would be difficult," she said. At the time, Betsey was living in Cambridge, Massachusetts, as a fellow at the Kennedy School of Government at Harvard. She met with Bill during a campaign stop in Manhattan. "We walked through some of the things again," she said. "One of the things I asked him about was Gennifer Flowers, and again he told me there was absolutely nothing to it. He knew that things he did as governor would be coming under attack, his previous campaigns, both his record in the state as well as questions about his character and women, and he wanted to be able to respond."

In the first week of April 1993, Betsey moved back to Arkansas and began assembling files in bankers' boxes for the task ahead. Within a tight circle of the campaign staff, Betsey's operation became known as "The Defense Department," and Wright was sometimes referred to as the secretary of defense. As journalists or Republican opponents made new allegations, she would examine the relevant files, determine the facts to whatever extent possible, show the underlying materials to someone in the top command of the campaign, and a response would be fashioned.

After Bill's election as president on Tuesday, November 3, 1992, "we were told to clear out headquarters in Little Rock by that Friday," Wright recalled. (Some members of the staff stayed on.) She had been working with about two thousand boxes of materials, she later estimated, and left almost all behind to be sealed up, catalogued, and put in storage with the rest of Bill's gubernatorial records.

"There were a number of things that I thought too sensitive to be left in those general files and I took them home to my house—about eight or nine big boxes, and a few smaller ones, including my working files on Clinton's father, on Gennifer, my working files on Whitewater, a bunch of personal letters to Bill, material from detectives, a lot of internal staff memos that could be misinterpreted . . . anything I didn't think belonged in the archives. Out of context a lot of that stuff was deadly. I had staff memos [about Whitewater] that had been read by people who didn't know anything about it, who thought that they [the Clintons] had probably committed crimes unknowingly, and I should have torn it all up. I mean I shouldn't have kept it. I should have just destroyed it." She said she sent an inventory of the contents of those boxes—probably fifteen in all—to Bruce Lindsey.

Shortly thereafter, Wright received a call from Lindsey saying that he and Webb Hubbell wanted the boxes turned over immediately to Hubbell. "This is when Bruce and Webb got to be idiots about not trusting me with the files and thinking they had to get them," she said. Hubbell said it was not about lacking trust in Wright. More likely, Lindsey wanted to be sure that the files were in the custody of a lawyer who could claim privilege as counsel to the Clintons.*

According to Hubbell, during the holiday season of 1992–1993, "there was a conversation among several people—Mack [McLarty] was involved, Bruce, I'm not sure who else," about what was to be done with the files. Bill was the President-elect, but caution was in order.

Hubbell was asked to get the files from Betsey, along with four or five handwritten index cards of Betsey's listing what was in the boxes. There were no records from the Rose Law Firm, said Hubbell, "only what Betsey had accumulated in the nine or ten months she was running this defense department—all from the attorney general's and governor's files,

---

*Lindsey failed to respond to my inquiries over a period of several years.

and her own research." Wright delivered the boxes to him at the Rose Law Firm offices. "I then took them to my house and they stayed in my house in Little Rock until all our furniture and stuff and the whole family moved up to Washington in May." His son, Walter, drove them to Washington, and the files were unloaded into the basement of the Hubbell home in Spring Valley.

Hubbell said he paid no notice to them until Hillary phoned the evening the Clintons, the Hubbells, and the Fosters were to have dinner together, in June. Vince and Webb had been unable to find the records Hillary had phoned about, pertaining to Bill's father and his only recently revealed marriages to other women before Virginia. After the difficult dinner with the Fosters at the Italian restaurant that night, Hubbell found in his basement the records Hillary was looking for. Hillary had seemed surprised that Hubbell now had all of Betsey's sensitive files from the campaign, he said.

ON NOVEMBER 5, David Kendall met with Bernard Nussbaum, Bruce Lindsey, Bill Kennedy, Jim Lyons, and the Clintons' Arkansas counsel, Steve Engstrom. It was decided at that meeting that Hillary and Bill needed a lawyer in private practice to handle Whitewater matters, and Kendall was hired. The Whitewater story had returned to the news with Susan Schmidt's story in the *Washington Post* about the RTC's investigation of Madison and Andrea Mitchell's reporting.

Hubbell said he got a call in mid-November from Kendall, who said, " 'I understand you have the Betsey files, could you look and see if there is anything related to Whitewater?' " Hubbell recalled. "And I did. I put it in a big envelope. I told him I had those thirteen boxes, or fifteen, and he said, 'I think we ought to get them.' " Meanwhile, said Hubbell, "we had discussions with Bernie and others about needing to protect the privilege, to make sure they were in the hands of private counsel for the Clintons, and ultimately I was told that Kendall and Barnett had been hired."

At 2:30 p.m. on November 20—the day Hillary's health care bill was finally introduced in Congress—Kendall and several young attorneys arrived in two station wagons at Hubbell's home to take possession of the files. They went into the vault at the Williams & Connolly offices that contained other Clinton material and were logged in: "five larger Banker's boxes, ten smaller Miracle boxes, and a small metal two-drawer check file."

Not long afterward, Betsey Wright was asked to come to the vault and explain the contents to Kendall, who developed a considerable appreciation for her judgment and organizational abilities. Over the next five years, some of the material would be given to the special prosecutor's office and congressional investigators when a subpoena was specific enough to match something in the files; material was denied on the grounds that it fell under the attorney-client privilege. According to lawyers familiar with these matters, Kendall was tenacious about guarding the contents of the files from intrusive investigation.

After Hubbell had been questioned a second time by Starr's investigators, they began asking questions about "Betsey's boxes." "I explained they were with Kendall," he said. "They were asking the same question in different ways, not that they thought the holy grail was necessarily in there, but they seemed skeptical about the attorney-client privilege."

According to Betsey Wright, Clinton lawyers, and White House aides, the danger from the files was always the nature of their contents in a volatile political atmosphere far more than any likelihood of criminal liability—though many documents undermined public statements by the White House and by Hillary. Today, the files remain locked in the same vault.

A few weeks after the files had been moved from Hubbell's basement to Williams & Connolly offices, Hillary had told Maggie Williams—as recorded in Roger Altman's notes—"I didn't want anyone poking around twenty years of our lives in Arkansas." With the records safely in the vault, that would be very difficult.

AFTER STARR had been shamed into staying in his post, his zealous determination to find any criminal wrongdoing by the Clintons became manic. With the likelihood of prosecution of Hillary extinguished, he began an unrestrained inquiry, under Ewing's direction, into every nook and cranny of Bill Clinton's sexual past. The logical nexus of his inquiry was the contingent of state troopers who had helped *The American Spectator* in its story. The FBI agents and prosecutors took the troopers through lists of women who might have had relationships with Clinton. Particular attention was paid to Paula Jones, and the fact that—with her case allowed to go forward by the Supreme Court—there would be a stream of witnesses giving depositions in the case. The reinvigorated investigation in Arkansas was referred to in the Office of the Independent Counsel as the "Trooper Project." In Washington, some of Starr's top deputies were dismayed by the line of inquiry, and the desperation that seemed to be attending it. Hillary's greatest fear, of course, had always been that Bill—and their journey—would somehow be undone by his assignations with other women from his past.

· · ·

IN MID-SEPTEMBER, Hillary and Bill traveled with Chelsea to Stanford for freshman orientation week. Young Secret Service agents assigned to protect her would pass for students, live in a dorm room near hers, and hang back to the maximum extent possible. Chelsea's room, shared with another freshman woman, was impossibly small, and Hillary tried finding ways to rearrange the furniture to create more space. Bill, improbably, had gotten hold of a wrench that he used to disassemble and reassemble her bed so it could be moved. On the day they departed to return to Washington, Chelsea's parents were suffering from empty-nest syndrome; they were disoriented, teary, nostalgic, sad, and proud. In a month Hillary would turn fifty.

In expectation of an emptier house, Hillary and Chelsea had bought Bill a dog. After studying breeds and looking at pictures, they decided on a Labrador as being the right size and temperament for the White House and the president. For Christmas the previous December, they had found a three-month-old chocolate Lab puppy who loved Bill and vice versa. He was named Buddy, in favor of a slew of other names that included Arkinpaws and Clin Tin Tin.

Now, with Chelsea gone, Hillary and Bill turned to each other. Those who saw them together noted a renewed closeness, and—with some breathing space now that they were almost certain Hillary would not be indicted—a lessening of tension in the White House. Hillary said she still "lit up" when Bill entered the room, that they were best friends. Their confidences to each other were their own, and almost never did they share them with others. Though they had, in her words, "our share of problems," they continued to make each other laugh. She professed to be certain that their laughter and mutual caring would carry them through the second term.

17

The Longest Season

Starr . . . would undoubtedly take it as far as he could.

—Living History

THE *WASHINGTON POST* headline across page one in its editions of Wednesday, January 21, 1998, was shocking: "Clinton Accused of Urging Aide to Lie." Bill had spent a tense night and early morning on the phone with Vernon Jordan, Bob Bennett, Bruce Lindsey, David Kendall, and Betty Currie, talking about the story and trying to keep his legal ducks aligned. Hillary said later he nudged her awake just after 7 A.M. and sat on the edge of their bed. "You're not going to believe this," she quoted him telling her, but there were "news reports" blanketing the Internet and airwaves as well, that he had had an affair with a young White House intern named Monica Lewinsky and had asked her to lie about it to Paula Jones's lawyers. Starr had been granted authority from Attorney General Reno to broaden his already vast investigation to determine if criminal charges against the president were justified. Bill and Jordan had tried to find a job in the private sector for Lewinsky, twenty-four; but Starr was out to prove that this was to buy her silence about a sexual relationship, the existence of which Bill had denied under oath.

Bill explained to Hillary—each would say later—that he had "encouraged" the intern when she came to him seeking job advice, that he had tried to be helpful, and that she had misunderstood or misinterpreted his willingness to help. They had only spoken a few times. There was no affair, nothing untoward. Years later Hillary would write that she had little trouble believing Bill because he had often been accused of such things groundlessly. In *Living History* she wrote that she quizzed Bill over and over on the matter that morning, and Bill continually said he did nothing "improper," though he could imagine how his actions might be "misread." We have only the sanitary and skeletal accounts of Bill and Hillary with which to judge the severity of the interrogation.

For Hillary, the investment in the truthfulness of Bill's explanation was nothing less than a lifetime's savings. Everything, including the presidency and their marriage, was at stake; she understood that immediately. She also knew that Bill's staggering negligence meant they were about to endure an inquiry incomparably worse than anything before.

She had to take on an effective and supportive defense of her husband and she settled on empathy: Bill was always reaching out to people he could help, she would make clear. He had told Hillary that he had tried "to minister" to the intern, who was both troubled and needy, and had come on to him.

Later, many friends of the Clintons were incredulous that Hillary could have believed Bill's story—initially and, more incomprehensibly, over the next seven months. But failure to accept Bill's explanation would have meant the total collapse of her world. She had already borne the brunt of six years of vicious pursuit by people like those pushing the Jones case and feeding the Starr investigation; she permitted herself to believe these were just more politically motivated attacks. She wrote that she repeatedly challenged her own assumptions as the "Lewinsky imbroglio," as she called it, played out.

Later that morning, Bill told a friend that he doubted his presidency would survive the week. He feared a stampede in which Democrats, urged on by the press, would join Republicans in demanding his resignation. If the president shared this assessment with Hillary, it has never become known. But events were moving so swiftly by the time she had left the White House at 10 A.M. for a convocation speech at Goucher College in Baltimore that she could easily imagine such a scenario. George Stephanopoulos, who had resigned from the White House staff immediately after the November 1996 election, was already talking on an extended edition of the *Today* show about the possibility of the president's impeachment, as was Sam Donaldson on *Good Morning America*. The networks went into special programming as their news anchors, in Cuba to cover a historic meeting between the pope and Castro, hurried to the Havana airport and chartered back to their stateside chairs on the set.

As the pressure intensified, Hillary was already planning how their presidency could be saved. She knew she was once again the key to their potential survival. She understood that everyone would be rigorously examining her words and actions, looking to her for clues. With aides already walking around the West Wing dazed, it was essential that, first, she and Bill be seen carrying on with their daily routines, and second, that it be made clear they intended to fight back. She did not mention it in *Living History*, but as Bill told a friend, he knew his marriage was now at stake, too.

Less truthfully, he told one of his principal aides that morning, "Well, this girl, she kept flirting with me. She kept coming on to me. But it was innocent. I mean I hugged her at events . . . but that was it." "And that was the line," said the aide. "And it stood up pretty well for a while. And a lot of us wanted to believe that that's all it was. . . . And she [Hillary] wanted to believe it. I mean how could you not?"

Later, Hillary would write: "I will never truly understand what was going through my husband's mind that day." Only he could explain "why he felt he had to deceive me and others." He did, in his own memoir: "I was deeply ashamed . . . and I didn't want [the truth] to come out. I was trying to protect my family and myself from my selfish stupidity."

The prevarication required for his survival as president and as Hillary's husband was extensive, beginning with the lie he'd already told Jones's lawyers about his relationship with Lewinsky. He didn't have the options that most middle-aged men branded as adulterers had: to work it out in the privacy of the marriage, seek counseling, get a divorce, enroll in a twelve-step program.

Since Hillary's withdrawal from the West Wing, credible rumors about Bill's flirtations with several women had become increasingly frequent, especially in the previous year and a half. Lewinsky was hardly unknown to the president's aides, many of whom had been concerned and suspicious about her easy access to the Oval Office, facilitated by Betty Currie. How far he had gone with the women, however, was strictly a matter of conjecture.

At a 9 A.M. meeting in the Oval Office, Bill told Erskine Bowles and Bowles's top deputies, John Podesta and Sylvia Matthews, that he'd had no sexual relationship with the intern and denied asking anyone to lie. "When the facts come out, you'll understand," he said. The meeting was fraught. Bowles, one of Clinton's best friends, had followed the president's orders and asked Podesta to help Lewinsky find a job, knowing little about their relationship. He was repulsed simply by the thought of Bill's alleged behavior, its possibility, and wanted nothing to do with defending him. He would concern himself thereafter with the institutional business of the presidency, speaking to the president only about policy and staff matters.

Around the same time, Hillary phoned Sidney Blumenthal and told him that the president was being falsely accused. She repeated Bill's explanation of events.

In years to come, there would be a lot of learned commentary about how much better off Bill would have been had he absorbed the supposed "lesson" of Watergate: that the cover-up is worse than the crime. Therefore, went this reasoning, a confession by Clinton that day or sometime during the following week would have been accepted within the political system, the president would have been censured by Congress, Starr would have desisted, and the matter would have gradually passed.

But, as Clinton recognized, the idea of transfiguring this principle to his relationship with Monica Lewinsky was absurd. Confess, he was all but certain, and he would be finished as president and as Hillary's husband. The Watergate cover-up had been an essential element of Nixon's larger crimes, far more egregious than approving a single break-in, because it was intended to keep investigators from the explosive cache of "White House horrors" (as his attorney general, John Mitchell, called them), of grievous constitutional abuse of the electoral and national security systems of the country. Bill Clinton confessing to the nation about a predatory affair with a bosomy woman-child employee barely seven years older than his teenage daughter was a different matter altogether. The attitude of the post-Watergate press and Congress, especially Speaker Gingrich's House, did not augur for the confessional, but rather the stake.

Dick Morris called the president at 11:25 A.M. "You poor son of a bitch," Morris said he told the president. "I know just what you're going through." The two hadn't spoken since Morris's resignation.

"I didn't do what they said I did, but I did do something," Morris, in sworn testimony, quoted Clinton as telling him. "I've tried to shut myself down . . . sexually, I mean. . . . But sometimes I slipped up, and with this girl, I just slipped up." When Morris recommended that Bill ask the country for "forgiveness," the president suggested he take a poll on the idea, though it was unclear what it was that would be forgiven. Bill met with aides that morning in the Cabinet Room, to discuss the themes of his State of the Union address, scheduled the following Tuesday. He was "ashen," and altogether distracted, said Mark Penn, who had succeeded Stan Greenberg as the Clinton pollster. There were no discussions about how the scandal might affect the speech. People present were almost whispering; one said later that he wasn't even certain there would be a State of the Union address.

Hillary had been asked to speak at Goucher on civil rights—it was the day after Martin Luther King's birthday—by Taylor Branch, a part-time professor there and the Clintons' good friend since the summer of George McGovern's campaign. Branch's wife, Christy Marcy, worked for Hillary. During the train ride to Baltimore, Hillary and her entourage were in a special parlor car reserved for them. David Kendall reached her there by telephone with more information: he had been called the previous week by journalists asking about another woman whose name had come up in the Jones litigation—a circumstance, Hillary said later, Kendall judged potentially problematical at the time but not cause for serious concern. Kendall told her that on January 16, Janet Reno had written the supervisory three-judge panel recommending that Starr's jurisdiction be expanded to include the Lewinsky matter and possible obstruction of justice.

A logical sequence of events must have fallen into place for Hillary as she processed this information. Bill had been interviewed under oath in the Paula Jones case the previous Saturday, January 17, at the White House, and spent many hours preparing for his testimony. Hillary had wished him luck, embraced him, and then waited in the residence for him to return. He had been upset and worn out when he got back upstairs, Hillary wrote, and made clear to her his resentment and disgust for what he regarded as a farcical process. Though they had plans to take Erskine Bowles and his wife to dinner downtown as thanks for his White House service and to convince him to stay on for the rest of the year, Bill wanted to cancel and, instead, the two of them had a quiet dinner at home. She told a radio interviewer that the next day they both stayed home (in fact, they had gone to church) and that she had busied herself with domestic chores, including cleaning out closets.

Hillary declined to take several phone calls from the president during the train ride after Kendall's call, according to an aide.

Her speech at Goucher was covered by more reporters than Hillary had seen at any of her events since her Pink Press Conference. The mob at the train station was even larger as she prepared to depart Baltimore. She responded unhesitatingly to the reporters who were shouting questions about whether she believed her husband this time. She was calmly assertive, almost matter-of-fact. "Absolutely," she said.

Hillary was aware that morning that whatever the facts, tens of millions of Americans, and many millions more around the world, were once again discussing her humiliation and (as she described it) asking how she could get up in the morning and be seen in public. She cited Eleanor Roosevelt's observation that a woman in political life must "develop skin as tough as rhinoceros hide."

Upon her return to the White House in the late afternoon, she went upstairs to the residence and phoned Sidney Blumenthal, who had become a kind of alter ego for Hillary, especially since the death of Vince Foster. Bill had summoned Blumenthal to the Oval Office while Hillary was at Goucher and recounted to him a much more detailed version of the story he'd told Hillary. He'd been obviously nervous, pacing behind his desk. Lewinsky had "made a sexual demand on me," said the president, and when he denied her advances, she threatened him. He felt like a character in *Darkness at Noon*, the president explained. He said it was hard for him not to try to help people in need.

Blumenthal wanted to know whether Bill had ever been alone with Lewinsky. They had always been within sight or hearing of someone, the president said. He was no longer the straying kind. He had hurt people in the past, but those days were over.

"I had never seen him this off-balance before," Blumenthal recalled. "I was used to seeing him in the Oval Office as a master of policies, facts, and ideas, the judge of arguments, always in control. Now he described himself as being at the mercy of his enemies, uncertain about what to say or do. In that Oval Office encounter I saw a man who was beside himself."

Blumenthal said he recognized later that Bill had probably told him such an elaborate tale because "I was close to Hillary and there was nothing more important to him at that moment than protecting his marriage." Correctly, Bill knew they would compare notes.

There followed—in a very personal conversation with Hillary, according to Blumenthal—her root explanation of Bill's underlying difficulties, and how it figured in his encounters with Lewinsky: the pathology of Bill's family background. That cumbersome inheritance constantly intruded on his ability to keep out of trouble, she believed; his unrestrained "empathy" was a consequence of his close relationship with his mother, an overly compassionate and open woman, and from growing up "fatherless and poor," and battling his violent, alcoholic stepfather. Bill was always helping people in difficulty, and his reaching out to Monica Lewinsky was "another example [of] this unusual ability of his to connect," said Hillary.

Blumenthal told Hillary that he had spoken to David Brock, formerly the Clintons' implacable foe who, as she already knew, had of late become Sidney's secret source of information about what their enemies were doing. "I had been telling her about him all along," Blumenthal said. "His revelations [of] the lines of influence underlying the scandal, the cause and effect, intent and action" clarified matters. Thus, "on the first day," according to information supplied by the author of the original Troopergate story, "both Hillary and I knew about what she would soon call the vast right-wing conspiracy."

Blumenthal, once a journalist of some distinction, shuttled between the Clintons from the time the Lewinsky story exploded until the impeachment had been overcome, armed with the latest battlefield reports culled from Brock and online databanks of what the other side might be doing, and fitting their machinations into the flow charts of the vast right-wing conspiracy. Presidential aide Rahm Emanuel had given Blumenthal the nickname "G.K.," for Grassy Knoll, suggesting conspiracy theories on a scale with John F. Kennedy's assassination.

Blumenthal first met the Clintons at a Renaissance Weekend in Hilton Head, South Carolina, in 1987. At the time, he was a reporter for the *Washington Post* and was eager to be introduced to the Arkansas governor. During the weekend, Clinton told Blumenthal about his political ambitions. While covering the 1992 campaign he began a friendship with Hillary. They were both from Chicago and educated on the East Coast. She told him about her "difficulties" being a working woman and campaigning for her husband. When the Clintons arrived in the White House, Blumenthal was *The New Yorker*'s Washington correspondent, and his coverage of the administration brought him into its inner orbit. Some of the pieces he turned out were embarrassing, from a journalistic point of view, in their puffery, and many were unusually insightful. Blumenthal left *The New Yorker* and, not long thereafter, began helping Bill write some of his speeches. In May 1997 Clinton asked him to work directly in the White House, with the title of assistant to the president. Over the ten years Blumenthal had known the Clintons, he had gained the trust and friendship of both. Unlike Vince Foster, his relationship with the first lady was premised on a keen political and intellectual sense. He believed the plot against the Clintons was "a Cataline conspiracy" such as Cicero had put down when Cataline tried to overthrow the Roman Republic.

While the Clintons' lawyers were in their offices downtown trying to assemble a plausible legal narrative, Blumenthal was in his corner office in the West Wing, observing the daily chaos. He made notes on the legal activities, the public relations, the comings and goings of aides (including himself) as they marched to and from their own lawyers' offices and in and out of grand jury rooms and sweaty interviews with minions of the special prosecutor, the FBI, and even Starr himself.

Blumenthal's totally politicized version of what was occurring—a putsch by right-wing forces who had already taken over Congress, the evangelical churches, talk radio, the think tanks, and many other institutions, in his view—became the one Hillary accepted and perfected, and which accorded with all her preconceptions. The two of them spent hours together, fitting together the pieces of the conspiracy. It had the advantage of considerable underlying truth. Bill's outrageously self-destructive behavior, in this narrative, played right into the hands of Starr, Gingrich, and other powerful right-wingers and their shock troops who had opposed the Clinton presidency and were now at the gates of the White House ready to pull its occupants out forcibly. The Clintons were being attacked even though Bill had *not* had sex with this latest woman to throw herself at him (at least according to Blumenthal's and Hillary's line of reasoning); he'd simply gone too far with his "empathy," gotten her jobs, given her gifts. Hillary, Blumenthal, the White House staff, the lawyers, the Democrats on the Hill had to demonstrate that this was yet another politically inspired attempt to take advantage of the president's weaknesses and turn them into further cause for undoing the Constitution and allowing this "independent" counsel to run wild as if the United States were a banana republic. If they failed to make the case, Bill, Vernon Jordan, and Betty Currie (and doubtless there would be others) might well be facing perjury charges, maybe obstruction of justice, and, in the president's case, the likelihood of impeachment.

One of their most active opponents, Richard Mellon Scaife, regarded as the Daddy Warbucks of the conspiracy by Sidney and Hillary, was, coincidentally, coming to dinner at the White House that very evening, for a fete the president and first lady were hosting to thank major contributors to the White House Endowment Fund, which had raised $25 million to pay for renovations of the Executive Mansion and preservation of its historical artifacts. She and Blumenthal joked about whom Scaife would be seated next to, perhaps Blumenthal, she suggested.

That afternoon, the president had been scheduled to do three previously scheduled interviews—with PBS, NPR, and *Roll Call*, the Capitol Hill newspaper—about his upcoming State of the Union address. The first, with Jim Lehrer, was carried live shortly after 3:30 P.M. by all the networks. Beforehand, Bill had been strategizing by phone with Kendall and vowed not to allow Starr to drive him from office. Bill later said he felt that if he could survive the furor for two weeks, "The smoke would begin to clear," and Starr's tactics would then become more transparent to the press and public, enabling "a more balanced" view to prevail. But right then, as he noted, the pressure was unimaginable and "the hysteria was overwhelming." As Bill sat down to begin the interview, Buddy—still a puppy—refused to move from next to the president's chair. The broadcast was delayed while Bill pulled Buddy outside and left him in the care of an aide. Inevitably, Lehrer's first question was about Lewinsky.

"There is not a sexual relationship, an improper sexual relationship, or any kind of improper relationship," said the president. To another question, he said, "I did not ask anyone to tell anything other than the truth. There is no improper relationship."

Watching in his office on the CBS lot in Los Angeles, Harry Thomason was dumbstruck at how weak the president's presentation had been. Bill seemed unsure of himself, halting. On air, reporters were already pointing out the president's use on several occasions of the present tense. Thomason immediately phoned Hillary. She asked how fast he could get to Washington. He caught the first flight out of Los Angeles in the morning and, for the next thirty-four days, took up residence on the third floor of the White House. Bill, meanwhile, had taken immediate note of his present-tense problem, and stated unequivocally in the two interviews following Lehrer's that there *had been* no sexual relationship. Still, he had looked less than convincing or steady during the three sessions with the press.

In keeping with Hillary's business-as-usual directive, there were no outward signs at that evening's reception and dinner that she and Bill were overly concerned about the day's events. Scaife stood in line to shake hands with Hillary and Bill and pose for a photo with the president. The Clintons with great forbearance managed looks of perfect civility. In the receiving line, Hillary extended a spur-of-the-moment invitation to entertainment executive Frank Biondi Jr. and his wife, Carol, to spend the weekend at the White House, in the Lincoln Bedroom. The Biondis were part of Hillary and Bill's special coterie of New York and Hollywood friends, but they were surprised at the invitation. "My first instinct was just to say, You don't want to have houseguests," said Carol, but Hillary acted "just like nothing was going on. And I said, 'Oh, we'd love to.'"

At 1:15 A.M. Dick Morris called to tell Bill the results of a poll he'd commissioned. The country's citizens would not be very accepting of a confession, he concluded. Bill was not surprised. "Well, we just have to win," Morris said Bill told him.

The next morning Hillary began calling staff members to shore them up for a fight. She was taking charge of the battle. Part of her strategy was to ensure that most of the president's aides focused on Bill's goals for the second term. With her approval, it was decided that the president's case would be controlled by Kendall, presidential counsel Charles Ruff, who had been one of the senior Watergate prosecutors, and a cadre of lawyers from Williams & Connolly and the counsel's office. Political aides and the White House press office would no longer participate in legal strategy meetings; they would get their information from the lawyers and Hillary.

Mark Penn was among the first she contacted. "She called and said to make sure that I would help get the White House moving, not dealing with the scandal per se, but . . . making sure the White House was focusing on policies and that there was a 'public opinion desk.' " She wasn't very specific, but Penn initiated a series of strategy sessions to review "where the public was, how our communication was being received." They became regularly scheduled weekly events, which the first lady would often attend in the coming months.

Mark Gearan, who was also phoned by Hillary that morning, took it as "her call to arms . . . sort of, Let's go! Put on your armor. People felt good for a moment." People liked hearing it because it was a weird day." The word "weird" would reappear in the accounts of many White House aides of the coming days.

In spite of the fact she had been lied to, it took Hillary less than two days to correctly figure out how events would proceed. She shared her assessment with Blumenthal in the first lady's study in the residence, while Bill rehearsed his State of the Union address in the theater, on Saturday, January 24: Starr and the Republicans would push the situation to its ultimate political limit. "Step by step she described the train of coming events," recalled Blumenthal. "Starr would write a report and refer it to the House, calling for impeachment"; the Republicans would follow through with a majority vote to impeach; Bill Clinton would stand trial in the Senate, the outcome dependent on whether he could hold Democratic support. Hillary expressed her regret that she no longer had her notes from working on the Nixon impeachment investigation. She asked Blumenthal if he would "help her," but what she really seemed to have in mind was that he stay by her side for the struggle ahead. "I replied that I'd be there all the way through," said Blumenthal. Then she began calling Democratic leaders, letting them know she was behind her husband 100 percent, shoring up their support as well for the fight ahead.

The State of the Union address could be a great opportunity for the president, or a disaster. During a break in the rehearsal, Bill asked Penn, Harry Thomason, and Blumenthal, who had joined a group of some twenty aides downstairs in the White House theater, whether he should make some sort of statement about the scandal in his address to Congress and the nation Tuesday. They all said no.

The firestorm outside was beyond containment. Washington had never seen such a media frenzy, in which fact, speculation, gossip, and rumor about a momentous event all seemed to carry equal journalistic weight—on the air, in print, and on the Internet. The seamy subject underneath it all was not just sex, but presidential sex, with the kind of detail that, in itself, could be ruinous, and certainly would leave lasting scars. On Friday, ABC News reported that Lewinsky had kept a blue dress in her closet with the president's "bodily fluids" on it as proof of their sexual relationship, and that the special prosecutor had taken possession of it. When Erskine Bowles heard of that, he bolted from a meeting saying, "I think I'm going to get sick." While Bill practiced his speech, out on the White House lawn Wolf Blitzer was reporting on CNN that presidential aides inside were discussing the possibility that Clinton might resign. Hillary was again not watching television, or reading the papers, and when Harry Thomason—who was watching, almost constantly—would hear her footsteps, he'd turn off the TV.

Thomason believed the president, if only to buy time for things to calm down, had to unequivocally deny a sexual relationship with Lewinsky forthwith, and say that he was getting on with the country's business. Clinton had told him, as he had almost everyone on his senior staff by now, that no such relationship had existed. Thomason wanted Bill to say the same thing publicly, to emphasize it with the same assertiveness that he had shown to some friends and aides in private. To the president's great disadvantage, the Lehrer interview was being rerun endlessly, as commentators analyzed his sentence structure and his body language. Blumenthal was inclined to agree with Thomason. He went back upstairs to the residence to put the question to Hillary. Hillary was not insistent, "just assenting," reported Blumenthal when he returned to the White House theater with a verdict.

The Clintons had previously planned to screen a movie, *The Apostle*, that night at Camp David for friends, with the film's stars, Robert Duvall and Farrah Fawcett, in attendance. Now it was decided to serve supper and show the movie at the White House, with about thirty people invited, including the Biondis. When Bill entered, the crowd suddenly hushed, except for one woman who clearly didn't realize he had arrived and was overheard saying, "I would. Wouldn't you?" "They were totally into the movie"—about an evangelical preacher—said Frank Biondi. "Bill was humming the hymns, tapping his foot to the songs. Neither one of them seemed particularly preoccupied. We both commented how amazing it was, they just enjoyed the night." They were trying, with great difficulty, to keep up appearances.

During the evening, Bill huddled with Democratic congressman Jim Moran of Virginia, away from the others. Bill convinced him that he had not had sex with Lewinsky, as the congressman dutifully told the press. Bill also pulled aside Senator Robert Torricelli of New Jersey, and asked him whether he'd be able "to fulfill my term as president." "It was clear to me, he was of the judgment it might not be sustainable," Torricelli said.

Despite Clinton's attempt to convince him there had been no sexual affair with Lewinsky, Torricelli didn't buy it.

The lawyers were opposed to Thomason's suggestion that the president make another public statement about the scandal, but the question seemed to be decided by the deteriorating situation in the press and as expressed in the private comments of members of Congress. The country was transfixed with the details and the characters: Bill, Hillary, Monica, Starr, Vernon Jordan, Betty Currie, Paula Jones, and the women who had set Lewinsky up—the press was reporting—to entrap the president: Lucianne Goldberg, a devout right-wing, Clinton-hating author of trashy novels and a sometime book agent, and Linda Tripp, who had once worked in Vince Foster's office and, after befriending Lewinsky, taped her calls and shared the details with Goldberg.

On ABC's *This Week*, George Will pronounced the Clinton presidency "deader really than Woodrow Wilson's after he had a stroke." Sam Donaldson, on the same broadcast, said it was not certain that the president would be able to get through the next week without being forced to resign.

Tim Russert, host of *Meet the Press*, put the president's survival odds at 50–50. Matt Drudge, founding editor of his eponymous right-leaning Web site and a guest on the show, said "There is talk all over this town [that] another White House staffer is going to come out from behind the curtains this week. . . . There are hundreds, hundreds [of other women] according to Miss Lewinsky. . . . We're in for a huge shock that goes beyond the specific episode. It's a whole psychosis taking place in the White House." Drudge was the changing face of American journalism, and his appearance on the oldest of the weekly television interview shows confirmed that the country was in some new place now.

It was Super Bowl Sunday. While most of America watched the Denver Broncos beat the Green Bay Packers, FBI agents questioned Ashley Raines, a White House employee and friend of Lewinsky, about what she had heard the president say on the intern's answering machine.

THE NEXT MORNING, Hillary and Al Gore were scheduled to preside over a ceremony in the Roosevelt Room to preview a child care program that the president would announce to Congress on Tuesday night. Fifty people were crowded into the room, among them several senators and a phalanx of officials from the Department of Education. After almost an hour of by-the-book speeches and encomiums by the first lady, the vice president, foundation presidents, and local parents and teachers, Gore suddenly said, "I am very pleased to introduce America's true education president and the greatest champion of working parents and working families that the United States of America has ever known: President Bill Clinton."

The president, after prolonged cheering from the surprised attendees, spoke for ten minutes or so—knowledgeably and compellingly, as ever—about education, and what the administration was doing for children. "Now I have to go back to work on my State of the Union speech," he said. "I worked on it till pretty late last night." Then he paused. Neither Harry Thomason, who was monitoring the proceedings on a closed-circuit screen in a West Wing office, nor Hillary was sure what Bill was about to say.

He leaned into the microphone and his voice intensified: "But I want to say one thing to the American people. I want you to listen to me. I'm going to say this again." He was left-handed, but on this occasion he pointed with his right index finger, jabbing it vigorously four times in front of the cameras as he enunciated what he wanted to get across: "I did not have sexual relations with that woman, Miss Lewinsky." He stabbed the lectern with his finger. "I never told anybody to lie, not a single time, never." Pause. "These allegations are false. Now I need to go back to work for the American people. Thank you." And he walked off.

HILLARY, BILL, and Kendall were on the same strategic page: There would be no compromise, no cease-fire. Blumenthal conducted and collected copious research on almost every aspect of the political, professional, and private lives of Starr, his prosecutors, the Paula Jones gang, the Republicans in Congress who were, already, talking about impeachment, and "the elves," which was what he called the individual mercenaries of the right (and sympathetic reporters) who fed the vast anti-Clinton conspiracy, as he saw it. Given the frequent hypocrisy, misinformation, disinformation, and conflicts of interest exhibited by the other side, this was an extremely fruitful area of exploration.

It was clear that only Hillary could staunch the hemorrhage at this point, and she had to do it soon.

On Tuesday morning, January 27, Hillary kept her scheduled interview with Matt Lauer on NBC's *Today* show. She had agreed to the interview months before; it was meant to coincide with that evening's State of the Union address. Hillary and Blumenthal had been preparing for almost a week. She was, noted Blumenthal, "the most important person" who hadn't been heard from, except for a few words on a train platform. Vernon Jordan had already plowed some ground for her, on January 22, the day after the original *Washington Post* story. "I want to say to you absolutely and unequivocally that Ms. Lewinsky told me in no uncertain terms that she did not have a sexual relationship with the president," he read in a statement. "At no time did I ever say, suggest, or intimate to her that she should lie." It was hard to believe that such a towering figure in Washington as Jordan would get himself mixed up in obstructing justice. If Hillary could cast similar doubt on the notion in terms of her husband, as well as credibly suggest how and why he had gotten innocently involved with Lewinsky in the first place, she might at least stop the precipitous erosion of support for the president and change some of the terms of public debate. "Hillary had to walk a fine line," noted Blumenthal, appearing neither as "a warrior or a wounded bird." He suggested she talk about "professional forces at work whose only purpose is to sow division by creating scandal."

By then, Blumenthal and Hillary had more inside information, from their mole, David Brock. Brock had had dinner with Laura Ingraham, the conservative radio talk-show host, and Alex Azar, a Washington lawyer who had left Starr's staff and now was "part of the clique of elves," as Blumenthal put it. Azar had supposedly revealed to Brock that he'd learned Starr didn't have a case because the prosecutor's elaborate plan to entrap the president had fallen apart. Brock said Starr had wanted Lewinsky to wear a wire that would enable the FBI to tape Jordan and the president talking together, presumably about getting her a job to keep her quiet about the affair. "Now they think they won't prove the crime. They'll just have an affair story," Brock had reported. Consequently, Starr now wanted to produce "a public uproar" sufficient to force Clinton from office. The scenario allegedly contemplated by the prosecutor was the same Hillary had presupposed.

Had Hillary and someone like Blumenthal, perhaps, rather than Ira Magaziner, been as resourceful and careful with health care reform as she was with the attempt to identify and expose the vast right-wing conspiracy, history might have been quite different.

Sitting across from Lauer in a pants suit, gesturing emphatically, hair perfectly coiffed, Hillary unflinchingly defended her husband. After a few pleasantries, Lauer got down to it.

"There has been one question on the minds of people in this country, Mrs. Clinton, lately, and that is, What is the exact nature of the relationship between your husband and Monica Lewinsky? Has he described that relationship in detail to you?" Lauer asked.

"Well, we've talked at great length, and I think as this matter unfolds, the entire country will have more information. But we're right in the middle of a rather vigorous feeding frenzy right now. And people are saying all kinds of things, and putting out rumor and innuendo. And I have learned over the last many years, being involved in politics, and especially since my husband first started running for president, that the best thing to do in these cases is just to be patient, take a deep breath, and the truth will come out. But there's nothing we can do to fight this firestorm of allegations that are out there."

Lauer wanted more specific information about what the relationship *was* between Lewinsky and the president. "He has described to the American people what this relationship was not in his words. . . . Has he described to you what it was?"

"Yes," Hillary said. "And we'll find that out as time goes by, Matt. But I think the important thing now is to stand as firmly as I can and say that, you know, the president has denied these allegations on all counts, unequivocally. And we'll see how this plays out. I guess everybody says to me, how can you be so calm? Or how can you just, you know, look like you're not upset? And I guess I've just been through it so many times. I mean, Bill and I have been accused of everything, including murder, by some of the very same people who are behind these allegations. So from my perspective, this is part of the continuing political campaign against my husband."

Lauer explained to the first lady that there had been reports that she had taken over the White House defense against the charges and that she was Bill's "chief defender."

"Well, I certainly am going to defend my husband," Hillary said. "And I'm certainly going to offer advice. But I am by no means running any kind of strategy or being his chief defender. He's got very capable lawyers and very capable people inside the White House, and a lot of very good friends outside the White House."

James Carville had said "this is war between the president and Kenneth Starr," noted Lauer. "You have said, I understand, to some close friends that this is the last great battle and that one side or the other is going down here."

"Well, I don't know if I've been that dramatic," said Hillary, ". . . but I do believe that this is a battle. I mean, look at the very people who are involved in this. They have popped up in other settings. This is—the great story here for anybody willing to find it and write about it and explain it is this vast right-wing conspiracy that has been conspiring against my husband since the day he announced for president. A few journalists have kind of caught on to it and explained it. But it has not yet been fully revealed to the American public. And actually, you know, in a bizarre sort of way, this may do it."

Hillary and Blumenthal had been rehearsing the conspiracy comments right up until about ten minutes before the show. Blumenthal had given Hillary the perfect story line. There was plentiful truth in what Hillary was saying, if you just forgot about the sex part. The legal risks remained, but Hillary was successfully, confidently, presenting a plausible alternative narrative to Starr's unrelenting attempts to establish that her husband was a degenerate, and therefore not entitled to hold the office of the presidency.

Hillary said her husband had been wounded by his own generosity, his desire to help people in need: "I've seen [Bill] take his tie off and hand it to somebody," Hillary responded to Lauer's question about whether it was possible that her husband had given gifts to Monica Lewinsky. "I have known my husband for more than twenty-five years, and we've been married for twenty-two years. And the one thing I always kid him about is that he never meets a stranger. He is kind. He is friendly. He tries to help people who need help, who ask for help. So I think that everybody ought to just stop a minute here and think about what we're doing. And it's not just what we're doing in terms of making these accusations against my husband. But I'm very concerned about the tactics being used and the kind of intense political agenda at work here."

In the White House, Hillary's mother and brothers and their wives, as well as Roger Clinton and some family friends, were in the Solarium watching the first lady's appearance. Dorothy was proud that her daughter was displaying a "You tell them!" attitude, as she had in punching out the neighborhood bully when she was a child. The family members watched the replays all afternoon and flipped through the channels to evaluate the news coverage. "Everyone was yelling at the television," remembered Dorothy's daughter-in-law Nicole Boxer. But there was also discussion and some speculation about how Bill had gotten into such a situation. "We had the TV on and everyone was sitting around on the couches, and just venting and getting it out and going over scenarios [of] How could this happen?" said Boxer. "And with every new report, we all were making commentary. . . . 'Oh, we can defend against this.' And at some point I decided to say that I know he didn't do it . . . but if he did, he should admit it. . . . And as soon as I get these words out of my mouth, Roger flies off the couch at me with his finger in my face and says, 'How dare you? He didn't do it. You're crazy! . . . What do you know?'" Nobody intervened, said Boxer, and she began to cry while the president's brother went on to rant at her. Eventually, Dorothy consoled her.

Hillary's brothers believed the Lewinsky allegations were perhaps true; they had assumed for years that their brother-in-law's wandering ways with women had not ceased altogether when he became president. They kept the opinion to themselves and their wives.

Later that afternoon, Hillary returned to the White House and headed to the Solarium. Harry Thomason was among those gathered who cheered her arrival. "I guess that will teach them to fuck with us," said Hillary.

PERHAPS NEVER BEFORE had a peacetime State of the Union address been so anticipated, and for reasons having little to do with what the president thought the actual state of the union was at that moment. Rather, there was far more interest in the state of the president, and what, if anything, he would say about the scandal swirling around him, whether he said it in words or in body language. And, if he did not address the subject, was that some kind of message in itself?

In the event, the president did not mention Monica Lewinsky. Instead, in a calm, focused, and direct voice he declared: "We have more than fourteen million new jobs, the lowest unemployment in twenty-four years, the lowest core inflation in thirty years. Incomes are rising, and we have the highest home ownership in history. Crime has dropped for a record of five years in a row, and the welfare rolls are at their lowest level in twenty-seven years. Our leadership in the world is unrivaled. Ladies and gentlemen, the state of our union is strong." That said nothing, of course, about the state of the presidency or the president.

In the next hour and fifteen minutes he talked about big plans: targeted tax cuts and new programs to help working families, to improve education and child care. "Now if we balance the budget for next year, it is projected that we'll then have a sizable surplus in the years that immediately follow," Clinton said. "What should we do with this projected surplus? I have a simple, four-word answer: Save Social Security first. Tonight I propose that we reserve 100 percent of the surplus, that's every penny of any surplus, until we have taken all the necessary measures to strengthen the Social Security system for the twenty-first century."

On that count, Clinton won ovations from both sides of the aisle. Said one Democrat: "The speech reminded us why the president stays popular through everything that's hit him."

Hillary, who had earned Bill a stay of execution, was pleased with the speech. She thought it had reinforced the message she was trying to get him and the White House to convey: they would not be deterred; the business of the nation went on with great success; the lawyers would take care of the Lewinsky business; he had a loving wife who not only accepted his explanation, but had recast the whole attack on her husband. As the *New York Times* wrote the next day:

While no proof has been offered to support Hillary Rodham Clinton's allegations that a "vast right-wing conspiracy" is behind the accusations of sexual impropriety imperiling her husband's presidency, several figures in the case against President Clinton have common ties in conservative groups and causes. Monica S. Lewinsky's alleged account of a sexual relationship with the president was steered to the Whitewater independent counsel, Kenneth W. Starr, by two lawyers, George T. Conway 3rd of New York and James W. Moody of Washington, who have been active in conservative causes.

"Part of my duty as good soldier, first knight, was to try to get the right story out," said Blumenthal. "I felt I had to go into a journalistic mode, but I couldn't be a journalist myself. I could suggest information. . . . " This was certainly the case with Conway and Moody, who had been steered to Blumenthal by Brock. The *Times* story noted that Starr, Conway, Moody, and others were members of the Federalist Society, an organization of attorneys who were dedicated to reversing "liberal" dominance of the law and the judiciary.

At the time the Lewinsky story broke, Chelsea was at Stanford. Hillary and Bill did not know how she would withstand this latest and most personal crisis of their married life; the political ramifications, the possibility they might be forced to leave the White House, would weigh on her, they knew. Now, like her mother, there would inevitably be an element of humiliation that she would have to endure.

There had been some question, during the frenzy of the previous week, of whether Hillary, almost immediately after the State of the Union speech, would go ahead with a planned trip to Davos, Switzerland, to attend the World Economic Forum, where she was scheduled to speak. In the end, Hillary decided to go and that Chelsea should come home on Friday, January 30, and spend the weekend at Camp David with Bill and the Rodham family—her mother and brother Tony, and his wife, Nicole. Bill could then talk to Chelsea, do the necessary explaining beyond whatever comfort they had both been able to convey to their daughter by telephone.

Chelsea was visibly upset through the weekend, and the crisis atmosphere, personal and political, hardly abated. Bill's concern and guilt about the situation he had provoked was evident. He was on and off the phone almost constantly, though he took time out for a round of golf.

The rest of the family hovered over Chelsea. She was unusually quiet, aloof, distant, not herself. For much of the weekend, the family watched movies in silence. Meanwhile, following a well-received speech at Davos, Hillary went skiing in the Alps, returning to Washington on Tuesday, February 3.

Hillary, through the next weeks, stayed in regular touch with old friends by phone. Many called to see how she was holding up; others she called. Hillary would invariably change the subject from herself, or what she and Bill were going through, and instead discuss the lives of her friends, they said later. She had done this kind of thing over the years whenever her world had been shaken. It seemed to help her keep her equilibrium. People who did not know her well suggested her solicitousness was premeditated, intended to win favor or find its way into the press. That does not seem to have been the case.

Nancy Bekavac had been expected at the White House as Hillary and Bill's guest the week the Lewinsky story broke, but she called to cancel—on Wednesday, the same day Bill had awakened Hillary with the news—leaving a message that she had a *personnel* emergency. The next morning Bekavac received an urgent call from Hillary, who had received a message that her friend had had a *personal* emergency. "And she said, 'Oh! We never have those in Washington,' " Bekavac recalled. "And the two of us just laughed. I said, 'God, what are you doing wasting your time calling me when you got these other things to do?' And she said, 'Waste my time? You're a friend, I'm worried about you. Bill's worried about you. We expected to see you last night, and I got this message, and he said, "You got to call." ' . . . So, I told her about my personnel problem. And, I said, 'What about you? How are you?' She said, 'I'm sure everybody out there thinks this is the worst day of my life. But the day isn't any different from any other day since we got to the White House.' " The two joked about the photo of Hillary in her bathing suit dancing with Bill on the beach in Hilton Head, South Carolina, that ran in newspapers across the country during their Christmas vacation.

Bekavac was nearing the end of a 120-day sabbatical from the presidency of Scripps College. "[Hillary said], 'Tell me the very best thing about your sabbatical.' Okay, here it is. Four months, no pantyhose. . . .

"I hung up the phone and I thought, in what has to be the worst week for any first lady in recorded history of humankind, she's made me feel better," said Bekavac. "She's made me feel happy. And I don't think I did a goddamn thing for her."

．　．　．

A WEEK AFTER her appearance on the *Today* show, a *Washington Post*/ABC poll showed that 59 percent of Americans believed that "Clinton's political enemies are conspiring to bring down his presidency." Bill had achieved the highest approval ratings of his presidency—67 percent of Americans approved of his performance as president.

During a February 6 press conference with British prime minister Tony Blair, Bill addressed Hillary's claim of a vast right-wing conspiracy for the first time. "Now you know I've known her for a long time, the first lady," Bill said. "And she's very smart. And she's hardly ever wrong about anything. But I don't believe I should amplify her observation in this case."

Newsweek was working on a cover story for its February 9 issue to include a two-page chart under the title "Conspiracy or Coincidence?" The artwork was professional, but it looked something like the diagrams Blumenthal was constantly refining, with links between twenty-three prominent luminaries and institutions of the ultraconservative constellation—politicians, lawyers, publishers, think tanks, fund-raisers, contributors—that helped feed the Starr investigation.

Finally, the campaign by Hillary and Blumenthal to turn the media tables on Starr was breaking through: Lars-Erik Nelson, the chief Washington correspondent of the New York *Daily News*, wrote about the gullibility of the capital press corps and its acceptance of Starr's "slander"; the *Minneapolis Star-Tribune* published a series about the Arkansas Project and Richard Mellon Scaife; the coverage of the Associated Press became critical of the prosecutor's tactics, yet balanced; the reporting of the online magazine *Salon* and *The New York Observer*, both representative of new journalistic directions, was as focused on the independent counsel as on the president and the White House. And in the *Boston Globe*, columnist Pat Oliphant wrote critically about how the Washington press corps had generally "overreached the facts in mad pursuit of an actual or circumstantial witness to White House sex," accusing the *Washington Post, The Wall Street Journal,* the *New York Times,* the *Dallas Morning News,* ABC, and *Newsweek* of abandoning traditional standards of fairness.

Meanwhile, Starr was investigating Blumenthal for obstruction of justice in his criticism of the special prosecutor's investigation, and had subpoenaed him to appear before the same grand jury investigating the president. "In essence, I was being accused of speaking to the press," Blumenthal said. He was willing to be judged guilty of pointing out Starr's abuses "to as many journalists as I could."

For the White House state dinner in honor of Tony and Cherie Blair,

Hillary decided to seat Newt Gingrich to her left and Blair to her right. She was hoping to get a reading on the speaker's thoughts about Starr's charges, and gauge his reaction to the drumbeat of impeachment commentary. Gingrich, she had decided, was "the key"; without his go-ahead it would be difficult for the impeachment train to reach its destination.

Much of the conversation at the table was about foreign affairs—Bosnia, Iraq, NATO expansion. Gingrich was aware that the Clintons and the Blairs had become close, and he admired the prime minister, if not the more liberal of his policies. Gingrich took the initiative himself—as the story was told by Hillary to Bill—and said, "These accusations against your husband are ludicrous. . . . Even if it were true, it's meaningless. It's not going to go anywhere." Hillary was surprised and pleased. Perhaps Gingrich was more complicated and less predictable than she had given him credit for. He was also, unbeknownst to her or even Blumenthal or Brock, at the time having an affair with a member of his staff twenty years younger than himself, for whom he would eventually leave his wife.

IN THE PAST, Hillary and Betsey Wright had succeeded in silencing or undermining the claims of many of Bill Clinton's women, and many who weren't but claimed to be so. That option was now closed off, lest Hillary or Wright risk another go-round with Starr over obstruction of justice.

The new details leaking steadily—many deliberately from Starr's office and Paula Jones's lawyers—about the president and Monica Lewinsky, and what they may have done while in each other's company, lent a certain plausibility to the accusations of other women, including those whose stories had previously been branded as false or misguided. One, Kathleen Willey, appeared on *60 Minutes* on March 15 to sensational effect, accusing the president of groping her. She said that Clinton had lied in his deposition in the Paula Jones case when he described a meeting between the two of them. "Too many lies are being told," she said. "Too many lives are being ruined. And I think it's time for the truth to come out." When Willey, a Democrat and volunteer at the White House, had asked Clinton for a staff job in 1993, she said, the president groped her in a meeting in the Oval Office and took her hand and put it on his genitals. Clinton had said in his deposition in January that he recalled their meeting but he denied anything sexual occurred. "When she came to see me [about her family's financial difficulties and whether he could help her get a paid position at the White House] she was clearly upset," he said. "I did to her what I have done to scores and scores of men and women who have worked for me or have been my friends over the years. I embraced her, I put my arms around her, I may have kissed her on the forehead. There was nothing sexual about it."

Willey was among a list of witnesses the Jones lawyers had called to support their claim that the president had a pattern of harassing and forcing himself upon women, and whom Starr's investigators were now interviewing. Despite Hillary's aversion to watching TV or reading the papers, Willey's story infiltrated the shield the first lady and her aides had created to keep her from hearing the seamier details of ongoing developments. Once again, she had to confront the effects of her husband's "empathy"—regardless of the specifics of what had transpired between Bill and Willey. Willey's testimony was eventually rendered legally useless to Starr because, like Bill Clinton, she had been untruthful under oath in the Jones case about events in her own private sexual life.* The special prosecutor never considered bringing a charge of perjury against her, unlike the president.

Four days after Willey appeared on television, Gingrich and Representative Henry Hyde, the chairman of the House Judiciary Committee, sent a Republican staff delegation to the special prosecutor's office to sift through the evidence and get Starr's judgment on whether there would be enough there to justify an impeachment inquiry.

This was a moment Starr had been waiting for, and he told the delegation that the evidence of obstruction of justice and perjury against the president was mounting and voluminous. Moreover, the details of Bill's assignations with Lewinsky were, in Starr's judgment, demeaning to the presidency to the extent that neither the Congress nor the American people would want him in office, once disclosed. (When some of his deputies questioned the relevance of the lascivious details and language Starr chose to include in his report to Congress, the prosecutor replied, "I love the narrative," and refused to expurgate it.)

The impeachment locomotive was now gathering steam. Hyde would at various times have doubts about the wisdom of continuing down the impeachment track, especially because Bill Clinton's popularity remained high, but from this point forward Gingrich had no hesitancy. Despite what he had told Hillary at the dinner for the Blairs, he had experienced a change of heart very soon afterward, or hadn't meant what he'd said at the time. And whatever his unease about the possible disclosure of his

---

*In addition, her former friend Julie Hiatt Steele later testified to lying when she corroborated Willey's account of the alleged groping incident and had said that Willey had told her about it on the same day it had supposedly occurred. Steele also admitted before a grand jury that she had actually heard about the purported incident four years later. Starr indicted Steele for obstruction of justice but later dropped the charges.

own marital problems, he subsequently enunciated a distinction: Bill Clinton had lied under oath while Gingrich had merely failed to live up to his own high standards and God's. "The president of the United States got in trouble for committing a felony in front of a sitting federal judge," he said of Bill Clinton's impeachment. "I drew a line in my mind that said, 'Even though I run the risk of being deeply embarrassed, and even though at a purely personal level I am not rendering judgment on another human being, as a leader of the government trying to uphold the rule of law, I have no choice except to move forward and say that you cannot accept . . . perjury in your highest officials.' "

Even the speaker's own aides believed that sheer grandiosity was part of Gingrich's enthusiasm for impeachment, given the nature of his ambitions, whether to take down the president or one day replace him. A bizarre rumor was circulating through the speaker's staff, which was first reported publicly by journalist Elizabeth Drew, and which Blumenthal seized on shortly after Gingrich had received Starr's heads-up. Drew, in an interview with *Salon* magazine, said:

> Speaker Gingrich is talking to, and has been talking to over a period of time, close associates about the idea of impeaching both Clinton and Gore. It goes as follows: Gingrich believes that the report will be so tough that Clinton will be impeached [and removed or driven from office]. The thinking then goes that Gore, as his successor, will pardon Clinton. This, of course, leaves Gore in place as the incumbent president, which is not something the Republicans wish to have happen. So once Gore has pardoned Clinton, Gingrich's thinking goes, the Congress will impeach Gore for having pardoned Clinton. As one of these close associates of Gingrich said to me, "You can't have a Clinton strategy without a Gore strategy."
>
> I know this seems wild. . . . I'm simply reporting what the Speaker of the House [the next in line for the presidency, under the Constitution, after the vice president] has been talking about.

With Gingrich now known among his colleagues to be relishing the chance to have Clinton impeached, other Republicans felt more comfortable in their extreme advocacy. Senator John Ashcroft said he believed Willey's story was "credible" and that "we are now not just dealing on the basis of rumors and suspected leaks. We have sworn affidavits from a variety of settings." And Republican whip Tom DeLay, himself as ethically challenged as any leader in the House of Representatives in decades, stated that the "faith the people have put in President Clinton has been violated time and again. . . . I cannot think of a better way to bring on formal congressional proceedings than to go on hindering, obstructing and belittling the judicial proceedings now under way." *

Hillary tried to remain calm and in control. She told one friend about a book she had been reading by Myra McLarey on "the earthy stoicism of rural women."

DURING THE FIRST five years of the Clinton presidency, Diane Blair would stay at the White House every month or two for several days. That was how she and Hillary kept in touch. Visiting late at night, after the first lady's official duties were over, "We can do gossip. We can do parents. We can do the whole bit," she explained in 1999. But in the previous year of Lewinsky and impeachment, 1998, Diane spent much less time at the White House, "because I was a coward. There were things I didn't want to discuss with him, and I didn't want to discuss with her. I was upset and I was blue and I was angry. And, I wanted to be a friend, but I wasn't sure what was the best way to be a friend to her." Diane, unlike Hillary, had made her own supposition early on about Bill and Lewinsky: "That he'd probably done something really stupid."

Blair was present enough, though, to see that "the joy went out of the White House. You could just feel this, and even though there were denials about particulars, and this, that, and the other, it was clear that something had happened, which was wildly inappropriate, and which was foolish. I'm not even sure at what point Hillary began having darker and darker suspicions about what did and did not occur." But by spring, her certainty was being shaken. Hillary had stopped reading newspapers "way back, in the early days of the administration," said Blair. "They made her angry. She found them trivial. . . . And I was shocked sometimes. I'd come in from Fayetteville, Arkansas, and I would know a lot more about, you know—I read the *Times* and the *Post*, and a whole bunch of other things, that I would know a lot more about certain things that were going on than she did, just because she hadn't read them. . . . And knowing this, it was a very awkward time to be a good friend because I didn't want to be the one to tell her something that everybody was chatting about on the Internet, that she literally was not aware of."

Diane was "as open to her as she wanted to be to me during that year. But we never really discussed it. I would ask, 'How are you doing?' in a

---

*In September 2005, a Texas grand jury indicted DeLay for conspiracy after a lengthy campaign finance investigation. He and two other associates were accused of illegally directing corporate donations to Republicans in the Texas legislature. He resigned from his position as majority leader in June 2006, and from the House.

general way. 'How are you feeling? Why don't you come down [to Arkansas]. Let's go take a trip.' . . . I mean I was trying to do that. But I did not force her to talk about the whole situation because I didn't how much she knew. I didn't know how much she wanted to know."

Like her mother, Hillary has said, she rarely reveals her innermost feelings to even the closest of friends.

"She would call me," said Diane, "but she never called and said, 'What should we do? I'm going insane. I don't know what to believe.' Nothing. And when the other shoe dropped the week of his grand jury testimony—and it was clear that there had been a relationship with Lewinsky. . . . She could not talk to anyone." For days.

FRIENDS OF the Clintons have long noted that when Bill has most needed Hillary's support, his attention and affection toward her flourishes. This was evident during their eleven-day tour of six African nations, starting March 22. Later, Hillary would write about a romantic interlude sitting alone with Bill in the back of a boat floating down the Chobe River in Botswana. They had seen elephants, hippos, eagles, crocodiles, and a mother lion and her four cubs that day. Though some critics denounced the tour as a way to divert attention from the Lewinsky scandal, the trip had been planned well before, and was to be the longest of the Clinton presidency. Bill had wanted to visit sub-Saharan Africa since his youth and now they were traveling to Ghana, Uganda, Rwanda, South Africa, Botswana, and Senegal to talk about economic development, environmental concerns, democracy, and human rights. No president had ever visited any of those African countries while in office.

It was true, though, that both were happy to get away from the internecine warfare of Washington, the unceasing rumor, speculation, and incessant talk of sex. And though Hillary's aides believe her veil of denial was lifting before the trip, she seemed able in this setting to put aside a large measure of the tension and seething. Moreover, they were visiting a part of the world where she had been before, and where her reputation was enormous, and mercifully disconnected from the tribal warfare back home.

On most of their previous foreign trips together as president and first lady, Hillary was forced by tradition to play the role of presidential wife, with each of her days filled with ceremonial tours and meetings that often meant relatively little to her. She frequently chafed at the schedules Bill's handlers arranged for her and was not much fun to be around. Her travels abroad of the past three or four years, without Bill, produced their own unique kind of expectation, excitement, and satisfaction. Now, on this trip, she was able to be a guide to him. As the traveling press noted, he needed her. She was the recipient of his rapt attention, and he was solicitous.

In Senegal, on April 1, the president took a call from Bob Bennett. Judge Susan Webber Wright, whom Bill had appointed to the federal bench but whose handling of the Jones case had won him no measure of comfort, had at last dismissed Paula Jones's suit on the grounds that it lacked legal merit. "This is fantastic," Clinton said, and though there was consensus that he should not gloat, Fox News managed to film an exuberant Clinton from outside his hotel window, with a cigar in his mouth, beating an African drum.

Bill and Hillary's shared belief about the paramount moral and political importance of human rights was reflected in their itinerary and their discussions with African leaders and ordinary citizens alike. In South Africa, they spent many hours with then president Nelson Mandela, who took Bill to Robben Island, the notorious gulag where Mandela had spent eighteen years imprisoned for sedition, and from which he plotted the liberation of his country. Bill was also insistent on stopping in Rwanda before they left the continent for home, though it had not been on the original itinerary. Clinton would say later that his failure to act to stop the genocide in Rwanda, where almost one million people died in 1993–1994, was his greatest regret as president. At the Kigali airport, where they stopped for a few hours (the only arrangement the Secret Service would permit), he and Hillary met with several dozen people who had come to tell them how their mothers, fathers, children, and siblings had been slaughtered. Bill acknowledged to them that his decisions contributed to the mass killings in the country, and that the international community, and the nations of Africa, had failed a basic human obligation. "We did not act quickly enough after the killing began. We should not have allowed the refugee camps to become a safe haven for the killers. We did not immediately call these crimes by their rightful name: genocide."

THROUGH THE SPRING and during the Clintons' Africa trip, Starr had been thrown on the defensive by intense criticism about leaks from his grand jury investigation. Kendall had filed a motion in court citing fifty broadcasts and newspaper reports that appeared from their attribution to be based on conversations with prosecutors, investigators, and others "close to the investigation." Starr was also getting little cooperation from Lewinsky's lawyers, and the Secret Service had asserted a privilege claiming that to interview agents who guarded the president would risk the president's protection. And the White House was claiming attorney-client privileges for Bruce Lindsey and other lawyers who had defended the Clintons, as well as for many documents. Starr was furious and decided to squeeze the White House again on the original Whitewater case. To her amazement, Hillary was again called to testify under oath, this time for almost five hours on April 25. "I never spent any significant time at all looking at the books and records of Whitewater," she said when shown financial documents relating to the investment. Twice she invoked the privilege that allows spouses not to answer questions about discussions with their marital partner.

James McDougal had died on March 8. Vince Foster was dead. Starr decided to put further pressure on McDougal's ex-wife, Susan, and on May 4, she was indicted on charges of criminal contempt for continuing to refuse to answer questions about Bill Clinton. Starr's grand jury also indicted Webb and Suzy Hubbell for tax evasion on $1 million of income Hubbell received before entering prison—charges that were later dismissed in a decision upheld by the Supreme Court, with a single dissenter: the chief justice.

BY MAY or perhaps June, the Clintons' closest aides noted an obvious change in the couple's interaction, even at official events. There was a chill they'd never seen before. They'd seen Hillary angry at Bill, but this was something entirely different.

In earlier years, the Clintons were demonstrably affectionate with each other in private. "They would hold hands," said one of Bill's deputies. "They would kiss. In the Oval, she'd come in and . . . stand and touch . . . she'd put her arms around him. . . . Everybody would sort of leave when they got together, just the two of them. There was a lot of affection."

By the end of July there was no demonstrable affection. In fact her disaffection was particularly notable at a memorial service for two police officers shot to death the previous winter when a deranged antigovernment protester tried to shoot his way into the Capitol. "Whatever part of the room Clinton moved in while we were in the holding room with other people, she moved to the opposite end," said an aide. "When she did this, it was so obvious. If he was going to go one way, she was going to go the other way. She deliberately did not want to be anywhere near him at all. She wanted nothing to do with him."

"I think she handled it as a very personal situation," said Mary Mel French, a friend of the Clintons from Arkansas and chief of protocol at the State Department during the Clinton administration. During this period, the messages and visits from members of her prayer group were becoming more frequent, though she is not known to have confided in anyone. It was around this time that Hillary learned from David Kendall—neither has ever disclosed the exact date in late July—that Starr had negotiated an immunity deal with Monica Lewinsky to tell her story to the Whitewater grand jury.

Starr had also informed Kendall that he intended to subpoena the president to testify before the grand jury. Kendall and the other lawyers were adamantly opposed to allowing him to testify, on grounds that the target of a criminal investigation should never testify before a grand jury and instead plead his Fifth Amendment rights. Hillary told Kendall and Bill that she believed he had to testify, that the massive "political pressure" left them no choice. As when she had opposed settling with Paula Jones, her vote on this crucial matter would be the one that counted. Hillary later claimed she was not unduly concerned about it, that there was no reason for her to fear what Bill would testify to.

This claim of unconcern is striking given their lawyers' understanding of the dangers. Starr's questions to Bill in a grand jury appearance would undoubtedly be difficult. Starr had asked for a blood sample from Bill. Kendall thought it was conceivable Starr was only trying to bluff and unnerve Bill, Hillary wrote. It is hard to believe that by then she did not suspect that the purpose of the blood test was to match Bill's DNA against the purported stains on Lewinsky's by-then infamous blue dress.

There was another reason Kendall did not want Bill to testify. If the president evaded Starr's attempt to bring about his impeachment, Kendall believed the prosecutor would attempt to indict him after he left office. Lawyers did not want their clients to be confronted in court with answers pried by a grand jury with its almost limitless latitude in asking questions. But another midterm election was approaching, in which the chance for Democrats to pick up seats in Congress would surely be adversely affected if, after claiming innocence for seven months, the president were to refuse to testify. A Democratic electoral tide might mitigate against impeachment.

On August 6, Lewinsky told her story to the grand jury under a grant of immunity and the threat of perjury charges being filed against her if she were not truthful. Bill Clinton knew he was trapped. Starr issued a subpoena for the president to testify on August 17. There was no room left to maneuver. He would have to tell his wife—and the world—that he had lied. He would have to explain to Hillary that the story he told her seven months earlier about his relationship with Lewinsky did not accurately describe what had transpired and was not what he would soon tell the grand jury.

Bill went to Linda Bloodworth-Thomason on Friday, August 14, to ask whether she might talk to Hillary first. She flatly declined.

On Friday night, according to Hillary, Bob Barnett came to the White House to meet with her in the Yellow Oval Room on unrelated business, ostensibly, and to see how she was holding up. By then, Barnett was the essential Clinton family adviser, moving easily between Hillary and Bill, strategizing with his law partner Kendall, handling personal and financial matters for the president and first lady, negotiating her book contracts, and, increasingly, trying to get reporters not to write unfavorably about the Clintons, or not write about them at all. He could be intimidating.

Hillary said Barnett asked her if she was worried. What if there was more to the story than she knew?

Hillary said she told Barnett that she didn't believe there was more to it, that she had continued to ask Bill—over and over again—if he had been truthful with her.

In her telling, Barnett persisted: she had to consider the possibility that some of what Bill had said was a lie.

"My husband may have his faults, but he has never lied to me," she said she replied.

That statement speaks for itself.

BARNETT HAD prepared the ground that Linda Bloodworth-Thomason had refused to tread. He also did nothing to dissuade the *Washington Post* and the *New York Times* from publishing stories in their weekend editions that said the president was considering changing his story: by now Bill's lawyers wanted him to admit what had occurred, and feared he might, at the last minute, continue to stonewall or perjure himself before the grand jury, to save his marriage, his presidency, or both. "President Weighs Admitting He Had Sexual Contacts," read the *Times* page-one headline.

Early on the morning of August 15, a Saturday, Bill woke Hillary. "This time he didn't sit by the bed," she wrote. He told her that the situation was "much more serious" than he'd previously admitted, that he now would have to testify that he and Lewinsky had had an "inappropriate intimacy." What had occurred was "brief and sporadic." He was pacing to and fro as he talked. Seven months before, he hadn't told her because he knew how hurt and angry she'd be; and he was ashamed.

Hillary wrote, in *Living History:* "I could hardly breathe. Gulping for air, I started crying and yelling at him, 'What do you mean? What are you saying? Why did you lie to me?' I was furious and getting more so by the second. He just stood there saying over and over again, 'I'm sorry. I'm so sorry. I was trying to protect you and Chelsea.' "

Until then, she insisted, she had believed only that he had acted ridiculously for paying attention to Lewinsky, and that she had remained convinced that he was being treated unfairly. She was now "dumbfounded, heartbroken and outraged that I'd believed him at all."

"She should have killed him on the spot," said Sara Ehrman. Later, Sara, Diane, Dorothy Rodham, and Hillary would all speak privately of Hillary's "heartbreak," and how it figured in her eventual decision-making: both to try to hold the marriage together and to seek a seat in the United States Senate.

Hillary insisted that Bill tell Chelsea himself that "he had lied to her, too." Both Hillary and Bill were now aware that their marriage might not survive, that there might be "an irreparable breach," she wrote. She said his eyes had filled with tears when she'd insisted he tell Chelsea.

There had been days when the Clinton White House was out of kilter, but with the possible exception of the day the Lewinsky story had broken, no one could remember a day as disorienting as the one of the president's grand jury testimony. Only the lawyers had any idea of what Clinton was going to say in his testimony (and they worried he might go off-script), and no one—including Bill—knew what he was going to say publicly afterward. His speechwriters and other aides had taken the initiative to draft a post-testimony address to the nation, but Bill had hardly looked at it.

Blumenthal, who was in Italy for a European conference on the "Third Way," the anti-ideological political movement that Bill Clinton and Tony Blair had championed, phoned Hillary. As much as he wanted to respect her privacy, he recognized that they had to be considering the obvious political questions. She agreed. She told him that the president would be " 'embarrassed,' " by having to testify before the grand jury, "but that was for him to deal with." Blumenthal's assessment of what had occurred between Hillary and Bill reflected his closeness to her, but was also accurate, if slightly hyperbolic: "Hillary had hoped against hope that her husband had reformed himself, that whatever agony she had gone through earlier in her marriage had been resolved. Now she was discovering that it was not over. . . . In a way, this blow to her pride made her in the eyes of many a more accessible and sympathetic figure. As she steeled herself, she drew warm concern. Her private relationship with her wayward husband had a magnified effect through her every word and gesture."

UNSURE WHETHER his marriage would survive, Bill wanted his testimony to do as little as possible to undermine it further. It would be conducted in the White House Map Room, a private sitting room on the ground floor that FDR had used to follow combat reports in World War II. Starr had withdrawn his subpoena after Bill voluntarily agreed to testify, in the presence of his attorneys, with the entire proceedings tape-recorded and with a live feed to the grand jurors in the courthouse. Four hours had been allotted for the session. Bill was determined to run out the clock on his interrogators, and play to the camera—and the country: he did not doubt that, grand jury secrecy notwithstanding, eventually the tape would be made public.

Overreaching as it might seem, he saw the possibility of turning the tables, in the long run, on his tormentors and Starr. He was a master of words, as he would prove once again. They were literalists and flatfoots and haters. His answers were lengthy, and he almost always took the question and turned it upside down. When they mentioned the Paula Jones case, he challenged its relevance and identified its political purpose: "They just thought they would take a wrecking ball to me and see if they could do some damage." The Jones suit, he noted, had been "funded by my political opponents."

The first questioner was Starr's deputy Robert Bittman: "Mr. President, were you physically intimate with Monica Lewinsky?"

What followed led to a presidential locution as famous in its day as "Fourscore and seven years ago" had been: "It depends on what the meaning of 'is' is," said the president.*

He read from a prepared statement in which he admitted "inappropriate intimate contact" with Lewinsky, which "did not consist of sexual intercourse," and did not "constitute sexual relations" as defined in a long list of terms he had been read at his deposition in the Jones case in January. He addressed the grand jury, and whoever else would eventually be watching the tape: "I'll bet the grand jurors, if they were talking about two people they know, and said they have a sexual relationship, they meant they were sleeping together; they meant they were having intercourse"—not oral sex. "In an effort to preserve the dignity of the office I hold," he told Bittman, looking down at his prepared notes, "this is all I will say about the specifics of these particular matters."

Literally hours were spent trying to pin the president down on what

---

*In the Jones deposition, Robert Bennett had represented to the judge and the lawyers for Jones that "there is no sex of any kind in any manner, shape or form" between the president and Lewinsky.

Now Clinton was asked by a prosecutor, "Wouldn't you agree, this was an utterly false statement?" Clinton smiled. "It depends on what the meaning of 'is' is. . . . If 'is' means is and never has been, that's one thing. If it means there is none, that was a completely true statement." A few minutes later, he added, "I was not trying to give you a cute answer to that."

was sex and what wasn't, on what kind of sex it was that he'd had with Lewinsky (he kept saying he wouldn't talk about specifics); he had told Vernon Jordan that "there was no sexual relationship with Monica Lewinsky, which was true," and on and on.

He took numerous opportunities to characterize the methodology of Starr and his investigation, and to remind his audience that he was the president of the United States, with official duties. "I don't have a perfect memory of all these events that have now in the last seven months, since Ms. Lewinsky was kept for several hours, four or five of your lawyers and four or five FBI agents, as if she were a serious felon, these things have become the most important matters in the world. At the moment they were occurring many other things were going on."

He offered a soliloquy on the Clarence Thomas–Anita Hill testimony, concluding "I believed that they both thought they were telling the truth," trying to demonstrate that there could be two honestly held interpretations of whatever had occurred. The prosecutors kept asking about "touching her breast, kissing her breast, or touching her genitalia." They did not look or sound good on tape.

Starr was the final questioner, asking three times about the claims of executive privilege the White House had utilized, trying to show a pattern of stonewalling—with only twelve minutes remaining until the 6:30 completion scheduled for Bill's testimony. Starr had never been a criminal prosecutor before his appointment as independent counsel, and, as had been evident for two years, it showed. Bill filibustered. He did not want to put the presidency at risk of being weakened. "Most of my time and energy in the last five and a half years have been devoted to my job. I have also had to contend with things no previous president has ever had to contend with. . . . And during this whole time, I have tried as best I could to keep my mind on the job the American people gave me."

When Starr asked for more time, Kendall declined.

DURING BILL'S TESTIMONY, Hillary remained in the Solarium as aides wandered in and out with drafts of the statement Bill would make on national television later that night. She had asked Harry Thomason that morning if he would get in touch with James Carville, who was in Brazil.

"Hillary thinks it's a good idea if you came," said Thomason. "It's going to be a pretty tough day. . . . I think she'd feel better if you were kind of hanging around."

Carville went straight to the Solarium. "It was like somebody had died," he said. Usually when he saw Hillary, she was smartly dressed, her hair nicely styled, and she'd have makeup on. This time, if she had any makeup on, it wasn't noticeable, and her hair was pulled back in a pony-tail. "She'd obviously been crying," Carville recalled. "She asked me to sit by her. . . . Just, 'Come sit with me.' "

At the end of his testimony, Bill went to the residence to shower and have something to eat. She caught a glimpse of him and she could tell he was infuriated. Otherwise, she avoided him. He went back to talk to the lawyers and speechwriters who were working on his statement. "I don't think he was anxious to go in that room [where Hillary was]," said Carville. "It was a pretty somber thing."

When Carville was leaving about 8 P.M. to appear on *The Larry King Show*, a draft of a statement for Bill's speech to the nation was circulated. Hillary did not want to review it. "Her mind was elsewhere," said Carville. Some members of the staff were debating whether, in his address to the nation, Bill should attack Starr or simply acknowledge his inappro-priate relationship with Lewinsky and apologize. Chelsea was listening. Finally "out of habit, maybe curiosity, perhaps love," Hillary said later, the first lady joined the group working on the statement: Bill, Chuck Ruff (the White House Counsel), Mickey Kantor, Rahm Emanuel, the Thomasons. The television had again been turned off in deference to her. She asked how things were going. It became clear that the president hadn't yet determined what he should say, that he was flustered and get-ting angrier. Time had been reserved with the networks for him to go on the air at 10 P.M. Bill saw the chance to attack Starr and the unfair-ness of the investigation, the unconscionable abuse by Starr of his posi-tion, but there were differing views as to how far he should go. He was getting more frustrated. Suddenly, Hillary interjected, "Well, Bill, this is your speech. You're the one who got yourself into this mess, and only you can decide what to say about it." That was all the advice she gave before she left the room.

Though it was a necessity that the speech include an apology, Clinton was anything but sure that he'd taken the wrong tack over the previous months. He told a friend later that he was certain he'd saved his job by lying in the first days.

Bill began his television address by saying he had testified truthfully to the grand jury, "including questions about my private life, questions no American citizen would ever want to answer. Still, I must take com-plete responsibility for all my actions, both public and private."

He then went on to explain his earlier testimony in the Paula Jones case. "As you know, in a deposition in January, I was asked questions about my relationship with Monica Lewinsky," he said. "While my answers were legally accurate, I did not volunteer information. Indeed, I did have a relationship with Miss Lewinsky that was not appropriate. In fact, it was wrong. It constituted a critical lapse in judgment and a personal failure on my part for which I am solely and completely responsible." He continued: "I misled people, including even my wife. I deeply regret that."

Bill then launched into an attack of Ken Starr. "This has gone on too long, cost too much, and hurt too many innocent people. Now, this matter is between me, the two people I love most, my wife and our daughter, and our God. . . . I intend to reclaim my family life for my family. It's nobody's business but ours. Even presidents have private lives. It is time to stop the pursuit of personal destruction and the prying into private lives and get on with our national life."

Most of his political advisers thought his harsh words for Starr were a mistake, and the overwhelming commentary of broadcast journalists and politicians, including some Democrats, was immediately negative in the extreme. The consensus was that the president hadn't been nearly contrite enough. Republicans were demanding that he resign immediately or face impeachment by the House and conviction by the Senate. Senator Moynihan called the speech "not adequate" because of the president's lack of an apology and because he spoke about Starr. "What were we doing hearing about the special prosecutor?" Moynihan said on an Albany radio station.

About ten minutes after Bill's speech ended, the phone in Blumenthal's hotel room rang: it was the president, asking for his reaction. Blumenthal responded, "It was all right." When Hillary asked, he repeated the words. Clinton said he was pleased with the speech. "Hillary also approved. That was the most important thing of all." While Blumenthal talked with Carville and Mark Penn, he could hear the president and Hillary "bantering" in the background. "They were still working as a team," he concluded. "Without that, nothing was possible."

Hillary directed her office to issue a public statement affirming her commitment to their marriage and her love for her husband. "She believes in the president and her love for him is compassionate and steadfast, and she's very uncomfortable with her personal life being made public." She may or may not have consciously meant all of that, but for the moment it would do. She had to prepare herself for the onslaught ahead.

The next morning, Hillary, Chelsea, and Bill left for their summer "vacation" on Martha's Vineyard. Hillary's eyes were hidden by sunglasses, her face void of expression, as they walked across the South Lawn to Marine One. Chelsea was between her parents, holding hands with each.

"Chelsea, I think, was taking care of her mom mostly at that point," an aide accompanying them said. The helicopter ride to Andrews Air Force Base and the plane ride to the Vineyard were tense. The small plane—to accommodate the short airstrip at the Martha's Vineyard airport—was crowded. Secret Service agents sat between the family and a couple of pool reporters at the rear of the plane. "It was awkward," said the aide. Chelsea and Hillary talked quietly as the president, seated in front of them, seemed to be contemplative, with good cause: in addition to his personal crisis, a cruise missile strike was being planned against Osama bin Laden and his training camps in Sudan and Afghanistan. The timing of one of the launches was to be in concert with a meeting bin Laden was believed to have called with his lieutenants in Afghanistan. For a while, Bill glanced at a mystery novel he'd brought along.

A delegation of friends—among them Vernon Jordan, Carly Simon, and real estate developer Richard Friedman, their host—were awaiting them at the airport. Hillary held back while Chelsea and Bill were embraced with hugs all around. She looked numb. Said one of those who had greeted him, Bill "looked at me, his eyes, he's got those big, soft eyes of his and he looked at me and all of a sudden he choked up and said, 'You know, it's been something really bad going on.' . . . He was sad and serious."

Later, Bill recalled, "I spent the first couple of days alternating between begging for forgiveness and planning strikes on al-Qaeda." Hillary slept upstairs, Bill downstairs on the couch. When she did speak to Bill she was usually in a tirade. She later wrote that she was disconsolate, profoundly sad, disappointed, and angry. She sensed she and Bill both felt abandoned. They had arrived at 5 P.M. on Tuesday and did not venture off Friedman's expansive property until Wednesday night, for Bill's birthday dinner at Vernon and Ann Jordan's home. Every other summer, when they'd been on the Vineyard for his birthday, the dinner had been a huge celebration, with bands, and dozens of friends. This time it was only the Jordans and the Clintons; Chelsea left after dessert to be with her friends. Hillary said she hated being trapped with Bill on the island.

During the day, Bill either played with the dog or spent time alone when he wasn't meeting with advisers in a separate guesthouse on the property that aides used as an office. Usually after a major speech or juncture in his presidency, Clinton would reach for the phone and begin taking a survey about how he'd done. This was no exception. Several times he called Bob Torricelli, the New Jersey senator, in the middle of the night. "[He said] that he was in real pain. I said to him . . . 'You know, you've done a bad thing, but you didn't kill anybody. You didn't violate the Constitution. You made a serious mistake. But if you put it into the context of your entire life, the good things you've done and the bad things, we'll all survive.' "

"Well, when I make a mistake, I make a big one," the president replied. Torricelli thought Clinton was so far down that it was necessary to reassure him again: " 'You're still a remarkably good man when you balance the good and the bad.' He was a man in agony. . . . He genuinely and deeply loves that woman. He is entirely devoted to her, and worships her. I could hear the pain in his voice, and it wasn't about politics, it wasn't about the legal fight that was ensuing. His pain was about what happened to her."

Bill gave the final order at 3 A.M. on August 20 to go ahead with the strike against bin Laden, and later that day made the announcement to reporters at a school gym in Edgartown, on Martha's Vineyard.

He then flew back to Washington for a televised address from the Oval Office to explain his decision. "Our target was terror. Our mission was clear—to strike at the network of radical groups affiliated with and funded by Osama bin Laden, perhaps the preeminent organizer and financier of international terrorism in the world today." After Bill's address, several polls indicated that Americans supported his decision but were suspicious about the timing. To his great disadvantage, a brilliant, dark cinematic comedy, *Wag the Dog*, about a fictional president ordering the bombing of a convenient enemy state to distract the nation's attention from his other problems, had been released in 1997 to great success.

Hillary, meanwhile, said she was touched by the efforts of friends. She had lunch with Katharine Graham (by now retired as the publisher of the *Washington Post* though still its chairman), which neither woman was known to have discussed afterward. Graham's late husband had committed suicide in 1963—he had been diagnosed with manic-depression—after having an affair with a young woman who worked for him. But it would have been in character for Graham to be direct in discussing the situation compassionately with Hillary and drawing out a response. Hillary and Chelsea went sailing with Walter Cronkite. Jackie Kennedy had died in 1994; now her companion, Maurice Tempelsman, took Hillary sailing on his yacht one evening. He talked about Jackie, said Hillary, and how much he missed her, and his understanding of how hard the life of the late first lady had often been. He told Hillary he hoped she could forgive Bill, that he really loved her.

Meanwhile, she called Diane Blair. "She was very apologetic about not having called, and she said she just couldn't talk about it, but she knew that I was thinking about her, and she was trying to think her way through," said Diane. Hillary told her that she was aware that "a lot of people thought I just should have thrown his clothes off the Truman Balcony and kicked him out of the house, but you know, it's just not that easy. It's just not that easy."

Bill returned to the Vineyard on Friday. Hillary was still in no mood for forgiveness, but it was the first time they began talking again. They took some walks together, on woodland paths where they wouldn't be spotted by photographers. Bill noted later there was only a little "thaw," and with Chelsea as well.

Bill Styron described both Hillary and Bill as looking "shell-shocked" through their time on the Vineyard. He said Hillary was "devastated" and "had to fight just to maintain her composure" at a large dinner party one evening at the home of friends. "Everyone sensed the awful strain they were going through," when they finally ventured out in public. There had been an awkward moment at a reception when law professor Alan Dershowitz proceeded to give the president "a pompous lecture that he hadn't used his head in the legal sense."

"I remember an awful sense of strain and distress," said Styron. "Yes, she was estranged from him . . . both were almost play-acting at being together. I was troubled by the fact that I was looking at someone trying to keep her composure in the most intense and restrained way."

During his conversations with Hillary, said Styron, she raised the subject of either Bill getting counseling for his sexual compulsions or the two of them having some kind of outside family counseling. "They were struggling with the idea of seeking some kind of help, I mean who wouldn't?" But the problem was the obvious one: "Presidents in trouble go to see Billy Graham or some such. In America you have to seek counsel from a preacher if you are a president. If it's not Billy Graham, it's Jesse [Jackson]. But plainly Clinton was far too intelligent not to know he needed to go beyond presidential preachers. . . . Given my limited knowledge, they must have struggled so horribly with the sense they needed some kind of outside help from nonreligious sources."

Both Hillary and Bill, during the Vineyard visit, talked to Styron about the unrelenting campaign against them by Republicans and the right wing—notably Starr and the network of "that Pittsburgh nut," a reference to Richard Mellon Scaife, that the Clintons believed was feeding Starr. They were certain that, from the start, Starr's investigation and the unrelenting efforts of their other enemies were intended to drive them both from the White House.

Hillary's bearing and character, especially during this stay on the Vineyard, had made a deep impression on Styron. "She's plainly a woman of great sensibility and intelligence," he believed. But it was the whole person of Hillary that so impressed Styron, including her perseverance and her resilience.

"She is a woman who has seen the depths of human experience. I mean good God, the crisis she went through must have been just stupefying. . . . It's just amazing she's weathered all these incredible storms and survived so well—and maintained this staunch relationship between the two of them, what I assume is this staunch relationship, even today."*

In Washington the calls for the president's impeachment or resignation had gathered strength and neared crescendo. The fact that the president hadn't been "contrite enough" in his four-minute address to the nation was chipping away his potential Democratic support. Word was leaking from Starr's office that the independent counsel was completing his report to Congress and would be sending it soon. Dick Gephardt, the Democratic leader of the House, described impeachment as a real possibility. One Democrat after another took to the microphones to condemn the president's lying and irresponsibility, and his seeming inability to look at his own actions rather than Starr's at the crucial moment. The Republicans now seemed dead-set on the impeachment path—if he couldn't be forced to resign first. Bill's political aides were trying to put out the fire, calling around town and promising that the president would show more contrition when he returned, that he understood he hadn't said enough about his own conduct. But they were also looking at, and citing, the polls: the president's approval rating was holding steady at 62 percent, almost the highest of his presidency.

By the end of their stay on the Vineyard, said Hillary, they had made some slight progress in their relationship. As hurt as she was, she said later, the hours spent alone over the past ten days had reaffirmed that she loved him. They were returning to "a new phase in a never-ending political war." She hadn't yet decided whether she would "fight for my husband and my marriage, but I was resolved to fight for my president."

LATE IN THE AFTERNOON of September 9, 1998, the Office of the Independent Counsel formally conveyed its report and a referral on impeachment to the House Judiciary Committee. The TV networks were alerted by Starr's new deputy for public relations. The official report—445 pages containing 110,000 words, and thirty-six boxes of supporting materials—would be delivered in two vans to the sergeant-at-arms of the House, who would be waiting by the Capitol steps at

---

*He said this in the third year of Senator Hillary Clinton's first term.

3:45 P.M. to receive it. The progress of the vans was followed on live TV, from the air and the ground, with solemn commentary by the network anchors.

Starr's report suggested that there were eleven grounds for impeachment, including perjury, obstruction of justice, and abuse of office. The word *sex* was used 581 times in its pages.

In the case of Richard Nixon, the independent counsel had made no suggestions about impeachment or any other matter entrusted to the Congress under the Constitution. Rather, he had submitted the voluminous factual findings of his investigation without extraneous comment or recommendation.

John Podesta, the deputy White House chief of staff, worried that defection by someone high in the administration could bring the house down in terms of political support on the Hill and among ordinary citizens. On September 10, Clinton gathered cabinet members and a few selected members of the White House staff in the Yellow Oval Room of the residence to apologize for lying to them and the public. Bill said he would atone for the rest of his life for what he had done. He also talked at length about his enemies. The response from the cabinet was mixed. Some followed Bill's lead and quoted scripture; others wanted to bolt from the room; still others rebuked the president, most severely Donna Shalala and, obliquely, Madeleine Albright, the two women in the cabinet who had defended him the previous January, saying they believed his explanation.

According to Albright, Clinton said that "the reason he had done it was that he had been in a rage for the past four and a half years. He had been a good actor and had put on a smile but had been angry throughout. He talked in that vein for some time without making eye contact, with me or anyone else—then stopped. As he spoke I felt lost. . . . I wasn't sure he had really apologized. . . . I also didn't understand the rage. . . . It felt weird and typical."

"I thought the meeting was about confronting him and making it very clear that what he did was wrong," Donna Shalala said. "And he seemed to think that he could just come in and apologize and that was it. And I suddenly realized that . . . he thought that his behavior was private, and that you separate the two. . . . I just think public figures have to be extremely careful about their private actions and that they set the tone, and I told him that. I just told him that I wanted him to reassure me that he understood that leaders were also moral leaders. He gave me a strange answer. He said, 'By your standard we should have elected Nixon instead of Kennedy.' And I think everybody was mortified at his answer, but most people didn't say a word because they weren't quite sure what the meeting was about. . . . Not many people seemed willing to look him straight in the eye and say that."

Shalala said that Hillary did not speak to her about the episode but that "I wasn't sure she got it either. . . . Within two weeks . . . she and everybody else around her were still talking conspiracies. They were still convinced it was a conspiracy. I'm convinced to this day that they don't get it," she said in 1999. By 2006, said Shalala, "They got it."

HILLARY WAS PREPARING for the worst, based on Kendall's assessment that Starr's report would contain a detailed narrative of what had happened between Bill and Lewinsky. Starr, and now Henry Hyde, had refused to let Kendall see the report in advance of its public release. On September 10, the House Rules Committee unanimously recommended its release. Just after noon the next day, the full House voted 363 to 63 to release the full report and the supporting documents. Within an hour it was posted on the Internet.

Starr wanted the most explicit report possible, he said, to demonstrate how much work the investigation had done. He was proud of the narrative. A few members of Starr's staff had resisted the kind of report that was transmitted. Brett Kavanaugh, one of his principal deputies (later named a federal judge by President George W. Bush), had argued that "the narrative shows how pathetic Clinton is. . . . He needs therapy, not removal. . . . Our job is not to get Clinton out. It's just to give information." But Starr's purpose was transparent, and many of his deputies agreed; a few even said it aloud: they wanted to humiliate the both of them, Hillary and Bill, *and* drive them from town. They believed there was sufficient evidence to impeach Clinton for perjury and obstruction, but if the Congress wasn't willing to impeach and convict him, the full tale was so abhorrent and disgusting, Starr was banking, the country would be repulsed and demand that Clinton go.

That afternoon, the country was transfixed: the contents of the report were beyond the wildest expectations of the White House lawyers, the network anchors, Democratic members of Congress who had been kept in the dark (unlike Hyde and a few Republican leaders who knew what was coming), and certainly the millions of Americans—including Chelsea Clinton—who were reading excerpts on the Internet.

The president's relationship with Lewinsky was recounted in lurid, semi-pornographic detail designed to strip Clinton of all respect and render a picture of him as a sex-obsessed degenerate or pervert. The blue dress had been only a preview: there was the phone sex, cigars as sex toys, the president masturbating in a closet, receiving oral sex while he talked to congressional leaders.

"This is about trying to destroy me as a person," Bill told his friend Terry McAuliffe. James Carville's outrage was, as always, quotable: "The core of the entire conspiracy lies in a few blow jobs. No phone was tapped, no one's office burglarized, no tax return audited. You can't elevate a blow job to anything more than a blow job." Much of the report cited raw grand jury evidence that, under the Constitution, could never have been used in a court case without cross-examination of witnesses.

Meanwhile, Bill continued what some of his aides variously described as the "contrition tour" or his "repentance tour"—they believed the attitude was genuine—seeking forgiveness, retreating into the arms of preachers and confessing his sins, and trying to stay in office.

Hillary went to work.

ON SEPTEMBER 17, 1998, Betsy Ebeling and Diane Blair were both staying at the White House to give Hillary moral support.

"So Hillary had us for five days," said Betsy. "I mean I had only seen the president once since August 17, and it had to have been terrifying for him to know that his wife and her two best friends were coming together that weekend," which was also the weekend that House Republicans and Democrats were arguing over whether to release the videotape of the president's grand jury testimony, and other taped evidence, including phone calls between Monica Lewinsky and her confidante Linda Tripp.

Though the president and his wife were "moving on separate schedules without doing more than briefing each other," said Diane, she didn't doubt, even then, that they would remain together. "I mean it's love, but it's also [that] they're dependent upon each other, and have been for over twenty-five years in ways the rest of us can only begin to understand if we have that kind of marriage ourselves."

The visit, said Betsy, was "surreal," and highly revealing of Hillary's way of coping.

"It was business as usual," said Betsy. "She was very busy. Very busy. But also Hillary wanted to make sure Diane and I had things to do: could we do this, and could we meet for dinner?—while people on the Hill were dueling on releasing the tapes. And we had no idea how much she knew of what was going on because she was not reading newspapers, and she was not watching TV. . . . Hillary was out doing three or four events in the afternoon. Diane and I sat up in the Solarium that afternoon trying to figure out what we were going to do, and I think we finally decided that we would just go with whatever cues she was giving us, and whenever the three of us got together we would have a good time and, if she wanted to," only then would they discuss the Lewinsky turbulence.

The day before, unbeknownst to Diane and Betsy, Stevie Wonder had attended a state dinner in honor of Czech president Václav Havel. "And, evidently at some point," said Betsy, "he came up to Hillary and said, 'I have had this song going through my head for the last couple of days, and I cannot complete the song unless you help me with the words.' So she said, 'Send me a tape, I'd be more than happy to listen to it.' And, he said 'No, no. You don't understand. I will not leave Washington until you give me the right words.' So she arranged for him to come upstairs.

"When the phone rings up in the Solarium it's Capricia Marshall, Hillary's secretary, saying, 'Hillary would like you and Diane to join her this evening at six o'clock in the residence. Stevie Wonder is coming to sing.' Diane and I are in my room and we have the TV on—no one has said to us, no, you can't watch TV. It's very quiet in the house. Very quiet. I mean this is a pretty intense atmosphere staff-wise, and the help, and throughout the house—nobody is talking. And we're standing in this room and we have the TV on waiting to hear when they're going to announce that they're going to release these tapes, when the phone in my room rings again. . . . 'Mr. Wonder's here, you've got to come down.' 'Okay.'

"So we go down, and there's nobody there. You know, the two of us standing near the piano. We're looking around. And I said, 'Oh my gosh, think of the stuff they'd have to move if they have to leave here.' I mean it was just . . . it was very weird timing, and we were very emotional. And all of a sudden in comes Capricia, and then in comes Stevie Wonder . . . like one of the most handsome men I have ever seen, and his manager, and his teenage son, who's about six-foot-two. You know: Walkman, the whole bit. Introductions all the way around.

"And then in comes Hillary, she's late, and we sit down. And he sits at the piano, which she assures him has been tuned that day. She's the hostess, so she sits next to him, in a chair by herself. Diane sits with the son. I sat with the manager. And Stevie starts to talk about why he is here, and what he is doing. . . . So he sits down, and plays this song, the whole theme of it being forgiveness . . . and every once in a while he'll go 'da-da-da-da,' because he doesn't have the words. And I'm watching Hillary sitting in this chair while Diane and I are just lost. . . . And, unbeknownst to us, she had paged the White House photographer to come up, who gets a 911 call. Well, he has no idea what's going on. The photographer comes up and Stevie now is singing this song with his heart, and this beautiful melody, and it's all about what forgiveness is, and Hillary has moved her chair all the way over now to where she is right next to the piano. He finishes the song . . . and, I mean I have never heard anybody put it into words, and with such feeling. He obviously touched her, but she was dry-eyed. I don't know how she did this. He finishes the song, and they talk about the nature of forgiveness. And what it does for the soul." Contrary to Betsy's account, Hillary, in a brief mention in *Living History*, says her eyes had filled with tears.

Stevie proceeded to play a second song, also about forgiveness—"No One Walks on Water"—which, for a while, Diane thought was "No One Likes Cole Porter."

"So, Diane is laughing at this point and I'm looking at her. It's like, 'What is your problem?' So, he finishes that song as well, and Hillary looks over at us and she says rather jokingly, 'I have to run to this event, but I hope you will stay and cheer my friends up.' "

Wonder did not want Hillary to leave yet. He had an idea, which Hillary did not mention in her eleven-line account of the musical interlude in *Living History:* "His idea was that they would write this song together, and the royalties would go to women's shelters. So off Hillary goes to this event, and before she leaves she looks at both of us and she says, 'Now don't go out. Don't be out late because I'm going to be home and we'll sit up tonight. Have a good time.' And that was pretty much what the weekend was like. . . .

"Truthfully between the two of us, I never saw her angry. There's other ways of expressing anger."

THE FOLLOWING DAY, September 18, Congressman Jim Moran of Virginia called Hillary. "If you were my sister, I think I'd just grab him, pull him behind the house, and break his nose," he told her.

She sounded happy to hear from him. Bill had regarded Moran as a crucial Democratic ally, assuring him back in January that he hadn't been involved with Monica Lewinsky. Moran had believed him and stuck with him, until a television interview on September 8 in which the congressman said, "The fact is that he lied to the American people as he did in the court. I think that that is a major problem that is going to undoubtedly necessitate impeachment proceedings." Now he told Hillary that her husband was "a philanderer" and "a liar." As much as Moran respected Bill's abilities and commitment to public service, he was "offended at what he's done to you, not to mention all the people who supported him."

Hillary responded that rightist elements opposed to what Bill had been trying to do all his life were behind the impeachment drive. It was important for the country that they not win, she said. They talked for another fifteen minutes. Moran agreed to back off for the moment.

Hillary said she had become the general in charge of Bill's defense and that she believed in him.

She was braced for the inevitable release of Bill's videotaped grand jury testimony, which the House agreed to that same afternoon. News stories, perhaps based on a few transcribed excerpts of the session and leaks from the Office of the Independent Counsel, suggested that the tape would show him erupting and snarling at the prosecutors.

The release of Bill's taped grand jury testimony, on the afternoon of September 21, was a turning point in the history of the Clinton presidency. The networks initiated a thirty-second delay in their transmissions to enable excision of sexual content, if necessary. But what viewers saw was something far different than anticipated, and enough felt offended by the prosecutors' conduct—and the release of the videotape itself—to change the dynamic of the struggle. There was something prurient about what Starr and the Congress were doing that seemed to offend more people than Clinton's conduct had. At least that was what the polls were showing.

Bill had been delivering a televised speech to the United Nations about the threat of international terrorism when the networks cut away to the videotaped report. Some networks showed a split screen—the U.N. delegates on their feet giving the president an ovation on one side, the president testifying on the other—while the audio feed was about touching breasts and all the rest.

In the White House the next evening, Nelson Mandela, who had attended the U.N. session, spoke of his love for the president. "We have often said that our morality does not allow us to desert our friends. And we have got to say tonight, we are thinking of you in this difficult and uncertain time in your life."

If Mandela could forgive, Hillary would write later, she could try; but it was difficult, no matter how eminent the role models.

"You could feel the deep gasps, the strain, the personal anguish," said Melanne Verveer, who was at Hillary's side more than anyone in this period. "This was not something that was hidden. . . . The public got some sense of it when they were together. But it was very hard on her. Getting on the helicopter or at events . . . this was something that really was very painful. And to have to work it out personally, whatever that took, with every fiber of your being and you have to know you're a public figure and the world was watching . . . not just the country was watching, the world was watching."

Earlier than most of the media, Hillary sensed the ground shifting outside Washington. It went beyond the polls. In individual congressional districts, and in states with competitive Senate races, she detected a desire for compromise, for a decent end to the national soap opera in which she was forced to play a starring role.

Perceptions of the first lady were changing, too. Many saw her handling herself under the most difficult circumstances imaginable with dignity and fortitude. There were some, too, who believed she was acting as an unfortunate role model for women, that she should have packed up and left him.

She saw her basic work as campaigning for Democratic candidates. If the Democrats made an impressive showing in the midterm elections in November, the Republicans would have to take note, she believed, and pull back from their fervid campaign for impeachment and removal of Bill from office. The president, meanwhile, was making headway in peace negotiations between Israel and the Palestinians.

"Grace strikes us when we are in great pain and restlessness," Paul Tillich had said in his classic sermon that she'd first heard from Don Jones. "It happens; or it does not happen." She said she was continuing to take one day at a time and see what transpired.

She kept to her own schedule of events, giving speeches, traveling both in the United States and abroad. She raised funds for Democratic candidates across the country. She campaigned for California senator Barbara Boxer, Arkansas Senate candidate Blanche Lincoln, and Representative Charles Schumer in his effort to unseat Senator Al D'Amato of New York, who had chaired the Senate Whitewater hearings. Even in the South she drew huge crowds, and when she left a state or campaign district, polls showed that the Democratic candidate had invariably benefited. "She was on fire," said Boxer's daughter Nicole, Hillary's sister-in-law. "She was the most popular woman in the country and the most popular principal to have out on the road to campaign for you."

Hillary attended rallies and gave speeches in twenty states. When she was diagnosed with a blood clot in her leg and had to take blood thinners, she didn't stop campaigning. "We have to send a very clear signal to the Republicans in Washington that Americans care about the real issues," she said. In mid-October, Bill managed to conclude a budget deal on Capitol Hill, resulting in the first federal surplus in three decades.

The midterm elections were less than three weeks away. Gingrich was predicting a Republican pickup of twenty-two seats in the election on the strength of anti-Clinton, pro-impeachment sentiment. "I will never again, as long as I am speaker, make a speech without commenting on this topic," he had pledged.

One of the ads ordered by the Republican National Committee pictured a series of mothers proclaiming, "What did you tell your kids?" Yet an NBC/*Wall Street Journal* poll on October 29 showed that 68 percent of the country was dissatisfied with the way Congress was handling impeachment. The negative reaction wasn't all against Republicans, though; Democrats in Congress hadn't come up with a unified front themselves. Some favored censuring the president as a means of staving off impeachment and meting out more measured punishment; others favored negotiating rules for an impeachment inquiry that would slow down the process and introduce an element of fairness that wasn't evident in the Republican approach yet.

James Hansen of Utah, one of the Republicans dedicated to impeachment, had said the previous week on a radio talk show, "Well, over 90 percent [of Republicans] are saying impeach. They're saying censure, they're saying all kinds of crazy things. Some are saying assassinate. I'm not saying that."

The full House, with thirty-one Democrats in support, had voted overwhelmingly earlier in the month to authorize a formal impeachment investigation by the Judiciary Committee. With that vote, Dick Gephardt predicted, "We're going to win by losing." The November elections, the White House hoped, could bring a compromise that would put the matter to bed without the inquiry going forward. Clearly, most Americans did not think the punishment of impeachment fit the crime—whatever the crime was.

The disconnect between the country at large and Washington was huge, as Sally Quinn noted in a 3,700-word (almost a full page) essay in the *Post* on November 2, one day before the election. "With some exceptions, the Washington Establishment is outraged by the president's behavior," and "want some formal acknowledgment that the president's behavior has been unacceptable . . . not just for the sake of the community, but for the sake of the country and the presidency as well . . . while around the nation, people are disgusted but want to move on," she wrote. "Certainly Clinton is not the first president to lie. But the scope and circumstances of his lying enrage Establishment Washington. . . . If Washington is a tribe, then the president is the tribal chief. He cannot be seen to dishonor the tribe." Many of the locals, she declared, "are offended that the principles that brought them to Washington in the first place now seem to be unfashionable or illegitimate." She suggested Clinton "resign" to spare the capital "any more humiliation."

Clinton's aides were thrilled with this further evidence of the hypocrisy of the self-proclaimed ruling class of the town. They brought him a copy of the article. He proudly kept it on his desk.

On election night, Bill and his aides ate pizza in John Podesta's office while getting the returns and exit polls by phone and on the Internet. Hillary, deputy counsel Cheryl Mills, and Maggie Williams waited for the returns in the White House theater and watched the film version of Toni Morrison's novel *Beloved*, about a black woman brutalized by men.

On election day, the Democrats picked up five seats in the House, shrinking the Republican majority from 223 to 211. In the Senate, the 55 to 45 Republican majority held. The results were bizarre, both for a lame duck presidency and the extraordinary circumstances of the election itself. Most of the journalistic experts had agreed with Republican predictions of large gains in the House and an increase in the GOP majority in the Senate. The last time the president's party had picked up seats in a second term was 1822. Hillary believed the Democrats could have done even better had they been unified and adamant against impeachment.

Barbara Boxer, whose seat had been considered endangered, won. In New York, Schumer defeated D'Amato, to Hillary's great satisfaction. Almost as satisfying, in North Carolina, Senator Lauch Faircloth was defeated. Faircloth, of course, was believed by Hillary to be complicit in the hiring of Ken Starr.

That Friday, New York's other senator, Pat Moynihan, taped an interview in Manhattan with longtime TV newsman Gabe Pressman. It was scheduled for Sunday broadcast. Moynihan said he would not run for a fifth term, two years hence. Later Friday night, the news already all over town, Charles Rangel, the Harlem congressman and one of the president's most ardent supporters, phoned Hillary to tell her and to ask her to consider running for Moynihan's seat. He thought she could win. Ten months earlier, Judith Hope, the chairwoman of the state Democratic Party, had told Hillary she didn't believe Moynihan would run in 2000 and had already urged her to consider it.

Hillary said later that she told Rangel she didn't want to pursue it, that, obviously, there were other matters for her to resolve in her personal and political life. Rangel's recollection is that she had been less unequivocal, and had left the door open ever so slightly. Over the next two weeks, *Time* magazine conducted a poll that showed Hillary's approval ratings at the highest they had ever been—70 percent, double the percentage at the time of the defeat of the health care initiative.

NEWT GINGRICH was now both terrified and furious that his extramarital affair with a congressional aide might be revealed in the upcoming impeachment fight. Many in his party blamed him for the election disaster. Three days later, Representative Robert Livingston of Louisiana declared he would challenge Gingrich for the speakership. In a conference call to the entire Republican membership after realizing his support was evaporating, Gingrich announced he was resigning as speaker and from the House. It was a remarkable end for the "Contract with America," his revolutionary and controversial brainchild for governmental change and reduction, and a nasty departure for its author. He headed home to Georgia, where not long after, he joined his girlfriend and left his wife. The undercurrent of unease and discontent among Republicans was the big story but a complicated one. Behind the scenes, Henry Hyde had told Kendall and Charles Ruff that, without a bipartisan majority, he didn't believe impeachment should move forward, and that perhaps an alternative—censure, most likely, and/or an admission by Clinton that he had lied—could succeed.

Bill and his White House political and legal staff had reason to think that the election returns might stave off the appetite of House Republicans for impeachment. Partly to eliminate any further troubles, the president settled the Paula Jones case on November 13 for $850,000 ($475,000 was covered by insurance). There could now be no appeal from the dismissal of the suit or other action arising from it. Hillary said she knew, with the wisdom of hindsight, that not settling with Jones early on had been a terrible error.

Despite the dismal Republican showing in the midterm election, few of its incumbents in the House seemed to lose their hunger for impeachment and whatever other punishment they could mete out, even though they doubted the Senate would vote to convict. And the White House, as late as the third week of November, was still talking about censure. But Gingrich's deputy, Tom DeLay, was now the real Republican power in the House. Known as "the Hammer," he controlled perks, campaign funds, and an ideological agenda that, in terms of disdain for the Clintons, was even more extreme than Gingrich's. He had no intention of giving an inch.

On November 19 Starr testified before the Judiciary Committee—the main witness in its four-week impeachment "inquiry." (Hillary had spent eight months working on the impeachment investigation of Richard Nixon before hearings had even begun.) In enumerating the charges against Clinton, Starr said that his investigation had found no grounds for articles of impeachment in the Travel Office affair, or an investigation into the improper use of FBI files by White House employees that had once achieved "Filegate" status. Congressman Barney Frank asked when Starr had arrived at those conclusions.

"Several months ago."

The congressman asked why the exoneration had been withheld until

after the election, "when you were sending a referral with a lot of negative stuff about the president and only now . . . give us this exoneration."

Starr's answer was full of legal hems and haws, finally amounting to
an acknowledgment that his office was responsible only for supplying
derogatory—not exculpatory—information to Congress, in his view.

AMONG DEMOCRATS, there was a growing sense that Hillary was
"mechanically defending Bill but not engaged," as one of the capital's
Democratic elders put it.

Whatever her role earlier, Hillary was now less a day-to-day player in
the White House strategy sessions. Several people tried to engage her in
the process, but to no avail. "I would make a point of trying to reach out
to her and tell her what's going on because I knew she cared," said Greg
Craig, her old friend from law school days, and a special counsel at the
White House for impeachment matters. "And then she would call back
with thoughts. But by and large she was pretty much detached from the
entire enterprise. . . . She appeared at one residence meeting very early
on. In my tenure there I never saw her again. And those residence meetings were every week except when the president was traveling. . . . It
wasn't that she was disinterested, though. She was interested, but she was
detached. . . . If you raised something about the process with her, she
would respond appropriately and intelligently, and she would have a
view. Did she deal herself in? No. Not in the way I've seen her do when
she's traveling nationally."

The midterm campaigning had enabled her to get out of Washington and the White House, to be with her own staff and the people she
felt close to. She did not relish plunging back into strategy sessions with
her husband's aides, and all the painful reminders of what had occurred
during the first seven months of the year, when she had led the fight to
save him. Many of her aides noted the change. This was still a delicate
period in the Clintons' relationship. To some she seemed emotionally
overwhelmed—understandably. Though many still speculated as to
whether Hillary would divorce Bill, those closest to them thought the
possibility remote. "This is how it is," Tony Rodham told his wife,
Nicole, "and they will always be together. You have two people that love
each other. There is no doubt."

"I think you have to go through a personal process and a public
process, and I don't pretend to know what all they tried to do to begin to
patch things up and work at it," Melanne Verveer said around this time.
"But there's been distance. And clearly it's not been without effort on
both of their parts to try to heal the rupture. But I think they also both

recognize that nobody can understand anybody's marriage, that these people have had a hell of a lot in common for a long, long time, and I'm not sure that either of them can imagine their lives separate from each other." Fitfully, they began to get to know each other again.

There seemed to be an expectation in the White House that logic would prevail too in terms of resolving the impeachment question, that the new Republican leadership would desist, especially if they read the polls. This ignored an important fact of Washington life: perpetual incumbency. Fewer than 50 House seats out of 435 were usually competitive each election, and those that were in 1998 were already decided; the gerrymandered congressional redistricting meant most members' seats were almost for life if they wanted them, assuming they didn't go to jail or get caught at something that particularly offended their constituents. And it was even more true for Republicans than Democrats. Democratic gains or Bill Clinton's high poll numbers didn't affect the feelings of certain Republican members toward Hillary and Bill. They still despised them. They had nothing to lose, in their view, by voting for impeachment. And the Republican base, the shock troops that turned out the votes and raised the money, especially the evangelical right, fed off Clinton-bashing. Why stop now when they had a chance to succeed in all they had dreamed of? Moreover, if impeachment succeeded, there was still a possibility that a few important Democrats might bolt, and bring enough votes with them to convict.

Such realizations, inexplicably, were slow in coming in the West Wing. "We in the White House were living in denial," as Blumenthal said. He told Hillary it was almost certain they would be able to make enough votes to stop impeachment. "That never occurred to me," she said. By Thanksgiving, the reality had penetrated the staff, and last-ditch efforts to find a means of compromise with the Republicans fell through. Greg Craig had publicly stated that the White House was open to some kind of censure or rebuke short of impeachment. Bill's staff counseled that, if he would publicly admit he had lied, he might be able to get a vote of censure. But Kendall continued to counsel him to never admit to a crime, and the lawyer's calculation that Starr or some successor might pursue him after he left office was not unfounded.

Now the clock was running out on the president. On December 11, the Judiciary Committee approved four articles of impeachment for referral to the full House of Representatives. Each vote was along party lines, 21 to 16 and 20 to 16. The first article was for "providing perjurious, false and misleading testimony to the grand jury."

Hillary and Bill flew to the Middle East the next day for a four-day trip. The strain between them was evident. By now, Hillary had begun expressing her concern to a few close friends that the Clinton presidency—her legacy and Bill's—was going to be judged on the impeachment of her husband and what led to it, and the investigations that from the start had spun beyond control.

On December 16, the day after their return to Washington, the president's military and intelligence team advised that there was only a small "window" to attack sites in Iraq where U.N. inspectors suspected Saddam had stockpiled weapons of mass destruction or was working on their production, as well as other military assets. The Islamic holy month of Ramadan was approaching.

The beginning of the bombing campaign forced the Republican leadership to delay the House debate on impeachment. Republican congressman Joel Hefley said that the bombing "is a blatant and disgraceful use of military force for his own personal gain." It was one of many similar statements. The Senate majority leader, Trent Lott, said the "timing and the policy" were both "subject to question." Missiles and bombs were still striking Iraq when the impeachment debate began on December 18.

Finally Hillary broke what was being regarded as a week of public silence about the efforts to remove Bill from office. She delivered a statement on the South Portico. The reporters' stories the next day noted that she looked tired and uncomfortable and almost severe. "I think the vast majority of Americans share my approval and pride in the job the president's been doing," she said. "We in our country ought to practice reconciliation and we ought to bring our country together." It was an enigmatic moment.

The next day, Saturday, December 19, before the votes on the articles of impeachment were to begin, Hillary met with the Democratic caucus at Dick Gephardt's request. Her statement the previous day had seemed less than a rousing endorsement for her husband. Though it was a foregone conclusion that the Republicans had the votes to impeach Bill Clinton for high crimes and misdemeanors, it was important to keep defections to a minimum, to lessen the chance that Democratic senators might vote to convict the president, leading to his removal from office.

Now she was "as defiant as the day she blamed the Monica Lewinsky scandal on a 'vast right-wing conspiracy,' " the *New York Times* reported. She told the closed meeting that she was there in part as "a wife who loves and supports her husband." Republicans were intent on "hounding him out of office" because they opposed his agenda. "You all may be mad at Bill," she told them. "Certainly I'm not happy with what my husband did. But impeachment is not the answer." Nor would her husband resign.

The Republicans that morning were producing unexpected drama. Six weeks had passed since Newt Gingrich had announced his abdication and prepared to leave town. While Hillary was meeting with the Democrats, Gingrich's successor as speaker, Robert Livingston, fifty-five, a member of Congress for twenty-two years, met with his party's caucus and announced that he had been unfaithful to his wife. "I have on occasion strayed from my marriage," he told them. "I sought marriage and spiritual counseling." Livingston had come to this juncture by virtue of the pornographer Larry Flynt, owner of *Hustler* magazine. In the midst of the Lewinsky-impeachment madness, Flynt had decided to challenge what he recognized as the hypocrisy of political Washington, especially (but not limited to) those pursuing Bill Clinton. Flynt had taken out a full-page ad on October 4 in the *Washington Post* offering up to $1 million to any woman who could prove that she had had a sexual relationship with a married member of Congress or high-level government official. The ad produced results. During Flynt's "investigation" of a respondent's claim, Livingston's wife, Bonnie, had called the pornographer and begged him not to print the details of her husband's affair in the magazine.

When the House opened its proceedings on the floor that morning, Livingston was the first to speak on the upcoming vote for impeachment. He addressed the president: "Sir, you have done great damage to this nation. . . . I say that you have the power to terminate that damage and heal the wounds you have created. You, sir, may resign your post." To that, Democrats, aware of Livingston's statements to the party caucus, shouted that Livingston should resign. "I can only challenge you in a fashion that I am willing to heed my own words," he resumed. "But I cannot do that job or be the kind of leader that I would like to be under the current circumstances. So I must set the example that I hope President Clinton will follow. I will not stand for Speaker of the House on January sixth." Those in the chamber were shocked. He had already groveled before his colleagues and admitted he had "strayed" from his marriage. Wasn't that enough? Livingston's colleagues were quick to differentiate between an affair and perjury.

The White House sensed great potential danger in what was happening. Gephardt had disappeared from the floor to confer with the president's aides, and soon a statement was issued in Clinton's name urging Livingston to reconsider. He didn't, and soon after, like Gingrich, resigned from the House. Finally, after two hours off the floor, Gephardt reappeared and spoke in the well of the House. He called Livingston "a worthy and good and honorable man," which brought a standing ovation on both sides of the aisle. Such were the ways of Washington in this longest season.

The House rejected Gephardt's parliamentary maneuver to force a vote on censure, 230 to 204. Acting on their prearranged plans, the

Democrats then marched out of the chamber as voting began on Article I, gathering on the steps of the Capitol to stage a brief protest rally, then turning around and parading back in before the fifteen-minute voting period expired.

On nearly a party-line vote, the House of Representatives passed two articles of impeachment, one for obstruction of justice and the other for lying under oath. Rather than hang his head in defeat, Bill joined Hillary and a slew of Democrats in the Rose Garden, as Al Gore praised the president. The House had done "a great disservice to a man I believe will be regarded in the history books as one of our greatest presidents," he said. This was a carefully orchestrated show of combativeness, to counter Livingston's suggestion that the president resign. The idea was to turn defeat into victory, and in a sense it worked. But there was the larger picture: the wreckage of what had seemed such a promising and idealistic presidency six winters before, and the young president and his brilliant wife who would change the face of governance in the capital. On their way outside, Hillary and Bill Clinton had barely spoken, and the tension between them was visible for all to see.

THE OUTCOME of the president's trial was, given the drama that had preceded it, relatively uneventful. The ceremonial proceedings, the chief justice in his Gilbert and Sullivan robes, the attempts at majestic oratory with their undercurrent of sex, were insipid. It was a low moment in the history of the American presidency, and even lower in terms of a United States Congress already on its way to becoming an institution that ignored its constitutional responsibility as a co-equal branch of government. Nor had the judicial system performed its assigned role without favor. The verdict was as expected, and Bill was acquitted after a five-week trial. The vote on the first article of impeachment was 55 to 45, with no Democrats joining Republicans favoring conviction for perjury; and 50 to 50 on the second article of impeachment on obstruction of justice (seventeen votes shy of conviction), with no members of the president's party voting to convict. The chief justice mercifully gaveled the proceedings to a close at 12:39 P.M. on February 12, 1999.

As the proceedings ended, Hillary Rodham Clinton had already begun considering whether she aspired to the same United States Senate that had just acquitted her husband.

18

A Woman in Charge

*The most difficult decisions I have made in my life were to stay married
to Bill and to run for the Senate from New York.*

—*Living History*

WHILE THE SENATE was voting on the articles of impeachment, Harold Ickes had spread out a large map of New York state and shown Hillary what was involved in running. There was something particularly defiant about choosing this moment to begin her decision-making in earnest. She had put off more serious consideration while the impeachment process hurtled forward, perhaps in part because, without the stigma of impeachment, she and Bill might still have had a chance to accomplish some of their goals, and redeem some of the promise of their journey. But even then, it was hard to imagine that they wouldn't be remembered primarily for what Bill had done with Monica Lewinsky, and Hillary with health care, and the personal drama they had put on for the nation and the world to watch. Now, Bill looked like the lamest of lame ducks, whatever his popularity ratings. Her anger and pain were still raw.

She and Ickes pored over the map. Ickes enumerated the problems that lay in her path. He pointed to, and they discussed, towns and cities, tiny hamlets, the boroughs of New York City. New York had almost twenty million citizens, and 54,000 square miles that a candidate for the Senate would have to traverse from the Great Lakes to the Canadian border to Fire Island. She had done a lot of campaigning over the years, but nothing similar to this. There would be so much to learn. She had no experience in the internal politics of New York: its ethnicities, outsized personalities, unions, cultures, suburbs, its broken rust-belt economy upstate, and, in New York City, Wall Street and the toughest press corps in the country, reporters who could spot a rube a mile away.

There were many reasons she shouldn't run, and Ickes laid them out. She wasn't from New York. She had never lived there (she and Bill had decided, though, not long after his reelection in 1996, that they would move at the end of his presidency to New York City and divide their time between Manhattan and Arkansas, where Bill would build his library). No woman had ever won office in New York in a statewide race. The press would live up to its reputation. Republican attacks on her in New York would be vicious. And she was still first lady, with official unofficial duties, so how could she be fully involved in such an exhausting campaign?

RUNNING FOR public office had virtually never been on Hillary's agenda. Only when she briefly trifled with succeeding Bill as governor of Arkansas, in 1990—after their marriage had almost ended, and his depression was so great that he had little interest in continuing in the job—had she considered it. Until then, and after she and Bill reached the White House, she had repeatedly told Diane Blair that she had no interest in elected office. In truth, she had never much liked campaigning, until she found her own voice and, to her surprise, connected with voters as her own distinct person in the 1998 off-year elections, in the gritty precincts that had been her husband's natural habitat. She had asked the voters to elect Democrats not to save Bill's presidency, but rather to support her ideas of constitutional governance and stand against the criminalization of the Clintons' politics, which was how she categorized what Starr, D'Amato, Faircloth, Gingrich, and those aligned with them had done. Every poll that Mark Penn had taken showed that the voters were responding to Hillary as a woman whose values they now seemed to appreciate. Her experience had been almost totally different from campaigning with or for Bill, as an adjunct of his agenda. While virtually everyone else caught up in the Lewinsky business had been diminished or, to some degree, discredited, only Hillary seemed to gain in stature. By the time her husband went on trial in the Senate, every opinion poll indicated that she had become widely admired in a way that Bill wasn't, by both women and men—as a result of *her conduct*. As he was struggling to stay in office, she was coming into her own.

"Very specifically we would say to each other over the years, 'You can have as great or greater impact by doing things other than elective office,' " Diane Blair said. When she visited the White House, she and Hillary—disguised in a hat or with her hair pulled back behind a headband—would sneak off (with the Secret Service hovering) to Rock Creek Park or the C&O Canal towpath for long walks. On one of these during "a particularly hard week" early in the second term, Diane asked, " 'Well, if you had your druthers right now, what would you really like to do?' And Hillary said, 'I would like to be in a think tank. I can see a room just loaded with books, next door to a library, and time to really just think hard about some of these policy issues. I just don't feel like I have time to really mentally engage with some of the things that I know are out there.'

"She did not say, 'Oh, I'd like to be a United States senator, or I want to be a governor.' What she said was, I want to be a policy woman. Until right now [1999], she has not seen elective office as the path that she had ambitions for in any way." Hillary had never previously felt the need to assert her own "legitimacy," separate from the single voice of her and Bill's journey. Now, with Bill having squandered so much of what was to have been their presidency, she felt differently.

One of the Clintons' closest aides believed that what was propelling her toward running was "the wrecking of their work, not just the humiliation." Actually, she wanted to undo both.

"Prior to this—the impeachment, Lewinsky—she was looking forward to having some semblance of a private life," Deborah Sale said around this time. "And being the senator from New York affords you none. That is something that could hold her back." Sale noted that Bill Clinton wanted her to run. "He thinks she deserves a chance to be her own individual person. Now if she chose a different way, he would support it, too. But being the senator from New York . . ."

Talking with Bill about whether she would run for the Senate was a kind of therapy in itself. (They also began weekly marital counseling together with a therapist; only a few members of their staffs were aware of it.) Hillary wrote that gradually they both allowed the tensions to fade. Their relationship was beginning to mend.

Along with Donna Shalala, Ann Jordan, Maggie Williams, and many other friends and advisers, Blair tried to dissuade Hillary from running for the Senate.

Hillary made the decision slowly, deliberately, analytically. Her decision-making process was different from Bill's. Ann Stock, her social secretary, noted that "when you look at her making this decision . . . every bone in her body says, Yeah, I'd love to do that. But, the introspective person says, Yeah, but I need to examine all parts of this."

The Lewinsky episode was critical not just to the Clintons' marriage but to Hillary's evolution as a politician. She was married to the most skilled politician of the age, yet there was no denying he was also experiencing the greatest presidential free-fall of the twentieth century, apart from Richard M. Nixon's. Until the day of impeachment when she met with Democrats on Capitol Hill, Hillary had not realized how much Bill was despised—there really was no other word for it—by many of his own party in Congress. She would never put herself in that position, she resolved.

BY THE LATE spring of 1999, she seemed ready to run, but one substantial impediment remained: the incumbent senator, Pat Moynihan, who had never been warmly inclined to Hillary. His wife, Liz, despised what she regarded as Hillary's lack of straight talking and dealing. Mandy Grunwald had worked for Moynihan and became an intermediary for Hillary. She tried to convey Hillary's attributes and vulnerabilities to Pat and Liz. Moynihan was not a liberal in the sense of traditional Democratic politics, nor was Hillary. He was an academic, and she would have been comfortable in the same role.

Moynihan was never one to personalize fights or hold grudges, but Hillary's willingness to demonize her enemies had left him with lasting caution about her. He also was a realist and could see the appeal of her candidacy. Moreover, Hillary had learned a lot in seven years in the White House. She was not going to make the same mistakes. He respected her mind. He accepted what was becoming inevitable. Terry McAuliffe had already promised to help raise the $25 million necessary to fund a winning campaign. He thought Hillary could win. Mark Penn's polls also were positive.

On July 7, she stood beside the senator at the Moynihans' nine-hundred-acre farm in Pindars Corner, in rural northwest New York State. Two hundred reporters were there to cover the event. She announced her candidacy. "I intend to be spending my time in the next days and weeks and months listening to New Yorkers," Hillary said. Bill visited an Indian reservation in South Dakota that day. "Now," said Hillary, "I suppose the question on everybody's mind is, Why the Senate and why New York and why me? All I can say is I care deeply about the issues that are important in this state, that I've already been learning about and hearing about." It wasn't totally clear if she was talking about the state or the issues.

DIANE BLAIR was not surprised at Hillary's decision to run. "Being a U.S. senator gives her an ongoing forum in which to pursue the agenda she's always been interested in ever since I've known her." Diane, Sara Ehrman, and Deborah Sale, among many of Hillary's female friends, were sure she would win. They certainly understood her strengths and her desires; perhaps most important, they sensed her determination to redeem her own legacy.

"I would say that right now most everybody in her life is simply a means of getting where she has to go," Sara Ehrman said while Hillary was considering whether to run. By then Sara worried that Hillary's Christian progressive optimism was in danger of devolving into arrogance—"God is on my side can be arrogance"—though it was easy to forget something basic about both Clintons: an irrevocable commitment to public service. "I'm not saying she's an unethical person, because she's definitely not," said Ehrman. "But everything and everybody is now part of the package of getting them there, getting them—her and the president—there for the greater good." Where Sara had once seen something pure in Hillary, now, after the Clintons' joint trial in the capital city, there seemed something . . . conventional. But she saw her old friend accurately as still being "on a mission." "Hillary still believes that she's going to shape the world. She's going to have a place to do it, and if Gore isn't elected, I have no doubt that in 2002 she'll start thinking about running for the White House."

Whatever else Bill was, he was a practical politician. Hillary welcomed his expertise. In *Living History*, she wrote that they both knew that in running for office she would be on her own as she had never been before. But they were up for building a new kind of partnership. In his memoirs Bill said he was ready to be the able assistant she had once been to him. The role reversal was fascinating.

A whole new dynamic had entered the country's political culture. The first lady's motives were the focus of frenzied debate. Was her marriage now based on love or political expediency? Was she a victim or an enabler? Could she be a forgiving person? Was she running to remove a political stain or because she truly wanted to be in the Senate? Did she want to be president? And ironically: Had the impeachment of Bill Clinton made possible a Clinton dynasty in American politics?

By the time she had declared her candidacy for the Senate, she had arguably become a more polarizing figure than he, inflaming the politics of gender in a way not seen since the first days of radical feminism in America, and perhaps not since the suffrage movement. The Republican Party at the turn of the twenty-first century existed for two overarching purposes: to elect a president and to defeat Hillary Clinton and Clintonism.

. . .

THE FEATURE OF Hillary Clinton's campaign for the Senate that proved brilliant, and the model for her subsequent politics, was the "listening tour."

Under the guise of trying to learn the concerns and complaints of constituents, and to offset the "carpetbagger" effect, she did the opposite of a lifetime's instincts: she restrained her tendency toward unequivocal advocacy and the assertion of her own strongly held views. Instead, she "interviewed" the voters; she made sure not to offend, and she told voters largely what they wanted to hear. In the poll-driven 2000 campaign for the Senate there was hardly a single noteworthy position she embraced that put her at odds with the core constituencies she sought. One principle was beyond compromise, though she enunciated it in the context of her own traditional values: a woman's right to choose.

Getting the nomination of the Democratic Party was easy. Congresswoman Nita Lowey, who had been planning on seeking Moynihan's seat, stepped aside. In the general election campaign, Hillary was blessed with the Republican opponent she drew. New York City mayor Rudy Giuliani had savored running against her, but he self-destructed in a marital scandal at the same time he was diagnosed with prostate cancer. Representative Rick Lazio of Long Island became the Republican nominee, and he was out of his league.

Lazio, well funded and backed by the national Republican apparatus and many of the Clintons' old foes, tried to paint Hillary into a liberal corner, but it didn't work. In debates, Hillary won on points, style (if not quite *To Kill a Mockingbird*, then having a certain charm of her own), and a platform that was perfectly tailored to crafting an electoral majority among the state's myriad constituencies, especially upstate, long Republican territory but ill-served by a Republican governor who allowed its economy to stagnate.

What was particularly striking in Hillary's campaign was how it contrasted with the view of leadership she had long embraced and demanded of others. She had sometimes worried that Bill's triangulation (the term was actually Dick Morris's) and centrist balance was too contrived, not principled enough. The leaders she admired were those who had shown the courage to challenge the conventional wisdom—Goldwater, Margaret Chase Smith, Saul Alinsky, Eleanor Roosevelt. In New York she felt risky, unequivocal advocacy would threaten her chances.

In a sense, her "listening tour" was similar to how Dick Morris had guided Bill's campaigns—a method of surveying and polling that established what voters wanted, and what would offend their sensibilities. This became her approach as a candidate.

On November 7, 2000, she won overwhelmingly, 55 percent to 43 percent.

NOT REDEMPTION, but something else awesomely powerful could be felt among several thousand congregants in the National Cathedral attending the funeral on December 16, 2000, of Charles Ruff, the gentle man who, from his wheelchair, had so eloquently and ably defended Bill Clinton in his trial before the Senate. Something ineluctable passed in the great nave of the cathedral that day, and for those called to witness, the capital city beyond seemed a changed place when they stepped into the sunlight outside.

Ruff lived an exemplary life in the pit that is political Washington, and the capital's judges, journalists, members of the bar and of Congress (of both parties), and not a few humble citizens, had turned out to pay their deepest respects. The eulogy, delivered by the president, was off-key. Clinton could not bring himself to properly thank Ruff for the *personal* service to him, not just during Ruff's defense in the Senate, but as Clinton's counsel through the most perilous months of his presidency. The impeached president instead couched his funereal salute in terms of what Ruff had done for the nation during the recent unpleasantness, as if Clinton's role had been totally incidental to the danger to the country and its institutions.

Viewed from the row behind where Bill and Hillary were seated for the service, their lack of physical or emotional contact throughout the ninety-minute memorial was almost painful to observe. Then, as the congregation began to recess, all eyes seemed to turn to Hillary, and suddenly her presence became the single focus of attention in the cathedral. Cameras trained on her, not him. Congressmen came up to shake her hand and kiss her cheek. Old friends embraced her tightly and wished her well. Strangers stared. To her side, the president stood comparatively ignored, diminished in the commotion over his wife, even a little lost. A new era could be glimpsed at the creation: Hillary was glowing, perfectly turned out, a woman in Washington at the center of the nation's attention, a woman unique in its history.

ON THE SAME DAY as Ruff's funeral, Simon & Schuster, a unit of the Viacom media conglomerate, announced that it would publish a memoir by Hillary of "her years as first lady." The announcement ended a week-long bidding war among publishers, presided over by Bob Barnett. In the end, Hillary would receive the second biggest nonfiction book advance in history, $8 million, slightly less than the sum paid to Pope John Paul II. "As far as I am concerned," said former senator Bill Bradley, "what she did in signing a book contract is no different than what Newt Gingrich did."

In 1995, under duress as a result of a House Ethics Committee investigation, Gingrich had returned a $4.5 million book advance from a publishing house controlled by Rupert Murdoch, whose representatives frequently lobby the Congress on behalf of his media interests, seeking tax breaks, exceptions to anti-monopoly laws, and other relief from customary governmental regulation. The Senate, unlike the House, which changed its rules after the Gingrich book controversy, permits income derived from book contracts that reflect "usual and customary" industry practices.

Hillary's contract was anything but "usual and customary," according to Common Cause and the Congressional Accountability Project, which suggested that she forsake an advance on the book and accept only sales-based royalties, on the grounds that the arrangement posed an obvious conflict of interest. The contract, as reported, was particularly favorable to Hillary in that she would receive up to half her negotiated advance upon signing; large advances are usually doled out over the length of a contract tied to stages of progress in the writing. The *Washington Post* and the *New York Times* both published editorials questioning the ethics of the arrangement. "The deal may conceivably conform to the lax Senate rules on book sales," said the *Times*, but it is "an affront to common sense."

The deal was negotiated before Hillary took her Senate seat, but its royalty provisions were later approved by the Senate Ethics Committe. The matter nonetheless recalled the kind of shortcutting she'd been accused of in the commodities trading uproar, raising again the notion that rules for other people didn't necessarily apply to her.

Predictably, Republican senators said Hillary was beginning her Senate career with the same approach to the law that afflicted the Clintons in the White House.

DESPITE THE FACT that Vice President Gore had been integral to the Clinton presidency and its considerable successes, he had chosen to distance himself from Bill and Hillary Clinton during his 2000 presidential campaign, to their chagrin. They had hoped that his election, with

Hillary's, would stand as a powerful repudiation of the impeachment and the politics that fueled it. Bill and Hillary both believed, as did many astute political analysts, that Gore's strategy had probably cost him the election. But he had wanted to make an implicit statement that he disapproved of Bill's conduct—his aides were *explicit* about his reasons—and the Clintons' ethical lapses.

On December 12, the Supreme Court, in a 5–4 decision, with Justice Rehnquist leading the majority, had dismissed the Gore campaign's attempt to obtain a recount of the disputed Florida results, and George Bush became the president-elect. On January 3, 2001, as vice president and, as specified by the Constitution, the presiding officer of the United States Senate, Gore swore in Senator Hillary Rodham Clinton of New York.

There was no precedent for her arrival as a freshman senator. She was still living in the White House, still the first lady of the United States. Her presence totally overshadowed that of the other ninety-nine members. They could see on that first day that she was a senator apart, a national figure, with a national constituency already. Those who had served in the chamber for decades (a few since the days when pages attended to cuspidors stationed at each entrance to the floor) understood this was something unique. In the coming weeks and months, people in the galleries largely ignored the other senators if Hillary was on the floor. They pointed at her. On the Capitol subways that link the House and Senate wings, passersby came rushing up to her for autographs, while other, longtime senators, considered the uncommon commotion. From her first days on the Hill, Hillary had a galvanizing effect on hundreds of women who worked there. Usually blasé at the presence of mere politicos, they followed her through the halls, asked her advice, filed applications to join her staff.

For the first time since she had left Washington to join Bill Clinton in Arkansas in 1974, Hillary's slate was her own to keep clean. This was a new beginning. She was now truly a woman in charge.

But soon thereafter, on the Clintons' last day in the White House, January 20, 2001, only hours before they were to go to the Capitol for the swearing-in of George W. Bush, Bill's controversial last-minute pardons set off her fury again—at him. The most offensive of the pardons was of Marc Rich, a fugitive financier whose excesses were the epitome of 1980s greed. His avenue to a pardon was the largesse of his ex-wife, Denise, who had contributed $1 million to Democratic causes, including $450,000 to the Clinton presidential library fund, and as an R&B songwriter gave him entrée into a glitzy New York party world that would enrich his post-presidential life. Other powerful friends and aides of the

Clintons had pleaded Rich's case, including former White House deputy counsel Jack Quinn and Beth Dozoretz, the treasurer of the Democratic National Committee and a close friend of Hillary.

While Rich had found favor, Webb Hubbell had not. A pardon would have given him the opportunity to resume the practice of law. He had not personally sought a pardon nor sent emissaries; old colleagues had told his family nonetheless they expected Bill to issue a pardon. When he didn't, Hubbell, his wife, and his children were devastated.

Meanwhile, it was discovered that Hillary's brother Hugh—who in 1994 had run a quixotic campaign for senator from Florida—had been paid $400,000 to lobby for a pardon and commutation of a prison sentence for a client/acquaintance, which the president did not grant, for evident reasons. By then the Rodham brothers had been in the news far more than their sister had hoped. "My family can be very demanding and I apologize for that," Hillary had said after a previous incident involving her brother Tony, who had screamed at White House aides insisting that a friend get a free ride on the first lady's plane when she was campaigning through Florida on Hugh's behalf. In 1999 the Rodham brothers had formed a company to sell hazelnuts grown in the former Soviet republic of Georgia; that led to a demand by Bill's national security adviser, Sandy Berger, that they dismantle their effort. "They're like mama's boys," a former Clinton aide told the *New York Times*. "It's a very odd family dynamic. They seem to feel, 'We've been out there, we've been in this fishbowl, we're not getting anything.' Mrs. Rodham [Dorothy] is always telling Hillary, 'You're not doing enough for your brothers.' "

HILLARY'S ABILITY TO adapt to new circumstances, until she had reached the White House as first lady, had almost never betrayed her. Its success was never more apparent than her first year on Capitol Hill. She had returned to form. She approached almost every aspect of her job opposite the way she had in the White House. When she was assigned a freshman's office in the Capitol basement, she happily accepted it and waited patiently for better quarters, though she could have immediately asked for more space given the size of her constituency. Her modesty, a word not often associated with Hillary, was appreciated by her Senate colleagues, though her grandiosity beyond the chamber as an outsized fund-raiser for her party and Democrat sui generis was a genuine political phenomenon of 2001. With the proceeds of her book deal, she and Bill purchased a $3 million house at the end of a forested cul-de-sac adjacent to the British embassy, which became the nexus of her political operations outside her official office.

On Capitol Hill, she was deferential. The first senators she sought out for conversation, for co-sponsorship of small but useful legislative initiatives, for prayer, for a drink, or for lunch in the Senate dining room tended to be those who had opposed the Clintons most vigorously, some of whom had voted to impeach or convict Bill: Orrin Hatch, Lindsey Graham, Sam Brownback.

She was determined to show them how serious she was. From the moment she was elected, it was widely expected that Hillary would become the bull in the Senate china shop. Instead, she inched her way to the head of the Democratic class by dint of study, speaking carefully and in measured tones. She didn't seek the limelight. (It came to her.) Her tenure as a senator was an extension of the listening tour that helped get her elected. She fetched coffee for her male colleagues, remembered who took cream or sugar, and carried it off with a touch of self-mockery. Hillary's sense of humor, over the next few years, gradually returned.

She learned the ways of the Senate. She identified who her enemies were, or those of her husband, and waged a campaign to win them over, or at least neutralize them. That was the internal institutional strategy. The external strategy was to show her constituents that she wouldn't let them down. She worked particularly hard for those who didn't support her, as if to prove to them that she wasn't who they thought she was. Her small-steps policy in the Senate reflected what she had learned from her husband's car tag experience in Arkansas: she would not forget the day-to-day needs of her constituents while promoting her larger ambitions. She was pleasantly surprised to find that addressing the problems and concerns of the millions of her constituents who lived in upstate New York was often similar to her Arkansas experience. Her representation on behalf of New Yorkers was effective, smart, and bold. Her initial committee assignments were Labor, Health Education, and Pensions; Environment and Public Works; and Budget, all of which enabled her to direct funds to her home state.

On the Democratic side, her first courtesy call was to Senator Robert Byrd of West Virginia, the dean of the institution, its self-appointed historian and guardian of tradition (and the most effective facilitator of federal largesse to a senator's home state of the past half-century). West Virginia was littered with Byrd-villes, Byrd FBI buildings, Byrd-funded military bases, Byrd federal records facilities, and the best federally maintained road system in the nation.

Hillary had always relished being a star pupil and teacher's pet, and she excelled at playing those roles in the Senate. Though Byrd had years before refused to rescue her health care plan and put it into the federal budget bill (thus effectively guaranteeing its death), she now decided that he had not acted out of enmity or ideological opposition. Rather it was senatorial tradition and the sanctity of the budget process, as he saw it.

A Democratic colleague touted Hillary as "a workhorse, not a show horse," which was the kind of filly Byrd appreciated. Still, she set up a brain trust that included former cabinet secretaries, and national security and economic advisers to the president.

She also joined the Senate's most exclusive, and private, prayer group, an acknowledgment by, among others, the most conservative of her fellow senators that they accepted the genuineness of her religiosity. They knew this because several of their wives had already been members of Hillary's women's prayer group while she was first lady.

For all her advances, the most surprising aspect of her first term was that she did little in the Senate that drew much attention as making a difference beyond New York. In fact, save for her support of the war in Iraq, she kept a low profile on many issues of great national import. She diligently sought to avoid controversy. She had spent her whole career looking at the big questions; now she seemed to be taking a more narrow view, resembling in some ways the former senator from her state whom she had despised, Senator Alfonse D'Amato, known as Senator Pothole. She delivered.

More than most senators, the 9/11 attacks radically altered Hillary's agenda. In office only nine months, she and New York's senior senator, Charles Schumer, became the city's most effective advocates for money and services from Washington. Partly through her relationship with Senator Byrd, $20 billion in recovery funds were set aside in the budget for the city. "We're in real trouble, and it's going to take a lot to put the city back together. Can you help?" she was quoted as asking him in a September 12 phone call.

"Count me in as the third senator from New York," Byrd reportedly told her.

ON OCTOBER 10, 2002, the Senate voted to authorize President Bush to use force against Iraq and Saddam Hussein. That day, Hillary took to the Senate floor and delivered a long speech. In part she said:

> Because bipartisan support for this resolution makes success in the United Nations more likely, and therefore, war less likely, and because a good faith effort by the United States, even if it fails, will bring more allies and legitimacy to our cause, I have concluded, after careful and serious consideration, that a vote for the resolu-

tion best serves the security of our nation. If we were to defeat this resolution or pass it with only a few Democrats, I am concerned that those who want to pretend this problem will go away with delay will oppose any UN resolution calling for unrestricted inspections. This is a very difficult vote. This is probably the hardest decision I have ever had to make—any vote that may lead to war should be hard—but I cast it with conviction.

And perhaps my decision is influenced by my eight years of experience on the other end of Pennsylvania Avenue in the White House watching my husband deal with serious challenges to our nation. I want this president, or any future president, to be in the strongest possible position to lead our country in the United Nations or in war. Secondly, I want to ensure that Saddam Hussein makes no mistake about our national unity and for our support for the president's efforts to wage America's war against terrorists and weapons of mass destruction. And thirdly, I want the men and women in our armed forces to know that if they should be called upon to act against Iraq, our country will stand resolutely behind them.

As it became obvious to Hillary and other Democrats who supported the war's authorization that the Iraq adventure was becoming a catastrophe, her tone and her words changed, though later than many of her Democratic colleagues. "If I had known then what we know now, there would never have been a vote and I never would have voted to give the president the authority," she said in the winter of 2007.

She has since claimed that she didn't expect the United States to go straight toward war when she cast her vote; rather, that the president would endeavor to do what was necessary to get United Nations arms inspectors back into Iraq to determine Saddam's WMD capabilities. "Well, I've said that he 'misused' the authority granted to him," she said in 2006. "When I spoke at the time of the vote I made it very clear that this was not a vote for preemptive war; this was a vote, I thought, that would enable diplomacy to succeed because we would have a unified front between the president and our Congress to go to the Security Council to try to get the inspectors back in. Obviously we now know, in retrospect, that the president and vice president and his team probably didn't intend for the inspectors to do their work."

At the time, according to former national security officials of the Clinton administration, Hillary was being advised on matters concerning Iraq by her husband and Sandy Berger, his national security adviser. Both felt she should support the president in the vote. Soon aferward, Richard Holbrooke also joined her national security advisory group, which continued to help her work through her statements and position on the war.

"Her perspective is of someone who lived and worked in the White House for eight years [as] one of the two right hands to the president, who understands the seriousness of intelligence—not just that available in 2002 and 2003, but available for a decade about weapons of mass destruction and other forms of repression in Iraq," said a former member of the Clinton administration. "She is familiar [with], and was prone to accept, the president saying, 'We know things we can't say . . . that suggest that this is a dangerous regime to the world.' She had been around when her husband bombed the guy because of WMD."

Though few other senators mistook the vote for anything but an authorization for Bush to invade Iraq without going back to the United Nations, Hillary insists she had a different, literal understanding of what the legislation said, and that Bush would honor it. "That's what Bush said in his speech in Cincinnati on October 7," she said. "They called me to the White House on October 8 and gave me another briefing. When I got back to my office, [National Security Adviser] Condi Rice called me and asked if I had any questions. I said, 'Look, I have one question: If the president has this authority, will he go to the United Nations and use it to get inspectors to go back into Iraq and figure out what this guy has?' [Rice replied,] 'Yes, that's what it's for.' Privately and publicly, that was the argument they were making."

According to officials in both the Bush administration and Hillary's entourage, there was a conversation between the two women about the meaning of the vote. But that is where the agreement ends, with Bush aides claiming Rice gave no such guarantee and Hillary's camp saying Rice did.

"You are not dealing here with two people with great reputations for candor," noted a disinterested former aide to President Clinton.

IN THE THIRD year of her term Hillary succeeded in her effort to be appointed to a seat on the Armed Services Committee—highly unusual for a first-term senator. The first thing she did as a member was to pay a courtesy call on Secretary of Defense Donald Rumsfeld.

It is clear from conversations with her advisers that Hillary's membership on the Armed Services Committee was intended to be the centerpiece of her new credentials for the presidency. She meant to become a defense intellectual, muscular in her approach, a master of the arcana of policy, weaponry, and strategy that would both serve her if elected, and help her get there by eliminating voters' fears about a woman being commander in chief. She had fought the crippling effects of Bill's weak credentials in this area and was resolved (and advised by her husband, among others) to strengthen her position. She assumed from the start that she could count on the liberal wing of the Democratic Party in the pocket of her pants suits; the challenge would be to win over swing voters, Republican moderates (and she believed they existed, the more so as the presidency of George W. Bush veered toward both debilitating incompetence and terminal mendacity).

Part of the excitement of a Hillary candidacy was the contemplation of how a new Clinton presidency would work with a woman in charge, and a former president, her husband, behind her. There is no doubt that the Clinton journey continues to be a joint enterprise. As for the state of her marriage, its reality is something known—as always—only to her and Bill Clinton, and their friends seem no more sure than long ago if the perception of the Clinton union by one of the partners is the perception of the other.

By the time of Hillary's campaign for reelection to the Senate in 2006, she had recruited a staff ready for a presidential campaign, a huge fundraising apparatus and war chest, and a strategy to quickly eliminate serious opposition for the Democratic nomination. The strategy, by all accounts, anticipated for far too long military success in Iraq, and a postwar ability to satisfy America's interests without great sacrifice.

"Her handling of the war issue subjected her to the kind of broader examination that she wasn't expecting," said a former Democratic senator, an admirer. "It put her in the position of looking backward, not forward, of caving to conventional wisdom instead of moving in the direction of new leadership, new ideas, being bold. Hillary stands for very good things on almost all of the other, traditional issues. Women's rights, child care, health care, minimum wage, etc. She's studied a lot of them. She is a very good senator, one of the best. But the war revealed something about her that she may not be able to get past: the idea that she is a throwback to another time, that she is looking like a tired version of herself."

One of her former White House aides observed, "I don't know how anything in her life can be deep or honest because she's tied herself in to stay with Bill. . . . So everything is seen from this kind of warped perspective, in a way. She can no longer be honest about what she actually feels, so it is hard to know if she's being honest about what she says she thinks."

Another aide referred to her very visible position on flag-burning:
"The only major thing I can remember her doing is the flag-burning

statute. That is evidence of the old Dick Morris/Bill Clinton 'triangulation,' looking for the opportunity to break away from Democratic Party orthodoxy, which is a good idea. But she might have picked something significant; it's not as if flag-burning on the streets of America is a national problem. As a constitutional question it leads you to wonder if she really believes people should go to jail for burning the U.S. flag. I can't believe somebody who graduated Yale Law School believes people should be prosecuted and put in jail for burning the American flag."

A long-time associate of the Clintons, with whom Hillary has consulted in her quest to return to the White House, said: "She has a very plausible case for president. She had an eight-year supergraduate course in the presidency, a progressive platform. But she should have been more probing and aggressive by this stage, not looking back." He paused. "Besides, I'm not sure I want the circus back in town." This may be a succint expression of her biggest obstacle.

HILLARY'S MEMOIR, *Living History*, was published in June 2003.

"It was a campaign document," her deputy press secretary in the White House, Neel Lattimore, had said about her first book, *It Takes a Village*. It was meant to define her in unexpected ways. *Living History* was likewise meant to be a campaign document. It is a very revealing document, but not in the sense she intended.

Since her Arkansas years, Hillary Rodham Clinton has always had a difficult relationship with the truth. She is hardly different from most conventional politicians in this regard. But she has always aspired to be better than conventional; *Living History* was meant to demonstrate that. But judged against the facts, it underlines how she has often chosen to obfuscate, omit, and avoid. It is an understatement by now that she has been known to apprehend truths about herself and the events of her life that others do not exactly share. *Living History* is an example of that.

In her artfully crafted public utterances and written sentences there has almost always been an effort at baseline truthfulness. Yet almost always, something holds her back from telling the whole story, as if she doesn't trust the reader, listener, friend, interviewer, constituent—or perhaps herself—to understand the true significance of events.

Hillary values context; she does see the big picture. Hers, in fact, is not the mind of a conventional politician. But when it comes to herself, she sees with something less than candor and lucidity. She sees, like so many others, what she wants to see.

In *Living History*, for example, she fails to note the common view of many of her friends from childhood and members of her extended family that her father was verbally and mentally abusive of her mother, and that other women might have chosen to walk out of such a painful marriage. Instead, Hillary alludes to the "difficult" nature of her father, as if he were merely a complicated curmudgeon. Never does she mention the traumas she endured during her husband's final, desultory term as the governor of Arkansas, which led her to consider divorce five years before the Clintons came to Washington.

To get caught up in the wave of one's time and to experience it and even try to influence its course is to live history. This, Hillary Clinton has done. But to tell history is something else again. *Living History* was intended to get on the record an acceptable version of events that would render the past reasonably explicable, blur the edges, put the past behind her, and allow her to move on with her airbrushed persona, regardless of election results.

As a girl and then as a woman, Hillary has almost always been desperate to be a passionate participant and at the center of events: familial, generational, experiential, political, historical. Call it ambition, call it the desire to make the world a better place—she has been driven. Rarely has she stepped aside voluntarily into passivity. Introspection, however, has not been her strong suit; faith in the Lord, and in herself, is.

Three pillars have held her up through one crisis after another in a life creased by personal difficulties and public and private battles: her religious faith; her powerful urge toward both service and its accompanying sense (for good or ill) of self-importance; and a fierce desire for privacy and secrecy. It is the last of these that seems to cast a larger and larger shadow over who she really is.

On January 20, 2007, Hillary Rodham Clinton announced her candidacy for president of the United States, fourteen years to the day after Bill Clinton was inaugurated as the nation's forty-second president. "Let's talk. Let's chat. Let's start a dialogue about your ideas and mine," she said. She chose to make her announcement over the Internet, in a video, sitting on a living room couch—alone. "I'm in, and I'm in to win," she said on her Web site.

Increasingly, what Hillary serves up for public consumption, especially since setting her sights on the Senate and the presidency, is usually elaborately prepared or relatively soulless. This is the true shame.

Hillary is neither the demon of the right's perception, nor a feminist saint, nor is she particularly emblematic of her time—perhaps more old-fashioned than modern. Hers is a story of strength and vulnerability, a woman's story. She is an intelligent woman endowed with energy, enthusiasm, humor, tempestuousness, inner strength, spontaneity in private, lethal (almost) powers of retribution, real-life lines that come from deep wounds, and the language skills of a sailor (and of a minister), all evidence of her *passion*—which, down deep, is perhaps her most enduring and even endearing trait.

As Hillary has continued to speak from the protective shell of her own making, and packaged herself for the widest possible consumption, she has misrepresented not just facts but often her essential self.

Great politicians have always been marked by the consistency of their core beliefs, their strength of character in advocacy, and the self-knowledge that informs bold leadership. Almost always, Hillary has stood for good things. Yet there is often a disconnect between her convictions and words, and her actions. This is where Hillary disappoints. But the jury remains out. She still has time to prove her case, to effectuate those things that make her special, not fear them or camouflage them. We would all be the better for it, because what lies within may have the potential to change the world, if only a little.

A NOTE ON SOURCES

Interviews

From the start of work on this book, in 1999, both Hillary and Bill Clinton told me on several occasions they would welcome being interviewed by me. In the end, both formally declined; through their spokespersons they said they did not wish to favor one of several books being written about Hillary.

Their closest friends and associates, however, are the primary sources for this book, especially those who have had the most proximity to Hillary during and since her childhood. Many agreed to be interviewed on the record. Others asked that they not be identified in the text or notes. I interviewed more than two hundred people and am grateful to each one of them. Of those who can be identified, I owe several special gratitude.

I would especially like to thank Betsy Johnson Ebeling for the many hours, patient explanations, and careful recollections she shared with me in discussing Hillary's early family life and the years in Park Ridge, and her continuing close friendship with Hillary, particularly in the year of the Monica Lewinsky scandal. I would also like to offer special thanks to Betsy's husband, Tom.

Of all the classmates, friends, and teachers I interviewed from the Wellesley years, Geoffrey Shields, Hillary's boyfriend for almost the whole period, was invaluable in helping me understand the young woman who arrived at age seventeen still unformed and left with so many of the essential elements of her adult character in place. Geoffrey also shared with me a number of Hillary's letters to him from the period—some quoted herein—that offer useful insights into her psyche, her seriousness, her ebullience, and her capacity for fun and risk-taking. I am particularly grateful for his observations about Hillary's family life, and his recollections of the time he spent with her parents.

At Yale Law School, Hillary and Bill Clinton formed a lasting friendship with Nancy Bekavac, an extraordinary woman who now serves as president of Scripps College in California. Her recollections and insights into the character of each, her familiarity with the details of their courtship and Hillary's hesitancy in marrying Bill, and her enduring relationship with them both—not to mention her humor—were sources of great help to me.

The late Diane Blair has often been described by Hillary as the closest friend of her adult life. Her contribution to this book is evident throughout its pages, based both on our extensive conversations in Fayetteville, Arkansas, and on the material from her seminal interviews with virtually every major participant in the 1992 Clinton presidential campaign. Those interviews were conducted for a book she planned to write, were transcribed verbatim from tape, and fill four large binders, each three inches thick, that are the property of the Diane Blair Trust, and which were made available to me by Jim Blair, who was Diane's husband. The book was never written. Tragically, Diane died in June 2000, an enormous loss to Hillary, and to all those lucky enough to have known her well. Because of her own senior position in the campaign and the trust in her by those interviewed, there is great candor and coherence in the accounts. Hopefully, when the definitive story of the Clinton campaign and presidency is written, those binders will be even more fully utilized.

Jim Blair shared his recollections and thoughts with me about every aspect of the lives of Hillary and Bill Clinton, in dozens of hours of interviews and less formal conversations in Fayetteville, and in many, many phone calls over the years. I sincerely thank him for all of it.

Betsey Wright met Hillary Rodham and Bill Clinton during George McGovern's presidential campaign of 1972, and found Hillary so impressive that she went to Washington shortly thereafter to advance the role of women in American politics generally, and, more specifically, Hillary, who she hoped and believed would one day be president. Along with the Blairs, no person knows more about every aspect of the Clintons' personal and political lives during their twenty years together in Arkansas than Betsey, who was Bill's chief of staff when he was governor, installed in the job by Hillary. Their trust in her abilities and discretion in those years was total, and well placed. I made several trips to Arkansas to interview Betsey, and she gave me an automobile tour of the state that furthered my understanding of the Clintons' story. Betsey's role in the 1992 campaign was essential: she assembled and kept the records of those aspects of the Clintons' past that formed the factual basis for their responses during the next eight years, when they had to answer questions of government investigators and journalists alike. David Maraniss, Bill's most prescient biographer, once mentioned the "love-hate" relationship between Bill and Betsey. I have tried to describe both that relationship and its effect on Hillary's life through these pages.

Dick Morris, the other essential figure in the Clintons' political lives during the Arkansas years and the White House years from 1993 to 1996, is obviously elemental to the story in these pages. Beyond his animus to the Clintons these days, in talking with me he had many invaluable recollections and facts at his command that could either be confirmed by other sources or are presented here as his personal insights and put in context. I owe him and Eileen McGann, his wife, my thanks.

Webb Hubbell and his wife, Suzy, have been especially generous in sharing their time and recollections with me. My understanding of Hillary's relationship with Vince Foster borrows heavily from their knowledge, and Webb sat through long interviews with me on several occasions in Washington, about—among other things—the Arkansas years, the Rose Law Firm, the Clinton governorship, the transition, and the first year of the Clinton presidency. I cannot thank them enough.

Deborah Sale, who grew up in Arkansas, has known Bill Clinton since his younger years, and Hillary since she met Bill at Yale. Her recounting of her friendship with both has been a reference point that I placed great trust in, and I owe her special thanks for her help, as well as my respect for the discretion she showed in discussing the lives of her friends with me.

Nicole Boxer, the former wife of Hillary's brother Tony, agreed to several interviews with me, and provided insights into the Rodham family and life in the White House residence, in both the early part of the presidency and the period of the special prosecutor's investigation of the Monica Lewinsky affair.

Oscar Dowdy, Hillary's first cousin, offered a perspective on her early life and her family that deserved examination, and my thanks for his help.

Donna Shalala and Robert Boorstin were enormously helpful in my understanding of Hillary's attempt at health care reform.

Special thanks to the late Dick Atkinson, Peter Edelman, Sara Ehrman, Mark Fabiani, Anne Henry, Jean Houston, and Bernard Nussbaum, all of whom described periods and incidents in the lives of Hillary and Bill Clinton in great detail and with unique understanding.

I also owe special thanks to the following individuals for their particular areas of insight or expertise:

Oxford and onwards: Robert B. Reich and Richard Stearns; Arkansas: Woody Bassett, Ernie Dumas, Connie Fails, Ann Pincus, Senator David Pryor, and Molly Raiser; Washington and Congress: former senators Bill Bradley and Robert Torricelli, Senators John McCain and John Kerry, and Lawrence O'Donnell; the 1992 campaign and White House: Roger Altman, Don Baer, Richard Ben-Veniste, Marcia Berry, Erskine Bowles, James Carville, Lanny Davis, Rahm Emanuel, Mark Gearan, David Gergen, Richard and Doris Kearns Goodwin, Stan Greenberg, Terry McAuliffe, Mike McCurry, Mack McLarty, Lissa Muscatine, Roy Neel, Mark Penn, John Podesta, the late Ann Richards, Ann Stock, Robert Strauss, and Melanne Verveer; special friends: Frank and Carol Biondi, Ellen Chesler, Richard Friedman, Jim Hart, Carly Simon, and the late William Styron.

Anonymous Sources

Many of the people I interviewed, including some who worked most intimately with Hillary or Bill Clinton in Arkansas, the White House, and on their legal defense, asked not to be identified. I am indebted to them all.

Books and Articles

A great many words have been written about Hillary Rodham Clinton, a condition explained both by the force of her personality, her unique position in our politics and our culture, and the information age in which we live.

A full bibliography of the books and articles I consulted in writing this book appears elsewhere, and quotations from them are listed in the Notes section. (One of my corollary objectives during interviews was to obtain the assessments of the people who know Hillary and Bill Clinton best about what has been written about the Clintons—and especially to help determine what printed information is reliable and what deserves to be discarded or contradicted. In cases where I have cited material from sources that raised doubts in my mind, I confirmed the information elsewhere.)

I want to note in particular several important and essential texts:

- *First in His Class* by David Maraniss (1995) is the essential starting point. It is indispensable almost as much in what it says about Hillary as about Bill Clinton, its main subject. The book ends with Clinton's announcement for the presidency in 1991.
- *Hillary's Choice* by Gail Sheehy (1999). Hillary has been zealous about guarding her correspondence and keeping it from journalists and authors. Happily, Sheehy obtained portions of perhaps the most essential letters of the earlier part of Hillary's life—the correspondence between the Rev. Don Jones and Hillary. Likewise, Sheehy's reporting on the Park Ridge years contains important contributions to the record.
- Donnie Radcliffe's *Hillary Rodham Clinton* (1993) was undertaken as Bill Clinton's presidential campaign began. The book is particularly useful because Hillary and others were interviewed by Radcliffe when, relatively at least, they were more apt to be candid than in later years.
- George Stephanopoulos's *All Too Human* (1999) is notably even-handed and candid, and reflects his closeness to Bill Clinton, as well as his difficult relationship with Hillary during the 1992 campaign and the first four years of Bill Clinton's presidency. It is essential to understanding the Clinton years.
- David Gergen's *Eyewitness to Power* (2000), by the man Hillary was (initially) happy to see supplant Stephanopoulos in influence, is a particularly useful addition to the record.
- James B. Stewart's *Blood Sport* (1996), and *The Hunting of the President* (2000), by Joe Conason and Gene Lyons, are best read or consulted in tandem: they are two extensively reported books that consider the Clintons' finances, the investigation by Kenneth Starr, and their coverage by the mainstream press. Conason and Lyons castigate Stewart at times in their indictment of Starr, the *Washington Post*, the *New York Times*, and other news outlets covering Whitewater, but both books represent important contributions to understanding what happened to the Clintons in Washington.
- Sidney Blumenthal, in *The Clinton Wars* (2003), has given us an indispensable record of his conversations with Hillary and Bill during the Lewinsky period, as well as his unique analysis and reporting on the vast right-wing conspiracy and the Starr investigation.
- *Shadow*, by Bob Woodward (1999), is also about other presidencies affected by the shadow of Watergate, but it is especially valuable with regard to Hillary and Bill in that it is based on interviews conducted during and immediately following the Lewinsky/Starr/Clinton engagement—while memories were fresh, and before extraneous political considerations caused some people to change or mute their accounts.

- David Brock's *The Seduction of Hillary Rodham* (1996) must be considered in the light of its author's ongoing political conversion, but it contains some very useful reporting that nails down parts of the Clintons' lives.
- *The System*, by Haynes Johnson and David Broder (1996), is the indispensable account of Hillary's health care debacle.
- Connie Bruck's profile "Hillary the Pol," which appeared in the May 30, 1993, issue of *The New Yorker*, is a masterful piece of reporting to which all journalists writing about Hillary eventually return for some basic information.
- Robert B. Reich's *Locked in the Cabinet* (1997) is that rare Washington memoir— genuinely candid and filled with good humor, with some important insights into the political raison d'être of the Clintons, and their ambitions.
- Elizabeth Drew's *On the Edge* (1994) is invaluable in understanding how the Clinton presidency got off to such a difficult start, and the mind-set of its principals.
- Dick Morris's *Behind the Oval Office* (1999) is a reissued account of a memoir first published in 1997. It is therefore invaluable, because most of it represents his memories and analysis unclouded by the ideology and animus of his later published works.
- *The Survivor*, by former *Washington Post* White House correspondent John F. Harris, is a well-written and solidly reported overview and analysis of the Clinton presidency.
- Another *Post* reporter, Peter Baker, is the author of *The Breach: Inside the Impeachment and Trial of William Jefferson Clinton*, a compelling and extensively reported account.
- Webster Hubbell's *Friends in High Places* is an unusual and essential text in terms of understanding parts of the Clinton journey, and is notably introspective.
- In *A Vast Conspiracy*, Jeffrey Toobin fills in important information about Harry Thomason and Linda Bloodworth-Thomason, especially in the period surrounding Bill Clinton's grand jury appearance.
- Garry Wills's essays in *The New York Review of Books* during the Clinton years are particularly insightful. Generally speaking, the extensive commentary and reporting in *The New Yorker* likewise was unusually perceptive.
- Michael Tomasky's *Hillary's Turn* is a full-blown and well-reported account of the 2000 Senate campaign.
- On first ladies generally, see Carl Sferrazza Anthony's *First Ladies* and for sections on Hillary in particular, see Kati Marton's *Hidden Power*.
- Michael Isikoff's *Uncovering Clinton* is a useful look at the journalistic process during the Clinton Wars.
- *The Clintons of Arkansas*, compiled and edited by Ernest Dumas in 1993 and published by the University of Arkansas Press, has contributions by old friends and colleagues of Hillary and Bill, including Diane Blair, William T. Coleman III (Bill's Yale housemate before he met Hillary), and Woody Bassett.
- I have commented briefly on *Living History* by Hillary Rodham Clinton in my last chapter, and more extensively about it and Hillary's book *It Takes a Village* earlier in the narrative. The principal value of *Living History* is as insight into how Hillary sees herself and wants the story of her life to be told. It is often at variance with my reporting, other books, and with newspapers and periodicals as well.
- The first half of *My Life* by Bill Clinton is reflective, fascinating, well-written, and often admirably candid about the early life of its author. Watching his politics evolve in those early pages is even inspiring. His admiration and love for Hillary suffuse the Arkansas and law school years. Unfortunately, he rushes through the presidential years. His account of the Lewinsky affair, Starr, and the impeachment period, makes important points about the Independent Counsel's investigation, while eliding over what was happening inside the White House from his perspective.

NOTES

Prologue

6 She had never . . . on the prowl: Author's interviews with Jim and Diane Blair, Dick Morris, Betsey Wright.

7 Robert S. Bennett . . . intertwined: Author's interview with confidential sources.

7 Hillary, too . . . with Lewinsky: Author's interview with Betsey Wright.

7 That afternoon . . . to resign: Author's interview with confidential source.

Chapter 1: Formation

13 "He was rougher than . . . as could be": David Maraniss, *First in His Class* (New York: Simon & Schuster, 1995), p. 320.

13 "Don't let the . . . your way out": Author's interview with Betsy Johnson Ebeling.

13 "She would never . . . had it": Ibid.

13 "golden boy": Hillary Rodham Clinton, *Living History* (New York: Simon & Schuster, 2003), p. 5.

14 She fulfilled . . . grandchild: Author's interview with Linda Bloodworth-Thomason.

15 Her favorite movies: Ibid.

15 "character building": Author's interview with Betsy Johnson Ebeling.

15 "How would you . . . Miss Smarty Pants": Author's interview with confidential source.

15 "Competitive, scrappy fighters": Martha Sherrill, "Mrs. Clinton's Two Weeks Out of Time: The Vigil for Her Father, Taking a Toll Both Public and Private," *Washington Post*, April 3, 1993, p. C1.

15 "pragmatic competitiveness": Marlene Cimons, "Hugh Rodham, First Lady's Father, Dies," *Los Angeles Times*, April 8, 1993, p. 7.

16 "Hillary's mom . . . own home?": Author's interview with Betsy Johnson Ebeling.

16 "I could go . . . earn it": Author's interview with Betsy Johnson Ebeling.

16 "basically a Democrat": Clinton, *Living History*, p. 11.

17 "He was a bullshit artist": Jerry Oppenheimer, *State of a Union* (New York: Harper-Collins, 217), p. 42. And confirmed by author's interview with Oscar Dowdy.

17 "hard-headed, often gruff": Clinton, *Living History*, p. 4.

17 Hugh was afflicted by self-doubt: Ibid.

17 "Dad was . . . in my life": Quote confirmed by Rodham's ex-wife Nicole Boxer. Appeared originally in Jerry Oppenheimer, *State of a Union* (New York: Harper-Collins, 2000), p. 44.

20 Mother and daughter . . . and ran: Author's interview with Betsy Johnson Ebeling.

20 "They eat . . . as well": Judith Warner, *Hillary Clinton: The Inside Story* (New York: Signet, 1993), p. 17.

20 "cheapskate": Author's interview with confidential source.

20 "the SOB": Author's interview with confidential source.

21 "should have completed the other one": Martha Sherrill, "Growing Up in a Chicago Suburb: A Good Girl, Getting Better All the Time," *Washington Post*, January 11, 1993.

21 "Occasionally he . . . loved me": Hillary Rodham Clinton, *It Takes a Village* (New York: Simon & Schuster, 1996), p. 156.

21 "not one to spare the rod": Ibid., p. 155.

21 "critical . . . kindhearted": Sherrill, "Mrs. Clinton's Two Weeks Out of Time," p. C1.

21 Tony seemed to . . . too physical: Author's interview with Betsy Johnson Ebeling, Nicole Boxer, and confidential sources.

21 "Hugh was . . . his father": Author's interview with a confidential source.

21 "Tony, on the . . . younger child": Author's interview with confidential source.

22 "They got ridden . . . years old": Author's interview with confidential source.

22 "was the girl . . . loved that": Author's interview with Betsy Johnson Ebeling.

22 " 'Little Hillary' . . . about it": Sherrill, "Mrs. Clinton's Two Weeks Out of Time," p. C1.

22 "Learning for earning's sake": Donnie Radcliffe, *Hillary Rodham Clinton* (New York: Warner, 1993), p. 205.

22 "Learning . . . learning's sake": Warner, *Hillary Clinton*, p. 13.

23 "Do you . . . or do?": Clinton, *It Takes a Village*, p. 147.

23 Dorothy's mother . . . and children: Clinton, *Living History*, p. 2.

23 "I'd hoped so . . . find out": Clinton, *Living History*, p. 3.

24 "My [step]grandfather . . . her mother": Author's interview with Oscar Dowdy.

24 "I have nothing . . . Rosenberg": Seth Gitell, "Meet Hillary Clinton's Grandmother," *Forward*, August 6, 1999, p. 1.

24 In the last years . . . for his wife: Author's interview with Nicole Boxer.

24 She also seemed . . . in himself: Ibid.

24 "weak and self-indulgent" . . . "disengaged from reality" . . . "be enchanting": Clinton, *Living History*, p. 4.

25 "They were both . . . loaned him money": Author's interview with Oscar Dowdy.

25 "I realized . . . laugh a lot": Author's interview with Betsy Johnson Ebeling.

25 Dorothy made her own . . . the children: Author's interviews with Betsy Johnson Ebeling, Nicole Boxer, Oscar Dowdy, confidential source.

25 "Mr. Difficult": Joyce Milton, *The First Partner* (New York: William Morrow and Company, 1999), p. 15, and confirmed by family sources.

25 "Maybe that's . . . with *him*": Martha Sherrill, "The Education of Hillary Clinton," *Washington Post*, January 11, 1993, p. B1.

25 "It was drummed . . . we did": Author's interview with Nicole Boxer.

26 "children without . . . seas": Clinton, *It Takes a Village*, p. 40.

26 "I grew up . . . *Best*": Ibid., p. 20.

26 "the stability . . . growing up": Ibid., p. 27.

26 Hillary's first boyfriend . . . or so she said: Author's interview with Geoff Shields.

26 As a child . . . treatment of her: Clinton, *Living History*.

26 "Love the sinner . . . have been wrong": Author's interview with confidential source.

27 "kind of the . . . down again": Author's interview with confidential source.

27 "Hillary hates the . . . puritan line": Author's interview with confidential source.

27 Dorothy and Hugh . . . he became: Author's interview with confidential sources.

27 "Dorothy is the . . . her daughter": Author's interview with Linda Bloodworth-Thomason.

27 "be either her . . . in different situations": Author's interview with Betsy Johnson Ebeling.

28 Dorothy wanted to . . . beekeeper in Auckland. Author's interview with Dick Morris.

28 "There's no room . . . cowards": Clinton, *Living History*, p. 12.

28 "I can play with the boys now": Ibid.

28 "Imagine having this . . . bring it back": Gail Sheehy, *Hillary's Choice* (New York: Ballantine, 1999), p. 26.

29 "Who is this . . . looked like": Author's interview with Betsy Johnson Ebeling.

29 By her own account . . . underdeveloped: Clinton, *Living History*; Sheehy, *Hillary's Choice*; and author's interview with Betsy Johnson Ebeling.

29 "I was immediately . . . with her": Sheehy, *Hillary's Choice*, p. 26.

29 "absolutely political . . . wasn't cool": Ibid.

30 "slinging mud . . . apple pie": Ibid., p. 37.

30 "against several . . . elected president": Clinton, *Living History*, p. 24.

31 "We were ignorant . . . like ours": Author's interview with Betsy Johnson Ebeling.

31 As Hillary's school life . . . on weekends: Ibid., and Clinton, *Living History*.

32 "Sister Frigidaire": Martin Kasindorf, "Meet Hillary Clinton: She's Raised Hackles and Hopes, but One Thing's Certain: She'll Redefine Role of First Lady," *Newsday*, January 10, 1993.

32 "He didn't want . . . or time": Author's interview with Betsy Johnson Ebeling.
32 Betsy and others . . . boys: Ibid.
32 "You don't need . . . a bike": Ibid.
33 Hillary's father . . . awful driver. Author's interview with Betsy Johnson Ebeling.
33 "Looking at it . . . is so modest": Maraniss, *First in His Class*, p. 254.
33 "practice date": Author's interview with Betsy Johnson Ebeling.
33 "[He] put her . . . the date": Ibid.
33 "She didn't like . . . with men": Sheehy, *Hillary's Choice*, p. 72.
34 "I also understood . . . his heart": Clinton, *Living History*, p. 162.
34 "She's a prude . . . Chicago suburbs": Author's interview with Lissa Muscatine.
34 "[My family] talked . . . with God": Clinton, *It Takes a Village*, p. 171.
35 "rabble rouser": Ibid., p. 23.
35 "Vanity asks the . . . it Right?": Martin Luther King Jr., Speech, "Remaining Awake Through a Great Revolution," in Sheehy, *Hillary's Choice*, p. 36.
36 "Hillary's faith is . . . a Methodist": Author's interview with confidential source.
36 "She elevates her . . . malice": Author's interview with confidential source.
36 "freethinking . . . mind": Sheehy, *Hillary's Choice*, p. 34.
36 "Can you . . . compassionate misanthrope?": Ibid., p. 53.

Chapter 2: A Young Woman on Her Own

39 "She and I . . . could accomplish": Bruck, "Hillary the Pol," *The New Yorker*, May 30, 1993.
39 "it is *not* . . . both ways": Author's interview with confidential source.
39 Hillary's time at . . . prevailed: Clinton, *Living History*. And author's interview with Betsy Johnson Ebeling.
40 "February depression . . . middle-class America": Sheehy, *Hillary's Choice*, pp. 53–54.
40 She had begun . . . after meeting a young man: Ibid., p. 54.
41 Its thesis, based . . . their husbands and children: The description is adapted from the *Encyclopedia Britannica*.
41 "not to be . . . wives": Radcliffe, *Hillary Rodham Clinton*, p. 57.
41 "You don't have . . . they don't": Author's interview with confidential source.
41 "psychic space": Clinton, *Living History*, p. 29.
42 "There was a . . . minor chord?": Author's interview with confidential source.
42 "She was neither . . . take note": Bruck, "Hillary the Pol."
42 "I would argue . . . social reform": David Brock, *The Seduction of Hillary Rodham* (New York: Simon & Schuster, 1996), p. 11.
42 "It seemed . . . relatively by": Author's interview with Greg Craig.
43 "Hillary was in . . . seen it": Ibid.
43 "reflected what you . . . manifested itself": Author's interview with Peter Edelman.
44 "I was testing . . . the church": Radcliffe, *Hillary Rodham Clinton*, p. 69.
44 "Look how . . . a Negro": Ibid.
44 "She already . . . popular": Bruck, "Hillary the Pol."
45 "not always easy . . . very insistent": Radcliffe, *Hillary Rodham Clinton*, p. 65.
45 "not in extremism, but in moderation": http://www.riponsociety.org/history.htm.
45 "extremism in the defense . . . no virtue": Bart Barnes, "Barry Goldwater, GOP Hero, Dies," *Washington Post*, May 30, 1998.
46 "It is really . . . rest for nature": Hillary Rodham Clinton, letter to Geoff Shields, provided by Shields.
46 "went steady . . . in love": Author's interview with Betsy Johnson Ebeling.
47 "two feet rule": Clinton, *Living History*, p. 33.
47 "she was attractive . . . dancer": Sheehy, *Hillary's Choice*, p. 45.
47 "The best place . . . about it": Hillary Rodham Clinton, letter to Geoff Shields, provided by Shields.
48 "was healthy . . . respect": Author's interview with Geoff Shields.
48 "devoted to the . . . care": Christian Brothers Academy literature.
48 "my boyfriend": Sheehy, *Hillary's Choice*, p. 69.

48 "an intense love affair . . . like her father": Ibid., p. 64.
49 "we always used birth control": Ibid., p. 69.
49 "personally very conservative": Maraniss, *First in His Class*, p. 256.
49 "for both . . . awakening": Charles Kenney, "Hillary: The Wellesley Years," *Boston Globe*, January 12, 1993, p. 65.
49 "She was very . . . decisions": Ibid.
50 "adopting a . . . political activist": Maraniss, *First in His Class*, p. 256.
50 "whether someone . . . heart liberal?": Ibid., p. 257.
50 "Some people . . . civil rights": Ibid.
50 "She was more . . . you win!": Ibid.
50 "very interested . . . politics": Ibid., p. 255.
50 "saved city": Maraniss, Ibid.
50 "See how . . . becoming": Ibid.
51 "from ideas . . . desire": Author's interview with Geoff Shields.
51 "Miss Rodham questions . . . with them": Kenney, "Hillary: The Wellesley Years," p. 65.
51 "I can't believe . . . happened?": Ibid.
51 "They each expressed . . . second objective": Ibid.
53 "I can't stand . . . it!": Kenney, "Hillary: The Wellesley Years," p. 65.
54 "Hillary would step . . . to do": Bruck, "Hillary the Pol."
54 "She presented her . . . mind": Radcliffe, *Hillary Rodham Clinton*, p. 73.
54 "Fight Now, Pay Later": Ibid.
54 "Instead of . . . be made": Ibid.
55 Near the end . . . John Wayne: Clinton, *Living History*, p. 36.
55 The Democratic convention . . . with war . . . the two . . . said Ebeling: Author's interview with Betsy Johnson Ebeling; Clinton, *Living History*, p. 37.
56 "It was kids . . . open": Author's interview with Betsy Johnson Ebeling.
56 "that our government . . . own people": Ibid.
57 "She kept the . . . discuss it": Martha Sherrill, "Hillary Clinton's Inner Politics: As the First Lady Grows Comfortable in Her Roles, She Is Looking Beyond Policy to a Moral Agenda," *Washington Post*, May 6, 1993, p. 1.
57 "the science of revolution . . . maximum feasible participation": Brock, *The Seduction of Hillary Rodham*, p. 16.
57 "started out . . . big difference": Maraniss, *First in His Class*, p. 257.
57 "might make . . . difference": Alan Schechter, cited in Maraniss, *First in His Class*, p. 257.
57 "I basically argued . . . years": Sherrill, "Hillary Clinton's Inner Politics," p. 1.
58 "There was no . . . all of us": Ruth Adams, Wellesley College Commencement Speech, May 31, 1969.
58 "empathy": Hillary Rodham Clinton, Wellesley College Commencement Speech, May 31, 1969.
58 "coercive protest": Ibid.
58 "I find myself . . . impossible, possible": Ibid.
59 "We are . . . of living": Ibid.
59 "She said it. . . . too far' ": Maraniss, *First in His Class*, p. 259.
59 "a very strange . . . ideas": Clinton, Wellesley College Commencement Speech.
59 "the one word . . . distrusted?": Ibid.
60 "that mutuality of . . . for people": Ibid.
60 "In many ways . . . as mine": Clinton, *Living History*, p. 40.
60 "My entrance into . . . bygone age": Clinton, Wellesley College Commencement Speech.

Chapter 3: Love and War at Yale

61 "both passionately share . . . each other": Connie Bruck, "Hillary the Pol."
61 "sharing of values . . . of them": Author's interview with Deborah Sale.
61 "Hillary was interested . . . change most of the world": Ibid.

62 "ultimately Hillary . . . 1970s": Ibid.
62 "The political . . . married him": Author's interview with confidential source.
62 "In fact . . . to run": Author's interview with confidential source.
63 "with Bill . . . zeal": Bruck, "Hillary the Pol."
63 "Well, first . . . any more women": Clinton, *Living History*, p. 38.
63 "We were awed . . . our class": Maraniss, *First in His Class*, p. 248.
63 "knew she wanted . . . recognition": Bruck, "Hillary the Pol."
65 "You had an . . . impressive": Author's interview with Peter Edelman.
65 "was at war with its own people": Clinton, *Living History*, p. 44.
65 "This, the first issue . . . problems": Brock, *The Seduction of Hillary Rodham*, p. 28.
66 "for too long . . . possible": Clinton, Wellesley College Commencement Speech.
66 "were not . . . of people": Brock, *The Seduction of Hillary Rodham*, p. 28
66 "the grim Connecticut . . . ghetto": Ibid., p. 30.
66 "University and the . . . Campus": Ibid., p. 32.
66 "Lawyers and Revolutionaries . . . Justice": Ibid.
67 "I personally . . . in U.S.": Ibid., p. 30.
67 "Come to New . . . Day": Ibid., p. 31.
67 "All power to . . . peace": Ibid.
68 "far more . . . to the left": Radcliffe, *Hillary Rodham Clinton*, p. 92.
68 "There was a . . . young woman": Sheehy, *Hillary's Choice*, p. 78.
68 "Burn Yale . . . police state tactics": Brock, *The Seduction of Hillary Rodham*, p. 31.
69 "the largest assemblage . . . witnessed": *Yale Daily News*, May 2, 1970.
69 "illegal and unconstitutional": Clinton, *Living History*, p. 46.
69 "not disruption or 'revolution' ": Ibid.
69 "the unconscionable expansion . . . waged": Ibid.
70 "Here we are . . . run us?": Radcliffe, *Hillary Rodham Clinton*, p. 95.
71 "You really . . . for them": www.womenshistory.about.com.
71 "starving, hungry . . . a person": Mission of the Children's Defense Fund Action Counsel.
72 "Of course": Radcliffe, *Hillary Rodham Clinton*, p. 96.
72 "Women administer . . . politics": http://www.senate.gov/artandhistory/history/minute/First_Woman_Both_Houses.htm.
73 "I always liked . . . done": Radcliffe, *Hillary Rodham Clinton*, p. 96.
74 "a personal turning point": Carole Bass, "Rights of Passage," *Connecticut Law Tribune*, October 12, 1992.
75 "I began to . . . play": Radcliffe, *Hillary Rodham Clinton*, p. 98.
75 "a more suitable family": Clinton, *Living History*, p. 49.
75 "child citizens": Clinton, "Children Under the Law," *Harvard Educational Review*, 1974.
76 "believes that twelve . . . slavery": Patrick Buchanan, Speech, Republican National Convention, Houston, August 17, 1992.
76 "one of the . . . decades": Garry Wills, "H. R. Clinton's Case," *The New York Review of Books*, Vol. 30, No. 5 (March 5, 1992).
76 "I want to . . . children": Clinton, "Children Under the Law."
76 "Falling in. . . . Clinton": Sheehy, *Hillary's Choice*, p. 76.
76 "was the wild . . . existence": Ibid., p. 83
76 "He was the . . . of me": Ibid., p. 76.
76 "I was afraid of us": Ibid.
78 "It is always . . . voice": Maraniss, *First in His Class*, p. 232.
78 "I'd never seen . . . on me": Author's interview with Nancy Bekavac.
79 "While law school . . . a while": Bill Clinton, *My Life* (New York: Knopf, 2004), p. 181.
79 "One day . . . woman": Ibid.
79 "And Hillary came . . . didn't take": Author's interview with Robert Reich.
79 "looking more . . . scholar": Clinton, *Living History*, p. 52.
80 "little by little . . . acquaintance": Radcliffe, *Hillary Rodham Clinton*, p. 100.
80 "politely excused myself": Ibid.

80 "chicken coop": Sheehy, *Hillary's Choice*, p. 71.
80 "went for a long walk . . . your friends": Clinton, *Living History*, p. 53.
80 "was much more . . . suggest": Ibid.
80 "I remember begin . . . was going": Author's interview with Nancy Bekavac.
81 "They were very . . . Bill!": Maraniss, *First in His Class*, p. 247.
81 "he cared deeply . . . disconnected": Ibid.
81 "My response . . . charming": Author's interview with Deborah Sale.
81 "looked like a hippie": Maraniss, *First in His Class*, p. 248.
81 "Their values are . . . quick": Author's interview with Deborah Sale.
82 "I just liked . . . thing": Bruck, "Hillary the Pol."
82 "The Bill Clinton . . . the tactician": Gergen, *Eyewitness to Power* (New York: Simon & Schuster, 2000), p. 297.
82 "He can astonish . . . surgeon": Clinton, *Living History*, p. 53.
83 "The reason she . . . McCarthy era": Author's interview with Robert Treuhaft.
83 "two were . . . communists": Ibid.
83 "All I can . . . wasn't": Brock, *The Seduction of Hillary Rodham*, p. 33.
83 "at Treuhaft . . . California": Clinton, *Living History*, p. 54.
84 "fierceness . . . the room": Author's interview with Stan Greenberg.
84 "she has a . . . he has": Author's interview with Dick Morris.
84 "But is that . . . someone?": Maraniss, *First in His Class*, p. 263.
85 "Hillary was . . . *Mockingbird*": Ibid., p. 264.
85 "We were . . . high-mindedness": Author's interview with Sara Ehrman.
86 "Fearless": Ibid.
86 "I'd call it . . . her side": Ibid.
86 "Bill Clinton tapped . . . she's free": Sheehy, *Hillary's Choice*, p. 85.
87 "You really saved our relationship": Maraniss, *First in His Class*, p. 277.
87 "more focused . . . questions": Radcliffe, *Hillary Rodham Clinton*, p. 114.
87 "Bill and I talked . . . to Bill": Maraniss, *First in His Class*, p. 277.
87 "women were . . . force": Ibid.
87 "It was a nascent . . . world": Ibid.

Chapter 4: Making Arkansas Home

88 "There are . . . infidelity": Author's interview with confidential source.
90 "I never doubted . . . friends": Hillary Rodham Clinton, "Good Marriages Are More Than a Piece of Paper," *Arkansas Democrat-Gazette*, October 8, 1995, p. 2.
90 "Yankee": Clinton, *Living History*, p. 63.
91 "What are you . . . Oh, you know . . . her here": Author's interview with Max Brantley.
92 "When I learned . . . something": Ibid.
93 "the perfect place to live": Clinton, *My Life*, p. 202.
93 Clinton had always . . . for them: Clinton, *My Life*, p. 202.
93 "would be a high-wire operation": Ibid., p. 209.
93 "head and . . . more experience": Ibid.
95 "disapproved of what . . . Little Rock": Ibid., p. 211.
96 "you have to . . . small pond": Maraniss, *First in His Class*, p. 316.
96 "besotted . . . light up": Ibid., p. 313.
96 "come in some . . . someday' ": Ibid.
97 "You don't understand . . . It's not": Author's interview with Bernard Nussbaum.
97 "She started calling . . . to fill": Maraniss, *First in His Class*, p. 319.
98 "I was very . . . women": Author's interview with Betsey Wright.
98 "about broke down . . . miserable": Maraniss, *First in His Class*, p. 321.
98 "There were girls . . . our lives": Author's interview with Betsey Wright.
98 In Washington . . . their work": Maraniss, *First in His Class*, p. 312.
99 "Hillary came dressed . . . Arkansas": Ibid., p. 317.
99 "She didn't care . . . great time": Radcliffe, *Hillary Rodham Clinton*, p. 125.

99 "Well, how long . . . you out": Maraniss, *First in His Class*, p. 319.
100 "Clinton for Congress": Ibid., p. 320.
100 "the Yankees in the Cadillac": Ibid.
100 "least [because] . . . wanted": Norman King, *Hillary: Her True Story* (New York: Carol, 1993), p. 46.
101 "But you know . . . not to": Martha Sherrill, "The Rising Lawyer's Detour to Arkansas: At Wellesley, She Found Her Calling; At Yale, She Met Her Future," *Washington Post*, January 12, 1993.
101 "chiefs": Maraniss, *First in His Class*, p. 307.
102 "evil": Maraniss, Ibid., p. 310.
103 "With the unexpected . . . a chance": Clinton, *Living History*, p. 69.
106 "brilliant and dazzling": Author's interview with Sara Ehrman.
106 "You are crazy": King, *Hillary: Her True Story*, p. 53.
106 "at sea about . . . to be": Maraniss, *First in His Class*, p. 316.
106 "Why on earth . . . future?": Clinton, *Living History*, p. 69.
106 "Are you sure . . . no . . . anyway": Ibid., p. 63.
107 "My friends and. . . . as well": Radcliffe, *Hillary Rodham Clinton*, p. 136.
107 "I was just appalled": Ibid., p. 137.
108 "He's not home . . . camping": Clinton, *Living History*, p. 71.
109 "She was moving . . . twenty": Author's interview with Deborah Sale.
109 "All business": Maraniss, *First in His Class*, p. 328.
109 "If you were . . . laid-back": Author's interview with Woody Bassett.
109 "unusual ability. . . . bottom line": Maraniss, *First in His Class*, p. 328.
110 "We walked over . . . impressed me": Author's interview with Diane Blair.
111 "somebody like me . . . the smallest . . . We both . . . dress code": Ibid.
112 "We'd go out . . . ground": Ibid.
112 "There would be . . . done that": Ibid.
112 "There is a . . . insult": Author's interview with Max Brantley.
113 Though Hillary became . . . walking down the road: Maraniss, *First in His Class*, p. 335; author's interview with Betsey Wright.
113 "They would constantly . . . each other": Sheehy, *Hillary's Choice*, p. 113.
113 "Send John Paul . . . own": Maraniss, *First in His Class*, p. 333.
114 "the Boy": Sheehy, *Hillary's Choice*, p. 135.
114 "Our organization went . . . entire staff": Maraniss, *First in His Class*, p. 335.
114 "No! You don't . . . [to Washington]": Ibid., p. 336.
115 "It was the goddamn money": Ibid., p. 337.
116 "oddly elated": Author's interview with Nancy Bekavac.
116 "We know how . . . time": Ibid.
116 "Sit down. We sit here": Ibid.
116 "This is Australia . . . it's not me": Ibid.
117 "She's the one that . . . they did": Author's interview with confidential source.
117 "They're not whole . . . be doing": Author's interview with Deborah Sale.
118 "I went into a funk": Clinton, *My Life*, p. 228.
118 "Well, Bill has . . . again": Author's interview with Jim Blair.
118 "happier with Bill . . . right direction": Clinton, *Living History*, p. 70.
118 "Oh hell . . . get divorced": Author's interview with Jim Blair.
118 "Whether I *wanted* . . . want that": Author's interview with Ann Henry.
119 "She wouldn't call . . . disrupted": Ibid.
119 "That's right . . . the marriage!": Ibid.
119 "I had lost . . . Arkansas": Clinton, *My Life*, p. 236.
119 "wasn't Mars . . . foolishness": Maraniss, *First in His Class*, p. 344.
119 "All we ever . . . argue": Ibid., p. 342.
119 "run Hillary . . . go": Ibid.
119 "He was surprised . . . he isn't": Author's interview with Betsey Wright.
120 "pray that it's . . . for me": Sheehy, *Hillary's Choice*, p. 119.
120 "Don't worry . . . support you": Ibid., p. 120.

120 "That's not to say . . . found her": Author's interview with confidential source.
120 "Well, I bought . . . by myself": Clinton, "Good Marriages Are More than a Piece of Paper," p. 2.
120 "I really started . . . like her": Author's interview with Betsey Wright.
121 "I think she . . . her heart": Author's interview with Deborah Sale.
121 "holding hands . . . in love": Sheehy, *Hillary's Choice*, p. 122.
121 "looking more at life . . . itself": Maraniss, *First in His Class*, p. 344.
121 "This will be fine": Sheehy, *Hillary's Choice*, p. 122.
122 "Who will give . . . Mr. Rodham": Clinton, *Living History*, p. 75.
122 "It was like . . . district": Author's interview with Ann Henry.
122 "Hillary Rodham will be your Waterloo": Sheehy, *Hillary's Choice*, p. 122.
123 "a person in my own right . . . sacrificial wife": Quote confirmed by Anne Henry. Appeared originally in Roger Morris, *Partners in Power*, p. 188.
123 "significantly improve the . . . Arkansas": Ernest Dumas, *The Clintons of Arkansas* (Fayetteville: University of Arkansas Press, 1993).
123 "minimum prison sentences . . . office": Ibid., p. 10.
123 "fair utility . . . privacy": Ibid., p. 9.
123 "Character, Competence, and Concern": Ibid.
124 "she was to . . . to women": Author's interview with Betsey Wright.
124 "a pilgrimage": Clinton, *Living History*, p. 77.
125 "slipped into . . . water": Author's interview with Jim Blair.
125 "an insulated big town . . . careers": Webb Hubbell, *Friends in High Places* (New York: William Morrow, 1997), p. 49.
126 "she not only . . . here": Author's interview with Woody Bassett.
126 "She could recite . . . absorbed it": Author's interview with Richard Stearns.
127 "It was Hillary . . . doesn't care": Bruck, "Hillary the Pol."
128 "[Vince] came back . . . for a job": Hubbell, *Friends in High Places*, p. 46.
129 "How will we . . . pregnant?": Ibid., p. 50.
130 The atmosphere . . . made her more attractive: Brock, *The Seduction of Hillary Rodham*, p. 81.
130 "At first, she . . . about her": Ibid..
130 "She was on . . . all day": Ibid.
130 "Hillary won their . . . like them": Hubbell, *Friends in High Places*, p. 4.
130 "In our morning . . . to others": Ibid., p. 53.
131 "But if she . . . to shreds": Ibid., p. 64.
131 "The real secret . . . either": Ibid., p. 65
131 "rat's ass": Clinton, *Living History*, p. 80.
131 "amazingly nervous": Hubbell, *Friends in High Places*, p. 60.
132 In December, a month . . . of the restaurant: Clinton, *My Life*, p. 246.
132 "get on board early": Maraniss, *First in His Class*, p. 351.
134 "our prevailing acquisitive corporate life": Clinton, Wellesley College Commencement Speech.
135 Even before Hillary . . . talked politics: James B. Stewart, *Blood Sport*, (New York: Simon & Schuster, 1996), p. 69.
135 "best person": Maraniss, *First in His Class*, p. 370.
136 "I made my . . . trader": Author's interview with Jim Blair.
136 "I was watching . . . going on": Ibid.
136 "I thought I . . . unreal": Ibid.
138 Finally, Hillary got . . . through Smith: Stewart, *Bloodsport*, p. 84; author's interview with Jim Blair.
138 "that all you . . . nation" Clinton, *My Life*, p. 255.
138 "A short trip . . . graveyard": Ibid.
139 "I'd like to be . . . Washington": Dick Morris, *Behind the Oval Office* (Los Angeles: Renaissance, 1999), p. 46.
140 "She had a . . . politics": Author's interview with Dick Morris.
140 Morris perceived . . . accomplishments": Dick Morris, *Rewriting History* (New York: HarperCollins, 2004), p. 73.

140 "She has much . . . defensive": Bruck, "Hillary the Pol.":
140 "She did not do . . . speeches": Ibid.
141 "People thought . . . name": Brock, *The Seduction of Hillary Rodham*, p. 81.
141 Despite the name issue . . . for only two days: Maraniss, *First in His Class*, p. 356.
141 Frank Lady . . . maiden name: Clinton, *My Life*, p. 255.
141 "the ArkoRomans": Ibid., p. 73.
142 "Talk about the . . . ERA!": Clinton, *My Life*, p. 257
142 "Okay . . . noted later: Ibid.
142 "the 31-year-old . . . politics": Howell Raines, "New Faces in Southern Politics: Women, Young and 'Outsiders,' " *New York Times*, July 3, 1978, p. 4.
142 "be perceived . . . backward": Ibid.
143 "Diamonds and Denim": Sheehy, *Hillary's Choice*, p. 118.
143 "The whole theme . . . sophisticated": Ibid.
143 "Our vote was . . . state": Brock, *The Seduction of Hillary Rodham*, p. 89.
144 "among the most . . . my life": Clinton, *Living History*, p. 82.
144 "Hillary was very . . . wife": Bruck, "Hillary the Pol."
144 "She thought . . . speak": Ibid.
144 "no concessions to . . . distant": Ruth Marcus, "Now, 'A Different Kind of First Lady,' " *Washington Post*, January 20, 1993, p. 20.
145 "she didn't want . . . irritant": Author's interview with Betsey Wright.
146 "For as long as I . . . help them": Maraniss, *First in His Class*, p. 359.
146 "He was left . . . it all": Ibid., p. 439.
147 "Think about who . . . stage": Sheehy, *Hillary's Choice*, p. 133.
148 "Bill was like a . . . advantage": Bruck, "Hillary the Pol."
148 "appearances were more . . . on": Maraniss, *First in His Class*, p. 425.
148 "a quiet humiliation" Author's interview with confidential source.
149 "I don't think . . . child": Sheehy, *Hillary's Choice*, p. 132.
149 Since very early . . . in Bermuda: Clinton, *My Life*, p. 272.
150 He would have discovered . . . getting pregnant": The description and footnote are taken directly from http://medpics.findlaw.com.
150 "Think of a baby . . . tight": Clinton; *It Takes a Village*, p. 8.
151 Fifteen minutes . . . Bill to hold: Clinton, *My Life*, p. 273.
152 "I never wanted . . . end": Ibid.
152 "designated worrier": "Clinton at Yale," *New York Times*, October 14, 2001, p. 7.
152 "mystified": Clinton, *Living History*, p. 85.
152 "Chelsea, this . . . we can": Ibid.
153 "We may . . . wise": Maraniss, *First in His Class*, p. 375.
153 "The feminist I . . . heroic": Sheehy, *Hillary's Choice*, p. 133.
153 "had assumed . . . baby' ": Hubbell, *Friends in High Places*, p. 78.
153 "Hillary began . . . due to her": Ibid., p. 79.
154 "I must say . . . election": Walter Isaacson, " 'We're Hoping That We Have Another Child,' " *Time*, June 3, 1996.
156 "I could sign . . . justify one": Clinton, *My Life*, p. 65.
157 "Governor Bill . . . Rodham": Clinton, *Living History*, p. 92.
157 "It showed . . . me": Ibid., p. 91.
157 "She still . . . aura": Author's interview with Jim Blair.
157 "Baby": Sheehy, *Hillary's Choice*, p. 134.
157 "You have to look . . . accomplish": Maraniss, *First in His Class*, p. 381.
157 "Well shit, General . . . fault?": Ibid., p. 378.
158 "You're fucking me": Ibid., p. 79.
158 "might actually lose": Clinton, *Living History*, p. 90.
158 "she believed very much . . . of stuff": Author's interview with Dick Morris.
158 "more creative and realistic": Maraniss, *First in His Class*, p. 382.
159 "We were brought up . . . system": Ibid.
160 "devastated": Clinton, *Living History*, p. 90.
160 "Bill's eyes were . . . seen them": Hubbell, *Friends in High Places*, p. 87.
160 "From then on . . . demanded it": Ibid., p. 86.

160 "He was half-laughing . . . Bowling": Dumas, *The Clintons of Arkansas.*
160 "He couldn't face . . . life": Author's interview with Deborah Sale.
160 "She basically . . . path in life": Ibid.
160 "People said . . . the time": Ibid.
161 "They now have . . . nothing": Author's interview with Ann Henry.
161 "a trainer to . . . the track": Maraniss, *First in His Class,* p. 391.
161 "It was like . . . jubilation": Author's interview with Betsey Wright.
161 "the Valkyries": Maraniss, *First in His Class,* p. 427.
162 Hillary and Bill combed . . . her garage: Clinton, *Living History,* p. 91.
162 "the lobby of . . . designs": Morris, *Rewriting History,* p. 48.
162 "the only track . . . darkness": Maraniss, *First in His Class,* p. 390.
162 "Hillary had . . . Lord": Brock, *The Seduction of Hillary Rodham,* p. 147.
163 "Bill obsessed on . . . for himself": Author's interview with Max Brantley.
163 "He really felt . . . something": Author's interview with Betsey Wright.
163 "The apolitical firm . . . into leaving": Hubbell, *Friends in High Places,* p. 88.
163 "Vince was just born middle-aged": Stewart, *Blood Sport,* p. 121.
163 "I was born . . . age forty": Ibid., p. 121.
164 "I don't think . . . lover": Author's interview with Webb Hubbell.
164 "He loved Hillary . . . business": Author's interview with confidential source.
164 "I looked around . . . physical": Author's interview with Nancy Bekavac.
165 "Bill, they didn't . . . get it": Morris, *Rewriting History,* p. 81.
165 "My Daddy Never Had to . . . Twice": Clinton, *My Life,* p. 295.
165 "Chelsea's second birthday . . . chance": Ibid.
165 "She was out . . . something": Author's interview with Woody Bassett.
166 "would sacrifice some of . . . expediency": Author's interview with Jim Blair.
166 "We had a long . . . her husband": Hubbell, *Friends in High Places,* p. 103.
166 "I don't have to change . . . Clinton": Michael Kelly, "Again: It's Hillary *Rodham* Clinton. Got That?," *New York Times,* February 14, 1993, p. 33.
166 "I teared up . . . throat": Brock, *The Seduction of Hillary Rodham,* p. 152.
166 "She understood that . . . anymore' ": Bruck, "Hillary the Pol."
166 "the inner qualities of people": Clinton, *Living History,* p. 91.
166 "really taking his . . . this over": Author's interview with Dick Morris.
167 "she jumped all . . . have it": Brock, *The Seduction of Hillary Rodham,* p. 154.
167 "Frank White would probably . . . win": Ibid.
170 "When you lead in . . . thicket": Maraniss, *First in His Class,* p. 407.
171 "We [Hillary and . . . do it right": Dumas, *The Clintons of Arkansas,* p. 103.
171 "This guarantees that . . . else": Radcliffe, *Hillary Rodham Clinton,* p. 203.
172 "Well, fellas, it looks . . . Clinton!": Sheehy, *Hillary's Choice,* p. 153.
172 The Arkansas Department . . . twenty-six years: Brock, *The Seduction of Hillary Rodham,* p. 168.
172 "the real heart": Ibid., p. 170.
173 "She made it . . . schoolteachers": Ibid., p. 169.
173 "The first purpose . . . doesn't": Ibid., p. 161.
173 "a small price . . . deserves": Maraniss, *First in His Class,* p. 413.
173 "walking through a . . . understand' ": Brock, *The Seduction of Hillary Rodham,* p. 171.
174 In Arkansas, a generation . . . and science: Maraniss, *First in His Class,* p. 456.
174 "thus far, the . . . encouragement": Brock, *The Seduction of Hillary Rodham,* p. 174.
176 "whatever it might be": Clinton, *Living History,* p. 97.
176 "Don't commit . . . talk": Author's interview with Bernard Nussbaum.
176 "Hillary, I know . . . early?": Stewart, *Blood Sport,* p. 240.
177 "The rumors about Bill . . . face": Hubbell, *Friends in High Places,* p. 136.
177 "What was at . . . would be": David Broder, "The Press After the Stakeout: Questions of Policy, Record—and Character—Need to Be Better Explored," *Washington Post,* May 12, 1987, p. 19.
177 "infidelity issue . . . tread": Maraniss, *First in His Class,* p. 440.

178 "He was using Hart's withdrawal . . . all about": Author's interview with Max Brantley.
178 "Hillary had long ago . . . with them": Author's interview with Betsey Wright.
178 "huge schisms": Ibid.
178 "when Hillary did really drastic things": Ibid.
179 "I just thought . . . issue": Ibid.
179 "all of the women . . . often": Ibid.
179 "This was a . . . know about": Ibid.
179 Mickey Kantor . . . the same": Maraniss, *First in His Class*, p. 441.
179 "If people had . . . right": Sheehy, *Hillary's Choice*, p. 177.
180 "I need some . . . father was": Clinton, *My Life*, p. 334.
180 "Finally I felt . . . ambitions": Ibid., p. 335.
181 "there was an . . . fooling around": Author's interview with Betsey Wright.
181 "The Numb and the Restless": Tom Shales, "The Numb and the Restless," *Washington Post*, July 21, 1988, p. 1.
182 "overburdened": Author's interview with Betsey Wright.
182 Hillary, pinned in . . . Give it": Ibid; Maraniss, *First in His Class*.
182 "She was going . . . and bars": Author's interview with Betsey Wright.
182 In the immediate . . . lobby": *The Tonight Show Starring Johnny Carson*, July 1988; Clinton, *My Life*, p. 342–3.
183 "I succeeded beyond . . . imagination": Ibid.
183 "No marriage . . . experience": *Glamour* magazine, cited in Brock, *The Seduction of Hillary Rodham*, p. 233.
183 "having a severe midlife crisis": Maraniss, *First in His Class*, p. 450.
183 "Bill, you're crazy . . . about it": Author's interview with Betsey Wright.
183 "he was playing . . . affair": Ibid.
184 "I was switching . . . I talked . . . was different": Ibid.
185 "He would wait me out": Clinton, *Living History*, p. 61.
185 "And that he . . . with Hillary": Author's interview with Betsey Wright.
185 "explained why I . . . leaving": Ibid.
185 "I said, 'Nancy . . . yours again' ": Ibid.
185 "in trying to calm . . . depressed": Ibid.
185 "business dynamics . . . problem": Ibid.
186 "because she kept . . . family": Ibid.
186 "I was perfectly . . . for me": Ibid.
186 "I don't think he's . . . common": Author's interview with Dick Morris.
187 "We were doing . . . to me": Author's interview with Diane Blair.
187 He continued to surreptitiously . . . Jenkins: Author's interview with confidential source.
187 "dithering and depressed": Maraniss, *First in His Class*, p. 452.
188 "I just don't . . . Yeah": Author's interview with Jim Blair.
188 "negotiation . . . Senate": Author's interview with Betsey Wright.
188 "The conclusion that . . . identity": Author's interview with Dick Morris.
189 For weeks before . . . Gennifer Flowers: Maraniss, *First in His Class*.

Chapter 5: The Prize

192 "That's one where . . . amazing": Bruck, "Hillary the Pol."
193 "I think you . . . arguments": Bob Woodward, *The Agenda* (New York: Simon & Schuster, 1994), p. 17.
194 "The sudden movement . . . excuse be?": Peter Goldman, Thomas M. DeFrank et al., *Quest for the Presidency 1992* (College Station: Texas A&M University Press, 1994), p. 31.
195 "Propeller-Head": Ibid., p. 44.
195 "All of you are . . . concerned": Ibid.
195 "Like nearly anybody . . . or not": Maraniss, *First in His Class*, p. 461.

196 "Mr. Clinton received . . . emphatically": Godfrey Sperling, "Don't Underestimate Hillary," *Christian Science Monitor,* July 1, 2003, p. 9.

196 "God, I hope they . . . into": Maraniss, *First in His Class,* p. 463.

197 "This campaign is . . . effective?": Diane Blair, interviews conducted for unpublished book. Copyright, the Diane Blair Trust.

197 "Probably Hillary . . . creative": Ibid.

198 "Cut the crap, Governor": Clinton, *My Life,* p. 368.

199 "One of our problems . . . Watergate": Roger Morris, *Partners in Power* (Washington, D.C.: Regnery, 1996), p. 203.

199 "I think that Hillary . . . to do": Diane Blair, interviews conducted for unpublished book. Copyright, the Diane Blair Trust.

199 "She doesn't look . . . battle": Author's interview with confidential source.

200 "From my perspective . . . together?" Goldman, DeFrank et al., *Quest for the Presidency 1992,* p. 90.

200 "If we don't . . . down": Ibid., p. 96.

200 "just go for it . . . backs": Ibid., p. 95.

200 Now that strategy . . . as a politician: Goldman, DeFrank et al., *Quest for the Presidency.*

201 "It took a lot . . . Chelsea": Clinton, *Living History,* p. 106.

201 "She steeled herself . . . for that": Author's interview with Robert Reich.

201 "He beckoned the producer . . . his face": Theodore H. White, *The Making of the President* (New York: Black Dog & Leventhal, 1961), p. 351.

201 "If the wife comes . . . wimp": Martha Sherrill, "The Retooling of the Political Wife: Her Final Test: How to Handle Scandal," *Washington Post,* January 13, 1993, p. 1.

201 "Intellect in a woman is unbecoming": Clinton, *Living History,* p. 106.

202 "You know, I'm . . . for him": Hillary Clinton, Interview, *60 Minutes.*

202 "I didn't mean to . . . about that": David Zimmerman, "Wynette Wants Clinton Apology," *USA Today,* January 29, 1992, p. 2.

202 "She seemed like . . . sorry": David Zimmerman, "Wynette Gets Clinton's Apology," *USA Today,* January 30, 1992, p. 2.

202 "The undercurrent . . . ambition": George Stephanopoulos, *All Too Human* (New York: Little, Brown, 1999), p. 92.

203 "I came in . . . term": Author's interview with Stan Greenberg.

203 "How aggressive to . . . fighter": Ibid.

203 "was listening": Ibid.

203 "It was very . . . what occurred": Ibid.

203 "I don't mean . . . destiny": Ibid.

203 "Her attitude was . . . analysis": Ibid.

204 "You know, sometimes . . . with them": Ibid.

205 "The minute you hear . . . sentence": Stephanopoulos, *All Too Human,* p. 93.

205 "I think he's . . . business": Goldman, DeFrank et al., *Quest for the Presidency 1992,* p. 194.

205 "Let me tell you . . . my wife": Ibid.

205 "I'm saying I never . . . Never": Ibid., p. 195.

206 "Sure. Ask her anything you want": Ibid., p. 196.

206 "I suppose I could . . . change": Dan Balz and Edward Walsh, "Clinton's Wife Finds She's Become Issue: Arkansas Lawyer Denies Impropriety but Vows to Rethink Her Role," *Washington Post,* March 17, 1992. p. 1.

206 "Hillary problem . . . disease": William Safire, "The Hillary Problem," *New York Times,* March 26, 1992, p. 23.

206 "were inundated with calls . . . got worried": Diane Blair, interviews conducted for unpublished book. Copyright, the Diane Blair Trust.

207 "The Lady Macbeth of Arkansas": Sherrill, "The Retooling of the Political Wife," p. 1.

207 "Yuppie Wife from Hell": Ibid.

207 "Bill Clinton Love Tapes": Ibid.

207 "Gennifer & Bill . . . Apartment": Ibid.

207 "Hillary Clinton . . . in a tank": Ibid.

207 "for herself . . . power": Felicity Barringer, "The President-Elect's Wife; Hillary Clinton's New Role; The Job Description Is Open," *New York Times*, November 16, 1992, p. 1.

207 "More than Nancy . . . American people": Goldman, DeFrank et al., *Quest for the Presidency 1992*, p. 662.

208 "a softer, natural . . . look": Howard Kurtz, "Portraits of a First Lady: Media Strive to Define Hillary Clinton," *Washington Post*, November 21, 1992, p. 1.

208 "zipped her lip": Ibid.

208 "allowing handlers to . . . own": Margaret Carlson Washington, "A Different Kind of First Lady," *Time*, November 16, 1992.

208 " 'Elect me and . . . feminism": Patrick Buchanan, Speech, Republican National Convention, August 17, 1992.

208 "It was hard . . . things around": Diane Blair, interviews conducted for unpublished book. Copyright, the Diane Blair Trust.

Chapter 6: A Transitional Woman

210 "something dirty . . . gloves": Maraniss, *First in His Class*, p. 385.

211 "I said it's . . . fire her": Author's interview with Dick Morris.

211 "but the better . . . out well' ": Ibid.

213 "would talk about . . . upside down": Author's interview with Ernie Dumas.

213 "He talks to her . . . constructively": Author's interview with Deborah Sale.

213 "They don't do . . . passionately": Radcliffe, *Hillary Rodham Clinton*, p. 229.

214 "looks like America": Cathleen Decker and Sam Fulwood III, "Clinton Courts Voters—Like a True Democrat," *Los Angeles Times*, July 2, 1992, p. 15.

214 "I will give you a. . . . Asian-Americans": Ibid.

214 "I would be . . . ever seen": Karen Ball, "Clinton Knows His Message Isn't Getting Out," Associated Press, May 22, 1992.

215 "If you really. . . . politics": Author's interview with Robert Reich.

216 "He didn't . . . circumstances": Author's interview with Deborah Sale.

216 "Economics and trade . . . to go": Ibid.

217 "made most of her big mistakes": Author's interview with confidential source.

217 "overrating the win": Author's interview with confidential source.

217 "This is victory . . . seize it": Author's interview with confidential source.

217 "I mean, that . . . pretty deep": Author's interview with confidential source.

217 "It's as if . . . grade class": Author's interview with confidential source.

218 "Mostly, [these] people . . . crazy": Author's interview with Donna Shalala.

218 "I suspect that there . . . with her": Author's interview with confidential source.

219 Jordan—handsome . . . president's: Author's interview with confidential source.

219 "I don't know that . . . any walls": Maureen Dowd, "The New Presidency: Boxes Bulging with Decades of Clinton's Life Await Journey into History," *New York Times*, January 14, 1993, p. 11.

220 "I told Susan that . . . president-elect": Author's interview with Roy Neel.

221 "a cabinet that . . . America": Decker and Fulwood, "Clinton Courts Voters," p. 15.

221 "She advised me . . . years": Gwen Ifill, "Clinton Wants Wife at Cabinet Table," *New York Times*, December 19, 1992, p. 8.

221 "I'm not prepared . . . long": Richard L. Berke, "The Other Clinton Helps Shape the Administration," *New York Times*, December 14, 1992, p. 6.

221 "She knows more . . . us do": Ifill, "Clinton Wants Wife at Cabinet Table," p. 8.

222 "They assume that . . . path": Author's interview with Donna Shalala.

223 "had always been . . . their way": Ibid.

223 "That was the . . . its face.' ": Ibid.

223 But more than Bill . . . campaign": Author's interview with confidential source.

224 "I spent so. . . . culture": Clinton, *My Life*, p. 467.

224 "Washington is largely.... untruths": Leslie H. Gelb, "Foreign Affairs, Untruths . . . ," *New York Times*, October 27, 1991, p. 15.

225 "The concept of service has little . . . chase": Sidney Blumenthal, cited in *Roll Call*, August 16, 1993.

226 She asked if . . .": Stewart, *Blood Sport*, p. 237.

226 "I'm looking for you . . . trouble": Bob Woodward, *Shadow* (New York: Touchstone, 1999), p. 228.

227 "He's a great guy": Stewart, *Blood Sport*, p. 242.

227 "We'll build a firm": Ibid., p. 241.

227 "What's the worst . . . true": Ibid.

227 "the last woman standing": Ruth Marcus and Michael Isikoff, "Clinton Withdraws Baird's Justice Nomination," *Washington Post*, January 22, 1993.

Chapter 7: Inauguration

230 "You and Mrs. Clinton . . . children": Laurie Asseo, "Stars Toast Clinton at Gala Drenched in Music and Laughter," Associated Press, January 20, 1993.

230 "remembering Kennedy Inaugural. . . . East Room": Author's personal notes.

230 Meanwhile, Jack Nicholson . . . the World": *Time*, February 1, 1993; author's notes from the event.

231 "made a mistake. . . . better": David Lauter, "Clinton's In-Laws Drop Corporate Party Plans," *Los Angeles Times*, January 15, 1993, p. 24.

231 "the Monsters": Author's interview with confidential source.

231 "We're now dealing . . . appear": Lauter, "Clinton's In-Laws Drop Corporate Party Plans," p. 24.

231 "They didn't think . . . stopped": Charles R. Babcock and Michael Weisskopf, "Change of Party, Same Game: Fund-Raising Keeps Its Prominence," *Washington Post*, January 15, 1993, p. 1.

231 "labor of love": Lois Romano, "The Reliable Source," *Washington Post*, January 20, 1993, p. 3.

231 "a contribution to . . . efforts": Ibid.

231 "There had been . . . to wear": Cathy Horyn, "First Lady Says She'll Pay for Clothes," *Washington Post*, January 21, 1993, p. 12.

232 "We must care . . . of Carter": Author's interview with confidential source.

235 "was the most . . . lifetime": Nell Henderson, "Clinton Leads Nation in Paying Homage to King," *Washington Post*, January 19, 1993, p. 1.

235 "Welcome to your new house": Ann Devroy and Ruth Marcus, "Clinton Takes Oath as 42nd President Asking Sacrifice, Promising Renewal: 'Era of Deadlock and Drift Is Over,' " *Washington Post*, January 21, 1993, p. 1.

235 "Good to see . . . luck": Ibid.

236 "Avoid this crowd . . . That's right . . . already": Sheehy, *Hillary's Choice*, p. 222.

236 George and Barbara . . . chandeliers: Author's interview with Robert Reich.

236 "would share so . . . burdens": Rev. Billy Graham, Invocation, Presidential Inauguration, Washington, D.C., January 20, 1993.

238 Hillary returned to her seat: Patt Morrison, "Purely Human Moments and Capital's Pomp," *Los Angeles Times*, January 21, 1993, p. 1.

238 "For he that . . . everlasting": Ibid.

238 "This beautiful capital . . . people": Bill Clinton, Inaugural Address, Washington, D.C., January 20, 1993.

239 "seemed very much . . . done": *Washington Post*, January 20, 1993.

239 "a blue unidentified . . . head": Maureen Dowd and Frank Rich, "The Boomers' Ball: Picking Up the Perks of Presidential Power," *New York Times*, January 21, 1993, p. 11.

239 "the tan tourniquet . . . neck": Ibid.

240 "Does she represent . . . important?": John J. Goldman, "Visit Multiplies Hopes at N.Y. School," *Los Angeles Times*, January 27, 1993, p. 5.

240 Do you think the. . . . 8%: Ibid.

240 "most Americans object to . . . herself": Diane Duston, "Hillary Clinton's Traditional Seat at Swearing-In Belies Her Future Role," Associated Press, January 20, 1993.
242 "Does Hillary . . . what": Jacqueline Trescott, "Marathon Man: Clinton's Long Night," *Washington Post*, January 21, 1993, p. 4.
242 "the painting with . . . seen": Clinton, *Living History*, p. 128.

Chapter 8: Settling In

245 "I wouldn't have . . . he did": Author's interview with confidential source.
248 "Her ground zero . . . you": Author's interview with Joe Klein.
248 "They really . . . here": Author's interview with Harold Ickes.
249 "Because the president . . . advisers": King, *Hillary: Her True Story*, p. 192.
249 "breaking decades of tradition": Robert Pear, "Settling In: First Lady, Hillary Clinton, Gets Policy Job and New Office," *New York Times*, January 22, 1993, p. 1.
250 "So where are . . . Zoë?": Stephanopoulos, *All Too Human*, p. 109.
251 "No, he can't do that": Ibid.
251 "the hidden hand . . . law": Maureen Dowd, "White House Memo: Hillary Clinton's Debut Dashes Doubts on Clout," *New York Times*, February 8, 1993, p. 14.
253 Was there anything . . . didn't: Author's interview with Bernard Nussbaum.
254 "focus like a laser . . . economy": Elizabeth Drew, *On the Edge* (New York: Simon & Schuster, 1994), p. 138.
254 "I compare it . . . control": Joe Klein, "Eight Years: Bill Clinton and the Politics of Persistence," *The New Yorker*, October 16, 2254.
254 "We didn't come here . . . Republicans": David Gergen, *Eyewitness to Power* (New York: Simon & Schuster, 2000), p. 277.
255 "Rubin was terrified . . . thing": Author's interview with confidential source.
259 "He's a hell . . . them": Michael Kelly and Maureen Dowd, "The Company He Keeps," *New York Times*, January 17, 1993, p. 20.
259 "She is much . . . this?" Author's interview with Harold Ickes.
259 "a little bit . . . dear": Author's interview with Robert Reich.
259 "my politics are . . . mind-sets": Sherrill, "Hillary Clinton's Inner Politics," p. 1.
260 "It's not true . . . responsibility": Bruck, "Hillary the Pol."
260 "a very practical . . . 1993": Author's interview with Dick Morris.
261 "Well, I want to . . . Ever": Stephanopoulos, *All Too Human*, p. 112.
261 "He's not one . . . to": Michael Kramer, "The Political Interest: Still Waiting for Bill's Call," *Time*, February 1, 1993, p. 37.
261 "one gray hair to another": John F. Harris, *The Survivor* (New York: Random House, 2005), p. 82.
261 "If I find . . . not": Stephanopoulos, *All Too Human*, p. 121.
262 "hard and fast . . . attack": Christopher Connell, "In Health Reform Aftermath, Delay Seen as Reason for Clinton's Loss," Associated Press, September 7, 1994.
262 "Bentsen, Rubin . . . programs": Author's interview with Donna Shalala.
263 "that sealed it forever": Author's interview with Melanne Verveer.
264 "She was a normal . . . fishbowl": Ibid.
264 "I don't go out . . . too": Radcliffe, *Hillary Rodham Clinton*, p. 261.
265 "With Chelsea, she is . . . too": Bruck, "Hillary the Pol."

Chapter 9: Portrait of a First Lady

267 "The sheets are damp": Robert Reich, *Locked in the Cabinet* (New York: Vintage, 1998), p. 49.
267 "George Stephanopoulos was reminded: Stephanopoulos, *All Too Human*, p. 130.
267 The weekend retreat . . . one another: Author's interview with Stan Greenberg.
267 "We were the . . . insulin": Author's interview with Dick Morris.
267 "someone to help . . . something": Ibid.
270 "Bill said 'Stay . . . dinner": Ibid.

271 bare-shoulder, black . . . dress: Clinton, *Living History*, p. 139.
272 "every woman who . . . transition": Marian Burros, "Hillary Clinton's New Home: Broccoli's In, Smoking's Out," *New York Times*, February 2, 1993, p. 1.
272 "We're trying to . . . ideas": Ibid.
272 "I can't say I'm very pleased": Marian Burros, "High Calories (and Chef!), Out at White House," *New York Times*, March 5, 1994, p. 6.
272 "I think she's . . . sense": Burros, "Hillary Clinton's New Home," p. 1.
273 "certain box, traditionalist or feminist": Clinton, *Living History*, p. 140.
273 "that people could . . . other": Ibid.
273 "because of the . . . smoking": Burros, "Hillary Clinton's New Home," p. 1.
274 "aggression": Author's interview with Dick Morris.
274 "taking the fight . . . the enemy": Ibid.
274 "When she does . . . it": Ibid.
274 "Unlike him she's . . . albino": Ibid.
274 "Her spiritual mysticism . . . sense": Ibid.
275 "He works in . . . over it": Author's interview with confidential source.
275 "She's not a creative . . . advocate": Author's interview with Dick Morris.
275 "He's always taking . . . work": Ibid.
275 "substantive . . . doesn't": Ibid.
275 "playing the part . . . pursued": Ibid.
275 "she definitely has . . . attack": Ibid.
276 "to savage women . . . I believe . . . Interns . . . I think . . . her much": Ibid.

Chapter 10: A Downhill Path

279 "penitentiary": Author's interview with presidential aide.
279 "Eagle": Harris, *The Survivor*, p. 32.
279 "Why can't I do what I want?": Ibid., p. 33.
280 "Re-elect Bush": Ibid., p. 34.
280 "Seems First Lady . . . hubby's": Bill Zwecker, " 'Hot' Rumors Dog Clintons," *Chicago Sun-Times*, February 19, 1993.
280 "Just in case . . . bedrooms": Ibid.
281 "We've got to . . . you": Paul Richter, "White House Denies Secret Service Spat," *Los Angeles Times*, March 30, 1993, p. 11.
281 (Later, Zwecker . . . security."): Stewart, *Blood Sport*, p. 248.
281 "too naive and . . . Arkansas": Ibid.
281 "the client": Ibid. And author's interviews with Webb Hubbell and confidential sources.
281 "I'm afraid if . . . sorry": Stewart, *Blood Sport*, p. 236.
282 "I was angry . . . glory": Peter J. Boyer, "Life After Vince," *The New Yorker*, September 11, 1995.
282 "This is gold": Hubbell, *Friends in High Places*, p. 255.
282 "I could never go back": Ibid., p. 202.
282 "Were the team . . . be": Ibid., p. 193.

Chapter 11: Health Care

284 "If I don't get . . . President": Harris, *The Survivor*, p. 20.
286 "People work best . . . discipline": Dana Priest, "Putting Health Care Under a Microscope," *Washington Post*, April 16, 1993, p. 1.
287 "They would take . . . operation": Brock, *The Seduction of Hillary Rodham*, p. 346.
287 "Compromise didn't come . . .": Stephanopoulos, *All Too Human*, p. 301.
287 "Any bill that . . . usual": Bruck, "Hillary the Pol."
288 "We know how . . . campaign": Ibid.
288 "Among Clintonites, it was . . . nostrums": Gergen, *Eyewitness to Power*, p. 307.
288 "Hillary believed . . . it": Author's interview with Lawrence O'Donnell.

288 "We may have been . . . involved": Haynes Johnson and David S. Broder, *The System* (New York: Little, Brown, 1997), p. 132.

288 "There's just nothing . . . need": Author's interview with Lawrence O'Donnell.

289 "The President has already . . . right": Drew, *On the Edge*, pp. 193–94.

289 Hillary's stature with . . . deteriorating: Author's interview with confidential source.

289 "Let's revisit this": Drew, *On the Edge*, p. 307.

290 "the rules in . . . opposition": Johnson and Broder, *The System*, p. 120.

291 "George Mitchell and Dick . . . [idea]": Woodward, *The Agenda*, p. 121.

291 "because the budget . . . enough": Author's interview with confidential source.

291 "All of our efforts . . . America": Johnson and Broder, *The System*, p. 121.

292 "That would be like . . . have": Eleanor Clift and Mary Hager, "Health Care: Covert Operation," *Newsweek*, March 15, 1993, p. 37.

292 "obscure law": Clinton, *Living History*, p. 153.

292 "was no longer . . . fixed": Author's interview with Webb Hubbell.

292 "I think the . . . sued": Hubbell, *Friends in High Places*, p. 193.

293 "Instead of a . . . indeed": Ibid.

293 "Webb, I told Hillary. . . . litigation": Author's interview with Webb Hubbell.

293 "Fix it, Vince! . . . all": Hubbell, *Friends in High Places*, p. 212.

293 "She was the . . . relationship": Author's interview with Webb Hubbell.

294 "She was furious . . . to do": Author's interview with Sara Ehrman.

Chapter 12: The Politics of Meaning . . . and Family

295 "When he turned . . . him?": Sheehy, *Hillary's Choice*, p. 233.

295 "He was mean, mean, mean": Author's interview with confidential source.

296 "leaning": Dana Priest, "White House Considers Requiring Individuals to Buy Health Insurance," *Washington Post*, March 29, 1993, p. A6.

297 "emphasis on personal . . . church": United Methodist News Service, September 16, 1992.

298 "When does life . . . end?": Hillary Rodham Clinton, Remarks, Liz Carpenter Lecture Series, University of Texas, Austin, April 7, 1993.

298 "crisis of meaning . . . soul": Ibid.

299 "struck down with . . . time": Ibid.

299 "Much of the energy . . . God": Sherrill, "Hillary Clinton's Inner Politics."

299 "He said the following . . . 'The eighties . . . 'I don't . . . That . . . win": Clinton, Remarks, University of Texas.

300 "[T]he debate over . . . Instead . . . this tumor . . . *We need* . . . ourselves": Ibid.

300 "remolding society": Ibid.

301 "Who will lead us . . . to do": Ibid.

301 "We are, I . . . are?": Ibid.

301 "provide decent, affordable . . . How do . . . system": Ibid.

302 "What do our . . . questions": Ibid.

302 "To fill that spiritual vacuum . . . treated": Ibid.

303 "He never told . . . all right": Clinton, *Living History*, p. 163.

303 "Lord, they loved . . . politics": Richard L. Berke, "Clinton Eulogizes Father-in-Law with Humor at Little Rock Service," *New York Times*, April 10, 1993.

304 "That was it for . . . hypocrisy": Author's interview with Bill Bradley.

304 "didn't hold grudges . . . life": Author's interview with Lawrence O'Donnell.

305 "In this first . . . government": Drew, *On the Edge*, p. 136.

305 "I want to thank . . . Hillary": Ibid., p. 137.

Chapter 13: The Cruel Season

307 "You keep telling . . . plan": Author's interview with confidential source.

307 "You could see . . . in": Author's interview with confidential source.

307 "Her attitude was . . . too": Author's interview with confidential source.

308 "we did give . . . no one": Author's interview with Donna Shalala.

309 "It was hard . . . once": Ibid.

309 "if the numbers . . . to do": Woodward, *The Agenda*, p. 199.

310 "Are these people . . . economics": Ibid., p. 200.

310 "I love this stuff": Harris, *The Survivor*, p. 20.

310 "The difference between . . . forever": Author's interview with Bob Boorstin.

310 "Some mornings she . . . awakenings": Author's interview with confidential source.

310 "The person on . . . over it": Sheehy, *Hillary's Choice*, p. 139.

311 "Does he need . . . enemies": Author's interview with confidential source.

311 "Bill's women problems . . . was": Author's interview with Betsey Wright.

312 "Once the impeachment . . . turn": Ibid.

313 "looks thinner than . . . House": Phyllis C. Richman, "Eschewing the Fat with Hillary: A New Point of 'Lite' at the White House," *Washington Post*, December 1, 1993.

316 "Do I know her?": Marian Burros, "Social Scene: A Highly Sensitive Post Is Filled by the Clintons," *New York Times*, January 12, 1993, p. 18.

316 "Who would ever . . . changed": Author's interview with Ann Stock.

316 "treated the White . . . house": Ibid.

317 "They don't care about people": Author's interview with confidential source.

317 "I think where . . . Arkansas": Author's interview with Ann Stock.

317 "He understands why . . . action": Drew, *On the Edge*, p. 92.

317 "I'm more interested . . . about": Radcliffe, *Hillary Rodham Clinton*, p. 251.

317 "You have to . . . today": Author's interview with Terry McAuliffe.

317 "It was a . . . push": Author's interview with Ann Stock.

317 "they ran it from a war room": Ibid.

318 "The mentality of . . . In social . . . last-minute": Ibid.

318 "We've got to . . . supper": Ibid.

318 "I mean, Bill . . . them": Ibid.

318 "I don't have . . . do": Ibid.

319 "When the President . . . anything": Ibid.

319 "I'm not doing . . . do": Ibid.

319 "That's part . . . charities": Ibid.

319 "They want to . . . it": Ibid.

319 "It was somewhat a . . . Quinn": Ibid.

320 "Beware of Washington": Sally Quinn, "Beware of Washington," *Newsweek*, December 28, 1992, p. 26.

320 "For Hillary Clinton . . . so high": Ibid.

320 "Making Capital Gains . . . Rules": Sally Quinn, "Making Capital Gains: Welcome to Washington, but Play by Our Rules," *Washington Post*, November 15, 1992.

320 "Think of it . . . them": Ibid.

321 "She must know . . . She should not . . . She should not . . . reality": Quinn, "Beware of Washington," p. 26.

322 "[Bill], was a little . . . honest": Author's interview with Rahm Emanuel.

322 "We were in a . . . storm": Hubbell, *Friends in High Places*, p. 185.

322 "The real test . . . friends": Ibid., p. 201.

323 "The Travel Office is . . . like": Author's interview with confidential source.

324 "Jesuitical lying": Author's interview with confidential sources.

324 "White House Project": Brock, *The Seduction of Hillary Rodham*, p. 368.

324 "best and brightest": Ibid.

324 "get the most appealing visuals": Ibid.

324 "image of the . . . Mickey Mouse": Ibid.

325 Now that Clinton . . . 'Thomason' name recognition": Ibid., p. 369.

325 "These guys are . . . Lader": Harris, *The Survivor*, p. 38.

325 "Harry was more . . . hill": Drew, *On the Edge*, p. 17.

325 "Stay ahead": Brock, *The Seduction of Hillary Rodham*, p. 374.

325 "good [press] story": Ibid.

325 "very interested": Report of the Independent Counsel.

326 "lavish lifestyles": Brock, *The Seduction of Hillary Rodham*, p. 374.
326 "highest levels": Ibid., p. 375.
326 "Are you aware . . . Office?": Report of the Independent Counsel.
326 "Oh, well, good . . . it": Ibid.
326 "HRC generally appeared . . . cloture": Brock, *The Seduction of Hillary Rodham*, p. 375.
326 "Harry says his . . . slots": Ibid., p. 376.
327 "mismanagement and possible misconduct": Report of the Independent Counsel.
327 "Well, this is a . . . it": Ibid.
327 "Well, I had . . . antennae": Stewart, *Blood Sport*, p. 263.
328 Though the White . . . an hour: Drew, *On the Edge*, p. 174.
328 "Ooh, I'm going . . . stand": Ibid., p. 183.
329 "a distant cousin": Stewart, *Blood Sport*, p. 265.
329 "We need to . . . interest": Brock, *The Seduction of Hillary Rodham*, p. 382.
329 "At the time . . . Harry . . . control": Report of the Independent Counsel.
330 "Hillary Clinton . . . Wonk": Nita Lelyveld, "In America's Magazines, Hillary Clinton Gets (A Teeny Bit), More Personal," Associated Press, May 8, 1993.
330 "Hillary Rodham Clinton . . . that?": Margaret Carlson Washington, "At the Center of Power: The First Lady Wants More Than Clout," *Time*, May 10, 1993.
331 "The Incredible Shrinking President": Michael Duffy, "That Sinking Feeling; Is Clinton Up to the Job?," *Time*, June 7, 1993.
331 "Her words were . . . target": Gergen, *Eyewitness to Power*, p. 298.
331 "You don't need it . . . it": Author's interview with Wendy Smith.
331 "You know, your staff . . . well": Author's interview with confidential source.
331 "Everybody [was] just . . . is": Author's interview with confidential source.
331 "She was very nervous about the press": Author's interview with confidential source.
332 "I said [in response] . . . at": Author's interview with confidential source.
332 "the outside": Author's interview with confidential source.
332 "a national staff . . . staff": Author's interview with confidential source.
332 "probably the first . . . judgments": Author's interview with confidential source.
332 "mind doing all . . . do": Author's interview with confidential source.
333 "Bill Clinton can be . . . it?": Gergen, *Eyewitness to Power*, p. 265.
333 "I didn't want . . . will": Author's interview with David Gergen.
333 "She was very . . . Washington' ": Ibid.
333 "If he's asking . . . comfortable": Ibid.
334 "In the new . . . rarity": Gergen, *Eyewitness to Power*, p. 264.
334 "One felt that . . . loyalty": Author's interview with David Gergen.
334 "She'd say, 'That . . . time' ": Author's interview with Dick Morris.
334 "She was very . . . her": Author's interview with Roy Neel.
334 "own little subculture": Clinton, *Living History*, p. 133.
334 "camaraderie": Ibid., p. 133.
334 "Kool-Aid drinkers": Author's interview with confidential source.
335 "They think because . . . happen": Author's interview with confidential source.
335 "Based on everything . . . But it . . . When there . . . Basically . . . And there . . . it?": Author's interview with confidential source.
337 "At the time . . . Diet": Hubbell, *Friends in High Places*, p. 232.
337 "carelessness about following the law": *Wall Street Journal*, editorial, June 17, 1993.
337 "No doubt Mr. Foster . . . attention?": Ibid.
338 "We suspect that . . . off": *Wall Street Journal*, editorial, June 24, 1993.
338 "Why was notice . . . president?": *New York Times*, editorial, July 11, 1993.
339 "I made mistakes . . . group": Stewart, *Blood Sport*, p. 283.
339 "I'm sure . . . defeat": Hubbell, *Friends in High Places*, p. 258.
339 "Vince had her heart . . . herself": Author's interview with confidential source.
339 "He was completely out . . . her": Author's interview with confidential source.
340 "The mores on . . . affair": *Wall Street Journal*, editorial, July 19, 1993.

340 Foster declined . . . two days later: Clinton, *My Life*, p. 531.
340 "I can't believe . . . Let's hope . . . know?": Stewart, *Blood Sport*, p. 29.
341 "I'm okay . . . home": Hubbell, *Friends in High Places*, p. 25.
341 "Of a thousand . . . Vince": Author's interview with confidential source.
341 "extraordinary sense of . . . family": Stewart, *Blood Sport*, p. 298.
341 "As I tried to explain . . . happen": Harris, *The Survivor*, p. 75.
342 "Webb, did you . . . with health care . . . have": Hubbell, *Friends in High Places*, p. 254.
342 "was messed up": Ibid.
343 "We shouldn't have . . . It would've . . . asked": Ibid.
343 "I know you're being . . . I could . . . advice": Ibid., p. 255.
343 "Hillary saw us . . . When are . . . Italian": Ibid., p. 232.
343 "Hillary said that . . . before": Ibid., p. 233.
344 "Hillary asked if . . . boxes": Ibid., p. 234.
344 "Webb, you all . . . coming": Ibid.
344 " 'Oh, I'm sorry' . . . 'So am I . . . Vince": Clinton, *Living History*, p. 175.
344 "sulk": Hubbell, *Friends in High Places*, p. 234.
344 "It was so . . . away": Ibid.
344 "opened up some . . . lament": Ibid.
344 "A Song for You. . . . mine": Clinton, *Living History*, p. 177.
345 "I can't deal . . . it": Stewart, *Blood Sport*, p. 306.
345 "destroyed": Author's interview with confidential source.
345 "I think she . . . that": Author's interview with confidential source.
345 "She was so . . . there": Author's interview with David Gergen.
345 "that the actions . . . life": Clinton, *Living History*, p. 173.
345 "automatic pilot": Ibid., p. 178.
345 "private": Ibid., p. 179.
345 "sheer willpower": Ibid.
345 "She often weighed . . . evil": Author's interview with Dick Atkinson.
347 "pretty seriously off on the wrong track": Richard Harwood, "Over the Heads of the Press," *Washington Post*, August 16, 1993, p. 17.
347 "got the impression . . . I recall . . . Hillary was . . . She absorbed . . . They were . . . House": Author's interview with William Styron.

Chapter 14: Not a Crook, Not a Degenerate

349 "campaign story . . . work": Author's interview with Mark Fabiani.
349 "it was reasonable . . . Clintons": Ibid.
351 "help conceal earlier . . . governor": Jeff Gerth and Stephen Engelberg, "U.S. Investigating Clinton's Links to Arkansas S&L," *New York Times*, November 2, 1993, p. 20.
352 "From [the Clintons' . . . solidified it": Author's interview with Harold Ickes.
353 "He was this . . . him": Author's interview with Betsey Wright.
353 "He was working . . . Yes": Author's interview with Jim Blair.
354 "And at one . . . weren't": Author's interview with Betsey Wright.
354 "It was a . . . this": Ibid.
355 "Before this death . . . death": *NBC Nightly News*, November 11, 1993.
355 "Whitewater became the . . . down": Stephanopoulos, *All Too Human*, p. 245.
355 "The *Post* was . . . documents": Ibid., p. 226.
356 "I don't want . . . on": Stewart, *Blood Sport*, p. 354.
356 "We can't just . . . it": Ibid., p. 353.
356 "They have managed . . . anything": Author's interview with Betsey Wright.
356 "I don't have a . . . Hillary": Stephanopoulos, *All Too Human*, p. 227.
356 "Saying her name . . . treated' ": Ibid.
356 "On this issue . . . veto": Ibid.
357 "She would get . . . There was . . . saying": Author's interview with Dee Dee Myers.
357 "These are my . . . to": Harris, *The Survivor*, p. 105.

357 "As you know . . . documentation": Stewart, *Blood Sport*, p. 355.
358 "strong-armed": David Brock, "Living with the Clintons: Bill's Arkansas Bodyguards Tell the Story the Press Missed," *The American Spectator*, January 1994.
358 "Hillary Watch": Ibid.
358 "Basically I think . . . hotel": Author's interview with Betsey Wright.
359 "was on a . . . later": Ibid.
359 "They were all . . . them": Ibid.
359 "Bruce was not . . . answers": Ibid.
359 "Bill had told . . . situation": Ibid.
360 "very much alone": Clinton, *Living History*, p. 208.
360 "I thought we . . . do": Author's interview with Mack McLarty.
360 "My first thoughts . . . much": Clinton, *Living History*, p. 194.
360 "was deep in . . . days": Gergen, *Eyewitness to Power*, p. 308.
361 "I cannot recall . . . that": Ibid., p. 309.
361 It is a federal . . . weeks: For a fuller account, see Drew, *On the Edge*, p. 382.
361 "The allegations are . . . him": Drew, *On the Edge*, p. 383.
362 "about the crafts . . . having": Lois Romano, "The Reliable Source," *Washington Post*, December 23, 1993.
362 "I find it . . . feelings": "White House: Clinton Told Money Offered Troopers to Talk of Affairs," Associated Press, December 21, 1993.
362 "smear artist . . . facts": Frank Rich, "Journal: David Brock's Women," *New York Times*, January 6, 1994.
363 "I Was a Conservative Hit-Man": David Brock, "Confessions of a Right-Wing Hit Man," *Esquire*, July 1997.
364 "the most bizarre . . . administration": Drew, *On the Edge*, p. 384.
364 "I think I'm going to throw up": Ibid.
364 "Clinton Papers Lifted After Aide's Suicide": Jerry Seper, "Clinton Papers Lifted After Aide's Suicide: Foster's Office Was Secretly Searched Hours After His Body Was Found," *Washington Times*, December 20, 1993.
364 "Foster's office was . . . found": Ibid.
364 "a man who . . . Roger)": Drew, *On the Edge*, p. 384.
366 "It was Hillary . . . tension": Bruck, "Hillary the Pol."
367 "Sadly, the Whitewater . . . it": Stewart, *Blood Sport*, p. 371.
368 "I accidentally found some . . . all": Author's interview with Betsey Wright.
368 "I told her . . . And I . . . There's going . . . Well, I . . . lawyer?": Ibid.
368 "Assuming we did . . . forthcoming": Stephanopoulos, *All Too Human*, p. 230.
369 Whitewater overshadowed . . . indictment": Brock, *The Seduction of Hillary Rodham*, p. 401; Fiske report.
369 "Mother called me at . . . her go": Clinton, *My Life*, p. 567.
370 "showed more affection . . . other": David Maraniss, "The Woman Who Shaped the President Dies in Her Sleep," *Washington Post*, January 7, 1994, p. 1.
370 "I hate to even . . . hand now": Bob Dole, interview, *CBS This Morning*, January 7, 1994.
370 "background noise": Clinton, *Living History*, p. 211.
370 "utterly stricken": Ibid.
370 "It is in the . . . reauthorized": Carolyn Skorneck, "White House Decries 'Cannibalism' in Attacks on Clinton," Associated Press, January 7, 1994.
371 "I just have to. . . . town": Carolyn Skorneck, "Reno Rejects Dole Suggestion of Political Interference," Associated Press, January 8, 1994.
371 "You know, I've . . . mother": *The Hotline*, January 10, 1994.
371 "Clearly, she had . . . come": Gergen, *Eyewitness to Power*, p. 299.
372 "Kendall would not . . . know": Author's interview with Betsey Wright.
372 "Turn over the . . . hide": *The Hotline*, January 10, 1994.
372 "If it comes . . . is": Ibid.
373 "I have nothing . . . trip": Drew, *On the Edge*, p. 406.
373 "You had your . . . trip": Ibid.

373 the scene had . . . don't": Clinton, *Living History*, p. 215.

373 He cited . . . us": Stewart, *Blood Sport*, p. 373; author's interview with Bernard Nussbaum.

373 "I've lived with . . . institution": Woodward, *Shadow*, p. 237.

373 "Mr. President, one . . . earth": Ibid.

374 "If you create . . . beyond": Ibid., p. 238.

374 "terrible precedent, basically . . . decision": Clinton, *My Life*, p. 573.

374 Hillary went . . . noose": Woodward, *Shadow*, p. 239; author's interview with Bernard Nussbaum.

374 "whether any individuals . . . way": Stewart, *Blood Sport*, p. 399.

375 "I want you . . . over": Woodward, *Shadow*, p. 242.

Chapter 15: Truth or Consequences

376 "I'm telling you . . . that": Terence Hunt, "Clinton Defends Wife, Self: 'No Credible Charge' in Whitewater," Associated Press, March 7, 1994.

376 "try and explain . . . of": Howard Kurtz, "ABC News Plunges into Whitewater," *Washington Post*, February 11, 1994.

377 "How do you counter . . . You don't . . . Are you . . . I blow . . . teenagers": Stewart, *Blood Sport*, p. 418.

377 "Don't Pillory Hillary": Dan Balz, "GOP Assailed for Attacks on Clintons," *Washington Post*, March 12, 1994.

377 "Her integrity and . . . issue": John King, "While Defending Clinton, Democrats Have Whitewater Jitters," Associated Press, March 11, 1994.

378 Under this intensifying . . . investment": Stewart, *Blood Sport*, p. 415.

378 "Top Arkansas Lawyer . . . $100,000": Dean Baquet, Jeff Gerth, and Stephen Labaton, "Top Arkansas Lawyer Helped Hillary Clinton Turn Big Profit," *New York Times*, March 18, 1994, p. 1.

379 "numerous people": Stewart, *Blood Sport*, p. 417.

379 "There was no . . . *Times*": Ibid.

379 "committed to a . . . destruction": Ruth Marcus, "Clinton Angrily Denounces Republicans: Party Is 'Committed to Politics of Personal Destruction,' President Says," *Washington Post*, March 15, 1994.

379 "Have you taken . . . I think there . . . I've also . . . wrong": Stewart, *Blood Sport*, p. 420.

380 "I don't think . . . answered": Author's interview with confidential source.

380 "Yes, I do . . . I think if my . . . me": "Excerpts from Hillary Clinton's News Session on Whitewater," *New York Times*, April 23, 1994.

381 "she essentially reverted . . . so": Author's interview with Roger Altman.

381 "She started off . . . often": Ibid.

382 "Whitewater is evaporating . . . office": Stewart, *Blood Sport*, p. 420.

382 "She felt good . . . her": Robert Reich, interview, *PBS Frontline*.

382 "They are peeling . . . issue": John King, "While Defending Clinton, Democrats Have Whitewater Jitters," Associated Press, March 11, 1994.

383 "they can't stand . . . attack": Richard L. Berke. "Party Attacking Clintons' Critics," *New York Times*, March 13, 1994, p. 25.

383 "to have a . . . reverse": Author's interview with confidential source.

383 "I swear to God, it didn't happen": Woodward, *Shadow*, p. 255.

384 "I begged him and . . . her": Author's interview with Jim Blair.

384 "Impeach Hillary": Lloyd Grove, "It Isn't Easy Being Right: At the Conservative Confab, Out of Sorts About Who's in Power," *Washington Post*, February 14, 1994.

384 "The whole scene . . . before": Stephanopoulos, *All Too Human*, p. 266.

384 "It's wrong that a woman . . . to me": Stewart, *Blood Sport*, p. 389.

384 "a cheap . . . trick": Ibid.

385 "Only after Mr. Clinton . . . relief": Ibid., p. 390.

385 "she was begging . . . D.C.": Author's interview with Betsey Wright.

385 "tolling agreement": Stephanopoulos, *All Too Human*, p. 272.

385 "distinguishing characteristics": Neil A. Lewis, "Material Hints of Assistance in Jones Case," *New York Times*, October 27, 1998.

389 "After a review . . . investigation": Text provided by the Associated Press, June 30, 1994.

389 "essentially those expected . . . probe": Douglas Jehl, "First Whitewater Report Pleases Clinton Advisers," *New York Times*, July 1, 1994, p. 16.

390 "really fucking crazy": Author's interview with confidential source.

391 "the Republican and their . . . Justice": Clinton, *Living History*, p. 243.

391 "eat his hat": Ibid., p. 244.

392 "appoint a new . . . remain": Jerry Seper, "Reno Seeks a Change in Fiske's Status," *Washington Times*, July 2, 1994.

392 "It is not . . . conflict": Michael J. Sniffen, "Fiske Replaced as Whitewater Prosecutor by Starr," Associated Press, August 5, 1994.

393 "Western wear . . . problems": Jeffrey Toobin, *A Vast Conspiracy* (New York: Random House, 1999).

393 "Everybody else has . . . done": Woodward, *Shadow*, p. 270.

394 "Our competitiveness, our . . . care": Drew, *On the Edge*, p. 302.

394 "Every American would . . . companies": Ibid., p. 303.

394 "I find her . . . self-righteousness": Author's interview with Bob Boorstin.

395 "In the very . . . husband": Johnson and Broder, *The System*, p. 183.

395 "I am pleased . . . last": Ibid., p. 184.

395 "I'm here as . . . nation": Bruck, "Hillary the Pol."

395 "Kevorkian prescription for . . . women": Johnson and Broder, *The System*, p. 185.

395 "Her thoughts sound . . . Marxists": Ibid.

395 "as exciting as possible . . . I'm sure . . . "We'll do . . . "You and . . . I have . . . understated": Ibid.

396 "Not since Eleanor . . . easily": Ibid., p. 184.

396 "I hope my mother is listening": Mike Feinsilber, "She Made Her Case in a Lawyerly Manner," Associated Press, September 28, 1993.

396 "Hillary Rodham Clinton . . . solution": Adam Clymer, "The Clinton Health Plan Is Alive on Arrival," *New York Times*, October 3, 1993.

396 "It's a long . . . superstar": Mary McGrory, "Capital Hillary," *Washington Post*, October 3, 1993.

396 "It was, in a way . . . they were": Maureen Dowd, "First Lady Takes Stage, Ending Era on the Hill," *New York Times*, September 29, 1993.

396 "If Ira Magaziner . . . destroyed": Johnson and Broder, *The System*, p. 186.

396 "My colleagues who have . . . at it": Karen Tumulty, "Health Care Math Leaves Critics Puzzled," *Los Angeles Times*, September 11, 1993.

396 "fantasy": Johnson and Broder, *The System*, p. 351.

396 "I can't believe they're . . . unprecedented": Karen Ball, "Sorting Through the Competing Health Care Bills: A Primer," Associated Press, October 11, 1993.

396 "until the legislation is complete": David S. Broder and Dana Priest, "As Momentum Slows, Clintons Said to Be Eager to Submit Health Care Bill," *Washington Post*, October 14, 1993.

397 "I don't remember . . . happen": Author's interview with Roger Altman.

398 "you to get . . . sit down": Johnson and Broder, *The System*, p. 132.

398 "It's certainly possible . . . common": Paul Richter and Edwin Chen, "Clinton, Aides Hit the Road to Push Health Care Plan," *Los Angeles Times*, September 24, 1993.

398 "The Government may . . . all": Johnson and Broder, *The System*, p. 205.

399 "The Government caps how . . . way": Adam Clymer, "Hillary Clinton Accuses Insurers of Lying About Health Proposal," *New York Times*, November 2, 1993.

399 "thousands of pages": Clinton, *Living History*, p. 192.

399 Once the Clintons . . . health care reform: Johnson and Broder, *The System*, p. 234.

400 "Whitewater and Health Care": Ibid., p. 276.

400 "The administration, the Democrats in . . . Washington": Harris, *The Survivor*, p. 149.

400 The decision to . . . buses rerouted: The account of the Reform Rider campaign is based on *The System* and *Living History*, p. 245.

401 "to use the . . . House": David E. Rosenbaum, "A Republican Who Sees Himself as a Revolutionary on the Verge of Victory," *New York Times*, July 24, 1994.

401 "It is time . . . bill?": Gergen, *Eyewitness to Power*, p. 302.

401 "willingness to compromise . . . Government": Judy Keen, "Health-Plan Backers in GOP Targeted," *USA Today*. June 1, 1994.

402 "impossible": Ibid.

402 "to win conservative . . . 1996": Ibid.

402 "Foley said absolutely not . . . through": Klein, "Eight Years."

403 "schizophrenic": Author's interview with confidential source.

404 "a creative pollster . . . strategist": Clinton, *Living History*, p. 251.

404 "how the Clintons . . . defeat": Morris, *Rewriting History*, p. 96.

405 "This guy is terrible . . . crawl": Author's interview with Robert Reich.

405 "she had been . . . '80": Ibid.

405 "I cut the deficit . . . Arkansas": Morris, *Rewriting History*, p. 97.

405 "confirmed": Clinton, *Living History*, p. 256.

406 "fighting to get . . . agenda": Johnson and Broder, *The System*, p. 516.

406 "Solid South": Ibid., p. 552.

407 "deflated and disappointed": Clinton, *Living History*, p. 257.

407 "My view is Hillary . . . unforgivable": Author's interview with Lawrence O'Donnell.

407 "When your purpose . . . opposition": Johnson and Broder, *The System*, p. 615.

407 "campaign-think": Ibid.

408 I don't know . . . spiral": Author's interview with David Gergen.

408 "I was profoundly . . . public": Clinton, *My Life*, p. 630.

408 "it was a matter . . . that": Author's interview with David Gergen.

408 "We weren't moving after . . . incoherent": Author's interview with Donna Shalala.

408 "My friends (closest . . . I think . . . Morris replaced . . . deferential": Author's interview with David Gergen.

409 "he pushed her . . . anything": Author's interview with Dick Morris.

409 "she literally withdrew . . . staff": Author's interview with Harold Ickes.

409 "She didn't trust . . . wicked witch": Ibid.

410 "I had a . . . her": Author's interview with Dick Morris.

410 "[A]s Clinton withdrew from . . . Morris": Stephanopoulos, *All Too Human*.

411 "To help get . . . loss": Morris, *Rewriting History*, p. 98.

411 "I told the . . . weak": Ibid.

411 "draft avoidance, the . . . prone": Ibid.

411 "There was nothing . . . him": Ibid.

412 "her outspokenness before . . . start sending . . . 1970s": Ibid., p. 99.

412 "miracle deck": Marianne Williamson Web site.

413 "humanistic psychology": www.jeanhouston.org.

413 "the Mystery School . . . potential": Ibid.

414 "scholar . . . Capacities": Ibid.

414 "For the Healing of America . . . equally": Colleen O'Connor, "Prayers for the World: Marianne Williamson Writes About Making Amends," *Dallas Morning News*, January 7, 1995, p. 1.

414 "positive . . . negative": Author's interview with Jean Houston.

414 "low point": Ibid.

414 "did the major guiding . . . visions": Ibid.

414 "psychologist . . . types": Ibid.

415 "experts in two . . . me": Clinton, *Living History*, p. 264.

415 He responded that . . . for the country: Author's interview with Jean Houston.

415 "He respected him . . . Republicans": Ibid.

415 "battered . . . tormented": Ibid.

416 "I thought about . . . life": Martha Sherrill, "Eleanor Roosevelt, in Bronze: Hillary Clinton Joins in Benefit for N.Y. Statue": *Washington Post*, February 22, 1993, p. 1.

416 "conversations": Ibid.
416 "How did you put . . . way?": Author's interview with Jean Houston.
416 "I was essentially . . . books": Ibid.
416 "My whole life . . . capacity": Joseph Berger, "Performing Séances? No, Just 'Pushing the Membrane of the Possible,' " *New York Times*, June 25, 1996, p. 13.
416 "design for the . . . Christ life": www.jeanhouston.org.
417 "act as if ": Author's interview with Jean Houston.
417 "hostile messages": Ibid.
417 "convention of New Age guru authors": Ann Devroy, "New Age 'Guru to the Glitterati' Advised Clintons," *Washington Post*, January 11, 1995, p. 4.
417 "personal growth guru . . . thinking": Ibid.
417 "lacks a sense . . . go": Ibid.
417 "could be evaluated . . . mischaracterized": Clinton, *Living History*, p. 263.
419 "My first responsibility . . . to do": Kenneth T. Walsh, "Being There for Bill," *U.S. News & World Report*, February 27, 1995, p. 36.
419 "I wished I was . . . Department": "First Lady to Spend 2 Weeks in S. Asia," *USA Today*, March 20, 1995.
419 "some of the last . . . childhood": Clinton, *Living History*, p. 268.
419 "my conviction that . . . globe": Ibid., p. 269.
420 "being rocketed forward . . . abandoned: Ibid., p. 271.
421 "The first lady . . . nuts": Ibid., p. 287.
421 "Washington just can't . . . power": Ann Devroy and Charles R. Babcock, "Gingrich Foresees Corruption Probe by a GOP House; Party Could Wield Subpoenas Against 'Enemy' Administration," *Washington Post*, October 14, 1994.
421 "corruption": Ibid.
422 Not long before . . . anything better: Woodward, *Shadow*, p. 367.
423 "You're supposed to . . . Presumably . . . But then . . . And I . . . silence": Author's interview with Betsey Wright.
424 "He and his mother . . . things": Ibid.
424 "I never talked . . . point": Ibid.
424 "In his handwriting . . . up' ": Ibid.
424 "Why did you . . . anymore?": Sheehy, *Hillary's Choice*, p. 260.
424 "That was in . . . But . . . What . . . He controls . . . police": Ibid.
425 "David Maraniss is . . . up": Author's interview with Betsey Wright.
425 "Well, there was . . . that' ": Ibid.
426 "I felt I was . . . him?' ": Ibid.
426 "Are they coming . . . Yep . . . are": Ibid.
426 "Bill Bennett, Bill . . . it": Ibid.
426 "I ended up . . . since": Ibid.
427 "She was mad . . . race": Author's interview with Dick Morris.
428 "I would talk . . . empty": Ibid.

Chapter 16: Truth or Consequences (2)

429 "not for anyone else . . . it": Author's interview with Mark Fabiani.
429 "centralize": Clinton, *Living History*, p. 222.
429 "Hillary was clearly . . . disadvantage": Author's interview with Mark Fabiani.
430 "was another iteration . . . changed": Ibid.
430 "we talked about . . . it": Ibid.
430 "like him very . . . meeting": Ibid.
430 "instincts are horrible . . . mind": Ibid.
430 "The president wasn't . . . her": Ibid.
430 "She is so tortured . . . today": Ibid.
431 "never seemed to . . . about": Ibid.
431 "keep your eye . . . forward": Ibid.
431 "very later in . . . McDougal": Ibid.
432 "personal": Woodward, *Shadow*, p. 282.

431   Fabiani and Sherburne . . . shouldn't open.": Author's interview with Mark Fabiani; Woodward, *Shadow*, p. 285; Senate Committee Report; and Michael Isikoff, "The Night Foster Died," *Newsweek*, July 17, 1996.

433   "bobbing and weaving . . . bored": David Maraniss, "The Hearings End Much as They Began," *Washington Post*, June 19, 1996.

433   "irrational hope that . . . there": Susan Schmidt and Sharon LaFraniere, "Senators Hear 2 Stories on Foster Office Search: Officer, First Lady's Aide Differ on File Removal," *Washington Post*, July 27, 1995.

434   "personal files": Woodward, *Shadow*, p. 282.

434   "very little sense": Schmidt and LaFraniere, "Senators Hear 2 Stories on Foster Office Search."

434   "Everything that happened . . . plot": Ibid.

434   "burn bag": Ibid.

435   "after a few . . . staff": Ibid.

435   "I had assurance . . . covered": Author's interview with Betsey Wright.

435   "I had approached . . . embarrassing": Ibid.

435   "the Tom and Daisy . . . be' ": Joe Klein, "The Body Count," *Newsweek*, August 7, 1995, p. 34.

437   "China's hospitality": Clinton, *Living History*, p. 303.

437   "push the envelope": Ibid., p. 302.

437   "shaping up as . . . sentiment": Ibid., p. 299.

437   "It is a violation. . . . will": Hillary Rodham Clinton, Remarks to the United Nations Fourth World Conference on Women, Beijing, China, September 5, 1995.

438   "may have been . . . life": "Mrs. Clinton's Unwavering Words," editorial, *New York Times*, September 6, 1995, p. 24.

438   "It kind of . . . issues": Author's interview with Lissa Muscatine.

439   "insisten[t]": Woodward, *Shadow*, p. 294.

439   "Foster regularly informed . . . staff": David Watkins draft memo, "Response to Internal White House Travel Office Management Review," House Government Reform and Oversight Committee.

440   "soul-cleansing . . . possible": Ibid.

440   "hell to pay . . . wishes": Ibid.

440   "There was a cover-up here": David Johnston, "Memo Places Hillary Clinton at Core of Travel Office Case," *New York Times*, January 5, 1996.

440   "distress": Ibid.

440   "The White House . . . discovered": Susan Schmidt and Toni Locy, "Travel Office Memo Draws Probers' Ire; Ex-aide Contradicts Hillary Clinton on Firings," *Washington Post*, January 5, 1996.

440   "troubling pattern that . . . Clinton": Ibid.

442   "and she says . . . over": Ibid., p. 298.

442   "Well, let's go . . . got": Ibid.

442   "Madison Guaranty . . . History": Ibid.

443   "Why would we . . . along?": Ibid., p. 304.

443   The records turned . . . separate days": Woodward, *Shadow*, p. 301.

443   "confirm what we . . . rest": Ibid.

443   "[It] could have . . . records": Author's interview with confidential source.

444   "everybody sort of thought . . . her?": Author's interview with confidential source.

444   "People are nervous . . . argument": Author's interview with confidential source.

444   "one of her . . . here": Martha Brant, "Life in Hillary Clinton's 'Village': In a Shadow of Scandals, First Lady Pursues Her Activism with Zeal of a Missionary," *Austin American-Statesman*, January 9, 1996.

444   "It was a . . . children": Author's interview with Neel Lattimore.

445   "Saint or Sinner?": Martha Brant and Evan Thomas, "First Fighter," *Newsweek*, January 15, 1996.

445   "First Fighter": Ibid.

445   "congenital liar": William Safire, "Blizzard of Lies," *New York Times*, January 8, 1996, p. 27.

445 "a more forceful . . . nose": "Columnist Strikes Back at President: Snowballs at 40 Paces," Associated Press, January 10, 1996.

445 "Mrs. Clinton, instead . . . questioned?": Clinton, *Living History*, p. 330.

445 "Oh, I ask myself . . . them": Ibid.

445 "You know, a month . . . certainly": Ibid., p. 331.

446 "every document we had": *The Diane Rehm Show*, January 15, 1996.

446 "Oh my God, we didn't": Ibid.

446 "mistaken": Ibid.

446 "All the work. . . . goods": Author's interview with confidential source.

446 "something deeper . . . work": Richard Bernstein, "A Few Hints on Nurture from the First Lady," *New York Times*, February 5, 1996.

446 "There is no . . . children": Hillary Rodham Clinton, "The War on America's Children," *Newsday*, March 12, 1995.

447 The chapter headings: Clinton, *It Takes a Village*, pp. 128, 121, 69, 302, 20.

447 "strong feelings about . . . quits": Ibid., p. 43.

448 "We're lucky we . . . afterwards": Ibid., pp. 105–6.

448 "constructive citizenship": Author's interview with confidential source.

448 "civil society": Author's interview with confidential source.

448 "generational challenges": Author's interview with confidential source.

448 "Raising children, like . . . perspectives": Clinton, *It Takes a Village*, p. 203.

448 "Safety-minded parents . . . reach": Ibid., p. 131.

449 "You know, turning . . . community": Author's interview with confidential source.

449 "Give me a . . . friend?": Author's interview with confidential source.

449 "many people . . . might leave someone out": Clinton, *It Takes a Village*.

450 "I don't think she [Hillary], . . . extent": Author's interview with Betsy Johnson Ebeling.

450 "straight out of . . . *Best*": Clinton, *It Takes a Village*, p. 20.

450 "a visible, daily . . . village": Ibid., p. 26.

450 "if illness or . . . family": Ibid.

450 "pitching in": Ibid.

450 "The adults around . . . consequences": Ibid., p. 132.

450 "Parents should be . . . accidents": Ibid., p. 133.

450 "The actual writing . . . ghostwritten' ": Barbara Feinman Todd, "Ghost Writing," *The Writer's Chronicle*, September 2002.

451 "As I was . . . to me": *A Book of Nonsense Verse* (New York: Little, Brown), 1973.

452 "I can't take . . . I?": Sheehy, *Hillary's Choice*, p. 310.

452 David Kendall reached . . . grand jury: Woodward, *Shadow*.

452 Hillary was traveling . . . against her: Author's interview with Melanne Verveer.

452 "discouraged and embarrassed . . . retained": Clinton, *Living History*, p. 334.

452 The presidential election . . . before then: Author's interview with Mark Fabiani and confidential source.

452 As she prepared with . . . an indictment: Author's interview with confidential source and Mark Fabiani. Kendall never directly told the other lawyers he believed Hillary would be indicted. Rather, Hillary confided his assessment at various points to others.

453 "When I say . . . that": Author's interview with Mark Fabiani.

453 "Hillary had run . . . this": Author's interview with confidential source.

453 "It was no . . . matter": Author's interview with confidential source.

453 "Carolyn Huber . . . important": Author's interview with confidential source.

454 "This really goes . . . on": Author's interview with confidential source.

455 "The billing records . . . crude": Author's interview with confidential source.

455 "that she was . . . work": Author's interview with confidential source.

455 "The biggest mistake . . . cared": Author's interview with confidential source.

456 Her intent—and effect . . . over and over": Author's interview with Mark Fabiani, confidential sources; Clinton, *Living History*.

456 "mystified": Woodward, *Shadow*, p. 316.

456 "after all these years": Clinton, *Living History*, p. 336.

456 "Some people made . . . forthright": Author's interview with confidential source.
457 "I, like everyone else . . . efforts": Francis X. Clines, "Hillary Clinton Tells Grand Jury She Cannot Account for Records," *New York Times*, January 27, 1996.
457 "angry, agitated, worried": Author's interview with confidential source.
457 "It was her . . . basically": Author's interview with confidential source.
457 "She became very . . . media": Author's interview with Mark Fabiani.
457 "Starr wasn't the . . . stuff?": Ibid.
457 "Every morning at . . . enough": Author's interview with confidential source.
457 "The rest of . . . investigation": Author's interview with confidential source.
458 "She just got . . . that' ": Author's interview with Mark Fabiani.
458 "And Kendall was . . . say": Ibid.
458 "What she's very good . . . awful": Ibid.
458 "went fairly far down . . . hand": Ibid.
458 " 'You can take . . . Go ahead' ": Ibid.
458 "Mostly she was . . . happened": Ibid.
459 "Well, okay, go . . . shake": Ibid.
459 Kendall had told her . . . stop at nothing: Author's interview with confidential sources.
459 "We had all . . . nothing": Author's interview with confidential source.
459 "damaged goods": Author's interview with confidential source.
459 "I would meet . . . there": Author's interview with Dick Morris.
459 "There was a . . . election": Author's interview with confidential source.
459 "it was understood . . . it": Author's interview with confidential source.
460 "Why didn't Bill . . . well": Author's interview with confidential source.
461 "college night": Clinton, *Living History*, p. 340.
462 "push millions of . . . accountability": Marian Wright Edelman, "Say No to This Welfare 'Reform,' " *Washington Post*, November 3, 1995.
462 Hillary had never . . . of the welfare system: Clinton, *Living History*.
463 "with minimal changes": Clinton, *Living History*, p. 368.
463 "Why should a huge . . . to": Author's interview with Lynn Cutler.
464 "I was in favor . . . street": Author's interview with Carl Anthony.
464 "final decision meeting": Stephanopoulos, *All Too Human*, p. 419.
464 "after the failure . . . pushy": Ibid.
464 "critical first step": Clinton, *Living History*, p. 369.
465 "principles and values": Ibid.
465 "a bridge to the future": Clinton, *My Life*, p. 723.
465 "brilliant engineering of Clinton's comeback": Stephanopoulos, *All Too Human*, p. 422.
465 "Dick's gone bad . . . down": Ibid.
466 "like a robot": Clinton, *Living History*, p. 375.
466 "raising our daughter . . . And it . . . It takes . . . It takes Bill Clinton": Hillary Rodham Clinton, Speech, Democratic National Convention, Chicago, Illinois, August 26–29, 1996.
467 Hubbell had been . . . Asian firms: Hubbell had known James Riady and his father Moctor Riady since another Rose Law Firm's partner had made an investment with the Lippo Group in the early 1980s. Upon resigning from the Justice Department and before publicly acknowledging any wrongdoing, Hubbell became a consultant to a number of clients who gave him retainers for advice on how to deal with Washington business.
467 "You take, you take": Harris, *The Survivor*, p. 270.
467 "like a subway . . . gates": Ibid.
467 "no one around here": Ibid., p. 269.
468 "You never felt . . . horrors": Author's interview with Melanne Verveer.
468 "was out to get the Clintons . . . There's a lot . . . But do you . . . obvious?": *The NewsHour with Jim Lehrer*, September 23, 1996.
468 "They were the . . . over": Bob Woodward, *Shadow*, p. 336.
469 "social meetings": Ibid., p. 341.

470 "Here we had made . . . relief": Ibid.
471 "unburdening": Author's interview with Melanne Verveer.
471 "a real sense of liberation": Ibid.
471 "I would not . . . better": Lois Romano, "The Win Blows in Little Rock: Dancing in the Streets for City's Favorite Son," *Washington Post*, November 6, 1996.
473 "Now that I'm . . . worst": Author's interview with William Styron.
473 "this was the . . . they did": Ibid.
473 "despised": Clinton, *Living History*, p. 396.
473 "extreme conservatives": Ibid.
473 Clinton later said . . . the words: Clinton, *My Life*.
473 "You're nearly as pretty . . . mama": Ibid., p. 395.
474 Gingrich seemed . . . she suggested: Clinton, *Living History*, p. 395.
474 "help shape": Ibid., p. 380.
475 "about how she . . . years": Author's interview with Doris Kearns Goodwin.
475 "felt a certain . . . embattled": Ibid.
475 "This was not . . . covered": Ibid.
475 "She thought the . . . second term": Ibid.
476 "I thought, Oh, my . . . that": Ibid.
476 "During the '92 . . . goes up": Ibid.
476 "She was talking . . . efforts": Ibid.
476 "Why not get . . . image": Ibid.
476 "If they . . . personally": Ibid.
476 "Because Eleanor was . . . deserved": Ibid.
477 "Your departure will . . . investigation": Woodward, *Shadow*, p. 351.
477 "Deep down inside . . . now": Ibid.
477 "As Fiorello . . . mistakes": Ibid.
477 Bill said later he didn't know: Clinton, *My Life*, p. 746.
477 Hillary was traumatized . . . a sitting president: Author's interviews with confidential sources on the Independent Counsel's staff. And Woodward, *Shadow*.
478 All the time . . . he said: Author's interview with Betsey Wright, Webb Hubbell, and confidential sources among Clinton's lawyers.
483 In mid-September . . . second term: Clinton, *Living History*, p. 393; confidential sources on the White House staff.
483 "our share of problems": Ibid.

Chapter 17: The Longest Season

484 "Clinton Accused . . . Lie": Susan Schmidt, Peter Baker, and Toni Locy, "Clinton Accused of Urging Aide to Lie: Starr Probes Whether President Told Woman to Deny Alleged Affair to Jones' Lawyers," *Washington Post*, January 21, 1998, p. 1.
484 "news reports": Clinton, *Living History*, p. 440.
485 She also knew . . . motivated attacks: Author's interview with Diane Blair, Jim Blair, Deborah Sale, confidential White House sources. Blumenthal, *The Clinton Wars*, p. 339; Clinton, *Living History* p, 441.
485 "Lewinsky imbroglio": Clinton, *Living History*, p. 441.
485 Later that morning . . . his resignation: Author's interview with confidential sources.
485 As the pressure . . . at stake, too: Clinton, *Living History*, p. 442, and author's interview with confidential sources.
486 "Well, this girl . . . not?": Author's interview with confidential source.
486 "I will never truly . . . day": Clinton, *Living History*, p. 441.
486 "why he felt . . . stupidity": Clinton, *My Life*, p. 774.
486 "When the facts . . . understand": Erskine Bowles testimony from Independent Counsel Report.
486 Around the same time . . . events: Clinton, *Living History*; Blumenthal, *The Clinton Wars*.
487 But, as Clinton . . . matter altogether: Author's interview with confidential White House sources and Clinton friends.

487 "You poor . . . through": Independent Counsel Report.
487 "I didn't do . . . up": Ibid.
487 "forgiveness": Author's interview with Dick Morris.
487 "ashen": Author's interview with Mark Penn.
487 David Kendall reached her . . . closets: Clinton, *Living History*, p. 442.
487 "Absolutely": John F. Harris, "FBI Taped Aide's Allegations: Clinton Denies Affair, Says He 'Did Not Urge Anyone' to Lie," *Washington Post*, January 22, 1998, p. 1.
489 "made a sexual demand on me": Sidney Blumenthal, *The Clinton Wars* (New York: Farrar, Straus & Giroux, 2003), p. 341.
489 He said it was hard: Ibid., p. 340.
489 They had always been within sight: Ibid., p. 342.
489 "I had never seen . . . himself": Ibid.
489 "I was close . . . marriage": Ibid., p. 343.
489 "empathy": Ibid., p. 339.
489 ". . . fatherless and poor . . . connect": Ibid.
489 "I had been . . . phase": Ibid., p. 340.
489 "His revelations [of] . . . conspiracy": Ibid.
490 "G.K.": Don Van Natta Jr., "White House's All-Out Attack on Starr Is Paying Off, with His Help," *New York Times*, March 2, 1998, p. 12.
490 Blumenthal first met . . . its inner orbit: Blumenthal, *The Clinton Wars*, p. 5.
490 "a Cataline conspiracy": Blumenthal, *The Clinton Wars*, p. 340.
491 "The smoke would . . . clear": Clinton, *My Life*, p. 775.
491 "a more balanced": Ibid.
491 "the hysteria was overwhelming": Ibid.
491 "There is not . . . relationship": Bill Clinton, *The NewsHour with Jim Lehrer,* January 21, 1998.
490 Blumenthal's totally politicized . . . she suggested: Blumenthal, *The Clinton Wars*, p. 340; Clinton, *Living History*, p. 449; author's interview with confidential sources.
492 Watching in his . . . the White House: Toobin, *A Vast Conspiracy*, p. 246; Clinton, *Living History*, p. 444.
492 "My first instinct was just . . . to' ": Author's interview with Carol Biondi.
492 "Well, we just have to win": Independent Counsel Report.
492 The next morning . . . and Hillary: Author's interview with confidential sources.
492 "She called and said . . . being received": Author's interview with Mark Penn.
493 "her . . . for a moment": Author's interview with Mark Gearan.
493 "Step by step . . . impeachment": Blumenthal, *The Clinton Wars*, p. 367.
493 "help her": Ibid.
493 "I replied that . . . through": Ibid.
494 "I think I'm going to get sick": Ibid., p. 325.
494 Thomason believed the . . . with a verdict": Author's interview with confidential sources; Toobin, *A Vast Conspiracy*, p. 251; Blumenthal, *The Clinton Wars*, p. 370.
496 The president, after . . . about to say: Author's interview with confidential sources; Toobin, *A Vast Conspiracy*.
494 "to fulfill my . . . sustainable": Author's interview with Robert Torricelli.
495 "deader really than . . . stroke": *This Week*, January 25, 1999.
495 "There is talk . . . House": Howard Kurtz, "In a Blizzard of Allegations, Did the Media Throw Caution to the Wind?," *Washington Post*, January 27, 1998.
495 "I am very pleased . . . Clinton": U.S. Newswire, January 26, 1998.
496 "Now I have . . . night": Ibid.
496 "But I want to say . . . again": Ibid.
496 "I did not have . . . you": Ibid.
496 Hillary, Bill, and Kendall . . . area of exploration: Blumenthal, *The Clinton Wars;* author's interview with confidential sources.
496 "the most important person": Blumenthal, *The Clinton Wars*, p. 373.
496 "I want to say . . . lie": Ruth Marcus and Thomas B. Edsall, "Jordan Gives Beleaguered President His Presence," *Washington Post*, January 23, 1998, p. 1.

497 "Hillary had to walk . . . scandal": Blumenthal, *The Clinton Wars*, p. 373.

497 "part of the clique of elves": Ibid., p. 368.

497 "Now they think . . . story": Ibid.

497 "a public uproar": Ibid.

497 "There has been . . . Well, we've . . . He has . . . Yes . . . chief defender . . . Well . . . this is . . . Well . . . I've seen . . . at work here": *Today*, January 27, 1998.

499 "You tell them!": Author's interview with Nicole Boxer.

499 "Everyone was yelling . . . What do you know?' ": Ibid.

499 Hillary's brothers believed . . . their wives: Author's interview with Nicole Boxer; author's interview with confidential source.

500 "I guess that . . . with us": Toobin, *A Vast Conspiracy*, p. 258.

500 "We have more . . . strong": Bill Clinton, State of the Union address, January 27, 1998.

500 "Now if we . . . century": Ibid.

500 "The speech reminded . . . him": Alison Mitchell, "Republicans Seek to Seize High Ground as Democrats Begin to Rally Around President," *New York Times*, January 28, 1998.

501 "While no proof has . . . causes": Tim Weiner and Jill Abramson, "In the Case Against Clinton, Some Links to Conservatives," *New York Times*, January 28, 1998.

501 "Part of my duty . . . information": Blumenthal, *The Clinton Wars*.

501 There had been . . . February 3: Author's interview with confidential sources and Nicole Boxer.

501 "And she said . . . House' ": Author's interview with Nancy Bekavac.

502 "[Hillary said], 'Tell . . . I hung up . . . for her": Ibid.

503 "Clinton's political enemies . . . presidency": Richard Morin and Claudia Deane, "President's Popularity Hits a High: Majority in Poll Say Political Enemies Are Out to Get Him," *Washington Post*, February 1, 1998.

503 "Now you know . . . case": Blumenthal, *The Clinton Wars*, p. 397.

503 "Conspiracy or Coincidence": "Conspiracy or Coincidence?," *Newsweek*, February 9, 1998.

503 "overreached the facts . . . sex": Thomas Oliphant, "The Witness Who Wasn't," *Boston Globe*, February 17, 1998.

503 "In essence, I was . . . as I could": Blumenthal, *The Clinton Wars*, p. 411.

504 "the key": Clinton, *Living History*, p. 450.

504 "These accusations against . . . anywhere": Ibid.

504 "Too many lies . . . come out": Pete Yost, "Clinton Says He Told the Truth About Willey Encounter," Associated Press, March 16, 1998.

504 "When she came . . . it": Deposition of Bill Clinton, January 17, 1998, District Court of the United States for the Eastern District of Arkansas.

505 Four days after . . . once disclosed: Author's interview with confidential sources and Office of Independent Counsel.

505 (When some of . . . expurgate it): Woodward, *Shadow*, p. 454.

506 "The president of the . . . officials' ": Ben Evans, "Gingrich Tells Christian Group of Affair," Associated Press, March 9, 2007.

506 "Speaker Gingrich is talking to . . . I know . . . talking about": Jonathan Broder, "Gingrich's Impeachment Scenario," *Salon*, April 29, 1998.

506 "credible": Guy Gugliotta, "House Republicans Wary of Plan for Starr Panel," *Washington Post*, March 20, 1998.

506 "we are now not . . . settings": Ibid.

506 "faith the people . . . underway": Ibid.

507 "the earthy stoicism of rural women": Sheehy, *Hillary's Choice*, p. 305.

507 "We can do . . . bit": Author's interview with Diane Blair.

507 "because I was . . . stupid": Ibid.

507 "the joy went out . . . as open . . . to know": Ibid.

508 "She would call me . . . to anyone": Ibid.

508 Later, Hillary would . . . talk of sex: Clinton, *Living History*; author's interview with confidential sources.

509   "This is fantastic": Author's interview with confidential source.

509   "We did not act . . . genocide": "Clinton's Painful Words of Sorrow and Chagrin," Associated Press, March 26, 1998.

510   "I never spent any . . . Whitewater": Steve Barnes, "McDougal Trial Sees Mrs. Clinton's Videotape," *New York Times*, March 17, 1999.

510   "They would hold . . . affection": Author's interview with confidential sources.

510   "By May . . . him.": Author's interview with confidential source.

510   "I think she handled . . . situation": Author's interview with Mary Mel French.

511   Hillary told Kendall . . . against impeachment: Author's interview with confidential sources; Clinton, *Living History*, p. 465.

511   Bill went to Linda . . . declined: Toobin, *A Vast Conspiracy*, p. 310.

511   Hillary later claimed . . . : Clinton, *Living History*, p. 465.

512   "My husband may . . . to me": Ibid.

512   "President Weighs Admitting . . . Contacts": Richard L. Berke, "President Weighs Admitting He Had Sexual Contacts," *New York Times*, August 14, 1998.

512   "This time . . . bed": Clinton, *Living History*, p. 465.

512   "much more serious": Ibid., p. 466.

512   "inappropriate intimacy": Ibid.

512   "brief and sporadic": Ibid.

512   "I could hardly . . . Chelsea' ": Ibid.

513   "dumbfounded, heartbroken . . . at all": Ibid.

513   "She should have . . . spot": Author's interview with Sara Ehrman.

513   "he had lied to her, too": Clinton, *Living History*, p. 466.

513   "irreparable breach": Ibid.

513   "Third Way": Blumenthal, *The Clinton Wars*, p. 459.

513   " 'embarrassed' ": Ibid., p. 461.

513   "Hillary had hoped . . . gesture": Ibid.

514   "They just thought . . . Mr. President, were . . . It depends on . . . inappropriate intimate contact . . . I don't have . . . I believed that . . . Most of my time . . . gave me": Independent Counsel Report.

515   "touching her breast . . . genitalia": Ibid.

515   "Hillary thinks it's . . . around": Author's interview with James Carville.

515   "It was like . . . died": Ibid.

516   "She'd obviously been . . . with me' ": Ibid.

516   At the end . . . his statement: Clinton, *Living History*, p. 467.

516   "I don't think . . . somber thing": Author's interview with James Carville.

516   "Her mind was elsewhere": Ibid.

516   "out of habit . . . love": Clinton, *Living History*, p. 46.

516   "Well, Bill, this . . . it": Ibid., p. 468.

516   "including questions about . . . As you know . . . This has gone . . . life": Bill Clinton, Speech to the Nation, August 17, 1998.

517   "not adequate": Dan Balz, "Hill Democrats View Speech as a Failure," *Washington Post*, August 20, 1998.

517   "What were we . . . prosecutor?": Ibid.

517   "It was all right": Blumenthal, *The Clinton Wars*, p. 465.

517   "Hillary also approved . . . of all": Ibid.

517   "bantering": Ibid.

517   "They were still . . . possible": Ibid.

517   "She believes in the . . . public": Ruth Marcus, "First Lady 'Committed' to Her Marriage: Aide Says President 'Misled' His Wife on Lewinsky Relationship," *Washington Post*, August 19, 1998.

518   "Chelsea, I think . . . point": Author's interview with confidential source.

518   "It was awkward": Author's interview with confidential source.

518   "looked at me . . . serious": Author's interview with confidential source.

518   Hillary slept upstairs . . . no exception: Clinton, *My Life*, p. 803; author's interview with confidential sources.

519 "[He said] that he was . . . survive' ": Author's interview with Robert Torricelli.
519 "Well, when I . . . one": Ibid.
519 " 'You're still a . . . to her": Ibid.
519 "Our target was . . . today": "Clinton's Words: 'There Will Be No Sanctuary for Terrorists,' " *New York Times*, August 21, 1998, p. 12.
519 He talked about Jackie . . . : Clinton, *Living History*, p. 470.
519 Hillary and Chelsea . . . really loved her: Clinton, *Living History*, p. 470.
519 "She was very . . . easy": Author's interview with Diane Blair.
520 Bill returned to . . . as well: Author's interview with friends of the Clintons'.
520 "thaw": Clinton, *My Life*, p. 805.
520 "shell-shocked": Author's interview with William Styron.
520 "devastated . . . composure": Ibid.
520 "Everyone sensed the . . . through": Ibid.
520 "a pompous lecture . . . sense": Ibid.
520 "I remember an . . . way": Ibid.
520 "They were struggling . . . sources": Ibid.
520 "that Pittsburgh nut": Ibid.
520 "She's plainly a . . . intelligence": Ibid.
521 "She is a . . . today": Ibid.
521 "a new phrase . . . president": Clinton, *Living History*, p. 471.
522 "the reason he . . . typical": Madeleine Albright, *Madam Secretary* (New York: Hyperion, 2003), p. 452.
522 "I thought the meeting . . . say that": Author's interview with Donna Shalala.
523 "I wasn't sure . . . get it": Ibid.
523 Hillary was preparing . . . Clinton go: Author's interview with confidential source on Clinton defense team; Office of Independence Counsel; Woodward, *Shadow*.
523 "the narrative shows . . . information": Woodward, *Shadow*, p. 453.
523 That afternoon, the . . . on the Internet: Ibid., p. 465.
524 "This is about . . . person": Harris, *Survivor*, p. 351.
524 "The core of the . . . blow job": Woodward, *Shadow*, p. 475.
524 "So Hillary had . . . weekend": Author's interview with Betsy Johnson Ebeling.
524 "moving on separate . . . ourselves": Author's interview with Diane Blair.
524 "surreal": Ibid.
525 Account of Stevie Wonder episode from author's interview with Betsy Johnson Ebeling.
526 "If you were my . . . nose": Peter Baker, *The Breach: Inside the Impeachment and Trial of William Jefferson Clinton* (New York: Scribner, 2000), p. 104.
526 "The fact is that . . . proceedings": Ibid.
526 "a philanderer": Ibid.
526 "a liar": Baker, Ibid.
526 "offended at what . . . him": Ibid.
527 "We have often . . . your life": John F. Harris and Juliet Eilperin, "Clinton Allies Seek Compromise on Hill: GOP Pursues Vote on Inquiry; Lawyers Cite Starr's Omissions," *Washington Post*, September 23, 1998, p. 1.
527 "You could feel . . . watching": Author's interview with Melanne Verveer.
528 "Grace strikes us . . . happen": Clinton, *Living History*, p. 470.
528 "She was on fire . . . for you": Author's interview with Nicole Boxer.
528 "We have to . . . real issues": Clinton, *Living History*, p. 471.
528 "I will never . . . topic": Ceci Connolly and Howard Kurtz, "Gingrich Orchestrated Lewinsky Ads," *Washington Post*, October 30, 1998.
529 "What did you tell your kids?": Ibid.
529 "We're going to win . . . losing": Toobin, *A Vast Conspiracy*, p. 336.
529 "With some exceptions . . . humiliation": Sally Quinn, "In Washington, That Letdown Feeling," *Washington Post*, November 2, 1998.
530 On election night . . . by men: Harris, *The Survivor*, p. 353.
531 Behind the scenes, Henry . . . .could succeed: Hyde's Illinois district included Park

Ridge. A few weeks later it would be revealed—as a result of research by journalists initiated by the White House—that Hyde had a five-year adulterous affair in the 1960s. The revelation lead to an apology for his "youthful indiscretions."

532   "mechanically defending . . . not engaged": Author's interview with confidential source.

532   "I would make a point . . . nationally": Author's interview with Greg Craig.

532   The midterm . . . no doubt": Author's interview with White House sources and friends of Hillary Clinton's.

532   "This is how . . . doubt": Author's interview with Nicole Boxer.

532   "I think you have . . . each other": Author's interview with Melanne Verveer.

533   "We in the . . . she said": Blumenthal, *The Clinton Wars*, p. 498.

533   "providing perjurious, false . . . jury": Articles of Impeachment; As Delivered to the Senate by House Judiciary Committee Chairman Henry Hyde, January 8, 1999.

534   "is a blatant and disgraceful . . . gain": Steve Gutterman, "Most Coloradans Support Military Action in Iraq; Many Question Timing," Associated Press, December 17, 1998.

534   "timing and policy . . . subject to question": Helen Dewar, "Lott Retreats from Criticism of Airstrikes: Senate Majority Leader Calls for 'United Front' a Day After Questioning Attack's Timing," *Washington Post*, December 18, 1998.

534   "I think the vast majority . . . together": James Bennet, "Clinton Reported as Very Troubled," *New York Times*, December 19, 1998.

534   "as defiant as . . . the answer": Melinda A. Henneberger, "Clinton's Top Defender Rallies Troops at Front," *New York Times*, December 20, 1998.

535   "I have on . . . spiritual counseling": Blumenthal, *Clinton Wars*, p. 547.

535   "Sir, you have . . . your post": Ibid., p. 550.

535   "I can only . . . January sixth": Ibid.

535   "a worthy and . . . man": Peter Baker and Juliet Eilperin, "Clinton Impeached: House Approves Articles Charging Perjury, Obstruction; Mostly Partisan Vote Shifts Drama to Senate," *Washington Post*, December 20, 1998.

536   "a great disservice to . . . presidents": Blumenthal, *Clinton Wars*, p. 552.

Chapter 18: A Woman in Charge

538   "Very specifically we would . . . office": Author's interview with Diane Blair.

538   "a particularly hard week . . . She did . . . in any way": Ibid.

539   "the wrecking of . . . humiliation": Author's interview with confidential source.

539   "Prior to this . . . New York": Author's interview with Deborah Sale.

539   "when you look at . . . of this": Author's interview with Ann Stock.

540   Mandy Grunwald had worked . . . was becoming inevitable: Author's interview with confidential sources.

540   "I intend to . . . about": Adam Nagourney, "Hillary Clinton Begins Pre-Campaign in a New Role for Her," *New York Times*, July 8, 1999.

541   "I would say . . . White House": Author's interview with Sara Ehrman.

544   "her years as first lady": David Kirkpatrick, "Hillary Clinton Book Advance, $8 Million, Is Near Record," *New York Times*, December 16, 2000.

544   "The deal may . . . sense": "Mrs. Clinton's Book Deal," Editorial, *New York Times*, December 22, 2000.

545   But soon thereafter . . . at him: Author's interview with confidential White House sources.

546   "My family can . . . that": Todd Purdum, "Siblings Who Often Emerge in an Unflattering Spotlight," *New York Times*, February 23, 2001.

546   "They're like mama's . . . brothers' ": Ibid.

548   "a workhorse not a show horse": Helen Dewar, "Clinton Tries to Be Just Another Freshman," *Washington Post*, December 6, 2000.

548   "We're in real trouble . . . Count me in . . . York": Joshua Green, "Take Two," *The Atlantic Monthly*, November 2006.

548 "Because bipartisan support . . . And perhaps . . . behind them": Hillary Rodham Clinton, Speech to the U.S. Senate, October 10, 2002.

549 "If I had . . . the authority": Cal Thomas, "Hillary Is No Bill," *Sun-Sentinel* (Fort Lauderdale, Florida), February 7, 2007, p. 25A.

549 "Well, I've said that . . . their work": Green, "Take Two."

550 "Her perspective is . . . WMD": Author's interview with confidential source.

550 "That's what Bush . . . were making": Green, "Take Two."

550 "You are not . . . candor": Author's interview with confidential source.

550 It is clear . . . her position: Author's interviews with Hillary Clinton's campaign aides.

551 "Her handling of . . . herself": Author's interview with confidential source.

551 "I don't know . . . thinks": Author's interview with confidential source.

551 "The only major . . . flag": Author's interview with confidential source.

552 "It was a campaign document": Author's interview with Neel Lattimore.

553 "Let's talk . . . mine": "Senator Clinton's Statement About Her Candidacy for President," Associated Press, January 20, 2007.

553 "I'm in . . . win": www.hillaryclinton.com.

BIBLIOGRAPHY

The bibliography includes only those books and articles cited in the notes.

Books

Albright, Madeleine. *Madam Secretary.* New York: Hyperion, 2003.
Baker, Peter. *The Breach: Inside the Impeachment and Trial of William Jefferson Clinton.* New York: Scribner, 2000.
Blumenthal, Sidney. *The Clinton Wars.* New York: Farrar, Straus & Giroux, 2003.
Brock, David. *The Seduction of Hillary Rodham.* New York: Simon & Schuster, 1996.
Clinton, Bill. *My Life.* New York: Knopf, 2004.
Clinton, Hillary Rodham. *It Takes a Village.* New York: Simon & Schuster, 1996.
———. *Living History.* New York: Simon & Schuster, 2003.
Cook, Blanche Wiesen. *Eleanor Roosevelt.* New York: Viking, 1999.
Drew, Elizabeth. *On the Edge.* New York: Simon & Schuster, 1994.
Dumas, Ernest. *The Clintons of Arkansas.* Fayetteville: University of Arkansas Press, 1993.
Gergen, David. *Eyewitness to Power.* New York: Simon & Schuster, 2000.
Goldman, Peter, Thomas M. DeFrank, Mark Miller, Andrew Murr, and Tom Mathews, *Quest for the Presidency 1992.* College Station: Texas A&M University Press, 1994.
Harris, John F. *The Survivor.* New York: Random House, 2005.
Hubbell, Webb. *Friends in High Places.* New York: William Morrow, 1997.
Johnson, Haynes, and David S. Broder. *The System.* New York: Little, Brown, 1997.
King, Norman. *Hillary: Her True Story.* New York: Carol, 1993.
Klein, Joe. *The Natural.* New York: Doubleday, 2002.
Maraniss, David. *First in His Class.* New York: Simon & Schuster, 1995.
Milton, Joyce. *The First Partner.* New York: William Morrow, 1999.
Morris, Dick. *Behind the Oval Office.* Los Angeles: Renaissance, 1999.
———. *Rewriting History.* New York: HarperCollins, 2004.
Morris, Roger. *Partners in Power.* Washington, D.C.: Regnery, 1996.
Oppenheimer, Jerry. *State of a Union.* New York: HarperCollins, 2000.
Radcliffe, Donnie. *Hillary Rodham Clinton.* New York: Warner, 1993.
Reich, Robert. *Locked in the Cabinet.* New York: Vintage, 1998.
Schmidt, Susan, and Michael Weisskopf. *Truth at Any Cost.* New York: HarperCollins, 2000.
Sheehy, Gail. *Hillary's Choice.* New York: Ballantine, 1999.
Stephanopoulos, George. *All Too Human.* New York: Little, Brown, 1999.
Stewart, James B. *Blood Sport.* New York: Simon & Schuster, 1996.
Toobin, Jeffrey. *A Vast Conspiracy.* New York: Random House, 1999.
Warner, Judith. *Hillary Clinton: The Inside Story.* New York: Signet, 1993.
White, Theodore H. *The Making of the President.* New York: Black Dog & Leventhal, 1961.
Woodward, Bob. *The Agenda.* New York: Simon & Schuster, 1994.
———. *Shadow.* New York: Touchstone, 1999.

Articles

Asseo, Laurie. "Stars Toast Clinton at Gala Drenched in Music and Laughter." Associated Press, January 20, 1993.
Associated Press. "Columnist Strikes Back at President: Snowballs at 40 Paces." January 10, 1996.
Associated Press. "Senator Clinton's Statement About Her Candidacy for President." January 20, 2007.

Associated Press. "White House: Clinton Told Money Offered Troopers to Talk of Affairs." December 21, 1993.

Babcock, Charles R., and Michael Weisskopf. "Change of Party, Same Game: Fund-Raising Keeps Its Prominence." *Washington Post*, January 15, 1993, p. 1.

Baker, Peter, and Juliet Eilperin. "Clinton Impeached: House Approves Articles Charging Perjury, Obstruction; Mostly Partisan Vote Shifts Drama to Senate." *Washington Post*, December 20, 1998.

Ball, Karen. "Clinton Knows His Message Isn't Getting Out." Associated Press, May 22, 1992.

———. "First Lady Opens Health Hearings: Wows Lawmakers, Answers Doubts." Associated Press, September 28, 1993.

———. "Sorting Through the Competing Health Care Bills: A Primer." Associated Press, October 11, 1993.

Balz, Dan. "GOP Assailed for Attacks on Clintons." *Washington Post*, March 12, 1994.

———. "Hill Democrats View Speech as a Failure." *Washington Post*, August 20, 1998.

Balz, Dan, and Edward Walsh. "Clinton's Wife Finds She's Become Issue: Arkansas Lawyer Denies Impropriety but Vows to Rethink Her Role." *Washington Post*, March 17, 1992, p. 1.

Baquet, Dean, Jeff Gerth, and Stephen Labaton. "Top Arkansas Lawyer Helped Hillary Clinton Turn Big Profit." *New York Times*, March 18, 1994, p. 1.

Barnes, Bart. "Barry Goldwater, GOP Hero, Dies." *Washington Post*, May 30, 1998.

Barnes, Steve. "McDougal Trial Sees Mrs. Clinton's Videotape." *New York Times*, March 17, 1999.

Barringer, Felicity. "The President-Elect's Wife; Hillary Clinton's New Role: The Job Description Is Open." *New York Times*, November 16, 1992, p. 1.

Bass, Carole. "Rights of Passage." *Connecticut Law Tribune*, October 12, 1992.

Bennet, James. "Clinton Reported as Very Troubled." *New York Times*, December 19, 1998.

Berger, Joseph. "Performing Séances? No, Just 'Pushing the Membrane of the Possible.' " *New York Times*, June 25, 1996, p. 13.

Berke, Richard L. "Clinton Eulogizes Father-in-Law with Humor at Little Rock Service." *New York Times*, April 10, 1993.

———. "The Other Clinton Helps Shape the Administration." *New York Times*, December 14, 1992, p. 6.

———. "Party Attacking Clintons' Critics." *New York Times*, March 13, 1994, p. 25.

———. "President Weighs Admitting He Had Sexual Contacts." *New York Times*, August 14, 1998.

Bernstein, Carl. *Washington Post*.

Bernstein, Richard. "A Few Hints on Nurture from the First Lady." *New York Times*, February 5, 1996.

Boyer, Peter J. "Life After Vince." *The New Yorker*, September 11, 1995.

Brant, Martha. "Life in Hillary Clinton's 'Village': In a Shadow of Scandals, First Lady Pursues Her Activism with Zeal of a Missionary." *Austin American-Statesman*, January 9, 1996.

Brant, Martha, and Evan Thomas. "First Fighter." *Newsweek*, January 15, 1996.

Brock, David. "Confessions of a Right-Wing Hit Man." *Esquire*, July 1997.

———. "Living with the Clintons: Bill's Arkansas Bodyguards Tell the Story the Press Missed." *The American Spectator*, January 1994.

Broder, David. "The Press After the Stakeout: Questions of Policy, Record—and Character—Need to Be Better Explored." *Washington Post*, May 12, 1987, p. 19.

Broder, David S., and Dana Priest. "As Momentum Slows, Clintons Said to Be Eager to Submit Health Care Bill." *Washington Post*, October 14, 1993.

Broder, Jonathan. "Gingrich's Impeachment Scenario." *Salon*, April 29, 1998.

Bruck, Connie. "Hillary the Pol." *The New Yorker*, May 30, 1993.

Burros, Marian. "High Calories (and Chef!), Out at White House." *New York Times*, March 5, 1994, p. 6.

———. "Hillary Clinton's New Home: Broccoli's In, Smoking's Out." *New York Times,* February 2, 1993, p. 1.

———. "Social Scene: A Highly Sensitive Post Is Filled by the Clintons." *New York Times,* January 12, 1993, p. 18.

Cimons, Marlene. "Hugh Rodham, First Lady's Father, Dies." *Los Angeles Times,* April 8, 1993, p. 7.

Clift, Eleanor, and Mary Hager. "Health Care: Covert Operation." *Newsweek,* March 15, 1993, p. 37.

Clines, Francis X. "Hillary Clinton Tells Grand Jury She Cannot Account for Records." *New York Times,* January 27, 1996.

Clinton, Hillary Rodham. "Children Under the Law." *Harvard Educational Review,* 1974.

———. "Good Marriages Are More Than a Piece of Paper." *Arkansas Democrat-Gazette,* October 8, 1995, p. 2.

———. "The War on America's Children." *Newsday,* March 12, 1995.

"Clinton at Yale." *New York Times,* October 14, 2001, p. 7.

"Clinton's Painful Words of Sorrow and Chagrin." Associated Press, March 26, 1998.

"Clinton's Words: 'There Will Be No Sanctuary for Terrorists.' " *New York Times,* August 21, 1998, p. 12.

Clymer, Adam. "The Clinton Health Plan Is Alive on Arrival." *New York Times,* October 3, 1993.

———. "Hillary Clinton Accuses Insurers of Lying About Health Proposal." *New York Times,* November 2, 1993.

Connell, Christopher. "In Health Reform Aftermath, Delay Seen as Reason for Clinton's Loss." Associated Press, September 7, 1994.

Connolly, Ceci, and Howard Kurtz. "Gingrich Orchestrated Lewinsky Ads." *Washington Post,* October 30, 1998.

"Conspiracy or Coincidence?" *Newsweek,* February 9, 1998.

Decker, Cathleen, and Sam Fulwood III. "Clinton Courts Voters—Like a True Democrat." *Los Angeles Times,* July 2, 1992, p. 15.

Devroy, Ann. "New Age 'Guru to the Glitterati' Advised Clintons." *Washington Post,* January 11, 1995, p. 4.

Devroy, Ann, and Ruth Marcus. "Clinton Takes Oath as 42nd President Asking Sacrifice, Promising Renewal: 'Era of Deadlock and Drift Is Over.' " *Washington Post,* January 21, 1993, p. 1.

Dewar, Helen. "Clinton Tries to Be Just Another Freshman." *Washington Post,* December 6, 2000.

———. "Lott Retreats from Criticism of Airstrikes: Senate Majority Leader Calls for 'United Front' a Day After Questioning Attack's Timing." *Washington Post,* December 18, 1998.

Dowd, Maureen. "First Lady Takes Stage, Ending Era on the Hill." *New York Times,* September 29, 1993.

———. "The New Presidency: Boxes Bulging with Decades of Clinton's Life Await Journey into History." *New York Times,* January 14, 1993, p. 11.

———. "White House Memo: Hillary Clinton's Debut Dashes Doubts on Clout." *New York Times,* February 8, 1993, p. 14.

Dowd, Maureen, and Frank Rich. "The Boomers' Ball: Picking Up the Perks of Presidential Power." *New York Times,* January 21, 1993, p. 11.

Duffy, Michael. "That Sinking Feeling; Is Clinton Up to the Job? As a Staff Shake-up Begins and His Four-Month Approval Ratings Dip to Record Lows, Americans Are Starting to Wonder." *Time,* June 7, 1993.

Duston, Diane. "Hillary Clinton's Traditional Seat at Swearing-In Belies Her Future Role." Associated Press, January 20, 1993.

Edelman, Marian Wright. "Say No to This Welfare 'Reform.' " *Washington Post,* November 3, 1995.

Evans, Ben. "Gingrich Tells Christian Group of Affair." Associated Press, March 9, 2007.

"Excerpts from Hillary Clinton's News Session on Whitewater." *New York Times*, April 23, 1994.

Feinsilber, Mike. "She Made Her Case in a Lawyerly Manner." Associated Press, September 28, 1993.

"First Lady to Spend 2 Weeks in S. Asia." *USA Today*, March 20, 1995.

Gelb, Leslie H. "Foreign Affairs, Untruths . . ." *New York Times*, October 27, 1991, p. 15.

Gerth, Jeff, and Stephen Engelberg. "U.S. Investigating Clinton's Links to Arkansas S&L." *New York Times*, November 2, 1993, p. 20.

Gitell, Seth. "Meet Hillary Clinton's Grandmother, Della Rosenberg: The Feisty Wife of a Yiddish-Speaking Jewish Immigrant: Family Secret's a Boost for Her Senate Chances." *Forward*, August 6, 1999.

Goldman, John J. "Visit Multiplies Hopes at N.Y. School." *Los Angeles Times*, January 27, 1993, p. 5.

Green, Joshua. "Take Two." *The Atlantic Monthly*, November 2006.

Grove, Lloyd. "It Isn't Easy Being Right: At the Conservative Confab, Out of Sorts About Who's in Power." *Washington Post*, February 14, 1994.

Gugliotta, Guy. "House Republicans Wary of Plan for Starr Panel." *Washington Post*, March 20, 1998.

Gutterman, Steve. "Most Coloradans Support Military Action in Iraq: Many Question Timing." Associated Press, December 17, 1998.

Harris, John F. "FBI Taped Aide's Allegations: Clinton Denies Affair, Says He 'Did Not Urge Anyone' to Lie." *Washington Post*, January 22, 1998, p. 1.

Harris, John F., and Juliet Eilperin. "Clinton Allies Seek Compromise on Hill: GOP Pursues Vote on Inquiry; Lawyers Cite Starr's Omissions." *Washington Post*, September 23, 1998, p. 1.

Harwood, Richard. "Over the Heads of the Press." *Washington Post*, August 16, 1993, p. 17.

Henderson, Nell. "Clinton Leads Nation in Paying Homage to King." *Washington Post*, January 19, 1993, p. 1.

Henneberger, Melinda A. "Clinton's Top Defender Rallies Troops at Front." *New York Times*, December 20, 1998.

Horyn, Cathy. "First Lady Says She'll Pay for Clothes." *Washington Post*, January 21, 1993, p. 12.

The Hotline, January 10, 1994.

Hunt, Terence. "Clinton Defends Wife, Self: 'No Credible Charge' in Whitewater." Associated Press, March 7, 1994.

Ifill, Gwen. "Clinton Wants Wife at Cabinet Table." *New York Times*, December 19, 1992, p. 8.

Isaacson, Walter. "We're Hoping That We Have Another Child." *Time*, June 3, 1996.

Isikoff, Michael. "The Night Foster Died." *Newsweek*, July 17, 1995.

Jehl, Douglas. "First Whitewater Report Pleases Clinton Advisers." *New York Times*, July 1, 1994, p. 16.

Johnson, David. "Memo Places Hillary Clinton at Core of Travel Office Case." *New York Times*, January 5, 1996.

Kasindorf, Martin. "Meet Hillary Clinton: She's Raised Hackles and Hopes, but One Thing's Certain: She'll Redefine Role of First Lady." *Newsday*, January 10, 1993.

Keen, Judy. "Health-Plan Backers in GOP Targeted." *USA Today*, June 1, 1994.

Kelly, Michael. "Again: It's Hillary *Rodham* Clinton. Got That?" *New York Times*, February 14, 1993, p. 33.

Kelly, Michael, and Maureen Dowd. "The Company He Keeps." *New York Times*, January 17, 1993, p. 20.

Kenney, Charles. "Hillary: The Wellesley Years." *Boston Globe*, January 12, 1993.

King, John. "While Defending Clinton, Democrats Have Whitewater Jitters." Associated Press, March 12, 1994.

Kirkpatrick, David. "Hillary Clinton Book Advance, $8 Million, Is Near Record." *New York Times*, December 16, 2000.

Klein, Joe. "The Body Count." *Newsweek*, August 7, 1995, p. 34.

———. "Eight Years: Bill Clinton and the Politics of Persistence." *The New Yorker*, October 16, 2000.

Kramer, Michael. "The Political Interest: Still Waiting for Bill's Call." *Time*, February 1, 1993, p. 37.

Kurtz, Howard. "ABC News Plunges into Whitewater." *Washington Post*, February 11, 1994.

———. "In a Blizzard of Allegations, Did the Media Throw Caution to the Wind?" *Washington Post*, January 27, 1998.

———. "Journalist in the Crossfire: David Brock Decries Personal Attacks by Columnists." *Washington Post*, January 13, 1994.

———. "Portraits of a First Lady: Media Strive to Define Hillary Clinton." *Washington Post*, November 21, 1992, p. 1.

Lauter, David. "Clinton's In-Laws Drop Corporate Party Plans." *Los Angeles Times*, January 15, 1993, p. 24.

Lelyveld, Nita. "In America's Magazines, Hillary Clinton Gets (A Teeny Bit), More Personal." Associated Press, May 8, 1993.

Los Angeles Times, January 21, 1993, p. 1.

Maraniss, David. "The Hearings End Much as They Began." *Washington Post*, June 19, 1996.

———. "The Woman Who Shaped the President Dies in Her Sleep." *Washington Post*, January 7, 1994, p. 1.

Marcus, Ruth. "Clinton Angrily Denounces Republicans: Party Is 'Committed to Politics of Personal Destruction,' President Says." *Washington Post*, March 15, 1994.

———. "First Lady 'Committed' to Her Marriage: Aide Says President 'Misled' His Wife on Lewinsky Relationship." *Washington Post*, August 19, 1998.

———. "Now, 'A Different Kind of First Lady.'" *Washington Post*, January 20, 1993, p. 20.

Marcus, Ruth, and Thomas B. Edsall. "Jordan Gives Beleaguered President His Presence." *Washington Post*, January 23, 1998, p. 1.

Marcus, Ruth, and Michael Isikoff. "Clinton Withdraws Baird's Justice Nomination." *Washington Post*, January 22, 1993.

McGrory, Mary. "Capital Hillary." *Washington Post*, October 3, 1993.

Mitchell, Alison. "Republicans Seek to Seize High Ground as Democrats Begin to Rally Around President." *New York Times*, January 28, 1998.

Morin, Richard, and Claudia Deane. "President's Popularity Hits a High: Majority in Poll Say Political Enemies Are Out to Get Him." *Washington Post*, February 1, 1998.

Morrison, Patt. "Purely Human Moments and Capital's Pomp." *Los Angeles Times*, January 21, 1993, p. 1.

"Mrs. Clinton's Book Deal." *New York Times*, editorial, December 22, 2000.

"Mrs. Clinton's Unwavering Words." *New York Times*, editorial, September 6, 1995, p. 24.

Nagourney, Adam. "Hillary Clinton Begins Pre-Campaign in a New Role for Her." *New York Times*, July 8, 1999.

New York Times, editorial, July 11, 1993.

Norris, Michele L. "A Celebration That 'Took on a Life of Its Own.'" *Washington Post*, January 17, 1993, p. 1.

O'Connor, Colleen. "Prayers for the World: Marianne Williamson Writes About Making Amends." *Dallas Morning News*, January 7, 1995, p. 1.

Oliphant, Thomas. "The Witness Who Wasn't." *Boston Globe*, February 17, 1998.

Pace, Eric. "Hugh Rodham Dies After Stroke; Father of Hillary Clinton Was 82." *New York Times*, April 8, 1993.

Priest, Dana. "Putting Health Care Under a Microscope: In Clinical Detail, Clinton Task Force Analyzes and Argues Its Way Toward a Reform Plan." *Washington Post*, April 16, 1993, p. 1.

———. "White House Considers Requiring Individuals to Buy Health Insurance." *Washington Post*, March 29, 1993, p. 6.

Purdum, Todd. "Siblings Who Often Emerge in an Unflattering Spotlight." *New York Times*, February 23, 2001.

Quinn, Sally. "Beware of Washington." *Newsweek*, December 28, 1992, p. 26.

———. "In Washington, That Letdown Feeling." *Washington Post*, November 2, 1998.

———. "Making Capital Gains: Welcome to Washington, but Play by Our Rules." *Washington Post*, November 15, 1992.

Raines, Howell. "New Faces in Southern Politics: Women, Young and 'Outsiders.' " *New York Times*, July 3, 1978.

Rich, Frank. "David Brock's Women." Journal, *New York Times*, January 6, 1994.

Richman, Phyllis C. "Eschewing the Fat with Hillary: A New Point of 'Lite' at the White House." *Washington Post*, December 1, 1993.

Richter, Paul. "White House Denies Secret Service Spat." *Los Angeles Times*, March 30, 1993, p. 11.

Richter, Paul, and Edwin Chen. "Clinton, Aides Hit the Road to Push Health Care Plan." *Los Angeles Times*, September 24, 1993.

Romano, Lois. "The Reliable Source." *Washington Post*, January 20, 1993, p. 3.

———. *Washington Post*, December 23, 1993.

———. "The Win Blows in Little Rock: Dancing in the Streets for City's Favorite Son." *Washington Post*, November 6, 1996.

Rosenbaum, David E. "A Republican Who Sees Himself as a Revolutionary on the Verge of Victory." *New York Times*, July 24, 1994.

Safire, William. "Blizzard of Lies." *New York Times*, January 8, 1996, p. 27.

———. "The Hillary Problem." *New York Times*, March 26, 1992, p. 23.

Schmidt, Susan, and Tony Locy. "Travel Office Memo Draws Probers' Ire; Ex-aide Contradicts Hillary Clinton on Firings." *Washington Post*, January 5, 1996.

Schmidt, Susan, Peter Baker, and Toni Locy. "Clinton Accused of Urging Aide to Lie: Starr Probes Whether President Told Woman to Deny Alleged Affair to Jones' Lawyers." *Washington Post*, January 21, 1998, p. 1.

Schmidt, Susan, and Sharon LaFraniere. "Senators Hear 2 Stories on Foster Office Search: Officer, First Lady's Aide Differ on File Removal." *Washington Post*, July 27, 1995.

Seper, Jerry. "Clinton Papers Lifted After Aide's Suicide: Foster's Office Was Secretly Searched Hours After His Body Was Found." *Washington Times*, December 20, 1993.

———. "Reno Seeks a Change in Fiske's Status." *Washington Times*, July 2, 1994.

Shales, Tom. "The Numb and the Restless." *Washington Post*, July 21, 1988, p. 1.

Sherrill, Martha. "The Education of Hillary Clinton." *Washington Post*, January 11, 1993, p. B1.

———. "Eleanor Roosevelt, in Bronze: Hillary Clinton Joins in Benefit for N.Y. Statue." *Washington Post*, February 22, 1993, p. 1.

———. "Growing Up in a Chicago Suburb: A Good Girl, Getting Better All the Time." *Washington Post*, January 11, 1993.

———. "Hillary Clinton's Inner Politics: As the First Lady Grows Comfortable in Her Roles, She Is Looking Beyond Policy to a Moral Agenda." *Washington Post*, May 6, 1993, p. 1.

———. "Mrs. Clinton's Two Weeks Out of Time: The Vigil for Her Father, Taking a Toll Both Public and Private." *Washington Post*, April 3, 1993, p. C1.

———. "The Retooling of the Political Wife: Her Final Test: How to Handle Scandal." *Washington Post*, January 13, 1993, p. 1.

———. "The Rising Lawyer's Detour to Arkansas: At Wellesley, She Found Her Calling; At Yale, She Met Her Future." *Washington Post*, January 12, 1993.

Skorneck, Carolyn. "Reno Rejects Dole Suggestion of Political Interference." Associated Press, January 8, 1994.

———. "White House Decries 'Cannibalism' in Attacks on Clinton." Associated Press, January 7, 1994.

Sniffen, Michael J. "Fiske Replaced as Whitewater Prosecutor by Starr." Associated Press, August 5, 1994.

Sperling, Godfrey. "Don't Underestimate Hillary." *Christian Science Monitor,* July 1, 2003, p. 9.

Todd, Barbara Feinman. "Ghost Writing." *The Writer's Chronicle,* September 2002.

Trescott, Jacqueline. "Marathon Man: Clinton's Long Night." *Washington Post,* January 21, 1993, p. 4.

Tumulty, Karen. "Health Care Math Leaves Critics Puzzled." *Los Angeles Times,* September 11, 1993.

Van Natta, Don, Jr. "White House's All-Out Attack on Starr Is Paying Off, with His Help." *New York Times,* March 2, 1998, p. 12.

Wall Street Journal, editorial, June 17, 1993.

Wall Street Journal, editorial, June 24, 1993.

Wall Street Journal, editorial, July 19, 1993.

Walsh, Kenneth T. "Being There for Bill." *U.S. News & World Report,* February 27, 1995, p. 36.

Washington, Margaret Carlson. "At the Center of Power: The First Lady Wants More than Clout. She Wants to Have a Life Too. Can She Find the Formula?" *Time,* May 10, 1993.

———. "A Different Kind of First Lady," *Time,* November 16, 1992.

Weiner, Tim, and Jill Abramson. "In the Case Against Clinton, Some Links to Conservatives." *New York Times,* January 28, 1998.

Wills, Garry. "H. R. Clinton's Case." *The New York Review of Books,* Vol. 30, No. 5, (March 5, 1992).

Yale Daily News, May 2, 1970.

Yost, Pete. "Clinton Says He Told the Truth About Willey Encounter." Associated Press, March 16, 1998.

Zehren, Charles V. "Whitewater Hearings on Tap." *Newsday,* July 7, 1995.

Zimmerman, David. "Wynette Gets Clinton's Apology." *USA Today,* January 30, 1992, p. 2.

———. "Wynette Wants Clinton Apology." *USA Today,* January 29, 1992, p. 2.

Zwecker, Bill. " 'Hot' Rumors Dog Clintons." *Chicago Sun-Times,* February 19, 1993.

Author Interviews

Roger Altman

Carl Anthony

Dick Atkinson

Don Baer

Woody Bassett

Nancy Bekavac

Lloyd Bentsen

Richard Ben-Veniste

Marcia Berry

Carol Biondi

Frank Biondi

Diane Blair

Jim Blair

Linda Bloodworth-Thomason

Tom Boggs

Bob Boorstin

Robert Borosage

Erskine Bowles

Nicole Boxer

Bill Bradley

Max Brantley

Connie Bruck

Dale Bumpers

James Carville

Ellen Chesler

Greg Craig

Lynn Cutler

Lanny Davis

Oscar Dowdy

Ernest Dumas

Betsy Johnson Ebeling

Tom Ebeling

Peter Edelman

Sara Ehrman

Rahm Emanuel

John Emerson

Mark Fabiani

Connie Fails

Barney Frank

Mary Mel French

Richard Friedman

Andrew Friendly

Kelly Crawford Friendley

Al From

Mark Gearan

David Gergen

Doris Kearns Goodwin

Richard Goodwin

Bibliography

Stan Greenberg
Jim Hart
Ann Henry
Jean Houston
Webb Hubbell
Harold Ickes
Mickey Kantor
John Kerry
Joe Klein
Neel Lattimore
Terry McAuliffe
John McCain
Mike McCurry
Eileen McGann
Mack McLarty
Bob McNeely
Brian McPartlin
Dick Morris
Lissa Muscatine
Dee Dee Myers
Roy Neel
Bernard Nussbaum
Lawrence O'Donnell
Kevin O'Keefe

Leon Panetta
Mark Penn
Ann Terry Pincus
John Podesta
David Pryor
Molly Raiser
Robert Reich
Ann Richards
Robert Rubin
Deborah Sale
Donna Shalala
Geoff Shields
Carly Simon
Wendy Smith
Richard Stearns
Ann Stock
Robert Strauss
William Styron
Robert Torricelli
Robert Treuhaft
Melanne Verveer
David Wilhelm
Betsey Wright

Other

Adams, Ruth. Commencement Speech, Wellesley College. May 31, 1969.
Articles of Impeachment: As Delivered to the Senate by House Judiciary Committee Chairman Henry Hyde, January 8, 1999.
Bernstein, Carl. Personal notes.
Blair, Diane. Interviews conducted by Diane Blair for unpublished book. Copyright, the Diane Blair Trust.
Bowles, Erskine. Testimony from Report of the Independent Counsel.
Buchanan, Patrick. Speech, Republican National Convention, Houston, Texas. August 17, 1992.
CBS This Morning. January 7, 1994.
Christian Brothers Academy literature.
Clinton, Bill. Inaugural Address. January 20, 1993.
Clinton, Bill. Interview, *The NewsHour with Jim Lehrer.* January 21, 1998.
Clinton, Bill. Speech to the Nation. August 17, 1998.
Clinton, Bill. State of the Union address. January 27, 1998.
Clinton, Hillary. Interview, *60 Minutes.*
Clinton, Hillary Rodham Clinton. Letter to Geoff Shields, provided by Geoff Shields.
Clinton, Hillary Rodham. Remarks, Liz Carpenter Lecture Series, University of Texas, Austin. April 7, 1993.
Clinton, Hillary Rodham. Remarks to the United Nations Fourth World Conference on Women, Beijing, China. September 5, 1995.
Clinton, Hillary Rodham. Speech, Democratic National Convention, Chicago, Illinois. August 26–29, 1996.
Clinton, Hillary Rodham. Speech to the U.S. Senate. October 10, 2002.
Clinton, Hillary Rodham. Statement of Hillary Clinton.
Clinton, Hillary Rodham. Commencement Speech, Wellesley College. May 31, 1969.
Clinton, Hillary Rodham. Wellesley College senior thesis.
Fiske Report.
Graham, Rev. Billy. Invocation, Presidential Inauguration. January 20, 1993.

King, Martin Luther, Jr., Speech, "Remaining Awake Through a Great Revolution," in
  Sheehy, *Hillary's Choice* (New York: Ballantine, 1999), p. 36.
Mission Statement, Children's Defense Fund Action Counsel.
NBC Nightly News. November 11, 1993.
The NewsHour with Jim Lehrer. September 23, 1996.
Reich, Robert. Interview, *PBS Frontline.*
Report of the Independent Counsel.
This Week. January 25, 1999.
Today. January 27, 1998.
The Tonight Show Starring Johnny Carson. 1988.
United Methodist News Service. September 16, 1992.
White House transcript. January 26, 1998.

Web Sites

Marianne Williamson Web site.
www.hillaryclinton.com.
www.jeanhouston.org.
www.riponsociety.org/history.htm.
www.senate.gov/artandhistory/history/minute/First_Woman_Both_Houses.htm.
http://icreport.loc.gov/icreport/

ACKNOWLEDGMENTS

Knopf vice president and senior editor Jonathan Segal, an incomparable editor in my view, has lent a guiding hand and been a patient teacher since I began work on this book seven years ago. He meticulously read draft after draft of its various sections, commenting on them and gently moving me towards my destination, and edging me onto the narrative path I sought. Once I was on it, he cleared away the obstacles I put in my own way (no matter how attached I was to some of them) and enabled me to better understand the character of my subject and put her story in its present context. He also became a cherished friend.

Four remarkable young assistants helped me with the research and every other aspect of the project. This book could not have been written without them and without the good humor that accompanied their diligence, dedication, and skill. I am indebted to them: Stacy Atlas Kerzner, Amanda Ely, Kristina Goetz, and Carmen Johnson.

At Knopf, I found a group of people who care about books in a way that to me feels unique: dedicated to maintaining the underlying values of a great tradition, and committed to cherished ideals and principles. As I discovered, part of the tradition is familial at Knopf (or, as Hillary might say, it takes a village), and begins with chairman and editor in chief Sonny Mehta, whose extraordinary faith in this project I am deeply grateful for.

I owe special thanks to several people at Knopf: Lydia Buechler, the copy chief, who shepherded the book through the copyediting and proofreading with great care and enthusiasm, and never a word of complaint through seemingly endless hours of work; Anke Steinecke, vice president and associate counsel, for her diligence and rare legal skill that helped strengthen the manuscript; Paul Bogaards and his promotion staff; Nina Bourne, a friend of many, many years who I was never lucky enough to work with until now; Kyle McCarthy, who as Jon Segal's assistant became an integral participant; Carol Shookhoff, who typed the manuscript and made helpful suggestions along the way; Fred Chase, a copyeditor whose skills and great care I came to hold in awe; Carol Carson, Knopf's art director; Avery Flück, the production manager; Virginia Tan, the book's designer; and Carol Janeway, the wonderful foreign rights director.

My agent, Owen Laster, of William Morris, is likewise rooted in the best traditions of his craft; he recently retired, but leaves a standard that is a tribute to his geniality and consummate professionalism.

Special thanks to Louis Plummer, Doug Hill, and Kate Griffin of PhotoAssist; and Dr. John Barrie for his insight and help.

I could not have completed this book without the help and isolation of Yaddo, a remarkable institution that gives writers and artists a contemplative opportunity to proceed and succeed. I was introduced to Yaddo by my friend Suzy Crile. There, I made another great friend for life, Elena Richardson, Yaddo's president. I cannot give enough thanks to Candace Wait, her husband, Charles, and Kathy Clarke, all of whom are dedicated to Yaddo's mission.

For thirty-five years now Bob Woodward and I have conducted an ongoing dialogue about our work and our lives—a source of great satisfaction.

I owe special thanks to my sons, Max and Jacob Bernstein, who had reached the age during my work on this book where their encouragement and criticism were both helpful and loving at the same time; special thanks also go to Thea Stone. My thanks also to my sisters, Mary Bernstein Hunter and Laura Bernstein Ikonen. My parents, Al and Sylvia Bernstein, both died before the book was finished, but their ideals inform all that I believe in. My mother, through the eight years of the Clinton presidency, worked as a volunteer in a group of retired women who sorted and helped answer Hillary's routine mail; she is not the source of a single word in this book. I miss her and my dad more than words can say.

I want to express my love and constant gratitude to Christine Kuehbeck, my wife, at whom I wonder every day. She is the person to whom I look for wisdom I find nowhere else; that has been especially true in every aspect of this book. Christine read these pages with a woman's eye. She raised questions and posed notions that would never have occurred to me—as she always does. She brings unusual insight and perception to all the subjects we endlessly discuss, and brings those qualities—and her unabashed enthusiasm—to the whole of our lives together.

INDEX

Index

A NOTE ABOUT THE AUTHOR

Carl Bernstein, with Bob Woodward, shared a Pulitzer Prize for their coverage of Watergate for the *Washington Post*. He is the author, with Woodward, of *All the President's Men* and *The Final Days*, and, with Marco Politi, of *His Holiness: John Paul II and the History of Our Time*. He is also the author of *Loyalties*, a memoir about his parents during McCarthy-era Washington. He has written for *Vanity Fair* (he is also a contributing editor), *Time*, *USA Today*, *Rolling Stone*, and *The New Republic*. He was a Washington bureau chief and correspondent for ABC News. He lives with his wife, Christine, in New York.

A NOTE ON THE TYPE

This book was set in Janson, a typeface long thought to have been made by the Dutchman Anton Janson, who was a practicing type-founder in Leipzig during the years 1668–1687. However, it has been conclusively demonstrated that these types are actually the work of Nicholas Kis (1650–1702), a Hungarian, who most probably learned his trade from the master Dutch typefounder Dirk Voskens. The type is an excellent example of the influential and sturdy Dutch types that prevailed in England up to the time William Caslon (1692–1766) developed his own incomparable designs from them.

Composed by North Market Street Graphics,
Lancaster, Pennsylvania
Printed and bound by R.R. Donnelley and Sons,
Harrisonburg, Virginia
Designed by Virginia Tan